AMERICAN GLASS

Other books from
the pages of *Antiques*

Constance Greiff, Ed., *Great Houses from the
Pages of Antiques*

Eric de Jonge, Ed., *Country Things from the
Pages of Antiques*

Howard Herschel Cotterell, Adolphe Riff and Robert M. Vetter,
National Types of Old Pewter

AMERICAN GLASS

Volume I·BLOWN AND MOLDED
Edited, with an introduction by Marvin D. Schwartz

Volume II·PRESSED AND CUT
Edited, with an introduction by Robert E. DiBartolomeo

WEATHERVANE BOOKS
NEW YORK

Cover photograph, courtesy The Corning Museum of Glass,
Corning, New York: bowl, South Jersey or Pitkin factory,
Conn., late 18th C.; candlestick, South Jersey, possibly Wistarberg, ca. 1740-1780; sugar bowl with cover, South Jersey,
possibly Wistarberg or Glassboro, ca. 1775-1800.

Back cover photograph, courtesy The Corning Museum of Glass,
Corning, N.Y.: Group of five lacy pressed glasses: sugar-
bowl with cover, shallow bowl, plate, cup plate and salt.
United States, New England, ca. 1830-45.

Contents

INTRODUCTION

Glass collectors have benefited from informative articles appearing in The Magazine *Antiques* since its inception in 1922. Through the years the magazine has enabled collectors to keep up with the latest news on discoveries of rarities as well as the newest research on significant glasshouses. Reading through the roster of authors reveals a surprising number of pioneer connoisseurs and researchers who made original contributions in *Antiques*. Gregor Norman Wilcox, Harry Hall White, Lura Woodside Watkins and, most important of all to American glass collectors, George McKearin and his daughter Helen, all introduced new ideas in *Antiques*. While some developed their thoughts more fully in books, others were satisfied with what appeared in the magazine, and went on to pursue other interests. Whatever their approach, the articles they contributed offer both solid facts and some of the more intangible feelings that must be learned by collectors serious in their pursuit of American glass.

This group of articles is an ideal primer for the aspiring collector because it reflects the thinking, along with all the possible doubting, that is crucial for the connoisseur. The articles fall into the two categories essential to the collector. On the one hand, they offer the body of facts that determines the activities of key glasshouses. On the other hand, they reveal the kind of glass Americans made, and illustrate the broad range of forms that was produced.

Interestingly enough, if one were to complain about something that *Antiques* has missed, it would be new information on the glasshouses operated by the legendary Henry William Stiegel. Since Frederick Hunter's book on Stiegel appeared in 1914, there has been very little serious work on the first of the colonial glassmakers to attract collectors. Illustrations of examples in private collections, however, have pointed the way to the ever-narrowing group of objects the connoisseurs feel safe in attributing to Stiegel. Another subject not covered in this collection is the production of America's earliest glasshouses. While any number of researchers have found records of glass-making activity in the seventeenth century, there are no glass examples that early which can be proven to be American, so there have been no articles covering the earliest efforts.

American blown glass is a field that scares too many potential collectors who worry because it is so easily copied that it is difficult to distinguish old glass from new. They forget that, although glass does not show age and it is possible to reproduce a lot of forms with ease, the metal used in the early glass is distinctive. Anyone willing to look at the fine pieces that are illustrated through the years in *Antiques* will see the more important forms and learn to distinguish the typical metals. Mexican and Bohemian reproductions are made of a metal that has impurities added artificially, and their regularity makes that clear to the educated eye. Many of the most questionable examples are suspiciously plain and unimpressive and a view of those safely attributed will help the collector to see what he should seek.

The history of American glass scholarship has been short. The 1920s saw key efforts to establish the dates and locations of active makers of blown glass. It was not until then that enthusiasts began to realize that some of the most fascinating examples of blown glass were nineteenth rather than eighteenth-century products. At the beginning of the century, any wonderful example of green glass from a New Jersey source was thought to have been produced at the glasshouse Caspar Wistar founded before 1740. Then George McKearin pointed out that early American glass included types that were made as late as 1900. Now it is known and accepted as fact that fairly simple techniques were used for glassmaking by a few craftsmen all through the nineteenth century. As in the case of American folk sculpture, prime examples of fairly recent origin are now prized.

Establishing the broad range of time that blown glass was important has been one function of the *Antiques* articles. Basic research has uncovered the fact that the bottle and glass manufactories spotted over the country were responsible for a repertory of blown glass objects made by techniques well-known to craftsmen of the eighteenth century and earlier. Whether bowls and pitchers, vases and plates, were end-of-the-day whimsies or a profitable side-line for a local market is open to question. That the objects were an activity of men who were busily mass-producing utilitarian glass, primarily window glass and bottles, is now an accepted fact. The more colorful bottles, the flasks with commemorative illustrations in relief, are an area for collectors that has attracted many who also like the more simple blown glass. Here, again, reproductions have caused confusion. In the 1920s, when the bottles first became expensive collectibles, fakes were made. Now careful looking is needed to avoid mistaking recent for old.

American blown glass is a broad field. To begin with, it includes a wide array of fairly primitive pieces but it also includes the more sophisticated work that was made to be used in elegant interiors. Collectors have to decide what appeals and the direction they prefer.

Using bottle or window glass for bowls and the other more decorative objects is an approach that some Americans took from the earliest days of documented glassmaking until the very end of the nineteenth century. These efforts are characterized by ornament made of applied gathers of molten glass tooled into a pattern before cooling. These motifs are frequently called "lily pad" and the effect is related to that achieved in German and Northern European glasshouses in the seventeenth and eighteenth centuries. The origins of the technique must have been continental, but Americans developed a particular manner and design when they tooled gathers of glass.

Birds and more abstract finials tooled into shape on clear colorless glass are another aspect of work in the German tradition. The glass metal is as fine and colorless as any made in the Old World for fine table wares. The decoration, on the other hand, has the roughness associated with work in the early German tradition of greenish "field" glass.

Overall diamond patterns on colored or clear glass made with a part-size mold have been traced to English sources. Stiegel was the first American to use such molds. He probably learned the technique when he visited Bristol, England, where it was popular. The men he trained may have spread the method, but it would have been as easy for emigrating English craftsmen to have brought the techniques with them. However it happened to spread, this English approach was used for making glass in many parts of the country after the Revolution.

Green and brown bottle glass has been used for more decorative pieces in New York and New England. Some of the activity was early, but glasshouses documented in the nineteenth century were producing flasks molded in part-size molds as well as other obviously later wares. These centers are often best understood after studying the research published in *Antiques*.

After Stiegel and Wistar, the third most important name in American glass is J. F. Amelung. The New Bremen Glassmanufactory he founded in the vicinity of Frederick, Maryland, was the first ambitious undertaking after the Revolution. Evidence from the excavations, as well as examples found in the area, reveal how this glasshouse assimilated English and German elements into a distinctively American output. The tooled decoration, engraved ornament and molded forms were used in new designs. Later, other Maryland and Pennsylvania glasshouses made similar pieces.

The use of colorless glass was a part of the American tradition that is seen at its best in work from Pittsburgh and Massachusetts. In the early nineteenth century both centers produced fine glasswares. Many of their craftsmen were from England and Ireland and worked in the English tradition making extravagant blown pieces with some tooled decoration, but cutting was an important decorating technique.

Glass blown into a full-size mold, the type called blown-three-mold, was made just about everywhere there were glasshouses in the 1820s and up to about 1850. Although not unknown in the Old World, this technique was particularly popular in the United States. It is interesting to see how it varied regionally and to see how its origins can be traced to both cut glass and ancient Roman models. While the research is fascinating, even more important are the examples that are shown. They make it clear that designers of the molds were very much aware of historic inspiration, but followed an esthetic that was special. The appeal of blown-three-mold glass is based on its superficial crudeness, the curious roughness that makes it apparent that blown-three-mold is a type of blown glass.

Whatever one's interests in glass are, developing an appreciation takes studying the facts and examples. The articles that follow offer the reader the opportunity to acquire the insights required to get the most out of American glass.

Marvin D. Schwartz

AMERICAN GLASS

An important acquisition

by the

Corning Museum of Glass

BY HELEN McKEARIN

RECENTLY THE CORNING MUSEUM OF GLASS acquired a significant cross-section of the George S. McKearin collection of American glass. This event is one impossible for me to consider dispassionately or impersonally: the collection and the museum are both too tightly woven into the fabric of my own studies, knowledge, and appreciation of glass. The truism that comparison is essential to knowledge has been made more viable for me by each: by my father's collection in the area of American glass; by the museum in the wide range of glass through the ages. The museum has brought together glass from all ages and countries of its origins and has presented, as has no other institution, its consecutive history. Thus it has re-emphasized for me the fact that American glass cannot be *known* by glass made in the United States only, and that more than a speaking acquaintance with its predecessors and contemporaries is requisite.

In the museum's plan for developing its library devoted to glass in all its aspects and for assembling its collections of glass the role of comparison was a primary consideration. Its importance became even more apparent as I catalogued the initial collections of glass in 1950-1951, using data supplied by students in the fields of foreign and ancient glass and to be found in the library, even then probably the most comprehensive in existence. Though the museum opened with limited collections, that is, limited in relation to the possible representation, it contained examples of the principal chronological, geographical, and technological categories through the ages from 1800 B.C. to the mid-twentieth century. These, in conjunction with the library's well-illustrated literature on the subject, were the foundation of a structure for comparative and specialized glass studies. That structure has been rising steadily. During a brief existence of five years library and collections have been expanded considerably, and new acquisitions of glass, mainly in the foreign and the ancient groups, have heightened the quality of the already exciting exhibits.

Now, on the museum's fifth anniversary, the American collection, which from the inception has formed the largest national group, is enriched by two hundred and fifty-five outstanding and carefully selected examples from the McKearin collection. All but a few of these pieces were among those chosen by my father and me to illustrate our book *Two Hundred Years of American Blown Glass*. That, within their categories, so very many of the pieces were, in our experience, unique in one feature or more of form or decoration, in hue of color or color itself, was in most instances fortuitous rather than designed. Our final choice was not governed by the rarity which was a quality of nearly every piece but by a plan for those visual and verbal comparisons and contrasts which are the cement binding our bits of knowledge into a coherent whole. Today at the Corning Museum of Glass, most of these pieces may be studied and seen in the *glass*. With the new acquisition—to my mind one of impressive quality—American glass in all its variety is represented by more than seventeen hundred examples. But more: to student and curious visitor, Corning offers the most comprehensive collection of American blown glass now available in any museum.

DISTINCTIVELY AMERICAN PATTERN-MOLDED GLASS

The purple salt, one of two recorded in the color, was blown in the German checkered-diamond pattern presumably used by Amelung at New Bremen, 1785-1795, and later in the Midwest where several Amelung blowers practiced their art. The eighteenth-century shape is more slenderly proportioned than known European prototypes. The extremely rare swirl-ribbed salt shows an early ninetenth-century Midwest version of the double-ogee form. The unique yellowish-green bowl (Mantua, Ohio, 1822-1829) illustrates the survival of eighteenth-century forms in the repertory of some blowers in midwestern bottle- and window-glass houses. The blue bowl, one of two in this form and color, is peculiarly Midwestern in its type of double-dome cover combined with nineteenth-century galleried rim, spherical body, and short-stemmed petaled foot.

1. Aquamarine free-blown plate with lily pad Type II, one of two recorded; individual piece fashioned from window or bottle glass at either the Redford or the Redwood Glass Works, northern New York, circa 1831-1850. Diameter 7½ inches.

2. New York State aquamarine free-blown sugar bowl, an article rarely decorated with lily pad; unique in combination of unusual features: lily pad Type II on bowl *and* cover; as knop stem, a hollow ball, containing 1829 silver half-dime; another, containing 1835 silver half-dime, on cover supporting chicken finial. Height over all, 11 inches.

3. Eighteenth-century free-blown bowl; only one recorded in clear olive-green lead glass with threaded rim and applied straight-sided table-ring, the last seemingly not used in the nineteenth century. Diameter 6⅝ inches.

4. Midwestern swirl jug, one of two recorded in "quart" size blown from brilliant light-amber bottle glass and pattern-molded in ribbing expanded and swirled to the left; short neck with flat rolled-over collar; applied handle with crimped end. Capacity 1 quart, 3 ounces. Height 6⅝₁₆ inches.

5. Dark olive-amber Pitkin bottle, pattern-molded in fine broken-swirl ribbing typical of flasks produced in late eighteenth- and early nineteenth-century eastern bottle houses; only recorded Pitkin bottle of taper shape, with narrow flattened shoulder, flaring neck, and sheared lip. Height 5 inches.

6. Deep amethyst eighteenth-century-type pocket bottle in the rare daisy-in-hexagon pattern, one of three pattern-molded designs believed to be Stiegel originals for, as yet, no *exact* counterpart has been identified in any foreign glass. Capacity 12 ounces. Height 4⅝ inches.

7. Amelung "Tobias and the Angel" tumbler, a gift to the wife of John Frederick Amelung of the New Bremen Glassmanufactory near Frederick, Maryland; inscription *"Happy is he who is blessed with Virtuous Children. Carolina Lucia Amelung, 1788"* arching over a handsome but somewhat overpowering frame for a vignette depicting Tobias and his guardian angel. In the interest of his design, the artist, like others before him, took liberties with the episode in the Book of Tobit: Tobias' little dog runs before instead of behind, and the fish whose gall was to cure Tobit's blindness is intact. Height over-all, 11⅞ inches.

8. The "Hornet and Peacock" decanter commemorating the fifteen-minute naval engagement in the War of 1812; made by Charles Ihmsen (glass manufacturer in Pittsburgh's Birmingham district) for his son-in-law, John Leaugeay, whose initials are engraved within leaf sprays; a rather rude engraving depicts the Yankee *Hornet* standing by the sinking English *Peacock* while two boats bring survivors to the victorious American ship; not only unique in decoration but the only recorded engraved glass of historical significance in that war period. Over 2 quart capacity.

9. Masonic flask (McK GIV-3, pint); light-amber lead glass with amethyst streaks; shaped and decorated in a full-size two-piece mold, at the Keene-Marlboro-Street Glass Works, New Hampshire, circa 1815-1820; obverse: Masonic emblems; reverse: United States coat of arms above oval frame enclosing *J.K.B;* as a flask from this particular mold, comparatively scarce; in coloring, extremely rare.

10. Blown-three-mold pitcher, only one recorded in wisteria-colored lead glass; patterned in the same quart-decanter mold as the decanter No. 11 and finished by blowing and manipulation; in pattern (McK III-5 with sunburst Motif I), obviously inspired by 1810-1830 cut glass as were so many of the geometric patterns which represent a probable American development in blown-molded glass since neither England nor Ireland seems anxious to acknowledge this adoption of the full-size piece mold for production of tablewares. Height 6⅝ inches.

11. Blown-three-mold quart decanter with stopper, the only footed red-amethyst decanter recorded from the GIII-5 mold attributed to the Boston and Sandwich Glass Works.

On the checkerboard of glass,

creations of blowers in our bottle- and window-glass houses—

free-blown individual pieces with and without applied ornamentation—

meet the challenge of their commercial counterparts,

blown and decorated to pattern by craftsmen

in the tableware manufactories.

1. South Jersey pitcher, olive-amber bottle glass with deeply imbedded opaque white looping and draggings, a technique from antiquity now believed not to have been practiced in the United States until about 1825. Height 6⅝ inches.

2. Colorless lead-glass pitcher, typically Midwestern in form, from the Pittsburgh area, circa 1815-1835; dip-molded sunken panels on body below an engraved leaf and flower circlet; on neck another circlet also characteristic of the region; hollow, blown handle. Height 5⅝ inches.

3. Bottle-glass candlesticks, rarities in glass of South Jersey type: *Center,* tall "black" glass, one of six blown about 1860 at the Westford Glass Works, Connecticut. Height 7⅛ inches. *Left,* red-amber, from one of the Stoddard, New Hampshire, bottle houses, 1842-1860, unique in form and color. Height 5 inches. *Right,* extremely rare "black" glass miniature, fashioned in one of the New York or Connecticut glasshouses, 1800-1850. Height 3½ inches.

4. *Right,* unique candlestick with composite knopped stem including a cylindrical column with crude dull and clear red twists; colorless non-lead glass; quite probably eighteenth-century American. Height 10 inches. *Left* Midwestern candlestick, brilliant colorless lead glass; bold air-twist in shaft, typical of the Pittsburgh area, probably fashioned before 1825. Height 9⅝ inches.

5. Handled vase with lily-pad Type II on body, threaded neck and rim; only lily-pad vase recorded in clear light-olive-toned amber bottle glass; fashioned in a New York State glasshouse, first half of the nineteenth century. Height 6¼ inches.

6. Blown-three-mold vase or celery glass, colorless lead glass, attributed to New England, circa 1820-1835; slender deep bowl of rare small size supported by applied flaring pedestal foot, molded for pattern and shaped by blowing and manipulation; the bowl's pattern GII-18 obtained in a decanter mold, and the foot's GII-21, in a tumbler mold. Height 6⅜ inches.

7. South Jersey handled free-blown lamp of brilliant aquamarine bottle glass, fitted with two-wick tin and cork whale-oil burner; attributed to the Isabella Glass Works about 1848-1850; unique in shape among the lamps which are rarities in the South Jersey tradition. Height 7⅛ inches.

8. Blown-three-mold colorless lead-glass lamp, the only recorded example having a globular font in geometric pattern GII-18, button-knop stem, and saucer base in GII-20; as a lighting device a rarity in blown-three-mold; attributed to the New England area, possibly from the New England Glass Works, circa 1820-1830. Height 5¼ inches.

9. Deep amber bottle-glass free-blown covered bowl; unique in form: small bowl with sides tapering from rounded bottom inward to deep galleried rim; cover, tall as bowl, with double-ogee sides, top sloping up gently to ball knob supporting chicken finial; attributed to Connecticut, circa 1810-1820. Height 7¾ inches.

10. Unique late eighteenth-century two-handled covered bowl of non-lead colorless glass; deep cup-bowl with shallowly engraved leaf sprays on sides, supported by short knop stem rising from sloping circular foot; nearly flat-topped set-in cover with unusually large "peacock" perched on ball knob; attributed to the Baltimore-Philadelphia area. Height over all, 7¹¹⁄₁₆ inches.

11

12

11. Tall wine goblet, free-blown from olive-amber bottle glass; one of few recorded stemmed drinking glasses in the South Jersey tradition, unique in conical bowl tapering sharply to stem of three knops graduated from large to small at center of heavy circular foot with wide under-folded rim; attributed to the Keene-Marlboro-Street Glass Works, circa 1816-1825. Height 7 5/16 inches.

12. Rare wine goblet blown from a heavy gather of non-lead glass of dark greenish cast; eighteenth-century "German" form having six small tears in the bowl's thick base, large hollow inverted baluster, and high domed foot; attributed to the New Bremen Glassmanufactory of John Frederick Amelung and Company, circa 1788. Height 8 inches.

13. New York State cruet or decanter-jug, free-blown from aquamarine bottle or window glass probably in the mid-nineteenth century; form unique among individual pieces; pear-shape with wide-spaced spiral thread on upper part, wide high slightly flaring rim with pouring lip, broad tapering three-rib strap handle. Height 8¼ inches.

14. Extremely rare cruet and stopper blown from purplish amethyst non-lead glass; ovoid body, pattern-molded in wide-spaced vertical ribs tapering into cylindrical neck with narrow flange and high arched lip; hollow handle; from Pittsburgh area, circa 1820-1850. Height over all, 9¼ inches.

13

14

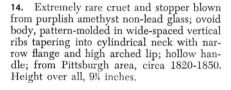

15

16

15. Unique oval bowl on standard, attributed to South Jersey, first half of the nineteenth century; free blown from clear deep olive-green glass; bowl ornamented only by single heavy thread below slightly flaring rim, resting on appropriately heavy merese (the "button" between bowl and stem); turned stem rising from narrow step on flat circular foot. Height about 9½ inches.

16. Unique blown-three-mold colorless lead-glass bowl on standard composed of short stem with large flattened globular knop and sloping circular foot; bowl patterned in Boston and Sandwich decanter mold in GIII-5, expanded and shaped by manipulation, applied rim of deep sapphire-blue; circa 1825-1835. Height 6 7/16 inches.

Motifs and patterns are referred to by the system used in American Glass, *the monumental work by Miss McKearin and her father, George S. McKearin. All illustrations, including the color plates, are by courtesy of the Corning Museum of Glass.*

FOLK ART IN AMERICAN GLASS

Five unique examples of individual rendering and interpretation within the framework of centuries—old traditions of glassblowing and ornamentation by glass applied to itself and tooled. They illustrate several decorative devices in the South Jersey tradition: the crimped foot and lily pad Type I on the South Jersey creamers, the larger (height about 3½ inches) being the only example with a double band of lily pad; lily pad Type II, on the New York State witch ball; a picot-edged wavy band (extremely rare form), on the New York State footed deep bowl; leaf prunts, on the South Jersey mug. All are of the first half of the nineteenth century.

The Melvin Billups glass collection

BY PAUL N. PERROT, *Director, Corning Museum of Glass*

DURING THE LAST FEW DECADES there has been a major redistribution of the world's glass heritage. Most of the great private collections which had been formed in the late nineteenth and early twentieth centuries have been either transferred to public ownership or dispersed at auction. Since the second World War the major public collections, whose growth had been stunted during the conflict, have been attempting to fill gaps in their holdings, while new specialized institutions have been formed, such as the Musée du Verre, Liège, the Corning Museum of Glass in Corning, New York, the Haaretz Museum in Tel Aviv, and the Pilkington Museum in St. Helens, England. In addition, new private collections have arisen, some with fanfare and others discreetly, taking advantage of the opportunities created by a general resurgence of interest. Hence it can be said that there is more concern about the history of glass at present than ever before: this is evidenced by a tremendous increase in the number of publications devoted to glass and by an attendant almost staggering increase in the value of glass objects.

Among the new collectors Melvin P. Billups has been one of the most active and also most retiring. His period of acquisition extended roughly from 1950 to 1960. As opportunities arose, with an unerring eye he seized them and, heeding the advice of those who had specialized in the more complex aspects of glass history, he gradually developed a very comprehensive collection. It presents a panorama of the history of glass extending from the eighteenth dynasty in Egypt to the late nineteenth century in America.

Obviously, this survey cannot do justice to Mr. Billups' collection. It does, however, convey something of its richness, of Mr. Billups' critical eye, and of his modesty in seeking to represent objectively the full sweep of glass history rather than only spectacular achievements. It is the collection of a gentleman who has attended to its growth with loving care; who consistently has shied away from any form of publicity; and who, mindful of the public trust which in a sense any important private collection represents, has selected the Isaac Delgado Museum of Art in New Orleans as its eventual final repository.

No collector, however impartially he may act, can help but introduce within his collection personal preferences,

Attributed to the glassworks of Henry William Stiegel, Manheim, Pennsylvania, c. 1765-1774. *Left to right:* bottle in amethyst glass blown in a 5-diamond-daisy mold; height 5 inches; ex coll. *George S. McKearin.* Covered sugar bowl, lid and bowl blown in an 11-diamond mold; height 6½ inches. Emerald green footed bowl, blown in a 15-diamond mold; height 4¾ inches. Opalescent creamer blown in a 19-diamond mold; height 4 inches; ex coll. *Charles C. Woolfe, George S. McKearin. All illustrations are from the collection of Melvin P. Billups; photographs by Raymond F. Errett.*

Attributed to John Frederick Amelung's glass manufactory at New Bremen, Maryland (1784-1795), on the basis of the quality of the glass and analogy with the checkered-diamond fragments found on and around the glasshouse site. Clear flask blown in a 7-checkered-diamond mold; height 5 inches. Green flask blown in an 8-checkered-diamond mold; height 6¾ inches. Deep blue salt, with tooled foot, blown in a 7-checkered-diamond mold; height 2⅞ inches. Goblet of clear grayish glass (originally with cover) engraved with floral ornaments surrounding the initials *C. G. C.*; probably after 1788; height 8¼ inches.

South Jersey type. Sugar bowl of clear glass with greenish tinge, lily-pad decoration on bowl and cover and chicken finial; height 5¼ inches; possibly southern New Jersey, probably second quarter nineteenth century. Green lily-pad pitcher; height 5⅝ inches; probably from a New York State glasshouse, second quarter nineteenth century. Basket of clear glass with greenish tinge, with chicken on top of handle; height 5½ inches; attributed to southern New Jersey, first half nineteenth century. Olive green bowl with lily-pad decoration; possibly New Hampshire, second quarter nineteenth century; height 3⅝ inches.

and one of the strongest aspects of the Billups collection is its large group of American glasses. It includes some of the rarities in Stiegel-type glass, several glasses by John Frederick Amelung, and an impressive cross section of the South Jersey tradition in New York State. In addition it is particularly rich in Midwestern and blown-three-mold glass. Mechanically pressed glasses, though represented, particularly by cup plates, do not match the other categories in rarity and impressiveness, for it is

the manipulative aspects of glassmaking rather than its industrial development that appeal to Mr. Billups.

One hundred pieces from the Billups collection were shown in the exhibition *A Decade of Glass Collecting*, held at the Corning Museum of Glass in 1962 and published in a catalogue of the same title. The collection has not been otherwise publicly presented as an entity until now. A second article will show examples of the Continental glass.

South Jersey type. Creamer and sugar bowl with ball stopper in two shades of pale green; height 4⅝ inches, 6⅜ inches (with cover); New York, Saratoga Glass Works, c. 1844-1860; ex coll. *Dr. Kline*. Candlestick in aquamarine glass; height 9⅛ inches; attributed to southern New Jersey, purchased from a direct descendant of Jonathan Haines, who founded the Waterford Glass Works at Waterford, New Jersey; possibly made at that factory between 1824 and 1828.

South Jersey type. Baptismal cup of aquamarine glass with four handles; height 3⅞ inches; southern New Jersey or New York State, second quarter nineteenth century. Mug of yellowish green glass with threading and strap handle; height 6⅛ inches; southern New Jersey, possibly late eighteenth century — probably early nineteenth century. Candlestick of green glass with heavy swirled ribbing at base of socket; height 8¼ inches; southern New Jersey, first half nineteenth century. Creamer of aquamarine glass with handle at right angle to the spout; height 3¾ inches; southern New Jersey, second quarter nineteenth century.

Attributed to Pittsburgh. Footed cup with conical body of blue, slightly grayish glass; height 5⅝ inches; probably Pittsburgh, first half nineteenth century. Sugar bowl of amethyst glass, the bowl and cover patterned in a 12-rib mold; height 6⅜ inches; Pittsburgh, second quarter nineteenth century; ex coll. *Mrs. Frederick S. Fish, George S. McKearin*. Mug of deep blue glass with spout and strap handle; 5¾ inches; probably Pittsburgh, first half nineteenth century. Footed bowl with eight pillar-molded ribs in amethyst glass; height 3¾ inches; Pittsburgh, first half nineteenth century; ex coll. *Walter P. Chrysler*.

Midwestern glass. Baptismal font of deep blue glass with pincered trailing on stem; height 6 inches; Pittsburgh area, first half nineteenth century; ex coll. *Mrs. Henry Ford Sr*. Deep amber sugar bowl patterned in a 24-rib mold with cover blown in a 10-diamond mold; height 6¾ inches; probably Zanesville, Ohio, Glass Works, c. 1815-1830. Vase of pale blue glass patterned in a 16-rib mold with applied pincered decoration on handles and body; height 6¼ inches; probably Zanesville Glass Works, c. 1815-1830; ex coll. *Al Flesh*. Inkwell patterned in a 19-rib mold; height 2 inches; Midwestern, possibly Kent, Ohio, second quarter nineteenth century.

Pattern-molded glass. Sugar bowl of amethyst glass patterned in a 20-rib mold with plain cover and twisted finial patterned in an 18-rib mold; height 6½ inches; Midwestern, probably Pittsburgh, first quarter nineteenth century. Light green sugar bowl, the cover plain, the body patterned in an 18-rib mold; height 7½ inches; attributed to New Geneva Glass Works of Albert Gallatin, c. 1797-1807. Pale blue flask double patterned in a 16-rib mold; height 6½ inches; Midwestern, second quarter nineteenth century. Light green pitcher double patterned in a 24-rib mold; height 3⅝ inches; probably Zanesville Glass Works, c. 1815-1830. Deep yellow green cup with handle double patterned in a 24-rib mold; height 3 inches; probably Zanesville Glass Works. c. 1815-1830.

Historical flasks. Green concentric eagle flask in McKearin pattern GII-76; height 7⅝; Keene, New Hampshire, Marlboro Street Glass Works, 1815-1824. Amethyst Washington-Taylor flask in pattern GI-37; height 8¼ inches; Philadelphia, Dyottville Glass Works, c. 1847-1848. Violin flask of amethyst glass is pattern GIX-43, marked J. R. & SON; height 7 13/16; Pittsburgh, John Robinson and Son, c. 1823-1845; ex coll. *Dan C. Meek.*

Blown-three-mold glass. Light green decanter in pattern GII-6; height 7¾ inches; Kent, Ohio, glasshouse of Parks, Edmunds and Parks, c. 1824-1833. Green pitcher in pattern GII-33; only five pieces in this pattern are known; height 5¾ inches; Mantua, Ohio, 1821-1829. Deep blue creamer in pattern GIII-24; height 4 inches; probably Boston & Sandwich Glass Company, c. 1825-1835. Bottle of clear glass with light bluish tint, patterned in a hat mold, GIII-23; height 3⅞ inches; probably Boston & Sandwich Glass Company, c. 1825-1835; ex coll. *George S. McKearin.*

Blown - three - mold glass. Clear celery vase in pattern GII-18; height 8½ inches; New England area, 1825-1835; ex coll. *William W. Wood III, W. M. Van Winkle.* Amethyst sugar bowl in pattern GII-32, the cover patterned in a 16-rib mold; height 6 inches; Midwestern, c. 1825-1835, ex coll. *Neil C. Gest.* Olive green bowl in pattern GII-6; height 3¼ inches; probably Kent, Ohio, glasshouse of Parks, Edmund and Parks, 1824-1833; ex coll. *George S. McKearin.* Brilliant green sugar bowl in pattern GIII-16, the cover plain; height 5½ inches; Keene, New Hampshire, Marlboro Street Glass Works, c. 1815-1835.

Blown - three - mold glass. Clear flask in pattern GIII-23; height 5 inches; probably Boston & Sandwich Glass Company; c. 1825-1835. Light blue witch ball in pattern GIII-16; diameter 5¼ inches; Keene, New Hampshire, Marlboro Street Glass Works, c. 1815-1835. Sugar bowl and cover of wisteria glass, the bowl in pattern GIII-5, cover GIII-6; height 7 inches; probably Boston & Sandwich Glass Company, 1825-1835; ex coll. *George S. McKearin.* Blue flask in pattern GII-24; height 4¾ inches; New England area, c. 1825-1835; ex coll. *W. M. Van Winkle, William W. Wood III, Hiram Norcross, Richard Loeb, George S. McKearin.* Amethyst salt with galleried rim in pattern GII-18; height 2½ inches; New England area, probably Boston & Sandwich Glass Company, c. 1825-1835. Canary yellow miniature decanter in pattern GIII-12; height 2¾ inches; Boston & Sandwich Glass Company, c. 1825-1835.

American blown glass in the Seigfred collection

BY JAMES ROSE

IT IS IMPOSSIBLE to do justice in a short article to the large and comprehensive collection of American glass formed by Ellen and Earl Seigfred. I have dodged the issue here by concentrating on its blown glass with special attention to examples from the Midwest, in which it is particularly rich. Only cursory coverage is given to its admirable specimens from other areas and none to its historical flasks, cup plates, salts, or lacy, pattern, and art glass.

Dean Seigfred, who is dean emeritus of the College of Fine Arts of Ohio University, has asked me to discuss the glass and not its owners, but I cannot resist expressing my astonishment that so impressive a group could have been assembled in so short a time. While the Seigfreds began collecting many years ago, they confined their early efforts to pattern glass, and they bought their first piece of blown glass only eight years ago. Their success, which is not much more than hinted at here, is a tribute to their perseverance, dedication, and, above all, perception and good judgment.

Inevitably, most of the objects illustrated here are well-known forms: standard rarities that need no comment beyond the statistical data given in the captions. A few pieces demand more extensive consideration either because they are unpublished or, in two cases (Figures 4c and 7a), because they are unusual examples of what superficially appear to be common forms whose inclusion in a group of rarities needs explanation.

First is the charming inkwell, Figure 3b. To my knowledge, its form is unique. Its metal strongly resembles that of Redwood and Redford, and, although I would not want to go on record as to a specific source, there is no doubt in my mind that it was made in New York State.

Second is the globular bottle, Figure 4c. Many similar bottles have turned up in Ohio, but few of them are of such exceptional form and grace. The present-day collector often tends to overvalue color and, indeed, the Seigfreds have many similar bottles in varying shades of amber and citron which, in the market place, would prove more valuable than the bluish-green one shown. The emphasis here is on the classic shape.

Third is the extremely rare mug, Figure 6b. But one other, and that imperfect, is known. The use of a hinged mold to form the diagonal ribbing (the mold seam can be seen plainly in the illustration, angling its way from southwest to northeast) is a recent, and surprising, discovery. In the simpler, diagonally ribbed design from the same hinged mold but without the embellishment of vertical ribbing, several pieces exist: a couple of chestnut flasks, a crimp-footed bowl, two creamers, and a pitcher. On the basis of a few find-spots, not the best of evidence, the Pittsburgh area seems a more likely place of origin than Zanesville.

The next rarity is Figure 7a. Club-shape bottles are not normally ranked very high in collectors' minds, but here we have one with thirty-two ribs *and* a terminal ring. So far as I know, it is the only such specimen extant. If others exist, I should be glad to hear of them.

The tiny amethyst cruet, Figure 7c, seems to be unique in color if not in form. It was blown in a sixteen-rib mold, as were a few (very few) similarly small, presumably Mantua cruets. These, however, are in light green or yellow-green. Mantua is known to have made amethyst glass and, while the shade encountered here is not precisely the cloudy color so typical of that factory, it is close to it. I have not seen this curious collar sag on any other piece, but I have little doubt as to its origin.

The last of the unpublished rarities is the little dark olive-amber pan, Figure 9c. Its dimensions are the same, and it is very likely the one mentioned by the McKearins in *American Glass* (chart, p. 304), where it is described as "the only one known." To my knowledge, it has not been illustrated before; it certainly merits that tribute.

Fig. 1. *(left to right)*

a. Footed salt of grayish-blue glass in checkered-diamond pattern, height 2⅞ inches; traditionally attributed to Amelung's Maryland glass factory, 1784-1794.

b. Bottle of amethyst glass in a pattern of diamonds over vertical ribbing, height 5½ inches; probably made at Stiegel's glassworks in Pennsylvania, third quarter eighteenth century. *Ex colls.* George S. McKearin, Richard S. Aldrich.

c. Covered mug of clear glass, copper-wheel engraved with a griffin and tulip within a medallion; height over all, 11¾ inches. Possibly Stiegel, probably third quarter eighteenth century. *Ex coll.* Helen Hammond Adams.

d. Bottle of amethyst glass in diamond-daisy design, height 4¾ inches; probably Stiegel, third quarter eighteenth century.

e. Covered sugar bowl of deep blue glass, both bowl and cover in an expanded diamond pattern; swirled finial; height over all, 5½ inches. Stiegel type and probably Stiegel, third quarter eighteenth century.

Fig. 2.

a. Jug in aquamarine glass with applied handle and crimped foot, height 7¼ inches; probably South Jersey, 1825-1835.

b. Bowl and pitcher of clear glass with opaque white loopings; height of pitcher 7 inches, diameter of bowl 8½; probably South Jersey, probably mid-nineteenth century.

c. Gemel bottle of green glass of sage tone with applied quilling on its vertical seams and with a crimped foot, height 7½ inches; probably South Jersey, possibly the Ohio River area where a few similar bottles were made; 1825-1835.

d. Pitcher in a medium green glass of gray tone with applied handle and crimped foot, height 6¼ inches; probably South Jersey, 1825-1835.

Fig. 3.

a. Lily-pad (Type II) pitcher of deep amber glass with applied handle and circular pad foot, height 5 11/16 inches. *Ex coll.* George S. McKearin, who attributed it to Ellenville, New York, c. 1836.

b. Inkwell in brilliant aquamarine glass with its original stopper, height 6 inches; probably New York State, second quarter nineteenth century.

c. Mug in dark olive-amber, or "black," glass with applied handle, height 5 inches; probably Saratoga, New York, mid-nineteenth century.

d. Lily-pad (Type III) pitcher with applied handle and applied foot, in light green glass, height 6 inches. *Ex coll.* George S. McKearin, who attributed it to Mallorytown, Ontario; c. 1830. Published: George S. and Helen McKearin, *American Glass*, Pl. 67, No. 8.

e. Vase in dark shaded amber, one of a pair, height 8 inches. *Ex coll.* George S. McKearin, who attributed it to Ellenville, New York. Published: McKearin, *op. cit.*, Pl. 65, No. 4 or 6.

Fig. 4.

a. Globular bottle in dark amber glass, melon fluted in a 24-rib mold, height 7 inches; probably Zanesville, Ohio, second quarter nineteenth century.

b. Pan of brilliant light green glass patterned in a 10-diamond mold and with infolded rim, height 1¾ inches, diameter 5½; probably Zanesville, second quarter nineteenth century. *Ex coll.* Miles A. Smith. Published: *Journal of Glass Studies*, Vol. II, p. 123.

c. Globular bottle in slightly cloudy bluish-green glass blown in a 24-rib mold and swirled to the left, height 7½ inches; probably Zanesville, second quarter nineteenth century.

d. Chestnut-shape flask of golden-amber glass patterned in a 10-diamond mold, height 5⅜ inches; probably Zanesville, second quarter nineteenth century.

All illustrations are from the collection of Dean and Mrs. Earl C. Seigfred; photographs by Keith Hackleman.

Fig. 5.

a. Jug in medium amber glass with applied 2-rib handle, height 5½ inches; probably Zanesville, second quarter nineteenth century.

b. Miniature globular bottle in aquamarine glass patterned in 24 ribs swirled slightly to the left, height 4¾ inches; probably Zanesville, second quarter nineteenth century.

c. Covered sugar bowl of medium amber glass, double-dome lid, cover and bowl each with 24 vertical ribs; height 7 inches over all; probably Zanesville, second quarter nineteenth century. *Ex coll.* Neil C. Gest.

d. Flip (a modern term for this large tumbler form) in light bluish-green glass, its 24 ribs tightly swirled to the right; height 5 11/16 inches; probably Zanesville, second quarter nineteenth century.

e. Urn-shape footed salt in dark amber glass, height 3½ inches; probably Zanesville, second quarter nineteenth century.

Fig. 6.

a. Chestnut-shape flask of medium darkish amber glass, its 24 ribs tightly swirled to the left; height 5⅜ inches; probably Zanesville, second quarter nineteenth century.

b. Mug of medium green glass, doubly patterned in the so-called broken-swirl design, the diagonal, but not the vertical, ribbing formed in a 24-rib hinged mold; applied hollow handle; height 4⅝ inches; possibly Zanesville, probably Pittsburgh, second quarter nineteenth century.

c. Grandfather flask of reddish amber glass in a 24-rib broken-swirl pattern, height 8¾ inches; probably Zanesville, second quarter nineteenth century.

d. Grandmother flask of deep golden amber glass with 24 vertical ribs, height 7 inches; probably Zanesville, second quarter nineteenth century. *Ex coll.* L. Earl Dambach.

Fig. 7.

a. Club-shape bottle of aquamarine glass patterned in a 32-rib mold and swirled to the right; terminal ring; height 8½ inches; probably Mantua, Ohio, 1821-1829.

b. Bowl of light green glass with a slightly yellowish tinge, patterned in a 15-diamond mold; height 1¾ inches, diameter 5¼ inches; probably Mantua, 1821-1829.

c. Cruet bottle of amethyst glass patterned in a 16-rib mold and swirled to the left, height 5½ inches; probably Mantua, 1821-1829.

d. Blown-three-mold decanter of light bluish-green glass in the McKearins' GII-6 pattern, with its original "lollypop" stopper; height 9 inches over all; probably Kent, Ohio, 1823-1834.

e. Covered sugar bowl of amber glass, rather dark in hue, and with 16 vertical ribs on the bowl; unpatterned flanged lid; height 5 inches over all; probably Mantua, 1821-1829. *Ex coll.* George S. McKearin.

Fig. 8.

a. Celery vase of clear glass with engraved festoon decoration above molded diapering instead of the usual gadrooning, height 8¼ inches; probably Pittsburgh area, early nineteenth century. Published: *Journal of Glass Studies*, Vol. VII, p. 133.

b. Covered sugar bowl of clear glass tinted amethyst in the heavier portions, with galleried rim and both bowl and lid patterned in a 15-rib mold; height 8 inches over all; probably Pittsburgh area, early nineteenth century. *Ex coll.* George S. McKearin. Published: McKearin, *op. cit.* Pl. 82, No. 4.

c Pillar-molded decanter of brilliant clear glass with eight blue ribs, height 12½ inches; probably Pittsburgh area, mid-nineteenth century.

d. Goblet of heavy, slightly smoky clear glass with a solid stem, its bowl engraved with the American eagle and 13 stars within a wreath; height 5½ inches; probably Pittsburgh area, early nineteenth century. A closely similar goblet in light green glass is in the collection of Melvin P. Billups.

e. Covered sugar bowl in clear glass, on a knopped stem and with a galleried rim, engraved with a cherry-and-leaf design; height 8 inches; probably Pittsburgh area, second quarter nineteenth century.

Fig. 9.

Blown-three-mold glass. a. Small tumbler of aquamarine glass blown in the inkwell mold GII-15 pattern, height 2⅝ inches; probably New England, second quarter nineteenth century.

b. Covered sugar bowl in clear glass, with galleried rim in pattern GII-18; height 6 inches over all; probably Sandwich, Massachusetts, 1820-1840.

c. Shallow pan of olive-amber glass blown in an inkwell mold, GIII-29, for pattern; height 1⅛ inches, diameter 3¾ inches; probably Keene, 1820-1840.

d. Creamer of deep blue glass patterned in a GIII-26 mold and with applied handle, height 4 13/16 inches; probably Sandwich, 1820-1840.

e. Chestnut flask of clear glass probably patterned in a half-pint decanter mold, pattern GIII-24; height 5½ inches; probably New England area, 1820-1840.

Fig. 10.

a. Creamer in a soft gray-blue glass with streaks of smoky amber, blown-three-mold pattern GI-29; height 4¼ inches; probably Sandwich, second quarter nineteenth century. *Ex coll.* George S. McKearin.

b. Flip glass in blown-three-mold pattern GII-18, height 5¾ inches; probably Sandwich, second quarter nineteenth century.

c. Vase of amethyst glass with twelve sunken panels; the so-called Stiegel type but possibly made at Sandwich, second quarter nineteenth century; height 7 13/16 inches.

d. Pint decanter in the blown-three-mold shell pattern, GV-8; height over all, 9½ inches; probably Sandwich, second quarter nineteenth century. *Ex coll.* George S. McKearin.

FIG. 1 — Amethyst, deep shade. Folded rim. 12 panels, rounded top, 4 ¾ in. Very pronounced ribs on sides and base. Deeply indented base. *Height*, 7 ¾ in. *Diameter of rim*, 5 ⅜ in. *Greatest diameter of body*, 4 ¹¹⁄₁₆ in. *Diameter of base*, 3 ½ in. FIG. 2 — Blue. Long panels, pointed at top. No available record of dimensions and other details. Figures 1 and 2 were found near Dundee, New York. FIG. 3 — Amethyst, much lighter in shade than Figure 1. 12 panels, pointed at top, 5 ½ in. Ribs blend into surface and are faint on base, which is not deeply indented. *Height*, 8 ¾ in. *Diameter of rim*, 4 ¹¹⁄₁₆ in. *Diameter of body*, 4 ¾ in. *Diameter of base*, 3 ⅝ in. FIG. 4 —

Deep cobalt blue. 12 panels, rounded at top, 4 ¾ in. Ribs fairly pronounced on sides, faint on base, which is slightly indented. Rim shallower than on preceding examples. *Height*, 8 ½ in. *Diameter of rim*, 5 ¹⁄₁₆ in. *Greatest diameter of body*, 5 in. *Diameter of base*, 3 ⅛ in. Purchased several years ago near Poughkeepsie, New York, for $5. FIG. 5 — Deep cobalt blue. 13 panels. *Height*, 7.43 in. *Diameter of rim*, 5.60 in. *Greatest diameter of body*, 5.90 in. *Collection of W. T. H. Howe.* FIG. 6 — Clear glass. 12 panels. *Height*, 8 ½ in. *Diameter of rim*, 5 in. *Diameter of base*, 3 ⅜ in. *Formerly in the Maclay collection*

A STUDY OF PANELED VASES

By GEORGE S. McKEARIN

Illustrations, except as noted, from the McKearin collection

I FEEL fairly free from risk of contradiction when I say the most romantic figure in the realm of early American glass is Henry William Stiegel — known as "Baron" Stiegel. The pinnacle he occupies in the history of glassmaking in America is due not only to the beauty of color, form, and decorative technique of the glass accredited to his glasshouse in Manheim, Pennsylvania, but also to the glamour and sweep of his achievements as a glassmaker in the struggling colonies of the new world, and to the poignancy of the final frustration of his ambition and his death in poverty and obscurity.

There were other romantic figures — probably many — in the development of glassmaking in America, but to no other was accorded the privilege of having such a biographer. I refer to the author of the book *Stiegel Glass*, published in 1915, an outstanding achievement in American biography. It is credited to Frederick William Hunter. The belief that the text was actually written by the late John B. Kerfoot is substantiated by comparison with Kerfoot's *American Pewter* and his earlier writings when literary editor of the original magazine *Life*.

As a beginner in collecting American glass, I pored for hours over the pages of this fascinating book. I once asked John Kerfoot if he and Mr. Hunter, in gathering material for the book and the glass illustrated in it, had any definite or incontrovertible evidence that any of the specimens illustrated were unquestionably Stiegel. He answered, "None." While wider knowledge and more intensive study in the field of American glass during the past twenty-five years have convinced us that many of the pieces illustrated in *Stiegel Glass* could not possibly have been produced in Stiegel's glasshouse, and that many others are identical with and indistinguishable from contemporaneous English and Continental glass, there are specimens shown that we feel can be definitely attributed to Stiegel.

In the early days of my collecting, it was the height of my ambition to own a Stiegel blue paneled vase like that illustrated as the frontispiece in Hunter's book. As I grew in stature as a collector, many paneled vases came to my attention. In color they were not confined to the deep, almost cobalt blue, of the Hunter vase, but appeared in other shades of blue, amethyst, emerald green, and clear glass. They showed variations in the shape of the body and in size, number, and details of the panels.

Long ago I reached the conclusion that a large percentage of these paneled vases were produced in the Sandwich glassworks. I have encountered several persons who seriously question the probability, even the possibility, that Stiegel ever made any of them. I recall one who stoutly maintained that they were purely Victorian. I have always accepted them as unquestionably American, because, as far as I can learn, they are virtually unknown in England or on the Continent, though similar paneled decoration is found on foreign pieces of other shapes. I have accepted the belief that Stiegel made such vases because available evidence seems definitely to support this conclusion. In the book *Stiegel Glass* occurs the statement, which Mr. Kerfoot personally confirmed to me, that he and Mr. Hunter found a fragment of one of these blue paneled vases when they made excavations on the site of Stiegel's second Manheim glassworks. Now, it is quite patent that the finding of one or a few fragments of a certain type of piece or pattern, in the course of excavations on a glasshouse site, cannot be accepted as conclusive evidence that similar pieces were a product of that particular glasshouse. However, other evidence must be considered in the case of this fragment which, by the way, can be seen in the collection of American glass in the Metropolitan Museum, and which appears to be identical in pattern with and similar in color to the Hunter vase.

To begin with, in contemporary newspapers, mostly of Philadelphia, appear advertisements, either Stiegel's own or those of his agents, listing various types of glassware he was making. Many terms, to us strange and unfamiliar, are used. Blue and plain flower pots are mentioned, possibly referring to flower vases. In the Manheim glassworks account books, in possession of the Historical Society of Pennsylvania, are shown a list for the year 1769 and another covering the period from January 1 to April 1, 1770, of glassware on hand at the Manheim glass store, out on consignment, or sold since the beginning of 1767. Some of the figures are in Stiegel's own handwriting. The list mentions blue flower jars. We cannot, I grant, be positive that *blue flower jar* or *flower pot* refers to the blue paneled vase, but it is a fair supposition, in view of other evidence. Let us summarize the evidence in support of the attribution.

First, Stiegel listed blue flower jars. *Second*, Hunter and Kerfoot excavated the fragments of a blue paneled vase on the site of the Manheim glasshouse. The depth at which it was found precludes the possibility of its being from some later source. *Third*, these paneled vases are unknown abroad. *Fourth*, there were no other glasshouses operating in America at the time, 1769-1774, or prior thereto, where it is at all likely that such vases were made.

[Stiegel had in all three glasshouses. In the first, at Elizabeth Furnace, actual blowing began on September 18, 1763. At his second glasshouse — his first at Manheim — the glassmakers began to work in the afternoon of November 11, 1765. In April 1769, he started to construct his second — larger and more pretentious — Manheim glasshouse. Around this glasshouse largely centers the Stiegel tradition, and it was the one which finally broke him.]

Therefore, I believe we are safe in accepting Hunter's conclusion that Stiegel made such paneled vases. However, as previously stated, I have for many years felt very sure that a large percentage of the paneled vases which have turned up were made elsewhere, copied after the Stiegel prototype, and most of them probably at the Sandwich glassworks. Since 1920, which marks the beginning of a widespread and growing interest in American glass, a large number of these paneled vases have turned up -- far too many for them to have been an exclusive Stiegel product.

In color and certain characteristics of the metal, many of these vases in blue, amethyst, and green appear to be identical with pressed lamps, vases, and candlesticks, as well as certain types of blown glass, definitely known to be Sandwich products.

About seventy to eighty per cent of the paneled vases have been found in New England and New York State, in localities where for years we have been finding in generous quantities various types of glassware known to be Sandwich products.

In an issue of the *Columbia Centinel*, published in Boston, September 21, 1825, Deming Jarves announced that his flint glass manufacturing in Sandwich was in full operation and that he was ready to receive and execute orders for any articles in that line.

For many years I have owned a clear paneled vase, identical in pattern and shape of the body, with some of the "Stiegel" paneled vases, but with longer neck and having, instead of the usual rolled-over rim, a gauffered or scalloped rim characteristic of the 1860-1870 period. I have recently seen another of these vases. Both were found in the vicinity of

FIG. 7 — Dark emerald green. No record of dimensions and other details. Found in home near Hudson, New York, fitted with pewter collar which originally had four prisms (*Fig. 8*). Present ownership unknown. FIG. 8 — The vase of Figure 4, wearing the pewter collar originally found on Figure 7. The prisms are an addition. FIG. 9 — Light blue. 12 panels, 4 5⁄8 in. *Height, 7* 15⁄16 *in. Diameter of rim, 5 3⁄8 in. Greatest diameter of body, 4 7⁄8 in. Diameter of base, 3 3⁄4 in. Collection of Mrs. Mitchell Taradash*

FIG. 10 — Blue. 12 panels, slightly diagonal, quite probably twisted in manipulation. *Height 7.037 in. Diameter of rim, 5 1⁄2 in. Greatest diameter of body, 5 1⁄2 in. Collection of W. T. H. Howe.* FIG. 11 — Clear glass. Flaring, gauffered or scalloped rim; heavy, molded horizontal rib or collar at base of neck. 12 panels, 5 in. Ribs pronounced on sides and base, which is slightly indented. *Height, 9 5⁄16 in. Diameter of rim, 5 3⁄4 in. Greatest diameter of body, 5 1⁄4 in. Diameter of base, 3 1⁄4 in.* Characteristically Victorian, of about 1860-1870

FIG. 12 (*above, left*) — Clear glass. Bulbous body flaring outward at base; different in shape from typical paneled vases. 12 panels with rounded tops, 3 3⁄4 in. Broad cylindrical neck and rolled-over rim. Ribs quite pronounced on body and on base. *Height, 6 1⁄4 in. Diameter of rim, 5 3⁄16 in. Greatest diameter of body, 4 5⁄8 in.* The only specimen of this adaptation of the paneled vase encountered by the author. Found in home near Poughkeepsie, New York. FIG. 13 (*above, right*) — Miniature vase, one of a pair. Amethyst. 9 panels, 2 7⁄8 in. Panels of mate are approximately 3 5⁄8 in. high. Other dimensions of both vases the same. *Height, 6 1⁄2 in. Top diameter, about 3 1⁄2 in. Diameter of base, about 2 1⁄4 in. Privately owned*

FIG. 14 (*below, left*) — Unpaneled. Amethyst, shaded, light below; striations in glass. Body almost straight sided. *Height, 7 1⁄2 in. Diameter of rim, 5 5⁄8 in. Greatest diameter of body, 4 7⁄8 in. Diameter of base, 3 5⁄8 in.* Circle of twelve petal-shaped indentations around pontil. FIG. 15 — Unpaneled, unusual shape. Color, amethyst. *Height, 8 1⁄2 in. Diameter of rim, 5 1⁄2 in. Greatest diameter of body, 5 1⁄4 in. Diameter of base, 3 5⁄8 in.* Base plain. *Collection of Doctor and Mrs. George Kamperman.* FIG. 16 — Unpaneled. Milky-white opalescent with bluish tone; pale turquoise on upper side of rim. Plain base. *Height, 7 1⁄4 in. Diameter of rim, 3 3⁄4 in. Greatest diameter of body, 3 13⁄16 in. Diameter of base, 2 1⁄4 in.* Note similarity in shape to Fig. 4

AUGUST 1939

61

Boston. On a number of paneled vases have been found pewter collars with glass prisms, which were fashioned to fit securely on the rolled-over rim. The first green paneled vase to be found, as far as I know, was fitted with such a collar, pierced with four equidistant holes for holding the prisms (*Figs. 7, 8*).

While these facts are not absolutely conclusive, they constitute strong evidence that Sandwich produced a large percentage of the "Stiegel" paneled vases. Some collectors and glass students with whom I have discussed this question have been inclined to disagree with my Sandwich attribution. They say, "If not Stiegel, why not New England Glass Company or some of the other early and mid-nineteenth-century glasshouses which operated in and around Boston and made flint glass, both blown and pressed?" It is, of course, possible, even probable, that paneled vases were made in other glasshouses of that period, or earlier. However, in the absence of more definite evidence I shall adhere to my Sandwich attribution for most of them.

[Furthermore, I have recently been informed that some fragments of such vases were found among the fragments of glass excavated on the site of the new and enlarged glasshouse which was built at the Sandwich glassworks in 1849. As yet I have not been able to confirm the report. However, the finding of a few fragments apparently showing similar

dishes likewise usually have twelve panels (See *Figs. 20, 21, 22.* Also *Stiegel Glass, Nos. 82, 83, 84, and 115*).

During a period contemporaneous with activity at Sandwich a great deal of clear-glass tableware in the way of pitchers, sugar bowls, compotes, vases, and so on was produced with a decoration of similar paneling, but usually the panels were much shorter than in the paneled vases. The number of panels was, again, usually twelve. A further decoration of engraving, by copper wheel, the design usually consisting of small, many-petaled, daisylike flowers and foliage, was frequently employed. A narrow band of leaf spray encircled the neck of many of the pitchers. The engraving on many of these pieces seems closely allied with that used on some of the finest Amelung pieces. Its technique appears to have been followed on vases, usually styled celery vases and frequently called Amelung, though of a form or shape quite definitely of a period several years later than the closing of the Amelung factory in 1794 (*Fig. 24*). It is quite probable that these vases and other similarly engraved pieces were blown at the Washington, District of Columbia glassworks (*c. 1806–1832*). The engraving characteristic of these Washington pieces recurs on known Pittsburgh pieces in conjunction with the short, slightly sunken oval-topped panels (*Figs. 23, 25, 26*).

I have enumerated these details in order to show the similarity be-

FIG. 17 (*below, left*) — Emerald green. Rim similar to that of paneled vases. Shape distinctly Victorian. *Height, 9 9/16 in. Diameter of rim, 6 1/8 in. Greatest diameter of body, 5 1/2 in. Diameter of base, 4 3/8 in. Collection of W. T. H. Howe.* FIG. 18 — Amethyst. *Height, 9 3/16 in. Diameter of rim, 5 7/16 in. Greatest diameter of body, 4 3/4 in. Diameter of base, 3 15/16 in. Collection of W. T. H. Howe.* FIG. 19 — Deep cobalt blue, very heavy glass. Shape almost identical with Figure 18, but smaller. *Height, 8 5/16 in. Diameter of rim, 4 3/16 in. Diameter of body, 4 in. Diameter of base, 3 3/8 in.*

FIG. 20 (*above, left*) — Clear paneled flip of the Stiegel type. 12 panels. Engraved above panels in floral design with conventionalized tulip, diamond-cut trelliswork filling its calyx. Paneled flips with this design are rare. *Height, 6 in. Top diameter, 4 3/4 in. Diameter of base, 3 in. Height of panels, 4 1/8 in.* FIG. 21 — Small rummer. Clear glass. Globular bowl with 12 slightly sunken oval-top panels. Ribbed, double-knop stem. Flaring circular foot. *Height, 4 1/4 in. Top diameter, 3 1/4 in. Diameter of foot, 2 9/16 in. Height of panels, about 2 in.* FIG. 22 — Small bowl. Clear glass. Flaring rim with welted edge. 12 slightly sunken oval-top panels. Ribs forming the panels quite prominent and extending on base to pontil mark. *Height, 1 13/16 in. Top diameter, 5 3/8 in. Diameter of base, 3 in.*

paneled decoration would not be conclusive, unless by comparison with actual specimens of paneled vases it could be shown they were from similar vases. They might be fragments from other paneled blown and molded tableware of which a wide variety of articles was produced in various glasshouses during the 1830–1850 period.]

I have seen four paneled vases in amethyst, in what, by comparison, we may call miniature size, but only one in blue. These miniatures have nine panels, while those of full size have either twelve or thirteen (*Fig. 13*). I have seen only one with full-size paneled body and short neck; it is clear glass (*Fig. 12*).

A few vases, similar in shape, but without the panel decoration, are found in amethyst and blue, but I have never seen or heard of one in green or clear glass (*Figs. 14, 15*). The vases illustrated in Figures 17, 18, and 19 are a type without panels which seems to be a sort of cousin to the paneled vases, with quite similar neck and rolled-over rim. Relatively few of these have been found, and they occur in blue, green, and amethyst, virtually identical in color to the paneled vases. I think they are probably Sandwich and fairly late, about 1840–1860.

As previously indicated, this decoration of slightly sunken panels, generally with rounded tops, is not peculiar to the Stiegel or Stiegel-type vases. It is found in eighteenth-century Stiegel-type flips and rummers (most of which are Continental or English), and on small dishes and bowls, also of the eighteenth-century type. These flips, rummers, and

tween the panel decoration of the Stiegel vases and flips and rummers of the same period, and the continuation of this paneling in tableware blown in Pittsburgh and other glasshouses which were contemporaneous with Sandwich. This form of decoration was undoubtedly used also at Sandwich and by the New England Glass Company.

The rolled-over rim or lip with plain edge is characteristic of the paneled vases. I have owned or examined close to one hundred and recall only one with folded or welted rim (*Fig. 1*). They vary in shape, height, greatest diameter of body, diameter at base, width and depth of the rim. In some, the rim turns down only slightly (*Fig. 4*). In others the down turn is almost at a right angle to the neck (*Fig. 1*).

The panels also vary in number and in shape. Most of the vases have thirteen panels, a few twelve. Usually the panels are rounded at the top (*Fig. 4*). Occasionally they are pointed (*Figs. 2, 3*). The vases occur in deep cobalt blue, deep sapphire, and light blue; amethyst, light and dark shades; deep emerald green and a lighter shade; and in clear glass. The plain vases occur in blue and amethyst. The plain amethyst vase of Figure 14 graduates from light to dark in different portions of the vase and shows decided irregular striations in the glass. It is heavier than most of the vases, either paneled or plain. On some of the plain vases there is a circle of twelve semi-diamond-shaped indentations around the pontil mark, on others the base is plain.

On the paneled vases there is a variation in the prominence of the ribs

62

ANTIQUES

forming the panels; in some they stand out only slightly from their surfaces. On all of them the ribs extend on to the base and to the pontil mark at the center. On some the ribs on the base show very faintly. The bases of some vases are more deeply indented than others.

While the evidence previously recited indicates that Hunter was probably correct in attributing paneled vases to Stiegel, I think the additional evidence clearly indicates that a large percentage of these vases were made in other glasshouses at a later date, and most of them at Sandwich. I do not think any particular shape of vase, or number or shape of the panels, or weight, can be designated as distinctly a Stiegel characteristic. Therefore, I would not attempt positively to attribute any particular vase to Stiegel. Yet, regardless of where they were made, these vases will always be highly prized and eagerly sought by collectors of early American glass.

CLASSIFICATION OF SHAPES

I have made the following classification of paneled vases according to shape. The six here listed seem to represent six distinct types, of which other

vases are variants. The plain vase of Figure 14 shows in the body from the shoulders down a straight-sided cylindrical form similar to Type V. The plain vase of Figure 15 is the only one I have seen in exactly this shape. The few vases with twelve panels which I have seen are all Type I or Type V.

I. Semi-ovoid body, rounding to short, broad neck, flaring slightly to rim (*Fig. 1*).

II. Body slightly more elongated and merging more gradually into a short, broad cylindrical neck, flaring slightly to rim (*Fig. 2*).

III. Body similar to II but with longer neck which tapers slightly to rim (*Fig. 3*).

IV. Semi-ovoid body tapering quite sharply to base, which is smaller than I, II, or III. Broad shoulders rounding to broad, cylindrical neck longer than I and II and flaring slightly to rim (*Fig. 4*).

V. Cylindrical body tapering slightly to base and rounding at shoulders which slope to broad cylindrical neck, flaring slightly to rim (*Fig. 5*).

VI. Body more nearly globular than I or IV, very broad at shoulders and tapering quite sharply to base. Broad cylindrical neck, similar to IV, flaring slightly to rim (*Fig. 6*).

FIGS. 23, 24, 25, 26 — Clear glass. Stemmed vase (*second from left*): cylindrical bowl, with flaring rim; gadrooned at base; double-knop stem; flaring circular foot. Engraved with swags, small daisylike flowers, and foliage. Typical example of vases frequently found in Maryland and Pennsylvania, and called Amelung, though shape and style are characteristic of period several years later than closing of Amelung's glassworks. Such items may have been made at the Washington, D. C., glassworks, operating from about 1806 to 1832. Style of engraving somewhat akin to authenticated Amelung pieces. *Height, 8 ½ in. Top diameter, 5 in. Diameter of foot, 3 11/16 in.* Low footed vase at left: *Height, 7 3/8 in. Top diameter, 5 in. Diameter of foot, 3 ½ in. Height of panels, 1 3/4 in.* This vase and the pitchers have 12 short, oval-top, slightly sunken panels. Engraved above panels with daisylike flowers and foliage in style reminiscent of Amelung technique and characteristic of Washington,

D. C., glassworks and of Pittsburgh work of 1830's. Ribs forming panels are pronounced; on the pitchers they continue on the base to the pontil mark, exactly as in "Stiegel" paneled vases. Pitchers have deeply indented base, hollow blown and applied handles. Narrow horizontal ribbing around upper part of neck and rim of Figure 25. PITCHER 25: *Height, 6 3/4 in. Top diameter, 4 3/8. Greatest diameter of body, 4 13/16 in. Diameter of base, 3 3/8 in. Height of panels, 1 3/4 in.* PITCHER 26: *Height, 6 5/8 in. Top diameter, 4 ½ in. Greatest diameter of body, 5 in. Diameter of base, 3 3/8 in. Height of panels, 1 ½ in.*

FIG. 27 (*below, left*) — Pitcher. Clear glass, quite heavy. 12 short, oval-top, slightly sunken panels, ribs prominent and continuing on deeply indented base. Hollow blown and applied handle. Wide molded horizontal ribbing encircling upper part of neck and rim. *Height, 7 ¼ in. Top diameter, 4 3/4 in. Greatest diameter of body, 5 1/8 in. Diameter of base, 3 ¼ in.* FIG. 28 — Pitcher. Clear glass with decided grayish tone, quite heavy. 10 short, oval-top, slightly sunken panels, ribs prominent and continuing on slightly indented base. Heavy molded horizontal ribs around upper part of neck and rim. Solid blown and applied handle with heavy central rib; impressed leaf decoration on base of handle where attached to body. *Height, 6 3/4 in. Top diameter, 4 1/8 in. Greatest diameter of body, 5 in. Diameter of base, 3 1/8 in.* FIG. 29 — Vase. Clear glass. Body bulbous at base; flaring rim. Short stem with angular central knop, flaring circular foot. 12 short, oval-top, slightly sunken panels around lower

part of body. Molded horizontal ribbing around rim. *Height, 8 5/8 in. Top diameter, 5 1/8 in. Greatest diameter of body, 4 in. Diameter of foot, 3 5/8 in.* FIG. 30 — Compote. Clear glass. Hemispherical body with flaring folded rim. Hollow stem with large hollow basal knop; flaring, stepped, circular foot. 12 oval-top, slightly sunken panels. Prominent ribs. *Height, 8 ½ in. Top diameter, 8 ¼ in. Diameter of foot, 4 ½ in.* Pitchers, sugar bowls and covers, vases, and compotes with such paneled decoration were made at Pittsburgh and undoubtedly at Sandwich, New England Glass Company, and other glasshouses during the period 1825–1850. FIG. 31 — Pitcher. Heavy, deep-green glass. Bulbous body. 8 short, oval-top, slightly sunken panels. Very prominent ribs which continue on base. Broad cylindrical neck, slightly flaring rim, and prominent, medium-arched lip. Solid handle. *Height, 4 in. Diameter of body, 3 ½ in. Top diameter, 2 in.* Previously owned in Maine. *Collection of Mrs. Margaret L. Bartholdi.* Top diameter of pitchers is across rim, not from lip to handle. Molded neck ribbing and handle decoration of pitchers 27 and 28 have 1830–1850 characteristics

American Glass Sugar Bowls

A Pictorial Guide for the Student

By Rhea Mansfield Knittle

ANTIQUES has always believed that an appropriate sequence of illustrations adequate in size will afford the student a clearer understanding of art objects than twice the amount of space devoted to verbal descriptions. Hence Mrs. Knittle has been asked to bring together and discuss a group of glass sugar bowls sufficiently comprehensive to furnish a background against which the collector may test his own finds in this particular field.

Unlike the collectors of no more than ten years ago, who viewed almost every specimen of old blown glass, regardless of type, as either Wistarburg or Stiegel, present-day students are hesitant to make dogmatic attributions. They are more inclined to speak of types than of specific factories, and even then are likely to consider their classifications provisional instead of absolutely assured. Until delvers in the fields of early American industry have come upon many another mine of information, attributions made on the sole basis of internal evidence must remain debatable.

Mrs. Knittle, indeed, is of the opinion that the time will never come when authorities on early American glass will make no mistakes. She argues that absolute documentation is too rare and existing data are too fragmentary to permit of infallibility on the part of even the most careful

Fig. 1 — Rare, sapphire-blue, blown flint glass, attributed to Stiegel (*c. 1767–1774*). *Height: 6 ½ inches*. Technique of making similar to Figure 2. Bowl elongated semispherical in shape. Domical cover; reamed edge; capped with pyriform finial vertically ribbed or spiraled. Example resembles the contemporary products of the Bristol factories of England, except for the lid. This domed effect is an early American form

students. It is, for example, unjustifiable to assume, on the ground of purely negative evidence, that a given glassworks confined itself exclusively to certain forms and techniques. Nevertheless, it does seem possible to classify early American glass according to certain quite easily recognizable peculiarities of form, technique, or detail of ornament, and to apply a general name to each class. This is the procedure that Mrs. Knittle has followed in her present treatment of sugar bowls. A large number of the specimens presented are authenticated as to precise source, and hence are reliable touchstones for testing unpedigreed items.

The bowls as pictured are in groups, representing glass typical of Manheim, Zanesville, Massachusetts, Pittsburgh, and Wheeling, West Virginia. As Mrs. Knittle suggests, future discoveries will make possible a more exact identification of the latter groups. The products of southern New Jersey, New York, and Ohio, outside of Zanesville, have been advisedly omitted, because of the limitations of space.

In a study of these well-authenticated illustrations, it will be seen that items in each group display certain features in common. Thus form and technique may combine with external history to furnish assistance in the determination of sources. — *The Editor.*

Fig. 2 — Very rare, cobalt-blue, blown flint glass, attributed to Stiegel (*1767–1774*). *Height: 5 ⅞ inches*. Both bowl and cover blown into a pattern mold, withdrawn from mold, and expanded by further blowing. Bowl diamond-faceted; semispherical body; flaring base merged into small, plain, circular foot. Cover, dahlia or Gothic-arch pattern; rather flat, with reamed edge (that is, folded under, as are all patterned Stiegel covers) extending over rim of bowl; capped with pyriform finial vertically ribbed or spiraled. This dahlia lid is rarer than that with diamond pattern. Item 203 in catalogue of the Garvan sale is similar.

Attributed to Stiegel because of: shape of bowl, which is curved at base, but not squat; size of circular foot, which is unusually small and slightly domed; shape of finial, perhaps the most outstanding characteristic — which, in American glass, is seldom found except on Stiegel sugar bowls.

Qualities that do not assist in deciding attributions include color and quality of the metal, which were not peculiar to Stiegel; resonance, which was achieved by other early American glassmakers; diamond pattern, which was produced by other houses, including those at Pittsburgh and Zanesville

Fig. 3 — Deep, muddy blue, blown flint glass, attributed to Stiegel (*1767–1774*). Shape similar to Figure 1, except that lid is pronouncedly domed. Metal devoid of pattern. Floral sprays etched and gilded on surface of bowl and cover — a known Stiegel method of decoration. Attribution rests on form, history, and satisfactory attribution of another piece almost a duplicate. All grades of glass, from bubbly, sand-pitted, bottle and cylinder glass to a superfine quality of flint, were blown at Stiegel's three furnaces

Fig. 4 — Very rare, superimposed or double-dipped clear cobalt-blue and opaque-white, blown flint glass, attributed to Bakewell of Pittsburgh (*c. 1815–1845*). *Height: about 7 inches.*

Formed by gathering on the end of a blow pipe molten opaque white metal, which, when partially cooled, was dipped into blue metal, and then shaped by blowing and manipulation. Straight-sided, rounding at bottom to attached base that flares into a spreading, circular foot. Lid domed; rim extending over edge of bowl; plain ball finial. Exceptional because of both height and construction of two layers of different colored glass. Probably the only sugar bowl of this technique known.

Attribution is based on ball-shaped finial; height of bowl and high-domed lid; use of opaque glass, which was prevalent in Pittsburgh; and history of the piece

Fig. 5 (below) — Very rare, brilliant blue, blown flint glass, attributed to Bakewell of Pittsburgh (*1815–1825*). *Height: about 6 ½ inches.* Blown into large diamond-faceted pattern mold and, after withdrawal, expanded and tooled into shape. Globular bowl, resting on unusual, spreading, scalloped base or foot; widely flanged at rim, in saucerlike fashion of Zanesville examples. In the recess thus formed fits double-domed lid capped by globular, snapped-off finial. Attribution rests on form: the shape and method of finishing finial, flanged rim, scalloped foot (the fact that it has a foot eliminates Zanesville attribution), rather squatty appearance; on the quality and color of the metal — Bakewell excelling in both; and on the history. Had been in the family of the original owners from *c.* 1824, when it was purchased in Pittsburgh, until it was sold in 1930. Fashioned from the finest metal, it is a rich, vibrant, medium shade of blue, not cobalt, sapphire, or ultramarine; neither is it any of the shades of blue typical of Stiegel's furnaces

Fig. 7 (below) — Cloudy blue, blown flint glass (*c. 1835–1865*). *Height: 6 ½ to 7 inches.* Trans-Allegheny form. Metal blown into perpendicularly fluted or ribbed mold, and expanded after withdrawal. Pear-shaped body, attached to medium high, spreading, unornamented, circular foot. Rim of bowl tooled into somewhat small saucerlike flange, into which cover fits. Cover continues and completes lines of bowl, and has reamed edge, with ball finial on short cylindrical stem. This form of sugar bowl is found in a wide range of shades and colors — blues, amber, amethyst, purple, green, and also clear glass. The shades of blue are more frequently found; the amethyst, purple, amber, and green are quite rare. Value depends on quality of metal as well as on color.

Attribution is not completely definite. Probably the type was blown at several of Pittsburgh's houses — Bakewell, Lyon, McKee — and at the Wheeling-Martin's Ferry works of Barnes, Hobbs & Company. It is a typical trans-Allegheny form. It may antedate 1835, and may be earlier than 1865, but was probably manufactured between those dates

Fig. 6 (above) — Very rare, cloudy or milky-white, blown glass, attributed to one of early Pittsburgh houses (*c. 1810–1835*). *Height: about 6 inches.* Both bowl and cover blown into a horizontally ribbed and vertically fluted mold, withdrawn, and expanded and tooled into their present form. Pattern known as the "broken swirl." Sides of bowl bend inward slightly at top, are rounded at base, and attach to a wide, flat, circular foot. Generally squatty effect. Lid tall and double-domed; wide rim; ball finial attached to short, cylindrical stem, and snapped off at the top (indicated by the mark left when pontil was snapped from the glass in the making. Scar was then polished to a smooth surface).

Attribution based on shape and method of finishing finial; domed lid; wide foot (a Mid-Western tendency in sugar bowls); squatty appearance (a Pittsburgh-Wheeling characteristic).

Several sugar bowls resembling this one in shape and pattern, which have been known during the last fifteen to twenty-five years, and have appeared in important glass auctions, were formerly attributed to Pennsylvania and New Jersey houses. At the time the existence of fine glass from Mid-Western houses was not realized

Fig. 8 — Rare, deep-amber, rather heavy glass, from Shepard & Company, Zanesville, Ohio (*1817–1837*). Bowl flares outward, curves in at neck, and is tooled abruptly outward and upward into a deep saucerlike rim. Semispherical lid is drawn out at top into an uneven, snapped-off, ball finial. Devoid of pattern. Probably originally rested on saucer base similar to that in Figure 9. Attribution is definite, since piece remained in family of maker until its purchase in 1929. Aside from source, attribution rests on finial peculiarities; high domed lid; wide extended rim of bowl; shape; and lack of a base proper.

All of the satisfactorily authenticated Zanesville sugar bowls, so far as known to me, are alike in their domed lids with ball finials, their sloping sides, rounded shoulders, flanged rims, and their lack of an attached base or foot

Fig. 9 — Rare, sea-green, bottle glass, from Zanesville (*1817–1847*). *Height: about 6 ¾ inches with saucer base*. Form of bowl almost duplicates that of Figure 8; rests on footed saucer, unquestionably blown as coaster for bowl, with rim flaring outward and heavily reamed; lid beautifully double-domed with spherical, snapped-off finial. This piece, like Figures 8 and 10, was found in Zanesville, where it was owned by members of the same family until 1930

Fig. 10 — Very rare, sea-green glass, from Zanesville (*c. 1817–1847*). *Height: about 6 ½ inches*. "Broken swirl" pattern, as in Figure 6. Blown into pattern mold perpendicularly ribbed and horizontally swirled, withdrawn, and tooled into present form. Shape somewhat similar to Figure 8, but with less irregular lid. Squatty body, curved in at neck, and expanded into wide, flanged, saucer-like rim. High, bell-like, domed lid drawn out into snapped-off finial. Found near Zanesville, and authenticated by technique and a duplicate never out of original family until purchased in 1929.

Probably every Zanesville sugar bowl originally rested on a footed, saucer-shaped dish blown from the same run of metal, used in lieu of an attached base. Rarely, as in Figure 9, the bowl is found with its saucer. At least three separate saucers, both patterned and plain, in green or amber, are known. It is believed that they were originally planned for use with sugar bowls

Fig. *11* (*above*, *left*) — Rare, clear (very rarely, blue), pattern-molded glass. Attribution uncertain (*1835–1865*). Possesses characteristics of pattern-molded glass of both Massachusetts and Wheeling, West Virginia. Finial, flanged rim, high dome, and pattern all conform to Wheeling technique. But the type is more frequently found in Massachusetts than in the Mid-Western glass district.
The fact should be noted that the Wheeling works of Hobbs, Barnes & Company was established by Massachusetts technicians

Fig. *12* (*above*, *right*) — Rare, clear flint glass, attributed to Massachusetts, Wheeling, or, because of the finial, Pittsburgh (*c. 1835–1865*). In technique similar to that of Figure 11, but pattern a variation. Cover, without design, domed, and with snapped-off finial

Fig. *13* (*left*) — Rare, brilliant cobalt-blue, flint glass, attributed to Massachusetts, Wheeling, or Pittsburgh (*1825–1845*). Metal unpatterned. Semiglobular dome of cover capped with an unusual finial composed of seven buttons of various sizes, applied one upon another

Fig. *14* (*right*) — Scarce, unpatterned, pear-shaped, clear flint glass, attributed to Wheeling-Martin's Ferry (*1850–1870*). Uncommon because of high, baluster-stemmed standard joining globular bowl and heavy, wide, circular foot. Domed cover finished with mushroom finial. Lack of color and late date detract from rarity. *Height: 10 inches*

Fig. 16 (below) — Scarce, rich cobalt-blue, flint glass, attributed to Pittsburgh (c. 1845–1865). Height: 9 ½ inches. Mechanically pressed into octagonal molds bearing two encircling rows of large, concave, oval impressions. Flaring sides; concave, octagonal standard; plain, circular, pressed foot; eight large, semi-oval scallops in a rim about the top of bowl, into which the lid rests. Upper section of double-domed lid semispherical, extending slightly over concave lower part; graceful, octagonal finial conforming in line with general shape of bowl and cover. Piece very pleasing, well proportioned, and of excellent material. Other items of similar pattern and shape bear Pittsburgh attribution or authentication

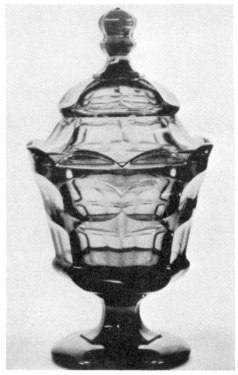

Fig. 15 (above) — Pressed, opalescent flint glass, from Hobbs, Barnes & Company, Wheeling (1850–1870). Both bowl and cover mechanically pressed in molds bearing two rows of large thumbprint, or paneled, depressions. Pressed circular foot. Double-domed cover extending over edge of bowl; pressed attached finial, mushroom shaped with concave stem.

This item unusual because of fiery opalescent color. Shape known also in clear glass, dark blue, and opaque white. An almost identical pattern was manufactured by the New England Glass Company, Cambridge, Massachusetts, and doubtless by Pittsburgh houses and at Sandwich

Fig. 17 (above) — Rare, amethyst-colored, fine grade, flint glass, attributed to the Mid-West, probably Wheeling or Pittsburgh (c. 1835–1865). Blown into perpendicularly fluted pattern mold, withdrawn, and expanded. Melon-shaped, with in-curved neck and flanged, saucerlike rim. Attached foot low, plain, and circular. Lid highly domed, graceful, with finial in form of flattened button resting on short, cylindrical stem. Rarity due in part to color. Pittsburgh houses probably made the preponderance of this type of sugar bowl

Fig. 19 (below) — Clear, mechanically pressed patterned glass, attributed to Pittsburgh, Wheeling, or Ohio, and included with this group as an example of the pressed-glass era of 1870–1880. Form excellent (compare Figure 2), but patterns conglomerate and decadent, and metal not flint but soda-lime. Unique in that pattern is impressed on the under side of the cover and flaring circular base, and on outside of bowl proper

Fig. 18 (left) — Clear, pressed glass, mechanically shaped in octagonal molds (1845–1865). Bowl flares outward; finished with elaborately scalloped rim; pressed base scalloped and circular; snake-skin background pattern; decorations large, rather decadent, pseudoclassical. Cover outstandingly peculiar in that palmettes are impressed on upper side, and diamond and semi-oval designs on under side. These forms alternate. Finial resembles dahlia and is concave in the centre.

Pattern made at both Sandwich and Pittsburgh, contemporaneously. Impossible to assign first use of design, whether to Lyon, Jarves, or Bakewell. Quality of metal varies in known examples; colors clear glass, fiery opalescent, sapphire blue, rich yellow. Fairly scarce in clear glass and blue; rare in other colors

Bowls & Pans: A Guide for Collectors *By* Rhea Mansfield Knittle

Fig. 1 — Pan Blown from Coarse, Bubbly, Bottle or Window Glass of Sea-Green (*1785–1795*). *Capacity: 1 quart; diameter across top: 8 inches*
Extremely wide base; large, rough pontil mark. Family attribution to John Frederick Amelung, Frederick County, Maryland, whose works were variously known to the trade as the "New Bremen Glass Works," "Etna Glass Works," "American Glass Manufactory," "Amelung's Glass Works." Purchased at Fredericktown prior to 1800 by great-grandmother of present owner. I have seen three pans attributed to Amelung, each with wide, flaring rim and plain edge. *Unusual because of attribution, age, relative scarcity*

Fig. 2 — Small Bowl Blown from Coarse, Thick, Sea-Green Bottle Glass Full of Sand Pits and Air Bubbles (*c. 1740–1800*)
Wide base; bulbous body, curving inward into a wide, cylindrical neck with plain edge; deep, depressed base and rough pontil mark. Definite attribution impossible. Several blown bowls of a later date, made from clear window glass, in shape almost identical with this, carry New Jersey attributions. Such shapes are unusual in crude bowls, and in their capaciousness give evidence of Dutch tradition. Some of the early South Jersey glassblowers were Dutch. But the New York Bayard-Bamper workmen also came from Holland. *Rare*

Fig. 3 — Medium Small Bowl Blown from Coarse, Thick, Deep Grass-Green Metal Full of Sand Pits and Air Bubbles (*1800–1808*)
The depression halfway up the sides of this outward-flaring piece is a departure from the usual form. Blown by A. Kohlenberg, Frederick County, Maryland, whose factory was called "New Glass Works" and "Glass Works Farm"; in original owner's family until 1930. *Unusual because of attribution, age, and relative scarcity*

Fig. 4 — Bowl or Pan Blown from Rather Crude, Sea-Green Bottle Glass Containing Numerous Air Bubbles (*1738–1780*)
Fairly heavy, reamed edge; sides slope vertically outward; pontil mark large but exceptionally neat for the period. Attributed by family documentation to the Alloway glassworks of Caspar and Richard Wistar. *Rare*

Fig. 5 — Large Milk Bowl Blown from a Rather Coarse, Light Grass-Green Bottle Glass Containing Sand Pits and Air Bubbles (*c. 1797–1817*). *Capacity: 2 gallons*
Base of bowl very wide; pontil mark large; sides flare gracefully toward folded rim, which is uncommonly deep and heavy. Attempts to suggest molded form are visible on lower part of this reamed edge, and signs of much usage are seen on top. The bowl was made at New Geneva, Pennsylvania, and is an excellent item of pioneer utilitarian glass. *Rare*

Fig. 6 — Large Milk Bowl Blown from Light-Green Window Glass (*1839–1850*). *Capacity: 2 gallons*
Shape similar to that of Figure 5. Grade of metal superior to that of previous illustrations, because better sand and more efficient fluxing were employed. Made by the Suncook, New Hampshire, Glass Works, which found the local sand unsatisfactory, and was forced to make hauls from the beds of the Maurice River in New Jersey. As a result of the expense involved, the operation of the plant was not of long duration. *Rare*

Fig. 8 (right) — MILK BOWL BLOWN FROM LIGHT-GREEN BOTTLE OR WINDOW GLASS (c. 1820–1830 or earlier). Capacity: 1 gallon
Form similar to Figure 7, but rim more deeply reamed and less flaring. Metal has sagged slightly in cooling.
Attributed to Wellsburg or Wheeling. Found in Panhandle section of West Virginia, and probably made at one of the early glassworks in this region when the state was a part of Virginia. Scarce

Fig. 7 (above) — SMALL BOWL BLOWN FROM COARSE, SAGE-GREEN GLASS, FULL OF SAND PITS AND AIR BUBBLES (1783–1830)
High, straight sides flaring slightly toward reamed edge. Rough pontil mark.
Blown at Pitkin Glass Works, Manchester, Connecticut, probably in earlier years of operation, and until recently in collection of the Pitkin family.
This glassworks also hauled sand from New Jersey river beds, using it for the better grades of metal. Desirable because of age and unusualness

Fig. 10 (left) — BOWL WITH HOLLOW-BALL COVER, BLOWN FROM VERY COARSE, HEAVY, DENSE, SAGE-GREEN GLASS (c. 1654–1767?)
Bowl curves gracefully outward from base to deeply and heavily reamed rim. Fairly large, plain, padlike attached circular foot.
Source unknown, but Dutch influence evident. Probably blown at an early Manhattan Island glass factory.
Use problematical. Rare

Fig. 9 (above) — MILK BOWL BLOWN FROM A GOOD GRADE OF LIGHT-GREEN BOTTLE GLASS (c. 1825–1845)
Similar in form to Figure 8, but manipulated with surer technique. Many milk bowls originally had hollow ball covers, blown for the purpose of keeping insects from the contents of the bowl — a serious problem in the days before screens and refrigerators. The balls were not for ornament, nor were they "witch balls" — an appellation incorrectly attached to the large majority of glass balls blown in our country. Attributed to Glassboro district, South Jersey

Fig. 12 (below) — MORTAR AND PESTLE BLOWN FROM BUBBLY, DENSE, AMBER AND SEA-GREEN BOTTLE GLASS (c. 1760–1830)
Shape similar to that of Figure 10, but edge not reamed. Bowl amber; attached to heavy, padlike green base. Pestle green. Attributed to South Jersey, probably from one of the early window- and bottle-glass houses of New Jersey district, or perhaps from an early Kensington district works near Philadelphia, which supplied chemists and apothecaries with considerable apparatus. Rare

Fig. 11 (left) — MILK BOWL BLOWN FROM A GOOD GRADE OF BLUISH-GREEN WINDOW GLASS (1831–1843)
Flaring sides slightly uneven. Reamed edge sagged during process of cooling. Large pontil mark.
Attributed to Redford, Clinton County, New York. This bluish-green metal is, in American glass, almost peculiar to the Redwood and Redford glassworks in New York. Known specimens of these factories bear witness to the expertness of John Foster, who was metal mixer at both of the establishments

Fig. 13 (above, left) — Bowl Blown from a Good Grade of Rich Green Bottle Glass *(1849–1859)*
Excellent form; graceful sloping sides, flaring outward toward rim; attached to raised, spreading foot. Both rim of bowl and edge of wide, circular foot reamed. Attributed to earliest period of operation of Lancaster, New York, Glass Works. *Unusual because of form*

Fig. 14 (above, right) — Bowl Blown from Light, Vibrant Green Glass *(c. 1844–1856)*
Superb form; deep and semispherical, with graceful, flaring rim and reamed edge. Attached foot is small, plain, circular, and rather heavy. Decoration achieved by dipping into hot metal the blowpipe on which was a gathering of slightly cooled metal, and by tooling or drawing out the second coating of glass into the wavelike pattern encircling the bowl.
Attributed to the Saratoga Mountain Glass Works, New York. Though the method of ornamentation is known as South Jersey technique because of its supposed introduction into America by South Jersey glassblowers, this piece and many of the finest surviving examples are known to have been fashioned by New York technicians who had migrated from the Glassboro district. *Rare*

Fig. 15 — Large Bowl Blown from Cobalt-Blue Flint Glass *(date problematical). Capacity: about 1 gallon*
Flaring, reamed rim; wide, raised, circular foot. Possibly a washbowl. Found in a border town along the Pennsylvania–Maryland line, it has been variously attributed to several early glasshouses in that vicinity. I do not believe it to be a Colonial American product. *Unusual because of color and size*

Fig. 16 — Bowl Blown from Excellent Quality of Rich, Deep-Toned Blue Glass with Purplish Depths in the Thicker Portions *(1830–1850). Capacity: over 3 pints*
Semispherical; delicately reamed edge; uncommonly small attached, circular foot. Attributed to Pittsburgh. *Unusual because of color and size*

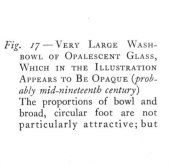

Fig. 17 — Very Large Washbowl of Opalescent Glass, Which in the Illustration Appears to Be Opaque *(probably mid-nineteenth century)*
The proportions of bowl and broad, circular foot are not particularly attractive; but color and quality of the glass and sweep of flaring rim are beautiful. Exceptional size and shape. Found in Massachusetts and attributed by a former owner to either Cambridge or Sandwich factory. *Unusual because of color*

Fig. 18 — BOWL OF SAPPHIRE-BLUE FLINT GLASS, WITH SLOPING, PLAIN, CIRCULAR FOOT
Metal blown in diamond-patterned mold and expanded after withdrawal. *Cf.* Figure 20. Glass of this color and pattern has been credited almost exclusively to Stiegel, *1767–1774*. But I believe it was produced also by Bakewell, Page and Bakewell, *c. 1815–1830*. *Unusual because of pattern*

Fig. 21 *(below)* — BOWL BLOWN FROM A PECULIAR SHADE OF DARK-BLUE, SOMEWHAT BUBBLY GLASS *(early nineteenth century)*
Metal blown into a fluted pattern mold and expanded after withdrawal until fluting broke near top. Attached, scalloped foot.
From the Pittsburgh district, it was undoubtedly made in a Pittsburgh or West Virginia factory. *Unusual because of pattern and foot*

Fig. 19 — MOLDED BOWL OF CLEAR GLASS GEOMETRICALLY PATTERNED *(c. 1825–1855?)*
Semispherical; reamed edge; circular patterned foot. In making, hot metal was blown into a full-sized, three-section, patterned mold, and not expanded after withdrawal (contrast Figs. 18, 20). Probably made in Massachusetts. Similar bowls have been found from about 6 to 12 inches across the top. *Unusual because of technique*

Fig. 20 — SO-CALLED BAPTISMAL BOWL OF COBALT-BLUE FLINT GLASS
Heretofore attributed exclusively to Stiegel, such pieces are now believed by some qualified students of early American glass to have been blown also in several Pennsylvania glasshouses and in Maryland. There is little doubt in my mind that the diamond-patterned, part-sized mold was employed at Manheim, New Bremen, Pittsburgh, Zanesville, and possibly in the Kensington district and the Panhandle section of West Virginia

Fig. 23 *(below)* — OFFHAND BOWL BLOWN FROM SEA-GREEN BOTTLE GLASS OF GOOD QUALITY
Semispherical; deeply reamed rim; attached small, scalloped foot. Attributed to Kearns or Carter and Woodruff of Zanesville. *Unusual because of scalloped foot*

Fig. 22 — ONE OF A PAIR OF BOWLS OF BEAUTIFUL, SEA-FOAM GREEN, ALMOST OPAQUE GLASS *(c. 1840–1860)*
This example differs in nearly every particular from all other American bowls I have seen. Shape unusual: flattened rim, with widely extended circular ring below it; attached flat, wide foot.
Hollow ball and foot are of clear, light-green metal whorled with rose and brownish-rose loopings. Attributed to a New York glassworks; undoubtedly an outstanding off-hand product. *Unusual because of form, ornamentation, and color*

Fig. 24 *(left)* — SEMISPHERICAL COMPOTE OR BOWL ON STEM OR STANDARD, BLOWN FROM MEDIUM-GREEN BOTTLE GLASS *(c. 1840–1855)*
Plain, flaring sides; attached, knopped stem; indented or crimped foot.
Made at Lockport, New York, glassworks. *Unusual because of form, stem, and foot*

Fig. 25 *(right)* — LARGE COMPOTE BLOWN FROM FLINT GLASS *(1845–1865)*
Flaring sides; plain rim; attached stem of clear glass and attached wide, plain, circular, clear-glass foot. Bowl double-dipped: inside amethyst, outside opalescent. Attributed to Pittsburgh. *Unusual because of superimposed color and technique*

Fig. 26 — LARGE MILK BOWL BLOWN FROM HEAVY, DEEP OLIVE-GREEN
BOTTLE GLASS (*1800–1820*). *Capacity: 2 gallons*
Sides nearly straight; base wide; edge deeply reamed. Attributed to the
Monongahela River district in western Pennsylvania. *Unusual because of
color and quality of the glass*, which differs from almost all other bowls in its
peculiar deep olive color and in its smooth, oily, glistening quality

Fig. 27 — LARGE BOWL BLOWN FROM GOOD GRADE OF HONEY-COLORED GLASS
(*c. 1817–1835*)
Deep, sloping sides; uneven reamed edge; deep pontil mark; broken swirl or
swirled and fluted pattern.
Attributed to Zanesville, Ohio. *Beautiful and unusual on account of color, size,
and technique*

Fig. 28 — SMALL BUT DEEP PAN BLOWN FROM BUBBLY, STRONG YELLOW-
GREEN GLASS (*c. 1817–1845*)
Spreading sides and reamed edge. Type found in Mid-Western glass district,
especially in eastern and southeastern Ohio.
Attributed to Portage or Muskingum County. *Desirable because of color*

Fig. 29 (*below*) — BOWL BLOWN FROM RICH, GOLDEN-AMBER GLASS
Shallow, sloping sides; deeply reamed edge. Blown into a vertically spiraled
or fluted pattern mold and expanded after withdrawal. *Unusually fine speci-
men because of color and technique.*
Family attribution to Maryland, but similar in technique to Zanesville glass.
Found in Ohio

Fig. 30 — PAN BLOWN FROM CITRON-COLORED GLASS (*c. 1817–1845*). *Diameter
at top: about 8 inches*
Sloping shallow sides; wide base, deeply rolled rim. Attributed to the Kramer-
Eberhart works at Greensboro, Pennsylvania, a Monongahela River district
factory. *Choice because of unusual and beautiful color*

Fig. 31 (*below*) — SMALL BOWL OR PAN, BLOWN FROM RICH AMETHYST FLINT
GLASS (*c. 1820–1840*). *Capacity: less than 1 pint*
Sloping sides; base with deep pontil mark; deeply folded rim. Attributed to
Pittsburgh. *Very rare because of color.* Modern spurious amethyst bowls and
pans are now occasionally found. This example is the only authentic old one
of its size known to me

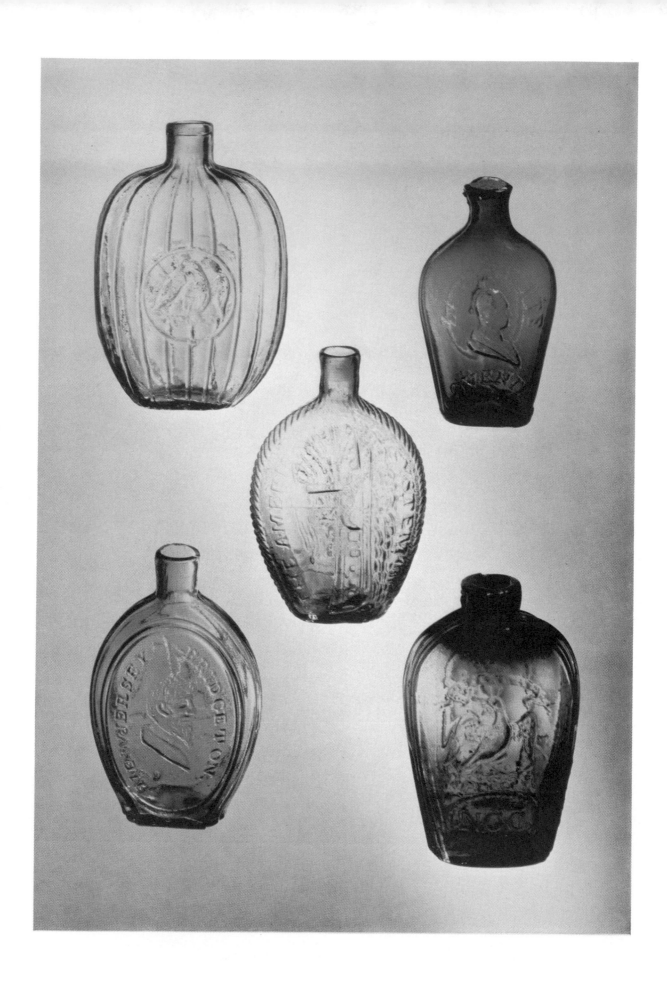

American pictorial flasks at the Corning Museum of Glass

BY PAUL N. PERROT, *Director of the museum*

Anchor and Pennant, golden amber; not previously charted. *Obverse:* anchor and BALTIMORE GLASSWORKS; *reverse:* phoenix and, beneath, RE-SURGAM. Baltimore, Maryland: Baltimore Glass Works, c. 1850. Height 7⅝ inches.

Masonic, olive amber. Masonic emblems on both sides. Attributed to Coventry, Connecticut: Coventry Glass Works; c. 1815-1830. Height 6¼ inches.

NO ONE HAS DONE MORE to further the collecting of American glass than the late George S. McKearin. He was one of the pioneers in this field, whose collecting fervor and tireless legwork were supplemented by an uncanny eye for quality and a skill in ferreting out the piece that would make a particular collection more complete. To his wide personal experience and the word-of-mouth traditions he sought out, his scholarly daughter Helen brought the results of her own research, a corpus of literary evidence and archival record—all of which, by proper correlation and interpretation, forms the very basis of history.

For almost forty years "Mac" avidly acquired, and, through constant sifting and exchange, made his home in Hoosick Falls, New York, the greatest repository of American glass. Since his death in 1958, many a custodian of an important collection of American glass has made a pilgrimage to Hoosick Falls in the hope of acquiring the missing links that would make his collection "great."

In 1950, when the collection of the Corning Museum of Glass was being formed, a large group purchased from George McKearin formed the backbone of the American section. In 1955, the addition of 253 pieces comprising practically all those owned by McKearin which had been published in *Two Hundred Years of American Blown Glass* made it the most comprehensive

facing page

Upper left: Eagle, green; not previously charted and only recorded example. Both sides similar. Origin unknown. Height 7 inches. *Upper right:* Lafayette, olive amber. *Obverse:* above bust, LA FAYETTE; beneath, COVENTRY C. T.; *reverse:* French liberty cap on pole; beneath, S & S. Coventry, Connecticut: Stebbins and Stebbins, c. 1824. Height 6⅞ inches. *Center:* American System, yellow green. *Obverse:* steamboat surrounded by THE AMERICAN SYSTEM; *reverse:* sheaf of rye surrounded by USE ME BUT DO NOT ABUSE ME. Probably Pittsburgh, Pennsylvania: Bakewell, Page, and Bakewell, c. 1824. Height 6⅞ inches. *Lower left:* Unknown man, light green. *Obverse:* bust surrounded by NEW JERSEY BRIDGETON; *reverse:* sailboat. Height 6⅞ inches. *Lower right:* Masonic, olive amber to olive green. *Obverse:* Masonic emblems; *reverse:* eagle and the letters N.G.C. Possibly Keene, New Hampshire: Marlboro Street Glass Works, c. 1815-1830. Height 7 3/16 inches.

collection on public display. This position has now been reinforced with the acquisition of 662 pictorial bottles and flasks from the McKearin collection. When *American Glass* was published in 1941, 398 flasks divided among ten groups had been charted by Helen McKearin. Since then, five other groups and 338 more flasks have been uncovered in her detailed census. Of these, 683 are now a part of the permanent display at Corning.

The origin of a great proportion of pictorial flasks is still unknown, though apparently a large number of glass factories were engaged in their production. Helen McKearin is currently engaged in a revision of the bottle section of *American Glass*, to include the 338 newly charted flasks, which will be published separately in the not too distant future. Until then the most complete sources of information are still: Stephen Van Rensselaer, *Early American Bottles & Flasks*, Peterborough, New Hampshire, 1926; George S. and Helen McKearin, *American Glass*, New York, 1941; Helen and George S. McKearin, *Two Hundred Years of American Blown Glass*, New York, 1950; Helen McKearin, *The Story of American Historical Flasks*, Corning, 1953.

The richness of the Corning group can only be suggested in these pages. For the specialist it will be a standard against which future discoveries may be checked. But for most of us these flasks will recall some of the events in nineteenth-century American history, testify to the ingenuity of our merchants and to the skill of our mold- and glassmakers, and bear testimony to the recognized popularity of their contents!

Left to right: Pike's Peak, light green; not previously charted. *Obverse:* prospecter walking with tools and bag; above, FOR PIKE'S PEAKE; *reverse:* prospector shooting deer. Probably Midwestern, after 1859. Height 7¼ inches. Lafayette, light green; not previously charted and only recorded example. *Obverse:* above bust, LA FAYETTE; *reverse:* Masonic emblem. Possibly Vernon, New York: Mt. Vernon Glass Works. Height 6 7/16 inches. Shield and Clasped Hands, aquamarine; not previously charted. *Obverse:* above shield, UNION; beneath, OLD RYE; *reverse:* eagle holding ribbon with letters A&DHC; beneath, PITTSBURGH. Pittsburgh, Pennsylvania: Alexander and David H. Chambers. Height 7 9/16 inches. Eagle-Draftee, acquamarine; not previously charted. *Obverse:* man in tail coat holding valise, facing rifle; issuing from his mouth a ribbon with the word DRAFTED; *reverse:* eagle. Origin unknown; Civil War period. Height 7½ inches.

Upper left: Columbia, aquamarine; only recorded example. *Obverse:* bust of Columbia; beneath, ASHTON; *reverse:* eagle; beneath, HOUGH. Probably Philadelphia: one of the Kensington glassworks; 1820's. Height 7½ inches. *Upper right:* Washington, green with amber tint; one of two recorded examples. *Obverse:* around bust, GENERAL WASHINGTON; *reverse:* eagle. Midwestern, Pittsburgh area, 1820's-1830's. Height 6¾ inches. *Center:* Lafayette, clear; only recorded example. *Obverse:* above bust, LA FAYETTE; *reverse:* Masonic emblems. Probably Mt. Vernon Glass Works; c. 1824. Height 6 7/16 inches. *Lower left:* Washington, colorless; not previously charted and only recorded example. *Obverse:* above bust, GENERAL WASHINGTON; *reverse:* eagle. Origin unknown; 1820's-1830's. Height 6¾ inches. *Lower right:* Andrew Jackson, light green; one of two recorded examples. *Obverse:* bust under arch surrounded by ANDREW JACKSON; *reverse:* eagle surrounded by WHEELING KNOX & MCKEE. Wheeling, West Virginia: Knox and McKee; c. 1824-1830's. Height 6⅞ inches.

Left to right: Railroad, olive amber; only recorded example. *Obverse:* horse-drawn cart with superimposed eagle. (Probably accidentally placed in mold a second time.) Surrounded by RAILROAD LOWELL. *Reverse:* eagle alone with stars. Coventry Glass Works, 1830's. Height 5½ inches. Masonic, olive green; not previously charted and only recorded example. *Obverse:* Masonic emblem; *reverse:* eagle. Marlboro Street Glass Works, c. 1815-1830. Height 7 1/16 inches. Cornucopia, olive green; one of two recorded examples. Cornucopia on both sides. Possibly Marlboro Street Glass Works, 1820's. Height 8⅛ inches. *In front:* American Eagle, peacock blue. *Obverse:* eagle; *reverse:* charter oak and LIBERTY. Origin unknown, probably 1820's or 1830's. Height 6⅝ inches.

Harrison, light green. *Obverse:* above bust, WM. H. HARRISON; *reverse:* log cabin. Midwestern, Pittsburgh, Pennsylvania, area; 1840. Height 6¾ inches.

Washington, sapphire blue. *Obverse:* above bust, LOCKPORT GLASS WORKS; *reverse:* bust alone. Lockport, New York, 1840's. Height 8 7/16 inches.

Left: Shield and Ring, dark olive green. Same design on both sides. Possibly East Hartford, Connecticut: either Pitkin or Mather Glass Works, c. 1815-1830. Height 7 1/16 inches. *Right:* Sunburst, dark olive green. Same design on both sides. Marlboro Street Glass Works, c. 1815-1830. Height 6⅞ inches. *Center top:* Shield and Clasped Hands, dark olive green; not previously charted. *Obverse:* above shield, UNION; *reverse:* eagle. Origin unknown. Height 8⅝ inches. *Center bottom:* Log Cabin, dark olive green. *Obverse:* NORTH BEND; *reverse:* TIPPECANOE. Mt. Vernon Glass Works, c. 1840. Height 5⅝ inches.

Pike's Peak, aquamarine; not previously charted. *Obverse:* prospector putting bottle to his lips; *reverse:* eagle. Probably Midwestern, after 1859. Height 8 15/16 inches.

Left to right: Sunburst, light green. Sunburst on both sides. Possibly Keene, New Hampshire: Marlboro Street Glass Works, or Vernon, New York: Mt. Vernon Glass Works; c. 1815-1830. Height 7 9/16 inches. Jenny Lind, aquamarine. *Obverse:* above bust, JENNY LIND; *reverse:* tree. Origin unknown; c. 1851. Height 9⅞ inches. American Eagle, aquamarine. *Obverse:* eagle; *reverse:* plain. Possibly Louisville, Kentucky: Kentucky Glass Works; after 1850. Height 10⅝ inches.

Left to right: Washington, pale green. *Obverse:* surrounding bust, G. G. WASHINGTON; *reverse:* above eagle, PITTSBURGH; beneath, F. L. Pittsburgh, Pennsylvania: Frederick Lorenz, 1820's-1830's. Height 6⅝ inches. Eagle, light green. Eagle on both sides. Midwestern, unidentified glasshouse. Height 6 7/16 inches. Andrew Jackson, aquamarine; unique in having a saucer lip. *Obverse:* surrounding bust, GENERAL JACKSON; *reverse:* eagle. Pittsburgh, Pennsylvania; probably John Robinson, c. 1824-1830. Height 6⅝ inches. Washington, light green. *Obverse:* surrounding bust, GENERAL WASHINGTON; *reverse:* eagle. Midwestern, unidentified glasshouse. Height 6⅝ inches. *In front:* American System, violet tint; only recorded example. *Obverse:* steamboat surrounded by THE AMERICAN SYSTEM; *reverse:* sheaf of rye, surrounded by USE ME BUT DO NOT ABUSE ME; beneath, B.P.&B. Pittsburgh, Pennsylvania: Bakewell, Page, and Bakewell, c. 1824. Height 6⅝ inches.

Left to right: Shield and Clasped Hands, corn-flower blue; not previously charted. *Obverse:* above shield, UNION; beneath, in frame, WM. FRANK & SONS, PITT.; *reverse:* flag, cannon balls, and cannon. Pittsburgh, Pennsylvania; William Frank and Sons. Height 7 9/16 inches. Columbia, cobalt blue. *Obverse:* bust of Columbia; *reverse:* eagle. Probably Philadelphia, Pennsylvania: one of the Kensington glassworks; 1820's. Height 7½ inches. American Eagle, olive amber. *Obverse:* eagle; *reverse:* cornucopia. Possibly East Hartford, Connecticut: Pitkin or Mather Glass Works, c. 1815-1830. Height 5⅞ inches. American Eagle, emerald. *Obverse:* eagle; *reverse:* cornucopia. Possibly Marlboro Street Glass Works, c. 1830. Height 6 9/16 inches. Scroll, light green; not previously charted and only recorded example. Same design on both sides. Origin unknown. Height 8 inches.

Left to right: Washington Monument, green; not previously charted and only recorded example. *Obverse:* monument; *reverse:* ear of corn surrounded by CORN FOR THE WORLD. Baltimore Glass Works. Height 7⅝ inches. Benjamin Franklin, yellow green; one of two recorded in this color. *Obverse:* around bust, BENJAMIN FRANKLIN; *reverse:* portrait of Thomas W. Dyott, surrounded by WHEELING GLASS WORKS. Wheeling, West Virginia: Wheeling Glass Works; 1830's. Height 6 7/16 inches. Zachary Taylor, deep green. *Obverse:* around bust, ROUGH AND READY; *reverse:* above eagle, MASTERSON. Midwestern, probably Pittsburgh, Pennsylvania, area; late 1830's-1840's. Height 8½ inches.

AMERICAN BLOWN WINES

By MARION BULL WHITING

Illustrations, except as noted, from the author's collection. Photographs by Redi Resk

THAT the subject of American wineglasses is largely obscured in clouds of uncertainty seems an unwarranted oversight on the part of glass collectors, especially in view of the fact that so much information about foreign drinking glasses is available. This neglect is due partly to the preference hitherto accorded historical flasks and bottles, the keen interest in offhand specimens, and, more recently, the popularity of pressed ware. Also responsible are the scarcity of records and the fact that many of the small glass factories were short-lived.

The very profusion of early bottles of every description, large and small, naturally leads to speculation anent the receptacles into which their contents passed for serving in public houses and in homes. Were they all brought from across the ocean? Why should we so readily credit glasshouses which imported at great expense Dutch, German, and English glassblowers, with producing merely crude bottles, milk pans, pitchers, and window glass, when the workmen hailed from countries where fine tableware in many forms was being made? To be sure, these artisans from the Old World encountered difficulties in the new country. Yet in spite of hindrances, both Stiegel and Amelung managed to turn out fine glassware. Fortunately, we have a small amount of direct evidence about some of the articles made by these two early houses.

Hunter's book *Stiegel Glass* shows a fragment of a cotton-twist stem which was excavated on the site of the Manheim works, and quotes lists taken from Stiegel's own records of the output of the factory. In the year 1770 he made hundreds of fine bulbed wines and fine beer glasses, as well as thousands of plain wine and beer glasses. He also made quantities of tumblers, mugs, cans, and large glasses. This list indicates that a wide range of forms was in use here, in a period when Europe was blowing molded, baluster,

FIG. 2 — DRINKING VESSELS

A, Hogarth measure or syllabub; probably English. Plain short stem; clear glass, showing a few grains of sand. *Height*, 3 1/4 inches. *B*, bar glass, American. Heavy, clear metal of decidedly yellow tinge. Found in the Hudson River valley. *Height*, 4 1/4 inches. *C*, Hogarth, probably English. Fairly clear glass. Twisted air-bubbles in the short stem. *Height*, 3 3/4 inches

FIG. 3 — TALL STEM WINES

A, early English, possibly Newcastle. Fine, heavy, dark metal with slight irregularities in glass. Well-balanced shape; domed and folded foot. Base of bowl is solid and contains a teardrop, as does the knop of the stem. An exceptionally fine glass. *Height*, 7 inches. *B*, wine showing Spanish influence, probably foreign. Glass clear with slight blue-gray tinge. Note solid base of bowl; molded, high-shouldered stem containing long teardrop; arched, folded foot

FIG. 4 (*right, above*) — KNOPPED-STEM TALL WINE, AMERICAN

Clear glass, slightly bubbled and irregular. Straight-sided flaring bowl. Elongated teardrops in stem. Foot fairly high and folded. A fine American glass, though lacking the sophistication of related English types. *Height*, 6 1/2 inches. MacIver Percival gives heights of analogous English glasses as 7 1/2 to 8 1/2 inches

FIG. 1 — MUG AND FLIP, AMERICAN

Both fairly light in weight. Metal of mug clear and slightly bubbly; crude wheel-engraved decoration. Stiegel type, showing German influence. *Height*, 4 1/4 inches. Flip is of very brilliant glass, slightly bubbly. Well-balanced six-color enameled decoration. Stiegel type, showing German influence. *Height*, 5 inches. *Flip from the collection of Mr. and Mrs. Drake H. Sparkman*

FIG. 5 (*left*) — OPAQUE-TWIST STEM WINES

German or Dutch type. *A*, glass clear but lacking brilliance and with slight greenish cast and some sand grains. Barrel-shaped bowl. Weak cotton-twist stem; exceptionally high-domed plain foot. *Height*, 6 1/2 inches. *B*, probably American. Clear glass with a few bubbles. Deep, straight-sided, flaring bowl. Weakly molded stem containing red center thread and thin white twist. Foot high and folded. *Height*, 6 3/8 inches. Not a well-proportioned glass. *C*, very clear glass. Foot plain. The small, straight-sided flaring bowl and straight stem with well-executed cotton-twist combine to make this a charming wine. *Height*, 5 3/4 inches. *B and C from the collection of Mrs. William Harvey Smith*

FIG. 6 — AMERICAN WINES
Showing varied types ranging from plain heavy to plain light with collar. *A* has molded bowl. *E* has engraved decoration and is a very pale green, similar in color to glass in the Metropolitan Museum attributed to Wistar. English influence is apparent. *Heights*, 4 ¼ to 4 ½ inches, about one inch less than analogous English glasses. *C* is considerably heavier, both in stem and foot, than the other examples. *D* has folded foot, often — though not infallibly — an indication of earliness

FIG. 7 — LATER TYPES OF PLAIN WINES
B, crude, with folded foot. Compare with fragments in Figure 10. *D*, bar glass with engraved palm-leaf design. Brilliant metal. A type found in central New York

FIG. 8 — SMALL WINES OR LIQUEUR GLASSES
A, teardrop in cut stem. *B*, plain, with long teardrop in stem and wide folded foot. *C*, facet-cut stem and engraved bowl. *A* and *C* show early type of cutting, popular in England, Holland, and France

FIG. 9 (*left*) — GROUP OF LATE WINES
A, bulbed stem. Bowl panel-cut, a later type of cutting than shown in Figure 8. *B*, gilded decoration on bowl. This glass is from a traveling liquor set which still carries the label of a New York City merchant listed in the 1835 directory. *C*, another type with cut panels

FIG. 10 — WINEGLASS FRAGMENTS
Excavated on the site of the Sandwich glassworks. *Left*, a typical form of about 1830–1840; compare with Figure 7, *A*. *Center*, four bases of wineglasses, some with folded foot. *Right*, stem of a ring-stemmed hock glass, of semi-opaque dove gray; and part of a late glass, though with folded foot.
From the collection of William Pennebacker

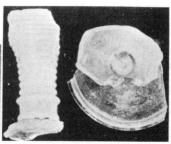

air-bubbled, and cotton-stem tall wines, as well as common wines.

Still another link in the chain of evidence comes from Sandwich, where several fragments of wineglasses have been found. These indicate that the welted foot was used at Sandwich at a relatively late date as compared with European practice. Furthermore, ring-stemmed hock or white-wine glasses of the type usually considered to be of Dutch provenance appear to have been made at the Sandwich factory (*Fig. 10*).

It is believed that O'Hara and Craig began blowing flint glass in Pittsburgh in 1802, though their output was probably small. In 1808 their example was followed by Bakewell and Page, who are credited with operating the first successful flint-glass factory in the country. The latter employed both French and English workmen and by 1817 were turning out quantities of fine blown tableware. The New England Glass Company, under Deming Jarves' leadership, made an excellent grade of flint glass, as did the Boston and Sandwich Glass Company at a slightly later date. But how may we recognize their products? What are the characteristics by which we may differentiate glass made in America from foreign glass?

The collection of foreign glass in the Metropolitan Museum of Art provides material on which to base comparative notes on general national characteristics of form, metal, and decoration, as a first step toward tentative authentication. The glasses here illustrated exhibit both resemblances to and differences from their foreign prototypes. Those specimens showing pronounced European characteristics in quality of metal, workmanship, and form are judged to be of alien origin. Pieces that show foreign influence but are of different metal, with variations in form, size, and work-

manship, are classed as American. Altogether, they fall into several distinct groups, taking into consideration shape and racial influence. They were collected from private sources in the Hudson River valley, near-by New York, New Jersey, and Connecticut, and cover the period from approximately 1750 to 1850, or perhaps slightly later.

It is difficult adequately to describe in cold print the characteristics of such a delicate substance as glass, and, unfortunately, there is no simple formula by which we may instantly recognize American glass. A few sign-posts mark the way, however. American glassmakers copied. Like all copies, their finished products diverged in one detail or another from the models. The following generalizations were arrived at from comparison of authenticated groups of American and foreign glasses:

1. American glass differs in quality from European. It is neither so heavy in weight as English flint glass, nor so light as the German, Dutch, or Venetian.

2. It possesses more brilliance than most Continental glass.

3. It is not so dark in tone as is much of the English.

4. American forms are, in general, decidedly simpler than those of Europe. American tall stem wines appear somewhat crude in comparison with fine English types.

5. American decoration is, on the whole, simple. It is likely to show merely a suggestion of the elaborate forms used abroad.

6. In enameled designs, clear, vibrant colors were employed for American glass, in contrast to the rather muddy, opaque shades common in Holland and Germany.

7. American stem wines seem to be uniformly smaller than their European prototypes.

PATTERN MOLDS AND PATTERN-MOLD GLASS

By HARRY HALL WHITE

Except as noted, illustrations from the Detroit Institute of Arts

CONCERNING early pattern molds and the glass blown in them, little published material is available, although pattern-mold glass is considered most desirable by many connoisseurs. In order to establish a definition of our subject, I quote the following pertinent characterizations:

Rib or diamond moulded: Patterns of straight or twisted lines or diamonds impressed on the surface of a glass by blowing it, while still plastic, in a mould. (Powell,[2] *p. 44.*)

Sometimes the ribs were started by incisions in a mould, but the vessel was delivered when its shape and size were only half complete. Inflation was continued after delivery and so the ribs were embodied in the surface of the vessel. (Thorpe,[3] *p. 16.*) Often, however, at an earlier stage of manufacture, the parison is given a pattern of ridges and furrows, or "corrugations," by being blown into a cylindrical or tapering mould of that form. The vessel is afterward fashioned into its final shape by free blowing and modelling, and the corrugations which it receives from the mould expand or contract according to the contours of the vase. . . . On the mould, of course, the corrugations are always vertical. They may be made curved or S-shaped on the vessel by sharply twirling it when on the blow-pipe. (Harden,[5] *p. 19.*)

The practical glassmaker provides this rather technical definition: "Offhand hollow ware with ornamental patterns secured by varying the wall thickness of the object with impressions taken from a mold." As *offhand* glass we classify objects given final form by the use of the chair, blowpipe, and punty, with such glassmaker's tools as marver, pinchers, shears, and calipers, but not by the aid of final form-producing molds. *Hollow ware*, of course, refers to all types of bottles, bowls, pitchers, jars, salts, and inkwells — the wide range of hollow objects made for

FIG. 1 — OFFHAND BLOWN COMPOTE
Green glass. Attributed to Zanesville, Ohio. *Height*, 8 ½ inches

FIG. 2 — THREE-MOLD DECANTER
Clear glass. Source unknown. *From the author's collection*

FIGS. 3, 4 — STIEGEL-TYPE AMETHYST POCKET BOTTLE AND EXPANDED THREE-MOLD PATTERNED BOWL
Clear glass. Source unknown

domestic use. The *patterns*, or final designs derived from the pattern molds, are many and greatly varied; their ultimate form is dependent on the skill of the operator. The term *pattern-mold glass* distinguishes the type from *blown glass* — plain objects blown without molded designs (*Fig. 1*).

A close relative of pattern-mold glass is our old friend, three mold. This is an ornamented glass, blown into a mold which produces both pattern and final form. Regardless of the number of the mold divisions, the type is still "three mold." Typical objects are clear patterned decanters (*Fig. 2*), pitchers, hats, and drinking glasses; deep olive-amber or green inkwells, hats, and Keene decanters. Three mold was originally mentioned in the queen's-ware and glass merchants' advertisements as "moulded ware." It represents an attempt, which characterized the period 1815–1845 in American glassmaking, to supply a low-cost ornamental glassware for a market unable to purchase costly cut glass. Eventually, it was forced off the market by the development of inexpensive pressed glassware.

A variant of three-mold glass actually encroaching on the pattern-mold field is the glassware patterned in a multipartite mold and expanded by blowing and manipulative processes of the offhand technique. Typical examples: so-called Stiegel daisy-in-square pocket bottles (*Fig. 3*); patterned tumblers, hats, or small pitchers, blown in Keene, Coventry, and Vernon inkwell molds; patterned bowls blown in Mantua and Kent decanter molds; patterned sweetmeats or bowls blown in Keene and Sandwich decanter molds (*Fig. 4*).

Add to this grouping such manipulative processes as: applied threads (*Fig. 5*), and the draping of supplementary gathers of metal on the blown surface in the so-called wave or lilypad pattern (*Fig. 7*); and you have included virtually all the processes used by the early American glassmaker in giving a decorated surface to the glass itself. (Compare, however, an alternate process of blowing in full-size molds, as described by Lura Woodside Watkins elsewhere in this issue. — *Ed.*) This, of course, is not to mention such ornamental processes as engraving, cutting, and enameling, nor does it refer to the ubiquitous pressed glass.

Glassmaking itself, the simple melting and shaping of crude pressed or padded ornaments and enamels, without inflation, goes back some three or four thousand

FIG. 5 — MOLD-BLOWN PITCHER IN RIBBED PATTERN

18-rib mold. Applied thread. Green glass. Source: Pittsburgh, Pennsylvania. *Height*, 5 ¾ inches

FIG. 6 (*right*) — FRAGMENTS OF SIXTEENTH-CENTURY PATTERN-MOLD GLASS
Left, diamond pattern. *Right*, broken-swirl pattern. Color, green. Source: Ellens Green near Rudgwick, Sussex, England. Excavated by S. E. Winbolt

FIG. 7 (*left and below*) — LILYPAD PITCHER AND BOWL

Pitcher, dark amber glass. Source: Stoddard, New Hampshire. In addition to the so-called "wave" or "lilypad" decoration made by draping gathers of metal on the blown surface of the glass, the pitcher has the secondary embellishment of applied threads around the neck. *Height*, 7 ⅛ inches. Bowl, aquamarine glass. Source: New York State. *Diameter*, 14 inches; *height*, 5 ½ inches

FIG. 8 (*below*) — RIBBED PATTERN-MOLD SUGAR BOWL

12-rib mold. Amethyst glass. Source: Pittsburgh district

years.[1] But the actual knowledge and use of the soap-bubble principle, the use of the blowing iron or tube, was possibly first used in the first century B.C.[1] Shortly following the discovery of the blowpipe came the technique of impressing designs on the soft gather of metal by placing it in contact with a cooler rigid form. Pattern molds were in use in the second and third centuries. In his *Art of Glassmaking* Peder Mannson, a Swedish monk who resided in Rome from 1508 to 1524, gave a perfect description of making pattern-mold glass: "A variety of copper moulds, ornamented inside, or with rims (*rander*, ridges). Into these moulds they first blow the glass and then take it out and blow it out wider."[4] In museum collections of ancient glass are specimens of this very early glass, molded ware exhibiting enviable skill in manipulation of form and application of handles.

I am fortunate to have, through the generosity of S. E. Winbolt,[4] fragments of a later date taken by him from Ellens Green near Rudgwick, Sussex, England (*Fig. 6*). A glasshouse was in operation there late in the sixteenth century. The Surrey-Sussex glasshouses were originally established by the Norman French early in the thirteenth century, and continued until competition with imported Venetian glass and London glass, coupled with royal edicts prohibiting the use of wood as glasshouse fuel, reduced their efforts to a minimum. These two fragments, originally light green in color, are free from surface oxide but do show a general inclusion of oxide and deepening color. The smaller fragment is in the diamond pattern found in American pieces, sometimes called ogive or lozenge; the object of which it was a part cannot be determined. The larger fragment is our broken swirl, broken rib, or transverse ridge. It was part of a small bowl at a point where the side joins the base.

There is a lack of uniformity in nomenclature for this glass. Let us consider, for instance, the simplest example of pattern-mold glass, the ribbed pattern. Powell[2] mentions it as "rib-moulded" (*Fig. 12, p. 9*), and "ribbed by moulding" (*Fig. 2, p. 2*). In his *Technical Terms* (*p. 44*) I find "Rib or diamond moulded." Thorpe[3] uses a much wider list of terms for this pattern and its process of making: "moulded fluting," "rib moulded," "blown ribs," "lining," "ribbed model," "ribbed decoration," "blown ribs straight." He writes: "One of the earliest of these operations was the lining of a vessel with blown ribs." Yet, despite variation in nomenclature, terminology, a constant tendency to mention this first pattern as "ribbed" is apparent. I recommend general adoption of the name.

The second type is likewise variously termed by the authorities. Powell[2] (*p. 56*) speaks of threaded decoration, "with spiral lines, produced by impressing vertical lines in the still plastic glass and twisting them." Thorpe[3] mentions this pattern as "writhen decoration," but proceeds to explain (*p. 16*): "Straight and vertical ribs were varied in several ways. A twist of the vessel at the moment of delivery from the mould gave the ribs a spiral movement." These clear descriptions of the method employed tend to justify the present American usage of the name *swirled pattern*, which is descriptive of both process and pattern (*Fig. 9*).

The third type, currently known as *broken-rib* or *broken-swirl pattern*, is less clearly defined by the authorities (*Fig. 10*). In fact, while I have seen it labeled "corn cob," "herringbone," "Pitkin type," "transverse ridge" and "interrupted rib," I have never read a description of the process. At length, however, I have pieced together the following analysis of the technique.

This very graceful and characteristic pattern was made by two insertions of the glass into a plain ribbed mold, with a twist of the gather after the first impression. The second impression "broke" the spiral lines formed by twisting the first impression. Close examination of objects in broken-swirl pattern in which the swirling is widely spaced will show the faint wavy trail of the first ribbed and twisted impression.

The fourth and last pattern in this group is the so-called diamond or ogive (*Fig. 11*). Powell [2] (*p. 52*) describes it, "moulded with shallow diamonds or with upright or sloping flutes." Pellatt [6] (*p. 112*) calls this pattern the "Venetian Diamond-Moulded," and implies considerable antiquity:

The old Venetian Diamond was formed by impressing soft glass in a metal mould, as follows: the first gathering, is solid, and afterwards covered by a second gathering, this is expanded by blowing in the usual manner, and being rewarmed, is blown into the projecting pillar-mould, and when further expanded impresses the Glass ball; the pillars are pinched together by the pucellas, at equidistant points, into the diamond form, one by one, until the whole of the projecting straight pillars become diamond pillars. Equally good effects are produced by modern Glassmakers in a more direct manner, by making brass open-and-shut, or dip moulds, so as to give at one operation the entire diamond impression, thus saving the tedium of forming each diamond separately with the pucellas.

Though I have seen pocket bottles and covered bowls in this pattern which were found in America, I have no evidence that the method of pincering a ribbed parison to make a diamond pattern was ever used here. The American diamond or ogive

FIG. 9 — SWIRLED PATTERN-MOLD GLASS

Aquamarine and green. Bottle, golden-amber glass. 24-rib mold. Source: Zanesville, Ohio

From the Detroit Institute of Arts and the author's collection

pattern was produced by the second process described by Pellatt. The process was long in use and is still current where glass hollow ware of this pattern is made.

The article *Migrations of Early Glass Makers* [7] traces the beginnings of these various processes in America. Though long attributed solely to Henry William Stiegel's glassblowers, we now know, from excavations made at nineteenth-century glasshouse sites in Ohio, that they were practiced to a considerable extent there.[8]

Miss Perie J. Abraham and Roy Watson recently discovered an actual set of old pattern molds which met specifications established by traditional description and illustration. According to

tradition, they had been at one time in use at the New Geneva Glass Works, founded by Albert Gallatin. Strengthening this tradition was an object that accompanied the molds: a branding iron for marking packing cases NEW GENEVA GLASS (*Fig. 12*). Though heavily oxidized it bravely exhibits legible marking.

Modern pattern or dip molds are variable to the extent that the blower may alter the number of ribs in the pattern. They are built with removable vertical blades in a cylindrical shell. The modern trade name, *optic*, is given to objects patterned in such molds. These old rib molds are of cast brass or bronze, so heavily coated with oxide, the patina that guarantees age, that they look almost black (*Fig. 12*). The larger has 20 ribs, the smaller 16 — important considerations that will assist in future identification of New Geneva glass. It is true that I have found in Ohio molds with the same number of ribs, but, in the case of the 16-rib mold at least, there is a sure means of differentiation.

In both of the New Geneva molds the ribs meet at a common point or center in the bottom of the mold; consequently the molded ribs will meet, similarly, at the bottom center of the patterned object, unless obscured by the

FIG. 10 (*above*) — BROKEN-SWIRL PATTERN-MOLD GLASS

Green, 20-rib mold. Source: Ohio

punty scar. From the fragments excavated at Mantua, Ohio, I discovered that the ribs did not converge on the base, but extended only to a terminal ring which generally encircled the pontil mark (*Fig. 13*). This ring is the one infallible earmark of a Mantua pattern-mold piece, whether in ribbed, swirled, or broken-swirl pattern. Likewise, 16-rib objects with ribs converging on the base may be identified as New Geneva products — if, of course, the quality of glass and the colors are true to type.

The differences between 20-rib specimens from New Geneva and from Kent, Ohio, where the works of Parks, Edmunds and Parks also used a 20-rib mold, are not yet established. In respect to other Ohio factories, while material from Zanesville glasshouse sites has not been available, it has been quite uniformly and logically agreed that Zanesville blowers consistently patterned their wares in a 24-rib mold. This conclusion, based on marked Zanesville flasks and repeated local finds in analogous colors and shades, seems to be supported by tradition. In this connection I gratefully acknowledge the assistance of Earl J. Knittle. Zanesville may have used other molds, but certainly the bulk of its rib pattern-moldglass has 24 ribs.

In Ohio I have also found pattern-mold bowls and flasks — pocket bottles — with 18, 32, and 48 ribs. The molds for the 18-rib pieces are unidentified. The 32- and 48-rib pieces were produced by double impressions from 16- and 24-rib molds. I

diamond mold should be useful in identifying its products: inside diameter, 1 ³⁄₁₆ in.; depth, 2 ⅝ in.; 16 short ribs in bottom of mold; 17 diamonds in bottom row, 16 diamonds in top row; 16 rows of diamonds, bottom to top; 8 diamonds in "chain height." The patterned halves of the mold are brass or bronze. The two handles and the link in the hinge are steel or iron, as are two pins securing the latter. The handles are riveted to the outer surface.

From the New Geneva area I had the good fortune to obtain a small glass pitcher (*Fig. 15*) patterned from this old diamond mold. It is a specimen of considerable character, in spite of the fact that the handle is missing except for the small attaching fold. The pitcher has 16 ribs converging at the pontil mark, and 8 diamonds in a vertical chain.

I have identified one additional diamond-pattern mold. It was used at Mantua, and shows 16 diamonds in a lateral chain.[8] Pocket bottles and bowls in this mold, in amber and green glass, are found in Ohio. The diamond-pattern pocket bottles, "Ohio Stiegel," generally attributed to Zanesville, have 10 diamonds in a lateral chain. They occur in all the glorious shades of olive green and amber (*Fig. 11*). Generally the patterns show 10 vertical ribs below the diamonds. Stiegel-type pocket bottles in amethyst show 28 diamonds and ribs, counted laterally (*Fig. 16*). The modern diamond-pattern pocket bottles produced in New Jersey have 12 diamonds in a lateral chain, with no ribs below (*Fig. 16*).

Much remains to be accomplished in the matter of mold identification. The material here presented is merely a progress report. Over a period of years I have recorded all rib, swirl, broken-swirl, and diamond-pattern mold glass that I have encountered. My notes list molds of from 8 to 48 ribs, most of which are yet to be identified.

REFERENCES

1. Dillon, E. *Glass*. London, 1907
2. Powell, H. J. *Glassmaking in England*. Cambridge, 1923
3. Thorpe, W. A. *English Glass*. London, 1935
4. Winbolt, S. E. *Wealden Glass*. Hove, 1933
5. Harden, D. B. *Roman Glass from Karanis*. Ann Arbor, 1936
6. Pellatt, A. *Curiosities of Glass Making*. London, 1849
7. White, H. H. *Migrations of Early Glass Makers*. ANTIQUES, August 1937
8. White, H. H. *The Story of the Mantua Glass Works*. ANTIQUES, December 1934, February, July, and November 1935

found both 16- and 32-rib fragments in the Mantua excavation, and was entirely mystified by the peculiarity of the multiple; recently, however, I found a footed bowl, in Zanesville amber glass, with 48 ribs. The pattern on the bottom gave conclusive evidence of double impression: the ribs were spaced "two by two." The glassblower had not been able to place the ribs of the second patterning exactly midway between the ribs of the first!

The third mold in this New Geneva group was as revealing as the other two. For years the exact method of producing the diamond pattern has been the cause of much speculation. Now, of course, it all seems simple — now that I have seen an actual old mold (*Fig. 14*). Modern molds are built in the same way. One now in the Mount Washington Glass Works at New Bedford, Massachusetts, very closely resembles the New Geneva mold, differing only in size and material; it is smaller and is made of steel.

The measurements of the New Geneva

FIG. 14 — NEW GENEVA DIA-
MOND PATTERN MOLD

Material brass or bronze. 16 diamonds

FIG. 15 (*right*) — DIAMOND PATTERN-MOLD PITCHER

Green glass. 16 diamonds. Source: New Geneva glassworks. *Height*, 2 ⅜ inches. *Base diameter*, 2 inches. *From the author's collection*

FIG. 11 (*below, left*) — DIAMOND PATTERN-MOLD GLASS

Amber and green. 10 diamonds in lateral chain. Source: Zanesville, Ohio

FIG. 16 — STIE-
GEL-TYPE AND
MODERN DIA-
MOND PATTERN-
MOLD POCKET
BOTTLES

Amethyst glass. *Left*, 28 diamonds and ribs. Source unknown. *Right*, 12 diamonds. Source: New Jersey. *From the author's collection*

AN ANTECEDENT OF THREE-MOLD GLASS

By LURA WOODSIDE WATKINS

Illustrations from the author's collection

THE first quarter of the nineteenth century is the dark age of American glassmaking. Although two major flint-glass works and several others of minor importance were established during that time, almost no authenticated specimens of their output have come to light. Research and excavation have given us a good deal of information about flasks and bottles of the period, but far less concerning tableware. The flint-glass houses, such as Bakewell & Company and the New England Glass Company, built their factories in cities and the sites are now inaccessible. All our knowl-

objects first blown at Sandwich. He was already acquainted with the process of its manufacture.

During the seven years preceding the opening of the Boston and Sandwich Glass Company, Deming Jarves was superintendent of the New England Glass Company at Cambridge. Previously, while a member of the Henshaw & Jarves firm, he had perhaps imported and sold molded salts and cruets, and his familiarity with such objects would certainly have suggested to his mind the possibility of manufacturing inexpensive substitutes for finer wares.

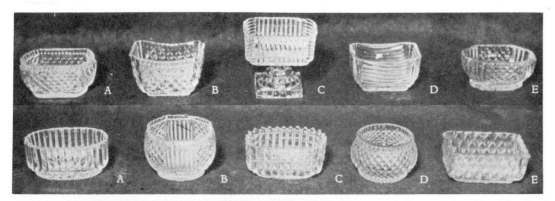

FIG. 1 — MOLDED SALTS

Top row, blown in full-size contact molds, rectangular or oval. Geometric patterns, chiefly diamonds and fluting. Note "fan-end" salt at left (*A*), as mentioned in a New England Glass Company advertisement of 1819. *Second row*, B, octagonal, with alternate panels of ribbing and diamond diapering. *D*, round, patterned with diapering; rayed base with central button. Both are well-known types. "Octagonal moulded salts" are mentioned in a New England Glass Company advertisement of 1819

FIG. 2 — MOLDED SALTS

Showing patterned bases of various types. The rayed base with central button of the second example from the right is found on a variety of other pieces, including the molded dishes and the sugar bowl illustrated on the following page

edge of their products must be gleaned from advertisements or from the occasional pieces of glass that may justifiably be attributed to one place or the other.

The loss to American glass history is the more to be regretted because our most characteristic type — molded glass made in imitation of cutting — came into vogue during those twenty-five years. Glass blown in full-size molds of two or three parts, according to the exigencies of form and pattern, was not uncommon, although not particularly favored, in Ireland at the end of the eighteenth century. Undoubtedly some of it found its way to this country. In our new democracy the use of fine tableware was not restricted to the upper classes; everybody wanted what had heretofore been more or less of a luxury. Cut glass, however, was still rather beyond the reach of the rank and file. For this reason, an imitation which connoisseurs today agree compares in artistic quality more than favorably with the hand-cut ware of the period became immensely popular.

Three-section-mold blown glass, in well-known geometric and baroque designs, seems to have been produced in quantity at a number of places after 1825. I say "in quantity" because the number of surviving specimens is so great in comparison with the amount of other American blown glass known to have been made as long ago as one hundred years that one can draw no other conclusion. Fragments of three-mold glass found on the Sandwich site prove that some, at least, and probably a great deal, of the clear and colored flint ware was turned out there (ANTIQUES, May 1939, *p. 240*). In fact, molded glass is mentioned in Jarves' list of

Jarves' temperament naturally turned toward mass production. Consequently, in the period when he was connected with the Cambridge company, several advertisements mentioning various kinds of molded glass appear. Some of it — hollow ware, such as tumblers, decanters, or pitchers — was probably the same type that he later made at Sandwich. Similar articles were, however, molded by a somewhat different process.

In making an object in a sectional mold, the workman, holding the gathering of glass on the blowpipe within the mold, expanded it by blowing until it received the impression of the design. The hinged mold was then opened, while the blower withdrew the glass, which still adhered to the blowpipe. His assistant, the "sticker-up," then attached to the base a punty rod, by which the object was held while the blowpipe was broken away from the mouth or open end. Shears and other tools were employed to trim and form the mouth or lip. The entire manipulation was carried on while the glass was hot and soft.

A heavy glass of similar surface texture, and even of similar patterns, was produced by a slightly different method. In this second process, the glass was usually blown in a one-part mold; the gathering on the blowpipe was dropped and pushed into it with some force, and a greater expenditure of breath was necessary to bring the thick walls of the bubble into contact with every part of the mold. When the blowing was accomplished and the object withdrawn, the overplus of glass at the top was expanded by blowing until it burst and fell away. After cooling, the jagged edges were cut away and the rim was then ground smooth on the cutter's wheel (*Fig. 3*). (See article by M. S. Dudley Westropp in ANTIQUES, December 1928.)

In molded glass made by the first process, it is possible to feel the design on the inside of the glass, corresponding to the figuration on the outside. In the second instance, this is not often possible, as the excessive thickness of the glass prevents the impression of the mold from being perceptible on the inner surface. There is usually, however, enough irregularity to enable one to distinguish such a mold-blown piece from a pressed one.

That glass molded in this way was a product of the New England Glass Company is first indicated by their advertisement in the *Boston Commercial Gazette* of October 4, 1819, where "moulded fan end Salts" are mentioned. In the following year "fan end and octagon moulded Salts" are noted (*Figs. 1, 2*). These two types of heavy salts are still fairly common in New England. Their manufacture continued throughout the 1820's — perhaps longer — and was not confined to the Cambridge factory. Jarves made molded salts for cutting in 1825, and before that the Irish glasshouses had sent to this country boat-shaped salts on standards.

Molded objects made at Cambridge before 1820 were quart and pint decanters, tumblers of various sizes up to one quart, castor bottles, liquor bottles, and pitchers. An advertisement in the *Boston Commercial Gazette*, of July 22, 1824, reads as follows:

NEW-ENGLAND GLASS COMPANY'S STORE
THE NEW-ENGLAND GLASS COMPANY have taken Store no. 3, South Row, lately occupied by Wing & Sumner, where they will receive orders for any kind of FLINT or CROWN GLASS, by wholesale or retail. They have now on hand and offer for sale as above, a great variety of Glass Ware of the following description, viz: — cut, plain, and moulded Decanters — cut, plain, and moulded Pitchers — rich cut and moulded, octagon, oval and round Dishes — rich cut and plain Sallad Bowls — Cellery Stands — Stand Lamps — Candlesticks with drops — elegant lustre cut Pedestals and arms — Astral Lamps with cut glass pedestals — Fountain Lamps with cut glass pedestals and founts — cut and plain Socket Lamps — cut, painted roughed and plain Entry Lamps, newest patterns — cut and moulded Salts, assorted patterns — cut and moulded Castor Bottles — cut, moulded, and plain Tumblers, Wines and Cordials — cut and plain Lemonades, Custards, Champaigns, and Clarets. Also, a general assortment of APOTHECARIES' and CHEMICAL WARES. Ware for exportation will be packed at factory prices — particular attention will be paid as to the matching of cut and plain glass. Any of the above Goods will be sold at wholesale or retail as cheap as at any store in Boston.

Persons wishing to furnish stores or public houses will do well to call and examine for themselves.

Boston, South Boston, Crown and Chelmsford Window Glass, wholesale or retail. Orders for Fan Lights or Bent Glass will be punctually attended to.

Also, Picture Glass as large as 22 by 28.

While the descriptions are ambiguous — molding and cutting could have been and, indeed were, features of one and the same object — still, the fact cannot be escaped that the molding process in some form was employed to make decanters, pitchers, dishes, castor bottles, tumblers, wines, cordials, and salts. Every one of these forms is known in three-mold glass, but, since salts of undoubted Cambridge origin molded by the second process are to be found, the question naturally arises whether any other articles were thus molded.

The answer is decidedly in the affirmative. I have found eight-sided dishes blown in one-part molds, and both large and small round dishes blown in tripartite molds. In their patterns of ribbing and diapering they closely resemble the salts. The thick, clear metal of which they are fashioned is ground smooth on the edge, leaving the pleasing irregularity of hand-workmanship.

FIG. 3 (*right*) — MOLDED DISHES
Rims have been ground to smooth away jagged edges. *A* shows three seam marks. The diapering and ribbing of *B* are not unlike some of the salt patterns. Both pieces have rayed bases

FIG. 4 — MOLDED SUGAR BOWL
Shape copied from a Staffordshire earthenware item, possibly by Deming Jarves. Shaped in sectional mold, though no seam marks are apparent. *Below, left*, end view of this unusual specimen, showing "fan-end" pattern, similar to salts of Figure 1. *Center*, side view, showing pattern of diapering and reeding, related to patterns of other pieces fashioned by the same process.

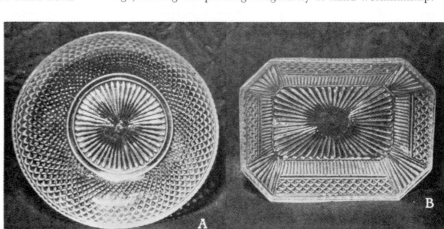

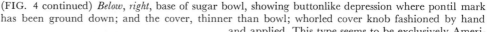

(FIG. 4 continued) *Below, right*, base of sugar bowl, showing buttonlike depression where pontil mark has been ground down; and the cover, thinner than bowl; whorled cover knob fashioned by hand and applied. This type seems to be exclusively American, and even in this country is rare. No English or Irish examples are known

The most unusual specimen of this heavy molded glass that I have seen is the sugar bowl of Figure 4. Its resemblance to the salts is noticeable; in other respects it represents a unique species. There can be no doubt that a Staffordshire earthenware sugar bowl was the prototype of this curious piece. One suspects that the idea of its construction may have originated in the fertile brain of Deming Jarves. It is not a type likely to have emanated from English or Irish sources. W. A. Thorpe disclaims it for England, and Mr. Westropp assures me that he has never seen or heard of such a piece in Ireland. In this country, as far as I have been able to learn, the only other perfect specimen is in the collection of George S. McKearin.

Although such a form must necessarily have been shaped in a sectional mold, the closest scrutiny fails to reveal any mold marks. The joints must have been cleverly fitted at the corners. The thickness of the rim (more than one-quarter inch) and its crooked slant may be clearly seen in the illustrations. The cover is of thinner glass, and the whorled knob is made by hand and applied. The base, as in the dishes and some of the salts, has a buttonlike depression where the punty mark would normally be.

The variety of salts molded in this manner is extensive enough to make the collection of them a pursuit in itself. C. W. Brown, in *Salt Dishes*, notes nearly fifty shapes and patterns. The greater number are rectangular or oval (*Fig. 1*). Octagonal salts with alternating panels of ribbing and diamond diapering and round salts with diapering only are well-known types. They have rayed bases with a central button (*Fig. 2*). Other geometric motives in diamonds, squares, or flutings occur on rectangular salts. Cutting was sometimes employed as elaboration, either in horizontal bands around the body or in points on the rim. With a slight amount of handwork it was thus possible to turn out a bit of glass that appeared at a little distance quite as brilliant as if entirely finished by cutting.

That this same type of molding was practiced at Sandwich is almost certain. One or two fragments of ribbed salts have been found, while Jarves, in his account book, mentions five-inch molded patty pans, molded salts for cutting, and oval, molded, eight-inch dishes. The patty pans could, of course, have been formed by expansion from a decanter mold; but, since it would be impossible to blow an oval dish in a three-part mold, the dishes of that shape must have been fashioned by the earlier process. As time went on and Jarves found the three-mold method more adaptable for making light and graceful glassware, he probably abandoned the old way of molding.

For many years these early products of American glassmaking have been neglected in favor of the more beautifully formed and finished three-mold glass. All examples are not equally attractive, but those pieces combining diapering and ribbing present a pleasingly varied surface, reflecting the light as lustrously as do the recognized three-mold types. They have perhaps not received the admiration they deserve because they have been confused with early glass patterned by pressing. Examination of the edge and of the characteristic blown texture should, however, enable one to distinguish the New England Glass Company type.

Three Mold Glass

By HELEN A. MCKEARIN

Illustrations from the private collection of George S. McKearin

THE age in which we live is, we are constantly informed, one of specialization; and each specialized line, be it of work or of play, has its own cant,—its own terms and names unintelligible to few but the initiated. As the insurance man puzzles us with his "risks" and "K. O.," the musician with his "counterpoint," and the architect with his "counter thrust," so the antique dealer with his "Old Blue," "Sandwich," and "Slipware" puzzles the neophyte in the throes of a developing antique complex. The foreigner with but an academic knowledge of English is no more mystified by reading that the "Yankees defeated the Red Sox" than many a budding dealer or collector by the phrase "three mold." Either the question, "What is three mold glass?" is daily asked, or the person in doubt assumes that any piece of glass on which three mold marks are found is the desirable article. There are some who have told me that they thought the term referred to the number of bands of decoration. The loose use of the term has given rise to confusion not only as to what kind of glass—pressed or blown—is meant, but also as to what type of three mold glass is of value to the collector. As a result many pieces of inferior quality and little value have been eagerly sought and acquired.

The term, three mold glass, like many phrases daily used in the antique world, is, one might say, a nickname for glass blown in contact, three section molds—one of those short-cuts in language for which we seem always to be looking. It is for these lovely, blown pieces of liquid luster that the discriminating collector of American glass is searching. The molds used in forming them were "full-sized"; that is, the size of the completed piece and of the mold was approximately the same. The molds themselves were made in three "hinged sections, and opened or closed at the will of the workman by means of a treadle or other lever."* Hence the term three mold.

The "gathering" of liquid glass on the blow pipe was blown into the mold on the inside of which the pattern was cut intaglio. In the blowing, the air forced the plastic glass into the form of the pattern in such a way that the finished piece, when taken from the mold, showed a depression on the inside to correspond to each protuberance on the outside.† The patterns of some pieces which I have found

Fig. 1 — THREE MOLD GLASS: GEOMETRIC
These examples illustrate the first class of the geometric type. They show wide vertical ribbing, which, in three of the examples, is combined with horizontal ribbing.

indicate that the design, instead of being cut entirely intaglio in the mold, was partially in bas-relief, which, of course, produced a fluting, or concavity on the outer surface of the piece blown in the mold.

The foregoing brings us to the consideration of typical—perhaps one could call them "tell-tale"—three mold patterns; for these patterns constitute a distinctive, even differentiating, feature of the glass. They may be classified under three heads, more or less arbitrarily chosen to aid in classification: namely, *geometric, arched,* and *baroque.*

Under the first head *geometric* the patterns are made up of one or more bands of decoration composed of one motif or a combination of motifs. There are five principal motifs used: (1) *Ribbing,* which may be vertical, horizontal, diagonal, twisted, or herringbone; (2) *Fluting;* (3) *Diamond Diapering;* an all-over pattern of diamond shaped protuberances; (4) *Sunbursts;* a square or rectangular frame with radii from a center to the sides; (5) *Diamond-in-the-Square;* square or rectangular frame enclosing a diamond usually equilateral. In the sunburst and in the diamond-in-the-square there are variations as to centers and corners.

The accompanying photographs illustrate some of the combinations forming what I have termed the geometric type. They, likewise, show a few of the articles made in three section molds.

In Figure 1 the pitcher is of the simplest pattern that I have found, wide vertical ribbing. On the mustard pots, the salt shaker, and cruet bottles one sees the use of horizontal ribbing also. In such patterns, in general, there is no uniform width or length to the ribbing; one finds wide and narrow, long and short. In Figure 2 a variation of ribbing, as well as a combination of decorative forms, is shown. The pattern seen here, a band of diamond diapering between bands of vertical ribbing, is, perhaps, the most common of all and explains the mistaken conception of three mold as three bands of decoration. From this picture, moreover, it may be seen that there is no standard width for the bands of the pattern.

In Figure 3 we have one of the most elaborate of the geometric patterns—three motifs—the herringbone type of ribbing, diamond diapering, and sunburst. The use of the sunburst motif, which this figure illustrates, to form

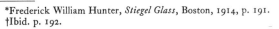

*Frederick William Hunter, *Stiegel Glass,* Boston, 1914, p. 191.
†Ibid. p. 192.

Fig. 2 — THREE MOLD GLASS: GEOMETRIC
In these, ribbing again appears, but it is not the same as that shown in Figure 1. It is, furthermore, used in combination with a broad band of diamond diapering.

medallions in a band of diamond diapering is the one we most often encounter. In a few patterns we find another use, also displayed in this illustration, that is, to form a band entirely of sunbursts. The herringbone ribbing is likewise shown. Although space does not permit a detailed treatment of the geometric patterns, the illustrations are sufficiently representative to furnish a basis for the recognition of other patterns.

The second and third groups—those which fall under the divisions arched and baroque—are each smaller than the geometric.

The patterns of the type called arched are so denominated because they are characterized by an arch motif, usually either Gothic or Roman. Figure 4 pictures decanters and a pitcher molded in the most ornate of the patterns in which the arch is the predominating feature; that is, this one is the most ornate which I have, as yet, found. I qualify my statement because new patterns are continually turning up.

The baroque group is sister to the arched. The term "baroque" has been chosen to signify that group of patterns which, in general, resemble the type of architectural decoration known as baroque or rococo. When used in reference to ornamentation, it calls to mind that Italian style composed of conspicuous curves, volutes, and scrolls; in short it is a highly ornate decoration. In Figure 5 appear two of the patterns which I have placed in the baroque class. The one at the right is the simplest, that at the left one of the most elaborate. Each is typical.

As I have stated, the patterns of three section, contact mold glass may be said to constitute one means of differentiating this type from other types of glass. In the pressed glass dishes, for example, one finds, as a rule, very elaborate, conventionalized floral and other baroque patterns which are more intricate than those designed for the blown pieces. The pressed glass patterns are usually on a stippled background such as is never encountered in the blown glass. Moreover, if one examines several pieces of the two kinds of glass he will find that the inner surface of the

pressed pieces is comparatively smooth; it does not follow the pattern. This same characteristic is common to other pieces of pressed, three mold goblets and similar articles, which have added to the obscurity connected with the name. Pressed glass pieces, likewise, lack the liquid luster of the blown glass. There are a few pressed three mold articles, such as decanters and cruet sets, which have a concave surface to correspond to convex and which have been molded into patterns similar enough to blown baroque to be mistaken for it unless one is very familiar with the two kinds of glass. In these pieces, however, the quality of the glass is so patently inferior that the resemblance goes no farther than the type of mold and the pattern. The blown articles have a living, liquid brilliance, but the pressed ones are like dead cut glass. Above all things, the fact which must always be kept in mind, and which cannot be over-emphasized, is that these patterns with which we have been dealing occur in the *blown*, contact, three mold glass, *not in the pressed*. The essential differences arise from the method of production.

Another type of glass with which the three mold has been confused is the pattern molded type. Pattern molded pieces, while somewhat the same in quality as the contact, are characterized by having no mold marks and by having an internal protuberance to correspond to an external one in the completed pieces.* Once in a while, a piece in typical three mold pattern is found on which no mold marks can be distinguished, and an inexperienced collector thinks it from a pattern mold. In event of finding such a piece the pattern can generally serve as a means of identification—together with the ear mark of the contact mold: that is, the relation of the convex to the concave surfaces. The absence of the mold marks may be due to "flashing"; that is, submitting to intense heat after taking from the mold, a process devised for the definite purpose of eliminating the marks.†

Occasionally one comes across a second digression from

---

*Hunter, *as before cited*, p. 196.
†Ibid. p. 198.

Fig. 3 — THREE MOLD GLASS: GEOMETRIC
One of the most elaborate of geometric patterns, the sunburst. It will be observed that this motif is here used in combination with vertical, horizontal and herringbone ribbing, and with fields of diamond diapering. The result is a rich and brilliant effect obtained by the skillful use of comparatively simple means.

type, pieces which, besides having no mold marks, have a perfectly smooth inner surface. When this occurs one must judge from the quality of the glass and from the pattern whether or not it be contact three mold, in which the thickness of the glass prevented the forming of the usual depression to correspond to the external protuberance.

The natural question which follows, "What is three mold glass?" is, "Where was it made?" The sources of contact three section mold glass constitute, at present, an antique nebula. They are largely a matter of conjecture and speculation. In *Stiegel Glass* the possibility that some, at least, of the finest specimens of three mold may be among the last efforts of Baron Stiegel is entertained. Today, however, students and collectors of American glass

Fig. 4 — THREE MOLD GLASS: ARCHED
Here is shown perhaps the most ornate development of the arched pattern, which is broken in the middle by horizontal ribbing. The twined serpents, forming a medallion on the decanters, constitute a fanciful touch in which an implied moral may be discerned. Stoppers show whorled ribbing.

Fig. 5 — THREE MOLD GLASS: BAROQUE
The pattern shown at the left is the most elaborate; that at the right the simplest. Each is typical.

generally accept the theory that three mold glass, in this country at least, is a later product than "Stiegel."

That certain olive-green and olive-amber decanters of geometric pattern were the product of the Stoddard factory in New Hampshire is reasonably well established. When excavations have been made on the site of the factory, fragments of this dark glass only have been unearthed. No specimens of clear, or of colored glass other than olive green and amber have ever been found at Stoddard, in so far as I have been able to ascertain. Nevertheless I have seen clear, flint glass decanters and pitchers identical in pattern with the known Stoddard, dark colored decanters. The conclusion that their source is common

seems, therefore, logical. Still, one cannot be too careful or cautious in attributing a piece of glass to a particular factory. The need for patient research and study before definite attributions can be made is urgent.

After all, although the knowledge of the birthplace of a given piece of glass may add to its interest from an historical point of view and to its commercial value, such knowledge cannot add one jot or tittle to its intrinsic beauty, wherein should be its inherent value. Three mold glass, wherever it may have been made, when viewed, in reality or in the imagination, awakens in the memory that much abused but happy verse of Keats,

"A thing of beauty is a joy forever."

THREE UNUSUAL EXAMPLES OF THREE MOLD GLASS
The pair of decanters, which hold about a pint and a half each, are a lovely shade of clear light green. The pattern is a rather unusual variety of the geometric type. It has a broad band of diamond diapering above and a similar band below a central band of vertical ribbing. On the shoulders is gadrooning. The stoppers are original, with fine, wide-spaced vertical ribbing on one side and fine horizontal ribbing on the other. The decanter in the center is also light green, showing a broad band of wide vertical ribbing with narrow horizontal ribbing above and below.

BLOWN-THREE-MOLD GLASS

A Condensation from
"Two Hundred Years of American Blown Glass"
by Helen and George S. McKearin

The glass here discussed was first treated as an independent type by Helen McKearin in ANTIQUES *for August 1924, where she established the names of the categories which are now generally accepted. Her further studies of this glass were recorded in* American Glass *(1941), in which the known patterns were numbered and charted. Pattern numbers used in the present article refer to that classification. The material presented here will appear in amplified form, fully illustrated, in the forthcoming book,* Two Hundred Years of American Blown Glass, *to be published in March by Doubleday and Company.*

BLOWN-THREE-MOLD—or to give it all the names by which it has been known, contact-three-section-mold glass, Stiegel, Stoddard, blown-molded, insufflated, three mold—is like a foundling left on a doorstep; no one knows its real name, if it ever had one. Since the glass was *not* a product of either the Stiegel or the Stoddard glasshouses, and the other names, in our opinion, are even more misleading, we continue to call it blown-three-mold, the name familiar for the past quarter of a century or more. It appears to have been more popular in the United States than in Britain and to have reached the peak of its production and popularity in the late 1820's.

Blown-three-mold glass has inherent identifying characteristics arising from its designs and the method of its fabrication. In general the glass, especially that blown from clear lead metal, has a liveliness of appearance akin to that of cut glass, though its liquid brilliance is to the brilliance of cut glass as the glow of polished pewter is to that of silver. Quality of metal, contours of pattern, and type of molding, all together determined the degree and quality of brilliance. But the method of molding determined the type of impression from the mold and therein lies one of the distinctive characteristics of the glass, namely, a softness and rounding of edges, and an impression less diffuse than on pattern-molded glass but less definitive than on cut glass or the later pressed glass.

Equally inherent characteristics, and more easily recognized, are the nature of the mold marks and the concavo-convex relationship of the inner and outer surfaces of a piece. Almost without exception, wherever there is a protuberance on the outside, there is a corresponding hollow on the inside. The mold marks are faint vertical ridges, about the width of a heavily penciled line. Frequently when reheating and manipulation were required, the marks were partially obliterated and so are difficult to locate. The mold marks may be two, three, or four in number, but are most commonly three.

About 150 characteristic patterns of blown-three-mold glass have been recorded and classified in three main groups according to the predominant motif: geometric, arch, and baroque. Since the type of ware was inspired by cut glass, many of the patterns, in the geometric group principally, faithfully reproduce those of cut glass and others are plainly derivative. The designers not only shuffled the old motifs for a new deal in combinations but also, it seems, originated a few patterns of their own, especially in the arch and baroque groups.

The patterns in the small arch group of about eight have either a Roman or a Gothic arch as the most conspicuous motif (*Fig. 1, left*). Decanters in one arch pattern and in four geometrics with the name of a liquor molded in the pattern have been recorded. Though this method of labeling was a logical step from the "ticket" necklaces for decanters, so far as we know these labeled decanters occur only in the American blown-three-mold glass, and in that they are rare.

The baroque patterns, about twenty-five in number, have simple arabesques and motifs such as hearts, palmettes, shells, and gadroonlike ribs (*Fig. 2*). Like the arch patterns, they are in comparatively high relief and the motifs of more generous proportions than those of the geometric. Also, whereas the geometric are tight and compact like the cut glass of the day, the arch and baroque are usually more free and flowing in line. The articles molded in the arch and baroque patterns were limited largely to decanters and pitchers, a few cruet bottles, and tumblers.

Geometric motifs, mainly rectilinear, form the patterns in the geometric groups. In a few a single motif has been used; in most, two or more, as a rule in horizontal bands. Ribbing predominates. Hardly more than half a dozen patterns have been recorded without ribbing in some one of its many forms: vertical, horizontal, herringbone, swirled, or spiraled; rounded or flat; broad or narrow; long or short. Vertical, horizontal, and diagonal flutes, also convex or concave circles and ovals as beading, have been used sparingly. The sunburst and diamond motifs are the most elaborate. There are three of the latter, each having a plain field and a ringed center; and eleven of the former. The sunbursts progress, or from a design point of view perhaps retrogress, from the simple sunburst with beams radiating from its focus, through nine steps to the most complex, the sunburst-in-square. Like their sunbursts, the geometric patterns seem to have progressed from utter simplicity of design to extreme ornateness, falling naturally into three groups on their way. Group I is composed mainly of flutings and ribbings; Group II, of ribbings or flutings and diamond diapering in bands or blocks (*Fig. 3*); Group III, of a

FIG. 1—*Left,* BLOWN-THREE-MOLD PITCHER (*c. 1815-1830*). Brilliant clear lead glass. Arch pattern GIV-6. Possibly the New England Glass Company. Height, 7⅜₁₆ inches. *Right,* BLOWN-THREE-MOLD PITCHER (*c. 1815-1830*). Clear lead glass. Baroque pattern GV-13. New England area. Height, 5¾ inches.

FIG. 2—*Left*, BLOWN-THREE-MOLD CREAMER *(c. 1825-1835)*. Sapphire-blue lead glass. Baroque pattern GV-14, sometimes called the *horizontal palm leaf*, one of the most elaborate of the baroque patterns. Boston and Sandwich Glass Company. *Center*, BLOWN-THREE-MOLD CREAMER *(c. 1825-1835)*. Light sapphire-blue lead glass. Baroque pattern GV-3. Height, 5⅛ inches. As far as we know, creamers and half-pint decanters are the only articles found in this pattern. No record is available as to the glasshouse in which this mold may have been used. *Right*, BLOWN-THREE-MOLD CREAMER *(c. 1825-1835)*. Cobalt-blue lead glass. Baroque pattern GV-8. Boston and Sandwich Glass Company. Height, 4½ inches. Quart, pint, and half-pint decanters, quart and pint pitchers, and creamers are known in this pattern.

diamond or sunburst motif in addition to the others *(Fig. 4)*.

From an analysis of the pieces and the surviving numbers there is no doubt that blown-three-mold, particularly in its geometric patterns, was a type of tableware made on a scale approaching mass production. There were decanters, from miniature to over a quart in capacity, bottles and carafes and their companion drinking vessels—cordials and punch cups, mugs and wines, goblets and tumblers from whiskey to flip glasses. There were dishes of many sizes; small plates, and bowls, large and small, with and without a foot or standard. There were preserve pots with cover and stand, celery glasses, pitchers from miniature to water size holding a quart or more, and sugar bowls, sometimes with matching creamers. In fact, there were most of the articles which the auctioneers and importers of fine cut glass after the War of 1812 and during the lush 1820's felt should be listed in their notices. And besides the table glass there were hats and inkwells, lamp fonts and night lamps, and individual pieces.

Most of these articles were fabricated from clear or colored flint (lead) glass, but an interesting minority were made from bottle glass. These last, as a rule, were drab olive-ambers and olive-greens, occasionally aquamarine and light greens. By far the greatest number of the flint-glass pieces were colorless, but there was a goodly proportion in blues, sometimes a light hue, sometimes a true sapphire, principally a deep purple-blue appearing amethyst when held to an electric light. Amethysts, true even when seen by daylight, and emerald greens were made sparingly. One or two pieces in canary yellow are known. Also there were pieces in odd tones like heliotrope and others defying description; whether they were achieved by intent or by accident is a question.

The present survey has been based on the examination of well over five thousand pieces of blown-three-mold glass. More than one thousand were analyzed to determine the molds in which they were patterned. That analysis established that more than 400 basic individual molds were used in their making. The basic molds for the production of all articles of tableware seem to have been bottle molds from gill to quart or more in size and in the various shapes and patterns for castors, cruets, and decanters; for bottle stoppers; and for tumblers from gill to large flip size, in barrel or cylindrical shape. Of course there were molds for a few other articles, for instance inkwells and lamp fonts. In one pattern alone (GII-18), having a band of diamond diapering between bands of vertical ribbing and a variety of base designs, we have determined more than fifty molds made for bottles, decanters, tumblers, castors, or inkwells. And these molds were used also to pattern such articles as salt cellars, dishes, hats, pitchers, sugar bowls, celery glasses, and bowls with and without foot.

In the fabrication of most articles of blown-three-mold

(other than the bottle and tumbler forms) the full-size mold was used to give the pattern, as were the dip and the part-size piece molds. The piece was fashioned mainly by offhand methods, its ultimate form shaped by manipulation, frequently having little resemblance to that of the mold in which it was patterned. Consequently the creation of a blown-three-mold sugar bowl, for example, took as much or nearly as much of the blower's time and skill as a pattern-molded bowl. Nevertheless, since so many of the articles, such as bottles and tumblers, necessitated little or no more handwork than the shearing of a rim or turning of a flange, blown-three-mold represented a considerable saving in labor and time for the glassmaker.

From the geographical distribution of the blown-three-mold glass which has been collected it would appear that it was a specialty of eastern rather than of midwestern glasshouses. It must have been included in the molded wares made and advertised by many of the glasshouses of its period which were devoted chiefly to the production of tablewares. Unfortunately, since most of them were in cities and towns, any physical evidence to be found on their sites has long since been destroyed. Fewer than a third of the recorded patterns and considerably fewer than a third of the recorded individual molds can be attributed to a specific glasshouse, and those largely because of excavations on factory sites.

The excavations of the late Harry Hall White on the sites of the glasshouses at Mantua and Kent, Ohio; Coventry, Connecticut; Mount Vernon, New York; and the Keene-Marlboro-Street works in New Hampshire, unearthed fragments in sufficient quantity to establish the certainty of production in a few geometric patterns. Those of Francis L. Wynn on the site of the Boston and Sandwich Glass Company's factory, combined with other determining factors, indicated that Sandwich produced the ware on a large scale in patterns falling in all three main groups. The output of the other proven sources may have been minuscule by comparison. Several of the patterns were used by more than one house. One mold in the pattern GII-33, having a band of diamond diapering between bands of vertical flutes, has been identified with Mantua *(Fig. 3)*, but this was not used at Mantua only. The same is true of the two patterns used at Kent. Three patterns (used principally for inkwells) have been identified with Coventry; five with Keene; four with Mount Vernon; and at least twenty-six with Sandwich. The commonest pattern in the entire category (GII-18) was common to all these eastern houses. Mount Vernon and Sandwich both used the geometric pattern of ribs and fan flutes *(GI-29)*, and both combined the sunburst-in-square with broad vertical and swirled ribbings in a comparatively simple pattern. Except for a slight difference in the treatment of the sunburst, their patterns appear identical. Other Sandwich

FIG. 3—BLOWN-THREE-MOLD FOOTED BOWL (c. 1822-1829). Clear, fairly deep green, non-lead glass. Pattern GII-33. Mantua Glass Works, Portage County, Ohio. Height, 5¼ inches. As far as we know, only five pieces of Mantua blown-three-mold glass have so far been recorded—this bowl, a quart pitcher, two quart decanters, apparently made without glass stoppers, and a large cover of the flanged set-in type for a bowl. (The pitcher, one decanter, and the large cover are illustrated on Plate 118, *American Glass*.) All are a similar color and patterned in a mold definitely known to have been used at the Mantua Glass Works. We have tested all but one decanter and found each is non-lead glass. Wear on the rim of the bowl indicates it may originally have had a cover. If so, it was undoubtedly similar to the one noted.

patterns show that factory's tendency toward elaboration in design.

At present only about a baker's dozen of all the remaining patterns can be attributed with any degree of certainty to either a glasshouse or a region. One geometric, one baroque, and three of the arch patterns (including Figure 1, left) undoubtedly were among those which the New England Glass Company used for its common run of wares. As the scarce pieces molded in the three geometric patterns GII-32, GIII-10 and 11 have been found almost exclusively in the midwest, these patterns were probably used by one or more of the midwestern houses specializing in tableware.

Seven other geometric patterns in Groups I and II were as British as they were American. However, if blown-three-mold glass was made in Ireland and in England, it was restrained in its number of patterns and motifs. Only ribs, or as the British call them pillar flutes, and diamonds were employed; such motifs as the sunbursts were not carried over from cut glass to the molded. Moreover, the forms and quantity produced were limited; not, certainly, because Britain did not have her classes unable to indulge in the luxury of cut glass but because their wants were met by other types of ware.

Blown-three-mold glass was in that twilight zone between the brilliance of craftsmanship and the darkness of mechanization in production of the ordinary wares. In another molded ware simulating cut glass, a type which preceded, followed, or developed concurrently with blown-three-mold, the glassmaker seems to have come even closer to a final transfer of craftsmanship from the glassblowers to the mold-makers. This was molded in patterns composed of simple motifs, principally shallow diamonds, usually in blocks or diaper bands as in blown-three-mold glass, and ribbings—chiefly vertical, horizontal, curved, sometimes forming a fan. Each piece was made from a generous gather of metal so that it was quite heavy, varying from an eighth to a quarter of an inch in thickness. And it looked stolid, as a rule quite

lacking the sparkle and life of the glass it imitated, perhaps because so much metal was used and its contours were rounded. In contradistinction to that of blown-three-mold glass, its inner surface was almost always even and smooth as on cut glass or the finest of the pressed glass. While an overwhelming majority of the pieces were made from clear glass, artificial colors were made occasionally. A few colored salts have been recorded. Apparently the output in the United States, at least, consisted mainly of salts, dishes, and covered bowls. The salts were of many shapes, with and without foot or standard; the dishes, round, oval, and octagonal; the covered bowls, globular with circular foot, or, rarely, rectangular in shape. The dishes were formed either in piece molds or shallow molds such as those used in blowing blanks for oval and octagonal dishes for cutting. Probably the molds for blanks gave some ingenious glassman the idea of having an incised pattern to simulate a cut design.

Among the many reasons for believing that production of this type of ware began before 1820 is the fact that by 1817 the oval, round, and octagonal cut-glass dishes were sufficiently popular to be mentioned specifically in auctioneers' and merchants' listings of imported glass. A sketch of one of the octagonal dishes was used by the New York City firm of glasscutters, Jackson and Baggott, at the head of their April 1819 advertisement announcing the opening of their store at 36 Maiden Lane. Molded fan-end salts, which undoubtedly belonged in this category of imitation cut glass, were among the articles listed in announcements in the Boston papers of the New England Glass Company's wares to be sold at auction October 6, 1819. In Ireland, we understand from M. S. D. Westropp, the authority on Irish glass, this type of molded ware was being made in limited quantities around 1830. It seems probable that in the United States little was made after mechanically pressed glass became popular. In 1829 at least six eastern glasshouses and four in the midwest were pressing glass on a commercial scale. Henceforth, as far as most of the non-luxury tableware and much of the ornamental glass was concerned, craftsmanship was to be in the hands of the moldmaker.

Illustrations from the McKearin collection, to be included in the book "Two Hundred Years of American Blown Glass," Doubleday and Company.

FIG. 4—EXTREMELY RARE BLOWN-THREE-MOLD BOWL ON STANDARD (c. 1825-1835). Clear lead glass, circular bowl with heavy applied rim of deep sapphire blue, short applied stem with large globular knop, and applied circular foot. Pattern GIII-5. Boston and Sandwich Glass Company. Height, 6⁷⁄₁₆ inches. *Photographs by Taylor and Dull.*

452

Fictions of "Three-Mold" Glass

By Helen A. McKearin

Note. — Artemas Ward once sagely remarked that it would be better to know less than to know so many things that are not so. That bit of philosophy prompted ANTIQUES to invite the writing of the following article, whose aim, as the reader will perceive, is primarily to reduce, if possible, the accumulated surplus of misinformation concerning a single popular type of glass. Its clear and accurate analysis of the differences in texture, aspect, and basic value between glass objects that have been blown in a mold and those which owe their form to mechanical processes, will repay careful study. Other articles of similar intention will follow. — *The Editor.*

AROUND the actualities of early American glass has accumulated an encrustation of misunderstanding and misinformation which the published results of diligent research have failed to dissolve. Errors of judgment, observation, and deduction, fables invented to meet the insistent demand of would-be collectors for specific factory attributions, and mythical stories of long standing, all contribute to the fabric of this obscuring envelope. To make the matter worse, articles are constantly being written which perpetuate the old-time fallacies; and even in some books accepted as authoritative, one finds them still repeated. To deal with each and every one in the space of a single article is impossible; but perhaps some of the toughest die-hards may be brought to the mat.

Just now some of the errors and myths clinging to the term "three-mold" as identifying a type of glass, merit special consideration.

In the first place, as a study of the origin and history of the term will demonstrate, "three-mold" should *never* be used in reference to any piece of *pressed* glass, even though that piece clearly shows three vertical mold marks. The term "three-mold," it ought to be remembered, is nothing more or less than an abbreviation of "blown contact three-section mold," a somewhat unwieldy title, which, to the best of my knowledge, was first used following the publication of *Stiegel Glass* by Frederick William Hunter, in 1914. It was a title evolved from Mr. Hunter's

descriptive phrases: "blown in full size, three-piece, contact molds" (p. 174), "full-sized contact molds" (p. 195), and "contact-mold-blown pieces" (p. 196). While conducting his studies in Stiegel glass, Mr. Hunter found many glass vessels which, he learned, had been formed by blowing molten glass into a full-size mold; that is, a mold of virtually the same size as the finished article. Such molds, he further learned, had been made in three sections, so hinged that they could be clamped together during blowing of the glass, and then opened to permit easy extraction of the molded object. The inner surfaces of these molds were cut in a pattern, which was impressed in the glass with which it came in contact. Stiegel molded pieces, on the other hand, were made quite differently. The globule of molten glass was first blown into a "small, open-top, pattern mold." Having thus received its preliminary form and pattern, the glass was taken from this mold, reheated, and expanded to the required size by blowing and shaping in the open. So Mr. Hunter differentiated between articles blown in a *full-size* mold and those blown in a *small open-top* mold, by calling the former "contact-mold-blown pieces" and the latter "pattern-mold" pieces.

Unfortunately, it must be admitted, these terms were not well chosen to identify two entirely different types of mold. For both the full-size mold and the small open-top mold have a *pattern* cut intaglio on their interior surfaces; and, in the process of blowing, this pat-

![Fig. 1 — Blown and Pressed Wine Glasses]

Fig. 1 — BLOWN AND PRESSED WINE GLASSES
a, Blown three-mold bowl. Stem and foot shaped "free-hand" and applied. *b*, Pressed glass in Palm, or Fern, pattern, showing three vertical mold marks from top to bottom. *c*, Pressed glass in Bellflower pattern, showing three vertical mold marks from top to bottom.

Fig. 2 — BLOWN THREE-MOLD WINE GLASS
Here the stem and foot have been drawn out from the bowl of the glass.

Fig. 3 — Blown Three-Mold Sugar Bowl
The foot has been independently blown in a small pattern mold; then expanded and applied to the bowl.

Fig. 4 — Blown Three-Mold Bowl
The foot has been independently blown in a three-section mold and applied to the bowl.

tern is transferred to the article by *contact* between the globule of glass and the sides of the mold. Hence, quite obviously, no matter what its size, any mold carrying an incised pattern is *both* "contact" and "pattern," and might be called by either name. The use of these words to designate two distinct types of molds should accordingly be discontinued. Similarly, the word "contact" is properly omitted from "blown contact three-section mold," leaving the entirely adequate term "blown three-section mold."

Mr. Hunter's book, however, brought the realization that "blown contact three-section mold" applied to those pieces of glass which had been blown in a full-size, three-section mold, and that such pieces could be identified by the resulting vertical mold marks on their sides. And, just as the popularity of this kind of glass increased, just so the term "blown contact three-section mold" became synonymous with fine quality and great desirability. It also came naturally to convey an implication of monetary value. Very soon, however, the full five-word designation was abbreviated to the familiar and convenient adjective "three-mold." But, by those who know their glass, this adjective is used only in reference to *blown* pieces.

To the initiate,

"three-mold" conveys the full significance of the longer name. Novices too often find it a pitfall. Forgetting the important, though omitted, word "blown," they accept as "three-mold" any piece of glass — whether blown or mechanically pressed — which shows three vertical mold marks. And the worst of this situation is that, while these novices mistake the application of the term, they never fail to remember its significance of desirability and quality. As a result, quite absurd importance and value are often attached to those mediocre mechanically pressed glass objects which, ever since the middle of the nineteenth century, have been made in three-section molds. Many an amateur has been humiliated, after showing his prized "three-mold" pitcher to an experienced collector, by hearing the casual remark, "Oh, yes. Rather nice for practical use. But, of course, the real three-mold is blown glass, not pressed."

As a matter of fact, the two types of molded glass — that *blown* in a three-section mold and that mechanically *pressed* in a more or less similar device, are so foreign to each other that it seems almost a crime to give them the same name. One might as properly insist that a rhinestone, because of superficial likeness, should be called a

Fig. 5 — Pressed and Blown Molded Glass
a, Ivy pattern salt, pressed in one piece. *b,* Geometric pattern salt, probably first blown in small tumbler mold and then shaped "free-hand" into a salt.

Fig. 6 — PRESSED AND BLOWN MOLDED PITCHERS
  a, Pressed Bellflower pattern; clearly impressed design; heavy handle. *b,* Arch and Fern pattern. Blown in a decanter mold, and the neck then expanded. Note lightness and grace of handle.

conspicuous mold marks.

Second, mold marks on blown three-mold glass differ from those on pressed glass not only in form but in position. For instance, the Bellflower wine glass in Figure 1, or any other pressed article which has a stem or foot, was usually made in one piece. Consequently the mold marks extend in a continuous line all the way from the top to the bottom. On the other hand, the wine glass in Figure 1, blown in a three-section mold, like any other blown three-mold article which has a stem and foot, was not made in one piece. The body, or bowl, was molded; afterwards the stem and foot were *added.* As these subsequently applied parts were not blown in a mold,

diamond. To tell the truth, there is not one point of similarity between the two kinds of glass I have mentioned, except the presence of mold marks.

The differences are manifold!

First, the mold marks are absolutely dissimilar. The mold mark on a mechanically pressed glass article is sharply defined. It looks like a tiny thread of glass applied to the piece after its formation.

The mold mark on a blown three-mold piece is very often difficult to locate! It is a very minute swelling in the piece itself. By a novice it might almost be mistaken for an imperfection in the glass. If you will take a pencil and draw a line on a piece of paper, using quite a bit of pressure; then turn the paper over, you will find a slight convexity on the reverse of your line. That is how a mold mark on a blown three-mold piece appears.

This radical difference in the character of the two marks follows naturally from two different methods of production. In *pressing* glass, the high pressure and rapid action of a metal plunger spread the sections of the mold very slightly and force the liquid glass completely into all crevices of the mold before any appreciable cooling can take place on the surface of the plastic mass. On the other hand, though in the *blowing* process the mold sections spread a little, the force of the blower's breath is much less than that of a plunger, and the expansion of the molten glass is consequently slower. Thus a slight cooling hardens the glass sufficiently to prevent its taking a sharp and definite impression from the mold. Furthermore, blown pieces were often "flashed" (reheated quickly) to obliterate or soften the

Fig. 7 (*right*) — PRESSED AND BLOWN MOLDED DECANTERS
  a, Pressed Horn of Plenty pattern. *b,* Blown geometric pattern. Here the difference between the incisiveness of the pressed pattern and the soft outlines of the blown is clearly demonstrated.

Fig. 8 — PRESSED AND BLOWN MOLDED PITCHERS
a, Pressed Wild Flower pattern; mold marks showing sharply from top to bottom. *b*, Blown geometric pattern. *c*, Pressed Westward Ho pattern. The pitcher *b* was first blown in a flip or tumbler mold and then shaped "free-hand" into pitcher form. Aside from its greater delicacy of pattern, the blown molded glass is far more free and spontaneous in form than pressed glass.

they, of course, show no mold marks. There are only two exceptions to this rule of applied, non-molded parts: (1), those pieces which have a stem and foot — or simply a foot — *drawn out* from the body itself; and (2), those to which a hollow foot, separately blown in a three-section mold or in a small open-top mold, has been added. The blown three-mold wine glass in Figure 2 illustrates stem and foot drawn out from the bowl; the pieces in Figures 3 and 4 show the hollow stem and foot separately blown in a mold and applied.

Third, the surfaces of the two types of glass are diametrically opposed in character. Where there are protuberances on the outside of a blown three-mold article, there are corresponding concavities on the inside, unless the glass is abnormally thick. The inside of a pressed piece, on the contrary, is always smooth, in no way following the pattern on the exterior.

In the blown glass, furthermore, there is never a distinct line of demarcation between the motives of the design. Instead, the parts of the pattern flow into each other. All angles formed by the junction of motives are slightly curved. In pressed glass the pattern is sharp, keen, almost excessively distinct in the separation of its parts. Pressed patterns approach to photographic clarity, whereas those of blown three-mold are diffused, and might be called impressionistic as compared with the pressed, as we see in Figures 6 and 7.

Fourth, pressed glass is an obvious *imitation* of cut glass. Blown three-mold displays an attractive adaptation of the patterns of cut glass. There is an æsthetic difference which may be appreciated, though it is almost impossible to demonstrate.

Fifth, an important distinction lies in the quality of the glass itself. While some pressed pieces are, perhaps, as fine in metal as any blown three-mold specimens, the majority are of far inferior fabric.

It must be kept in mind that the *only* pressed glass with

which we are here concerned consists of pieces pressed in a three-section mold. This is "late" glass, manufactured chiefly after 1850. The blown three-mold pieces were made, for the most part, before that date. If the two kinds of glass were both popular products made today, the blown three-mold would be found in the exclusive shops, the pressed at the "Five and Ten."

From the discriminating collector's point of view, the finest pieces of glass pressed in a three-section mold cannot compare in value, desirability, or beauty with blown three-mold. The heights of æsthetic or monetary value are seldom for the products of purely mechanical methods: they are for the handiwork of skilled craftsmen. Who would prefer the plaster frieze to the art of the sculptor? There is much the same sentiment toward glass. The human element is evident in blown glass, even that which has taken its pattern from a mold. It is absent from glass that has been pressed.

Having thus tried to explain what the knowing collector understands by "three-mold," I must in the end admit that the term itself is not entirely satisfactory. What then shall we employ as a substitute?

I do not feel that "insufflated," the latest designation for blown three-mold glass, will relieve our difficulties. In the first place, a careful comparison of the definitions given in various dictionaries shows that "insufflate," as a rule, is used in connection with medical or ecclesiastical matters. Secondly, even if accepted in its broadest possible sense, the word could be no more than an awkward substitution for "blown."

If we were insisting on scientific exactitude of description, we should have to revert to the long and awkward title "blown three-section mold." But why be pedantic? "Blown three-mold" is short, adequate and, to the majority of collectors, perfectly understood. Having been recognized in glass terminology, it should be retained.

Fig. 1 — *a*, SMALL MOLD-BLOWN SYRIAN-TYPE BOTTLE FROM CYPRUS (*early first century A.D.*)
    From the Metropolitan Museum of Art
    b, THREE MOLD-BLOWN PERFUME BOTTLES, FRENCH OR AMERICAN (*nineteenth century*). *From the collection of Frederic Fairchild Sherman*

Glass: Ancient and Antique

By HOMER EATON KEYES

IT WOULD appear that only within the past fifty years or so has any widespread interest been manifested in ancient glasses, other than such rare and impressive examples as the Portland vase, whose transfer from Italy to London in 1770 exercised so significant an influence upon Josiah Wedgwood's pottery designs. Oddly enough, more than a century was to pass before this monument of the Roman glassmaker's art was to stir emulative ambitions among the glassworkers of England. Meanwhile, the simpler household utensils of glass turned out within the Roman dominions, from the first to the fourth century after Christ, seem virtually to have escaped the attention of even the most ardent eighteenth-century admirers of classic culture and its expression in the domain of the arts.

How, then, are we to account for the extraordinary similarity observable between the domestic glasses produced in various parts of the Roman Empire more than

Fig. 2 — *a* (*above*), MOLD-BLOWN SYRIAN-TYPE JUG FROM CYPRUS (*early first century A.D.*)
From the Metropolitan Museum of Art

b (*right*), OFFHAND-BLOWN ALEXANDRIAN JUG (*fourth century A.D.*)
Compare lip form with that of the jug, *c.*
From the University of Michigan Museum

c (*left*), MOLD-BLOWN AMERICAN JUG (*early nineteenth century*)
Note vertical panels and recurrence of honeysuckle motive.
From the McKearin collection

d (*above*) MOLD-BLOWN AMERICAN DECANTER (*early nineteenth century*)
Note band of diapering and fluting of the body

Fig. 3 — a (left), MOLD-BLOWN SYRIAN SATYR MUG (first century A.D.)
From the Metropolitan Museum of Art
b (below), MOLD-BLOWN FRENCH FLASK (nineteenth century)
Clear glass, here filled with milk.
From the F. Brown collection

Fig. 4 — a (below), ALEXANDRIAN FLASK (fourth century A.D.)
Blown in ribbed mold; ribs subsequently dragged together with pincers.
From the University of Michigan Museum
b (right), AMERICAN MIDWESTERN FLASK (early nineteenth century)
Blown in ribbed mold; ribs subsequently dragged together with pincers.
From the McKearin collection

1500 years ago, and the wares turned out by the artisans in American glasshouses of the eighteenth and nineteenth centuries? The phenomenon is virtually inexplicable except on the assumption that certain traditions of glassmaking were handed down unbroken from master to apprentice through more than a thousand years of European history and, in due time, were carried to this country by immigrants from the smaller old-world glasshouses.

In so far as may be judged from their performances in the land of their adoption, these immigrant workmen were seldom adept in the art of making the finer table wares such as were in use among fashionable folk of England and the Continent. America's primary need of the moment was window glass, common bottles, and other purely utilitarian vessels. It was easier to find abroad and to attract to this country workmen capable of meeting this need than to lure others more proficient. Even when a manufacturer like Stiegel became ambitious to supply glass for the tables of American gentry, the quality of the resultant product never surpassed that which the peasant glassmakers of Europe were able to achieve.

What may be called "stylish" glass was not produced in

America until the 1800's had reached the beginning of their second decade. By that time the making of glass had become a fairly stable industry, thanks to a growing population, improved facilities for transportation, some aid from protective tariffs, and perhaps the substitution of corporate control for the previous vicissitudes of individual management. By this time "stylish" glass, both at home and abroad, was beginning to assume aspects of decadence that became increasingly apparent as the century advanced. Such glass is here outside our immediate concern.

But even while the great glasshouses in the neighborhood of Boston in the east and Pittsburgh in the west were beginning to accomplish a measure of sophistication in the forms and decoration of glassware, the ancient peasant tradition continued to dominate the conceptions of the workmen in small rural bottle- and window-glass factories, scattered here and there from the Atlantic seaboard to southern Ohio. When the help in such factories turned from their daily routine to shape offhand bowls, pitchers, mugs, and vases for their own use or that of their friends, they followed the precepts of their apprentice days, precepts which their masters in turn had been taught in youth.

Fig. 5 — a, ALEXANDRIAN GLASS (fourth century A.D.)
From the University of Michigan Museum
b, BOWL FROM MANTUA, OHIO (early nineteenth century)
Note folded rims, designed to strengthen exposed points of contact. From the collection of Harry Hall White

Fig. 6 — a and b (above), THREE ALEXANDRIAN
BOWLS (fourth century A.D.)
Note hollow pedestal in centre, crimped foot at
left and right.
From the University of Michigan Museum
c and d (left and right), MIDWESTERN BOWLS
(nineteenth century)
One with hollow pedestal, the other with
crimped foot

This conservative habit seems to have persisted in some localities until as late as 1850. By virtue of it, considerable quantities of nineteenth-century offhand-fashioned glasses possess characteristics that ally them not only with native products of the eighteenth century but with still earlier foreign wares whose ancestry is traceable to ancient Sidon in Syria, and the glasshouses of early Christian Alexandria. The opportunity for comparison afforded by the accompanying illustrations should adequately reinforce the verbal statement.

Less easily explained than the continuity of ancient tradition in the domain of offhand articles of glass is the early nineteenth-century revival of an old Syrian technique that had apparently been not only abandoned but virtually forgotten within five centuries after the birth of Christ. This is the process of shaping vessels by blowing glass in full-size separable molds. Examples of articles thus produced nearly 2000 years ago are here pictured beside others probably of American make dating from the early 1800's.

Here, of course, the factor of a long-standing habit of thought is eliminated. Hence we are forced to conclude that the late revival of what is popularly known as three-mold glass was due to some perspicacious manufacturer's museum encounter with an ancient object retrieved in the course of excavation. Whether originally made in Syria or by Syrian workmen in Rome, such articles were in their day exported to all parts of the known world and have been dug up unexpectedly in various places in Europe and in northern Africa.

Unfortunately, writers on English and European glass devote very slight attention to nineteenth-century mold-blown articles and to the circumstances, other than those of economic pressure, that first prompted a revival of their making. We know that the method involved was used in Ireland about the year 1800, and still more extensively in the United States. We know, likewise, that it is still relied upon by French manufacturers of fanciful liqueur bottles. In general, however, as a money-saving device it has been superseded by the far cheaper process of mechanical pressing. Today's manufacturers might well consider its possibilities for a type of decorative ware intermediate in cost between the expensive cut and engraved forms and the stolid progeny of the pressing machine.

Fig. 7 — a, SYRIAN FLASK (about 300 A.D.)
From the Metropolitan Museum of Art
b, NEW JERSEY PITCHER (nineteenth century)

Foreign Influences in American Glass

By Gregor Norman Humphreys

Note. — The author is indebted to the courtesy of the following individuals and institutions for the photographs used to illustrate this discussion: the Metropolitan Museum of Art, New York City, for Figures 1, *centre* and *lower right;* 2, *right centre* and *extreme right;* 4, *right;* 7, *right centre* and *extreme right;* the National Museum of Ireland, Dublin, for Figures 3, *left;* 4, *above;* George William Bierce, Cleveland, Ohio, for Figures 5, *left* and *above;* 8. From his own collection are Figures 1, *centre left, centre right, lower left;* 2, *extreme left* and *left centre;* 3, *right;* 6, *extreme left* and *left centre.*

EUROPEAN schools of design and technique in the glass-making craft were already firmly established when glass was first being made in America. Each country was expressing itself according to its temperament and its habits of life. The huge *Wilkommen* glasses, for example, are typically German, in answer to a national custom relative to the greeting of guests. The temperament of the English was well displayed in their fashioning of late seventeenth-century lead glass. Drawing often from the same sources (chiefly early Venetian) for inspiration, glassworkers of the various European nations nevertheless evolved objects quite dissimilar in style and workmanship.

Diverse Nationalities of American Glassworkers

It was emigrant workmen from established glasshouses of Europe and the British Isles who transplanted their craft in America. Naturally, each brought with him, in his blowpipe, as it were, the vernacular of his own country. To this primary circumstance may be traced the obviously cosmopolitan character of American glassware as a whole.

A summary of some of the earlier attempts at glassmaking in this country will give us some idea of the diversity of nationalities represented by the workmen here engaged:

1608	Jamestown, Va., Eight Poles and Germans
1620	Jamestown, Va., Italians
1654–55	New Amsterdam, Dutchmen
1739–80	Alloway, N. J. (Wistarberg), Imported Dutch workmen
1752–60	Braintree, Mass., German Protestants
1753–85	New Windsor, N. Y., Hollanders
1765–74	Manheim, Pa. (Stiegel), Experts from Bristol, England, Dutchmen, Germans, Irishmen, Italians
1771	Kensington, Pa., Englishmen, Dutchmen, Scotchmen
c. 1795	Pittsburg, Pa., Various factories employing: Irishmen, Englishmen, Frenchmen, Germans, Dutchmen

Six distinct schools of

glassmaking are represented in this list. Of each of these schools the characteristics were inevitably expressed in American glassware — sometimes in almost original purity, but often mingled one with another. Thus we find the most literal reproductions of traditional European forms and methods, side by side with an unmistakable American hybrid. Glassworkers were of a roving habit, and their constant meeting and mingling tended constantly toward a fusion of ideas.

Netherland Influence

One of the most clearly marked foreign influences in American glassware is that of the Netherlands style. Great numbers of our early glassworkers came from the present states of Holland and Flanders. They had developed, despite widespread contacts with the work of other countries (notably Germany), a style and technique much their own. They were especially proficient in the art of engraving.

In America, glass objects fluted vertically (*Fig. 1, centre left*), or spirally, were made after the Netherlands style. The American use of the sunken panel (*Fig. 1, lower right*), on drinking glasses and other hollow ware, appears to be another instance of borrowing from the same source. Glasses displaying these motifs are, for some reason, usually termed *Stiegel,* but other factories of Stiegel's time, and later, produced such pieces.

Clear glass objects, rimmed with blue (*Fig. 1, centre*), appeared at this period and again in the nineteenth century. This detail, also, was derived from the Netherlanders, who had used it at Liége in the second quarter of the eighteenth century. Two well-known patterns favored by engravers at the Stiegel factory, the tulip, and the basket of flowers (*Fig. 1, centre right*), are typically of the Netherlands.

A distinct Netherland-

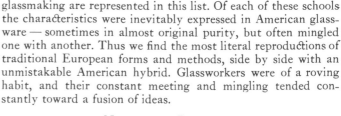

Fig. 1—Five American and Foreign Types (*last half of the eighteenth century*) Displaying details borrowed directly from the Dutch: (*centre left*) fluted bowl, folded foot; (*centre above*) clear glass, blue rim; (*centre right*) typical Dutch engraving much copied in America.
Foreign and American Glass (*Lower left*) English paneled goblet (Bristol?) in the Dutch taste; (*lower right*) American use of the same motif, style of Stiegel (*1765–74*).

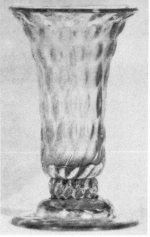

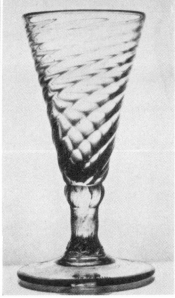

Fig. 2 — ABORIGINAL INDEBTEDNESS TO ENGLISH PRECEDENT
(*third quarter of the eighteenth century*)
The glasses left centre and right centre are reticulated; (*extreme left and left centre*) English pieces; (*right centre and extreme right*) similar American glasses in the Stiegel manner.

ish flavor obtains, too, in a certain type of glass largely accredited, in the past, to Wistarberg, but now known to have been made at numerous other factories, even as late as the middle of the nineteenth century.* We refer to objects on which have been superimposed shaped decorations consisting of glass either in the same color as that of the body or, more rarely, in another color. The "lily pad" design is a familiar designation of this type. Ware of this sort had been previously made in the Netherlands. Similar American productions, however, are in no sense of secondary importance: in color they are admirable, and they possess a charming naïveté of form and technique.

Glass of the Wistarberg and South Jersey type felt also a direct Venetian influence. Among examples of this glass are to be found scent bottles in pure Venetian manner. Again, we perceive the style of Venice in a detail of frequent use: the thin spiral thread of glass with which the necks of jugs or bowls, and the collars of bottles, were decorated.

    For significant data on glass of this type, see ANTIQUES, Vol. X, p. 274, Wistarberg and South Jersey Glass, by George S. McKearin.

Fig. 3 — IRISH PROTOTYPE; AMERICAN IMITATION (*first third of the nineteenth century*)
(*Left*) Irish cut decanter; (*right*) contact-molded decanter, presumably American.

The Netherlandish influence, it may be observed, was felt until comparatively late in our glassmaking history. Many of our South Jersey type pieces, probably a majority, are nineteenth-century products, though in an eighteenth-century style. The tendency to preserve a given style through a long period is characteristic of the early American glasshouses.

GERMAN INFLUENCE

Somewhat akin in feeling to Netherlandish types, German glassware was frequently imitated in America. The forms and proportions of objects often betray the German imprint. Stolidity of silhouette, and occasional floridity of decoration (as in enamels, on an object otherwise severe), are frequently the sign of German derivation.

The German influence upon American glassware is most strongly apparent in enameled pieces. American glassware, however, did not assume those monumental forms wrought in Germany by the Germans, of which highly decorative examples may be studied in the Metropolitan and Pennsylvania Museums.

The British Museum displays a German enameled tumbler, of the seventeenth century, in the more domestic manner employed at the American factories.* It bears a hunting scene, multicolored, closely related in character to American pieces made over a century later. A number of American pieces of this sort, almost literal translations, are illustrated by Hunter (*Stiegel Glass*). With the notable exception of nineteenth-century cut glass, such pieces probably offer the most striking example of the direct influence of foreign work upon the form and decoration of early American glass.

SPANISH INFLUENCE

To a lesser extent the Spanish taste is felt. Spanish enameling, though excellent, was of a different character, and we but seldom recognize its resemblance to American enameled wares (as in our comparatively late enamel-decorated and fluted mugs). Quantities of Spanish glassware, however, were exported to Mexico and to this country. Its influence is most noticeable in one instance: the typical Stiegel flip glasses of flaring shape, with sunken panels on the lower part of the body and with geometric or floral engraved borders above, may be almost exactly matched in Spanish prototypes.†

Fig. 4 — IRISH AND AMERICAN GLASS (*first third of the nineteenth century*)
The American "daisy-in-the-square" decanter (*right*), and similar "sunburst panel" pieces, derive from such Irish examples as the cut butter-bowl (*above*) with large cut diamonds and sunburst on diagonal panel in square.

ENGLISH INFLUENCE

In American glass are likewise discoverable evidences of what Hunter, in speaking of Stiegel glass, refers to as the "Bristol tradition" (*Fig. 2, right centre* and *extreme right*). Stiegel, as noted in the foregoing list of American factories, imported specialists from Bristol, England, who introduced the style of that glassmaking centre into the works at Manheim. Most of the English influence on American ware, other than the later cut glass, resulted in close approximations of the Bristol style. It is perhaps significant that this style has certain points in common with that of the Netherlands.

Traceable in large part to Bristol is the American sapphire blue glass, which well stands comparison as to color with any foreign metal. An advertisement in a recent issue of an English collectors' magazine pictures over a dozen pieces of colored glass — variously spiral-ribbed, vertically fluted, plain, enameled, and colored-edged — almost any one of which, were the group not clearly titled *Bristol*, would be instantly accepted by the average American collector as American glass, if not (and rashly) Stiegel.

The influence of Bristol and Nailsea is further apparent in the sworled glass produced in America for over a hundred years, until the post-Civil War period. Here, as well as in England, this treatment was used in the decoration of jugs, bottles, bowls, large hollow balls (used as jug and bowl covers), and so on. Clear glass might be streaked with serpentine lines, or sworls, of opaque

white, or colors; or the sworling might appear in colors on opaque white. The color was not applied, but was part of the actual composition of the metal, deriving probably from the early Venetian practice of using bands of opaque color (*filigree glass*) in the body of the glass.

ENGLISH-IRISH INFLUENCE

American collectors are very generally familiar with our contact-molded glass, produced by subjecting blown glass to the pressure of a patterned mold, usually in three sections (hence the alternate name, "three section mold glass").* This, clearly, is but the molded expression of the cut technique in which English and Irish factories were producing like patterns in the early nineteenth century.

Figure 3 shows the relationship. It illustrates the best known pattern, called, in the contact-molded wares, "quilted and ribbed," and, in the cut wares, "plain diamonds with fluting." Our contact-molded "daisy-in-the-square" and "sunburst," which are but variations in the same manner, also have an original model in Irish cut glass (*Fig. 4*).

It is not so well known, however, that contact-molded glass of this type was by no means exclusively an American product, but was made also by glassworkers in England and Ireland. M. S. Dudley Westropp illustrates a few such pieces of Irish make.†

FRENCH INFLUENCE

In another variation of the contact-molded group, ornately patterned, we meet French influence.‡ The manufacture, in America, of almost all glass of this type (contact-molded, that is) covers roughly the first half of the nineteenth century; and it was not until that time that American glass felt the French influence to any appreciable extent. In Figure 5 an American molded jug of pronounced Empire type is bracketed with a French candlestick of about the same period. The candlestick has a decided greenish tone in the metal, whereas the jug is of clearer crystal-like fabric; but, in so far as design and technique are concerned, the two might well have been made at the same place and time.

Most strongly is the French influence apparent in American glass of the Sandwich type,§ that lacelike pressed ware now known indiscriminately as "Sandwich," though made by numer-

*Illustrated in *Glass*, by Edward Dillon.
†See ANTIQUES, Vol. IX, page 143.

*For illustrations of this type, see ANTIQUES, Vol. VI, page 78, *Three Mold Glass*, by Helen A. McKearin.
†M. S. Dudley Westropp, *Irish Glass*; Plate XXXVII.
‡To these often somewhat flamboyant patterns the term Baroque has been applied. This, however, seems to be a misnomer, since in date and in style such patterns really belong in the Empire and post-Empire periods. In factory glass after 1840, we of course find reflections of the Louis XV revival, which infected all forms of decorative art.
§See ANTIQUES, Vol. VII, page 245.

ous other glasshouses. For this glass, which has a charm of a sort not too closely associated with good taste, the Sandwich factory is best known. The earlier blown and molded productions of the establishment have, unfortunately, received too little notice.

Later in its history, the Sandwich factory (and others engaged in the manufacture of similar ware) turned to Bohemian prototypes, undercut through colored overlays, in what is usually termed cameo style. At the same time, English and Irish cut glass was extensively copied by the cheap pressed method. Figure 8 is in the manner of much ware produced at that time, poorly mimicking the cut technique.

IRISH INFLUENCE

It is a curious fact that, though cut glass was being made in quantities by the English and the Irish, after, roughly, the middle of the eighteenth century, and though literally tons of this glass were shipped to America in the years following,* no great quantity of cut glass seems to have been made in this country much before the second quarter of the nineteenth century.

However, from that time on, American glassworkers more than made up for their previous delay. Pittsburg factories, and there were many at the time, produced such pieces as that of Figure 6, *left centre*, whose cutting may well be compared with the true Irish cutting shown beside it (*Fig. 6, extreme left*). The latter wineglass was recently purchased from a set of table glassware originally ordered from Waterford by General George H. Thomas. American factories repeated the Irish manner, also, in their use of cut and molded glass in combination. The foot of an object, for instance, might be left roughly molded, or cast, while the surface of the bowl and stem were entirely cut and polished. "Cast," "molded," and "pressed" glass, it must be remembered, are not one and the same thing.† The American cut glass was often

Fig. 5 — FRENCH AND AMERICAN EMPIRE
(*first quarter of the nineteenth century*)
The character and technique of the French candlestick (*left*) are clearly echoed in the American contact-molded jug (*above*).

exceedingly well done; and, when it closely follows Irish cuttings, only keen perception will distinguish the domestic from the foreign article.

CONCLUSION

The development of glassworking after about 1810 became more a matter of industry than of craft. Contact-molded and South Jersey-type glass are an exception, being a curious survival of the eighteenth-century manner rather than a typical nineteenth-century product. Some of the better cut glass, too, is commendable, as just stated. But the coarsely cut, the carelessly engraved, or the monstrously-designed pressed wares, whose name is legion, cannot address themselves to the attention of the serious collector. "Influences" felt in our later glassware are too often other than Classic.

A truly American vernacular, however, may be found in the earlier hybrids to which we have previously referred. Mixed types they are; but, under the integrating touch of the skilled glassworker, they become something more than any one of the several types they represent. Drawing freely from the English, the German, or the Dutch, to suit his fancy, the American glassworker welded his motifs together into a whole completely his own. It is this originality, brought to bear against the varied background of the craft of the period, which produced our early American glass.

In Figure 7 are pictured two glasses, of American make, which illustrate this point. The first (*right centre*) shows decided German influence in its general form, and in such details as the lip of the bowl. The stem, while finding some precedent in foreign work of earlier date (notably English-German), is more essentially a product of the maker's fancy. The foot, though high (in the English manner), shows a heaviness typical of American work, as elsewhere exhibited, in Figure 2, *right centre*. The color, green and amber, is of a quality identifiable with no country other than our own. Here is a glass of dignity and of good proportion, adapted to its purpose, and a natural outgrowth of existing conditions in our earlier factories.

The second glass (*Fig. 7, extreme right*), with its heavy tear stem and thick flaring bowl, is of a style commonly used in English taverns. Here we may trace English-Dutch influence. The engraving is of an early type, after the English, derived from

---

*See Irish Exports lists, *Irish Glass*, M. S. Dudley Westropp.

†The terms *cast*, *molded*, and *pressed*, as applied to glass, indicate three different processes of patterning the material.

Cast glass is cast in a mold very much after the manner of molten iron. When taken from the casting mold, it is liable to be rough, and to require subsequent careful polishing of surfaces and edges.

Molded glass, as the term is used in America, is glass which takes its form by being blown into a mold by lung power. The molten material thus assumes the form and pattern which have previously been cut in the metal of the mold. A pontil mark often remains on pieces thus produced; though this mark is fre-

quently obliterated, in fine pieces, by grinding. Molded glass was frequently blown in a mold smaller than the finished article was intended to be. Having taken form from the mold, the article in question was subsequently reheated, and then expanded by blowing in the open, during which process its shape underwent modification at the hands of the blower.

Pressed glass receives its shape and pattern by being forced with a mechanical plunger into a mold whose inner configuration the surface of the glass thus assumes. When the surface of the plunger is smooth and carries no pattern, the inside of pressed glass is smooth. Plates *may* show pattern on both sides.

Fig. 6 (Left) — WATER-
FORD AND PITTSBURG
(*early in second quarter
of the nineteenth cen-
tury*)
Our early Pittsburg fac-
tories made such pieces
as the glass at centre
left, cut after the manner
of the Irish Waterford
glass beside it.

Fig. 7 (Right) — AMERI-
CAN HYBRIDS
(*Right centre*) green and
amber, attributed to Wis-
tarberg, German-English
influences; (*extreme right*)
good Dutch-English type,
but with a curious double
foot, evidently an Ameri-
can innovation.

the Bohemian. But probably nowhere else shall we find a foot such as is used here. Its inspiration possibly comes from the English "Norwich" foot, composed of a series of two or three rising steps with flat, horizontal surfaces. The American work-man who blew this glass has achieved his effect in a decoratively harmonious manner. The keen-eyed collector will find, in his meanderings, many pieces illustrative of this American vernacular style. It is, furthermore, in pieces such as these that the highest interest of American glass, for the collector, at least, is discoverable.

Fig. 8 — AMERICAN PRESSED GLASS SALT (*second
quarter of the nineteenth century*)
In the Sandwich style, featuring the Irish cut "strawberry diamond" motif. French influence also shown
in rim and base.

BY THOMAS S. BUECHNER

Origins of American glass

THE STUDY OF AMERICAN GLASS, an enormous subject in itself, covers a rather small part of the whole history of glass. Many American-glass enthusiasts tend, nevertheless, to regard it as an independent phenomenon—a child without parents. The revelation that it is the sturdy offspring of normal parents and can trace its ancestry back to the time of the Pharaohs will not, it is hoped, come as a disappointment.

Glass in general has certain persistent and specific characteristics: it is usually molten when formed; it can be inflated by blowing air into it; it can be molded, painted, engraved, and so on. To the glassblowers of Syria nineteen hundred years ago it presented approximately the same problems as it did to the Stanger brothers a hundred and ninety years ago, and as it does to us today. This is the wonderful thing about the study of glass—through it we see how different people do the same thing, and how in doing it they express their respective cultures and civilizations. Best of all, it enables us to determine the relative merit of the solutions which the problems and possibilities inherent in glass have evoked.

The illustrations accompanying this article have been selected to emphasize the relationship of American glass to the glass of the rest of the world—a relationship of

Fig. 1. Left: South Jersey bowl, late eighteenth or early nineteenth century. Right: bowl, probably Tyrian, first or second century A.D. *Except as noted, illustrations are from the Corning Museum of Glass and photographs of Corning pieces are by John Kalinich.*

Fig. 2. Eighteenth-century sugar bowl, United States. *Henry Francis du Pont Winterthur Museum.*

Fig. 3. Covered bowl, South Germany, eighteenth century.

560

Left.
Fig. 4. German beaker, sixteenth century.

Right.
Fig. 5. South Jersey pitcher, early nineteenth century. *Presented to the Victoria and Albert Museum by the Corning Museum of Glass.*

quality, and not one of historical importance. The standards applied to American glass as part of the history of our nation are not, of course, affected by the achievements of the rest of the world: Amelung will always be important to us for having produced some of the finest eighteenth-century American glass, no matter how his product compares with contemporary Venetian or German pieces. It is when we remove the adjective "American" that we face the problem of relative quality.

Types of glass are a basic factor in judging quality, and color is of paramount importance. The fine greens and ambers of glass in our South Jersey tradition have been produced in primitive glasshouses since the time of Julius Caesar. The two bowls reproduced in Figure 1 are of approximately the same form and color; the one

on the left is a South Jersey piece made in the late eighteenth or early nineteenth century, the other was probably made in Tyre in the first or second century A.D. Seventeen hundred years and more than twice that number of miles separate these two pieces, yet they most certainly belong to the same glassmaking tradition.

Figures 2 and 3 demonstrate clearly the American glassmaker's debt to the Old World. The superb eighteenth-century sugar bowl in Figure 2 is a fine example of the best of the South Jersey type; the equally impressive bowl in Figure 3 was found in southern Germany. The fact that much of our early glass is folk art is well known, but its close affinity to the folk art of the countries from which it takes its inspiration is often ignored.

In Figure 4 we see one of our most cherished decorative devices, the lily pad, embellishing the base of a German glass made centuries before its counterpart was produced in America. This is an illustration of derivation rather than indebtedness. The glassmakers of this country developed the lily pad into a distinctive ornament far superior to the modest beginning displayed on this sixteenth-century beaker. It is possible to trace the lily pad back even further—there is a fine bottle decorated with this device, now in Teheran, which was made in Persia in the eleventh century A.D.

The two bottles in Figure 6 were both patterned in ribbed molds. Much of the glass made in midwestern America was decorated this way, and the number of ribs often indicates where a piece was made. The flask on the left was made in a twenty-rib dip mold; the other in a twenty-four-rib dip mold. The former is Midwestern, early nineteenth century; the latter, Islamic, before the tenth century.

This practice of inflating a gather of glass in a small patterned mold and then expanding it by blowing after removal from the mold was used extensively in early American glasshouses. It was also used in glasshouses virtually throughout the world, and in practically all major glassmaking periods. The most frequent design is

Fig. 6. Left: flask, midwestern United States, early nineteenth century.
Right: Islamic flask, before the tenth century.

561

Fig. 7. Left: hanging lamp, possibly Egyptian,
tenth century.
Right: flask, United States
(possibly Stiegel),
late eighteenth century.

Fig. 8. Blown-three-mold decanter,
United States (Sandwich), c. 1825-1835.

Fig. 9. Blown-three-mold amber glass beaker,
probably Syrian, second or third century A.D.

Fig. 10. Jenny Lind
two-part-hinged-mold
historical flask,
United States
(possibly Ravenna, Ohio),
1850's.

Fig. 11. Two-part-hinged-mold
beaker, Roman Empire,
second century A.D.

562

a repeat diamond pattern; certain more intricate designs may be peculiar to a specific country, or even an individual glasshouse. For example, the diamond-above-flute, daisy-hexagon, and diamond-daisy are thought to have been originated by Stiegel (McKearin, *Two Hundred Years of American Blown Glass*). Such details are a great help in tracing a glassmaking tradition, but even here it is not possible to claim complete originality. The flask in Figure 7, patterned in a diamond-above-flute mold, is possibly by Stiegel; the hanging lamp beside it, patterned in a diamond-below-flute mold, is probably tenth-century Egyptian.

American glass decorated by inflation in a hinged mold is of two main types: blown-three-mold, usually an abstract geometric pattern incised in the walls of a three- or more-part hinged mold; and two-part hinged-mold, usually carved with some commemorative patriotic portrait or symbol and known by the generic term "historical flask." Most of the devices in both these groups, particularly the historical flasks, are typically American,

but both types existed in antiquity. The blown-three-mold beaker with all-over bud or mollusk design alternating with raised dots (Fig. 9) was probably made in Syria in the second or third century A.D. Figure 11 shows a small beaker in amber glass, blown in a two-part hinged mold, which commemorates a gladiatorial combat held during the last half of the first century A.D.

The problem of separating the Continental from the American is familiar to every student of the decorative arts. The glass illustrated in Figures 12, 13, and 14 emphasizes the close relationship of our own work with that of the countries from which we drew traditions as well as craftsmen. These comparisons also suggest that the American version may sometimes represent an improvement over its prototype. Although America's contribution to glassmaking is generally assumed to be limited to the mechanical press and subsequent technical developments, it is possible that our glassmakers created a national idiom. We will never know unless we relate our own glass to that of the rest of the world.

Fig. 12. Left: wine or firing glass, United States (possibly Amelung), engraved; last quarter eighteenth century. Right: goblet, cut and engraved; Ireland, c. 1790.

Fig. 13. Left: bowl, United States (probably New England), c. 1830-1840; pressed in crossed-peacock-feather design. Center: cup, Roman Empire, third or fourth century A.D.; engraved in diamonds and ovals. Right: bowl or dish, England, c. 1830; cut in fans and diamonds.

Fig. 14. Left: tumbler, United States (possibly Stiegel), probably third quarter eighteenth century; multicolored peasant-type enameled decoration. Right: tumbler, probably German, second half eighteenth century; multicolored peasant-type enameled decoration.

563

GLASS AT THE FORUM

Foreign Influences in American Glass, I

By MALCOLM WATKINS

Last month we presented the first of a series of condensed transcripts of the lectures delivered at the 1949 Antiques and Decorations Forum at Williamsburg. The subject last month was ceramics. We here present the Forum lectures on glass. The speaker at the first session was Malcolm Watkins, Associate Curator at the U. S. National Museum, Smithsonian Institution; this account is published by permission. The speaker at the second session was Marshall Davidson, Editor of Publications at the Metropolitan Museum of Art.

THE TOPIC *Foreign Influences in American Glass* sounds like a subject for investigation by the Committee on Un-American Activities. As a matter of fact there is a nationalistic attitude today on the part of some collectors, who draw a line of demarcation between everything that is American, and therefore assumed to be good, and everything foreign, and therefore assumed not to be good. Needless to say, this is unscientific!

American glass did not emerge like a sort of Venus, risen from the colonial sea. When the manufacture of glass was introduced in America in the eighteenth century, it was part of and the result of a long traditional development. To understand this development we must look back on English glass, which in turn was a synthesis of many Continental influences stemming from Venice, France, Germany, and the Netherlands, spiced with English ingredients.

There were two factors contributing to this process of synthesis in English glass. First, the invention of lead glass by Ravenscroft about 1674 was an English contribution which introduced an entirely new sort of glass metal. Second, there was a sympathetic rapport between the English buying public, the sellers of English flint glass, and the manufacturers and blowers of the glass. Ultimately it was the English public that decided the forms English glass should take. The Glass Sellers Company gauged public taste and interpreted changes of fashion, and then transmitted their findings to the glass-makers. A truly English product emerged from this process.

Colonial America was in all things a reflection of England, even though at times only a pale reflection. Everyone who set himself up in society in the towns from Boston to Charleston tried to mimic English ways. It was natural that this tendency should be found in the field of glass as well as others.

Before 1675 English glass was in its infancy. Not much was made for export, and even if it had been conditions here were not such that there was a demand for fragile luxuries like glass in many households. There are occasional references to glass objects, but they are principally bottles. After 1680, however, we find a change. The lead-glass industry was getting into its stride in England, and glass was being imported here. From then on more and more glass came in, and it was more and more elaborate. Some quite elegant pieces were being produced in England, so ornate that they must have been purely decorative pieces, intended for display rather than use, but not many such pieces found their way to the American colonies.

As far as glass made here in the seventeenth century is concerned, we really cannot say much. We know that there were a few attempts to establish bottle factories and window-glass factories. At Jamestown in 1608 a factory was started, which lasted about a year and was reestablished about 1622.

When we come to the eighteenth century we discover something more exciting. In England we find handsome glass in fine proportions being made in the Queen Anne period. We also find that glass was introduced in unbelievable quantities to America. Newspaper advertisements are full of lists of glass after the early 1700's. These were mostly drinking glasses. In 1712 Bristol glass was advertised in Boston. In 1719 there was a shop selling glass exclusively there. By 1731 such pieces as decanters and punchbowls were advertised. Hogsheads and barrels of glass were sold in Boston right at the docks. Now and then some Spanish glass came in from Barbados, but about 99% of the imported glass was English.

Not all the glass imported in the early eighteenth century was purely utilitarian. Some of it was decorative as well. This was particularly true of the Bristol pieces made after 1750, in opaque white in imitation of Chinese porcelains and decorated by some of the same men who decorated Bristol porcelain. But the more elegant types of Continental glassware did not find their way here in any quantity until the nineteenth century.

The first glass made successfully in America, from a commercial standpoint, was that of Wistar, whose factory made bottle and window glass and other practical utensils from 1739 to 1780 without interruption. Wistar died in 1752, leaving an estate of $150,000, which was a tidy sum for that period and shows how successful his factory must have been.

VENETIAN WINEGLASS *(sixteenth century).* **City Art Museum, St. Louis.**

ENGLISH WINEGLASS *(c. 1700-1720).* **Victoria and Albert Museum.**

Who it was who introduced fine flint tableware into America as an American manufacture is still a matter of doubt. For all practical purposes, however, it was Stiegel, who came from Germany. In 1763 he was making glass at the Elizabeth Furnace in Pennsylvania and two years after that had built a large factory at Manheim. The first glass Stiegel made was bottle and window glass. It was not until 1769 that he suddenly came forth with glass of a fine type. He had gone to England in 1763, and almost certainly visited the London and Bristol flint-glass factories. He very daringly sought to compete with the English monopoly, and went at it wholeheartedly, establishing an agency and stores from Boston to Baltimore. He had 150 workmen at one time at Manheim, mostly German but a few Irish and English. Since he was competing with English glass of the period, the forms had to be very like those of England. He advertised, in fact, that his glass was equal to the best flint glass imported from abroad. Over and over we find this emphasis on comparison with English glass. In many cases it would indeed take an expert to distinguish between the English and Stiegel colored glass. We call most pieces "Stiegel type," since we cannot tell whether they were actually made by Stiegel.

In addition to making colored glass and plain flint glass, Stiegel also had enamelers and engravers working for him. Enameled Stiegel glass is definitely in the German tradition. Perhaps in these wares Stiegel was trying to please the local Pennsylvania Dutch market. Many enameled Stiegel pieces are closely related to German and Austrian enameled glass of the period. In the case of such pieces as well as of those decorated with shallow engraving, it is impossible to say how much of it was made by Stiegel, how much was imported, or how much was made by other American manufacturers.

Stiegel had competitors in the Philadelphia area. In 1771 the Kensington works challenged Stiegel's claim that his was the first flint-glass works in America. The list of their products was the same as Stiegel's and the English ware of the period. They also claimed that their glass was the equal of English flint.

Stiegel suddenly went bankrupt and his factory closed down. The war came, and glassmaking was in the doldrums. It remained for Amelung to come to America from Germany, with cash backing from a German concern and German workmen. The same pattern was repeated through the eighteenth century: each time a new factory was started, new foreign glassworkers were imported. Amelung established a factory called New Bremen in Frederick, Maryland, and began making glass in the German tradition. The range of his

BOTTLE *(c. 1730)*, a type commonly used at table, from which stemmed both the familiar cylindrical wine bottle and the table decanter of later days.

STIEGEL-TYPE PATTERN-MOLDED SAPPHIRE GLASS. The covered bowl is a type generally unknown abroad, possibly identifiable with "sugar boxes with covers" as advertised by Stiegel. *Photograph courtesy of Parke-Bernet Galleries.*

glass has only recently been revealed, by the archeological efforts of Dr. and Mrs. Martin Stohlman (see ANTIQUES, October 1948). They unearthed fragments showing that Amelung made bottle glass, chemical apparatus, window glass, all sorts of colored glass, and cut and engraved glass. Amelung's German glassworkers introduced the German tradition into commercial glass here in America to a greater extent than ever before. He had some of the best engravers working for him. The Germans always excelled in this technique, and we know that an exceptionally skilled engraver must have worked with Amelung. There is a famous pokal, now at the Metropolitan Museum, which was once thought to be a German piece, since it was found in Bremen. However, it is inscribed with the name of the New Bremen glassworks, and the date 1788, and was evidently sent to Bremen by Amelung to show what his New Bremen works could do.

The German tradition was perpetuated after Amelung closed in 1793. Many of Amelung's workers went to Pennsylvania. Gallatin backed a glassmaking enterprise at New Geneva, directed by Kramer, who was one of Amelung's former workmen. Numerous South Jersey factories also sprang up at this time, producing the traditional South Jersey type of pitcher with lily-pad decoration. To make this decoration the lower part of the piece was redipped in the glass and the second coating drawn up by tooling into liquid-looking strips. In Ohio at Zanesville the German tradition went on too, producing pieces that resemble those of Stiegel type. In fact, this glass is often called "Ohio Stiegel type."

Between 1790 and 1800 Frederick M. Amelung, son of the founder of New Bremen, established a glassworks in Baltimore. After 1802 the factory continued in other hands, and a whole group of celery vases with engraving reminiscent of Amelung work may have been made there. Perhaps some of Amelung's engravers wandered up to the Baltimore and Philadelphia areas.

The English tradition, dictated by the commercial market, continued as well. In Pittsburgh factories began to appear at the end of the eighteenth and beginning of the nineteenth century. O'Hara and Craig in 1797, Bakewell a few years later, in 1808, gave new impetus to the English tradition. There were English and Irish glassworkers at both these factories.

As the nineteenth century wore on, the change in taste—or the degeneration of taste—began to have an effect. The products of the Jersey City glassworks about 1824 show a greater massiveness, but the skill of workmanship is still as great as ever. The same thing is true of glass made in the

STIEGEL-TYPE ENGRAVED FLIP GLASS. Glass of this type, sketchily decorated with popular motifs, such as tulips, was in common use as tableware throughout the western world.

1820's at Pittsburgh and the New England Glass Company in Cambridge.

Cut glass was introduced into America as early as 1750 from England and continued to come in larger and larger quantities. In 1797 from Dublin alone to New York alone 240,404 pieces were imported, mostly drinking glasses. The cutting was imitated at Bakewell's factory and at Cambridge.

Then pattern molds were discovered, which could produce the effect of cut glass more cheaply. Thus came about the first three-mold glass. Sandwich picked up the three-mold tradition and made much of it in the 1820's and 1830's.

It was only one step beyond this to the introduction of glass pressing—an American contribution. Here the foreign influence was only superficial, and glass had indeed become a mass-production product. But pressed glass is another subject altogether.

STIEGEL - TYPE ENAMELED GLASS. Another example of the commodity tableware of the eighteenth century. *Collection of George L. Hammell.*

Foreign Influences in American Glass, II

By MARSHALL DAVIDSON

IN THE EARLY HISTORY of American glass there are two key dates: 1608 when the first glassworks was established at Jamestown, and 1788 when the first dated piece of American glass was inscribed. Evidence of what was made in this country between those dates is circumstantial. No physical remains from American furnaces during the intervening years can be definitely identified, despite the fact that at least a dozen glasshouses were set up, operated for a time, and, ultimately, abandoned. We know, from newspaper accounts, inventories, and such excavations as those undertaken at Williamsburg that glass was used with increasing frequency in America during that period.

Between those two dates, 1608 and 1788, a revolution was taking place in the living habits of the ordinary people of the western world. At the beginning of the seventeenth century the great hall of medieval tradition had its modest counterpart in the small colonial "hall," the room of all purposes. In the course of the next two centuries this tradition broke down into concepts which were novel then but which today we accept complacently—concepts of privacy, comfort, and efficiency within the home. Separate rooms with special functions appear. There was a parallel evolution of furniture. At the beginning of our period chairs were rare and rude; at the end they were common everywhere and made in a variety of convenient forms. Eating habits changed, too. Wooden plates were replaced by pewter, pewter in turn by earthenware—and forks replaced fingers. Though this

same transition went on everywhere, it was more rapid and complete in America than elsewhere.

AMELUNG POKAL, the first inscribed, dated American glass (1788). Engraved on one side *New Bremen Glassmanufactory North America State of Maryland* and on the other with the arms of the German city of Bremen and *Old Bremen Success and the New Progress.* The form is purely German. *Metropolitan Museum of Art.*

SOUTH JERSEY TYPE PITCHER. Aquamarine with lily-pad decoration.

Similar developments can be traced in glassware, which indeed might be considered as a barometer of living standards. From a precious rarity at the beginning of the seventeenth century glass became, by the end of the eighteenth, an ordinary commodity. The earliest colonists wanted and needed glass, largely for windows and bottles, and in response to growing demands glasshouses were built in several colonies. For numerous good reasons, however, they all failed. In the first place a glassmaker is in a different position from a furniture maker, a silversmith, or a pewterer. For a profitable venture glass must be made in some quantity. To make a single piece of glass is uneconomical. Furnaces, pots made of special clay, extensive equipment, and hired hands are needed—in short, a factory set-up. During the colonial period conditions did not favor the growth of factories. For one thing there was not enough venture money; for another, when land was free for the taking and manpower in great demand no man would long work for another. Imports, manufactured under more favorable circumstances abroad, streamed into the country. As a consequence, down to the end of the eighteenth century all the glass factories folded, one after another.

At the time of the first American settlements Venice was making the finest glass. Its exquisitely clear, soda-lime glass—the "crystal" of the day—represented a peak of perfection. All over Europe Venetian glass enjoyed international currency as a standard of quality, the same sort of currency the American dollar enjoys today. In the best circles abroad it was more desired than gold or silver. It was a time, let us remember, when English sea dogs were bringing home precious metals galore, plundered largely from the hapless Spaniards. A contemporary writer said, "It is a world to see in these our days, wherein gold and silver aboundeth, that our gentility, as loathing these metals (because of the plenty), do now generally choose rather the Venice glasses, both for our wine and beer, than any of these metals, or stone, wherein before time we have been accustomed to drink; but such is the nature of man generally, that it most coveteth things difficult to be attained." (A perfect description of a collector!)

The influence of Venetian glass pervaded all Europe. In England it was reflected in glass made as much as a century later. Someone has said the English have achieved their greatest successes in industrial design when in an effort to imitate something done on the Continent they failed. This is true in glass. In attempting to imitate the soda-lime glass of the Venetians, the English arrived at lead glass with a lustrous quality all its own, which became the crowning glory of English glass in the eighteenth century.

Early American factories made no effort to reproduce the fine glass objects which constitute most of the illustrations in books on European glass. There was neither the time nor the patronage, nor perhaps even the inclination, to develop the more elaborate forms which are the outstanding triumphs of European craftsmanship. In America glass practice reverted to fundamentals.

One of the most crying needs was for bottles. The typical bottle of the early eighteenth century was of a squat onion shape with a rim around the neck. These were customarily used at table as decanters. Since the colonists were hard drinkers, bottles were important. In 1763, for example, Massachusetts distilled a million and a half gallons of rum. It is commonly explained that most of the spirits were exported, but actually two-thirds were consumed right in New England.

In all eighteenth-century glasshouses bottles and window glass were the staple commodities. There was a certain affinity between the two. If you take a bottle in a molten state, fix the pontil rod at the bottom, open up the mouth and spin it at the end of a blow-pipe, you get a flat disk of glass that can be cut into window panes. Glass windows made of such spun disks—so-called crown glass—have certain peculiar characteristics. For one thing the surface of the glass as it was being made never touched any other surface, which left it with a special brilliance. Glass so made had certain irregularities which caught the sun and reflected it in many different directions, giving the pane a self-luminous quality. Then again, the process of spinning the glass rapidly on the pontil rod until it reached a relatively flat form, at which point it was cooled, resulted in an appearance of barely arrested movement which accounts for the lively surface of windows in old houses. Finally, the frequent addition of too much soda to the metal gave it a photo-sensitive quality, a tendency to change color in the sun, as we see in the purple windows on Beacon Hill in Boston and elsewhere.

Such glass was probably made at all American factories in the eighteenth century. What else they made we don't exactly know. Advertisements mention in addition "any sort of glass agreeable to directions."

OHIO PATTERN-MOLDED BOTTLE, twenty-four ribbed mold. *Collection of George S. McKearin.*

366

ANTIQUES

IRISH CUT-GLASS BOWL *(early nineteenth century)*. *National Museum of Ireland.*

AMERICAN BLOWN-THREE-MOLD GLASS BOWL, an obvious imitation of the imported cut-glass type shown at left. *Collection of George S. McKearin.*

Most colonial glassmakers came from Holland, Switzerland, England, and Germany and many of the factory owners were Germans. In Germany several traditions of glassmaking prevailed, taken over from the Venetians. One of these was enameling. The first enameled glass for the German market was probably made on order in Venice, but it was later produced in Germany. The designs were relatively crude, and the fact that it was a glorified peasant art is indicated by the illiterate (sometimes obscene) inscriptions. The better grades of German enameled glass were not imported to America in any quantity, but Bohemia developed a large export trade in enameled glass reduced to relatively simple types, with sketchy enameled decorations, which might be called the five-and-ten-cent-store glass of its day. It was distributed to such distant points as Persia, and may now be found in practically all the museums of the western world. In America only is it called Stiegel glass. We *do* know that Stiegel had enamelers working for him and must have produced glass of this type, but whether a given piece was made here or in Germany it is usually impossible to say.

Another German development taken over from the Venetians was the art of engraving on glass. This, too, was reduced to its common denominator in Bohemia and a kind of popular glass produced for country fairs and export. Engraved glass of this type was made in America too, but of any individual example we can only say that it may have been made in New York—or New Jersey—or Pennsylvania. Some types commonly identified as Stiegel, made of lead glass in various fine colors, closely resemble forms made at Bristol and other English glasshouses and commonly sold in rural areas. Occasional shapes found here seem, however, to be definitely American developments, quite possibly made at Manheim.

Stiegel failed during the "cold war" preceding the American Revolution. Not much glass was made during the Revolution. Amelung came to this country in 1784 with high hopes, bringing over 68 workmen. From the Amelung works comes the first inscribed and dated *(1788)* example of American glass that can be certainly identified. But though he spent $33,000, his enterprise failed, and his workmen went elsewhere.

We get clear evidences of a purely American style for the first time well after the Revolution. This was not developed deliberately; it simply evolved as a by-product of different conditions and materials. Glass made at Zanesville, Ohio, for instance, was produced by much the same techniques as those used traditionally, but the shapes, the metal, the colors are unmistakably American. A wide variety of native forms was produced in this midwestern area as well as in the east.

Excellent clear glass in the English and Irish tradition was turned out by factories in Pittsburgh and its neighborhood and shipped as far south as Mexico. (In the early years of the nineteenth century square-rigged ships were sailing from Marietta and other inland ports down the Ohio and Mississippi and across the Atlantic to points as far away as Italy.)

In addition to the efforts to reproduce imported glass pieces were made which were purely American in character, both by accident and design. Three-mold glass was developed in an effort to reproduce more cheaply the cut glass coming in from Europe. But though such glass is more or less derivative from cut-glass designs, in the color of the metal, the shapes, and the patterns it is far away from the cut-glass imports.

The growth of a native American tradition in glass shows a constant reference to basic forms and fundamental practices. Sturdy usefulness is a characteristic of the most typical glass made in this country. The history of American glass might be described as the evolution of a vernacular in glass design. Following the War of 1812 America went through a period of bumptious independence, and in that spirit the American glassmakers broke off more deliberately from tradition.

It is a good thing to remember that American glassmakers followed practices which had been in use for centuries. There are some rather startling parallels between what was done in this country and what had been done two thousand years before. For instance, we have seen that three-mold glass was made here to imitate cut glass as cheaply as possible; two thousand years before, the Romans did the same thing for the same reason. Another example may be found in glass fragments made before the Christian era which show many of the characteristics with which we are familiar in South Jersey pitchers—applied looped decoration, the reeds around the neck, the heavy form. There are many close parallels between nineteenth-century American and early Roman glass.

For two thousand years glass practices had not changed, up to the nineteenth century. The first and only radical revolution in glassmaking since the evolution of the blowpipe in the pre-Christian era was the mechanical pressing machine, invented in the late 1820's in this country. For the first time we find a brand-new technique. It marked the beginning of mass production and, in a sense, a culminating point in the American tradition of glassmaking.

Glass: English, Irish, or American?

BY PAUL N. PERROT, *Director, Corning Museum of Glass*

"MUCH OF THE GLASSWARE consumed in Ireland is imported, for our houses find the supply of the American market so much more lucrative and have so much of that trade that they think lightly of supplying the home consumption. The Houses of this city [*i.e.*, Dublin] which are in the American trade have generally orders for New York sufficient to occupy them entirely for two years." This often cited passage from Wallace's *Essay on the Manufacture in Ireland,* published in 1798, reveals one of the reasons for the economic struggles which dominated the American glass industry until the embargoes of 1806 and 1807: a constant flow of imports. Indeed, the hostility which led to the War of 1812 and the more stringent duties were not sufficient to halt this influx and large imports continued sporadically and, occasionally, clandestinely. After the war they increased even further, to the great discomfort of our glass producers.

That "Anglo-Irish" glass was so much in demand, in spite of a clear patriotic duty to buy American, cannot be explained only by its relatively low cost and plentiful supply and the high quality of its material. It satisfied preferences which had deep roots.

By and large, it is safe to say that the bulk of the glass which was used in the houses of our gentry until at least the third quarter of the eighteenth century, and in most cases considerably later, was imported either from England or, in limited quantities, from the Continent. The reason is of course plain. Until then there was no local source for luxury or even good glass, and when an indigenous industry finally emerged, it was judged in contemporary accounts to be "equal in beauty and quality to the generality of Flint glass imported from England." We were thus conditioned to importation and to emulating imports, and probably unaware of the minor differences between an "Irish" or an "English" provenance.

This is not astonishing, for the distinction is so difficult to make that a decade ago E. Barrington Haynes stated that Irish glass "was produced under the direction of English glassmasters, supported by English capital, and blown by English glassblowers from English materials" (ANTIQUES, March 1950, p. 197). Further, in spite of the

1.

2.

3.

Note: All objects attributed to England and Ireland were acquired from English or Irish collections. Their attribution is made on this basis as well as on stylistic considerations. All other objects were found in America and are attributed on the basis of circumstances of finding, ownership, history, style, and nature of the glass.

Except as noted, all illustrations are from the Corning Museum of Glass; photographs by Stanley Weisenfeld, Corning Glass Works.

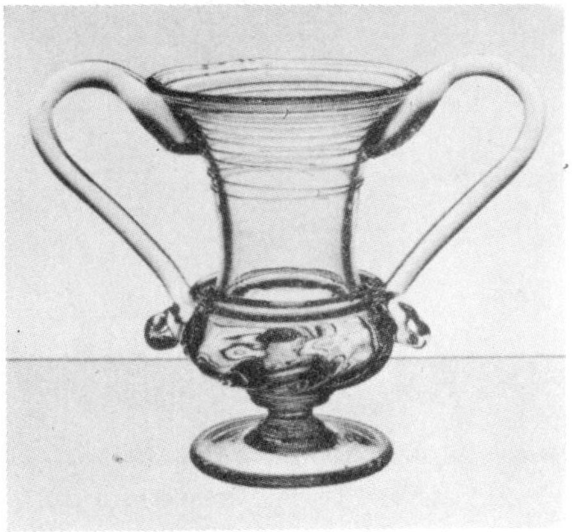

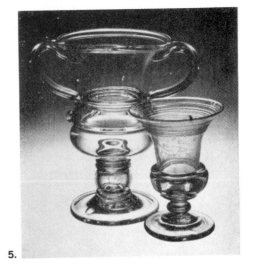

4.

5.

bulk of Irish imports, these seem to have been small in comparison to the quantities imported from Britain, as recorded in United States Treasury reports as well as in advertisements through the first quarter of the nineteenth century. However, it is possible that merchants found it expedient to omit the word Irish from advertisements, since English glass was considered the best.

During this period our industry became established on a firm commercial and financial basis. New factories were founded, particularly in New England and Pennsylvania, and the rigors of foreign competition were tempered by more realistic duties. It was natural for these firms to imitate what was and had been so fashionable during the preceding years as well as contemporary imports. It is astonishing that our glassmakers did not succumb entirely to this temptation and that eventually they developed indigenous styles and approaches which make much of nineteenth-century American glass a predominantly American expression.

No one to my knowledge has yet been able positively to identify American glasses which are exact copies of their Anglo-Irish prototypes. Yet, as seen in contemporary records, they were produced in quantities. Just as many so-called Stiegel enameled glasses found in the Corning collection and elsewhere were made in central Europe, many glasses previously identified as Anglo-Irish may have been made in our glasshouses or decorated in our

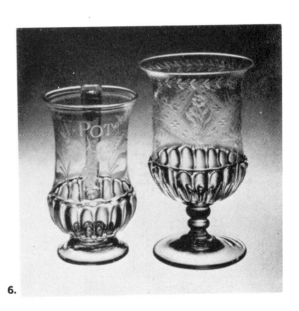

6.

Fig. 1. Sugar bowl, English, c. 1780 (lead glass).

Fig. 2. Sugar bowl, American, Stiegel type, c. 1770 (lead glass). Both this American bowl and the English one (Fig. 1) are in a rich sapphire blue glass, pattern molded and free blown. Though the number of diamonds differs and the foot of the English example is pattern molded while the American one is applied and tooled, there is an obvious affiliation in the choice of design and color. As far as is known, glass of this color was not produced in Ireland. The twisted finial on the cover of the American bowl does not occur on any Anglo-Irish pieces. It seems to be a Continental motif.

Fig. 3. Creamer, English, late eighteenth century (lead glass). Creamer, American (?), Stiegel type, c. 1770 (lead glass). Pattern molded respectively in fourteen- and fifteen-diamond molds; handles similar in form and treatment. The quality of the sapphire blue glass in the English example is high and it is relatively free of impurities, while in the other, which is light purple, the glass is extremely bubbly. Nevertheless, we have strong evidence that a practically flawless material was also produced in America at about the same time. While we can assume that this type of pitcher was made in America, it is possible that a large number of those surviving are English.

Fig. 4. Loving cup, Irish, eighteenth century (lead glass). *Photograph by David Hollander.*

Fig. 5. Loving cup, American (?), possibly New England Glass Company, c. 1835, with an 1810 George III coin in the knop (lead glass). Vase, American, South Jersey-type, Redford Glass Works, c. 1840 (non-lead glass). The similarity of these two examples to that in Figure 4, in spite of a century's gap, is striking. Had the Irish cup been found in America it would undoubtedly have passed for a New England product. The cup with the coin in the base is extremely close to one made at the New England Glass Company and dated, from its engraving, 1833. The custom of inserting coins of foreign origin was practiced by glassmakers in Europe over a long period of time and may also have occurred in America. However, the possibility that this cup is Anglo-Irish cannot be excluded.

Fig. 6. Tankard, English, c. 1790 (lead glass). Celery vase, American, possibly Pittsburgh, early nineteenth century (lead glass). The rib-molded base of the bowls, a motif which occurs in England from the late seventeenth century onwards, is produced by similar techniques. It became particularly popular in the Philadelphia and Pittsburgh areas. A foot of the same form is seen on the Irish mold-blown bowl in Figure 17.

7.

8.

9.

10.

11.

independent cutting establishments. Whether a test can be devised which will permit easy identification through physical means, remains to be seen. In the meantime, we can only speculate and turn our gaze to the more obvious differences which developed into American styles.

Though it has been stated that high-quality flint glass produced in America during the first quarter of the nineteenth century tends to be of a more brilliant metal than English or Irish, as well as slightly lighter in weight, the evidence is at best meager. These characteristics have been attributed to purer raw materials and more dependable sources of heat. Such criteria are, however, not sufficient in themselves: for example, Waterford's production at its best is remarkably clear and free of cast and many early Pittsburgh lead-glass pieces have a strong grayish cast.

A few of the patterns found in Irish mold-blown glass are very similar to the ones found in American pieces. When the former first appeared is not clear, nor do we know whether they evolved out of the ribbed pattern molds which were used mostly for the bottoms of decant-

ers and wineglass coolers, or whether they were due to the influence of American glasses blown in full-size piece molds. The latter, however, appears unlikely if we compare the vast number of individual patterns developed in America in the 1820's and 1830's to the very few found in Ireland. Had Ireland copied America one would expect her to have taken advantage of the vast decorative vocabulary we had developed in a few short years. If, on the contrary, we adopted a not too popular technique developed in Ireland, one might expect that it would have received the fullest possible exploitation in this country. On this slim circumstantial evidence it is probably safe to assume that Ireland gave the first impetus.

Conversely, though a hand press was used in Ireland and England at least as early as the last decade of the eighteenth century, there is no indication that the pressing machine as it developed in America was ever used in Ireland. We know that when it was introduced in England in the 1830's it was received with misgivings, and that its American origin was soon acknowledged.

Some of the illustrations reveal the kinship between Anglo-Irish and American glass. They show conclusively that our craftsmen were not satisfied with adapting borrowed motifs. They elaborated on them, and such combinations of motifs, for example, as the strawberry diamond and fan which are found on both English and Irish cut pieces seem to have been given a purely national flavor. Influences, however, were now to travel in both directions. Our new pressed-glass techniques revolutionized the market, making available to the masses ornate pieces at prices which everyone could afford. Europe started copying our techniques, and though we continued to look to England and the Continent for inspiration, our industry had come of age and had discovered its own idiom. By the early 1850's, as the last Irish factory was closing down after seventy years of great prosperity, America had become one of the leading glass producers of the world.

The author is indebted to Helen McKearin, who has generously given her advice.

Fig. 7. Decanter, probably American, possibly Amelung, c. 1790 (non-lead glass). Decanter, English, 1807 (lead glass).

Fig. 8. Firing glasses, probably American, possibly Amelung, c. 1790 (non-lead glass). Rummer, Irish, c. 1790 (lead glass). The decanter (Fig. 7) and the firing glasses were tentatively attributed by the late George S. McKearin to Amelung. He made the attribution with caution and probably based it mainly on the fact that they are of non-lead glass. It is possible that Amelung's commercial glasses were of this type. The extreme delicacy, almost weakness, of the engraving seen on one of the firing glasses and on the American decanter contrasts with the rather strong and not overly refined engraving characteristic of Amelung's presentation pieces. The Masonic firing glass is in this respect more typically an Amelung product.

Fig. 9. Decanter, Irish, Waterford, before 1799 (presumably lead glass). *Photograph by courtesy of the Victoria and Albert Museum, London. Crown copyright.*

Fig. 10. Decanter, American (?), early nineteenth century (lead glass).

Fig. 11. Decanter, American, possibly Pittsburgh, early nineteenth century (lead glass). This decanter and those in Figures 9 and 10 have so much in common that any categorical attribution seems inadvisable. The general proportions and the manner in which such details as the stars are executed strongly point to a common origin; flute-molding at the base and a few other details are the only major differences. This one has a slight grayish cast and motifs often found in the Pittsburgh area (see Fig. 6). The pressed mushroom stopper, a popular American type, though probably belonging to another decanter, is practically identical in form and technique to Anglo-Irish ones of the 1790-1830 period.

Fig. 12. Bowl, Irish, end of eighteenth century (presumably lead glass). A close prototype of the strawberry-fan designs in Figure 13. The characteristic turn-over at the lip is seldom found in America. This type of hand-pressed foot, almost an anachronism under such an elaborately cut bowl, may have fostered the development of more complex pressing devices in America around 1825. *Royal Scottish Museum, Edinburgh.*

Fig. 13. Sugar bowl and cup, American, Pittsburgh, possibly Bakewell, c. 1815-1835 (bowl, non-lead glass; cover and cup, lead glass). Pitcher, Irish, early nineteenth century (lead glass). Strawberry-diamond cutting was directly derived from the diamond design popular in England and Ireland (Fig. 12) at the turn of the century. The elaborate fan design so often found on Philadelphia and Pittsburgh pieces has the same origin, though it seems to have been developed to a far greater extent in America than in Europe. It occurs on a series of tumblers with sulphide inserts which may well be the ones made by Bakewell in 1824 and advertised in 1825 (Fig. 14).

Fig. 14. Tumbler, American, Bakewell, Page and Bakewell, 1824 (lead glass). Cup, American, probably Pittsburgh, c. 1820-1835 (lead glass).

12.

13.

14.

15.

16.

17.

Fig. 15. Pitcher, Irish, c. 1810 (lead glass). Urn, Irish, c. 1810 (lead glass). Pitcher, American, possibly Brooklyn Glass Works, John L. Gilliland, c. 1825-1835 (lead glass). The vast number of advertisements put out by glassmaking and glass cutting firms proves conclusively that much cut glass derived from "English" prototypes. This dependence is evident in these two pitchers. Though there are several important differences in the cutting and the general form, there is an obvious similarity of approach in such details as the cutting at the neck, the paneling beneath it, and the grooves on either side of the handles. Several pitchers published by Westropp are closer in shape to the American one, though the cutting on the lip of the latter appears to be more elaborate than is generally the case in Anglo-Irish examples. The high quality of the American metal in the second quarter of the nineteenth century is often attested to. In 1851 Gilliland received first prize for flint glass submitted to the London Exposition of that year.

Fig. 16. Decanter, American, possibly midwestern, c. 1830 (lead glass). Blown-three-mold in Pattern G 11-27 (McKearin, *American Glass*), one of the few designs which also appear on glass attributed to Ireland. It is similar to the Irish bowl in Figure 17, though the number of diamonds is different. *Henry Ford Museum.*

Fig. 17. Pitcher, American, Boston and Sandwich Glass Company, c. 1830. Compote, American, Boston and Sandwich Glass Company, c. 1825-1835. Decanter, American, probably Keene, New Hampshire, c. 1820. Compote, Irish, early nineteenth century (all of lead glass). Irish mold-blown glass, whether it developed before or after the American variety, had a very small decorative vocabulary mostly based on diamonds and ribs and was produced in small quantities, judging from the number of surviving examples. Westropp, in his article in ANTIQUES, December 1928, illustrates a decanter almost identical to this one except that the narrow bands have horizontal ribs instead of diamonds. Mold-blown geometric patterns such as those of the American pitcher and compote never appear in either English or Irish glass and can therefore be considered purely American contributions. Neither do we find "Gothic" and "baroque" designs, though there are vaguely reminiscent parallels to the latter on the Continent.

ON ATTRIBUTING AMERICAN BLOWN GLASS

FIG. 1

By GREGOR NORMAN-WILCOX

Illustrations from the collection of Mr. and Mrs. W. Dan Quattlebaum. Photographs by courtesy of Los Angeles Museum. Captions on page 74

SOMEWHERE in the earlier years of collecting, one begins to suspect that not every lyre-back chair is really Duncan Phyfe, or every blue jasperware vase Wedgwood — or every thin-blown jug of purplish cobalt glass a Stiegel piece. But the tendency to attach specific *names* to things is not readily outgrown. It prevails not only among beginners but also, too often, among experts. Especially in the field of early American glass it is well to ask what justifies an attribution. After all, the cobalt jug becomes no better in itself for being given a name. This article is an attempt to re-examine established facts, in the effort to determine how often we can, or should, attribute examples of American blown glass.

A generation ago any lilypad jug (*Fig. 4, E*) was called "South Jersey" or even "Wistarberg," because the technique was then believed to be peculiar to that region and to the eighteenth century. But now we know that others of the same type, as good or better, were made at many places in New England and New York State almost a century later.[1] A generation ago, too, it was easy to identify the wares produced by Stiegel — until we began to learn that much of this "Stiegel" glass had really been made in Ohio, and in 1850 instead of 1770. Indeed, we have received so many surprises of this sort that nowadays we hardly dare consider any particular metal, color, or manner of workmanship as necessarily characteristic of a certain source.

What may be called purely circumstantial evidence, once blithely accepted, is now in general disrepute. Not all the glassware found on Cape Cod is Sandwich. And a great many pieces have come from Manheim, the very site of the Stiegel works, without being Stiegel examples at all — perhaps without even being American. It is inconclusive to point out that much American glassware, until recent years, was discovered in the actual homes of old families — hence, undisturbed and archæologically intact! Even though such houses might have been next-door to an early glassworks, we are not warranted in supposing. Local markets were often of negligible importance; there was always more Stiegel glass in Boston or New York, no doubt, than ever at home in Manheim. Early factories sent their output far and wide, sometimes maintaining regular agencies in distant cities, or conducting annual auctions that were attended by dealers from everywhere.

All this is negative argument, to be sure; yet it is not written with destructive intent. Rather, it is an effort to explore at the start the principal pitfalls and problems, in order to clear the way for more hopeful discussion.

STYLE

The mistake commonest among glass collectors is that of assuming that the *style* of a piece can, in itself, establish a source and date. For example, the form and decoration of Figure 1, *D* may indeed represent Stiegel's manner of 1770 — but its style was also used in (English) Bristol glass of about the same time, and in Ohio pieces of sixty and seventy years later. The large jug of Figure 4, *B*

shows the opaque white sworling usually recognized under the name (English) Nailsea — yet Mrs. Knittle[11] tells us that in America this type was "made at nearly every flint-glass works, 1820–60." We have already remarked that the small lilypad jug (*Fig. 4, E*) would certainly have been attributed to New Jersey not many years ago — but here is an occurrence of the lilypad in New York State, while Mrs. Knittle[12] pictures others from New Hampshire and New York. ANTIQUES[8] shows still another, authenticated as a product of New London, Connecticut (*see also*[2]). So we may guess the folly of attempting to attribute American glass merely on the basis of its style. *Style*, meaning only the general form of a piece and the character of its decoration, is superficial, having little to do with other and intrinsic factors — the metal used, its texture, the technical processes employed, the color.

We must remember the effect of the "roving habit" of the early American glassworker. When business became slack or when wanderlust waxed strong, the workman gathered together his tools and moved on. Wherever he worked, his accustomed technique was expressed. His tools might produce at Zanesville precisely the imprint they had left at Greensboro a year before. The result was a continual exchange and repetition of styles, sometimes over wide areas and through long periods of time.[9]

Naturally, certain plain objects were produced everywhere. Bowls such as Figures 5, *D*, 6, *D*, and 7, *C* or plates like 4, *D* or cups as plain as 5, *A* and *C* belong to no specific region or period, and are unusual in almost no respect. Other pieces of somewhat more ambitious character though still unpretentious (*Figs. 3, E and 5, B*) display such simple features as might have occurred to anyone. Moreover, glassware does not consistently echo the orderly sequence of styles observable in silver or ceramics. Favorite types were used over and over, by glassworking father and son; any logical shape, or any easy mode of decoration, might continue to appear for a century or more.

Finally, it is well to remember, in studying glass or antiques of any other kind, that merely to look for resemblances between example and type is not enough. We must observe not only in what respects one piece is *like* another, but how it *differs*. The differences are the significant thing.

THE METAL

Glass, as everyone knows, is a processed combination of several ingredients, which must be mixed and fused under certain conditions. If the materials and the conditions never varied, we might always achieve the same result; but this is by no means the case. The purity of each ingredient, the precise proportions of one to another, the heat of the glass pot and the length of time allowed for "cooking," the manipulation of the molten metal as it is removed from the crucible and while it is being worked — each of these and other factors has an effect on the ultimate appearance of the glass itself. Slightest variations influence the weight or color, surface or texture, of the finished metal.

No two glasshouses produced exactly the same metal. But for that matter, no single glasshouse turned out its own metal twice just the same. Where so many factors were involved, no expenditure of pains could guarantee the result. How, then, can we surely identify a certain metal as the work of one factory? The answer is, we can't.

Perhaps we are asked to admire some thin and flinty bowl or cup while its owner, holding it aloft and tapping the rim with a pencil, listens for the resonant tone characteristic (he tells us) of Stiegel glass. Shall we remind him that many a piece made in 1920 will ring just as sweetly as Stiegel's? Resonance depends largely on the shape employed, and only partly on the material, regardless of age or source. Perhaps he says something, too, about the rich purple-blues and ruddy amethysts which you "can always tell" as the work of Stiegel. But we may assure him that Bristol glass and Ohio Stiegel are often of quite as rich and ruddy a hue.

Despite such doubts as these, the case for old glass has its affirmative aspects. We learn to know the softened "bloom" or patina all glass acquires with time — a surface oxidization resulting from long exposure to light and air — and we are not to be misled by modern handmade Mexican glass which lacks this patina, however much it may represent the Stiegel technique. We learn local peculiarities which distinguish certain early factories, such as the fact that Stoddard produced no clear glass because material in the vicinity was suitable only for bottle glass in dark colors. We learn how the metal itself may control the design, with the dark Connecticut bottle glass lending itself to coarse and casual types of work, or the brittle metal of Stiegel tradition making possible a greater refinement of detail. We do learn many general rules and specific facts; but also, we learn to be conservative in applying our knowledge.

TECHNIQUE

The pitfalls already indicated in connection with style and metal recur with consideration of technique. If we have observed the restless habit of the glassworkers during times of prosperity, and their forced migrations when glass making enterprises failed, we may guess the widespread distribution of their methods as well as their styles. We follow the Kramer family westward through the glasshouses of Maryland, Pennsylvania, and Ohio. The name of John S. Foster is associated with many a venture in Massachusetts, Vermont, and upper New York. And workers from New Jersey were scattered throughout New England, bringing Jersey traits to the northern area.

Where certain simple types of work were of universal occurrence, their technique was everywhere quite the same. A bowl such as Figure 5, D would be made in the same way at Westford, Connecticut, in 1870, as it was at Greensboro, Pennsylvania, in 1800. One "folded" edge looks like another, and there is no index to period in pontil marks or spiral ribbing.[3]

In glassmaking, we have to consider not only the fundamental points of technique shared by all American glass but also the long and curious survivals of certain distinctive modes and manners. Expanded pattern-molding (*Fig. 1, B, C,* and *D*) such as Stiegel used during 1765–1774 was still a favorite device in Ohio glass of the mid-nineteenth century. Pinched-on handles and threaded necks (*Fig. 1, B*), molded paneling (*Fig. 3, E*), tooled decoration (*Fig. 4, E*), and many another device persisted for more than a hundred years. Such effects were produced always in the same way — the same, indeed, as had been employed for similar work 2,000 years before! Any collection of ancient Greek or Roman glass will provide pieces quite as much in the "Stiegel" technique as

FIG. 6

FIG. 7

and familiar themes, and employing the technique to which his hand was accustomed. The late, oft-quoted J. B. Kerfoot described this tendency: "Three generations of these workmen continued for more than a hundred years to make . . . the same range of pieces, unaltered in form and indistinguishable in technique." [13]

Mrs. Knittle [12] (*p. 38*) assures us: "Summing up the matter, it should be said that one can seldom 'date' a piece of early American glass by form, design, color, or technique." And such considerations as form the basis of the present article lead toward the conclusion that this statement applies as well to *source* as to *period*.

anything that came from Zanesville.[10] We find clear glasses with the ("Stiegel") thread of blue at the edge, or others with the ("South Jersey") threaded neck, or others showing contact molding and expanded molding, among items made 1,500 years before the *Mayflower* first sighted the Massachusetts shore. It is even too easy to discover such resemblances. The differences (it might be repeated) are the things to notice.

In general, it may be said that the Jersey tradition of bold, "juicy" work spread toward the north, through New York State and New England, while the lighter Stiegel tradition was passing westward, into the glasshouses of the Pittsburgh area and Ohio. In this broad sense we do encounter regional types of work. But what we learn is not so much how to identify the technique or style of particular factories, as how to distinguish the various main *schools* of work. Very often, our attributions cannot go beyond that point. We may group the heavy lilypad jugs and bowls according to their type, whether Wistarberg or Stoddard, regardless of date. And we regard the more fragile Stiegel-type pieces (whether Manheim, Pittsburgh, or Mantua) simply as instances of another and dissimilar trend or school.

Attributions may sometimes be made with assurance, it is true, in the case of "offhand" pieces. These were the things produced after hours and off-the-record, when workmen were permitted to use the day's residue of metal for fashioning objects entirely to suit themselves. Jugs, mugs, vases, or bowls were styled according to the worker's fancy — forthright and utilitarian things, or whimsical novelties, designed as treasured personal gifts for wives and friends. While the commercial output of any factory lost its identity when it scattered, the unofficial offhand pieces carried personal associations long remembered.

Still, even in offhand work where the personal element was so strong, habit and tradition usually prevailed. Though the worker was free to follow his fancy, he found himself repeating favorite

THE ILLUSTRATIONS

FIG. I — FOUR CREAM JUGS, NOT NECESSARILY "STIEGEL"

Representing traditions of style and technique which persisted from the mid-eighteenth to the mid-nineteenth century, and from the seaboard westward to Ohio. *A* (sapphire blue, purplish in thicker parts) came from a family in East Orange, New Jersey, while *D* (same color, with reticulated molding) is from a house in Quaker City, Ohio. *B* (palest green, full of bubbles, with 22 spiraled ribs) was found in the New York City area. *C* (clear glass, 18 ribs) displays features sometimes occurring in Ohio work. Though Stiegel reminiscences are strong in *C* and *D*, these must be called "Stiegel type" or, at most, "Ohio Stiegel." *B*, of thin metal and light in weight, shows a curious blending of the technique commonly associated with Stiegel's name and the style considered characteristic of New Jersey. Nineteenth-century traits are observable in *A;* and all four pieces probably date within the first third of that century, despite their earlier implications. *Heights, left to right*, 5 ¼ in., 4 ¾ in., 4 ⅞ in., 4 ½ in.

FIG. 2 — WINEGLASSES, ATTRIBUTED TO AMELUNG (*1784–1795*)

If our attributions are at smaller risk of challenge where they concern so little-known an author as Amelung, we are then under the greater obligation to support our claims. In this instance, every evidence (of locale-where-found, of history, and of intrinsic features) points to Amelung.[5,6,11] In spite of such evidence, the pieces here shown offer surprises such as we encounter everywhere in our study of American glass. We have seen that Amelung could turn out first-quality metal, with engraved ornament unsurpassed in America at the time; yet here we discover two comparison-pieces of bubbly texture and dusky metal. The inference might be that these are early or experimental examples. Obviously we dare not be too dogmatic as to what a certain maker did, or did not, produce. We are reminded that neither metal, color, technique, nor style offers an invariable guide. *Height of each*, 5 ⅛ in.

FIG. 3 — GOOD AMERICAN GLASS OF THE EIGHTEENTH CENTURY

Pieces in the Stiegel (*1765–1774*) and supposed Bayard-Bamper (*c. 1752–1767*) traditions, though the same types undoubtedly were produced by contemporary glasshouses which are known little if at all. *B* and *D* are in pure, unassimilated style — the former English, the latter East German. Judged by their style alone, *C* might be Dutch, *A* German, the

ANTIQUES

twelve-paneled flip glass (D) Spanish. If Stiegel advertised his express intention of "competing with" the foreign wares, and if he sought workmen direct from European glassmaking centers, we cannot wonder that his output offers a literal echo of the things we know as European. While all these pieces are American, no one may pretend to place or date them beyond question. They exemplify a school of work widely followed during the late eighteenth century, and perhaps now beyond hope of positive attribution. *Heights, left to right,* 6 ½ in., 7 ¾ in., 4 ¾ in., 5 7/16 in., 6 in.

FIG. 4 — EARLY AND LATER, IN NEW YORK STATE

Of various metal, color, technique, and style such as found in, but by no means confined to, New York State. Features as early as the tooled lilypad (E), or as late as the opaque white sworling of B, suggest a range of dates at least through the first half of the nineteenth century. The colors are aquamarine, varying from the bluish thick-lights of the ball-covered cup (A) to the pale and bubbly metal of C, which was made so unsteady on its foot it was never thought worthy of being given a handle! If these pieces are characteristic of what *was* done in New York State (especially in the Saratoga region), we must remember that they are not types of work necessarily *limited* to that area. (Compare A with other ball-covered jugs and jars, also New York State.[2]) In style these pieces reflect the period *c.* 1760–1860, but their actual dates range only within the first half of the nineteenth century. We must not suppose that crudity is an indication of early work, or refinement of form and manner a later characteristic. *Heights, left to right,* 3 ⅜ in., with cover 5 in.; 8 in., 4 in., 4 7/16; *diameter of plate,* 5 ⅞ in.

FIG. 5 — MADE ALMOST ANYWHERE, FOR ALMOST A CENTURY

From New Hampshire to Ohio, from perhaps 1780 to 1860, examples of these types were made by many glassmakers, and their attribution is usually hazardous. C (pale aquamarine), was made between 1829 and 1850 at Suncook, New Hampshire; D, light-green milk bowl of the early nineteenth century, is from the factory founded by Albert Gallatin at New Geneva. (Compare this bowl and the smaller Ohio bowl, Figure 6, D, with illustrations in ANTIQUES.[4]) Unlike these two attributed pieces, A (of faulty but slick-surfaced, deep-green bottle glass, its edge folded inward) might have been made almost anywhere, at the turn of the century or as much as fifty years later. As for the rich reddish-amber flip, B, (with 24 molded ribs, turning to left near top), only guesswork could place this piece in the Zanesville and eastern Ohio area, about 1820. *Heights, left to right,* 4 ¼ in., 5 ¼ in., 3 7/16 in., 6 ⅜ in.

FIG. 6 — OHIO GLASSWARE (1815–1860)

B and C are from Zanesville, but the molded bottle, A, and the bowl, D, can only be assigned to "Ohio, first half nineteenth century." B is of pale purplish hue; this may be discoloration resulting from exposure to sunlight. Its 28-rib molding is sharply twisted to the left, but disappears toward the base. (Compare with Mantua-type jug.[7]) Swirled in the other direction, the 32-ribbed wine or strong-ale glass is of clear colorless metal and is engraved in block letters with the name R. WADDINGTON. Both of these we attribute to Ohio, probably to Zanesville, second quarter of the nineteenth century. A is a swirled broken-rib globular bottle (24 ribs) of deep golden amber; compare it and B with Figures 11 and 12, ANTIQUES.[4] D is an olive-amber bowl with everted and outward-folded edge. Though here called "Ohio glassware" for convenience, these really represent the general family of work prevailing in the triangle between Kent or Ravenna, the Monongahela, and Louisville. Their exact sources are probably conjectural, and their dates might range anywhere from *c.* 1815 to *c.* 1865. *Heights, left to right,* 7 ½ in., 4 ¼ in., 2 ⅞ in., 4 ¼ in.

FIG. 7 — PLAIN PIECES OF OHIO TYPE

Though A and E recall Staffordshire pottery forms of the 1830's and 1840's, the glassworker has modified the forms to suit his own medium, and has not added molding, tooling, engraving, or even the element of color to interrupt the subtle play of light across smooth surfaces. He has been satisfied with pleasing proportion and soft highlight. Therein lies much of the homely charm of common nineteenth-century blown glassware. The miniatures, B and D, are such things as early glassworkers made after hours for their own children. They repeat in delightfully small scale the shapes, details, and painstaking workmanship of full-size pieces. A, which we here place within the Ohio-Pittsburgh triangle, proposes a nice study in attributions. An almost identical sugar bowl in amethyst was pictured in the catalogue of the Herbert Lawton sale in 1931,[14] and described as a "Stiegel" piece. Mrs. Knittle, however, assigns to Pittsburgh itself (rather than to Ohio) certain features exemplified by both pieces.[4] Still another (contact-molded) sugar bowl, illustrated in the catalogue of the Hammond-Walker Collection, repeats these supposedly distinctive features (of foot, general form, flange, and lid), yet is accredited

by Miss McKearin "probably Sandwich." *Heights,* A, 7 ½ in.; B, 2 ¼ in.; *diameter,* C, 5 3/16 in.; *heights,* D, 2 in.; E, 7 ⅜ in.

If serious experts, qualified by years of research and handling of old glass, can thus employ the same criteria yet arrive at such varying conclusions, those less experienced may well be wary of the urge to attach names to what they see. Circumstances seldom warrant attribution, and where they do not, the label *Unidentified* is an honest and respectable confession.

REFERENCES

The Magazine ANTIQUES:
1. October 1926, pp. 274–280. *Wistarberg and South Jersey Glass,* George S. McKearin
2. February 1930, pp. 137–143. *A Glimpse of Early Glass*
3. August 1930, pp. 141–143. *A Pictorial Demonstration of Glassmaking*
4. December 1931, pp. 344–348. *American Glass Sugar Bowls,* Rhea Mansfield Knittle; also June 1932, pp. 264–268; and December 1932, pp. 224–228
5. September 1934, pp. 88–91. *Safe Clues in the Amelung Quest,* Homer Eaton Keyes
6. January 1935, pp. 7, 8. *Add to Amelung,* Editor's Attic
7. February 1935, pp. 64–68 and July 1935, pp. 30–33. *The Story of the Mantua Glass Works* — Harry Hall White
8. September 1935, pp. 101–103. *Connecticut Glass,* Charles B. Gardner
9. August 1937, pp. 64–67. *Migrations of Early Glassworkers,* Harry Hall White
10. August 1937, pp. 70–72. *Glass: Ancient and Antique,* Homer Eaton Keyes
11. February 1938, pp. 80, 81. *Another Inscribed Amelung Glass*

BOOKS:
12. *Early American Glass* (Century), Rhea Mansfield Knittle

CATALOGUES:
13. Dr. Pleasant Hunter Collection: Sale (1920), American Art Galleries. Notes by J. B. Kerfoot
14. King Hooper-Kaufman-Lawton Collections: Sale (1931), National Art Galleries

GLASS CENTER AT 1939 NEW YORK WORLD'S FAIR

This million-dollar, ultra-modernistic edifice, close to the thematic Trylon and Perisphere on Flushing Meadows, houses the interesting exhibits of the Owens-Illinois, Pittsburgh Plate, and Corning Glass Companies. Its huge tower of glass blocks, blue fins, and spiral helix and its "functional" architectural plan contrast dramatically with the picture of the Libbey Glass Company's "palace" at the 1893 Columbian Exposition, shown on page 78

AUGUST 1939

75

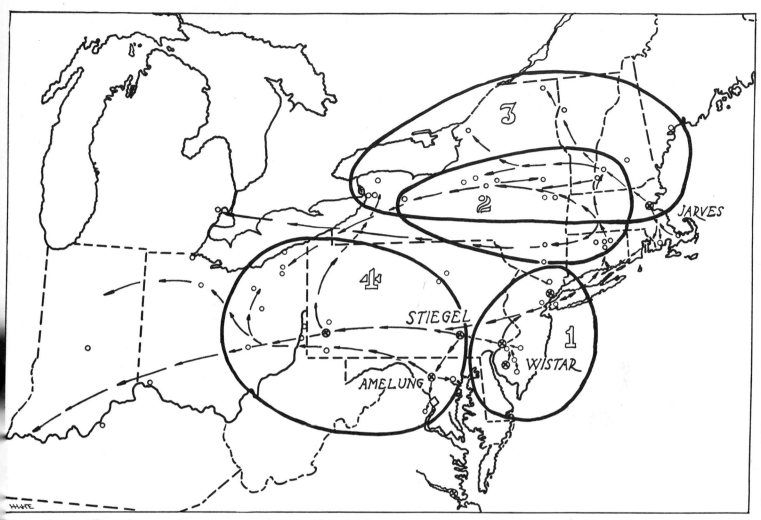

Fig. 1 — Areas of Early American Glassmaking and Lines of Worker Migration

Offhand-blown glass from Areas 1, 2, and 3 frequently shows evidence of a common kinship in form and modes of decoration. The reason for this is in part revealed by the lines of worker migration indicated on the map by arrows. The migration lines in Area 4 are less confused for they mark the direct course followed mainly by former employees of Stiegel and Amelung, who thus bore westward a technique more delicate than that commanded by the New Jersey workmen

Migrations of Early Glassworkers

By Harry Hall White

THE vagrant tendencies of American glassworkers in early days have become almost proverbial. Evidence of how individual artisans and occasionally whole groups of them were seized by the migratory urge crops up constantly, though often briefly and in disconnected passages, throughout the historical source material on our native glassmaking.

Sometimes this evidence is no more than a casual statement regarding an individual. Sometimes it is a vague hint or a suggestion, leaving much — generally too much — to the imagination. Again, on the other hand, we meet with clear and circumstantial accounts of mass movements. We are, for example, familiar with the romantic trek of Amelung men *en route* to Louisville, and the persuasive diplomacy that halted the journey at Gallatin's venture in New Geneva, Pennsylvania (Antiques for April 1928, *p. 290*). We have heard likewise of how crown-glass-makers were lured from Boston to Utica, New York (Antiques for July 1929, *p. 44*), and of how other men were shifted from Boston to the Union Flint Glass Works in Philadelphia. A less clearly documented but nevertheless quite unmistakable record of these and other migrations has been left to us in the distinctive forms and modes of ornamentation on blown glass that the traveling workmen produced in the localities where they paused during their journeyings or came permanently to rest. By way of obvious illustration of this record, we find that the so-called lilypad ornament — though employed in New Jersey, certain

parts of New England, and in several New York factories — is *not* associated with Ohio. Conversely, the ribbed and swirled patterns of the Midwest are not eloquent of Eastern origin.

The whole territory from which comes most of the blown glass still surviving from early days lies north of Virginia and stretches westward from the Atlantic seaboard into the state of Ohio. During the period of our concern — roughly from a little before the Revolution until the mid-1800's — this far-flung domain harbored four different traditions of glassware forms and modes of ornamentation, each confined to a particular area and each revealing its specific peculiarities most clearly in such typical objects as bowls and pitchers. To be sure, we must not try to fix the boundaries of these areas with perfect exactitude. Within all of them we shall encounter overlapping and conflicting types, particularly in the New England–New York State section. Nevertheless, it is an indisputable fact that the experienced observer can almost unfailingly identify the area from which a piece of early glass has come.

Perhaps arbitrarily, yet not without reason, we have chosen Area 1 as the earliest stable source of American blown glass. It is shown on the accompanying map as comprising lower New York, all of New Jersey, much of Delaware, and a scrap of eastern Pennsylvania. Its presiding deity, first in the flesh and later in spirit, was Caspar Wistar. Yet it would be a mistake to discount the influence of men from the old glasshouses of Manhattan, of which we know both so much and so tantalizingly little. New York City must have been a veritable cross-roads for artisan travel, and have contributed from its own overflow of imported Low Countries talent to the migratory streams that were moving north, south, and west.

AREA 1 is the source of bowls and pitchers in all the varying shades of green and amber. Later came the bicolored pieces and striated objects in the Nailsea fashion. The earlier pieces seem to occur in the deeper colors. Bowls and pitchers are found either plain or ornamented with dragged applications of glass in the so-called lily-pad design. They may exhibit a plain or crimped cast-on foot. (*Fig. 2.*)

It is believed that the bicolored looped patterns in this blown glass are not so early as was originally surmised. They are probably a nineteenth-century product and

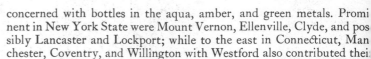

Fig. 2 — TYPICAL VESSELS FROM AREA 1, SOUTH JERSEY FORMS

a, Deep bowl, and pitcher, the latter with threaded neck and slightly crimped foot. *From the George S. McKearin collection*

b and *c* (*below*), Pitchers in striated aquamarine and opaque-white glass, "Nailsea style." *From the W. Griffin Gribbel collection*

d (*below*), Blue pitcher on slightly flaring foot. In form allied with pitcher *a. From the George Horace Lorimer collection*

(For color portrayals of Jersey glass, see Frontispiece of ANTIQUES for October 1926)

in no wise associated with Wistar. Investigations thus far conducted at Wistarberg confirm this opinion. That the early, rather high, straight-sided bowls were a product of Area 1 is substantiated by fragments from my excavations at the Wistar site in South Jersey. Variants of this type are to be found in Areas 2 and 4. We are likewise aware that Area 1 was not a large producer of tripartite-mold-blown glass; though during the development of its large industrial centres from 1810 to 1840 it is certain to have made some glass of that type.

Glassworkers from Area 1, men versed in the so-called South Jersey technique, moved in considerable numbers northward to glasshouses in Connecticut, New Hampshire, and New York. Likewise the perennial westward urge carried some of the New Jersey glass forms to western Pennsylvania and Ohio, as will subsequently be noted.

IN AREA 2, which embraces a good deal of New York State and not a little of New England, we find the majority of what we term, as a broad designation, the "bottle houses." These factories were primarily

concerned with bottles in the aqua, amber, and green metals. Promi-nent in New York State were Mount Vernon, Ellenville, Clyde, and pos-sibly Lancaster and Lockport; while to the east in Connecticut, Man-chester, Coventry, and Willington with Westford also contributed their quota of bottles and flasks. Of course, a few establishments in the area were chiefly occupied with window glass. Among these may be mentioned Utica, Vernon, Rock-ville, Woodstock, and Ontario at Geneva, New York.

The blown prod-ucts of this area, other than bottles, are many and exhibit a wide range of color and ornament. Oddly enough, however, the supply of bowls has been ungenerous, though such as were made are quite spe-cific in type, and hence easily recognized.

The colors of Area 2 glass are generally strong and the forms deep — an inheritance from Area 1. Pitchers from Keene exhibit the handsome lilypad motive more competently handled than is the case with the similar ornamentation in New Jersey. New York State bottle-house pitchers show a gradual departure from the ample lines derived from Area 1 toward the form of an inverted truncated cone. Area 2 turned out much tripartite-mold-blown glass in many colors and forms at Keene, Coventry, and Mount Vernon, but *not* at Stoddard, New Hampshire (ANTIQUES for June 1927, *p. 459,* September and November 1929, *pp. 193 and 394*).

AREA 3 has been laid out on the map to include the approximate lo-cations of the window-glass houses whose establishing marked the in-dustrial rise following the Revolution and the War of 1812, up to, say, the centennial year of 1876. Here in bowl and pitcher forms we again recognize an inheritance from New Jersey-trained glassmen.

The area in question inevitably overlaps Area 2, since no natural geographical boundary separates bottle houses from window-glass houses. On the other hand, a very distinct line of demarcation is to be found

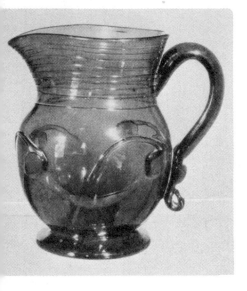

Fig. 3 — TYPICAL VESSELS FROM AREA 2, NEW YORK AND SOUTHERN NEW ENGLAND
a (left), Amber pitcher from Keene, New Hampshire; lilypad decoration. Compare 2a.
b (above), New York State and New England pitchers. Note conical body of middle item. a and b from the W. Griffin Gribbel collection
c (below), Green deep bowl with wide rim. From the George Kamperman collection

the color of the metal in their wares. Obviously bowls or pitchers from window-glass houses are in very light green, or in the nearest shade we have to the true aquamarine with its attractive bluish cast. This shade is frequently found in the glass of the Oneida Lake group: Cleveland, Vanistota, Bernhard's Bay. The northern group, in which Redford and Redwood are prominent, made a richer shade of very light green — but it was window glass. The lilypad pieces from the last-named factories are, without question, the finest items of our later blown glass.

Area 4 has yielded some of the most romantic and beautiful glass made in America. It here that our glasshouse craftsmen most nearly achieved a national type of blown glass. Here, in so far as our American production is concerned, several types of ornamentation were originated. Occasional pieces of similar imitation may have been made in houses outside this area, but not as a regular product.

Of the actual output of Stiegel and Amelung we have

little reliable information other than that derived from the inventories and advertisements of these two unfortunate captains of industry. The collapse of their short-lived enterprises spilled their craftsmen into the ever-westward-flowing stream of emigration. Some of these wayfarers found lodgment in the newly founded glassworks of western Pennsylvania. Others fared onward to dimly perceived goals in Ohio. Wherever they congregated they produced a unique type of glassware, quite different in both form and ornament from glass made in Areas 1, 2, and 3, though here and there we occasionally recognize the influences of the older Eastern forms — mostly in deep bowls. Pitchers and bowls from Area 4 may be plain or exhibit several modes of ornament, which, for lack of better designation, we may classify as *ribbed pattern*, *broken-rib pattern*, *swirled pattern*, and *diamond pattern*.

In addition to such patterns, Area 4 produced glass blown in tripartite molds. Just how much glass of this type and in what patterns the Pittsburgh

Fig. 4 — TYPICAL VESSELS FROM AREA 3
a, New York State pitchers with threading and lilypad decoration. From the W. Griffin Gribbel collection

Fig. 4 b, New York State bowl with lilypad decoration.
From the Detroit Institute of Art

Fig. 4 c, Aquamarine New York State bowl with lilypad decoration.
From the Detroit Institute of Art

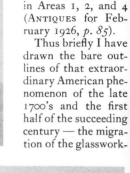

district contributed we do not at present know. Our dig at Kent and Mantua permitted the identification of two molds used in these communities. To date they have been exemplified in the various shades of country glass (ANTIQUES for February 1935, *p. 64*).

On the other hand, patterned pieces in swirled, ribbed, broken-rib, and diamond pattern occur in many

at Louisville, Kentucky, was established by men whose names are similar to those which may be found in the city directories in Areas 1, 2, and 4 (ANTIQUES for February 1926, *p. 85*).

Thus briefly I have drawn the bare outlines of that extraordinary American phenomenon of the late 1700's and the first half of the succeeding century — the migration of the glasswork-

Fig. 5 — TYPICAL VESSELS FROM AREA 4
a (above), Green swirled Ohio pitchers and salt. *From the Detroit Institute of Art*
d (below), Aquamarine broken-rib Ohio bowl. *From the Harry Hall White collection*
e (below), Diamond-pattern bowl, from Mantua, Ohio. *From the George E. Follansbee collection*
f (below), Stiegel-type creamer. *From the George S. McKearin collection*

Fig. 5b, Green Ohio bowl with scalloped foot. *From the Detroit Institute of Art*

Fig. 5c, Greenish-amber Ohio small bowl. *From the Harry Hall White collection*

shades of green and amber; the green group leans more toward the amber than toward the olive. The amber group, on the other hand, is unmistakably of the golden variety, often with a very deep amber quality. Both a good strong green glass and a true aquamarine were blown in Area 4. Particularly from the Pittsburgh district do we find blown pieces in vibrant amethyst and sapphire.

To account for the extremely wide range of color found in Area 4 we must remember that within this territory lies Pittsburgh, the great glassmaking district, as well as the lesser towns of New Geneva, Wheeling, Zanesville, Ravenna, Kent, and Mantua. Here ancient traditional knowledge rubbed elbows with pioneering experiment, and at times the twain became intimate.

In conclusion, it seems evident from information now at hand that migrations occurred from the two glass labor centres of Area 1 — South Jersey, Philadelphia, and New York City — not only westward but northward through the New England States and into New York State, that is to say, into Areas 2 and 3. From the two latter areas we may trace subsequent removals westward into Area 4, and even beyond into Michigan and Kentucky.

Due to the increasing industrial concentration at Pittsburgh, Area 4 drew heavily from the labor forces of the Eastern glasshouses. But the Pittsburgh district, in turn, contributed largely to the manning of glasshouses in other places. Lancaster, New York, was started by Pittsburgh men (ANTIQUES for October 1927, *p. 300*). The Kentucky Glass Works

ers. Why was it that the men who cherished the New Jersey traditions of form and decoration favored a route that carried them northward into New England and thence by wide detour into New York State? Why was it, again, that the harsh highway across the Alleghenies beckoned so compellingly to the refugees from the disasters that overwhelmed Amelung and Stiegel? We may but guess at an answer. But quite as remarkable as the migrations themselves, perhaps even more so, was the tenacity with which each group of workmen clung to the craft traditions in which they had been trained and which they seem to have transmitted virtually intact to their apprentice successors. So it was that, as they passed from place to place to pause for a little or to remain, they marked their way with shining memorials of glass in which the student of today may find not only a rare loveliness, but a reflection, caught and fixed beyond erasure, of history and of romance.

Editor's note. To the neophyte collector of glass the apparent multiplicity of forms discoverable in examples of early American ware seems too confusing to encourage attempts to associate an item with its source. Obviously, the first step toward the identification of specific items of glass must be that of relating them to clearly defined groups. We believe that Mr. White's article affords assistance in this direction. Quite as important, Mr. White explains why certain early glasshouses, though geographically separated, produced stylistically affiliated types of glass. — H. E. K

Fig. 1 — PROBABLY SOUTH JERSEY GLASS

Pitcher acquired in the neighborhood of the glassworks section of New Jersey; loving cup, in New Jersey; tall wine glass and ball, in Philadelphia; larger pitcher, in Virginia; goblet, in New Jersey. All are of a light, warm green color and, with the exception of the goblet, which appears to be unique, seem characteristic of the glass attributed to New Jersey.

Photograph by W. Coulbourn Brown from the collection of M. L. Blumenthal

Various South Jersey Operations

By RHEA MANSFIELD KNITTLE

THE largest beds of sand in New Jersey suitable for glassmaking were located about four miles below Millville. This Maurice River variety was shipped or hauled (frequently both) to more distant Jersey works, to Philadelphia, Boston, Hartford, New York, and Brooklyn, and even to early West Virginia glass industries. The pits were first opened nearly a hundred and fifty years ago. There were also large sand deposits of fairly good grade near Williamstown, New Jersey, which supplied each of twelve factories with one thousand tons per year.

Naturally, this prevalence of good silica beds accounted for the numerous little factories which, for a century or so from the Colonial period, attempted glass manufacture in the Jerseys. Many of these houses, however, blasted for only a short time. It may interest the collector and the industrialist to note that 2 ran for 2 years; 1 ran for 3 years; 2 ran for 5 years; 2 ran for 10 years; 4 ran for 20 years; 2 ran for 30 years; 1 ran for 35 years; 1 ran for 45 years. Other undertakings went to the wall within a few months after starting. The majority of glass manufacturing properties were continuously changing ownership or management.

Before 1855 the State of New Jersey depended upon her forests for fuel, and coal did not supersede wood for melting purposes until that year. Its introduction made possible the enlargements of the furnace pots to two or three times their former size and capacity.

The Honorable John T. Bodine, one of the greatest authorities on our early glass manufacturing methods, writing in 1883, stated:

The use of coal has made locations of glass factories at places other than upon water navigation in New Jersey very expensive. Even with railroads, the cost of freight in getting coal and materials to the manufactured products from the marketable points of Philadelphia and New York is about 9 to 10 per cent of the gross receipts of manufactured goods, while the only offset thereto is about 2 per cent, in the cost of sand, and wood for annealing the ware. Many of the New Jersey works have been located where wood could be used. If the locations were abandoned and the works removed to the large consuming points, the whole plant, so far as the building is concerned, would be lost.

Mr. Bodine wrote to a friend, in 1883:

I knew some blowers, when I was a small boy, that were then old men, and could make both bottles and window glass. I have been unable to fix a time when window glass commenced to be made in cylinder form. I personally know of cylinder window glass being made in 1827 or 1828 at Millville. I find that about 1812 a crown glass (window glass) factory was started up the Delaware (the Columbia).

As the New Jersey glassworks increased in number, the blowers, and frequently the managers, migrated from one factory to another. It was also not uncommon to find a financier or group of money lenders for such an enterprise simultaneously controlling five or six of these undertakings. The Whitneys, Woodward Warrick, Joseph Iszard, the Synnotts, Jacob Guggenheimer, and the Bodines loaned money or bought stock in this or that enterprise; and certain glasshouses were controlled by New York City groups.

Of Joseph Iszard, one of the Whitney-Warrick associates, John R. Downer writes:*

Joseph Iszard was himself a hard-working man, and he furnished employment to many others. Thus accumulating capital, he, in the latter fifteen years of his life, busied himself at setting money to work. An extensive borrower from various sources, private money-lenders, banks, the Glassboro loan and building association, and from those to whom he gave mortgages upon his properties, from time to time, he invested in new enterprises liberally, and in almost every instance wisely.

When the Gloucester County Bank, now the First National, Woodbury, was being organized, he subscribed to $2,500 capital stock, July 7, 1855, and when the bank opened for business, January 1, 1856, he was among the first borrowers, giving his note for $1,000, January 4, 1856, and was thereafter a heavy borrower from the new bank, securing credit upon notes of his own, and others, having them discounted, using the proceeds to promote his many financial affairs.

April 8, 1856, Joseph Iszard bought twenty shares of stock in the new local enterprise, the Glassboro Loan and Building Association,† and was, throughout the succeeding nine years, one of its largest customers, always ready to secure and employ the surplus cash of the building association paid in at its monthly meetings.

Mr. Downer continues:

While Joseph Iszard was not a glass manufacturer, he was an owner of glass factory properties, his memoranda showing that, on March 12, 1856, he sold the original Williamstown glass factory to Robert Wilson, for $3,500. This factory property had, for about fifteen years, been a problem, and a bone of contention among the various owners and lessees, particularly John Swope and his son-in-law Gabriel, Joseph Iszard, and John F. Bodine. It was by the strategy of the last named that the old factory, of which the Bodines owned three-eighths, and the Iszards five-eighths, finally became the property of Joel Bodine and his three sons, John F. Bodine, William H. Bodine, and J. Alfred Bodine. The old factory had been idle several years, falling into decay and depreciating in value, while the Bodines were running the new factory at Williamstown, which they had built opposite the old one, and another factory at Bridgeton which they operated, 1846–1855.

Fig. 2 — PROBABLY SOUTH JERSEY GLASS
Formerly in the Lawton Collection

Williamstown, called Squankum in its earlier days, first boasted a glass furnace in 1835. This Free Will Glass Manufactory was well named. Each stockholder wanted his own way, and the company was finally compelled to dissolve on account of constant friction before Iszard and his associates took it over. The new works erected by the Bodines was known as the Washington Glass Works,‡ while the output was handled by another member of the family, under the name of Thomas Bodine & Company, established at 807 Market Street, Philadelphia. The firm specialized in white and green druggists' glassware.

Says Mr. Downer, further:

The Iszards could not rent out the old factory, being five-eighths owners, and the Bodines could not operate it without the Iszards' consent; so at last, John

F. Bodine, now thirty-six years old and a glass manufacturer of fifteen years' experience, adopted a ruse to acquire all of the old factory. Secretly negotiating with Robert Wilson, the successful and well-to-do lumberman of Fries Mill, the latter made overtures to the Iszards ostensibly to purchase and start up the old factory, in opposition to the Bodines. John F. Bodine and Robert Wilson staged a public quarrel in the presence of the Iszards' local sympathizers, which lent color to the reality of the opposition and made it easier for the deal to be consummated. Wilson bought the works, paying $500 down, and four days later the entire purchase price, which, of course, was furnished by the wily John F. Bodine. Wilson, now owner of the Iszards' interest, speedily transferred to the Bodines, thus ending family squabbles over the old glassworks so far as ownership was concerned.

In the same year that the Iszards, Bodines, and Wilsons patched up their disagreements, Joseph Iszard bid in the struggling Milford glassworks at sheriff's sale for $4,900. Milford was known as Pendleton when Matthias Simmerman built the furnace, but is now known as Kresson. In other words, Pendleton, Milford, and Kresson glass are from one and the same place. (At times I wonder whether we shall ever get our native glass industry completely straightened out!)

From the spring of 1856 until the Civil War period, the glassworks was operated by Samuel Iszard & Company, the company being, in the main, Joseph Iszard and his son Ira. As was usual with these South Jersey attempts, their efforts met with failure, and Joseph had to protect his son Ira from creditors by entering a judgment against him.

Just as for the New York group which controlled the Atlantic glassworks, J. Huffsey & Company of Philadelphia acted as agent for the Iszard druggists' ware. It is believed that each of these houses made a Jenny Lind calabash bottle, which Huffsey wholesaled and retailed at Number 50 Fourth Street, Philadelphia. Huffsey was primarily an agent, not a manufacturer.

By the year 1882, the following early established factories in New Jersey had gone out of existence: Allowaystown, Columbia, Clementon, Tuckahoe, Hammonton, Jackson, Old Brooklyn, Estelville, Greenbank, New Columbia, Balsto, Crowleytown, Kaign's Point, Milltown, Bulltown, Lebanon, Westville, Jersey City, Elizabethport, Waterford, Medford, Camden, Milford, Riverside, Herman City, Winston, Malaga, Jansboro, Quinton.

It can readily be understood why attribution to a certain factory of an offhand piece of blown glass or even of the regular production made in New Jersey is a rather precarious procedure.

Note: I wish to thank Mrs. Louis G. Meade of Cleveland, Ohio, for giving me a copy of the article written by John R. Downer for *Our History Club* at Glassboro. Mrs. Meade was formerly Miss Emerald Iszard of New Jersey.

*A paper published by the Glassboro *Enterprise* in 1922.

†New Jersey was the first state to enact a law to incorporate building and loan associations. This was in 1847.

‡See the author's *Early American Glass*, pp. 358–360.

Fig. 1 — SOUTH JERSEY GLASS
The vase, late in form, is of a deep blue and is shown in color in the Frontispiece. The bowl, probably much earlier, is a clear, light shade of blue. The pitcher, made by one Joel Duffield at the Whitney Glass Works, while it is a nineteenth-century example, is a beautiful specimen of South Jersey glass.

Wistarberg and South Jersey Glass

By GEORGE S. McKEARIN

Illustrations from the author's collection

AS I look back about ten years, to the beginning of my interest in early American glass, the field was virtually divided into two principal sections — *Stiegel* and *Wistarberg*. Of course, there was Sandwich glass; also bottles and flasks — the former generally dismissed as pressed, late, and of slight interest and little value, and the latter as junk, which only a "loon-a-tick" would think of collecting.

There were a few pioneers in the field of American glass, like the late Alexander Drake and Edwin Atlee Barber, who collected flasks and bottles, appreciating, probably, the wide and beautiful range of colors and the interesting designs found not only in the earlier plain and pattern-molded flasks, but also in the whisky flasks and bar bottles appearing after 1812 and blown in two-piece molds, in which designs of historical, patriotic, political, and similar import were cut. Perhaps these pioneers in a field of collecting held in contempt by the discriminating (spelled with very large capitals and pronounced with great relish) collectors of early glass — so-called *Stiegel* and *Wistarberg* — sensed, dimly perhaps, that the lowly and despised flasks, many of which bear names of the glass factory in which they were made, might prove connecting links in proving fine pieces of Stiegel and Wistarberg to have been blown at a time and place far removed from the day and locality of Baron Stiegel and of Caspar Wistar and his son Richard.

As for Sandwich, likewise dismissed with a shrug of disdain by the discriminating collector (again large capitals) of early American glass, it came eventually into its own in so far as popularity was concerned; but even with the remarkable rage which developed three or four years back for the *lace* and *snakeskin* glass, colored lamps, candlesticks, cup plates, and the like, few collectors realized that some of the finest blown glass produced in this country was made at Sandwich, as well as at the plants of the New England Glass Company, and at certain Pittsburgh factories, which likewise made much of the pressed glass generally classified as *Sandwich*.

The exquisite contact three-section mold glass of the finest types and patterns, described in the brief article by Helen A. McKearin in the August, 1924, number* was, of course, generally collected by the early American glass collector of ten to twelve years ago; but it was quite generally, though erroneously, written and spoken of as Stiegel. It is interesting to note, in passing, that data which has come to hand during the past year or so identifies Sandwich as undoubtedly one source of some of the finest of this glass.

EARLINESS A MATTER OF TYPE, NOT OF DATE

So much in the way of very sketchy and general comments regarding the field of early American glass; and let me make clear at the outset — *when I speak of early*

*See ANTIQUES, Vol. VI, p. 78.

American glass I refer to type, pattern, decorative technique, and quality of glass, rather than to date. The collector of Americana does not think of the period from 1825 to 1860 as *early*, and chronologically it is not; but, in the field of American glass, many of the finest specimens, bearing every apparent indication of eighteenth century production, were blown in relatively obscure factories scattered throughout the New England states, New York, Pennsylvania, New Jersey, Ohio, Maryland, and that part of what was then Virginia but is now West Virginia, during the early and mid-nineteenth century period.

In the choicest collections, those privately owned and those in our museums, many of the best specimens of early American glass, referred to as *Stiegel* or *Wistarberg*, were actually produced during that much later period. Nor does this fact detract one jot or tittle from their interest or their beauty in form, color, and design; neither does it lessen their rarity.

WISTARBERG AN OVERWORKED TERM

With the possible exception of *Stiegel*, not any word in the realm of American glass has been as loosely used and greatly abused as *Wistarberg*. At first every fine piece of green, blue or amber glass too heavy to qualify under the supposed Stiegel distinctive quality of lightness in weight, and all those pieces with certain decorative characteristics, such as the crimped foot, threaded neck, and superimposed layer of glass tooled into a frieze-like effect sometimes called lily-pad, were Wistarberg. Collectors and museums bought and cherished them as such. South Jersey many of these specimens undoubtedly were, but I doubt that there

are half a dozen pieces of glass in existence which can be *authenticated* as the product of the factory of Caspar Wistar and his son Richard.

For years Boston pickers, traveling every week from Charles Street, gathered such pieces from private homes or from shops of small dealers throughout the highways and byways of Massachusetts, Connecticut, New Hampshire, New York, Pennsylvania, or wherever their quest for the antique led them. They were, quite naturally, not particularly interested in early American glass from the standpoint of study and investigation; and consequently expended little or no effort to secure information as to the history and probable origin of their finds. Collectors wanted Stiegel and Wistarberg, and, therefore, Stiegel and Wistarberg these pieces were.

We know quite definitely that the commercial products of the Wistar factory were window glass, bottles, snuff cannisters, and so on; and this is true also of the factory of Stanger Brothers, which started at Glassboro, New Jersey, about 1775, and of various other factories which came into being throughout South Jersey between 1775 and 1850.

The lovely bowls, pitchers, mugs, vases, candlesticks, and the like, which were blown in these factories, treasured and handed down to posterity, later to delight and enchant the collector of early American glass, were the products of individual workmen, blown offhand for themselves, their families or friends, in accord with the prevailing custom of permitting workmen to use for their own purposes the fag-end of the pot of molten glass. This same custom prevailed in practically every bottle or window-glass factory which operated between 1775 and 1850 throughout the

Fig. 2 — TYPICAL WHITNEY GLASS WORKS PIECES

All heavy, amber glass, similar n color and quality to the flasks which the Whitney people made for many a brand of whiskey in the days when good liquor was the rule — and cheiap.

New England states, New York, Pennsylvania, Maryland, Ohio, and Virginia, as well as in New Jersey.

The Emergence of "South Jersey"

About six years ago, at the time of the sale of Dr. Pleasant Hunter's last collection, in November, 1920, at the American Art Galleries, many thoughtful students of early American glass began to realize that not all of the glass called *Wistarberg* could possibly have been made in and survived from the original factory of Caspar Wistar and his son Richard. From that time on, therefore, glass of this type began to be spoken and written of under the more general term of *South Jersey*; but, naturally, many of the finest examples still were, and are today, referred to as *Wistarberg*. In an introductory note in the auction catalogue of Dr. Hunter's sale, J. B. Kerfoot writes most interestingly of South Jersey glass, and from him I quote as follows:

The first South Jersey glass factory was established near the village of Alloway, in Salem County, in 1739, by Caspar Wistar of Philadelphia; the small settlement that grew up around the works being known as *Wistarberg*. In 1775 another factory was started at what is now Glassboro by two of Wistar's workmen. Between then and the early 1840's a great number of factories—small and short-lived for the most part—were started throughout this section and along the Mulliga River; most of them established by Wistar workmen or their descendants, and all of them manned by workmen trained in the Wistar tradition and technique. Under this tradition the right to use the fag-end of each pot of molten glass for their individual purposes was a recognized perquisite of the workmen. And, as a matter of fact, practically all the pieces now collected as *Wistarberg* or *South Jersey* glass are of this latter origin, the commercial output of all these factories having consisted of window glass, bottles, snuff canisters and other similar hollow ware. Again and again, as a matter of proved and indisputable fact, three generations of these workmen continued for more than one hundred years to make for themselves and their friends the same range of pieces, unaltered in form and indistinguishable in technique. So that, so far as concerns these wholly true-to-tradition specimens, the attempted differentiation between *true Wistarberg* pieces and *South Jersey* pieces is utterly futile and meaningless. But, call them what we will and date them as we choose, their rarity remains the same. About 1850 a complete change of fashion seems to have taken place under the influence of which the earlier forms more or less wholly disappeared. Previous to this, but for how long back of 1840 it is not yet possible to say, slight modification of technical treatment and a decided fondness for color stunts had been creeping in, although the earlier *forms* were retained unaltered.

Old Forms Appear in Late Specimens

However, bear this in mind: while it is self-evident, when you find, say, a glass pitcher showing certain characteristics in shape or decoration which were not encountered in our china or silver before 1830, that the pitcher can hardly be earlier than that date, it is not at all unusual with glass, not the commercial product but that blown by individual workmen, to find very early forms or decorative features faithfully copied many, many years later. I know this to be true. I have specimens in which very early South Jersey characteristics are followed, but which I know to have been blown by individual workmen in New York and New England factories *after 1830*—pieces which would readily be accepted as early South Jersey, and, in some cases, even as Wistarberg.

What I am trying to set forth is that in the identification or attribution of early American glass there is not any royal road to learning. It is only the occasional and exceptional piece which may within itself tell its own story.

Generally speaking, it is not possible from the color, quality, form, or decorative technique of a piece of glass to determine the particular factory of its origin. Fortunately, however, for the student and real collector of American glass, one thing with respect to these individually blown pieces is generally true — they were owned and remained in the vicinity where the factory which produced them was located. Most of these factories operating between 1825 and 1860 were located in what were then, and still are, small villages or rural communities; and from the direct descendants of the men who worked in such factories or of the friends of the workmen, to whom individually blown pieces were given, it has been possible to obtain many interesting examples authenticated beyond a doubt as to the factory where they were produced.

The Reliability of Family History

Family history going back only one or two generations with respect to such pieces of glass found in the immediate vicinity of the factory is generally accurate with respect to the attribution. Thus, we have been able to classify with certainty interesting examples from the factories which were located at Keene, Stoddard, and Lyndeboro, in New Hampshire; Westford, East Willington, Coventry, and New London, in Connecticut; Redford, Redwood, Sand Lake, Saratoga, Cleveland, Bristol, and elsewhere, in New York; Whitney Glass Works, Isabella Glass Works, Waterford, Coffin & Hay, and others, in New Jersey.

However, when it comes to eighteenth-century factories, like that of Caspar Wistar and his son Richard, family history becomes, in most instances, a dangerous and uncharted sea upon which to embark for the port of attribution. The colors, shapes, and decorative features which we believe characterize pieces blown by individual workmen in the factory of the Wistars undoubtedly were reproduced by the same and other workmen in many later factories, and I do not know of any way of distinguishing a Wistarberg piece from a similar piece made years later in another factory. Hence, my expressed doubt as to there being in existence half a dozen pieces which can unquestionably be attributed to the Wistar factory.

Cases in Point

Let me illustrate: I have in my collection what has been for several years considered one of the finest and earliest of South Jersey blue glass bowls, with circular crimped foot. It was in the early collection formed by Messrs. Kerfoot and Hunter when they first became interested in Wistarberg glass. It passed into the hands of a well-known student and collector, was exhibited with other rare examples of South Jersey glass in the Metropolitan Museum, and was considered a Wistarberg piece. It had characteristics which have been held to distinguish the earliest South Jersey glass; yet, not very long ago, I secured its exact counterpart in everything except color, in another bowl — of beautiful clear amber — which has a well-authenticated history of having been blown by William Coffin himself, in the factory of Coffin & Hay, at Hammonton, New Jersey. *And that factory did not start until 1820.* This does not prove that the blue bowl was made in the factory of Coffin & Hay — it may be a Wistar piece — but it does

Fig. 3 — From Various South Jersey Factories

The pitcher and mug at the left are very similar, but made at different factories — the pitcher at the Whitney Works, the mug at the Isabella Glass Works, as was also the rare lamp at the extreme right.

The two light green pitchers were blown at Waterford, and are quite similar in color to the well-known *Union and Clasped Hands* flask, marked *Waterford*. It is interesting to learn that the Isabella Glass Works, which were located at New Brooklyn, New Jersey, were named after Isabella Stanger, daughter of the proprietor.

go to show that one cannot, from the evidence of the glass itself, say that certain pieces are, or are not, Wistarberg.

In one of the auction sales, a few years ago, appeared a dark amber pitcher with superimposed decoration of the so-called lily-pad type. It is, I think, the largest and one of the finest pitchers of that type and color in existence. Everyone seemed to consider it Wistarberg beyond a doubt. Just how they could be so certain, I could not figure out. I have seen pitchers similar in color and decoration which were made in New Hampshire factories. This particular pitcher showed signs of great wear, but I have seen just as great wear on a piece which I know to have been made after 1800. There was nothing in the way of history or record to connect the piece with the Wistarberg factory; in fact, it was picked up in New York state, far from the Jersey line, and there was no record of its having come from South Jersey. I am not speaking thus of the blue bowl or of the amber pitcher in any way to disparage them. To what particular factory you attribute them does not add to or take from either piece an atom of the beauty and rarity it possesses by and of itself. I merely wish to illustrate with respect to Wistarberg glass how impossible it is, in almost every instance, to prove the attribution.

General Terms Safest

With the more general term of *South Jersey*, we are treading on firmer ground: firmer, first, because the term is general, indicating a type of glass instead of examples of the product of one factory which ceased to exist at such an early date that attribution, based on any family history, becomes, in ninety-nine cases out of one hundred, an attempt to weave the fabric of identification to the pattern of one's own desire; and, secondly, because the general

term applies to the product of a large number of factories scattered throughout a certain section or district, operating, probably, with a continual interchanging of workmen and handing-down of methods and technique from father to son and grandson, so that, for generations, the same general shapes, colors, and decorative features were produced almost unaltered, though they were eventually modified more or less in keeping with the commercial glass, china, and metal ware of the day.

In the third place, we are on firmer ground because these factories came into being many years after Caspar Wistar's day. In like manner, they were engaged in the manufacture of window glass, or, as with most of them, of bottles, whiskey flasks, snuff jars, medicine phials, and such. Bowls, pitchers, mugs, and similar articles were not a commercial product, but were individually blown pieces, frequently, in fact generally, cherished and handed down in the families of the workmen who made them, or of the friends and relatives for whom they were made. Consequently they remained, as a rule, in the vicinity of the particular factory where they were produced, traveling only as the occasional family was uprooted from its native soil. Attribution based on family history going back only two or three generations does not become lost in the limbo of uncertainty which obscures practically every attempt at attribution to a specific factory as early as that of the Wistars.

Most South Jersey Glass After 1800

I think we must concede that by far the greater proportion of South Jersey glass, including much of the finest in quality and what we consider early in form and feeling, was blown *after 1800*. Prior to that date we have, I believe, only two factories to draw from — the original enterprise

Fig. 4—NEW YORK AND NEW JERSEY GLASS
The globular bowl with knopped stem and circular foot is New York State glass of South Jersey type and color. The straight-sided bowl is a very unusual shade of deep grass green, very yellow in tone. It is shown also in the Frontispiece.
The bi-colored pitcher is a late type. It was blown, probably in 1873, by a workman for his sweetheart—a cook in the employ of a Mr. Swinburn in Philadelphia. After a quarrel with her lover, this woman gave the pitcher to her employer, from whom it was acquired two or three years ago.

of Wistar, continued by his son Richard; and the factory at Glassboro, founded by the Stangers, which, after the failure and imprisonment for debt of the original founders, was, in 1781, acquired by Colonel Thomas Heston, and during the following years passed through various ownerships, until, in 1835, Thomas H. Whitney purchased an interest in the factory, which was then known as the Harmony Glass Works. *American Bottles Old & New*, by William S. Walbridge, and Barber's *American Glassware* give the Whitney date as 1837.

From about 1815 on there were many factories in the South Jersey districts, the advent of the hinged molds for producing fancy bar bottles and whiskey flasks having apparently given a great impetus to the business. It is among pieces produced by workmen in these factories (including, of course, the Stanger-founded glass works) and during this period, we must place the great bulk of our South Jersey glass. As a rule, specimens found in the section where these factories operated and showing typical characteristics in form, color, and decoration, may safely be accepted as South Jersey, even though we know that pieces similar in color and general characteristics to South Jersey glass were made in New York and New England factories of contemporary period. In case of many of these specimens — particularly those made in the bottle factories after 1820—family history may be accepted with a fair degree of safety, particularly when the source as well as the characteristics of the glass itself bears out the attribution. Unfortunately for identification as to specific factories, much fine South Jersey glass was picked up in the early days of American glass collecting when practically everything found in that section was called *Wistarberg*. Apparently the possibility that such early-looking pieces were blown by workmen in the various comparatively late

bottle factories was not sensed at the time. Hence the opportunity to secure specific attributions was, in most instances, irretrievably lost.

Many of the best of these South Jersey examples were dispersed during the Frederick William Hunter Sale in January, 1920. Some marvelous specimens were in the collection formed by Miss M. I. Meacham a few years ago. Some of them may well have been examples from the Wistar factory, or that of the Stangers. But these two collections have been scattered, and with very few specimens, in so far as I know, was any definite history supporting any attribution, handed on. Some of the finest examples were acquired by the Metropolitan Museum of Art in New York City and may be seen there.

Fortunately, from time to time, South Jersey pieces have been picked up there by an occasional collector or dealer interested in identifying the factory which gave birth to them; and such specimens are of great value to us in our study of American glass. I have been particularly fortunate in acquiring a few interesting examples with what I believe to be, in most instances, reliable attributions. In closing this article, I am going to illustrate a few such specimens which can be accepted as actually being South Jersey glass.

ILLUSTRATIONS

The color plate (*Frontispiece*) shows characteristic examples of South Jersey glass. The pitcher in the top row is a lovely shade of blue, light in tone — what I call a steely blue. It shows the modification in form and decorative technique which appeared toward the middle of the nineteenth century. The amber bowl next to the pitcher and the three pieces in the middle row are also shown in other illustrations accompanying this article. The vase at the right end of the top row is actually a dark olive amber, quite similar in shade to many of the pieces made at Keene and at

Fig. 5 — REDWOOD, NEW YORK, GLASS
Bowl and pitcher show typical South Jersey characteristics of decoration. They were blown at the Redwood Glass Works, Redwood, New York, not far from Watertown.

Stoddard, New Hampshire; Coventry and East Willington, Connecticut; and certain of the New York State factories. The blue bowl on circular, crimped foot in the bottom row is the one referred to in the text as having been in the early collection found by Messrs. Hunter and Kerfoot and considered a Wistarberg piece. Its amber counterpart beside it is the bowl said to have been made by William Coffin himself, in the factory of Coffin & Hay, founded at Hammonton, New Jersey, in 1820.

In Figure 1 are shown three pieces. In color they are typical South Jersey blues. The pitcher, with its threaded neck and crimped foot, is a particularly fine example and was made by Joel Duffield at the first Whitney factory — so says family history. By *first* is probably meant the factory of the period beginning in 1835 when Thomas H. Whitney purchased an interest in the glass works, as distinguished from the period beginning about 1842, when he acquired entire control and, with his brother Samuel A., formed the firm of Whitney Brothers and changed the name to Whitney Glass Works. The small vase is also a Whitney product. The bowl is a lighter shade of blue than either of the other pieces, and I do not know in what factory in South Jersey it was made; but it might easily be of a much earlier period.

The pieces in Figure 2 are also specimens from the Whitney Glass Works. They are a clear deep amber in color, and the vases, nine inches tall, while very rare and unusual, are — quite patently — relatively late.

Figure 3 shows some very interesting examples of South Jersey, all with specific factory attributions. The small doubled-colored pitcher at the left is of heavy glass, light green and opaque white, and was made at the Whitney Glass Works about 1850 by one Jacob Montcuef. The mug, similar in color and character of glass, was made at the Isabella Glass Works, New Brooklyn, New Jersey. The pitcher next it is typical South Jersey light green glass. It was made at Waterford, one of the bottle factories. This specimen is quite unusual in shape, the short squatty body resting on a crimped foot and merging into a very broad, cylindrical neck with flaring rim. The applied decoration is also unusual, a sort of wave-like effect covering just the very lowest part of the body, while three long filaments are carried

upward over the body and on to the neck in a form one can almost fancy as the heads and necks of long sea serpents arising from an uncharted and mystical sea of glass to leer at the poor investigator who has embarked upon an uncertain and danger-beset voyage of attribution. The taller pitcher, next that of my sea-serpent fantasy, is a lovely light green with turquoise tint. It is an attractive shape with heavy crimped foot. The simple decoration encircling the neck is similar to that of the pair of amber vases in Figure 2 and is, I think, late. This pitcher was made at Waterford. The lamp is a rare piece, turquoise green in color. It was made at the Isabella Glass Works, about 1840, by Julius Stanger, and was purchased from an heir and descendant, a Miss Stanger of New Brooklyn, New Jersey.

In Figure 4 is an interesting pitcher, showing a two-colored effect in light green and opaque white. It shows a late form and this is borne out by the coin dated 1873 imprisoned within the hollow of the stem. The bowl of straight-sided cylindrical form at the left is a very unusual rich yellow green color. I know nothing of its history other than it was found in South Jersey, but I have seen a similar bowl, of similar glass and color, which is attributed to the Isabella Glass Works. The sugar bowl at the extreme left is a beautiful shade of light green, with turquoise tint, typical South Jersey glass, *but I happen to know that it is a New York State product*, made probably at Redwood, Jefferson County, as it was found in the vicinity of that place. Originally it no doubt had a cover and I know that it had small applied looped handles on the sides, which were broken off.

In Figure 5 are a bowl and pitcher which, a few years ago, would have been accepted as unquestionably Wistarberg; but they are New York State glass, made at Redwood, fully one hundred years after Caspar Wistar founded his glass works. They are lovely light turquoise green in color. The bowl, resting on a circular foot, is very graceful in form and measures nearly twelve inches across the top. The pitcher, made to go with the bowl and matching it perfectly in color and decoration, holds fully two and one-half quarts.

In Figure 6 are two of the finest pitchers of this type I have ever seen. The color is even finer than that of the bowl and pitcher. The larger holds better than two quarts; the smaller

Fig. 6 — REDFORD, NEW YORK, GLASS

Typical examples of glass made at Redford, New York, near Plattsburg. The color is a lovely light green, turquoise in tone.

about a pint. They, as well as the plain bowl on circular foot at the left, were made at the Redford Glass Works, located in the little hamlet of Redford, not far from Plattsburg, New York. Let me say right here that as far as my own observation and study go, there is, generally speaking, nothing in the character and color of the glass itself to distinguish Redford pieces from Redwood or from those of several other New York State factories which came into existence during the early or mid-nineteenth century. I have

been extremely fortunate, however, in securing for my own collection many pieces found in the immediate vicinity of these various factories and purchased from families whose fathers or grandfathers worked in them. Such specimens, absolutely authenticated, have been of inestimable value to me in my study of American glass. In a later article I may tell readers of ANTIQUES more about glass of South Jersey type and characteristics made in New York State.

NOTE.— In conjunction with Mr. McKearin's contribution on South Jersey glass should be read the following article on the Wistars. Evidently, if we are to permit ourselves to speak of Wistarberg glass, we must do so in the full realization of the fact that we frequently mean glass made according to the Wistar tradition in many different places and during a period of more than a hundred years. As Mr. McKearin points out, it is probably better to classify such of this glass as has a reasonably well-known New Jersey origin as South Jersey, and at the same time to bear in mind that examples in aquamarine glass so similar in form and texture to South Jersey products as to be readily mistaken for them were made in other states of the Union.

Mrs. Sicard has derived her "Sidelights" from original sources in state and historical society archives, which she has carefully listed, though their individual indication seems scarcely necessary here.

For the benefit of the reader who has not at hand the material for immediately acquainting himself with the chief epochs in the history of glassmaking in earliest America, it may be observed that, almost from the beginning of Colonial settlements in this country, the need of glass both for glazing windows and for supplying household and table requirements was keenly felt. Strange, therefore, as it may seem that, in a rude and sparsely settled country, attempts should be made to manufacture a

product which, like glass, calls for the exercise of high technical skill and trained artistic sensibilities, it would appear that glasshouses of a kind were among the first industrial establishments erected.

The Jamestown Colony twice made ventures in glassmaking, first with Polish and German workmen imported for the purpose in 1608, and, again, in 1620. Both undertakings were short lived.

Salem, Massachusetts, boasted a glass-house that led a halting existence from 1638 to 1642, or thereabouts. The mid-seventeenth century witnessed some trials at glassmaking in New York City. But, while the need for glass was pressing, all these early attempts to supply it proved failures. Apparently they lacked both adequate capital and competent management.

Indeed, lack of these two requisites spelled the ruin, not only of the seventeenth century glass-houses, but of the vast majority of the small enterprises that sprang up in New England and the Middle States during the eighteenth century and the first years of the nineteenth. Caspar Wistar commanded adequate capital, and he was a born master of men. He started in life poor enough, as an immigrant lad of twenty-one years. But he shortly acquired both money and repute as a manufacturer of brass buttons. By 1739 he was ready to turn his attention to the industry of glassmaking, in which difficult field he was the first to achieve any real measure of success.— THE EDITOR.

Sidelights on the Wistars and Their Glass-House

By Hortense Fea Sicard

IN Philadelphia, May 9, 1724, a bill was passed as follows:

Entitled an Act for the enabling of John Cratho, Merch't, Caspar Wistar and Nicholas Gateau, to Trade and Buy and Hold Lands in this Province.

The Caspar Wistar referred to therein had come to this country when twenty-one years of age, and in the year 1717. He was a German Palatine, but, soon after settling in Philadelphia, he joined the Society of Friends and married a Quakeress. Wistar first engaged in the business of making buttons, and so assured was he of their quality that he gave with them a several-year guarantee. Whatever he attempted was carried out with marked success and his foresight led him to enter the glass industry.

July 31, 1740, letters to Thomas Hill, Secretary to the Lords Commissioners for Trade and Plantations, from one Charles Carkese, noted the erection of a glass works eight miles from the port of Salem in West Jersey by one "Caspar Wester, a Palatine, the glass house being brought to perfection so as to make glass."

By 1748 both Caspar and his son Richard were actively interested and at work. In the year 1752 the father died and Richard inherited the business.

The new owner lived in Philadelphia. Associated with him, and living about the year 1767 at the glass-house on Alloway's Creek, were Martin Halter and Hugh Blackwood. Later, though perhaps even during the above-mentioned period, Benjamin Thompson managed the manufactory. For two or more years after the elder Wistar's death, the business continued to grow, but the furnaces still turned out the same sort of crude glass.

It will be interesting for those of today who seek specimens of Wistar glass, to know how the product was regarded in Colonial times. Those persons who are not of the collecting fraternity, and who look askance when one muses on the charms of Wistarberg, who see nothing to enthuse over in the robust little bottles all so alike in shape, and who discover no beauty in the whorled or the double-dipped glass — such persons would no doubt agree with the ideas expressed by Governor Franklin.

June 14, 1768, writing from Burlington, New Jersey, to the Right Honorable Earl of Hillsborough in regard to the industries in the Colony, Franklin referred to the factory as one where were made "Bottles and very coarse Green Glass for Windows used only in some of the Houses of the poorer Sort of people".

The profits from this factory had been insufficient to induce others to follow in the glassmaking industry, although there had been at that time talk of others starting, since Parliament had laid a duty on glass. Notwithstanding this duty, however, Franklin considered that America would continue to secure glass from abroad, because fine glass could be made there cheaper than here.

It may have been this duty which encouraged Richard Wistar. It may be that from then on he imported a higher grade of foreign artisans to work exclusively for him in producing a greater variety of wares; or, again, it may have been that, in spite of the quality of American-made glass, Americans would not pay the price for the imported article as the Governor had so confidently expected. In any case, the factory thrived.

As for the work, a good share of it was turned out by men — many of them ex-soldiers — who spoke Dutch, French, and Portugese, but very, very little English; men often homesick for their native land, hugely dissatisfied, anxious to start at something for themselves, considered slaves, bound by a period of time to these Wistars. They were constantly deserting.

Richard Wistar was observing. The entire age for that matter was an observing age, and Richard Wistar could give the most minute details regarding men employed by him at the glass-house. He kept in touch with the intimate details of their lives as well as the interests of their families. No doubt, too, realizing that there would be desertions, with consequent loss of labor and money to him, he made especial effort at remembering the idiosyncrasies of his men. The following advertisements are of interest in this connection:

Twelve Dollars Reward. Run away on the Second of this Instant from the Glass House in Salem County West New Jersey, a Dutchman named Philip Jacobs, about Five Feet Six or Seven Inches High, light Grey Eyes, sandy Hair, thick Lips, speaks but little English; had on when he went away a blue Cloth Coat with Metal Buttons, red Plush Jacket striped Ticken Trowsers, good Shoes with large Brass Buckles and a Castor Hat about half worn; took Sundry other Things with him, also a Fiddle upon which he is much addicted to play; both his Legs are sore.
November 6 — 1767.   RICHARD WISTAR, Wistarburgh

Ten Dollars Reward. Run away from the Subscriber's Glass House in Salem County, West Jersey, a Dutch Servant Man, named ADRIAN BRUST, about 27 years of Age, 5 feet 7 or 8 inches High of a pale Complexion has short light Hair, two Moles on his left Cheek and on his right temple a Scar, also on one of his Feet near his Ancle which is but lately healed, and the Shoe mended where the Cut was. Had on when he went away an old Felt Hat, a lightish coloured Upper Jacket with Brass Buttons, this Country make, about half worn with a Patch on one of the hind Flaps where there was a Hole burnt; an under one with flat Metal Buttons, both of Linsey. Leather Breeches, Grey Yarn Stockings, good shoes with Brass Buckles, A good Shirt, and generally wears the Bosom Part behind.

A third advertisement refers to another "Dutchman" and describes certain blue-flowered buttons of metal, brass buttons, a Dutch pillowcase and a silk handkerchief, as well as a piece of linen for shirts, carried away by the deserter, who might further be identified by a scar located on the sole of his foot.

Two things in these advertisements are of particular interest: first, the gay buttons which Wistar was wont to describe as adorning the garments of his runaways; secondly, the men deserting were scarred. It may be that these men (ex-soldiers) bore the marks of battle; it may also be that they acquired their wounds through carelessness in their glass-house work.

While there is no record to prove it, Richard Wistar or

his manager may well have been the person responsible for the suppression of the fairs customarily held at Salem within a few miles of the glass-house. These events were considered most "inconvenient and unnecessary". Horse racing was held, and one may easily imagine how vigorously the men discussed John Budd's famous horse there at Salem. Swan was "a black horse, fifteen hands one inch high, one white foot, a snip on his nose and a small star on his forehead. Learnt to pace and goes fast as any horse in the continent—trots and gallops very light and runs fast. He is as handsome as any horse in America".

Fairs were unnecessary and inconvenient, but quite to be approved were the building of roads, erection of bridges, causeways, and so on. Benjamin Thompson was appointed to collect subscriptions in their behalf at the glass-house.

By 1771 visitors from remote sections were coming to the famed place at Allowaystown. William Shute and Jacob Paullin started a stage route between Piles Grove (adjacent to the glass-house) and Philadelphia. "Prices for passengers or lumber per 100 weight carried the whole distance into Piles Grove for three shilling nine pence and those gentlemen or ladies favoring them with their custom could depend on good usage and utmost care." These two above "humble servants" promised to carry them to the glass-house.

Then suddenly the business established after years of labor faced its most critical period, the Revolutionary War.

Wistars — Caspars, Richards, Daniels, Bartholemews, Williams, and Johns, all related to the Palatine Caspar — are mentioned frequently in the records of the Revolution. At first, on account of business or their Quaker religion, many were excused, only to take their places later in the different battalions of the Philadelphia militia. A letter from Colonel Samuel L. Miles, of New York, in November, 1776, to William Wister, Merchant in Philadelphia, mentions a Captain Wister as being there in New York.

Where hitherto he had steadily acquired land, by 1778–79 Richard Wistar was placing for rent and for sale various sections throughout West Jersey—lands rich in orchards of cherries, pears, apples, and plums; fertile meadows and vast beds of asparagus.* He was not even now a poor man, but he was past middle life and too worn by war to cope with the necessary readjustments. Before him was a dreary outlook for the glass industry. In 1780 Richard Wistar put the glass manufactory up for disposal.

The GLASS MANUFACTORY in Salem County West Jersey is for sale with 1500 Acres of Land adjoining. It contains two Furnaces with all the necessary Ovens for cooling the Glass, drying Wood etc. Contiguous to the Manufactory are two flatting Ovens in Separate Houses, a Storehouse, a Pot-house, a House fitted with Tables for the cutting of Glass, a Stamping Mill, a rolling Mill for the preparing of Clay for the making of Pots; and at a suitable distance are ten Dwelling houses for the Workmen; as likewise a large Mansion House containing Six rooms on a Floor, with Bake-house and Washhouse; Also a convenient Store-house where a well assorted retail Shop has been kept above 30 years, is as good a stand for the sale of goods as any in the County, being situated one mile

and a half from a navigable creek where shallops load for Philadelphia, eight miles from the county seat of Salem and half a mile from a good mill. There are about 250 Acres of cleared Land within fence 100 whereof is mowable meadow, which produces hay and pasturage sufficient for the large stock of Cattle and Horses employed by the Manufactory.

There is Stabling sufficient for 60 head of Cattle with a large Barn, Granery and Waggon House. The unimproved Land is well wooded and 200 Acres more of Meadow may be made. The situation and convenience for the procuring of Materials is equal if not superior to any place in Jersey.

For terms of Sale apply to the Subscriber in Philadelphia.— RICHARD WISTAR.*

Before he could sell the factory representing his lifework, Richard Wistar had passed away.

In the Chesterfield Friends' *Marriage Records*, on the seventeenth day of the tenth month, 1781, appears the marriage of John Wistar of Upper Alloways Creek, Salem County, son of Richard and Sarah deceased, to Charlotte Newbold of Mansfield, daughter of Clayton and Mary Wistar. Family witnesses of the ceremony included Mary B., Richard, Caspar, Jr., Thomas, Elizabeth, and Sarah. John continued with the factory for a time — then all record of it gradually ceases.

On January 15, 1799, one John Wister, Jr., merchant, married the "amiable" Jane Richards, both residents of Philadelphia, and one Robert Wharton, Esq., performed the ceremony.

There is one point not quite clear to Wistar admirers, and that is the relationship between Richard and the famous Dr. Caspar Wistar. The impression has been quite general, and was considered correct by the Editor of the New Jersey Archives, that Dr. Caspar was also a son of the founder of the glass industry who died in 1752; but this cannot be if we are to believe the following notice copied from *Niles' Weekly Register* of Baltimore for January 31, 1818:

Died at Philadelphia on the 21st. inst., Dr. Caspar Wistar age 56, a first rate physician and professor of Anatomy in the University of Pennsylvania. He has long been famous in the Medical world and was exceedingly well versed in the Sciences generally. His decease is a public calamity!†

Dr. Caspar was an author, and was at one time president of the Philadelphia Philosophical Society. A letter in regard to the appointment of an inspector of pearl ashes, dated March 31, 1790, is jointly signed by Drs. Hutcheson and Wistar, and the latter appears as "Caspar Wistar, junr."‡

A hundred years and more have passed. Where once stood the first successful flint glass manufactory of this country only a commanding buttonwood tree remains as sentinel. The objects from the Wistar glass-house are still being diligently sought for to be admired, cherished, and preserved. Their testimony is mute but none the less effective in regard to that tireless, sagacious, and most successful gentleman, Richard Wistar of Wistarberg.

---

*Hunter in his *Stiegel Glass* (Boston and New York, 1914, p. 158) observes that at the time of his writing some hundreds of acres of the old Wistarberg lands were still held by the family.— THE EDITOR.

Pennsylvania Journal, October 11, 1780.

†He may easily have been the grandson of the original Caspar. That there was a son Caspar, brother to Richard, appears in the will of the founder of the family.

‡*Philadelphia Magazine and Review of Information And Amusement*, January, 1799.

Safe Clues in the Amelung Quest

By HOMER EATON KEYES

THE *Bulletin* of the Metropolitan Museum of Art for June 1928 pictures and describes an important specimen of glass at the time recently acquired by the Museum. This specimen is a covered presentation goblet, or, as the Germans call it, *Pokal*, eleven and one quarter inches in height. Its form is similar to that of contemporary European goblets on a baluster stem, though in the particular instance rather excessive heaviness of stem and base in relation to the mass of the bowl tends to minimize the aspect of proud upstandingness which customarily characterizes German vessels of the *pokal* type.

Index to the authorship of this impressive object is discoverable in two inscriptions. On the obverse of the bowl are engraved the words, *New Bremen Glassmanufactory — 1788 — / North America, State of Maryland.* Engraved on the reverse appear the arms of the German city of Bremen and the legend, *Old Bremen Success and the New Progress.* The cover, which is surmounted by a knop, is ornamented with an engraved foliated scroll. In color the glass is described as being "clear white, with greenish tones appearing in the thicker portions of stem and base."

The piece was found in Bremen, Germany, where it was said to have reposed for upward of a century in the hands of a local family. Its inscriptions have been held to justify its acceptance as a memento of the ill-fated Maryland enterprise started, in 1784, by John Frederick Amelung of Bremen, Germany, and virtually abandoned in 1795. The story of the founder's high initial hopes and of his ultimate failure, as told at some length in Rhea Mansfield Knittle's book, *Early American Glass*, is again rehearsed by her in notes entitled *Rex Absolutus of the Monongahela*, which appeared in ANTIQUES for April 1928 and is further quoted in the Metropolitan Museum *Bulletin* above referred to. It receives amplification from Charles Messer Stow in *The Antiquarian* for December 1930. Its repetition here is unnecessary. Our present concern is with particular pieces of glass, not with the

external facts of the industrial history that lies behind them

The natural surmise regarding the Metropolitan goblet that it was a show piece made by Amelung in New Breme (near Frederick) and sent to his backers in old Bremen as token of the success of the new-world experiment. With th surmise the Attic must confess to having been, at the tim somewhat dissatisfied. In weight and contour the goblet question showed no evident correspondence to any oth surviving specimens of authenticated American glass. Furthe more, its engraved embellishments were so far superior to tho achieved by Stiegel, or, as it seeme by any other early American man facturer, as to raise questions. Was not possible — probable, even — th the Bremen item had been made Germany to celebrate the Maryla undertaking, rather than in Frederi to prove the triumph of the venture Or, granting the goblet's America origin, could convincing reasons be a vanced for believing that the singularl competent engraving was America rather than German handiwork?

Happily, all such doubts have bee set at rest by the advent Baltimore of a second im posing ceremonial gla vessel obviously related the Metropolitan examp and undeniably an Am lung product. The latte item, lately deposited the Baltimore Museum Art by Doctor Charles Fenwick of Baltimore, is family heirloom, havir been presented to the Do tor's great-grandfather a tribute from admirir friends. As may be see in the accompanying illu trations from inadequa photographs, this additic to the Amelung group in the form of a tall fli to which a surmountir domical cover with kno finial imparts dignity an proportion. The metal fairly heavy, thick by ha an inch at the strongl pontiled base. In some po tions of an almost smok hue yielding to cryst toward the top, it diffe from the faintly greenis glass of the Metropolita goblet.

The wheel-engraved de oration, while not quit

Figs. 1 and 2 — TWO VIEWS OF A COVERED GOBLET (*1788*)
Clear flint glass. The goblet bears engraved inscriptions which relate it to the ill-starred Amelung venture in New Bremen, Maryland. Comparison with other articles here illustrated affords convincing evidence that it was made in Maryland and sent to Germany as a token of industrial progress. *Height,* 11 ¼ inches.
From the Metropolitan Museum of Art, New York City

qual to that of
e Metropolitan
xample, is sur-
risingly good. On
e cover appears
foliated scroll,
till retaining
aces of gilding.
ne side of the
wer vessel dis-
lays a crown —
eminiscent of that
n the Metropoli-
n goblet — float-
ng beneath the
ords, *Floriat
ommercium.* Be-
w this, in turn,
xpands a wreath
f palms and flow-
rs from whose
idst a dove waves
hopeful sprig of
afage toward the
ame, *Charles Ghe-
iere.* Near the
ottom of the re-
erse two well-let-
red lines read:
*Iew Bremen Glas-
anufactory / the
0ᵗʰᵉ of June 1788.*
The overall
eight of the Balti-
ore cup and
over is 12½
ches; that of the
letropolitan gob-
t, 11¼ inches.
uch differences in the character of the two
ieces as occur are either observable in the
lustrations or have already been noted in this
omment. The fact that the Metropolitan
oblet exhibits a greenish tinge, as against a
noky quality in the Baltimore cup, is of no
reat moment. Neither may we be surprised
at the engraving on a master work to be ex-
ibited in the homeland is more carefully
rought than that on an article likely to be
ibjected to less critical inspection.

Turning now to points of resemblance, we
nd the most striking to be the almost identi-
al shape of the cover finials; the prevailingly
omical form of the covers themselves; the
anner in which an applied thread of glass
ipports these covers on the lip of the vessel
eneath, thereby obviating necessity for an
itegral overhanging flange; and, lastly, the
ose likeness in the lettering of the inscriptions.

ig. 5 — CASE DECANTER (1788)
    Clear flint glass. Made for Colonel Baker Johnson of
    Frederick, Maryland, and, in the manner of its
    engraving, clearly related to the presentation pieces
    of Figures 1 and 3 and the wine glasses of Figure 11.
    The stopper is modern. *Height,* 7½ inches.
    Formerly in the collection of Charles Ross Rogers

Figs. 3 and 4 — TWO VIEWS OF A COVERED CUP (1788)
    Clear flint glass. Presented to the great-grandfather of the present owner,
    Doctor Charles G. Fenwick of Baltimore. The engraved inscription quoted
    in the accompanying text clearly points to its making in the Amelung
    factory. For a time lent to the Baltimore Museum of Art, to the courtesy of
    whose director, Roland J. McKinney, ANTIQUES is indebted for photo-
    graphs. The cloudy aspect of the illustration is due to the photographer's
    application of a substance calculated to overcome troublesome reflections
    on the glass. *Height overall,* 12½ inches

(The Baltimore
cup has recently
been acquired
rather mysteri-
ously by an un-
named purchaser,
and has been
withdrawn from
view.)

The device of
an applied cover
thread or bead is
again observable
on a large sweet-
meat bowl that of
late has crept un-
announced into
the glass cases at
the Metropolitan
Museum, where it
is credited to
Amelung. A crude
example, is this
latest find, with
an ill-shaped foot
and plain circular
stem sustaining a
bowl shaped

somewhat like that of the Museum goblet and
surmounted by a knopped, domed cover whose
contour recalls the cover outline of the Baltimore cup. The glass is quite green in color and
full of bubbles. Its surface is devoid of ornament. The piece is, however, highly significant,
since its combination of forms employed in the
two ceremonial glasses already discussed satisfactorily certifies its source as Frederick. A
goblet, *sans* cover, of almost identical form,
pictured in Mr. Stow's article referred to
above, is there ascribed to a Frederick factory,
but not that of Amelung. Apparently three,
and perhaps four, independent glassmaking
establishments cropped up in the neighborhood
during Amelung's tenure or shortly after its
conclusion. To them have been credited some
extremely primitive articles of glass — far
cruder than the Metropolitan's sweetmeat
bowl, which, if not one of Amelung's commercial products, nevertheless unmistakably reveals peculiarities of general form and specific
detail observable in his more ambitious wares.

In the long run, however, Amelung's place
in the history of American glassmaking will be
determined not by his everyday performance,
but by his achievements in the realm of

superior articles for use and decoration. Here his notable contribution was the first wheel-cut engraving, worthy of the name, in America. Stiegel's flat, lightly ground silhouette patterns might as well have been produced by acid etching. Amelung's ornaments, on the contrary, are cut deeply enough to obtain effects of modeling and of brilliant contrast between sparkling lenslike areas of clear glass and their enframing bands of frosty texture. These characteristics are exemplified in the two presentation vessels of our discussion. They are again so apparent in the embellishment of a case decanter made and inscribed for Colonel Baker Johnson as to assure that piece safe harbor in the Amelung category.

But, in some respects, the most startling contribution to our knowledge of Amelung's capabilities is afforded by a small collection of heirloom glasses belonging to Miss Margaret B. Waesche of Washington, D. C. The first of this group is an engraved goblet on baluster stem supported by a saliently convex foot. The bowl exhibits engraved scroll and garland forms, in conception and execution quite similar to those occurring on the Metropolitan goblet and the Baltimore cup. On one side appears the name *C. Amelung* (for Caroline Amelung, wife of the glass master); on the other, the name *Metha Repold* and the date *d.16. Octo.1792*. Apparently this goblet was a presentation piece. Metha Repold was the wife of George Repold, prosperous citizen of Baltimore, and of German extraction. Portraits of the pair may be seen among the paintings preserved by the Maryland Historical Society.

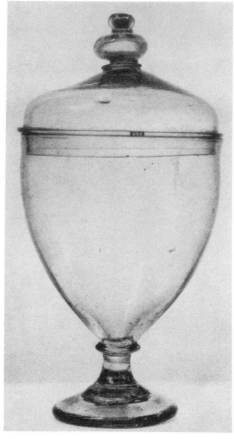

Fig. 6 — COVERED SWEETMEAT BOWL
In various details of form closely allied to the Amelung presentation pieces of Figures 1 and 3. Rather crudely made from bubbly greenish glass. *Height,* 15 inches.
From the Metropolitan Museum of Art

According to Miss Waesche, who ? descended from the Repolds and is th fortunate inheritor of many choice an cestral belongings, this Baltimore coupl were on terms of affectionate intimac with the Amelungs of Frederick, an were patrons as well as friends. Asid from other considerations, Metha Re pold's goblet is important as evidenc that, during at least four years of activity the Amelung factory maintained, an perhaps surpassed, its earlier standard of excellence. All its previously discovere dated pieces have been inscribed with th year *1788.* The recently revealed goble it will be remembered, is of *1792.*

What some may consider a still mor remarkable item in Miss Waesche's col lection is an eight-inch flip whose obvers carries the initials *G M R* (for George an Metha Repold) within a handsome en graved framing. But the really astonish ing feature of this flip is to be found o the reverse, where we encounter a vi gnette engraving of a tall Marylan farmhouse, standing in the shadow c trees and shrubbery, and with its roug foreground populous with domestic fow.

Several drawn wine glasses, evidentl the remains of a set, complete the toll c Miss Waesche's Amelung treasure. A may be seen in the accompanying illus tration, the form of the initials engrave upon them corresponds to that of th letters on the great flip. The surroundin wreath recalls, though it does not pre cisely resemble, that of the B. Johnson decanter, to whic reference has already been made.

Aside from the engraved articles here pictured and discussec

Figs. 7 and 8 — TWO VIEWS OF A PRESENTATION GOBLET (*1792*)
Clear flint glass. Given to Metha Repold by her friend Caroline Amelung, wife of the glass master. Aside from its revealing inscription, obviously related to other authenticated Amelung glasses. *Height,* 7 inches.
From the collection of Miss Margaret B. Waesche

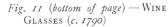

Figs. 9 and 10 (left and right) —
TWO VIEWS OF A FLIP GLASS
(c. 1790)
Clear flint glass, slightly smoky in thicker portions. Heavy base, strongly pontiled. Handsomely engraved scrolled medallion enclosing the initials of George and Metha Repold. The reverse ornamented with a landscape vignette, of which a detail is appended. *Height*, 8 inches.
From the collection of Miss Margaret B. Waesche

Fig. 11 (bottom of page) — WINE GLASSES (c. 1790)
Clear flint glass, somewhat bubbly in the stems. The engraved lettering is like that on the flip.
From the collection of Miss Margaret B. Waesche

nd the green sweetmeat bowl a the Metropolitan Museum, am unaware of any glasses nat afford conclusive internal vidence of having been made n Amelung's factory. To that urce tradition credits a numer of items seemingly too late n style and technique for cceptance, though they may epresent the output of the altimore works that sprang om the seeds scattered by the l wind that dismembered the ew Bremen plant. Others, rimitive alike in form and bric, while probably of Fredrick manufacture, were best cognized as testimony to attempts at reviving the glass inustry in or near the town of Amelung's glassmaking venture.

There are yet others hose claims to an Amelng pedigree must wait pon further documented discoveries. lope of that occurrence encouraged by the rprising advent of the altimore cup and of the estimably significant roup of glasses belongg to Miss Waesche. any event, the gratiingly extensive series f distinguished exmples that I have here een privileged to asmble is sufficient to arow an entirely fresh nd quite entrancing

light on the history of early American glassmaking. In the midst of this illumination, John Frederick Amelung stands forth a majestic figure, whose stature as creative artist and ingenious craftsman overtops that of his Colonial predecessors and his commercially more successful nineteenth-century followers.

The specimens of engraved flint glass here illustrated should be sufficient evidence of the quality of the products manufactured at the New Bremen plant to convince once and for all of the erroneousness of their belief those who have maintained that only primitive vessels, of crude bottle and cylinder glass, were made by Amelung. As Mrs. Knittle notes in *Early American Glass*, Mr. Boudinot, during the Congressional debate in 1790 concerning a loan to Amelung, stated that he considered the new Bremen glass "superior to any ever produced in America." Perhaps for the first time, this opinion is shown to be justifiable. Examples of Amelung's craftsmanship which have recently, and almost miraculously, been brought to light prove that, in this country, his glass stands second to none.

The search for New Bremen and the glass of John Frederick Amelung

BY IVOR NOËL HUME, *Chief archeologist, Colonial Williamsburg*

OLD BREMEN SUCCESS AND THE NEW PROGRESS were words of good cheer which in 1788 traveled the miles from an obscure and youthful Maryland settlement to the great maritime city of Bremen in Germany. A hundred and forty years later they were heard again in America when the magnificent covered goblet on which they were engraved was acquired by the Metropolitan Museum of Art. More important than the wishes of one Bremen to another was the additional engraved information that the glass was a product of the *New Bremen Glassmanufactory—1788—North America, State of Maryland.*

Just as the now famous Bremen pokal had publicized the achievements of John Frederick Amelung in 1788, it did so again in 1928. Because the goblet was of superior quality, impressive size, and, above all, the first recorded marked product of an American glasshouse, its discovery generated an interest in Amelung among collectors—an interest which has increased steadily through the years as each new piece has come to light.

Engraved items of unquestionable Amelung manufacture are now scattered through a number of private collections and museums, not the least of them the fine specimens in the Corning Museum of Glass. However, it has long been realized that the engraved pieces were not typical of the factory's output, and so, in 1962, an exploratory excavation on the supposed New Bremen site was undertaken by the Corning Museum, in association with the Smithsonian Institution and archeological personnel provided by Colonial Williamsburg. The object was simply to determine something of the size of the factory and to recover examples of its various products. If this venture proved informative a more complete excavation was to follow in 1963.

The site lies in virtually unblemished pasture land on Bennett Creek some nine miles from the town of Frederick, and at the foot of the impressive Sugarloaf Mountain outcrop. The approximate location had been well known for many years, and collectors from Washington, Baltimore, and elsewhere had dug numerous holes into it in a generally successful quest for examples of the factory's waste. But as these "treasures" were recovered without benefit of the techniques of modern archeology, the information obtained from them was limited and sometimes misleading.

John Frederick Amelung had arrived in Maryland from Bremen, Germany, in the summer of 1784, bringing with him sixty-eight workers and " . . . instruments for three different Glass Ovens," and he quickly established a substantial manufactory on part of a two-thousand-acre tract which spanned the Monocacy River and extended almost to the Potomac. By 1790 Amelung had acquired an additional one thousand acres and had erected another glasshouse; he employed between four and five hundred workers and, according to George Washington, the New Bremen project was manufacturing " . . . Glass of various kinds nearly to the amount of three thousand pounds value" per annum. However, in the spring of 1790 Amelung suffered a substantial fire loss (details of which are still in doubt) as well as financial setbacks occasioned by an alarming shortage of customers. Twice he appealed to Congress for financial help, and twice he failed to get it.

Five years later, in 1795, Amelung offered the bulk of his holdings for sale; but there were no takers. At the close of the year he was declared bankrupt, and although he had previously deeded his unmortgaged property to his son, it appears that New Bremen put out its fires and never reopened. A possible exception may have been the glasshouse on the one-thousand-acre tract, for this was, perhaps, acquired by one of Amelung's imported craftsmen, Adam Kohlenberg, who operated a factory on nearby Bear Branch into the early nineteenth century.

The site selected for the recent excavations lay in a meadow directly south of the still-surviving Amelung mansion. It was there that the amateur collectors had been best rewarded and it was there, too, that the remains of old stone-walled basements and other potentially interesting archeological features were to be seen. Most intriguing of the latter were two tree-capped mounds which seemed likely to conceal either structures or waste tips. Trenches cut through both subsequently revealed that the first did indeed contain a waste heap, while the second covered the stone-built foundations of a pair of fritting ovens.

Although, as I have said, the 1962 excavations were intended only to dig a few test trenches so as to determine the potential of the site, when the second cutting exposed part of a major structure the plan was changed to enable us to clear the whole of that feature. It was then found to be only the corner unit of a much larger building measuring in excess of 54 feet, 1 inch, by 53 feet, 7 inches, as the south and east walls had been traced for those distances by the time the excavation ended. A subsequent study of eighteenth-century Euro-

Aerial view of part of the Amelung glass-house excavated in 1963, showing the west melting furnace with its four wings, which are believed to have housed small fritting ovens. Beyond these foundations, to the right, can be seen the remains of a pair of annealing ovens, while in the top left corner stands the east melting furnace. The modern metal roof in the background covers the pair of fritting ovens excavated in 1962. *Except as noted, all photographs by courtesy of the Corning Museum of Glass.*

Aerial view of the pair of fritting ovens at the southeast corner of the glasshouse which were uncovered in the fall of 1962. The two angled projections represent the remains of the firing channels, only one of which has been emptied of the rubble which filled it when the building was abandoned.

pean glass factory plans indicated that the maximum size for such a building might be in the region of 71 by 47 feet—and our structure was already wider than that. Nevertheless, it was supposed that the sizes would be approximately the same and that the layout would be comparable, *i.e.*, a melting furnace in the center with workers' chairs around it, and ancillary ovens located in at least three of the four corners. The program for the continuance of excavation in 1963 was based on these probabilities. Unfortunately, however, we were using the wrong crystal ball.

The structure did run true to form in that it possessed a melting furnace with secondary units at the four points of the compass around it; but then the eighteenth-century designer confounded us by going on to repeat the entire pattern on a larger scale to the west, thus making the glasshouse twice as large as we had supposed. Measuring all of 112 feet, 9 inches, by 65 feet, 9 inches, it contained ten individually fired ovens, plus a probable four others built into the corners of the larger of the two melting furnaces. In all, there would seem to have been six fritting ovens, two working furnaces, one pot arch, six annealing ovens, one wood-drying room, two pot-making and storage rooms, as well as two more rooms which may have served for the temporary storage and packing of the finished products.

The remains of a light flask of clear nonlead metal, appearing slightly purple in transmitted light, oval in section, and without molded ornament. Height 6¼ inches. This important piece was found lying in the burned clay against the north wall of the east melting furnace. *Photograph by the author.*

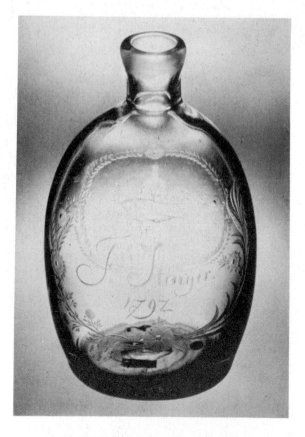

The Stenger flask, dated 1792, and undoubtedly made at New Bremen. Height 6¾ inches.

The foundations of the building were of local field stone, as were the walls. The generally slender construction of the walls at north and south indicates that they were of no great height, probably no more than six or eight feet. But these, coupled with the exterior walls of the more heavily built ancillary ovens, probably supported a massive wooden roof rising another twenty feet or so to the crest. Thus the excavated glasshouse might well have borne a striking resemblance to the one at Breitenstein in Bohemia illustrated in Jaroslav Vavra's *5000 Years of Glass-Making* (Prague, 1954, p. 17).

Because stones coated with glass were found built into the walls of the factory, it was evident that this could not have been the first glasshouse built at New Bremen. The archeological evidence also suggested that the building had ceased to exist by the time Amelung offered his manufactory for sale in 1795. Indeed it is possible that it burned in the fire of 1790 and that most of the stones were then salvaged and re-used elsewhere. If these tentative deductions are correct, the excavated building had a life of no more than five years.

Among the artifacts recovered were a few tools, including fragments of numerous blowing irons, a hammer used for breaking up old pots and retrieving cullet, also part of a heavy cast-iron rake possibly used for stirring frit. A much-worn stone ball was of particular interest in that it is believed to have come from a rotating or tumbling barrel used for grinding cullet or quartz. On the floor of the pot room was a quantity of still-plastic clay, samples of which have since been fired at the Williamsburg Pottery in Virginia and found to create a fine-grained body comparable in texture to that of the many fragments of pots or crucibles discovered on the glasshouse site.

More exciting, from the collector's point of view, was the recovery of great quantities of glass, many pieces of which can be safely claimed as products of the Amelung factory. Among the shapes represented were drawn-stemmed wineglasses (the majority with folded rather than plain feet), firing and dessert glasses, tumblers of widely varying sizes, tumbler or goblet lids, decanter and bottle stoppers, sugar bowls with ornamental handles, mugs or cans with handles, utilitarian bowls and pans, bottles, flasks, and window glass.

Two small engraved fragments were found, both paralleling motifs previously attributed to Amelung. Flask and tumbler pieces were discovered decorated with expanded ribbed molding, also with pattern molding in diamond and diamond-daisy designs. The base of a cut tumbler and various examples of cut-faceted and paneled stems were also found, though the latter gave a positive reaction when subjected to the hydrofluoric acid spot test for lead. It must be admitted that this is not a very reliable test, but of the many fragments tested, nearly all suggested an absence of lead in the metal. The few exceptions may represent old glass brought to the factory for remelting.

Particularly revealing was the wide range of colors represented among the fragments: different shades of green were used for flasks, common bottles, bowls, and some table glass; amber for molded bottles, bowls, and possibly for chestnut flasks; amethyst for sugar bowls, creamers, goblets, and small bottles; blue for sugar bowls, and for the ornamental handles and rims of clear mugs or cans. The clear table glass contained hints of

Two of three broken tumblers found amid a deposit of ground clear glass at the bottom of a burned barrel set in the glasshouse floor against the north wall. Height of left example, 4⅛ inches; height of right, 3¾ inches. *Photograph by the author.*

pale green, gray, and sometimes purple, indicating that Amelung had difficulty in producing a consistent metal—a fact which will continue to make it unwise to attempt to identify his products on the evidence of color alone.

No large inverted-baluster stems of the types used for the majority of the engraved goblets were among the pieces recovered. However, one fragment with a knop above an inverted baluster was found—a then somewhat old-fashioned style which occurs only on the Bremen pokal. Rather surprisingly, one piece of an air-twist handle was recovered, as also was an unfinished stem containing a six-strand opaque twist. One is tempted to suggest that Amelung might have been producing such ornamented pieces. But no opaque glass, either in rods or cullet, was found in the excavations. It may be significant that only one drawn-stemmed glass was found which contained a deliberately inserted tear, and this gave a positive reaction when spot tested for lead.

The many thousands of glass fragments have as yet received only a cursory examination, and it is expected to be some months before any final conclusions can be drawn. In the meantime, we must continue to treat the excavated material with extreme caution for fear of confusing old glass bought by Amelung for remelting with pieces actually produced at his factory.

As for the site itself, the digging has raised as many questions as it has answered—possibly more. But on the credit side the Corning-Smithsonian excavation project provided us with our first opportunity to study the complete plan of a major American glasshouse, and this in itself may indeed rank as an achievement of the first importance. Because Amelung's venture was on such a massive scale, however, we are left with the disturbing possibility that New Bremen still retains most of its secrets.

The "Tobias and the Angel" covered tumbler, made at New Bremen in 1788. Height (without cover), 8⅜ inches. Fragments of tumblers of this size as well as pieces of comparable lids were found in the excavations.

A conjectural reconstruction of the New Bremen glasshouse based on the excavated ground plan and on the exterior of a similarly proportioned factory building which was still standing in the late nineteenth century at Breitenstein in Bohemia. *Drawing by Richard Stinely of Colonial Williamsburg.*

A "new" Amelung tumbler

BY KENNETH M. WILSON, *Curator, Corning Museum of Glass*

As is frequently the case, one good thing leads to another. In this instance, an article published in Antiques in March 1964 has led to the discovery of an important piece of American glass (Figs. 1, 2): a heretofore unrecorded Amelung tumbler (in collectors' parlance, a "flip glass"). The identification of this piece was stimulated by Ivor Noël Hume's article *The search for New Bremen and the glass of John Frederick Amelung*, which included an illustration of the Tobias and the Angel covered tumbler in the Corning Museum of Glass (Fig. 3).

Shortly after his article appeared Mr. Noël Hume received a letter from a reader who said he had a glass of the same form as the Tobias tumbler, engraved with an eagle and shield and bearing on the reverse the engraved inscription *New Bremen Glassmanufactory/ 1792*. Mr. Noël Hume communicated this information to the Corning Museum, which, along with the Smithsonian Institution, had sponsored the 1962 and 1963 excavations of the New Bremen factory site under his archeological direction. Then the owners of the tumbler, Mr. and Mrs. Albert J. Henry, lent it to the Corning Museum for study and exhibition.

The tumbler's history, beyond the fact that it had been given to Mr. Henry's mother before World War II, is unrecorded. At that time it still had a cover similar to that on the Tobias and the Angel tumbler, but this was later broken, and unfortunately thrown away. Though it appeared immediately evident that the Henry piece was from the same family as other known Amelung tumblers, such as the Tobias and the Angel, the George Repold, and the one in the Garvan Collection at Yale, there were at first some reservations about its engraving, primarily because that of the main motif—an eagle with shield (Fig. 5)—seemed different from the engraving on any known Amelung example.

A subsequent detailed study of the engraving and comparison with various elements on known Amelung pieces (Figs. 4-10) leave no doubt that this newly discovered

Fig. 1. Recently discovered tumbler from John F. Amelung's New Bremen Glassmanufactory. It seems quite likely that the coat of arms on this tumbler was based on one of several coins of the period, *e.g.*: the Massachusetts copper cent of 1788 (Laurence Brown, *Coins Through the Ages*, Pl. X, No. 4); the Washington cent of 1791 (Joseph Coffin, *The Complete Book of Coin Collecting*, Pl. XI); or the New York Excelsior cent of 1787 (*ibid.*, Pl. XII). Height 8¾ inches. *Collection of Mr. and Mrs. Albert J. Henry; currently on loan to the Corning Museum of Glass.*

Fig. 2. Reverse of Fig. 1, engraved *New Bremen Glassmanufactory/ 1792*.

Fig. 3. The Tobias and the Angel covered tumbler, engraved *Happy is he who is blessed with Virtuous Children. Carolina Lucia Amelung. 1788.* Height without cover, 8⅜ inches. *Corning Museum of Glass.*

Fig. 4. Detail, left side of wreath on the Tobias and the Angel tumbler.

Fig. 5. Detail, obverse of the Henry tumbler.

tumbler is from the New Bremen Glassmanufactory. Not only are the composition and the floral and foliate motifs alike (Figs. 4, 5), but the manner in which they are engraved is consistent with that of all the other pieces examined. These included, besides those already mentioned, the Stenger flask, dated 1792; a goblet bearing the names *C. Amelung* and *Metha Repold*, also dated 1792; the pair of *George Trisler* goblets, dated 1793; the Bremen pokal at the Metropolitan Museum; and a tumbler owned by the Connecticut Historical Society (ANTIQUES, September 1964, p. 315). The leafy branch on which the bird is perched on the Henry tumbler, the two leafy branches on the Repold piece, and the four identical branches on the Tobias tumbler may be cited as examples of this consistency.

Though letters and numerals on these engraved Amelung pieces are in many cases identical, there are some slight variations. Minor differences also are apparent in the execution of certain motifs, such as the florets and stalks of wheat which occur on most of the engraved pieces. In a sense, these variations help to confirm the authenticity of the engraving on the Henry tumbler, for this examination revealed similar small variations in the design and execution of elements on other signed and definitely attributed Amelung pieces—for example, the short and long *s* on the pair of Trisler goblets and on the Repold tumbler, where of three wheat motifs two are identical and the third lacks its central stem or vein. These are

natural human variations, to be expected. In short, a skilled forger, to have successfully added the engraving to a plain tumbler at a later date, would have had to have access to at least a half-dozen known Amelung pieces and the opportunity to study them minutely—two conditions that did not exist.

121

Fig. 6. Detail, date on the obverse of the Stenger flask. *Corning Museum of Glass.*

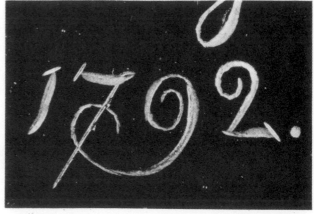

Fig. 7. Detail, date on the Henry tumbler.

Fig. 8. Detail, date on one of the pair of Trisler goblets. *Corning Museum of Glass.*

Fig. 9. Detail, the word *Bremen* on the Henry tumbler.

The engraving on the Henry glass is, in fact, more carefully done and of a higher quality than that on the Tobias and the Angel tumbler and other pieces in the Corning Museum, or on the Bremen pokal, even though the depiction of the eagle is somewhat awkward. This is notable in the words *Bremen* on the Henry tumbler, as compared with the same word on the Bremen pokal (Figs. 9, 10). Though at first glance they appear to be quite different, a more careful study shows they are of the same style and character but that the execution of the word *Bremen* on the Henry tumbler is much more sophisticated. This is especially true of the letter *B*, but the other letters in this word are also more refined.

Undoubtedly, the Henry tumbler was made as a presentation piece, and since its engraving is of a superior quality, it naturally leads one to wonder whether it was meant to be even more special than the usual presentation pieces, and to speculate for whom it was engraved. In this connection one cannot help recalling the goblets presented to George Washington in 1789 (ANTIQUES, April 1964, p. 448).

This important object is now on exhibition at the Corn-

Fig. 10. Detail, the word *Bremen* on the Bremen pokal. *Metropolitan Museum of Art.*

ing Museum of Glass, and the search for a link between the chief element of its decoration and a possible historical event continues. In addition, an intensive scientific study of the composition of known Amelung glasses is under way, which may provide new proof of the Henry tumbler's authorship.

New York State Glasshouses

Part I

By HARRY HALL WHITE

THE lament of one age is the delight of the next. Witness the regret expressed in the personal diary of DeWitt Clinton, in 1810, when, as member of a commission for the State which he was later to govern, he wrote:

August 16th, 1810, . . after the Oneida Reservation we entered the town of Vernon, in which three glasshouses are in contemplation; one has been in operation for some time. It is rather to be regretted that this business is overdone. Besides the glass introduced from Pittsburgh, and from a glasshouse in Pennsylvania, on the borders of Orange County, and glass imported from Europe, there are ten manufacturies in the State already, or about to be established.*

I have had the keen enjoyment of investigating the scant records and genealogies, and of visiting several of the sites of the old glasshouses mentioned in Clinton's journal. Some of my discoveries will be of interest to the collector.

As a member of the commission which was to report on the most eligible route for the Erie Canal, Clinton was in close touch with local industrial developments, and heard of plans and prospects, many of which were never developed outside the minds of their promoters. Of the glasshouses in the town of Vernon noted in his diary, only two succeeded in making sufficient glass to entitle them to mention by later historians, and to leave enough fragments to enable one to locate their old furnace sites.

However, when I examined the State records of incorporations, I found that, prior to 1810, four charters were granted by the State Legislature for making glass in Oneida County, in which Vernon Township is located. The concerns thus incorporated were: (*1*) the Oneida Glass and Iron Company; (*2*) the Oneida Glass Factory Company; (*3*) the Utica Glass Company; and (*4*) the Mount Vernon Glass Company. The following notes record my further investigations into the history of these enterprises.

The Life and Writings of DeWitt Clinton. By William W. Campbell. New York, 1849. p. 191.

VIEW OF THE MAIN STREET OF UTICA ABOUT 1810
From *America, Historical and Descriptive.* By J. S. Buckingham. New York, 1841, Vol. II, p. 258.

THE ONEIDA GLASS AND IRON COMPANY

This company, incorporated in 1809, was established at Taberg, New York, now a sleepy little village in Annsville Township, in the southern part of Oneida County. I have visited the place, interviewed the oldest living inhabitants, and searched the furnace site. But from no source could I obtain evidence that glass was ever actually made at Taberg. Thus, for once, both history and tradition checked — which is unusual. The site of the old furnace is at the edge of a low, but fairly steep, bluff, at whose foot parts of the early cupola now lie. This location evidently permitted wagon-hauling of fuel, flux, and ore to the level of the furnace-charging gate.

The products of the Oneida Glass and Iron Company, it seems, were always charcoal pig iron, and hollow ware — kettles, pots, and skillets. This pig iron was of a very fine grade. For its making Clinton ore was freighted, on the Chenango Canal, from Kirtland, New York. From this excellent grade of metal were made the billets which were later rolled into the sheet iron which has endured these many years in pierced lanterns, sconces, and the decorated tinware now treasured by us all.

At the time of its incorporation, the Company undoubtedly obtained the charter right to make glass should its iron production proved unsuccessful. In early charters or laws I have frequently found provisions allowing a manufacturer to make additional products, or to establish a glasshouse in an adjoining county in case the materials at the original location were found unsuitable. In any event, the Oneida Glass and Iron Company was a glass company that did not make glass.

THE ONEIDA GLASS FACTORY COMPANY

The petition of this second concern was allowed by the thirty-second session of the New York State Legislature, February 17, 1809. The promoters and first directors of the enterprise were: Watts Sherman, Abraham Varick, John Steward, Jr., Alexander B. Johnson, and Richard Sanger.* The local historian records a long list of subscribers to the company's stock, the amount of which was $100,000. Most of these optimists were Utica men, some of whom were later to become prominent in the early history of their city. At this time, however, Utica was but a village, about the size of Buffalo, with a thousand or twelve hundred inhabitants.

One man in particular, among the Glass Factory organizers and promoters, though not a Utican, is to be noted. This was Lawrence Schoolcraft, whose name is familiar to most students of American glass and glass manufacture.

When I first heard of Schoolcraft, he was mentioned as "the superintendent of a glasshouse near Albany"; but I have never been able to find a trace of him in Albany history. His interest in the Utica project, however, greatly assisted its promotion, though he took no active part in its management or operation. At a later date, with his son Henry Rowe Schoolcraft, he was to prove instrumental in the organization of a glasshouse at Keene, New Hampshire. He eventually settled in the town of Vernon, New York, where the records show that he was Justice of the Peace in 1826. He died there, in 1840, and is buried in the village cemetery. I have dwelt, at considerable length, on the history of this man and his connections at Utica, Vernon, and Keene, for reasons that will be apparent when the products of these various places are compared.

The Glass Factory Company purchased a factory site at Vernon, New York, seventeen miles west of Utica, "where the turnpike traverses the Skanandoa." A glasshouse was promptly erected and placed in operation under the management of Willett H. Shearman. So successful and so long was this man's guidance, that the factory became known as "Shearman's Works." Its product was marketed through a Utica dealer or agent, E. B. Shearman, evidently a relative of the manager.

In looking over Shearman's advertisements, I was impressed by the man's continual emphasis of the fact that he specialized in American products. His slogan was "Dealer in American Goods." Among these goods he lauds the merits of his "Oneida Window Glass." These old newspaper files reveal plenty of competition with Shearman's glass. They also show the activities of some of the rival glasshouses — some new names and some old friends, including: the Peterboro Glass Works, the Champlain Glass Works, the Ontario Glass Works, the Geneva Glass Works, the Pittsburgh Glass Company, and the New England Crown Glass Company.

Of course these different firms did not all leap into the market at the same time, but they came in sufficiently rapid succession always to afford keen competition. Nevertheless, the business of the Glass Factory Company grew, for, as the receipt of a new brand of glass was announced by a certain store or warehouse, Shearman would advertise that he had just appointed a new agent. The *Utica Patriot* for September 10, 1811, contains the statement:

The Pioneers of Utica, from the Earliest Settlement to 1825. By M. M. Bagg. Utica, New York, 1877. p. 273.

E. B. Shearman announces his appointment as agent for the Oneida Glass Factory, and deposits of glass with two dealers:

William Alexander, Little Falls, N. Y.
G. Huntington & Co., Rome, N. Y.

Note that this advertisement appeared in 1811; but Clinton, in his private journal of 1810, previously mentioned, states that he saw, in Little Falls, New York, good glass of local manufacture.

There is no documentary or other evidence to explain why the directors of the Glass Factory Company decided to quit their business. The fact is that they disposed of their real estate, and closed the Company's affairs August 18, 1836, thus ending the career of one of the first, and one of the most successful, of the early New York glasshouses west of Albany.

I found Vernon a pleasantly typical New York village, boasting several of the "untouched type of country store buildings." After suitable enquiry, I located the site of the glasshouse, about a mile from the village, on the Peterboro road that leads to the southward. Here, at the right of a four corners, lies a triangular piece of property, where formerly stood the Oneida Glass Factory Company's works. The site is now pasture land, for the old structure has been long since demolished. However, parts of the foundations and some masonry are yet to be seen. In and about the place, I found a good many fragments of glass; but a more thorough search might be possible if the land were under cultivation. It is unlikely that any saleable product other than window glass was made here. The majority of worked fragments which I found were in aquamarine, the regular factory run, unless an order was received for a lot of colored glass for a church or a public building. On such occasions, I surmise, those workmen who were sufficiently skillful would blow a few offhand pieces for friends and visitors. These interesting and sometimes beautiful pieces are eagerly sought by collectors, and, strange to say, bring high prices despite the fact that they defy classification or attribution as to either source or age.

THE UTICA GLASS COMPANY

Encouraged by the success attending the sale of stock in the Oneida Glass Factory Company, one of the stockholders, Peter Bours, and two other investors, John Stewart, Jr., and Seth Dwight, together with Hugh Cunningham and Benjamin Walker, in 1809, obtained from the State Legislature a special charter for the Utica Glass Company. A capital stock of $250,000 was offered for sale.

The Company proposed to manufacture crown glass, a grade of product superior to the cylinder window glass such as the Oneida Glass Factory Company was to produce. At that time crown glass was successfully made in this country only at Boston, Massachusetts; and the Utica Company promptly tried to secure the necessary workmen from that city. Deming Jarves mentions this attempt, but states that it was unsuccessful. The agent and the workmen who had been induced to break their indentures and leave the employ of the Boston Window Glass Company were arrested and returned to the Hub.*

* *Reminiscences of Glass Making*. By Deming Jarves. New York, 1865. p. 57.

About three miles north of Utica, on the Glass Factory Hill Farm, and on a road still known as the Glass Factory Road, the Company purchased a tract of land and erected suitable buildings. At this site I found many evidences of elaborate preparation. Some of the foundations of the old furnace are still to be seen, though, as is common in the case of ruins of the sort, much material has been drawn away for foundations of various buildings and for road-making.

I carefully searched the site and the surrounding territory, much of which was under cultivation, and obtained a very satisfactory gathering of glass. Among the pieces I found no evidence that the company made anything other than the intended product — crown glass — though the fragments of the rim, or extreme edge, of the large sheet obtained by the "crown method" are so suggestive of the edge of blown dishes that they might easily mislead the casual observer. The fragments found were all of a uniform, light aquamarine.

There was a great deal of speculation in the Glass Works stock, but the enterprise proved a failure. Expenses were high, and production low. What happens today, happened then. The Company struggled along in a hopeless effort to compete with the crown window glass of Boston. It was struggling in 1813, and in 1819 it advertised for glassblowers. In March, 1822, the plant and lands were leased to the Oneida Glass Factory Company of Vernon. So ended another of the early attempts — no bottles or flasks, though some of the inevitable offhand pieces may be in today's collections.

(To be continued)

New York State Glasshouses*

Part II

By Harry Hall White

THE MT. VERNON GLASS COMPANY

CONCERNING a glasshouse, it frequently happens that the more meagre the information which I secure, the more important to the collector it proves to be. Here is an instance. The Mt. Vernon Glass Company manufactured bottles and flasks, but left no available written records of the product or of the designs in which it was made. Local historians and recent writers have virtually ignored the concern.

The office library of the Secretary of State in Albany, New York, contains the *Private Laws of the State of New York* for the year of 1810. Chapter XVI of this volume records the petition of the organizers of the Mt. Vernon Glass Company — "Abraham Van Epps, William Root, Benjamin Pierson, Robert Richardson, Isaac Coe, Daniel Cook, Benjamin Hubbell, David Pierson and others." Five of these men were also stockholders in the Oneida Glass Factory Company. Their petition was granted at the twenty-third session of the Legislature, and was dated February 17, 1810. Five hundred shares at $250 each were issued. The following notice in the *Utica Patriot* for August 8, 1811, indicates that the stock was issued and partly paid for:

MT. VERNON GLASS WORKS
Stockholders' notice of installments unpaid, 50 days to pay the installments and interest, or forfeit the previous payments. Vernon, Aug. 8, 1811.

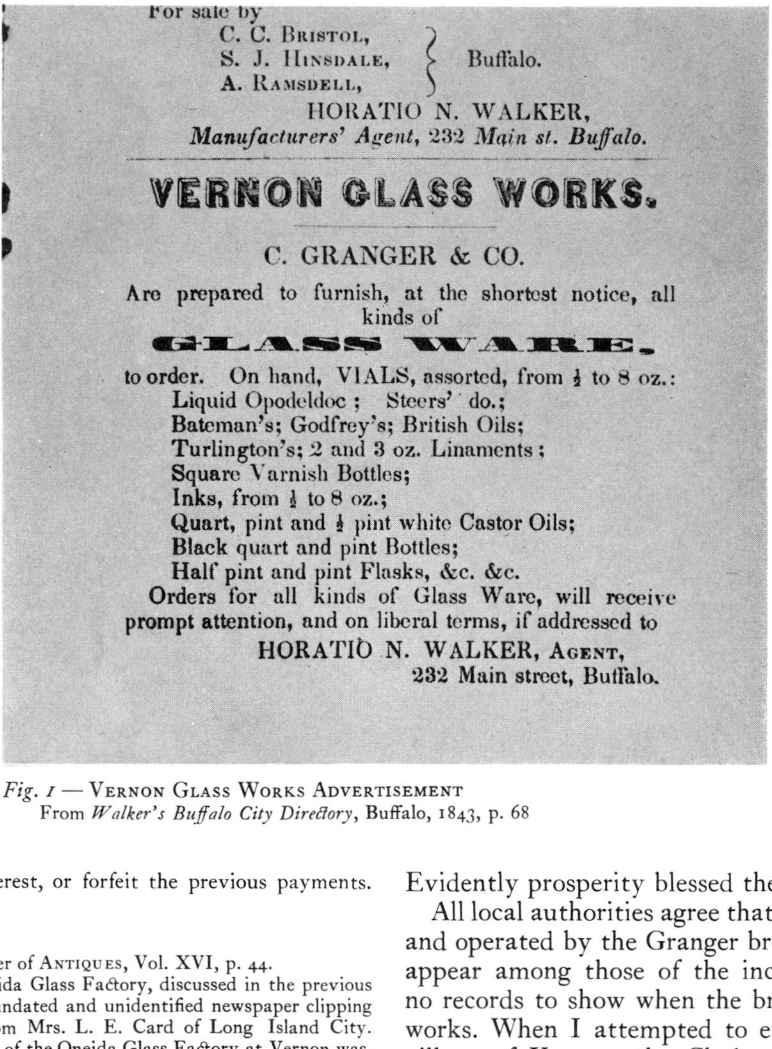

For sale by
C. C. BRISTOL,
S. J. HINSDALE, } Buffalo.
A. RAMSDELL,

HORATIO N. WALKER,
Manufacturers' Agent, 232 Main st. Buffalo.

VERNON GLASS WORKS.

C. GRANGER & CO.

Are prepared to furnish, at the shortest notice, all kinds of

GLASS WARE.

to order. On hand, VIALS, assorted, from ½ to 8 oz.:
Liquid Opodeldoc ; Steers' do.;
Bateman's; Godfrey's; British Oils;
Turlington's; 2 and 3 oz. Linaments ;
Square Varnish Bottles;
Inks, from ½ to 8 oz.;
Quart, pint and ½ pint white Castor Oils;
Black quart and pint Bottles;
Half pint and pint Flasks, &c. &c.
Orders for all kinds of Glass Ware, will receive prompt attention, and on liberal terms, if addressed to
HORATIO N. WALKER, AGENT,
232 Main street, Buffalo.

Fig. 1 — VERNON GLASS WORKS ADVERTISEMENT
From *Walker's Buffalo City Directory*, Buffalo, 1843, p. 68

It is apparent that the founding of the glasshouse occurred at some time before the incorporation, in 1810, for, during 1811, the following advertisement occurs in the *Utica Patriot:*

BOTTLE GLASS
The President and Directors of the Mt. Vernon Glass Company give notice that they continue to manufacture all kinds of Bottle Glass of a superior quality at their factory in the Town of Vernon in the County of Oneida.

Merchants, Traders, and Pedlars may be supplied at wholesale on liberal terms; with any quantity of
Porter)
Cider } Bottles
Beer)
of the usual size — and common bottles from ½ pint to four gallons.

Orders addressed and application made to David Pierson, Agent for the Company, at the said factory will be strictly attended to.
Wm. I. Hopkins, Sec.
Vernon, April 6th, 1811.

This is interesting but very general information, particularly in so far as flasks are concerned. Notices of stockholders' meetings occur periodically in the Utica papers; but no details appear regarding the company's product or the proprietors. Following the original purchase of land, in 1814, from William Root, ancestor of Elihu Root, the Mt. Vernon Glass Company continued to acquire property at intervals up to 1820, when the last transaction is recorded.*

Evidently prosperity blessed the enterprise.

All local authorities agree that this glasshouse was owned and operated by the Granger brothers. But no such names appear among those of the incorporators, and there are no records to show when the brothers took control of the works. When I attempted to examine the records of the village of Vernon, the Clerk advised me that, in 1836, when his father took over the books from the previous incumbent, the documents were found to have been destroyed by mice in the trunk where they had been stored.

---

*Continued from the July number of ANTIQUES, Vol. XVI, p. 44.

Note. — A side light on the Oneida Glass Factory, discussed in the previous part of this series, comes from an undated and unidentified newspaper clipping recently received by ANTIQUES from Mrs. L. E. Card of Long Island City. According to this item, the business of the Oneida Glass Factory at Vernon was, from 1813 to 1836, conducted by Willett Helar Sherman. Sherman was born in Exeter, New Hampshire, in 1792, worked for a time in Providence and Wickford, Rhode Island, and, at the age of twenty-one, moved to Vernon to take charge of the glassworks at that place. His wife was Catherine Ann Schoolcraft. James Schoolcraft Sherman, elected Vice-President of the United States in 1908, was a grandson of this pair. — *Ed.*

*The Index of Deeds to Corporations at Albany, New York, p. 120.

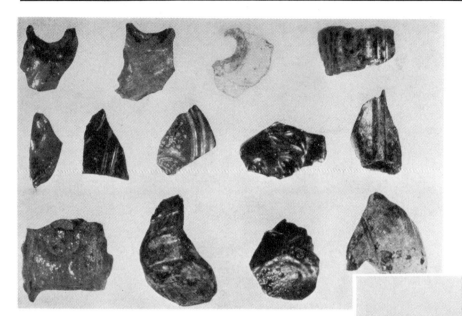

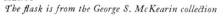

Fig. 2 — Half-Pint Cornucopia-Urn Flask and Fragments

The inhabitants seem to have been as careless in their use of the town name as they were with the Town Clerk's records. The place was usually spoken of as Vernon; but the corner stone of the local church is inscribed *The Mt. Vernon Presbyterian Church.* The *Gazetteer of the State of New York*, by Horatio Gates Spafford, A. M.,* reveals the following:

> In this town are four glasshouses, owned by three companies, two of which are incorporated. The glass manufactured here is of good quality. A part of this town is known by the name of *Mt. Vernon.*

The glass manufacturer evidently considered his

_____
* Albany, New York, 1813, p. 319.

Fig. 3 (below) — Pint Lafayette-Masonic Flask and Fragments
   The flask is from the George S. McKearin collection

establishment to be located in the mountless part of the community, if we may judge from the advertisement of the Buffalo agent, Horatio N. Walker, in the directory which he published in 1843, as *Walker's Buffalo City Directory (Fig. 1).* He treated himself to a good half page — as was proper to glass agent and publisher. Manufacturers were not always so fortunate in the choice of their representatives.

The site of this glasshouse was north of the village — I believe either outside the village limits, or in that part known as Mt. Vernon. I found this plot of ground now owned by a Mr. Whitmore, who gave me the privilege of snooping to my heart's content. Most of the location was now under cultivation, so that I had an excellent chance to search it. It had been used as a garden for thirty years, and, in the course of that time, a great deal of the rubbish such as I was after had been systematically culled from the surface, and conveniently dumped at the edge of a railroad right of way, thus saving me considerable time. I spent many pleasant days searching the land, the adjoining gardens, and this rubbish heap of possibilities. As I searched, many unexpected finds turned up. It is difficult to describe, to one who has not participated in a search of this sort, the extreme fascination of such discoveries.

When all the material was gathered, it amounted to a bushel and more. Washed, sorted, and classified, it revealed fragments of the following objects: a halfpint Cornucopia-Urn flask; a pint Lafayette-Masonic flask; a pint aquamarine Sunburst flask; a pint aquamarine Masonic flask; "Stoddard type" inkwell; pressed salt dishes; three-part-mold decanter; blown flint decanter; Chestnut bottle; flint cruets, bottles, and offhand pieces; snuff and black bottles, lettered and plain; aquamarine medicine and prescription phials; a pint Railroad flask.

A very comprehensive list, you will admit; but upon examination of the photographs of the fragments of the most important pieces you will concede the accuracy of the evidence. Let me illustrate and describe these various types.

Half-Pint Cornucopia-Urn Flask (*Fig. 2*)

This little flask, one of the most decorative of a long series, and a type frequently found, was produced at the Mt. Vernon works in olive-amber and in olive-green ranging almost to aquamarine. Possibly such flasks were made in aquamarine, but I found no fragments. The colors of the fragments shown run more to the green than to the amber. This flask is similar in type to that which I excavated at Keene, New Hampshire, in 1925.*

Pint Lafayette-Masonic Flask (*Fig. 3*)

Up to date, this variety, by reason of resemblance, has been attributed to the glasshouse at Coventry, Connecticut. It is true, of course, that some of this particular variety may have been made there as well as at Mt. Vernon; but I have now definitely established, beyond any question, that this unmarked flask was made at Mt. Vernon. It is of interest to note, in the workmanship and design of these Lafayette and DeWitt Clinton busts, the evident influence, or possibly I should say the copying, of the aristocratic and dignified mien characteristic of the work of that popular portrait artist, St. Memin. It is very clear that the mold-cutter used a St. Memin

* See ANTIQUES, Vol. XI, pp. 459–463.

Fig. 4 — Pint Railroad Flask and Fragments

profile of Lafayette for his model.*

The fragments shown exhibit shades of olive-amber ranging to olive-green, fairly light. The fragment in the upper left-hand corner contains the letter *L*. The piece immediately below shows the face of Lafayette's portrait. The specimen is otherwise without lettering.

Pint Railroad Flask (*Fig. 4*)

Discovery of these fragments at the Mt. Vernon works is not as surprising as it may at first seem. This flask was originally attributed to the Kensington Glass

* *Hawkers and Walkers in Early America*, by Richardson Wright, Philadelphia, 1927, pp. 134, 135.

Fig. 5 (below) — Three-part-mold Blown Inkwell and Fragments

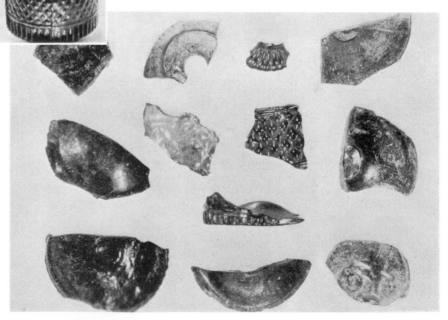

Works at Philadelphia, solely because of its resemblance to some other marked Kensington flask. I have never been able to obtain any other evidence favoring that attribution. In 1925 I established the fact that flasks of this type were made at Keene, New Hampshire. Thereafter I became increasingly certain that the more popular types of flasks were made at many glasshouses. This find at Mt. Vernon merely substantiates that judgment. I am, further, confident that fragments of the flask under discussion lie buried about several other works in operation between 1825 and 1850.

The fragments found at Keene, I now see, are of the variant having the larger lettering; while those at Mt. Vernon are from flasks bearing the smaller lettering —but not the small lettered variant on which the inscription is reversed.

These Mt. Vernon fragments are oxidized more than those secured at Keene, but when wet show their colors very well. Both olive-amber and olive-green, in all their varying shades, are among these pieces. There seems to be a tendency toward the olive-amber.

STODDARD TYPE INKWELL (*Fig. 5*)

Here is evidence that the three-part-mold blown inkwell

Fig. 6 — THREE-PART-MOLD BLOWN DECANTER AND FRAGMENTS

was a Mt. Vernon product. The patterns are fewer than at Keene, but the variation in color is greater. These pieces show olive-amber, olive-green, and green. The inkwell pictured was found in the vicinity.

FLINT AND OLIVE-GREEN THREE-PART-MOLD BLOWN DECANTER (*Fig. 6*)

The fragments pictured supply clear evidence for attributing this particular pattern to Mt. Vernon. It has long been surmised that such decanters, since they have been found in the locality, were made by a glassmaker in central New York; but precise knowledge of the works that produced them has hitherto been lacking.

They were made in both clear flint and deep olive-green. They invariably have the large, flanged neck, which seems to be quite characteristic of Mt. Vernon. Stoppers were furnished, but were not "ground in" in the three-part-mold pieces that I have encountered.

These stoppers may be seen, in various stages of making, in Figure 7. Some smaller clear flint finials likewise appear in that illustration. Further revelations from my bushel of fragments must be postponed to another month.

(To be continued)

Fig. 7 — FRAGMENTS OF SUNBURST STOPPERS
Showing completed stoppers, stoppers in process, stoppers of other types, finials, and knobs.

Fig. 1 — Mт. Pleasant Town Site in 1927

New York State Glasshouses

Mt. Pleasant

By Harry Hall White

A T THE conclusion of my studies of the Mt. Vernon glass-house site, in 1926, I set out to learn more of the Grangers who had there so successfully operated. I wished, in particular, to establish the date of their departure from Vernon, to verify their founding of the glasshouse at Mt. Pleasant, Saratoga County, New York, and to discover what had been the products of the latter enterprise. My findings are largely the result of correspondence with Mrs. Helen Granger Ely, a daughter of Gideon R. Granger; reference to a genealogical history, *Launcelot Granger*, by James N. Granger, published at Hartford, Connecticut, in 1893, by Case Lockwood and Brainard Company; and communication with various state and government offices and with the older inhabitants of Saratoga and its vicinity.

Nathan Granger was born at Suffield, Connecticut, in 1769. After the Revolution, he came to New York State and married Hannah Monroe of Greenfield, Saratoga County. Later, he removed to Vernon, Oneida County, where, settling as a merchant, he remained until his death, in 1836. He is buried in the cemetery adjoining the site of the Mt. Vernon Glass Works. Of six children born to him, three were boys: Charles, Oscar, and Gideon (*Launcelot Granger*, page 204).

During their boyhood, the most impressive occupation known to these younger Grangers was that of glass-making. In their home town, two glasshouses were in operation: the Oneida Glass Factory, and the Mt. Vernon Glass Works (ᴀɴᴛɪǫᴜᴇs for July and September, 1929). So the boys were apprenticed

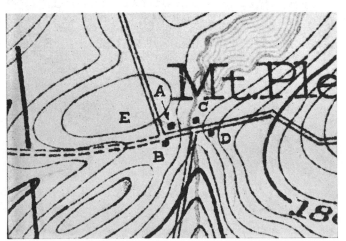

Fig. 2 — Map of Mт. Pleasant
Detail from *Saratoga Quadrangle, New York. U. S. Geological Survey,* edition of June, 1902; reprinted 1929.

to the trade, and eventually became practical glassmakers. But there are no records to show when they became interested in the Mt. Vernon Company. They are not among those listed as the original promoters of the undertaking, nor do their names occur in the notices inserted in local papers for the yearly meetings at which directors were appointed. Eventually, however, I found an advertisement of the works in which C. Granger & Company are given as the proprietors. This C. Granger was Charles Granger, the eldest of the three brothers.

Mrs. Ely writes me that the factory at Vernon was abandoned because of the increasing scarcity of wood fuel. At the time, she was five or six years of age; and, as she was born at Vernon in 1840, this would bring the closing date about 1845 or 1846. This agrees pretty closely with the fact that the last Mt. Vernon advertisement I have been able to find is that of 1843 in the Buffalo *City Directory*. The presence of the Oscar Granger family, in 1834, at Mt. Pleasant, where we have record of an addition to his family, suggests the possibility that this second brother was thus early preparing a new district for the anticipated move from Mt. Vernon. It is not surprising that he selected the fresh location on the forested slopes of Kayaderosseras Mountain in Saratoga County. His mother's former home was in Greenfield Township, in the same county, and the almost limitless supply of fuel in the neighborhood must have been common knowledge to the family.

The older inhabitants about Mt. Pleasant state that the village was settled in 1844.

They add that the proprietors of the glass concern were Oscar Granger, Walter S. Todd, and John W. James, operating under the name of Granger and Company. Mrs. Ely reports that the firm was known as James, Granger, and Todd. Further data are in agreement as to the fact that James and Todd remained in the firm but a short time, leaving the business to Oscar Granger and his nephew, Henry C. Granger, the latter a son of Charles Granger, proprietor of the Mt. Vernon works.

From the James family, the company took title to about 1,400 acres of woodland in the northwest corner of Greenfield Township. The title seems to have passed from John W. James and Sarah B. James to Walter S. Todd and Oscar Granger, in 1846 and 1847 (*County Land Records*, Ballston Spa, New York, Book ZZ, page 245). John W. James and Sarah B. James deed one twelfth of 1,000 acres to Oscar Granger; and, on August 5, 1848, Jessie James and Hannah James deed five twelfths of the same to Granger and Todd. This certainly is more specific than the vague statement in N. B. Sylvester's *History of Saratoga County*, published in 1878, which covers the whole story in the following paragraph:

Fig. 3 — ARCHÆOLOGY IN NORTHERN NEW YORK STATE
Excavations at Mt. Pleasant, 1927.

> About the year 1850, a glass factory was started on the mountain in the north-west part of the town. A little village of about one hundred inhabitants sprang up around it. It was named Mount Pleasant. Some years ago, the factory was moved to Saratoga Springs and the village followed it to its new location.

Communicating with the Bureau of the Census in the Department of Commerce at Washington, D. C., I learned that manufacturing statistics were first gathered in 1810, but that the returns for Saratoga County for that year are missing. Likewise, in the returns for 1820 and 1840, there is no mention of glass-making in Saratoga County. No provision for collecting industrial and manufacturing statistics was made in the census of 1830. Under date of 1850, however, I found:

> The Granger Company of the town of Greenfield, Saratoga County, — Mt. Pleasant is located in Greenfield — had a glass manufacturing plant employing on an average forty men and producing 7,200,000 bottles to the value of $18,000 per year.

Such, then, is the entire result of several years' correspondence with township, county, and state authorities, the Bureau of the Census, and various local historians and elder inhabitants. Nowhere do I find substantiation for the early date of 1801 which several recent writers have given for the establishment of a glasshouse in Saratoga County. N. Hudson Moore, in her *Old Glass, European and American*, is the only one who cites authority for this date. On page 280 of her book, she says:

> In a New York State gazetteer (1860) mention is made of a glass-works being established at Mt. Pleasant, Saratoga County, in 1801.

Yet, though I have examined everything available, from French's encyclopædic *Gazetteer of the State of New York* to the smallest gazetteer and Saratoga guidebook, I have been unable to discover the passage to which Mrs. Moore refers. If data concerning an 1801 glasshouse really exist, they must relate to another venture; not to the one I have under investigation. The facts which I have established are, in short, that the Grangers left Vernon, New York, for Mt. Pleasant, about 1844 or 1845, and, by 1849, were in substantial production — sufficient, at least, to receive recognition in the census reports of 1850.

Many conjectures and speculations might, at this point, be agreeably dwelt upon. Why should a going concern, C. Granger and Company of Vernon, after removal to Mt. Pleasant, New York, accept James and Todd as partners, even though temporarily? Why do we find Oscar Granger the leading spirit instead of Charles Granger, the apparent proprietor at Vernon? But, as suppositions add no value to facts, I shall adhere as closely as possible to the latter. Too much of our glass history is invention born of the necessity, or the eagerness, to meet demands for information, and hence depends more on plausibility than on proof. But one question certainly calls for an answer: what did the Grangers make at Mt. Pleasant?

Twice I have visited the site of their factory — in 1927 and in 1929. The view in Figure 1 gives a good idea of the charm of the locality. It was taken with the camera pointing up the road that leads eastward, over the mountain, to Porters Corners. The road at the left sweeps in from Batchellerville. (See map, *Fig. 2*.) Neither of these roads may be recommended for week-end excursions; they are virtually impassable.

On the corner, at *A* of the map, once stood the hotel and boarding house for glass men. It was known as the *Temperance House*. Here, quite appropriately, in 1884, Henry Ward Beecher addressed the community during his presidential campaign on the Prohibition ticket. Directly across the road, to the south, at *B*, rose the Granger home. From the extent of its stone foundations, I judge it to have been a substantial and pleasing structure, consisting of what was known as "a two story upright with wings." Its windows must have commanded a splendid outlook to the south. Back of the *Temperance House*, and a short distance up the road that leads to Batchellerville, are today the remains of the erstwhile combination church and school building.

Down the Porters Corners road and beyond Black Brook, on the left, a well-constructed building, *C*, still survives, though in advanced stages of ruin. The Granger home was doubtless quite similar to this building, with wings and pleasantly rambling additions. I found even its cellars lathed and plastered, and provided with an outside grade-level entrance toward Black Brook.

Fig. 4 — FRAGMENTS OF MINERAL WATER BOTTLES
Varieties, CLARKE & CO. NEW-YORK and C. W WESTON & CO
SARATOGA N. Y.

In the attic, I picked up several old bottles. At the rear of this house, large barns and stables accommodated the draft horses and oxen, for a glasshouse using wood for fuel was almost as much a lumbering operation as a glass factory. In fact, Mt. Pleasant operated a sawmill and box factory. Across the road from the stables, Archer's Store, *D*, supplied community needs; behind it, Black Brook paused in its flight down the mountain to turn the great wheels which now lie abandoned beside the stonework of the millhouse and penstock of the sawmill and box factory.

From this mill, boxes filled with bottles packed in mountain meadow grass were teamed down the mountain road. I am certain that my readers share my keen curiosity regarding the contents of those boxes.

Fig. 6 — FRAGMENTS OF BOTTLE
Lettered CONGRESS & EMPIRE SPRING CO SARATOGA N. Y. Large C.

I carefully searched all of the old buildings, the old foundations, and such indications of masonry as were visible, for evidences of glassmaking; but without reward. In fact, the only discoverable signs of such operations were a few chunks of slag uncovered in the roadway. Further study of my map revealed the fact that three of the four corners were occupied by buildings, or at least by foundations where buildings had been. These I had explored. The fourth was an empty mountain meadow, or hay field, which lay beyond a hedgerow and an immensely wide stone wall parallel to the Batchellerville road.

This unpromising field proved to be the site of the Mount Pleasant Glasshouse. During a systematic exploration of its topography, I observed a series of low swells or mounds, four or five in number, rather equally spaced along the stone wall. They were entirely too regular to be accidental. Pits sunk into them produced immediate results (*Fig. 3*). During my two visits, with the aid of several assistants, and in spite of the violent objections registered by a

Fig. 5 — SARATOGA MINERAL WATER BOTTLES

swarming population of mosquitoes and deer flies, I succeeded in excavating about a bushel of significant fragments. By significant fragments, I mean pieces showing designs, molded sections, or offhand manipulation. They were in sufficient quantity to enable me to state that the following bottles, flasks, and offhand pieces were part of the Mt. Pleasant product: mineral water bottles; bitters bottles; medicine bottles; chestnut bottles; railroad flask (horse and cart); cornucopia flask; and offhand items — the usual apprentice pieces, trials, and gifts.

MINERAL WATER BOTTLES

Judging by the relative quantity of their discovered fragments, mineral bottles formed a prominent, if not a major, part of the factory output. Several varieties are represented among my finds; but, since I do not collect this type of bottle, I lack complete specimens to illustrate some among them. The fragments in Figure 4 are from bottles like numbers 1 and 2 in Figure 5. In color, they are olive-amber and olive-green. Fragments of the third bottle in Figure 5 are to be seen in Figure 6. This is the later type, with which many are familiar. A similar bottle, but with a variant lettering, is represented by the fragments in Figure 7. I have no complete specimen of this. The inscription is CLARKE & WHITE. NEW YORK, with a large C in the centre. The fourth bottle in Figure 5 has been included here because it is a Saratoga mineral water bottle. I found it, however, on a glass heap at one of the glasshouse sites in South Stoddard, New Hampshire, which was also a large producer of such containers (*Early American Glass*, Rhea Mansfield Knittle. Chapter XLIII). Be not misled by its date, *1767*, which merely commemorates the year when the first white man imbibed Saratoga water for medicinal purposes (*Gazetteer of New York*, by J. H. French, 1860, page 592).

The bottles of Figure 8 are of a period prior to the operation of the Mt. Pleasant works. They are included here since they have a bearing on the subject of Saratoga mineral water bottles. Who made them, I do not know. But they are early, and bear the name of a spring-exploiting company that functioned between 1823 and 1833. The larger one, olive-amber in color, was taken from the

Fig. 7 — FRAGMENTS OF BOTTLE
Lettered CLARKE & WHITE. NEW YORK. Large C.

Note. The methods employed by Mr. White in obtaining information concerning the sites of early American glass factories, and his manner of assuring the correct identification of the products of these various establishments are, in all essentials, similar to the procedure of archæologists who burrow into the débris of the lost cities of Asia Minor or remove the overlying sands which hide the tombs of Egyptian Pharaohs. Carried out for the most part with no recourse to outside aid, and confined largely to sinking pits in promising locations, Mr. White's operations are necessarily conducted on a limited scale and at irregular periods. But, in their way, the results of his delvings are no less momentous than are the achievements of archæologists overseas. The latter group of delvers are performing the spectacular feat of establishing contacts with remote civilizations. Mr. White is doing his bit to give continuity to the history of America's art-industrial development. His is a scholarly undertaking that deserves recognition from scholars. — *The Editor.*

Fig. 8 — SARATOGA MINERAL WATER BOTTLES
Lettered LYNCH & CLARKE NEW YORK. Not made at Mt. Pleasant.

cellar below the Redwood Glass Factory office. But it was not made at Redwood. The smaller one, in olive-green, came from Akron, Ohio.

To afford an idea of the age of these marked specimens I am listing the dates of some of the Saratoga spring companies, taken from Dawson's *Saratoga; its Mineral Waters*, published in New York, in 1874.

CONGRESS SPRING

Lynch & Clarke	1823–33
Clarke & Company	1833–52
Clarke & White	1852–65
Congress & Empire Spring Company	1865–

EMPIRE SPRING

C. W. Weston	1848–61
D. A. Knowlton	1861–63
Saratoga Empire Spring Company	1863–65
Congress & Empire Spring Company	1865–

That persons interested in this branch of bottle collecting may be aided in making identifications, I have shown the mold numbers on the bottoms excavated (*Fig. 9*). All of these pieces are in strong olive-green.

(To be concluded)

Fig. 9 — MOLD MARKS ON THE BOTTOMS OF MT. PLEASANT MINERAL WATER BOTTLES. Numbers from 1 to 5, and letter B.

Fig. 1 — PARTIAL EXCAVATION ON THE MT. PLEASANT SITE

New York State Glasshouses

Mt. Pleasant

By HARRY HALL WHITE

In the July ANTIQUES Mr. White told in detail of his study of the Mt. Pleasant Glasshouse. By gathering information from descendants of the concern's operators, from government records, from genealogical history, and finally from excavations on the site, he has succeeded in piecing together a comprehensive account of the glasshouse's activities. In this issue he considers the various kinds of glassware made at Mt. Pleasant. — *The Editor.*

RAILROAD FLASK

The flask with the horse and cart and the toast *Success to the Railroad* appears to have been an important part of the Mt. Pleasant product. I was surprised and delighted with the large quantity of its remains that I unearthed — far more than I had been able to secure either at Keene or at the Mt. Vernon works. The Mt. Pleasant flask is the usual size, one pint, with obverse and reverse alike (*Fig. 3*).

It is evident that similar molds — those with the

Fig. 2 — FRAGMENTS OF RAILROAD FLASK

smaller, lighter lettering — were used at both Mt. Vernon and Mt. Pleasant. The fragments in Figure 2 are a few selected to show the design and lettering. It is unfortunate that the two glasshouses used the same, or at least similar, molds for so long a period. It is consequently impossible to fix the date when the design was discontinued at one place or the other. Indeed, I can find no differences between the railroad flasks produced at the two places. Their colors may serve to distinguish them, but lack of an

Fig. 3 — RAILROAD FLASK MADE AT MT. PLEASANT
From "Photographic Guide for Bottle Collectors," by H. H. White, 1928

Fig. 4 — CORNUCOPIA FLASK
Excavated at Mt. Pleasant, 1927

Fig. 5 — A Cornucopia Comparison

Left, Mt. Pleasant Cornucopia flask (note wide spot, or flaw, between two centre panels of urn on reverse); *right*, Cornucopia flask without flaw in centre panels. This flask agrees with fragments from Keene.

Flask at the left, from the collection of Ernest W. Young; flask at the right from "Photographic Guide for Bottle Collectors," by Harry Hall White

accurate nomenclature of colors and shades makes such differentiation a poor reliance.

The colors of the Mt. Pleasant fragments, based on the quantity of each excavated, rank as follows: *first*, deep olive-green; *second*, olive-amber; *third*, deep green; *fourth*, light amber. The Mt. Vernon fragments, on the same basis, are as follows: *first*, olive-amber; *second*, olive-green. The olive-green of the Mt. Pleasant pieces is very green; and, of course, all of the four colors occur in an endless number of shades.

CORNUCOPIA FLASK

The symmetrical little cornucopia flask occurs among these fragments in half-pint size only. The usual urn appears on the reverse. This brings me to an experience over which I have never ceased to rejoice. The most pessimistic and hardened addict will, at times, dream of the almost impossible chance of excavating an unbroken specimen. Such a dream came true for me at Mt. Pleasant. From the southwest side of the first mound, I extracted the flask shown in Figure 4. That was in 1927. I must admit that this find was one of the influences that led me to return in 1929. My resurrected flask is in olive-amber glass, very greasy, bubbly, and dark looking, even at its clearest. Its interior is heavily coated with a deposit of lime, some of which likewise clings to the exterior.

I have carefully compared both fragments and complete specimens of the cornucopia flasks from Keene and from Mt. Vernon to discover some characteristic whereby a Mt. Pleasant flask might be surely identified. While many slight variations occur, only one consistently appears in both the fragments and the flasks. The urn on the reverse of the Mt. Pleasant flask and fragments displays a slight widening between the two centre ribs that is not found in the fragments from Keene. Unfortunately,

Fig. 6 — Cornucopia Flask Fragments

Enlarged to show difference between Mt. Pleasant (*left*) and Keene (*right*)

my scraps from Mt. Vernon do not include the particular area containing this wide spot. When more pieces from that factory are available, I may find that, as in the case of the railroad flask, the same or similar molds were in use at Mt. Vernon and Mt. Pleasant.

I have enlarged the fragments the better to demonstrate this wide spot on the three pieces at the left (*Fig. 6*). The two pieces at the right, in the same illustration, are from Keene, and do not have this separation. The reverse of the cornucopia flask (*Fig. 5, left*) quite clearly displays the curious spot between the two central ribs of the urn.

The color or shade of the Mt. Pleasant fragments is nearly always deep olive-green. Almost no olive-amber fragments were found, though the complete specimen I so fortunately excavated is olive-amber.

MEDICINE AND BITTERS BOTTLES

Remains of these bottles among the fragments are quite plentiful, both offhand and molded, lettered and plain (*Fig. 7*). They reveal about the same form as the bottles made at Mt. Vernon. The colors are dark olive-amber, olive-green, and aquamarine. Of the bottles in Figure 11, the first on the left is marked B. FOSGATE'S ANODYNE CORDIAL. This little fellow is pontil-marked, and all the N's are cut backwards in the mold.

The snuff or drug bottle second on the left in Figure 11 is olive-amber. The majority of such bottles were unlettered, and seem to have been produced by every bottle house of the period.

The sarsaparilla bottle made for Doctor Townsend of Albany, New York, is well-known to everyone who has snooped through attics. Heavy and strong, it successfully withstands the crashes that bring more fragile and desirable glass to an untimely end. The specimen in Figure 11 is olive-green; the fragments excavated

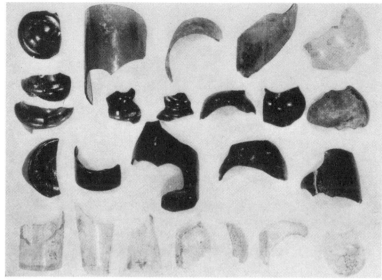

Fig. 7 — FRAGMENTS OF OFFHAND AND MOLDED MEDICINE BOTTLES

Fig. 8 — FRAGMENTS OF CORNU-
COPIA FLASK (*obverse*)

Fig. 9. — FRAGMENTS OF CORNU-
COPIA FLASK (*reverse*)

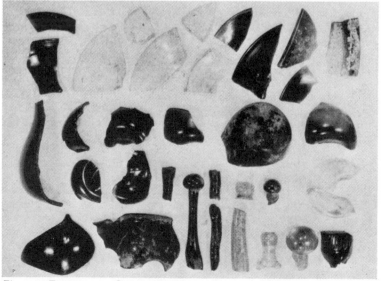

Fig. 10 — FRAGMENTS OF OFFHAND PIECES AND CHESTNUT BOTTLE

are both olive-green and olive-amber. None is pontil-marked.

The fourth bottle in Figure 11 is a choice little aquamarine medicine, as awkward as can be. The fragments show smaller sizes as well (*see lower row in Figure 7*). The fifth bottle was made in an unlettered cylindrical mold, which opened and shut like a flask mold, in two pieces, hinged at the bottom.

The fragments and objects in the lower row of Figure 12 are included here for the sake of their general interest. The first two are of heavy mold-blown glass. One is part of a hexagonal pickle bottle in olive-amber; the other, a heavy bottle or dish with a spherical lower part, approximately eight inches in diameter. This is in olive-green glass. The third fragment is a fraction of a cologne bottle, though I hesitate to state its use, since its color is olive-amber. Those I have seen with a label are aquamarine; in fact one I found in the attic of the boarding house is of this type, but smaller and in aquamarine. These fragments, however, are too insufficient in quantity to justify an authoritative statement that Mt. Pleasant produced them. The other objects in the lower row require no identification.

CHESTNUT BOTTLE

The remains of the sturdy old-time chestnut bottles in this gathering give the collector another milepost. At Mt. Vernon, the high proportion of chestnut bottle fragments offered reasonable evidence of large production of the type. At Mt. Pleasant the case was reversed. I found bits of the chestnut bottle so infrequently as to suggest that the factory soon ceased to make that form. A few fragments are to be seen in Figure 10. It is fair to conclude that when the more rugged mineral water and bitters bottles found favor as general containers, the manufacture of the chestnut bottle gradually declined.

The date 1840 may reasonably be accepted as constituting the latter boundary

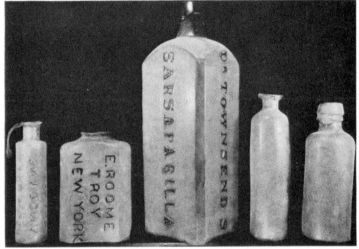

Fig. 11 — TYPES OF MEDICINE BOTTLES MADE AT MT. PLEASANT

of this, one of our most characteristic bottles. Regarding the time of its origin, I have no reliable information. The earliest date I can authoritatively assign is that of the glasshouse of Caspar Wistar, where I have excavated chestnut remains. Fragments are also to be found on the site of the Etna Glasshouse of the Johnsons, in Maryland, which operated about the time of the Revolution. It is stated that, amongst his wide variety and tremendous output, William Henry Stiegel also included chestnut bottles.

OFFHAND PIECES

Offhand glass is the only glass that one may be certain was made at every glasshouse, early or late — and still is made — wherever hand blowing is done. The pieces in Figure 10 are selected from many taken in the Mt. Pleasant finds. They represent dishes of various forms and gathers of glass intended for some decorative purpose. The most interesting item in this group is part of a gather of metal that had been patterned in an open top, vertically ribbed mold.

CONCLUSION

It is my opinion that my accumulation of bits from Mt. Pleasant does not include all of the types of bottles made there; for I believe that my excavations have emphasized the products of the factory's latter years. I have tried to be conservative. Where it is impossible to make a complete excavation, one is liable to be misled into drawing general conclusions from too few pieces. I have found that the ruins of old glass factories are inviting dumping grounds for community rubbish, some of which may easily be mistaken for evidence of local enterprise. But I think that my excavations afford us a safe and adequate conception of the products of the Saratoga Mountain Glasshouse at Mt. Pleasant, New York.

Fig. 12 — FRAGMENTS FOUND AT MT. PLEASANT
Upper row, fragments of sarsaparilla bottle; *lower row*, doubtful objects

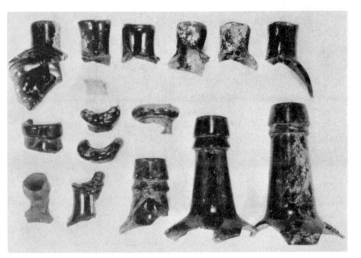

Fig. 13 — TYPES OF NECK FINISH AND COLLARS USED AT MT. PLEASANT
Showing the "general line" of the Mt. Pleasant factory

Fig. 1 — CLEVELAND (NEW YORK) GLASS WORKS (founded 1840)
From an advertisement issued by Caswell (1863–1877)

Fig. 2 — UNION GLASS COMPANY WORKS, CLEVELAND (founded 1851)
Virtually contemporary with the preceding print

The Glass Industry of Cleveland, New York

By MARY E. DAVISON

Illustrations from the author's collection

AT VARIOUS times between the close of the Revolutionary War and the mid-nineteenth century, glassmaking was undertaken in many rural districts of New York State. Several of the more important factories established during the latter part of this period either bordered on or were near Lake Oneida. Among these factories was that of the Cleveland Glass Works, so named because it was located in the village of Cleveland, in the township of Constantia, Oswego County. One James Cleveland, it appears, settled there in 1826, built the first store, and eventually persuaded the government to endow the place with a post office — and to appoint him to the postmastership.

In the year 1840 Anthony Landgraff selected Cleveland as the site of a glassworks. Landgraff was no tyro in the business of glassmaking. Born in Germany, he had come to America in 1812, and soon after his arrival had associated himself with one of the concerns already manufacturing glass in Vernon, Oneida County. Of these there were two: the Oneida Glass Factory Company, whose production was confined to

window glass, and the Mount Vernon Glass Company, which made a large variety of bottles and flasks. Probably Landgraff had gained his American experience with the first-named company. The surmise is suggested by the fact that when, in the mid-1830's, Vernon's wood supply became exhausted, the local bottlemakers migrated to Saratoga County, whereas the window-glass establishment went to Cleveland.

Landgraff's name does not appear among those of the personages who controlled either of the factories at Vernon. Once established in Cleveland, however, he won recognition as a forceful character, active, influential in all public enterprises, and so progressive in his ideas of glassmaking as to be subject to occasional ridicule. Nevertheless, he was a practical glassmaker, and, according to local tradition, made his own furnaces, pots, and many of his glassworking tools.

A booklet, *Historical Souvenir of Cleveland's Best Industry (1903)*, has this to say of Landgraff's works:

The new factory buildings were large and substantial for the times, but the

Fig. 3 — OFFHAND GLASS FROM THE CLEVELAND WORKS
Lilies, darner, dipper, chain; all in bluish aquamarine

melting furnace was only 6 x 8 feet on the inside, and the melting pots a little larger than good sized water buckets. . . . Their capacity was about three-hundred feet of glass, but as both double and single strength was then only half their present thickness, these ancient pots held only about one-hundred and fifty feet. The cylinders ranging all the way from 12 x 18 to 22 x 28 single and about the same double, were mere pigmies by the side of the huge rollers of to-day; but they were opened off-hand without the aid of pole or crane, so that the work was not so very light and easy as it would seem. Each blower gathered, blew, flattened and sometimes cut his own glass, and the tending boys (now gatherers), were merely water boys and roller carriers. In the intervals between blowings, the blower had to cut his own wooden block for blowing up the ball. Those were the days of long fires and many weary hours for the blower; but the wages were good even in those days — averaging more than a dollar a box — and the ways of living simpler and less exacting than now.

The manner of selling glass was in keeping with the character and primitive ways of those early days of small, local and independent manufactories. Oneida Lake was, in the middle of the last century, connected with the Erie Canal by a side-cut, and it was customary during navigation to load a canal boat and peddle [the glass] in the towns and villages along the canal from Troy and Albany to Lockport and Buffalo, often in the way of barter for store goods and other supplies.

The oldtimers of Cleveland tell how in the winter, before the railroad came to the village, the glass was loaded on sleighs and driven across frozen Lake Oneida to the railroad station at Canastota. When the lake ice was unsafe, the sleighs traveled by highway to Camden.

At the beginning of his venture in Cleveland, Landgraff brought his sand by boat from Vernon, but in 1841 he unearthed a sand bed close to his own works. This bed yielded a sand far superior to that which he had formerly been using or could obtain elsewhere, since it imparted exceptional brilliance to the glass of which it was a constituent part. This discovery led to the finding of other beds in the neighborhood and the consequent invasion of Cleveland

Fig. 4 — BOTTLES FROM THE CLEVELAND WORKS
So-called "gimmal," carafe, holster types. The middle item stands 13 inches high

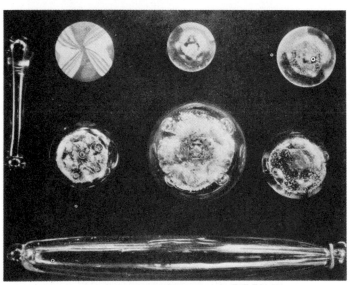

Fig. 5 — PAPERWEIGHTS, ROLLING-PIN, PESTLE
Oddly enough, the paperweights often enclose designs in colored or frosted glass, although produced in a factory specializing in window glass

Fig. 6 — GLASSBLOWERS AT WORK
The book in which this woodcut appears was published in 1836. Methods of glass-blowing, however, have remained virtually unchanged to the present day, and will, doubtless, continue unaltered.
From "The Book of Commerce by Sea and Land," Philadelphia, 1836

by additional glass companies, until the place became the centre of what, until recently, continued to be an important industry.

Incidentally, I may say that, for many years, quantities of Cleveland sand were shipped to distant factories in this country and in Canada, and that the substance still enjoys a considerable market. The metal of the reflecting mirror recently produced at Corning, New York, for Mount Wilson, California, embodies sand obtained in Cleveland.

Anthony Landgraff, with his four sons, Francis, Harmon, Gustavus, and Charles, and a son-in-law, George Cowerden, continued to operate the family glass business until 1861, when it passed into the hands of William Sanders, who, in 1863, sold his holdings to J. Caswell and Crawford Getman. The new owners conducted the plant with ability and success. In 1877 Caswell retired, leaving his long-time partner in control. Getman, who was a shrewd businessman, eventually took over the idle plant of the neighboring Union Glass Company (founded 1851), consolidated its operations with those of the old Landgraff works, and then, in 1889, sold the property to the United Glass Company.

The subsequent history of the plant is brief. After expending large sums to equip the old factory with every facility for making glass, the ambitious new owners found themselves unable to make a profit as well. Accordingly, in 1899 they sold out to the American Window Glass Company, which very soon abandoned the works. An attempt by local residents to resurrect the industry was made in 1902, but proved unsuccessful.

A map of Oswego County published in 1857 indicates three glass-factory sites in Cleveland — that of Anthony Landgraff and Sons (founded 1840), that of the Union Glass Company (founded 1851), and, about three miles to the west, on the lake road at Bernhard's Bay, that of the Empire Glass Company. As already remarked, the Union Glass Company was taken over by a successor to the Landgraffs. The tale of the

Empire venture is yet to be told. Nothing remains of its buildings save crumbling foundations, about which strewn fragments of glass are still in evidence. The land where the Union Factory once stood is now a grass-grown pasture, where browsing kine must pluck carefully to avoid mingling cullet with their cud. A large chimney, no doubt a monument to the defeated hopes of the United Company, towers above the few visible remains of the old Landgraff works. Nevertheless, the broken bits of glass that lie about on every hand testify to the quality of the Landgraff product; for they are even yet brilliant and reveal the limpid bluish-aquamarine hue for which Cleveland glass was famous.

All three companies built homes for their workmen. Some of these structures are standing and occupied today. The old company stores where the workers exchanged paper scrip for various personal and household supplies are no more. But specimens of the old scrip money are treasured by souvenir-minded Clevelanders.

PRODUCT

Apparently the commercial output of the Landgraff works was confined exclusively to window glass. Yet, as was the manner of the time, the workmen were accustomed to occupy their leisure with the making of offhand pieces. These men were, it is said, immigrants from Germany and the Low Countries, skilled in their craft. Thanks to their mode of amusing themselves, many attractive articles of glass passed into local homes to be carefully protected until the persuasiveness of the collector overcame the proprietary instinct. In color the early offhand items are prevailingly of aquamarine, quite strongly bluish in the thicker portions, but paling to a lighter hue where the glass is thinned. Hence it is easy to mistake a Cleveland example for a product of Southern New Jersey.

The old Cleveland workmen made a great variety of offhand things. The most

Fig. 7 — THREE-QUART AND THREE-PINT PITCHERS
The form of these pitchers and the threading of their necks ally them with items from other American factories where German workmen were employed

Fig. 8 — BOWL AND BALL (*Landgraff*); BOTTLE (*late period*)
The bowl has a welted lip

desirable are, of course, the pitchers and bowls (now very hard to find). Large examples of these vessels, as well as large bottles, are similarly finished at the base. Then there were rolling-pins, stocking darners, lilies, balls, chains, and other pleasing but quite useless trinkets, paperweights, and canes. The paperweights must have required the obtaining of special equipment not to be found in a window-glass factory. A specimen in my collection enshrines a varicolored flowerlike form in a body of pale aquamarine. Others reveal frosted motives centred in a deep aquamarine body. One harbors the initial A. and another L., for Anthony Landgraff (*Fig. 5*).

The canes, too, are often as multicolored as a stick of old-fashioned candy. In some instances the bright threads are applied to the surface of the stick, in others they occur as long spirals within. These canes occur in many forms, round, rectangular, hollow, solid. They may be plain or twisted, short or long. A veritable staff fully six feet from end to end is occasionally encountered.

Some offhand pieces were made during the late Cleveland period, after 1889; but they are inferior to their predecessors — paler in tint, lighter in weight, and less robustly attractive in form. I am confining my illustrations, with one exception, to the early and more admirable examples.

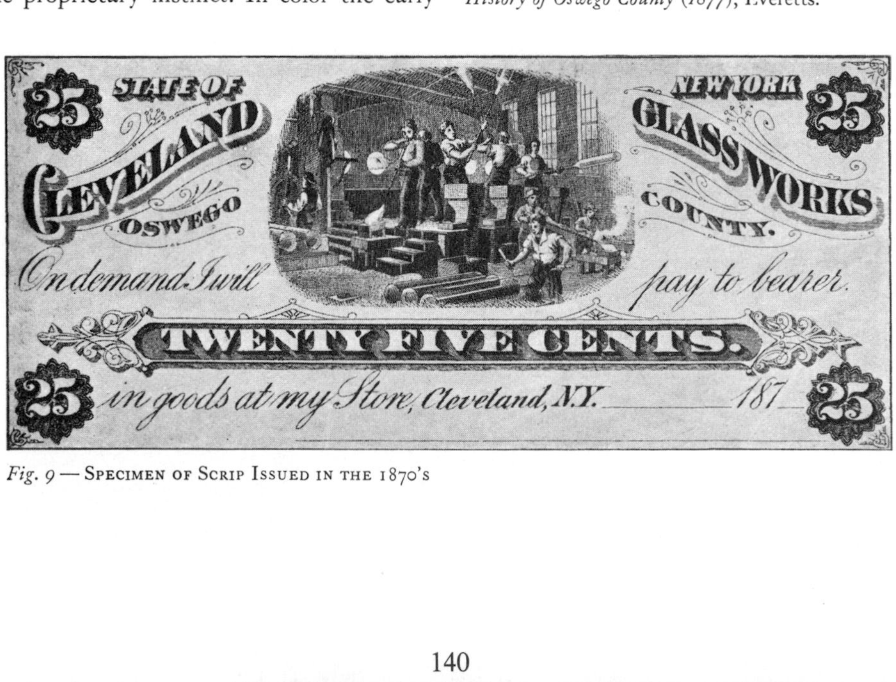

REFERENCES

Gazeteer of New York State, 1860.
The New Topographical Atlas, Oswego County, N. Y. (*1864–1865*).
History of Oswego County (*1877*), Everetts.
Landmarks of Oswego County (*1895*), Churchill.
History of Oneida County, N. Y. (*1878*).
Historical Souvenir of Cleveland (*1903*).
Glassblowers and members of the families of former glassblowers.
Regarding neighboring enterprises, see articles by Harry Hall White, ANTIQUES, July, September, and November 1929; July and September 1930; the Oneida, Utica, Mount Vernon, and Mount Pleasant works are discussed.

Fig. 9 — SPECIMEN OF SCRIP ISSUED IN THE 1870's

THE GLASS OF PETERBORO, NEW YORK

By MARY E. DAVISON

THE history of glassmaking in New York State is not complete without the story of the Peterboro enterprise, one of the earliest of its kind in central New York. The little town of Peterboro is situated in the center of Madison County, bordering on Oneida Creek. Among the pioneers who fought and worked their way into central New York after the Indians were subdued in 1779 was the Goff family from Hartford, Connecticut. According to the Goff genealogy, David Goff and a company of men from Hartford left their homes about 1783 to seek a place in this new country where they might start the manufacture of glass; their chief concern was to find suitable sand and a large supply of wood for the essential fuel. They proceeded up the Mohawk Valley from Albany, and settled in what was then a dense forest and is now known as Peterboro. There they began the making of window glass. Their products were shipped by oxcarts and prairie wagons to the near-by pioneer towns and as far east as Albany.

David Goff was born about 1757. He was honorably discharged from the Continental Army in 1781, and was one of those who survived that famous winter at Valley Forge. After coming to what is now Peterboro, he married a Miss Fowler. The thirteenth of their fourteen children, a son named Lyman, was born in 1805.

Stephen, the son of Lyman Goff and grandson of David, was born in 1833; his son, Ralph, was born in 1865, and is at present living in the old homestead near Merrelsville, not far distant from Peterboro. Ralph Goff remembers as a boy meeting Jerry Hoffman, a glassworker resident near Peterboro who reached the age of ninety-nine years. From him Ralph heard many stories of the early days when Hoffman and his brother and David Goff were making glass in Peterboro. The descendants of Jerry Hoffman kept in their possession for many years a collection of offhand pieces made by the Hoffman brothers.

In 1809 Peter Smith, a prominent promoter in the vicinity, appears on the glassmaking scene. Smith was an extensive landowner and merchant, and it was for him that Peterboro was

PETERBORO GLASS (1783–1830)

Mostly of varying shades of bluish green, except 3, 4, and 5, which are almost clear, and possibly of later date; 11 is likewise light, and filled with salt and bits of colored chintz for decoration. 8 appears broken off at the top but one edge is smooth; evidently an imperfect piece. Another piece almost identical with 6 is in the author's collection.

From the collection of Mrs. Hollis Ingalls

named. He financed a glassmaking enterprise that seems to have either succeeded or superseded the works started by Goff and others. In 1809 he wrote to Albany asking for a copy of the law governing the manufacture of glass; he received it April 17. Apparently he formed a company; letters have been found addressed to Soulden and Smith. Other persons interested in the venture were Smith's son, Peter Skenandoah Smith, Jonathan Turk, Abraham Turk, and R. M. Malcolm. An account of Peterboro glassmaking, given in *Madison County History* by J. E. Smith (*1890*), states that a glass factory was operated by Smith and Solon. Possibly the Soulden addressed in correspondence I have seen was the William Solon mentioned in the account as Smith's partner.

The Peterboro glassworks made cylinder glass in large quantities. At first the manufacturers drew their sand from the shores of Lake Oneida, which was some distance from the factory, but later they found suitable sand much more conveniently located, in Stockbridge.

De Witt Clinton, in his *Journal* for August 10, 1810, mentions a glasshouse operated in the town of Peterborough (old spelling), Madison County, New York, and writes of seeing a three-horse team from Albany loaded with sandstone for a glasshouse in Utica. He says, "The intelligent driver could not tell us from where it came, nor what it was for, nor for what use applied. It is a peculiar kind of sand-stone, infusible, obtained from Bolton, Connecticut, and it is used for the hearths of glass-houses. No other but infusible ones will answer for this purpose. When at Oswego we saw some stones of similar description, which it was supposed would resist fire, and were also intended for a glass-house in Oneida County."

Just what partnerships and reorganizations Smith's firm passed through I am unable to record in full, but contemporary correspondence offers hints that they may have been frequent. A letter from Lawrence Schoolcraft to his son Henry Rowe, dated from Vernon, New York, March 31, 1813, says, "At Peterboro new lords make new laws which causes trouble. Harry Cook was served with a writ while here by the Oneida Co., to gether with one of his bottle-mates, engaged in getting away workmen"; another, dated April 16, says, "Reports from Geneva and Peterborough works are both unfavorable. Disaster follows disaster, until it is difficult to say what will ensue" (quoted by Harry Hall White in ANTIQUES, February 1939, *p. 81*). A letter from Royal Johnson, dated *1814*, asks for his release from the company, offering to take some of his interest in glass stock and to assist "the new company" in any way possible for the sum of $500.

The voluminous correspondence of Peter Smith and his son Gerrit reveals, among other information, the fact that Gerrit Smith continued glassmaking on a larger scale than his father. Gerrit was born in Utica, New York, March 6, 1797; was one of the leading members of the American Anti-Slavery Society; and was elected to Congress in 1852.

December 8, 1819, Smith received a letter from Isaac Ten Eyck of Cazenovia, asking how soon the factory would be in operation, as he wanted some 7 x 9 glass. This glass may have been needed to equip the Ten Eyck mansion at Cazenovia, which was recently demolished. Again in 1819, mention is made of articles taken from the old glass factory to the new factory. So this year, perhaps, marks the beginning of a third period of glassmaking in Peterboro.

Records in Gerrit Smith's handwriting mention "Accounts. etc., pertaining to Glass Factory which I conducted by myself in 1819, 1820, 1821." November 23, 1819, Francis Galligher agreed to work for Gerrit Smith "whenever said Smith or superintendant of the Glass Factory required his services, to be at no expense to G. Smith for his board, liquor or otherwise. His wages ten shillings a day." Other workers were Stephen Bosworth, packer, who was mentioned in 1819; John Elting, stoker and wood-dryer, October 28, 1819; Benjamin Butler, stoker, August 23, 1820; John Pike, master-stoker and mixer, who was to receive $24.00 per month, one third in cash, remainder in goods from the company store — glass at $6.00 per box for 7 x 9, and other goods like wheat and corn at the prices of the day. Pike seemed to be favored, as he was to be given rent-free the best house that was vacant.

In *Blotter No. 1, Book of Charges (1819–1820)*, are at least sixty names of men who were no doubt employed by Gerrit Smith in the glass factory. In the year 1821 some of the workers were Isaac LaGrange; D. Abrahams; A. R. Soggs; John (Fritz) Hoffman, and Jeremiah (Jerry) Hoffman. August 21, 1821, a letter was received from A. S. Schoolcraft asking to work at the factory as an expert cutter, and the name P. (for Peter?) Schoolcraft occurs in connection with the factory. The full story of the Schoolcrafts' glassmaking activities was recounted by Harry Hall White in ANTIQUES for December 1938, *p. 301;* February 1939, *p. 81;* and April 1939, *p. 186.*

Smith purchased his diamond sparks from W. L. De Zing of Geneva, New York, insisting on securing the finest quality. He disposed of his glass through the firm of Trotter and Douglass of Albany, New York, who sold it to retail firms. Large quantities of glass were also sold to P. S. Mills and Company of New York City. In one letter to Smith this firm mentioned some criticism of the texture of the glass, and in a letter of later date they complimented him on the improvement in quality. Again, May 2, 1821, P. S. Mills wrote suggesting that Smith make a large quantity of glass 6 x 8, 10 x 12, and 8 x 10, and that it be free of specks and blisters and as clear white as possible. In the year 1821 the concern was making 750 boxes of glass a month, most of which was delivered to New York. From July 1820 to January 4, 1821, Trotter and Douglass had disposed of $4,788.18 worth of glass for Smith. The prices quoted May 16, 1821, were: 100 feet 7 x 9, $9.00; 10 x 12, $12.00; 8 x 18, $10.00.

Writing to Smith in 1821, Trotter and Douglass complained of bad business, saying they had made no sales of any consequence and had shipped to New York only a few boxes which they had on hand. They said that the Ontario Works and the Rensselaer Glass Works were filling the market with glass said to be of superior quality. In 1825 Gerrit Smith was advertising glass in the current newspapers. How much longer his works continued is not known, but certainly not later than 1830.

I have been able to locate the sites of only two glasshouses in Peterboro. One is but a short distance from the center of the town; all that remains is stone from the foundation and some rotted beams. The other is about two miles out, on what is called the Bliss farm. There a large building may be seen today, presumably part of the last works. I was fortunate to find at both sites some specimens of the glass that verify, as to color, the offhand pieces which have been credited to Peterboro. These offhand pieces, which are very rare, are mostly jars, bottles, deep bowls, or beakers. As far as I know no pitcher has ever been found. The glass here shown was bought by the present owner one piece at a time, over a period of several years, from the descendants of the Hoffman brothers. Another piece, almost identical with *6*, was found in a neighboring town, owned by the family of a former glassblower. Several other offhand specimens survive in a near-by village, but only about sixteen pieces can be safely attributed to Peterboro.

Peterboro glass can be distinguished by its deep bluish-green color. It seems to be much darker than examples from other New York State glasshouses. The bottles, jars, and bowls have pontils, but the entire bottoms of the pieces are rather bumpy and rough.

ACKNOWLEDGMENTS:

Doctor W. Freeman Galpin, Doctor Wharton Miller, Professor W. J. Davison, all of Syracuse University, Syracuse, New York; Mrs. Hollis Ingalls, Peterboro, New York; and Ralph Goff, Hoboken, New York.

REFERENCES:

Correspondence of Peter and Gerrit Smith, Syracuse University
Gazetteer of New York State, J. H. French
History of Madison County, New York, J. E. Smith
Life and Writings of De Witt Clinton, W. W. Campbell.

LANCASTER, NEW YORK, PITCHERS (c. 1850)
A. deep cobalt blue; *B.* aquamarine; *C.* light ultramarine blue; *D.* aquamarine; *E.* bicolored brilliant light turquoise blue with pale cornflower-blue threading. Note the thumb lug on the handles of *A* and *D.*
Pitcher E from the collection of Mrs. Frederick S. Fish; others from the author's collection

Authenticated Lancaster Glass

By ERNEST W. YOUNG

HAVING arranged his business and financial affairs at Lancaster, New York, where for the previous five or six years he had conducted a tavern, William Curtis set forth with his wife and two sons to take up a quarter section of land in southern Michigan. The destination was reached May 30, 1851. Journeying by water to Detroit and thence overland, the family had brought among their worldly possessions some carefully packed mementoes of their former home, cherished objects of the glassblower's art.

The five so-called *lilypad* off-hand blown pitchers shown herewith, together with two additional examples not shown, constitute the rather remarkable remnant of an original lot of eight. Their late owner — youngest son of William Curtis, sixteen years of age at the time of the Michigan migration, ninety years of age at the time of his death in 1925 — clearly remembered that the pitchers had been made by the glassblowers of the newly established glassworks at Lancaster, and that they had been used at parties and other festive occasions in his father's tavern as "creamers" — four blue and four green — placed at intervals down the long table. Whether the elder Curtis, like other Lancaster tradesmen, had been financially interested in Reed Allen Cox & Company, the son was not sure. In any event, he well remembered that the blowers and glassworkers had all boarded at the tavern, and he recalled the obvious pride with which the blowers had furnished the pitchers as chief decorations for the table.

In the accompanying illustration *A* is a deep cobalt blue; *C* a light ultramarine blue; *B* and *D* are aquamarine; while *E* is in the unusual bicolor combination of brilliant light turquoise with pale cornflower-blue threading. The range in height is from just under six to just over eight and one half inches. All exhibit an excellent quality of metal.

Together with the various and usual South Jersey implications

to be found on similar New York State off-hand blown glass, and the rather unusual bicolor combination of one of the pieces illustrated (also an occasional Jersey feature), the discerning glass collector will observe in two of the pitchers the characteristic, though highly infrequent, Jersey thumb lugs upon the upper hilt of the heavily molded handles. Amid all our blown glass there are but few pieces showing this thumb lug. (See Lawton sale, 1923, Number 340, and evidently the same piece in the Girl Scouts Exhibition, pictured in ANTIQUES for February 1930, page 137. A better example, McKearin's sale, 1931, Number 189.)

The detail was doubtless suggested by similar devices used over a long period of time on vessels from which to drink or pour, and in various materials such as pewter, or earthenware. Glass thumb lugs, when found, invariably signalize that coveted naïve vernacular which we have learned to associate with the best and rarest of our early South Jersey creations. Their appearance here is of considerable interest.

With the facts as given, these particular pieces, in contrast with the greater portion of our native blown glass, may, it seems evident, be quite accurately dated. Allowing for the erection of a building and the construction of a furnace and pots — probably started late in 1849 — and permitting some use of the pitchers before the Curtis migration in May 1851, we may feel sure that these pitchers were made in or at one or the other ends of the year 1850. It is not unreasonable to accept them as the work of some among the original eight blowers and other operators who, in 1849, left Pittsburgh to establish a factory in the newly incorporated city of Lancaster, New York.

In addition to whatever inherent interest they possess as pedigreed and dated Lancaster glass, these pieces afford a concrete example of the relative lateness of at least a portion of our socalled "early American glass."

Fig. 1—PITKIN GLASS
Two flasks showing right and left swirling; another, at right, vertical flutes crossed by diagonals. Strong, irregular line of demarcation between neck and body due to an extra coating of molten glass achieved by redipping the object in the melting pot during the process of shaping; evidently to add thickness and strength to the expanded sides of the piece. Inkwells also exhibit swirled decoration. Figured flask (half pint) shows spread eagle and cornucopia. In this size the initials *J.P.F.*, which occur on pint flasks, are omitted

Connecticut Glass

By CHARLES B. GARDNER

DESPITE the fact that several Connecticut glass factories operated successfully over a long period of years, such of their output as survives affords little to the collector of offhand blown glass. Since, however, from the beginning the workmen in these factories concentrated upon the manufacture of bottles and containers of various kinds, we are indebted to these establishments for some of our rarest flasks.

Pitkin

The earliest producing factory of which we know was operated by William and Joseph Pitkin at Manchester, Connecticut, between 1783 and 1830. Its output was in various shades of amber and olive green. From Germany the Pitkins introduced type of flask hitherto not made in this country, using the so-called half-post method in its manufacture. Flasks of this type a today generally known as "Pitkin flasks," despite the fact th virtually identical vessels were later turned out in Keene, Ne Hampshire, while similar forms were made in Ohio (*Fig. 1*).

The original Pitkins were usually both vertically ribbed an swirled, producing somewhat the aspect of corn on a cob. The is no means of distinguishing these Pitkins from the simil flasks made at Keene. In shape, color, and technique the tw products are the same. The Ohio Pitkins are usually large broader at the shoulder, the ribbing and swirls coarser, and t

Fig. 2 — TWO RARE PITKIN FLASKS
Left, pint amber; obverse: *Jared Spencer* on circular band surrounding bull's-eye, above Gothic tracery with quilting; reverse: the same except that circula band shows *Manchester Con. Right*, half pint amber; obverse: star over crossed keys; reverse, *G* framed by Masonic square and compasses.
From the collection of Thomas C. Wayland

Fig. 3 — COVENTRY GLASS
  Flasks: Lafayette; moon,
  star, and hourglass; De
  Witt Clinton; Masonic.
  Inkwells: diamonds
  above flutes; diamonds
  above larger diamonds

olors running from aquamarine to a variety of bright greens.
  Several of our choicest historical flasks must be credited to
this early Connecticut factory. The pint amber flask marked
.P.F. (J. P. Foster) under a spread eagle, reverse horn of plenty
ver *CONN*, and the half pint similarly decorated but unlettered,
re among the rarest (*Fig. 1*). So also is the pint amber flask
arked *Jared Spencer* on a circular band surrounding a bull's-eye
ver a conventional design and quilting; the reverse being the
ame, except marked *Manchester Con*. There are two additional
ariants of this latter flask. Another rare flask attributed to
itkin is the half pint amber, with five-pointed star over crossed
eys; reverse, *G* within Masonic square and compasses.

  A great part of the Pitkin output consisted of demijohns, both
arge and small, jars, and chestnut bottles. The factory's ribbed
nd swirled inkwells, both square and round, are rather unusual
nd hard to find. Of special interest to glass collectors is the fact
hat the ruins of this factory still stand, and are being preserved
y the Orford Parish Chapter, Daughters of the American
evolution, as a memorial to the Pitkin family for active par-
icipation in the struggle for liberty.

Coventry

The Coventry Glass Works, operating in Coventry between
he years 1813 and 1848, is credited with producing the first of

our historical flasks, which was turned out about 1824–1825 to
celebrate General Lafayette's triumphal visit to the United
States. This flask exhibits the bust of Lafayette on one side, while
the reverse portrays De Witt Clinton, at that time governor of
New York State, or, as an alternative, the Masonic arch or the
French liberty cap on a pole under stars. To Coventry likewise is
attributed the rare little half-pint flask bearing a moon and
seven stars suspended above a large five-pointed star, over an
hourglass with Masonic pillars on either side; reverse the same.
At Coventry, as at all the early factories, chestnut bottles, demijohns, inkwells, and snuff bottles were made.

  That patterns similar to the two three-mold inkwells here
illustrated were made at Coventry is attested by fragments
bearing both designs. One of these displays a broad band of
small diamonds covering the upper part of the vessel and separated by a narrow rib from a band of larger diamonds at the base.
The other is characterized by small diamonds, separated by a
narrow rib from a band of vertical flutes. The base is decorated
with concentric circles.

  It is surmised that window glass was also manufactured at
Coventry, but the only evidence to this effect is an aquamarine
Lafayette-Liberty Cap flask indicating that aquamarine glass
was at least attempted here. Amber was the prevailing color
achieved at this Connecticut glass factory.

Fig. 4 — SUNDRY FLASKS
  Left to right: Willington
  eagle; Westford sheaf of
  wheat; Union Glass
  Works, New London;
  New London eagle.
  *Illustrations, except as
  noted, from the author's
  collection*

Fig. 5 (left) — CONNECTI
CUT GLASS
Jars, snuff bottles, demi
john, and chestnut flasks
from various factories

Fig. 6 (below) — "LILY
PAD" JUG ON STEM
Green glass and closely
resembling certain South
Jersey pieces and their
New York State deriva
tives. The rather weak
support appears to be
the only feature indica
tive of relatively late
date. *From the collection
of Meade Minnigerode
Photograph by Duncan*

Willington

The product of the Willington Glass Works (*1815–1872*) is of little interest. Flasks from this factory were decorated with a spread eagle over a wreath, and were produced in quart, pint, and half-pint sizes. Around the ruins of the Willington factory may still be found the fragments of demijohns ranging in size from two quarts to five gallons. Apparently no clear glass was made here, if the lack of fragments of that nature be accepted as proof. The colors ranged from olive green and olive amber to a very brilliant red amber.

Westford

The Westford Glass Works (*1857–1873*) made the common unmarked quart, pint, and half-pint flasks as well as flasks decorated with a sheaf of rye or wheat. The colors were in various shades of amber, and the flasks are not particularly attractive. In his contribution to the glass section of the Girl Scouts Exhibition catalogue, September 1929, George S. McKearin pictures two heavy dark-amber candlesticks of "spool-turned" baluster shape as offhand specimens from Westford.

New London

The New London Glass Works (*1856–1874*), operating under various names, produced not only colored glass but aquamarine in the form of demijohns, jars, and flasks. The factory likewise turned out quantities of patent-medicine bottles. The standing eagle was used, as well as an interesting type of flying eagle.

Despite years of searching, exceptionally few pieces of offhand glass have been found from any of the establishments named. Aside from several pieces of the type in the possession of George S. McKearin, the only examples with which I am familiar were made at New London. One is a handsome sea-green lily-pad pitcher with knopped stem and slightly domed foot, which, were its origin not specifically attested,

would be ascribed to South Jersey. This pitcher was made for one John Ferguson, who was employed near the glass factory, for presentation to Delia Craig, from whose granddaughter the piece was obtained. It is now in the possession of Meade Minnigerode of Essex, Connecticut, to whom I am indebted for the excellent photograph (*Fig. 6*). With the pitcher was found an aquamarine bowl about six inches in diameter and five inches deep. The latter's long association with the pitcher suggests that it derives from the same source.

Fig. 7 — CONNECTICUT
GLASS
Offhand Connecti-
cut articles. The curi-
ous bottle with upper
and lower compart-
ments connected by
tubes is ascribed to
Coventry. The inkwell
is a Pitkin product
blown in a two-part
mold. Three sides ex-
hibit respectively the
initials *J.P.F.*, a bas-
ket of fruit, and an
eagle; the fourth side
is indistinct.
*From the collection of
George S. McKearin*

MORE LIGHT ON COVENTRY AND ITS PRODUCTS

PART I. *"Railroad" Flasks*

By HARRY HALL WHITE

FIG. 1 — COVENTRY-MADE "LOWELL RAILROAD" FLASK. Olive amber or olive green, half pint

FIG. 2 — FRAGMENTS FROM OBVERSE OF COVENTRY "LOWELL RAILROAD" FLASK

THIS is a progress report on what I have been able to discover concerning the glass produced at Coventry, Connecticut, from a study of fragments from that site. Surprisingly enough, no new data regarding the Coventry glassworks have been offered since publication of the facts gathered by local correspondents for Doctor Edwin Atlee Barber forty years ago.[1] These were summarized and well illustrated by Charles B. Gardner in ANTIQUES.[2]

My investigation of Coventry began after my excavation at Keene, New Hampshire, in 1926. Due to peculiar conditions at the Coventry site, I was unable to make a prompt and complete dig. Frequently in country sites there is a large enough deposit of refuse material to warrant a real excavation. At Coventry, however, after the destruction of the furnace the material was dispersed. Stone masons and brick layers came for their portion, while the small rubbish, in accordance with what seems to have been frequent practice, was used to dress and lighten the characteristic heavy loam soil of adjoining fields. On this account, the gathering of enough fragments to form a study of the Coventry product required a long time, many visits, and much patience. The heaviest deposit of usable material was on the Jesse L. Lee Farm. During the operation of the furnace, this property, like much of the adjoining land, was owned by principals of the Coventry company, the Chamberlins, Roots, and Turners. The property surrounding the traditional glasshouse site contained, of course, some suitable material, though the opening of a sand pit spoiled some of my chances there. Nevertheless, in the course of ten or twelve yearly visits, I succeeded, with the aid of the Lee children, in gathering a quantity of fragments. After carefully eliminating contemporary glass, I was able to establish satisfactorily and logically the attributions which follow.

Too great caution cannot be observed in making attributions based on fragments. It is evident that single fragments are accidents, two similar fragments a coincidence. Three or more fragments from one object must be found before even tentative attribution is justified. My conclusions regarding Coventry products

FIG. 3 — COVENTRY-MADE "RAILROAD" FLASK, REVERSED INSCRIPTION. One pint

FIG. 4 — FRAGMENTS OF COVENTRY REVERSED-INSCRIPTION "RAILROAD" FLASK

do not upset any long-established traditions, as some of my excavations have done. Certain groups of flasks have for years been known as New England types,[3] on the basis of provenance as well as of similarity to marked specimens. At last I can offer definite proof of the source.

A high percentage of the so-called *Railroad* series, which to date consists of nine easily recognizable types and variants, was made at Coventry. That the *Lowell Railroad* half pint (*Fig. 1*) was a Coventry product is attested by the fragments shown in Figure 2. Thus a much-studied flask with a considerable bibliography [4] finally finds its home.

The second Coventry *Railroad* flask has the inscription *Success to the Railroad* reversed from the normal placement. It has *Success* above the train (*Figs. 3, 4*). This is one of the rarer flasks of the *Railroad* series. The commonest is the Keene variant,[5] which is readily distinguished by having the largest letter size in the inscription (*Fig. 5*). Examples of this Keene variant occur most frequently in dark glass, in all shades of olive green and amber; in aquamarine are found Keene flasks with lettering nearly identical in form and placement, but showing a definitely lighter cutting in the mold (*Fig. 6*). In these the wagon wheels have an interesting peculiarity. The bottom of the wagon box runs parallel with the horizontal wheel spokes, forming double lines through the wheels. I have not seen this in a Keene dark glass bottle, though it does occur in the "reversed inscription" Coventry flask.

A variation of this so-called normal *Railroad* type, with the same inscription but smaller lettering and

FIG. 5 (*above*) — KEENE, NEW HAMPSHIRE "RAILROAD" FLASK. Identified by large-size letters of inscription. Amber, one pint

FIG. 6 (*left*) — KEENE, NEW HAMPSHIRE "RAILROAD" FLASK. Variant of Figure 5, with lighter-cut lettering. Aquamarine, one pint

FIG. 7 (*above*) — MOUNT VERNON GLASS WORKS, VERNON, NEW YORK, "RAILROAD" FLASK. Identified by smaller, lighter cutting of inscription than on products of other factories. Amber, one pint

FIG. 8 (*below, left*) — COVENTRY-MADE "RAILROAD-EAGLE AND STARS" FLASK. Amber, one pint

FIG. 9 (*below, right*) — FRAGMENTS OF COVENTRY "RAILROAD-EAGLE AND STARS" FLASK

different spacing, is from a mold used at some time at the Mount Vernon Glass Works, Vernon, New York (*Fig. 7*). This flask is frequently found in deep green and amber glass very full of bubbles. After 1844 the Grangers used the mold at Mount Pleasant, Saratoga County, New York.[6] I know of no better way of telling the Mount Vernon product from the Mount Pleasant than by color: the latter is green, the "Saratoga mineral-water bottle green." The Grangers' meal ticket while on Saratoga Mountain was making mineral-water bottles for the Springs. This differentiation is also borne out by the fragments.

The sixth in this series of attractive flasks is also a Coventry product (*Fig. 8*). The obverse has the usual inscription in the usual placement, but the reverse carries a spread eagle lengthwise of the bottle surrounded by seventeen five-pointed stars. Just why the mold cutter decided on seventeen stars is anyone's guess. The fragments show a few stars and several other details (*Fig. 9*).

Another Coventry *Railroad* flask is very like the preceding but shorn of its ornaments, the inscription and stars (*Figs. 10, 11*). This flask occurs in all of the usual Coventry colors but is seldom well blown and clearcut like the variant with inscription and stars. It is generally a strong, heavy bottle.

The so-called *Engine* variant (*Fig. 12*), attributed to Lancaster, New York, because of the frequency of its occurrence in that vicinity, completes the series. This flask is famous for the wide range of colors and shades in which it has been found. Though I was unable to

REFERENCES

1. *American Glassware, Old and New*, Edwin A. Barber
2. Antiques, September 1935, p. 102
3. Antiques, August 1937, p. 65
4. Antiques, February 1923, p. 72
5. Antiques, June 1927, p. 459
6. Antiques, September 1929, p. 195; September 1930, p. 220
7. Antiques, October 1927, p. 300
8. *Antique Fakes and Reproductions*, Ruth Webb Lee (p. 80)

Fig. 10 — Fragments of Coventry "Railroad-Eagle" Flask

Fig. 11 — Coventry-Made "Railroad-Eagle" Flask. Olive green, one pint

find fragments during my search at Lancaster,[7] its attribution is generally accepted.

An illegitimate foreign cousin of these flasks is the reproduction made in Haida, Czechoslovakia, which is available in many colors — aqua, green, amber, blue, and amethyst (*Fig. 13*). It is easily detected by the very prominent serration of the mane on the animal's neck, though this is sometimes removed by equally detectable grinding! The mold was made from an impression of only one side of the Granger mold, whose two sides differ slightly. Another reproduction is that of the *Lowell Railroad*, with either an eagle or Washington bust on the reverse. This flask has been made in New Jersey. Its general dissimilarity to any of the authentic flask groups should brand it as spurious. Since it has been recently exposed,[8] I shall not help to perpetuate it by further illustration.

In order that a check list of the known types and variants of the *Railroad* series of flasks may be available to the collector, I have compiled this study and photographic record. This series presents a rather overlooked field for the glass collector who specializes in flasks. Here the possibilities available to him are extended to include at least twenty different flasks within a single category. I know of no collection which comprises all the flasks in all the distinct color shades.

In addition to these *Railroad* examples which were made at Coventry, my investigation of fragments from the site has revealed that the factory made sundry flasks, historical and otherwise, and a variety of other blown and molded objects. In subsequent issues of Antiques I shall deal with these other Coventry products.

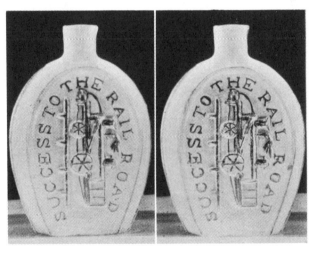

Illustrations from the author's collection

Fig. 12 (*above*) — Lancaster, New York, "Railroad Engine" Flask. Green, one pint

Fig. 13 (*right*) — Czechoslovakian Reproduction "Railroad" Flask. Identified by serrations of animal's mane, and by identical obverse and reverse

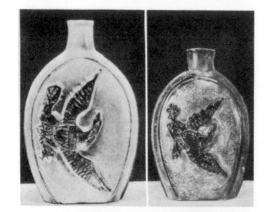

MORE LIGHT ON COVENTRY AND ITS PRODUCTS

FIG. 1—COVENTRY-MADE "SPREAD EAGLE" FLASKS. *Left*, amber, one pint. *Right*, olive green, half pint

PART II. *Flasks Other than "Railroad"*

By HARRY HALL WHITE

FIG. 2 (*below*) — FRAGMENTS OF COVENTRY HALF-PINT "SPREAD EAGLE" FLASK

IN ANTIQUES for October 1940 I told of my investigation of the glasshouse site at Coventry, Connecticut, and began a report of the conclusions regarding the factory's products which I had made from study of fragments excavated there. Of these products, Part I dealt only with flasks in the well-known *Railroad* series. In the present article I shall consider the other flasks made at Coventry.

Two flasks of strong character are the half-pint and the pint *eagle* flasks of Coventry (*Figs. 1, 2*). Both sizes have the spread eagle lengthwise on each side, obverse and reverse alike.

A pair of flasks that date from the Presidential campaign of General Andrew Jackson was made at Coventry. The half-pint size (*Fig. 3, left*) bears bas-relief profiles of Jackson and Washington, Jackson facing left and Washington facing right. On the pint size (*Fig. 3, right*), Andrew still faces left and George has followed his example. The cutting of these molds is shallow and the design on the

FIG. 3 (*right*) — COVENTRY-MADE "WASHINGTON-JACKSON" FLASKS. *Left*, amber, half pint. *Right*, amber, one pint. Identified by small lettering of inscriptions

FIG. 4 (*below*) — FRAGMENTS OF COVENTRY "WASHINGTON-JACKSON" FLASKS. *Left*, half-pint fragments. *Right*, pint fragments

FIG. 5 — KEENE, NEW HAMPSHIRE, VERSION OF PINT "WASHINGTON-JACKSON" FLASK. Note larger lettering than in Coventry analogue

the rounded outer ends of the sunburst rays (*Fig. 14*). The half-pint sunburst flask with rounded-end rays, while undoubtedly made at Conventry, did not show up in my gathering of fragments. However, fragments were found of a half pint with the rays sheared off more abruptly (*Fig. 15*).

A sunburst flask of different type was made at Mount Vernon (*Fig. 17*). When I first excavated there I found a few fragments but hesitated to make attribution (see ANTIQUES, November 1929, p. 394). By continued search I have since found confirming fragments. The flask is notable for its weight.

One of the joys of collecting flasks is the discovery of a rare known variation of an old flask. An even greater exhilaration comes to the discoverer of a new and unknown variant. Extended descriptions of differences between variants fail to give the details easily shown by photography. For that reason I have sought for brevity of text and offer instead as clear a guide to Coventry flasks and their analogues as the arts of photography and photo-engraving permit. In a subsequent article I shall consider Coventry products other than flasks.

fragments is consequently in low relief, so that details are nearly lost in Figure 3. The version of this flask made at Keene, New Hampshire (*Fig. 5*), is readily distinguished by the larger lettering of the inscriptions.

It is pleasant to find that the old favorite shown in Figure 6 was made at Coventry. The generous supply left for collectors indicates that it must have been made at other glasshouses as well, though I have been unable to find variants of this mold of the pint *cornucopia-urn*. The fragments show the designs with unusual clearness (*Fig. 7*). I found fragments of the half pint as well (*Figs. 8, 9*). This is a very charming little flask, and fortunately a quantity survives.

FIG. 6 (*below, left*) — COVENTRY-MADE "CORNUCOPIA-URN" FLASK. Amber, one pint

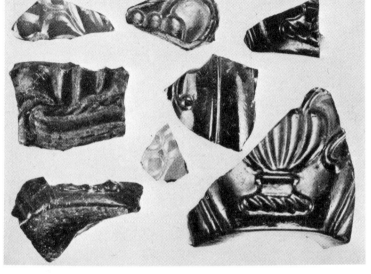

FIG. 7 (*above*) — FRAGMENTS OF COVENTRY PINT "CORNUCOPIA-URN" FLASK

FIG. 8 (*left*) — COVENTRY-MADE "CORNUCOPIA-URN" FLASK. Amber, half pint

FIG. 9 (*below*) — FRAGMENTS OF COVENTRY HALF-PINT "CORNUCOPIA-URN" FLASK

There is a long series of variants in this size, possibly eight or ten that I have segregated; some day I intend to unravel the tangle with the help of my fragments, and find out where else they were made.

Of course I found fragments of the marked Coventry flasks, the pint and half-pint *Lafayette-DeWitt Clinton* and the half-pint *Lafayette* (*Figs. 10, 12*). There are fragments of both in Figure 11, as well as some *Masonic* fragments, but not enough of the latter for me to determine accurately the entire design or to be certain that they were not just stray pieces.

New England produced a large crop of so-called *sunburst* flasks. A few were marked, such as the two Keene sizes, pint and half pint (*Fig. 13*). (See ANTIQUES, June 1927, p. 459.) But at Coventry accurate identification had to await analysis of the fragments (*Fig. 16*). The pint size matches the fragments; note

226

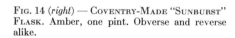

FIG. 10 (*above*) — COVENTRY-MADE "LAFAYETTE-DE WITT CLINTON" FLASK. Amber, one pint

FIG. 11 (*above, right*) — FRAGMENTS OF "LAFAYETTE-DE WITT CLINTON" AND "MASONIC" FLASKS. Found at Coventry

FIG. 12 (*right*) — COVENTRY-MADE "LAFAYETTE-DeWITT CLINTON" FLASKS. Aquamarine and olive green, half pint

FIG. 13 (*below*) — KEENE, NEW HAMPSHIRE, "SUNBURST" FLASKS. Olive green, half pint

FIG. 14 (*right*) — COVENTRY-MADE "SUNBURST" FLASK. Amber, one pint. Obverse and reverse alike.

FIG. 15 (*extreme right*) — COVENTRY-MADE "SUNBURST" FLASK. Olive green, half pint. Obverse and reverse alike

FIG. 16 (*below, left*) — FRAGMENTS OF COVENTRY "SUNBURST" FLASKS

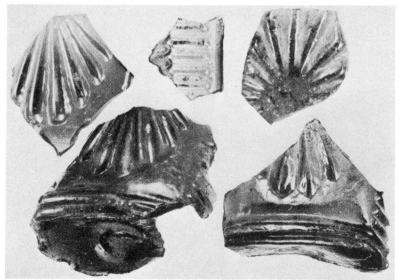

Illustrations from the author's collection; photographs by the author

FIG. 17 (*right*) — MOUNT VERNON GLASS WORKS, VERNON, NEW YORK, "SUNBURST" FLASK. Green, one pint, obverse and reverse alike. Frequently noted for its unusual weight

MORE LIGHT ON COVENTRY AND ITS PRODUCTS

PART III. *Miscellaneous Products*

By HARRY HALL WHITE

Editor's Note. This is the conclusion of Mr. White's report on the products of the glasshouse operated at Coventry, Connecticut, from 1813 to 1842. His attributions and analysis of Coventry glass are based on study of fragments that he excavated on the factory site. Parts I and II, on Coventry products, appeared in ANTIQUES for October and November 1940, and dealt with "railroad" and other flasks.

Except as noted, illustrations from the author's collection

SOME of the most interesting of New England glass products — quite unappreciated by the collecting fraternity — are the fascinating little inkwells blown in three-part molds. Long known as "Stoddard inkwells," they are now generally designated simply as "three-mold inkwells," on the evidence of my discoveries at Keene in 1923–1926. They are known to have been made at both Keene and Vernon (see ANTIQUES, June 1927, p. 462; November 1929, p. 394). Now the glassworks at Coventry, Connecticut, may be added as a source.

Figure 1 shows what I call Coventry Type I. This well has the conventional diamond pattern, with vertical reeding or ribbing below, and a plain base. It has no pattern between the upper edge of the diamonds and the flange about the opening. I have it in one size only, two and one half inches in diameter.

My Coventry Type II (*Fig. 2*) is a similar well but has five concentric rings on the base, counting the outside ring. Moreover, it has ribbing on the top, between the edge of the diamond pattern and the edge of the opening flange. I count forty-nine ribs in the small, two and one half-inch size. In the larger well of two and three quarter-inch diameter, the pattern is similar but the base rings are faint. The reeding or ribbing about the top face has a count of fifty-five or fifty-six, with one very wide rib at one of the three-mold marks.

The Coventry Type III has a slightly different pattern, or combination of diamond patterns (*Fig. 3*). The usual band of small diamonds is spread above a narrow band of larger diamonds which number fifteen at the base circumference. It has a plain base and plain top.

Here are three unmistakable Coventry patterns. To show the

FIG. 1 — COVENTRY TYPE I THREE-MOLD INKWELL

FIG. 2 — COVENTRY TYPE II THREE-MOLD INKWELL

FIG. 3 — COVENTRY TYPE III THREE-MOLD INKWELL

FIG. 4 (*below*) — FRAGMENTS OF KEENE, NEW HAMPSHIRE, THREE-MOLD INKWELLS. *Left group*, Keene Types I and II. *Center group*, Keene Type III. *Right group*, Keene Type IV

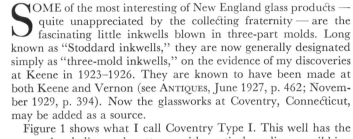

FEBRUARY 1941

79

153

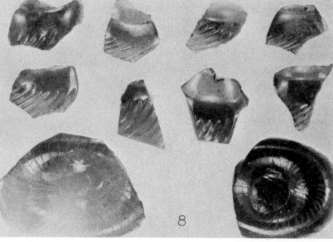

mold errors, cracks, breaks, and slight differences, on whose basis the minor variants may be catalogued. Search for such fine points adds immeasurably to the fascination of collecting these charming pieces.

Coventry also made inkwells of the so-called *Pitkin* type, more correctly termed the *half post* pattern-mold type (*Fig. 5*). That they were made in both right and left twist is evidenced by the fragments (*Fig. 6*).

Probably the term *half post* deserves explanation. This type of patterning was a German process, and was indeed sometimes called the German Method, while *half post* was possibly a more technical term used by the blowers themselves (*Encyclopædia Britannica*, 9th ed., p. 673). The gather of glass on a blowing iron was called a post, particularly after it had been shaped on the marver. A second gather of a partial coating of glass, extending as far as the neck, was called a half post. The edge of this coating gave the neck the appearance of having been inserted into the body of the piece, which gave rise to the incorrect expression, "inserted neck."

Flasks as well as inkwells were among the half-post products of Coventry, with both left and right swirling in plain and

FIG. 5 — COVENTRY-MADE HALF-POST AND PATTERN-MOLD INKWELLS. *From the collection of Charles B. Gardner*

FIG. 6 — FRAGMENTS OF COVENTRY INKWELLS MADE BY HALF-POST AND PATTERN-MOLD METHOD. Swirled and broken-rib patterns

FIG. 7 — FRAGMENTS OF COVENTRY LEFT-SWIRLED HALF-POST FLASK

FIG. 8 — FRAGMENTS OF COVENTRY RIGHT-SWIRLED HALF-POST FLASK

FIG. 9 (*below*) — COVENTRY-MADE HALF-POST BROKEN-RIB POCKET BOTTLE

differences between these and the Keene three-mold wells, let us review the latter (*Fig. 4*). Keene Type I has the conventional pattern, but has fourteen diamonds in the base circumference, is two and three quarters of an inch in diameter, and has a ribbed top face with forty-two ribs. Keene Type II is similar in pattern to Type I but has sixteen diamonds in the base circumference, is only two inches in diameter, and has thirty-eight top-face ribs. I have found this type in clear glass with standing neck. Keene Type III has a different pattern — four small diamonds in a square, with nine of these squares in the circumference; it has a plain base and a ribbed top face with forty-eight ribs; it is two and three eighths inches in diameter. Keene Type IV has the usual diamond pattern and ribbing below, while the base is patterned with ribs diverging from the punty to an outside ring or circular rib.

These, then, are the principal three-mold patterns of inkwells as made at Keene and Coventry. Collectors will eventually find

broken-rib patterns (*Figs. 7, 8, 9*). The majority were patterned with thirty-six ribs.

The balance of Coventry's products are what I have found, through excavation of many sites, to be those of the usual country glass-house — primitive types of offhand and molded utilitarian glass for the use of the homestead, the pharmacy, and the manufacturer of various liquids:

The omnipresent chestnut bottle (*Figs. 10, 11*).

Snuff bottles and jars, in half-pound, pound, and larger sizes. The majority

FIG. 10 — COVENTRY TYPE CHESTNUT BOTTLES

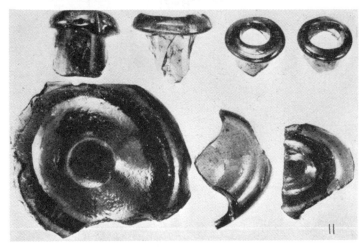

FIG. 11 — FRAGMENTS OF COVENTRY CHESTNUT BOTTLES. Half a peck of such fragments were found

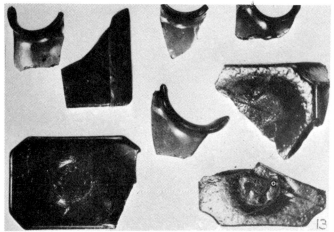

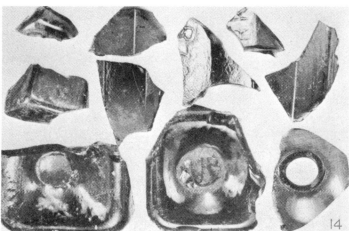

FIG. 12 (below) — COVENTRY TYPE SNUFF BOTTLES

FIG. 13 (above) — FRAGMENTS OF COVENTRY HALF-POUND SNUFF BOTTLE

FIG. 14 — FRAGMENTS OF COVENTRY POUND SNUFF BOTTLE, LETTERED

FIG. 15 — COVENTRY-MADE BOTTLE FOR "SWAIM'S PANACEA"

FIG. 16 — FRAGMENTS OF COVENTRY BOTTLE FOR "SWAIM'S PANACEA"

were plain, to carry a paper label (*Figs. 12, 13*), but some were blown in lettered molds (*Fig. 14*).

Bottles for "Swaim's Panacea," one of the numerous patent medicines and nostrums popular between 1825 and 1835 as a cure for all ailments (*Figs. 15, 16*).

Quantities of "drug store" cylindrical bottles, both offhand and molded (*Fig. 17*). These had neck finishes of three kinds: plain small flange, single serrated collar, and double serrated collar. I found fragments in three diameters: 1 ¼, 1 ⅝, and 2 ¼ inches.

The square shoe blacking or varnish bottle (*Fig. 18*), a constant product of New England glasshouses, including Coventry. The fragments indicate two sizes: 1 ½ and 1 ¾ inches wide.

Since the Coventry works operated over a long period (*1813–1842*), we are not surprised to find a wide variation in the types of neck finishing. The fragments (*Fig. 19*) reveal everything from the plain neck of a flask and varnish bottle to the rolled neck on snuff and drug bottles, the early flange, and the fully formed collar of one or two serrations or ridges.

Finally I come to the most difficult of all glasshouse material to classify, the offhand-blown material. Seldom do I find enough fragments so that I can reconstruct the complete form of an object. Nevertheless, the fragments of Coventry offhand are informative. They definitely show the threaded rim, the folded or reamed edge, and the plain, slightly thickened edge. Jars and pitchers seem to predominate. Figure 20 shows the bulbous column of a fine candlestick and a few patterned twists and pitcher handles. The glass from Coventry's pots covers a very wide color range of amber, green, olive green, olive amber, and aquamarine. Thus the collector may hope to find Coventry-made rarities in any of these shades.

FIG. 17 — FRAGMENTS OF COVENTRY CYLINDRICAL BOTTLES
FIG. 18 — COVENTRY-MADE SHOE BLACKING BOTTLES
FIG. 19 — FRAGMENTS FOUND AT COVENTRY. Showing wide range of neck finishes
FIG. 20 — FRAGMENTS OF OFFHAND-BLOWN OBJECTS MADE AT COVENTRY

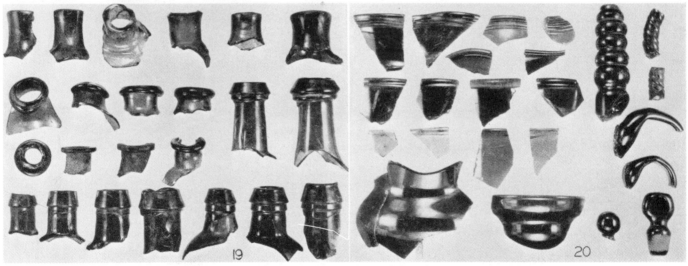

Keene, New Hampshire

By HARRY HALL WHITE

Illustrations from the author's collection

I. EXCAVATION AND DISCOVERY

FROM the standpoint of possible discovery, the site of an old glass factory occupies, in my mind, relatively the same position as an old attic. The uncertainty and the chance of unexpected revelations of treasure exercise a constant lure. In the exploration of an old factory location, one, and only one thing, is certain, namely: that the fragments of glass remaining there from the days of early activity are permanent and unchanging records. The timber of structures will decay, and metal work will corrode almost be-

Fig. 1 — FRAGMENTS OF KEENE "SUCCESS TO THE RAILROAD" FLASK, *(large lettering)*
The fragment in the lower left-hand corner is aquamarine glass.

yond recognition, but the bright fragments of the products of the place are certain to tell a truthful story.

Some sites are not accessible: one that I know of is now occupied by a railroad station, another by a business block, while a third has been washed away by the changing course of a river, forever denying the explorer the joy of discovery. Keene, however, offers happy exception to such melancholy cases. In consequence, while visiting that New Hampshire city, in March, 1925, I made enquiry regarding the sites of the old glasshouses.

Fig. 2 — TYPE OF "SUCCESS TO THE RAILROAD" FLASK, *(one pint, olive-amber)*

There were, once upon a time, as every collector knows, two prominent glass factories in Keene, the New Hampshire and the Keene Glass Works. A third works is reported to have been in operation for a short time, but I did not attempt to locate its site, which is recorded to have been on Gilsum Road. Instead, I devoted my time to the remains of the other two establishments.

The New Hampshire Glass Works was situated at the joining of Washington Street and Gilsum Road, on property since used, in part, by the city for its jail. While the history of this factory is common knowledge, its products, other than window glass, are little known. An examination of the gardens and open places about this old location failed to bring forth anything but specimens of aquamarine glass. These consisted entirely of fragments of window glass, drippings, pieces broken from blowpipes. Pieces of the old glass pots were also found. Nothing appeared to show that the works had ever made bottles or flasks.

This dearth of material, however, should not be accepted as conclusive evidence that the New Hampshire Glass Works confined itself exclusively to window glass. The discovery of the refuse dump may unfold another story.

The Keene Glass Works, on Marlboro Street, at one time operated by the well-known concern Perry and Wood, I next visited.* Fortunately, owing to the season, the gardens about this spot were practically free from vegetation, and the washing of spring rains had revealed a number of specimens of the broken product. After searching the grounds and securing a quantity of fragments, I bethought me to raise the floor of the barn on the premises, where, in days past, much refuse glass had been dumped. Here I found a mass of fragments firmly held in ice and frozen mud which the spring warmth had not yet thawed. I had to leave them there; any heat that I might have applied would have shattered them.

*For notes on this factory see ANTIQUES, Vol. V, p. 69.

September came before I was able to return. Meanwhile the old barn had been torn down; but an interested friend had saved the precious junk. This I added to my collection. To make more certain, I sunk several pits to the level of the original grade near the old works, and secured many good pieces, all confirming the indications of the material taken from the surface.

As may be surmised, great caution must be observed in drawing conclusion from such evidences. There is always the possibility of mistaking the refuse of subsequent generations for the product of the original occupant of a site. Experience and observation must safeguard against that. On the part of the research amateur there exists too strong a desire — if I may speak frankly — to *discover* something — new facts, startling ideas. The seeming necessity of discovery should not run away with good judgment.

II. The Nature of the Find

When my gathering of fragments was finally assembled, washed, and spread out for examination, I at once realised that something unexpected lay before me. After eliminating all doubtful pieces, and retaining only specimens sufficiently oxidized to carry assurance of age, or bearing recognisable decoration, I found, along with the well-known and accepted varieties of Keene glass, fragments of the following:

1. *Stoddard Type* inkwell.
2. *Pitkin Type* flask.
3. *Success to the Railroad* flask.
4. *Eagle-Cornucopia* flask.
5. *Urn-Cornucopia* flask.
6. *Eagle-Masonic N. E. G. Co.*, flask.
7. *Washington Portrait* flask.

Can a greater surprise be imagined? Before any conclusion could be drawn from these telltale fragments, many possibilities were to be considered. A workman at this glasshouse might have thrown away a broken flask of personal use, or my specimen might represent sample flasks discarded by the works. But the *quantity* of the specimens argued against either of these possibilities. I also discovered, upon further study, that these pieces were from flasks that had never been used; their bottoms were without wear. Evidently they were mainly from imperfect flasks, flasks not well blown — too thin at the shoulder, too thick at the base — and represented poor distribution on the part of the

gatherer. Then the possibility that these fragments were cullet* from other factories presented itself. But their shades of color matched those of known Keene examples too closely to admit of that hypothesis.

Even the most conservative doubter must, I think, admit that I had sufficient evidence before me to conclude that all these pieces represented types that, at some time, had been made at Keene.

III. Early Designations Faulty

Hitherto I had been content to accept the designations of these objects as they had been applied by early students of American glassware. Like the average collector, engrossed with accumulating types and their variations, I had given little thought to the accuracy of my information. We do not know the grounds upon which Dr. Barber and others long ago attributed the specimens of my recent discovery to Kensington, Coventry and Stoddard. It seems quite possible, however, since all are unmarked pieces, that such attributions were based upon hastily observed resemblances, or on memory, which offer the most unreliable evidence imaginable. In the case of glass, furthermore, the mere circumstance of similarity between an unmarked and a marked piece is far from giving proof of identical manufacture.

IV. Similar Flasks from Different Factories

Consider the matter of the popular type of *Scroll* flask. I have established the fact that this flask was made both at Louisville, Kentucky, and at Lancaster, New York, during the same period, — approximately 1850. While these flasks varied slightly in detail, the type remained the same. Other variants of this same type have since been found *marked* as the product of Pittsburgh and Wheeling factories.

Again, of the one pint *Eagle-Agriculture* flasks, one kind is marked *T. W. D.*, while the other is marked *J. Shepard & Co., Zanesville, Ohio.* Obviously Dr. Dyott and the Reverend Shepard purchased their molds from the same source. If an example of either of these flasks was found unmarked, it might easily be attributed to the wrong maker. Yet again, consider the long series of bottles, or decanters, of the *Jenny Lind* type. Their

Fig. 3 — Fragments of Two Types of Keene Sunburst Flasks
Among these fragments are pieces of a half-pint Perry and Wood, an aquamarine fragment of the same type, and pieces of a flask of a different variety, whose rays divide some distance from the center.

Fig. 4 — Keene Sunburst Flasks

*Broken glass from any source was purchased by early factories from itinerant peddlers and junk men and remelted. Such broken glass was called cullet.

molds are strikingly similar, but we all know that the flasks themselves were made at several different factories.

It becomes increasingly clear that molds of like type were in use in a number of different glasshouses during the same period. The early glassmakers were eager to take advantage of every popular type of flask to increase their sales. It was, without doubt, in those days quite as costly to express individuality and to attempt to educate the buyer to a new product as it is today; and I am certain that the manufacturers of the old time were not blessed, or cursed, with the dominating influence of high pressure advertising campaigns.

V. The Railroad Flask

Returning to the Keene fragments: Figure 1 shows several pieces from a *Success to the Railroad* flask, with horse-drawn cart. Of this type of flask as it was produced in different places there are, all told, six variants, as follows:

1. *The large lettering.*
2. *The smaller lettering.*
3. *The smaller lettering reversed.*
4. *The smaller lettering with eagle and stars on the reverse.*
5. *The horse and cart on the obverse, eagle on the reverse, without stars or lettering.*
6. *The horse and cart on the obverse and reverse without letting.*

Such flasks are found in many shades of several colors. *They surely were not the product of a single glasshouse.* But the molds are sufficiently alike in detail to suggest that they were all cut by the same moldmaker, or, at least, in the same shop. *The fragments found at Keene are from the variety having the large lettering (Figs. 1 and 2). These show three general colors—aquamarine, amber,* and *olive-amber.*

VI. The Sunburst Flask

The *Sunburst* type also develops a number of varieties representing different factories. Some of the molds for this pat-

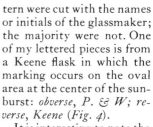

tern were cut with the names or initials of the glassmaker; the majority were not. One of my lettered pieces is from a Keene flask in which the marking occurs on the oval area at the center of the sunburst: *obverse, P. & W; reverse, Keene (Fig. 4).*

It is interesting to note the difficulty encountered by the mold cutter in getting the entire word *Keene* within the oval. Due to an error in judging the spacing of the letters, the final E is tacked to the letter N. This is best observed in the one pint size.

Among my fragments (*Fig. 3*) I found two varieties and three shades of the *Sunburst* flask: (1) the variety in which the rays diverge from the center in single lines; and (2) the variety in which

Fig. 5 — Fragments
a Fragment of Washington Portrait Flask (Amber).
b Fragment of Cornucopia Flask (Aquamarine).

the rays divide at some distance from the center. Two colors are present, amber and aquamarine, with the usual two shades of amber.

VII. Washington-Jackson — Eagle-Cornucopia — Urn-Cornucopia Flasks

Fragments of a portrait flask were found that check very closely with the Washington side of the *Washington-*

Fig. 6 — Eagle-Cornucopia Flask
Fragments of this type were found at Keene.

Jackson flask, in one pint amber (*Fig. 5*). The *Eagle-Cornucopia* one pint (*Fig. 6*), and the *Urn-Cornucopia* half-pint flask (*Figs. 7 and 8*) also occur in these specimens. All of these designs have long been attributed to various makers. Here, for the first time, I have found concrete evidence as to their place of manufacture. *This does not mean, how-*

Fig. 7 — Fragments of Urn-Cornucopia Flask (*half pint*)

Fig. 10 — FRAGMENTS OF "STODDARD TYPE" INKWELL
Fragments of inkwells showing five variations.

ever, *that they were made at Keene only.*

VIII. EAGLE-MASONIC FLASKS

Several varieties of the *Eagle-Masonic* flasks occur among my fragments. They are the well-known one pint amber *Keene-Masonic* flask, the half-pint amber *Eagle-Masonic* flask (*Fig. 9*), long suspected of being a product of the Keene works, and the pint amber *Eagle-Masonic* flask with five vertical ribs at the edge, marked *N. E. G. Co.* This lettering is quite faint on the fragments and is usually faint on the complete flasks. This has led to the readings— *N. F. C., N. E. G.*

IX. KEENE AND BOSTON AFFILIATIONS

The presence of fragments bearing initials of the New England Glass Company — *a Boston concern* — gave me pause, until I became better acquainted with the history of that company. It is recorded that they were glass cutters and makers of fine flint glass. They made both blown and pressed ware; their product and their reputation were both far removed from such a common article as an amber pocket flask.

Then I learned that the New England Glass Company is reported to have had affiliations with a Keene glasshouse at some period. I have not been able to verify this report; but it seems fair to infer, at least, that the Keene Glass Works made flasks for the New England Glass Company. My fragments of the type presumably made are in deep amber only. Since the flask is known in various shades of amber, aquamarine, and clear glass, it seems not improbable that Keene may have made the amber and aquamarine items and the New England Glass Company those in clear glass.

X. "STODDARD" INKWELLS

The inkwells of which I found fragments have heretofore been credited to the glasshouses at Stoddard, New Hampshire. Of the five varieties shown

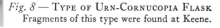

Fig. 11 — BROKEN AND PARTIALLY BLOWN PIECES OF DECANTERS

(*Fig. 10*), one is an offhand piece, another is pattern-molded after the manner of a *Pitkin* type flask, while the remaining three were blown in ornamented molds which, when opened, divided into three parts — a necessity, you observe, when an object having a circular cross-section was blown in a mold in which the ornamental design was deeply cut.

This last, loosely termed *three-mold glass,* is believed to have been the product of the general period 1815 to 1840; though these dates are not exact. I have authentic information concerning a three-part-mold decanter made in Ohio in 1821; also I have seen a three-part-mold syrup mug, fitted with a pewter hinged cap, on which was cast the inscription *PAT. 1855.* However that may be, the feeling exists among the best informed as to this particular branch of American glass that the three-part-molded inkwell was not a regular product of American glasshouses much after 1840.

Accepting this opinion as sound, without other evidence, it would seem, from the dates of the Stoddard glasshouses, that the patterned inkwells cannot have been made in those establishments. Stoddard's first works operated in a feeble manner subsequent to 1842, but several fresh starts and reorganizations were necessary before they really got under way in 1850. However, as for Stoddard, this is pure speculation; time will tell the story. I am certain that Keene *did* make these delightful little inkwells in many patterns and sizes. They vary considerably in finish at the neck, as this part of their marking was an offhand operation allowing some latitude for the individu-

Fig. 8 — TYPE OF URN-CORNUCOPIA FLASK
Fragments of this type were found at Keene.

ality of the finisher. The Keene Glass Works is, without doubt, but one of several works of the period that made such inkwells.

XI. PITKIN TYPE FLASKS

An attractive type of decanter appears among the fragments of Figure 11. The partially blown piece in the upper right-hand corner is an excellent example of the pattern impressed on a "gather" of

Fig. 9 — EAGLE-MASONIC FLASK (*half pint*)
The finding of fragments of this pattern at Keene indicates one place of its manufacture.

Fig. 12 — FRAGMENTS OF PITKIN TYPE FLASKS, FOUND AT KEENE

XII. SNUFF BOTTLES

The snuff bottle seems to have been a common product of this glasshouse. The colors appear to have been the usual shades of amber and olive amber.

I have included an illustration showing the varieties of neck finish found among these fragments. (*Fig. 14*). Among them will be recognized the necks of the snuff bottle, and of the flask with a "sheared neck," which was never sheared — ask a glassmaker. In the third specimen from the left in the bottom row, appears an interesting form of the plain neck. Here is a narrow beading molded on the neck without the addition of a thread of glass. The various forms of neck used on the "black bottles" made at Keene range from patent medicine size to demijohn dimension.

CONCLUSION

The safest conclusions that may be drawn from the foregoing discussion are: (1) that certain kinds of flasks enjoyed their periods of sentimental popularity; and that certain fashions governed the use of particular patterns of decanters, bottles, and inkwells. (2) That, during the period of each fashion, the same popular styles of glass were made by many different factories. (3) The factory at Keene produced a far greater variety of wares than it has hitherto received credit for. Among its products are certain inkwells and flasks which have hitherto been erroneously attributed to Stoddard.

metal in a pattern mold. Whether this is piece of a decanter or of a defective and unfinished *Pitkin* type flask, I have been unable to determine.

Pitkin type flasks were made at Keene, as the fragments show (*Fig. 12*). There are two varieties, the plain twisted or sworled, and the cross-ribbed or double-sworled. All such flasks were made by the "German method," or, as

Fig. 13 — PITKIN TYPE FLASKS
   This is the pattern of the flask of which fragments are shown above.

the glassmaker terms it, the *half post* method. What appears to be an inserted neck, and is frequently so referred to by the uninformed, is, in reality, but the lip of a second gathering of glass on the partially blown initial gathering. Any collector who has been at all careful in his study of glassmaking methods will realize the futility of attempting to *insert* a neck in a bottle or flask.

It is not remarkable that the beautiful and popular *Pitkin* type of flask should be found at Keene; it was made at many glasshouses, possibly at as many as made the well-known *Chestnut* type bottle. The many fragments of the latter bottle among my debris suggests that the type must have been a usual Keene product during a long period. It came in various shades of amber, and its homely, stolid shapes are always attractive.

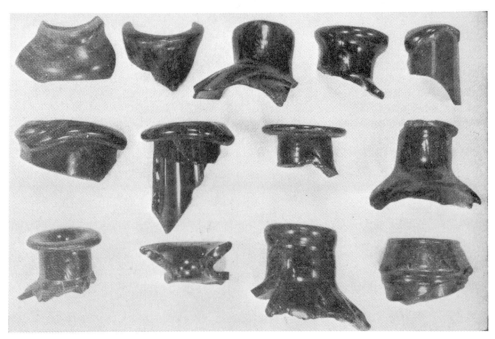

Fig. 14 — TYPES OF NECK FINISH

Stoddard Glass

By LURA WOODSIDE WATKINS

Except as noted,
illustrations from the collection of
C. Malcolm Watkins

GLASSMAKING in Stoddard represents the third stage in the eastward drift of the industry from Lake Dunmore, Vermont, through Keene and Stoddard to Lyndeboro. Lake Dunmore is linked to Keene by Henry Schoolcraft, who helped to found the former works and came to the New Hampshire town when the Vermont company failed. Stoddard's first glass manufacturer came from Keene and was followed, shortly after, by many others who were forced to look for work elsewhere after the closing of the Marlboro Street works.

No less than four different glasshouses were operated in South Stoddard and Mill Village between 1842 and 1873. These settlements are something over two miles apart. Mill Village, now the local centre, lies to the north. South Stoddard is today a mere crossroads. The irregular four corners at South Stoddard were called *The Box*, a name also applied to the old Gilson Tavern that stood on the spot for many years. *The City*, another designation for it, suggests the importance of the busy little forest community when the glasshouse was in operation.

Fig. 1 — C. B. BARRETT'S ADVERTISEMENT OF STODDARD GLASS
Perhaps more ambitious than conditions warranted. From the Portland Directory for 1869

South Stoddard: Joseph Foster's Works (1842)

Of the first attempt at glassmaking in Stoddard we know little more than what is told in a brief paragraph in Gould's *History of Stoddard*. This relates that Joseph Foster came from Keene in 1842, "built a furnace (of stone principally) in an old house west of Gilson's tavern, and ran it a short time, but having no capital, he failed in business. He afterwards built another 80 rods north of the village, but again failed." Nevertheless, Foster was still operating in 1849; he is listed as a maker of black glass bottles in the *New England Mercantile Union Directory* of that year.

Mill Village: Granite Glass Company

In 1846 a more successful venture was launched in Mill Village by Gilman Scripture, John M. Whiton, Jr., and Calvin Curtice, who put up a large factory there. All were men of some importance in the community: Scripture was a justice of the peace and selectman, and together the three partners ran the village store. Scripture, after the failure of his glass business, retired to Nashua, where he was distinguished by being chosen mayor of the city. Curtice also moved to Nashua, although he returned to Stoddard shortly before his death in 1882.

The first building of the company was burned to the ground during the winter following its erection, but was soon restored and glassmaking resumed. The concern was known as the Granite Glass Company. In 1849 it was listed in the New England Mercantile Union Directory as *C. Curtis & Co., black glass bottles*. By 1854 its output was "annually $2500 worth of bottles of various sizes and descriptions." The buildings stood on the high bank of a little stream on the south side of the road to Antrim, a location that is plainly visible from the main road to Keene.

Two years later Scripture, Whiton, and Curtice failed. The works were taken over by George L. Curtis, who had come to Stoddard from Windsor, New Hampshire, in 1847, and had since been connected with the firm as shipper or distributing agent. In partnership with B. F. Messer he continued to operate the establishment under its original style, *Granite Glass Company*. He also kept a store. When, after two or three years, the partnership was dissolved, Curtis carried on alone until 1872. His departure from Stoddard in that year seems to have marked the end of the Granite Glass Company. Eventually its buildings were burned; but the brick floors and the remains of the fire pots may still be discerned by those who will delve beneath the sod.

It is said that the Granite Glass Company owned two warehouses that were taken over by the South Stoddard Glass Company in 1860. These may have been the buildings erected by Foster in South Stoddard that were assigned to Scripture, Whiton, and Curtice after Foster's failure in 1850.

South Stoddard Glass Company

Glassmaking in South Stoddard really began in 1850 with the organization of a company of five men: Luman Weeks, Almon Woods, Ebenezer A. Rice, Nicholas Hill, and Frederick A. Gilson. On the southwest corner of the crossroads, at *The Box*, they erected a group of buildings that included a glasshouse, a large warehouse, and four tenements. Two years later they added a store. The advantage of proximity to the Box tavern, owned by Weeks and Gilson, and managed by Gilson, may have had something to do with their choice of location.

The following brief paragraph concerning Luman Weeks appeared in Guild's *County Gazeteer and Directory* for 1885:

Luman Weeks was born in Peru, N. Y., March 26, 1818. M. Cynthia Pike of Marlow, N. H., and

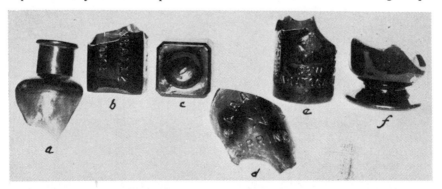

Fig. 2 — FRAGMENTS FROM SOUTH STODDARD
a. Neck of jar; *b.* Kimball's Jaundice Bitters; *c.* base of bitters bottle; *d.* Saratoga Spring; *e.* High Rock Congress Spring/ C & W/ Saragota N. Y. (pint); *f.* base of offhand vase

located in Stoddard in 1840. He drove the stage from Marlow to Hancock until March, 1844, then from Stoddard to Boston until 1850. He then built his glassworks at South Stoddard, and carried on the business for 23 years, manufacturing bottles, demi-johns, etc., and giving employment to a number of hands. He moved to Keene in the fall of 1873, where he has since resided. He has been selectman of Stoddard several times, and represented that town in 1864–5 and in 1873.

In 1852 Woods and Hill left the company, and a year later Rice sold out, leaving the firm as it afterwards remained — Weeks & Gilson, The South Stoddard Glass Company. Although it did not do so large a business as the factory in Mill Village, it continued successfully until 1873, when all glassmaking in Stoddard came to an end, partly as a result of the depression following the Civil War, and partly because a change in taste demanded containers of clear glass, which the Stoddard factories, limited as they were to local materials, were unable to produce. The warehouse, although filled to the roof with crates of bottles packed in hay, was abandoned. Weeks found it impossible to sell the stock for enough to pay the cartage to Keene, the shipping point. Much of it was given away.

A few years after the close of the factory, the building was maliciously fired and was burned to the ground, consuming at the same time the neighboring four tenements and the store. Frank L. Schultz, whose father, John Henry Schultz, "ran the melts" in the glasshouse, witnessed the conflagration. Although only a small boy at the time, he remembers vividly his excitement, which was occasioned partly by the fact that he and other youngsters of the neighborhood salvaged candy from the burning store.

Until recently it has been a simple matter to obtain specimens of the broken glass that tell so plainly the story of the last days

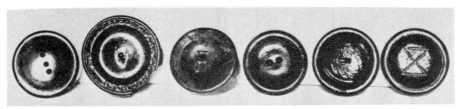

of glassblowing in South Stoddard. The site is now becoming overgrown with shrubbery and will soon be unidentifiable.

Mill Village: The New Granite Glass Works

The last glassworks to be founded in Stoddard was built, at the close of the Civil War, by the sons of Joseph Foster. It stood in Mill Village next to the present home of Mrs. Mary Lane. It is said that George Foster managed the business, while Charles and Wallace were practical glassblowers. A younger brother, Joseph, was also employed making wicker covers for demijohns and carboys. At some time before 1868, the Fosters sold out to Charles B. Barrett, who advertised the business under his own name in the Boston Directory of that year.

Barrett was a dealer in liquors and tobacco, with headquarters in Boston at 45 North Market Street and 45 Clinton Street, corner of Merchant's Row. He is said to have financed the glassworks. He advertised that he was the only glass manufacturer in New England who sold his own wares and could, therefore, give his customers the agent's commission. Barrett's factory burned down in 1871 and was never rebuilt.

Later History

By 1873 all glassmaking was at an end in Stoddard. Fogg's *Gazeteer of New Hampshire* for 1874 speaks of it reminiscently, saying that the glass manufactured annually in the town was worth $40,000, but that the glassworks were no longer in operation.

The natives of Stoddard perhaps did not altogether regret the passing of the industry from their village. They had never approved of the foreign workmen with their free and easy ways and their intemperate habits. Those among the glassblowers who were of American origin had come from Connecticut or from Keene. After the manner of their kind, when the Stoddard works

Fig. 3 — EXAMPLES FROM THE SOUTH STODDARD RUINS
a. Star Spring Co. Saratoga N. Y. (pint), reddish amber; *b.* reddish amber; *c. High Rock Congress Spring/ C & W/ Saratoga N. Y.* (quart), reddish amber; *d.* olive amber; *e. Kimball's Jaundice Bitters*, olive amber

Fig. 4 — SPRING-WATER BOTTLE BASES FROM SOUTH STODDARD RUINS
The second, shown carrying the mark *Weeks & Gilson, So. Stoddard, N. H.*, is rare. Only fourteen of these bottles are known

Fig. 5 — STODDARD INK BOTTLES
Octagonal; plain conical; sixteen-sided

closed the blowers wandered on to Lyndeboro or to factories in New York State. Persons still living can remember the days when the glasshouses were in full blast, with two hundred employees at work in the two factories, and the fires going day and night for at least six months in the year. Women as well as men were engaged in the industry, especially in making wicker covers, for which they were paid thirty-five cents each. Five or six baskets a day provided a wage that at the time was considered satisfactory. The glassblowers themselves received high wages, ranging from four to eight dollars a day, and even more in rush times.

Stoddard Products

The output of the Stoddard factories was entirely bottle or "black" glass. The color ranges from green or greenish amber through light and dark golden amber to a real mahogany color. The mahogany is a product of the Barrett works; a true green has been found at South Stoddard. None of the factories was ever successful in producing a lighter glass. The sand was procured from various places near at hand: from Centre Pond, and from pits near Munsonville and Antrim. History records that an employee of the Granite Glass Company, one Henry Whitman, aged seventeen, was buried under a sand bank near Antrim, where he was digging, and was instantly killed.

James D. Cutter, of Antrim, the oldest living man (1927) who blew glass in Stoddard, worked in all three glasshouses, and was familiar with their formulas. He says that the batch for bottle glass was made up of eight parts of sand, twelve of ash, and two of salt. Most of the Stoddard glass is full of bubbles — that of the Granite Glass Company markedly so. The glass from South Stoddard is clearer, and of a golden- or reddish-amber color rather than the greenish amber characteristic of the rival factory. The wavi-

Fig. 6 — FOSTER AND BARRETT PRODUCTS
Reddish-amber gallon demijohn and 8 ¼-inch jar

Fig. 7 — GRANITE GLASS COMPANY PRODUCTS
a. Spring-water bottle, greenish amber; *b.* and *c.* pint flasks, concerning which some discussion will be found in the text, amber; *d.* ship bottle, greenish amber

Fig. 8 — STODDARD LILY-PAD PITCHERS
Brilliant clear amber.
From the Herbert D. Mason collection

ness frequently seen in mold-blown bottles from Stoddard was caused by improper heating of the mold.

There has been considerable controversy as to whether three-part molds were ever used at Stoddard. Authorities now agree that this type of glassblowing was practiced in Keene, but probably not at Stoddard. If a piece of three-mold glass seems to have a Stoddard history, the chances are that it was made in a mold brought from Keene by some migrating workman, who may have used it on his own account. I myself have found a fragment of a sunburst flask, bearing the word *Keen*, in the waste pile of the Granite Glass Company, which illustrates the point that Keene molds did find their way to Stoddard. The older inhabitants of Stoddard know of no three-mold pieces made in Stoddard, though they have seen quilted and ribbed bottles that had been made elsewhere. Three-mold glass was certainly not a commercial product of the Stoddard glasshouses, and, according to evidence supplied by the best-informed investigators, it was not an offhand product.

The commercial ware of all three Stoddard factories was similar in kind, as may be ascertained by examining fragments found in the waste piles. The list of bottles that Barrett advertised shows the extent and variety of the shapes and sizes of containers manufactured. He mentions "Black, Green & Amber Ware" and "all descriptions of demijohns, flasks, wine, soda, mineral, ale, ink, blacking, bay water, cologne, hair oil, patent medicine, and all other kinds of bottles."

The ruins at South Stoddard yield remains of all sorts of ale bottles, mineral-water bottles — notably those made for the High Rock Congress Spring, and the Star Spring at Saratoga — bottles for Kimball's Jaundice Bitters, demijohns and carboys of different sizes, eight-sided ink bottles, and flasks. In addition to plain bottles of sundry shapes, the Granite Glass Company ruins afford fragments of sixteen-sided and plain conical ink bottles, snuff bottles, and eagle flasks. Not the least interesting relic is the base of a bottle marked *Weeks & Gilson, So. Stoddard,*

N. H. — the only mark that definitely establishes the firm name.

Several Stoddard flasks are identified by the factory mark. Four similar types of eagle flasks were the work of the Granite Glass Company: *a.* Obverse, eagle with shield on breast, ribbon in mouth, perched on arrows and olive branch, head to the left, above an oval with lettering *Granite Glass Co.*; reverse, the same, *Stoddard, N. H. b.* Obverse, same design, *Stoddard, N. H.* in oval; reverse, the same with no inscription. *c.* The same, with no lettering on either side. *d.* Dot in oval (½ pint).

All have sheared mouths and scarred bases. Stephen Van Rensselaer in *Early American Bottles and Flasks*, lists *a.* in pint and quart sizes, with the note that the final *d* in Stoddard is omitted in the larger size. I have found fragments of both *a.* and *b.* in the pint size. *C.* was made in one-half pint, pint, and quart sizes. It rarely occurs in olive green. Van Rensselaer also lists a similar half-pint bottle with a four-pointed star in the oval.

Perhaps rarer than the eagle flasks is a plain amber flask marked *Granite Glass Co.* on one side and *Stoddard, N. H.* on the other. This occurs both with sheared mouth and scarred base and with collared mouth and molded base (*Fig. 7*).

A third rare type of flask displays the American flag with thirteen stars on one side and the words *New Granite Glass Works* in a semicircle over *Stoddard, N. H.* on the other.

Fig. 9 — NEW GRANITE FLAG FLASKS
Olive amber, in pint and half-pint sizes, the latter extremely rare. *From the Herbert D. Mason collection*

Fig. 10 (above) — STODDARD JARS AND HATS
Centre jar, extremely thin, light amber; others of fine amber tint. *From the Herbert D. Mason collection*

Fig. 11 (below) — STODDARD OFFHAND PIECES
Probably by Matt Johnson, an English worker at Stoddard. *From the Herbert D. Mason collection*

Flag flasks were made both with sheared mouth and collared, in half-pint and pint sizes. H. E. Swain, who worked at The Box factory, is authority for the information that flag flasks were also made at South Stoddard.

While the bottle collector will find much of interest in the regular Stoddard output, the general glass collector will search more eagerly for those offhand specimens that were made by the glass-blowers for presentation pieces. A large variety of such articles has already been gathered by discriminating persons.

Most important of the offhand work are the large pitchers blown in Wistarberg style with a superimposed lily-pad decoration. They exhibit the persistence of a technique that had its origin more than one hundred years before, and was undoubtedly passed on from one glass-blower to another. The examples in Figure 8 were the work of Matthew (Matt) Johnson, of the Barrett works, noted for his skill in fancy blowing. The list of objects made in this way is a long one, and includes pitchers, bowls, jars, flower pots, hats, canes, rolling pins, balls, double flasks, salts, and scent bottles. An ink bottle with whorled tooling has been discovered in the South Stoddard ruins, and I have found at the same place the base of a large jar or vase.

The Granite Glass Company gave inkwells to grammar-school graduates. The wells were solid blocks of glass with an egg-shaped depression for the ink.

BLOWN THREE-MOLD DECANTERS AND INKWELLS
Patterns consist of bands of ingeniously varied geometrical forms, imitating those found on cut glass of the early 1800's. Decanters and inkwells thus ornamented have often been erroneously attributed to Stoddard, New Hampshire. The accompanying article explains this unfortunate mistake and endeavors to correct it

Dispelling the Stoddard Myth

By HELEN A. MCKEARIN

"When you have erred, be not afraid to correct yourself."

WHENEVER I hear blown three-mold glass called *Stoddard* — and the occurrence is all too frequent — my guilty conscience vibrates to the recollection of a paragraph in an article that I published thirteen years ago in ANTIQUES. Let me quote my erroneous statement: "That certain olive-green and olive-amber decanters of geometric pattern were the product of the Stoddard factory in New Hampshire is reasonably well established. When excavations have been made on the site of the factory, fragments of this dark glass only have been unearthed. . . . Nevertheless I have seen clear, flint glass decanters and pitchers identical in pattern with the known Stoddard, dark colored decanters. The conclusion that their source is common seems, therefore, logical. *Still, one cannot be too careful or cautious in attributing a piece of glass to a particular factory.*"

The only truth in that quotation lies in the last sentence. The rest is fallacious on several counts. (*1*) There were, in all, four factories at Stoddard, not one only. (*2*) Identity of pattern unsupported by other evidence does not constitute a logical basis for assuming a common source of manufacture. (*3*) Fragments of dark blown three-mold pieces had actually *not* been found on any Stoddard factory site.

Nevertheless, in 1924, and for a short time thereafter, most students, at least all whom I knew at the time, believed that geometrically patterned bottle-glass decanters and inkwells blown in full-size, three-section molds were products of the little New England village of Stoddard. It was my misfortune to perpetuate the belief by giving it the authority of print. Misplaced faith in two unsubstantiated rumors was responsible for this. For one thing, it was widely reported that local tradition, a positively hypnotic signpost usually pointing in the wrong direction, maintained that Stoddard had produced the glass in question. Likewise, it was said that excavations at Stoddard had yielded fragments of the blown three-mold bottle-glass decanters and inkwells in sufficient quantity to leave no doubt that they were a local product. Thus six geometric patterns came to be ascribed to Stoddard. Four of these, as follows, were found on inkwells: (*1*) Band of vertical ribbing below one of diamond diapering. (*2*) Band of diamond diapering between bands of vertical ribbing. (*3*) Narrow band of large diamonds below a wide band of fine

diamond diapering. (*4*) Band of vertical ribbing, above and below a band of equilateral diamonds, each framing four small diamonds.

The pattern of the so-called Stoddard pint decanters consists of four bands, as follows, beginning at the bottom: (*a*) vertical ribbing; (*b*) alternate rectangles of diamond diapering and sunbursts, the latter's rays framing a targetlike boss with a bull's-eye centre; (*c*) short diagonal ribbing to the right; (*d*) vertical ribbing. The pattern on the quart decanters differs from the pint in pointing its diagonal ribbing to the left, while its sunbursts exhibit a waffled centre. The Stoddard attribution was accepted for *bottle-glass* pieces *in these patterns only* and never for any articles blown from clear or colored flint glass.

To make assurance doubly sure, let me repeat that subsequent research has fully established the fact that no such patterns in any kind of glass were made at Stoddard. The later findings have been given ample publicity. But errors die hard. Indeed, the Stoddard name not only sticks to dark bottle-glass decanters and inkwells but has also been attached to nearly all pieces of glass molded in geometric patterns.

How has this come about? One of the many contributing factors is doubtless the attraction exercised by a maker's name or a factory attribution. The wish to know when and from which factory a piece came is perfectly natural. Such knowledge adds nothing to the intrinsic quality of an article, but it can impart an added historical or cultural interest. As a rule, considerations of value, monetary value, are involved. A specific factory attribution seems greatly to enhance the commercial value of any piece. And the enhancement is usually in direct ratio to the supposed importance of the factory. Without doubt labels or attributions can be transmuted into gold, or could have been until 1933. This state of affairs and the fact that most of us are prone to believe what pleases our imagination stimulate the adopting of hasty attributions based on rumor, conjecture, and specious reasoning.

Certainly wishful argument from similarities in the geometric patterns has contributed largely to the spread of the Stoddard myth. Probably the first step was to conclude that flint-glass articles apparently identical in pattern with those of bottle glass were blown in the same factory. I say "apparently identical" because after studying the patterns on over a thousand pieces of blown three-mold glass, and counting and measuring the individual units in the bands of these patterns, I know that similar arrangements may vary widely in the size and number of their motives. Patterns are identical only on pieces blown in one and the same mold. For example, clear flint-glass decanters in two shapes occur in the pattern employing the sunburst with waffled centre (*see illustration*). But the bottom band of one decanter will exhibit 81 fine vertical ribs about 1 ½ inches tall, while the corresponding band of another will reveal 84 fine vertical ribs about 1 ⅝ inches tall. This obviously means that the two decanters were blown in two different molds, which may or may not have been used in the same factory. But to return to the thread of our discussion: even identical patterns cannot be accepted as reliable evidence of a common source, since we have learned that mold makers sometimes supplied virtually identical molds to various manufacturers. Harry Hall White cites an example of this procedure in the case of the scroll or violin flasks. Mere similarity of pattern offers no real clue to source. South Jersey type glass and some of the pressed pattern glass exemplify this fact.

Having disposed of Stoddard attributions based on supposed similarities of pattern, we may re-examine the known Stoddard product. The fact that *no clear glass* was made at Stoddard has, of course, been frequently affirmed during the past few years, but apparently without much effect. Rhea Mansfield Knittle in her book *Early American Glass* (*p. 368*) tells us that "the silica about Stoddard precluded the possibility of clear-glass making," and "no clear-glass fragments have ever been unearthed from the glass-house ruins at Stoddard, and no examples of clear glass have ever been authentically attributed to the town." Lura Woodside Watkins says that one reason glassmaking ended at Stoddard in 1873 was that "a change in taste demanded containers of clear glass, which the Stoddard factories, limited as they were to local materials, were unable to produce" (ANTIQUES, August 1933, *p. 53*). Most important of all are the exhaustive excavations made by Herbert D. Mason at Stoddard. Not one scrap of clear glass did he find, so he has told me. Lastly, all the known products of the factory are flasks and similar articles of dark bottle glass in shades of green and amber. *It is therefore impossible that any blown three-mold articles of clear or colored flint glass would have been made at Stoddard.*

As for geometrically patterned bottle-glass decanters and inkwells, there is no factual basis for believing that any of the kind were the commercial product of any Stoddard establishment. In the first place, the first Stoddard glassworks was not in operation until 1842, by which time the popularity of what we call blown three-mold glass was undoubtedly on the wane. It is unlikely that a new venture would start off with old styles. Furthermore, Mr. Mason's excavations at Stoddard turned up not even fragments of three-mold pieces. In 1926 Rhea Mansfield Knittle said, "although certain decanters, inkwells, and hats were attributed to Stoddard until a year or two ago, it has since been ascertained that they were produced at Keene." Harry Hall White has proved by his excavations on sundry factory sites that some dark pattern inkwells were blown at Perry's Keene, New Hampshire, factory, others at Vernon, New York, and still others at Coventry, Connecticut. Incidentally, all three of these factories were operating contemporaneously. Lastly, Lura Woodside Watkins in her article on Stoddard glass in ANTIQUES for August 1933 remarks that "If a piece of three-mold glass seems to have a Stoddard history, the chances are that it was made in a mold brought from Keene by some migrating workman, who may have used it on his own account. . . . The older inhabitants of Stoddard know of no three-mold pieces made in Stoddard, though they have *seen* quilted [diamond-diapered] and ribbed bottles that had been made elsewhere. Three-mold glass was certainly not a commercial product of the Stoddard glasshouses."

I hope that this review of well-established fact and authoritative opinion will put an end to the longstanding Stoddard error. The commercial glass products of that town can lay virtually no claim to æsthetic charm. Among them were no pleasingly quilted decanters, no snug, cylindrical, diapered inkwells either of clear glass or of the sundry muddy green and olive glasses yielded by the sand of the neighborhood.

Note. For fairly recent studies of the glass of Stoddard, Keene, and New York State, see ANTIQUES for June 1927 (*Keene, New Hampshire,* by Harry Hall White); September 1929 (*New York State Glass Houses: Mt. Vernon,* by Harry Hall White); August 1933 (*Stoddard Glass,* by Lura Woodside Watkins).

Early Window Glass

QUESTIONS have come to us from sundry sources regarding the size of windows in early American dwellings, and more particularly regarding the dimensions of the panes of glass set into the frames. It is impossible to answer such questions categorically without a comprehensive investigation. It may, however, be noted that New England windows prior to 1700, perhaps even prior to 1725, were probably all of the casement type, with diamond-shaped panes set in lead. J. Frederick Kelly in his *Early Domestic Architecture of Connecticut* pictures such a window with panes measuring 4 ½ by 5 ¾ inches.

With the advent of double-hung windows, about 1725, Mr. Kelly tells us, came the use of rectangular lights measuring 6 by 8 inches. These dimensions were gradually increased. In 1754 the contract for building a house for John Townsend of Newport called for 7 by 9 inch lights. By the year 1800, 9 by 12 inch lights were in frequent use.

Thereafter, larger sizes were constantly available, though 7 by 9, 8 by 10, and 10 by 12 inch lights continued as stock production. From a résumé of advertisements, chiefly from Pittsburgh firms, generously supplied by Harry Hall White, it would appear that in 1803, 10 by 12 inch lights were the largest made. In 1847 lights 21 by 25 inches, and 24 by 30 inches, are advertised. In 1866, 32 by 44, and 40 by 60 inch lights are advertised. In 1872, the brownstone urban mansion might suffer panes 38 by 76 inches in dimension. In 1883, the Pittsburgh Plate Glass Company was advertising plate-glass sheets ⅜ of an inch thick and large enough for a show window with a 15 by 12 foot opening.

The sizes of early windows were to some extent regulated by the sizes of the lights available and by the number of lights per window. John Townsend's contract, for example, calls for 19 windows of 24 lights each; 9 windows of 18 lights each; and 4 of 12 lights each. The size of the lights was to be the same throughout.

It is perhaps fair to query whether progress in the technique of window-glassmaking and the consequent increase in the size of available lights was responsible for the continuous enlargement of window openings during the 1800's. Or, on the contrary, did changes in architectural design, accompanied by new ideas of suitable fenestration, first create a demand, which manufacturers hastened to fill?
— *H. E. K.*

BLOWN THREE-MOLD FRAGMENTS EXCAVATED AT SANDWICH

By HELEN McKEARIN

Except as noted, illustrations from the McKearin collection

THE idea that Sandwich was a large, perhaps the largest, producer of blown three-mold glass should not come as a surprise to anyone. It is an idea which has been entertained by students and collectors for a long time. In fact, for nearly twenty years some of us have believed it to be not a probability but a certainty. The basis for the belief has been founded on several types of evidence which in the space of this article can be presented only briefly.

Comparatively speaking, an extraordinarily large quantity of blown three-mold table and decorative glass, especially in the geometric patterns, has been found and collected, largely in the east. The number of surviving pieces and the range of patterns and articles point to its having enjoyed a great popularity. The approximate date of this ware has been fairly well established as between about 1820 and about 1840, possibly a little later. It is only logical to infer that blown three-mold was produced in factories of the period which were equipped to make, in fact, specialized in making, fine table and decorative wares. In consideration of all these

No. 2 — BLUE TOILET BOTTLE
Spiral ribbing, Type II

No. 3 — CLEAR FLIP
Wide band of vertical ribbing, Type I

No. 4 — CLEAR TUMBLER
Wide band of vertical ribbing, Type II. Note folded rim

No. 5 — COBALT-BLUE TOILET BOTTLE
Vertical ribbing, Type I

No. 7 — GRAY-BLUE HALF-PINT TOILET BOTTLE
Vertical ribbing, Type I. *Formerly in the Maclay collection*

No. 8 — CLEAR MUSTARD POT
Vertical ribbing, Type II, broad pronounced ribs

No. 9 — CLEAR CRUET BOTTLE
Vertical ribbing, Type II, broad pronounced ribs

No. 11, *b* — CLEAR SHAKER, LAZY SUSAN SHAPE
Broad, flat vertical ribbing, topped by horizontal ribs

No. 12, *b* — GRAY-BLUE HALF-PINT PITCHER
Wide band of broad vertical ribbing between horizontal ribbing, fan fluting

No. 13, *a* — CLEAR WHISKEY GLASS
Band of vertical ribbing, band of diamond diapering

No. 14 — CLEAR MINIATURE DECANTER
Band of vertical ribbing, one of alternate blocks of diamond diapering and sunburst with radii from small dot at focus

No. 15 — COBALT-BLUE TUMBLER AND FOOTED SALT
Band of herringbone ribbing, alternate blocks of diamond diapering and sunburst-in-square

No. 16, *b* — COBALT-BLUE QUARTER-PINT DECANTER
Band of herringbone ribbing, one of alternate sunburst-in-square and blocks of diamond diapering, band of sunburst-in-square, band of vertical ribbing

No. 17 — CLEAR CRUET BOTTLE
Band of herringbone ribbing, 3 sets of sunburst with radii from dot at focus, sunburst-in-rectangle, and rectangle of diamond diapering, band of vertical ribbing

factors, the proved progressiveness of Deming Jarves and his associates at Sandwich, and the known wide variety of Sandwich products, have made it seem inconceivable that the Sandwich factory did not produce blown three-mold glass on a large scale. Secondly, certain pieces, such as the vertically ribbed toilet bottles and the miniature decanters (*Nos. 5 and 14*), have been found in colors and glass identical with authenticated Sandwich pressed-glass pieces. Lastly, tradition and family history have attributed many pieces to the early days of the Sandwich factory. To cite an instance, one out of many, in 1920 a collector purchased from a life-long resident of East Sandwich a pair of half-pint decanters, in pattern like Number 12b, which were accompanied by the following affidavit: These blue bottles which I let you have were bought at the Sandwich Glass Factory when my mother . . . was four or five years old, and she was born in the year 1821. It was about the first glass that was made there and later skilled workmen from Europe were employed and much beautiful and artistic work was done. . . .

Now our belief in the Sandwich production of blown three-mold glass is strengthened by the important evidence of fragments excavated on the factory site.

In 1937 the Massachusetts Institute of Technology acquired a large collection of glass fragments which were excavated by Francis L. Wynn of Sandwich on the site of the first glasshouse building. The sorting of thousands of fragments was accomplished by Mrs. Lura Woodside Watkins and F. H. Norton, professor of ceramics at the Institute. Besides the fragments of innumerable pressed-glass articles and lacy glass of many types, they found that the collection included a large number of blown three-mold fragments. Details concerning the finding and locations of the fragments have already been given by Doctor Charles W. Green in his article on the identification of lacy-glass dishes and salts (ANTIQUES, August 1937, *p. 58*), and by Mrs. Watkins in her article on the cup-plate finds (ANTIQUES, September 1938, *p. 132*). It has been my privilege to study the fragments of blown three-mold glass.

While the fragments in the Institute collection, plus a small collection lent to me by Mr. Wynn, may not in themselves constitute *proof* of manufacture at Sandwich, they certainly are most important evidence. I understand that other fragments of blown three-mold are owned by a few private collectors, Mrs. Ruth Webb Lee, and the Sandwich Historical Society. It is probable that the complete collection would form a body sufficiently large to be regarded as *proof*. However, as I am one of those who have believed that a large proportion of the American blown three-mold patterns and glass originated at Sandwich, the fragments I have studied and the facts that they reveal concerning patterns and molds have turned belief into conviction.

Over one hundred patterns have been found on blown three-mold glass, but there has been little positive information as to where they were produced. The excavations and research of Harry Hall White prove that two patterns were blown in bottle glass at Coventry, Connecticut, and five at Keene, New Hampshire, in the Marlboro Street factory; that a geometric pattern was blown in bottle glass at Kent and another at Mantua, Ohio; and that at least three patterns were blown in bottle glass and clear flint at the factory of the Mount Vernon Glass Company at Vernon, New York. Not many out of over one hundred! Now the fragments owned by the Massachusetts Institute of Technology and by Mr. Wynn indicate many molds and patterns used at Sandwich. Moreover, they show a variety of colors: clear; blue in a wide range — cobalt, sapphire, grayish, and opaque light shades; greens, both light and deep, brilliant emerald; opaque white; canary; and opalescent — the last as used by Mrs. Watkins to mean "glass of all degrees of translucency which shows an opalescent fire when held to the light."

Before tabulating the results of my study of the Sandwich fragments I should like to make clear the distinction between pattern and mold. A pattern is a combination of given motifs; a mold (as the word is used in referring to pattern) is a *particular* combination or variation of the motifs in a pattern. For example, a band of diamond diapering between bands of vertical ribbing is a *pattern*. Incidentally, it is the commonest combination of the geometric motifs. There are over fifty *molds* cut in this pattern, and each differs from the others in one or more respects: size of the mold itself, number and size of the units composing the bands of the pattern, width of the bands, types of design on the base or bottom. Patterns are identical only on pieces blown in one and the same mold or, if such a thing is possible, in molds *exactly* alike. The same patterns were sometimes used in more than one factory. But, though one must allow for the possibility that identical molds may have been made for more than one factory and that a mold may have been carried from one factory to another, the probability is that each factory had its own molds for its patterns and that they differed from those used in other factories. Therefore, if it is established that a particular mold was used in one factory, the likelihood is that all pieces blown in that mold were made at that factory.

In my study of the Sandwich blown three-mold fragments I found there were many pieces too small to admit of any definite pattern identification or to give more than a slight clue to the pattern. Nevertheless, I have, I believe, been able to determine twenty patterns, and as well some of the molds in which they were blown. The accompany-

No. 20 — CLEAR QUART DECANTER
Arch and fern with snake medallion. *Formerly in the Maclay collection*

No. 21 — CLEAR QUART DECANTER
Star and ribbing. Pattern cut so that mold mark passes through ribs and rings. *Formerly in the Maclay collection*

No. 22 — BLUE HALF-PINT PITCHER
Band of heavy, short vertical ribs; equidistant alternating dots and trefoils; palm-leaf band, equidistant dots, guilloche, equidistant palmettes. Full-size *four-part* mold

No. 23 — CLEAR PITCHER
Contiguous beaded arches framing heavy ribs; palmettes at each spandrel; side of foot with serration-like ribs. Full-size *two-part* mold

ing illustrations of unbroken analogous examples are numbered to correspond with the following classification of fragments.

As I have stated, there were many fragments which, while they did not admit of definite pattern or mold identification, nevertheless provided clues to other patterns and motifs. There were many showing a combination of ribbing and diamond-diapering motifs in various sizes. Some showed the sunburst which has radii from focus. There were several bases, plain, with parts of sides showing 23 broad vertical ribs. These latter, in clear and in opaque white glass, may have been portions of inkwells or of cruet bottles. Also, there were a few fragments which may have been from a blown four-mold decanter, in the high relief characteristic of baroque patterns: a guilloche band between wide bands of gadrooning; 3 collar ribs on neck; 3 rows of 40 beads each between bottom and medial collar rib.

There has already been a great deal of speculation about the amber, olive-amber, and olive-green glass fragments of inkwells found at Sandwich. I understand that there are more in existence than the very few in the Massachusetts Institute of Technology collection. In the latter small group I found three inkwells, represented each in a different pattern. One was the type made at Coventry, Connecticut, the other two were of the types made at Keene, New Hampshire, as proved by Harry Hall White's studies and excavations. I consider it doubtful that they were made contemporaneously at Sandwich, especially since I have never found clear glass wells in these particular patterns or from these molds. However, as has been pointed out, there is always the possibility of a mold being taken from one factory to another. After the closing of the Marlboro Street factory at Keene and that at Coventry, Connecticut, the molds used for blown three-mold inkwells may have been acquired by the Sandwich factory. At any rate, the probability that inkwells in ambers and greens were blown at Sandwich cannot be ignored.

It is to be hoped that all the other fragments from blown three-mold glass which were excavated at Sandwich will be subjected to careful study and analysis. I feel confident that when this is accomplished many more patterns than those which I have tabulated will be identified.

PATTERN (*Read from bottom to top of piece*)	COLOR	ARTICLE	MOLD
Geometric Patterns			
1. Spiral ribbing. Type I (very fine)	Clear	Toilet bottle	(Probably) 49 ribs; concentric ring base, *i.e.*, pattern of concentric rings on base or bottom. Produced in various colors
2. Type II	Clear	Toilet bottle	(Probably) either 19 or 20 ribs; plain base. Produced in various colors
3. Wide band of vertical ribbing. Type I	Clear	(Probably) Flip	(Probably) 35 ribs separated at top and with petal-like termination; daisy base, *i.e.*, 8 deep diamond-shaped indentations, outer points of which are smaller than inner
4. Type II (fine)	Clear	Tumbler	(Probably) 50 fine vertical ribs, tops blending into plain band above; concentric ring base
5. Vertical ribbing. Type I	Clear	Toilet bottle	39 ribs extending on base to center and to collar rib at base of neck; fine ribbing between that and second collar rib about ½″ above. Produced in various colors
6.	Green Cobalt blue	Toilet bottle	39 ribs extending on base to center and to collar rib at base of neck. . . . Impossible to tell from fragments whether there is a second collar rib on the neck with ribbing between it and that at base of neck or extending beyond the second
7.	Emerald green Grayish blue Slatey blue Clear	Toilet bottle	34 ribs extending to collar rib at base of neck, narrow medial collar rib with ribbing above and below; ribs from body extend about 1/16″ on base to smooth center which is slightly sunken, giving a set-in look
8. Type II, Broad pronounced ribs	Clear	Mustard pot	18 broad rounded ribs extending to collar rib at base of neck and tapering on base to center
9.	Clear	Cruet bottles	18 broad rounded vertical ribs, collar rib at base of neck, finer vertical ribbing on neck to second collar rib; 18 ribs on base taper to small dot at center
10. Alternate broad flat ribs and fillet	Clear	a, Cruet bottle	12 vertical ribs, 6 broad flat and 6 fillet alternating; base, 6-petal daisy in relief
		b, Bird fountain with chicken finial	Same number of ribs as above
11. Broad, flat vertical ribbing, topped by horizontal ribs	Clear	a, Cruet bottle	10 broad flat vertical ribs; 4 horizontal collar ribs; plain base
		b, Cruet bottle or shaker (lazy susan shape)	Heavy horizontal rib, 10 broad flat vertical ribs, 4 horizontal ribs; base, 4 concentric rings around dot at center
12. Wide band of broad vertical ribbing between horizontal ribbing, fan fluting	Clear	a, Quart decanter Pint decanter ½-Pint decanter	No fragments of bases so molds cannot be determined
	Cobalt blue	b, ½-pint decanter or pitcher	3 horizontal ribs, 21 broad heavy vertical ribs, 2 heavy horizontal ribs, 12 fan flutes, collar rib; concentric ring base
13. Band of vertical ribbing, band of diamond diapering	Clear	a, Whiskey glass	54 fine vertical ribs, single horizontal rib, diamond diapering band: 2 high, 24 around; concentric ring base
		b, Cordial	Same mold
14. Band of vertical ribbing, one of alternate blocks of diamond diapering and sunburst with radii from small dot at focus	Clear	Miniature decanter	Band of 60 fine vertical ribs; 3 sunbursts (18 radii from small dot at focus) and 3 blocks of diamond diapering (3 high, 4 across) alternating and separated by a vertical rib, band of 45 fine vertical ribs; bands separated by a horizontal rib; concentric ring base
15. Band of herringbone ribbing, alternate blocks of diamond diapering and sunburst-in-square	Pale green Light amethyst Gray-blue Sapphire Clear	Hat, salt, or tumbler. (All three articles were made from this mold. On salts the band of herringbone becomes virtually a chevron, due to the elongating of the band during manipulation in forming the piece.)	15 panels of herringbone ribbing, 3 sunburst (16 radii from small sunken dot at focus)-in-square and 3 blocks of diamond diapering (4 high, 6 across) alternating and separated by a vertical rib; bands separated by a horizontal rib; concentric ring base

PATTERN	COLOR	ARTICLE	MOLD
16. Band of herringbone ribbing, one of alternate sunburst-in-square and blocks of diamond diapering, band of sunburst-in-square, band of vertical ribbing	Clear	a, ½-pint decanter or pitcher	15 panels of herringbone ribbing, 3 sunburst (24 radii from small sunken dot at focus)-in-square and 3 blocks of diamond diapering (5 high, 6 across) alternating and separated by a vertical rib, 2 horizontal ribs, band of 15 contiguous sunburst (10 radii from small dot at focus)-in-square, 48 fine vertical ribs; concentric ring base; bands 1 & 2 and 3 & 4 separated by a horizontal rib
	Blue	b, ¼-pint decanter or creamer	15 panels of herringbone ribbing, 3 sunburst (20 radii from small sunken dot at focus)-in-square and 3 blocks of diamond diapering (5 x 5); band of contiguous sunburst (8 radii from dot at focus)-in-square, 48 vertical ribs; bands separated by a horizontal rib; concentric ring base
17. Band of herringbone ribbing, 3 sets of sunburst with radii from dot at focus, sunburst-in-rectangle, and rectangle of diamond diapering, band of vertical ribbing	Clear	Cruet bottle or shaker	Nonagonal, panel of herringbone ribbing to each side; 3 sets of rectangular sunburst with 20 radii from dot at focus, sunburst (16 radii from small sunken dot at focus)-in-rectangle, rectangle of diamond diapering (6 high, 4 across), 54 fine vertical ribs; bands separated by 2 horizontal ribs; concentric ring base

Arch Patterns

PATTERN	COLOR	ARTICLE	MOLD
18. Contiguous Roman arches with spray of leaves rising from each spandrel	Clear	Tumbler	12 sunken panels under Roman arches, vertical spray of spikelike petals spring from spandrel and rise about 1 ¼″ above top of arches, three long spikelike petals rise at an acute angle to stem; base: 16 elongated diamond shaped indentations
19. Contiguous gothic arches with 2 sprays of leaves rising from each spandrel	Clear	Tumbler	12 sunken panels under gothic arches; 24 sprays of fine leaves, 2 springing from each spandrel and curving away from each other toward apex of arch
20. Arch and fern with snake medallion	Clear	Quart decanters Pint decanters	Bottom band: 6 double gothic arches over fern leaf, 2 herringbone ribs and triangle in 5 spandrels; 2 horizontal ribs; upper band: 6 alternate arch-over-fern-leaf and fern leaf; in one section the arch over fern in upper band is shorter and over an oval medallion (which breaks the horizontal ribs) formed by 2 snakes with heads meeting at center top, at center bottom bodies entwine into spandrel formed by two arches of bottom band; center of medallion: lattice and dots with scroll at each end (some molds had names of liquors); broad collar rib at base of neck; base: 24 ribs extend from body about 1″ on base, 3 concentric rings around small circle at center, ribs alternately large and small. The size of the motif varies with the size of the piece. Many fragments of the stoppers for these decanters both in quart and pint size, were found; they have a flat ribbed top (15 ribs) and swirled ribbing on curved sides (18 ribs)
21. Star and ribbing	Clear	Decanter, probably quart	(Probably) 31 flat square-topped vertical ribs about ¾″ high; 33 ½″ rings enclosing a 12-pointed star; 4 curved ribs between rings, 2 curving toward each ring; 21 broad flat square-topped vertical ribs. It is interesting to note that in the quart mold the pattern was so cut in the section that the mold mark passes through the ribs and the rings

Baroque Patterns

PATTERN	COLOR	ARTICLE	MOLD
22. Band of heavy, short vertical ribs; equidistant alternating dots and trefoils; palm-leaf band, equidistant dots, guilloche, equidistant palmettes	Clear		While parts of the principal motifs were among the fragments, it is impossible to determine from just which mold they came. I have records of four different molds for this pattern — qt., pt., and ½-pt. decanters. Except that one ½-pt. mold has a concentric ring base, the number of units is the same in all four molds; their variation is in the size of the units. (Decanters and pitchers were blown in this pattern) 22 broad ribs; equidistant dots and trefoils (4 of each); 8 units in palm-leaf band; 8 equidistant dots; 16 links in guilloche; 4 equidistant 5-petal palmettes. Full-size *four-part* mold
23. Contiguous beaded arches framing heavy ribs; palmettes at each spandrel; side of foot with serration-like ribs	Clear	(Probably) Pitcher	Only small fragments, but, so far as I have been able to ascertain, only pitchers have been blown in this pattern and they are from the same mold: 8 contiguous beaded arches (34 beads to an arch) framing 3 heavy ribs, the middle one longer than the others; 5-petal palmette rising from each spandrel; foot (molded with body), vertical side with 32 serration-like ribs which extend on base to 3 rings around dot at center. Full-size *two-part* mold

Stoppers

Tam o' Shanter, type used in toilet bottles: a, solid, fluted
                                                   b, plain, blown
Solid stepped button
Cast wheel, type used in miniature decanters: a, flat disc, 22 ribs from ring at center
                                                 b, " " , 19 ribs " " " "
Blown three-mold ball: a, plain top, vertical ribbing and diamond diapering on sides
                                                 b, ringed top, band of diamond diapering between bands of vertical ribbing
Blown three-mold stoppers for arch and fern decanters, see No. 20

PITTSBURGH GLASS

By LOWELL INNES

Part I.

Mr. Innes, assistant headmaster at Shady Side Academy, was a founder and first president of the Pittsburgh Early American Glass Club. His research has included excavation at the site of the first Gallatin venture.

THE IMPORTANCE, both economic and artistic, of the Pittsburgh district in glass is at last pretty well accepted. Utility window glass and hollow ware, made as early as 1797 at New Geneva under the aegis of Albert Gallatin, and at Pittsburgh itself at the O'Hara and Craig enterprise on Coal Hill, were being shipped down the Ohio and the Mississippi by the beginning of the nineteenth century. Another profitable market was the Great Lakes area and Canada, reached by way of the Allegheny: up Frenchmen's Creek to Le Boeuf, or Waterford; then overland to Presque Isle, one of the best shipping points on Lake Erie. A letter of November 1800 from Isaac Craig to James Naylor at Waterford, Pennsylvania, sets forth clearly the trade route to Queen's Town, Canada, prices a box of window glass at $14, and foretells by the quantity (40 boxes) that Pittsburgh was in the market to stay. Raw materials were reasonably available except for top-notch clay for the cooking pots, and this was usually carted over the Alleghenies from New Jersey or an importing seaport like Baltimore.

O'Hara and Craig attempted to begin flint-glass manufacture as early as 1800, but it remained for Benjamin Bakewell to broaden the field with his flint-glass manufactory in 1808. Then Pittsburgh embarked on most forms of eastern and Continental products. Rather a typical picture of the development of the industry comes from the year 1856. Of the 32 factories, 8 made flint-glass tableware (both blown and pressed); 2 produced black bottles; 8 turned out vials and drugware; and 14 were window-glass houses. The distribution of these products, if we judge from 1860, was about one fourth to the east and three fourths to the midwest and the west.

Pittsburgh was the first district to use coal and natural gas as heating fuels for the pots. With factories like Bakewell's (*1808–1882*), the first really successful flint-glass house carrying a general line, and with James B. Lyon & Company (*1848–1890*) given over mainly to pressed glass during the second part of the century, Pittsburgh could be sure of quality as well as production.

Nearly everyone has heard of President Monroe's order to Bakewell's in 1817 and President Jackson's in 1832 for fine cut glass to adorn the White House table. How many know that American glass manufacturers chose James B. Lyon & Company to represent the industry at the Paris Exposition of 1867? And when table glassware entered the realm of big business with the efficient adoption of the soda-lime formula, the Pittsburgh district led the field in production. Finally, the founding and the emergence of Pittsburgh Plate Glass as the most important company of its kind assured the locality of continued predominance. By the middle of the 1880's Allegheny County (Pittsburgh) had one third of all the capital invested in American glass, better than one fourth of the establishments, and one fourth of the production.

Considering the quality of Pittsburgh glass as well as its quantity, it is surprising that prior to 1940 collectors thought only in terms of Jersey, Stiegel, Amelung, Sandwich and Cambridge, and Ohio. Pittsburgh had never been granted a separate individuality except perhaps for a few examples of early hollow ware, marked historic flasks, heavy river-boat glass, pattern-molded sugar bowls, and late pressed tableware.

A stimulating exhibition of over 300 specimens of Pittsburgh glass was held in the fall of 1947 at the Historical Society of Western Pennsylvania. It was aimed to give a comprehensive view of the development of glass manufacturing techniques in the district and to reveal the shifting demands of the American public, modified, of course, by production costs and designs. That exhibition is the basis of this article.

The selection of specimens for the exhibition was governed by two important principles. First, Pittsburgh must be taken as a district, not as a city. The geography of the network of rivers and the existence of numerous small factories from New Geneva to Pittsburgh and Pittsburgh to Wheeling speak clearly of migratory workers, copied techniques, and moldmakers who respected the rights only of the immediate customer. The second principle, a corollary of the first, was that a type of glass current and popular at Pittsburgh but made at Brownsville or Wellsburg, for instance, deserved to be included.

Blown Glass — Earliest Type (Fig. 1)

The specimens illustrated were shown at the Carnegie Museum in January 1941 when the Pittsburgh chapter of the Early American Glass Club made the first attempt to trace Pittsburgh glassmaking in a public exhibition. These pieces, actually the counterpart of the earliest group in the 1947 Historical Society show, were supplemented by four important additions: a typical Gallatin-Kramer gemel bottle, a sturdy small green whiskey tester, and a couple of heavy amber bowls. Several new bulbous bottles have turned up, but all these pieces, even the tall green jars and useful milk pans, have become scarcer than hen's teeth. Soon after the show at a small antique auction near Waynesburg,

FIG. 1 — EARLIEST TYPES of off-blown or free-blown glass made in the Pittsburgh district, showing the influence of Gallatin workmen. (See also McKearin, *American Glass*, plates 45 and 46.)

Pennsylvania, a free-blown bulbous green bottle brought $27, even without actual Kramer authentication.

This illustration shows clearly the earliest types of functional free-blown glass, the blower using either the pale green of the window metal or the heavy amber of the early bottles. The preponderance of light green pieces is a fair guide to what was being turned out. The early green flips support this color evidence, too. The bull's-eye window light is somewhat deceiving, for the Pittsburgh district used the cylinder or rolled method of making window glass from the very beginning. Several of the O'Hara and Craig letters to the east place informal orders for small diamonds for cutting of the cylinder and flat sheet.

Easily the prize of the bottles is the squat one which has a seal on one side inscribed AL'TIN WO. The tall milk pan, however, should prove convincingly how impossible it is to authenticate without documentary or technical evidence. The bowl came from Fairchance, picked up by Miss Perie Abraham, before Neil Gest and Doctor Parke Smith began studying the Kramer family. (See their article in ANTIQUES, March 1939.) Possessing characteristics of Gallatin's New Geneva enterprise (*1797-1803*), it may nevertheless have been blown after 1807 at Greensboro, across the river, where Gallatin's German glassblowers moved the plant, or at the second New Geneva venture after the factory had been rebuilt in 1837 under Andrew and Theophilus Kramer. The other pans could have been blown at the same place or more likely at Brownsville, Perryopolis, Monongahela City, or Pittsburgh. This process of rebirth took place with most of the small factories such as Fayette City, Bridgeport, New Albany, and Belle Vernon.

The rolling pin, said to have been blown across the Monongahela from Pittsburgh (the present Southside) a hundred years ago, is of bluish glass. The only other color variation is the pale honey-colored witch ball in the upper left-hand corner, which has been popularly attributed to the third New Geneva venture.

Chronologically the next group of Pittsburgh glass should be in more sophisticated forms than those in Figure 1, such pieces as

would be functional — pitchers, sugar bowls, decanters, flips, salts, saucers, and a plate or two. These articles were undoubtedly made, but are now museum pieces or collector's items.

Letters from James O'Hara indicate prices of such pieces. In 1806 he listed pint tumblers at $1.60 a dozen; half-pint tumblers, $1.00 a dozen; pint flasks, $1.20 a dozen; quart bottles, $1.00 a dozen; half-pint decanters, $1.50 a dozen; quart decanters, $3.00 a dozen; pint decanters, $2.00 a dozen. In 1810 he itemized to Joseph Carson of Philadelphia gallon pitchers at $1.20 a dozen; half-gallon pitchers at $.80 a dozen; gallon jars, $.96 a dozen; quart jars, $.40 a dozen; pint jars, $.30 a dozen. There can be little doubt that all these items were made from ordinary unrefined metal. They were probably like Figures 4, 5, and 6 on the opposite page.

Cut and Engraved Glass (Figs. 2 and 3)

The next group, then, in time sequence is probably the cut and engraved flint. When Alex Wilson visited Pittsburgh in 1810 he wrote a letter stating that he had seen at Bakewell's a chandelier, highly ornamented and perfectly transparent. It was sold to a Mr. Kerr, an innkeeper, for $300 and hung suspended in his home for all to marvel at. From Fearon's *Sketches of America* (1818) comes a pertinent comment: "At Page and Bakewell's glass warehouse I saw chandeliers and numerous articles in cut glass of a very splendid description: among the latter a pair of decanters cut *from a London pattern* the price of which will be 8 guineas. It is well to bear in mind that the demand for these articles of elegant luxury lies in the western states. The inhabitants of eastern America being still importers from the old country."

A word of warning after that statement is not out of place. Not all glasshouses did their own cutting; many sent the blanks out. Inevitably Irish, English, and even French

ANTIQUES

FIG. 4 — FREE-BLOWN GLASS. The sugar bowl at right is characteristic of Pittsburgh free-blown shapes. That at left was favored at both Wheeling and Pittsburgh. The yellowish salt cup has a heavy bowl and folded foot.

patterns were followed throughout the century and were interchanged at first. No individual factory could keep a monopoly of design. By 1829 Bakewell's had three buildings, one for blowing, one for cutting, and one for storing glass, but primarily this concern had begun as a cut-glass project. William Peter Eichbaum of Bakewell's seems to have been the most skillful cutter working over a long period, yet a man named Jardelle, who had cut President Monroe's decanters and wines for the White House in 1817, also cut the commemorative vases presented to Lafayette in 1825.

As yet no documentary evidence has turned up on particular designs of engraved pieces, except those few in the Bakewell catalogue of 1875. Describing the copper-wheel method, Anne Royall says (*Pennsylvania or Travels Continued in the U.S.*, 1829): "The engraving is very neatly done, indeed surpassing any I have seen in the country . . . The machinery of these lathes is costly, $50.00 . . . The ware is also high, $5.00 a tumbler. The patterns are mostly obtained *from Europe* and the pattern executed when I was in, for beauty and taste was exquisite particularly a greyhound its head erect as though looking at something and though not an inch in length it was perfect and entire the eyes, ears, nose being life itself."

Free-Blown Glass (Figs. 4, 5, and 6)

When glassmen from the Amelung factory entered the Pittsburgh district through the New Geneva enterprise and gradually moved down the Monongahela, they continued the tradition of sturdiness in both stems and bases. Although we have no actual name records from the Stiegel craftsmen who must have tarried at Pittsburgh before their pattern-mold art was reborn in Ohio, it is only sensible to believe that some practiced blowing here. James O'Hara was constantly

FIG. 6 — FREE-BLOWN and pattern-molded examples. The swirled cruet and paneled vase were made by the pattern-mold method, which will be discussed in Part II of this article. The pitcher and covered compote are excellent examples of useful free-blown tableware of good design. (*Figures 1, 4, 5, and 6 courtesy of* Carnegie Magazine)

writing east for new hands. As early as 1805 he was corresponding with Nicholas Swerer of the Kensington Works at Philadelphia. On August 25, 1810, after the short and apparently unsatisfactory sojourn of Frederick M. Amelung in Pittsburgh, O'Hara wrote to Joseph Carson of Philadelphia in the hope of securing the following blowers, all trained in the eastern style: Francis Wolf, Jacob Stanger, Frederick Stanger, Randolph Button, John Bolton, and Lewis Ferdinand. By his description of each man and by his offer of a three-year agreement, O'Hara must have investigated them well. So let us imagine that the pear-shaped bowls which often distinguish the sugar bowls of Pittsburgh are inherited from Stiegel. Otherwise the free-blown forms would seem to have grown out of a new environment: an old art meeting current needs.

The clear flint pieces of off-blown glass for table use probably were not made in great quantities except for decanters and tumblers. All these pieces had hard daily use and few have come down to us. Clear, usually lead, metal prevails. All the bases sturdily support any weight. The stems, though frequently baluster, are strong rather than graceful. The handles are often broad enough to be hollow. An unobtrusive touch of individuality sometimes appears — a flat thumb rest at the top of the handle where it joins the body of cruet or pitcher. This is a slight depression, not the thumb latch seen particularly in earlier Continental and South Jersey pieces. The sugar bowls swell generously in a pear shape or round bubble, the domed covers sinking below a supporting rim. Tooling appears most frequently on rims of pitchers. Rarest free-blown types are small bowls, salt cups, and plates. The rich fullness of easy curves had replaced the stiff heaviness of early bottle and window-glass factories, where many of the offhand pieces created were blown after hours by workmen for their families rather than as standard products. The glassblower of 1865 used the same tools and techniques as his fellow of 1820. True, the quality of metal might be improved, the design might have become smoother, yet the variations may be so slight and so paradoxical that an experienced collector can err frequently.

(*To be continued*)

Editor's Note. Part II of this article will continue Mr. Innes' analytical discussion of the glass produced at Pittsburgh, based on the comprehensive exhibition which he arranged at the Historical Society of Western Pennsylvania. It will discuss items representing the pattern-mold and pillar-mold techniques.

FIG. 5 — FREE-BLOWN GLASS. Cobalt and clear, by Thomas Bovard (*c. 1830*).

FIG. 6 (*right*) — PATTERN-MOLDED and free-blown examples. The free-blown pitcher and covered compote at right were discussed in Part I. The swirled cruet and paneled vase at left are good examples of glass made by the pattern-mold method.

FIG. 7 (*below*) — PATTERN-MOLDED and free-blown examples. *left*, pattern-molded sweetmeat dish on high baluster stem. *Right*, blown sugar bowl on funnel base such as is often found on large covered compotes and baptismal bowls.

PITTSBURGH GLASS

By LOWELL INNES

Part II

Twenty years ago Rhea Mansfield Knittle, pioneer student of American glass, wrote in ANTIQUES: "When the complete history of the early glass industry of the Pittsburgh district is some day written, it will form one of the most illuminating, surprising, and stimulating contributions to the manners and times of the formative period of our country which could be embodied in printed form." Not till 1947 was a comprehensive exhibition of Pittsburgh glass held; then it was arranged at the Historical Society of Western Pennsylvania by Lowell Innes. His article, of which Part I appeared last month, is a major contribution to that still incomplete history.

Pattern Mold (Figs. 6, 7, 8, 9)

THE DATES for free-blown and pattern-molded pieces are highly uncertain — conservatively from 1810 to 1870. In a letter written July 30, 1805, to Frederick M. Amelung of Baltimore, James O'Hara says: "You are right in procuring the molds, I wish you to have them complete." O'Hara had just settled with Amelung to come to his factory in Pittsburgh. What these molds were remains shrouded in obscurity. As for other Pittsburgh mold patterns, the McKearins believe firmly in the 8-rib, 12-rib, and 15-rib molds of the Bakewell factory, and the prevalence of such pitchers, sugar bowls, and covered sweetmeats in our district supports their opinion.

Some problem pieces which have convincing geographical histories were included in the 1947 exhibit: the large ale with sunken panels and the brilliant diamond bottle (16 chain diamonds), both shown in Figure 9; also a Stiegel-type salt with 16 round diamonds, and a small diamond whiskey glass. Three sunken-panel pieces also appeared: a beautiful compote attributed by George McKearin to Philadelphia, Cambridge, or

Pittsburgh (see ANTIQUES, August 1939, p. 63, Fig. 30); the small globular sugar bowl (*Fig. 9*) and the 9-inch vase (*Fig. 6*). Our purpose was to raise questions.

Of course, the ribbed Pittsburgh cruets always grace a midwestern collection. A few swirled pieces were shown, but no broken swirl.

Before leaving the pattern-molded group, I quote from a recent personal letter of James Rose, a very astute and traveled glass authority: "I'm as sure as I can ever be that a lot of the fine stuff now assigned to Zanesville or, in the case of three-mold, Mantua was actually made down your way. Take those light green swirled or herringbone pitchers now attributed to Zanesville . . . they don't turn up around Zanesville but do between Wheeling and Pittsburgh and I, for one, don't think Zanesville could have had much success shipping glass into that district. Moreover, there's no doubt at all but that Pittsburgh made fifty pieces of glass to Zanesville's one, but until we get into a relatively late period (beginning with those amethyst, blue and clear sugars, creamers and compotes made in the 12-rib mold which seem to date about 1840 or a little earlier) we attribute nothing to Pittsburgh."

Using Mr. Rose's dictum we should also say a word about blown-three-mold. In ANTIQUES for November 1926 Harry Hall White stated: "At just what year the three-mold blown decanters were first made in Pittsburgh, there is no definite record; but it is safe to state that communication with eastern manufacturers was sufficiently close to allow the making of three-mold pieces in Pittsburgh shortly after their eastern production, say 1815 or 1820. I am confident that this will be proven by subsequent in-

46

ANTIQUES

FIG. 8 — PATTERN-MOLDED examples. Matching sugar bowl and creamer blown in a 15-rib mold. The smaller creamer of 8-rib mold, in a design typical of Bakewell workmanship, looks reasonably early, but was a wedding present in the mid-1860's to the wife of Doctor David McCarell of Hickory, Pennsylvania.

vestigation." No Pittsburgh collector of my acquaintance, however, believes the theory that blown-three-mold glass was made here, principally because it does not turn up in any quantity.

Pillar Mold (*Figs. 10, 11, 12*)

If any type of blown glass has been instantly and generally attributed to Pittsburgh by antique dealers, it is the heavy river-boat tableware so widely distributed up and down the Ohio and Mississippi valleys. Characterized by vertical ribbing, it is known technically as pillar-molded. The process of manufacture described by Apsley Pellat has been often quoted and is conveniently summarized in McKearin's *American Glass* (pp. 21, 22).

For a long time I believed that the weight of the piece and of the ribbing approximately determined the age — the lighter, the earlier. The heaviest and latest would be well characterized by the Victorian vases, which have a constant charm in spite of their decadence. My opinion was changed quickly a few years ago when the Gailey Wilsons of Hickory, Pennsylvania, showed me two well-authenticated pitchers, equally heavy and almost identical (*Fig. 10*). One was brought from Ireland in 1817 by Richard Hanna, Mr. Wilson's ancestor. The other, purchased from a member of the Duval glassmaking family, was blown at Wellsburg, West Virginia, about a hundred years ago.

Over a reasonable period my conviction has been strengthened that pillar molding came to America from England and Ireland. I am also convinced that this type of blowing was practiced up and down the rivers. The article on Kentucky glass by Jane Keller Caldwell in ANTIQUES (November 1947) fortifies that opinion, for collectors in Pittsburgh can produce numerous duplicates of all the pieces she pictured. An article in *Antiquarian* (October 1929, p. 13) by Charles Messer Stow shows cuts from a McKee catalogue (*c. 1859*), several of which are identical with the pieces attributed to Louisville. Thomas C. Pears III has shown me a map of the Ohio and Mississippi valleys which his father drew to indicate where Bakewell glass was sent, basing it on references in the letters of his great-grandfather, Thomas Pears. Some of the towns noted, like Lexington, are not even on the river. Several letters written in 1820–1822 describe the difficulties of being stranded in a miserable frontier town like Shippingport with a

FIG. 9 — PATTERN-MOLDED examples, possibly Pittsburgh. Large ale glass on hollow hour-glass stem, 12 panels. Pint decanter, 16 chain diamonds. Small sugar, thoroughly Pittsburgh in shape, 9 panels.

FIG. 10 — PILLAR-MOLDED PITCHERS, clear glass, virtually identical in weight and type but of widely differing age and source, as proved by family authentication. *Left*, made in Ireland before 1817; *right*, blown at Wellsburg, West Virginia, about 1848.

FIG. 11 — PILLAR-MOLDED EXAMPLES. Tall vase, a superb piece, is brilliant smoky amber. Decanter and creamer, cobalt. Cruet, clear glass, lightly designed, with narrow ribbing. The glass stopper is exceptional; pewter or cork were usual.

boatload of glass to dispose of. Yet it had to be sold, and one must feel that much of the Valley glass came from Pittsburgh. At present Canadian antique shops have many pillar-molded bottles and decanters, undoubtedly imported from England and Ireland. Geographical distribution cannot be regarded as final evidence.

The pillar-molded section of the 1947 exhibition was brilliantly impressive. Pitchers, compotes, cruets, vases, decanters, and bowls predominated. Without doubt their use in hotels and on boats made certain types common. Chiefly an 8-rib mold seemed to have been employed in Pittsburgh, though every once in a while 12 ribs may be found. This type of glass was made even past the turn of our century.

FIG. 12 — HEAVY-RIBBED pillar-molded examples in clear glass. Pitcher shown in McKee catalogue (c. 1860). Decanter (left) typical of so-called river-boat glass.

I have encountered pieces like the river-boat type which were made elsewhere. The closest approximations in pitchers that I have seen come from eastern Massachusetts.

A most fascinating puzzle is how to draw the line between conventional pattern molding and the obvious pillar ribs. The demarcation is as uncertain as the line between prose and poetry, because they always approach a common point. The small blue creamer in Figure 11 is a good example. In Pittsburgh proper it would be called pillar molding; outside, I think, pattern molding. Actual dating of molded pieces, too, is equally uncertain during the first sixty years of the nineteenth century.

Miscellaneous (Figs. 13, 14)

FLASKS. It is surprising today that Pittsburgh has no major collectors of flasks, surprising because the district must have shipped millions down the rivers and to the western territories. Of the fifteen included in the 1947 exhibit probably the best one for metal design and rarity was that illustrated in Figure 13. The others, mostly of the Civil War period, bore the starry pennon, clasped hands, eagle, Union flags, and cannon. A couple of Masonic ones broke the monotony, as did a late soda-water bottle. All were marked *Pittsburgh;* only the Bakewell and one other carried a firm name. The latter, a bluish aquamarine quart, was decorated with an upright flag on one side and a sturdy cannon on the other and was made at the little-known factory of William Frank & Son, which operated from 1854 on. Alan Frank, a great-grandson of William, now owns the flask.

DECANTERS AND TUMBLERS. Gorgeous color appeared in three blown-molded decanters: two, a canary yellow and an amethyst one, were *Ashburton* quarts; the third, a blue paneled *flute,* is shown in Figure 13, with matching tumbler and a whimsical plate made from a tumbler mold.

48

ANTIQUES

FIG. 13 — BAR WARE molded in *flute* pattern. A Bakewell catalogue (*1875*) shows similar pieces made by pressing. Cobalt blue except tall clear rummer beside decanter. *Right*, Half-pint scroll flask, green, marked B. P. & B. (*1824–1836*). (In 1824 the name was Bakewell, Page & Bakewell; in 1836 it became Bakewell, Pears and Company.)

LINED OR CASED GLASS. After seeing the marvelous blue-lined sugar bowl in the Garvan collection at Yale, one might rightfully expect multicolored glass from Pittsburgh. The specimens in our exhibit, three pitchers, were probably of the second half of the century, after the Austrian blowers had toured the States and influenced taste. One pitcher, very much like Figure 1, Plate 54, of McKearin's *American Glass*, is grey and opaque white. The second, heavier and more graceful in both bowl and handle, is of fiery opal covered with clear. The third, shaped conventionally like the second, has a rich amethyst lining, a white second layer, and a clear glass outer covering.

PRESERVING JARS. Three marked quart jars throw light on techniques. Two of them came from the McKee factory. The first, of clear metal, is completely free-blown, with a cover showing the seal impression *J. & F. McKee, Pittsburgh, Pa*. The cover has an absolutely smooth edge devised, we think, to seal itself against the top hermetically. The second McKee jar of aquamarine glass was blown into a two-part mold with *S. McKee & Co., Pittsburgh, Pa*. stamped on the bottom. The top of this jar was of tin fitting down into a glass shoulder around which hot wax was to be poured for the sealing. J. & F. McKee was the firm name in 1850, but within three years it had become McKee Brothers. According to Rhea Mansfield Knittle, S. McKee & Co. was an earlier organization than either J. & F. or McKee Brothers, but the blown-molded jar seems much later than the blown one spoken of above. The third jar, a crude citron one, is of the same design and technique as the later McKee jar and carries the impression *A. G. W. L. Pitts. Pa*. Probably it is from the mysterious Arsenal Glass Works of the Lawrenceville district. Charles Jeremy backed this enterprise, which seems to have folded after one year, 1865–1866, as far as evidence from the city directories guides us.

(*To be concluded*)

FIG. 14 — CASED-GLASS COMPOTE attributed to Pittsburgh. Bowl double-dipped: inside amethyst, outside opalescent. Attached stem and foot of clear glass.

Figures 6, 7, and 12 courtesy Carnegie Magazine. Items illustrated in Parts I and II from the following collections: Pittsburgh Chapter of the Early American Glass Club, Mr. E. R. Eller, Dr. Florence Kline, Mr. John J. Grossman, Mr. John H. Neelley, Mr. and Mrs. Robert Carew, Mr. and Mrs. Gailey Wilson, Mrs. Rhea Mansfield Knittle, and the author.

THE GLASSMAKING KRAMERS

By NEIL C. GEST and PARKE G. SMITH

THE MIGRATIONS of early glassworkers from the factories of Maryland and eastern Pennsylvania into the Pittsburgh region and thence westward into Ohio have been traced by the glass that has been found along their route. In ANTIQUES for August 1937, Harry Hall White discussed at length the course of these migrations, and the spread of influence from early glassmaking centers through certain well-defined zones. Little has been published, however, concerning the peregrinations of individual glassworkers. In the hope of partly filling this gap, we present a brief history of Johann Baltazar Kramer and his son, George. Kramer's name is associated with the Stiegel factory, with those of Frederick County, Maryland, particularly Amelung, and with the New Geneva and Greensboro works.

Our investigation of the glassmaker was prompted by discovery of several pieces of glass that may be ascribed to Kramer. It has been greatly facilitated by the courteous generosity of LeRoy Kramer of Chicago, who has put at our disposal genealogical data regarding Johann Baltazar Kramer and his descendants.

The first Johann Baltazar Kramer came to America from Germany on the good ship *Britannia*, landing at Philadelphia, September 18, 1773. Accompanying him were his brothers, Adam, George, and Martin. Of their activities during the first weeks after their arrival on these shores, little is known, but it was not long before Johann Kramer turned up at the glassworks of Henry William Stiegel. In the archives of the Historical Society of Pennsylvania are rec-

FIG. 1 — FLIP GLASSES
Left, taken to Ohio by George Kramer. Brilliant green. *Height*, 5 inches. *Right*, attributed to the Amelung factory. Clear flint glass, slightly smoky in thicker portions. Heavy base, similar to flip at left; sides more widely flaring.
From the collections of Parke G. Smith and Miss Margaret B. Waesche

ords of his continuous employment by Stiegel from October 23, 1773, to March 4, 1774, and of Stiegel's employment of Martin Kramer from the same October date until his death in January 1774.

Johann Baltazar Kramer married Margaretta Berta Volsin on January 18, 1775. Of that union six children were born. Three births are officially recorded in the Ger-

FIG. 2 — FLUTED "JELLY GLASSES"
Left, taken to Ohio by George Kramer. Brilliant green, full of bubbles. 24 ribs. *Height*, 2½ inches. *Right*, found near New Geneva. Blown in mold with 24 ribs.
From the collections of Parke G. Smith and Neil C. Gest

FIG. 3 *(left)* — WINE GLASSES
Left, taken to Ohio by George Kramer. Deep green. *Height*, 5 inches. *Right*, attributed to the Amelung factory. Clear flint glass. More refined in material and line than the glass at the left.
From the collections of Parke G. Smith and Miss Margaret B. Waesche

FIG. 4 *(right)* — SMALL TUMBLER
Taken to Ohio by George Kramer. Brilliant green. *Height*, 3 inches.
From the collection of Parke G. Smith

118

FIG. 5 — THREE BOTTLES
Taken to Ohio by George Kramer and now in the possession of his descendants. Like all pieces attributed to Kramer, they are made of brilliant green glass, typical of the products of New Geneva and Greensboro. The bottle at the right below is unusually heavy. The flask has a so-called sheared neck. The mouths of these bottles are reinforced. *Heights, left,* 8 inches, *lower right,* 9 ½ inches, *lower left,* 8 inches.
From the collection of Parke G. Smith

man Reformed Church of Frederick, Maryland: those of Margaret on September 2, 1775, Baltazar on October 10, 1777, and George on January 22, 1780. The will of Johann Baltazar Kramer, dated October 12, 1813, and filed in Fayette County, Pennsylvania, contains reference to the other three children: Polly, whose married name was Axton, Christiana (Kramer) Scott, and a son, Andrew, who appears to have been born March 26, 1790.

As Johann Baltazar Kramer was a glassblower it is reasonable to surmise that following the termination of his employment by Stiegel he might have sought work in one of the little-known glass factories near the German community in Frederick County, Maryland, which was not far distant. Although no extant records associate Johann Baltazar Kramer with the Amelung works, which were opened in 1784, we know that during the period of their activity he was in Frederick County, and that his family was on intimate terms with some members of the New Bremen community. Furthermore, it may be more than coincidence that at about the time when the Amelung project was meeting financial difficulties, Johann Baltazar Kramer left Frederick County. He is known to have been in Fayette County, Pennsylvania (New Geneva and Greensboro), in 1794.

An oft-quoted tale recounts that a group composed of Johann Baltazar Kramer, his son George, a relative, Christian Kramer, and friends, Louis Reitz, George Reppler, John C. Gabler, and Adolph Eberhart, accompanied by their families, met Albert Gallatin at Tomlinson's Tavern in Greenville, adjacent to Cumberland, Maryland, and that Gallatin persuaded them to join forces with him at the New Geneva, Pennsylvania, glassworks. Albert Gallatin, a Swiss, had in 1785 settled on the Monongahela River opposite Greensboro. The

FIG. 6 — PITCHER, GOBLET, AND CANDY JAR
Taken to Ohio by George Kramer and now in the possession of his descendants. All brilliant green. *Height of pitcher,* 8 inches. *Height of goblet,* 8 ½ inches; *diameter,* 5 inches. *Height of jar,* 11 inches

village that grew up around his home he named for his native city. Whether his meeting with the glassmakers was accidental or prearranged is a question. Since Gallatin was supplying the capital for a new glass factory, however, it seems likely that the meeting was prearranged so that he might employ blowers and workers. In any event, an agreement was reached, and glassmaking began at New Geneva late in 1794, according to a recently discovered newspaper article by James Ross, an early western Pennsylvania settler. The article gives details regarding the first operations and the subsequent construction of three plants, listing as workmen all those who had convened at Tomlinson's Tavern, and others added as business progressed.

The first works were small and equipped with only four pots. They were located near George's Creek, about a mile from the Monongahela and outside the village of New Geneva. The initial output of the new factory is believed to have consisted mainly of window glass and other forms of crown glass. A few years later, as the new country became more thickly populated, the original factory was abandoned and a new plant built at Greensboro, across the river. In the meantime, Albert Gallatin, who had been appointed Secretary of the United States Treasury by President Jefferson, had in 1803 sold his interests to a number of his associates and workmen. The principal purchasers appear to have been the Kramers, although George Teppert, John Gabler, and possibly all of the original Frederick County group participated.

About 1837, while the Greensboro plant was still active, a new plant was built at New Geneva, owned by Andrew Kramer, Theophilus P. Kramer, and Philip Reitz, all descendants of the original New Geneva group. The factory continued in operation until about 1857, when it yielded to the competition of increasingly numerous pressed-glass factories. Thus we find members of the Kramer family perpetuating the glassmaking tradition from the time of Stiegel's last attempt until after the middle of the following century.

In 1813 Johann Baltazar Kramer died. In 1818 or 1819 his son, George Kramer, left New Geneva with his family and traveled overland to the Ohio, down the river on a flatboat to the new community of Cincinnati, and again overland about forty miles to the north, where he settled in Oxford Township, Butler County, Ohio. Living today in Oxford is a Mrs. Martha Ellen (Herron) Emerick, now over ninety years of age, who is a granddaughter of George Kramer (son of Baltazar) and Barbara, daughter of Ludwig Kramer (not related to Baltazar). Mrs. Emerick remembers hearing her grandmother tell of attending the New Bremen school.

This implies that Ludwig may have worked in the Amelung factory, and suggests the possibility that Baltazar was likewise employed there. It may be pointed out that two Kramers appear in the list of Amelung's workmen, though their given names are not mentioned. Mrs. Emerick recalls that her grandfather, George Kramer, when he left New Geneva for Oxford, took a great deal of glass with him to use as a means of barter in his new home, and that after his death the pieces remaining were distributed among the grandchildren. Many items were given to Mrs. Emerick and are still either in her own or family possession. Of this group several are here illustrated, and credited to New Geneva and Greensboro on the basis of this family tradition.

The output of the earlier works with which the Kramers were connected seems to have been chiefly, if not exclusively, green glass. According to invoices and accounts in the possession of LeRoy Kramer, the Kramers produced a great deal of window glass and quantities of bottles. All the pieces here ascribed to them are of green glass. While fine amber and green quilted flasks, "grandfather" flasks, and various items in blue and amethyst have been credited to these factories, we have been unable to find a basis for their attribution either to New Geneva or to Greensboro. Many pieces have been found in that locality — unauthenticated, of course, though with plenty of local tradition — but they are milk bowls, bottles of various sizes, pans, an occasional creamer or salt shaker, many flip and toddy glasses, wines, a few sugar bowls, and so on. Many are no doubt offhand blown. There is little doubt that much glass of brilliant color and fine quality came from the Pittsburgh district, but we have no record that anything other than the typical greens came from New Geneva or Greensboro.

The pieces here attributed to the Kramers and their associates show a relationship to Maryland glass. In fact, on grounds of intrinsic evidence as well as tradition, it seems not unreasonable to suggest that Baltazar Kramer may have worked in the New Bremen factory. It is interesting to compare the flips and wine glasses shown at the left in Figures 1 and 3, and Amelung glasses shown beside them, which were discussed in ANTIQUES for September 1934 (p. 91). The former, to be sure, are not engraved. On the whole, they are of inferior metal, with numerous bubbles and impurities, and they seem to be less competently fashioned.

FIG. 8 — LARGE GREEN BOWL
Found within a few miles of New Geneva. Metal of finer quality than most pieces here illustrated; shape unsymmetrical; workmanship crude. *From the collection of Neil C. Gest*

FIG. 7 — BRILLIANT GREEN BOWL
Found in possession of a family for two generations neighbors of the Kramers; according to tradition, originally acquired from George Kramer. Note the characteristic bulge, which likewise occurs in candy jars and bowls attributed to the Kramers. *Diameter, 6 inches. From the collection of Parke G. Smith*

Worthy of comparison are the fluted glasses shown in Figure 2 and the sugar bowl of Figure 9. The two glasses and the body of the bowl are of the same height and all are patterned with twenty-four ribs. While one jelly glass of Figure 2 is of poorer quality and cruder workmanship than the other, the two may have been blown in the same mold. The sugar bowl differs from these glasses in contour, but its similarity in size and pattern indicates that it may likewise have been blown in the same mold and expanded above the base after removal from the mold. It is of the same deep, brilliant green as one glass of Figure 2 and was discovered in the same possession. Since one of the glasses of Figure 2 was taken to Ohio by George Kramer, these two related items may also be ascribed to New Geneva.

Eventually it may be possible to establish a definite standard for identification of Kramer-made glass. In the meantime, the pieces here illustrated and this résumé of the Kramers' activities are offered as a basis for further investigation and discussion. Certainly the rôle played by members of the Kramer family in the glassmaking history of this country was one of no little importance.

Note. A brief account of the glassworks at New Geneva and Greensboro is given by Rhea Mansfield Knittle in her book, *Early American Glass.* For further information concerning glass and glassmaking of the Monongahela River district, the reader may be interested to consult the following articles in ANTIQUES:

Rex Absolutus of the Monongahela, by Rhea Mansfield Knittle, April 1928 (*p. 290*)

The Distribution of Early American Glass, by Lura Woodside Watkins, July 1937 (*p. 11*)

Bowls and Pans: A Guide for Collectors, by Rhea Mansfield Knittle, June 1932 (*p. 264*)

References to Amelung and his glass occur in the Magazine in the articles listed above, and also as follows:

Safe Clues in the Amelung Quest, by Homer Eaton Keyes, September 1934 (*p. 88*)

Add to Amelung, January 1935 (*p. 7*)

Fresh Reflections on American Glass, February 1938 (*p. 80*)

ALBERT GALLATIN (*1761–1849*)
Statesman and financier, Secretary of the United States Treasury under Thomas Jefferson. Founder of the New Geneva glassworks and sponsor of the Kramers

FIG. 9 — COVERED SUGAR BOWL
Unusually deep brilliant green. Body of bowl blown in mold with 24 ribs; applied handles and 5-scalloped base; plain cover, pontiled under the swan which is annealed to top. Compare body of bowl with the jelly glasses shown in Figure 2: all have 24 ribs, are identical in color, and appear to have been blown in the same mold. Sugar bowl and glass at the right in Figure 2 were found in the same possession in a farmhouse about 30 miles from New Geneva, and according to tradition were made in a near-by factory.
From the collection of Neil C. Gest

FIG. 10 — WIDE-RIMMED BOWL OR PAN
Found near Greensboro. Unusual shape. Similar in quality of glass and workmanship to pieces here attributed to the Kramers.
From the collection of Neil C. Gest

The Lancaster Glass Works

By HARRY HALL WHITE

All photographs by the author, from specimens in his personal collection

HISTORY

THAT we have a fairly exact date for the establishment of The Lancaster Glass Works is possibly due to the fact that the enterprise had its beginning in the same year that the city of Lancaster was incorporated — 1849. For forty years prior to that year, the thriving young city of Pittsburgh, Pennsylvania, had been a training school for glassworkers, and had supplied many outside ventures with practical men. So it happened at Lancaster that the original plant was started by a group of operatives who hailed from Pittsburgh.

REED, ALLEN, COX AND COMPANY

Prominent among these men—eight in all—and evidently the promoter of the enterprise, was one Charles Reed. The group erected their establishment on what was, at that time, appropriately known as Factory Street, now named Court Street. It was a small affair, having a five-pot furnace, with pots not over twenty-four inches in diameter. The pioneer company apparently included some of the workmen, as it was styled Reed, Allen, Cox and Company.

REED, SHINN AND COMPANY

The duration of this first company's operations is not known. Some changes in make-up occurred for reasons which are not recorded. Evidently some of the founders of what was originally a coöperative company sold to a man by the name of Samuel S. Shinn; for the second recorded name of the firm is that of Reed, Shinn and Company.

JAMES, GATCHELL AND COMPANY

During the operations of this new firm a fire destroyed much of the works. This occurred in 1859. The plant was rebuilt at once, and continued under the same control until 1863, when Dr. Frank H. James purchased the interest of Shinn, and carried on the business with N. B. Gatchell under the firm name of James, Gatchell and Company. This partnership lasted until after the close of the Civil War, when James and Gatchell purchased the holdings of the remaining partners, and manufactured glass under their own names.

The Directory of 1866 shows their advertisement, in which it is stated that they manufacture "glassware of every description, with a large supply on hand." That advertisement sounds very familiar to anyone conversant with similar announcements of the period. One might almost think, from this uniformity, that they were syndicated. The wording is very clear in its implication of large scale production; but none of the surviving workmen, or the associates of the company, or the older inhabitants of Lancaster can recall any products of the establishment other than bottles and flasks — except for a period during the Civil War, when large quantities of telegraph insulators were made.

THE JAMES GLASS WORKS

The Directory of 1866 also gives the following names of the workmen employed:

Glass blowers	Pot maker	Machinist and Mold maker
J. D. Fry	Sherman Remington	Thomas Leary
J. J. Voll		
H. Kupper		
B. Myers		
J. Springer		

About this time the interests of Gatchell were purchased by Dr. James, and the works were then known as The James Glass Works.

Following the Civil War, Lancaster's production kept pace with the times. The day of the patent medicine was at hand, along with that of liquor camouflaged for the conscientious under the alias of "bitters." That the factory took advantage of this demand is evident when we examine the long list of medicine, bitters, and perfume bottles which it turned out.

In connection with the works under the operation of Dr. James was a company store where the employees might take merchandise as part or full equivalent of their wages. Consequently the proprietor at times allowed the purchasers of his glasswares to make payment in articles of value to the company store. Firearms, ammunition, footwear, and many other things were thus accepted in exchange. One of the old glassworkers recalls Dr. James' telling, with amusement, of a certain customer from Rochester, New York, a large purchaser of perfume bottles, who offered coffins in trade for bottles.

In the early days of Lancaster, the local glassworks were among the most prominent of the town's industries, and, for a long period — probably after the factory fire — the only fire apparatus in the town was owned by the glass company.

LANCASTER COÖPERATIVE GLASS WORKS

Dr. James retired in 1881, when his establishment was purchased by a company composed of the workmen of the plant, which was now styled The Lancaster Coöperative Glass Works, Limited. This carries the genealogy of the concern as far as the collector is interested to follow.

IDENTIFYING LANCASTER GLASS

It has been my good fortune to have an interview with Frank H. James, son of Dr. James, the former owner, who was associated with his father in the management of the works. Mr. James has given me much information regarding the factory's later products. Many details of the process of manufacture and of the product have like-

Fig. 1 (left) — SCROLL FLASK Sometime a product of the Lancaster Glass Works, (*one pint, aquamarine*).

Fig. 2 (right) — URN-CORNUCOPIA FLASK No inscription (*one pint, aquamarine*).

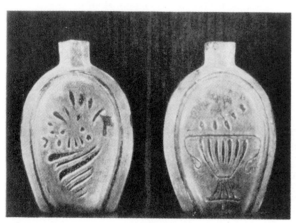

Fig. 3 (left) — URN-CORNUCOPIA FLASK No inscription (*one-half pint, aquamarine*).

Fig. 4 (right) — URN-CORNUCOPIA FLASK Reverse marked *Lancaster Glass Works, N. Y.* (*one pint; aquamarine*).

Fig. 5 (left) — LANCASTER BOTTLES Wishart's Pine Tree Cordial, Flora Temple, and C. W. Merchant.

Fig. 6 (right) — LANCASTER BOTTLES Warner's Tippecanoe Bitters, Drake's Plantation Bitters, and Barrel.

Fig. 7 (left) — WARNER'S SAFE CURE BOTTLES The one-half pint and clear glass bottles were evidently made at a later date and at another factory.

Fig. 8 (right) — LANCASTER GLASS ITEMS

wise been given by John G. Lumbrix, a practical glass blower, who started with the works in the fall of 1861. Of particular interest is the fact that the bottles and flasks named in the following list were identified by these gentlemen as having, at some time, been made in Lancaster. This does not mean that they were exclusively a Lancaster product. Similar molds may have been in use in other works at the same time. Then, as today, bottles were bought from the maker who could quote the best price, and frequently a source of supply was changed for this very reason.

BOTTLES AND FLASKS MADE AT LANCASTER

Bottles	*Flasks*
Hostetter's Bitters	Scroll
Dr. Fish Bitters	Traveller (Pikes Peak)
Plantation Bitters	Railroad with eagle
Burdock Bitters	Urn-Cornucopia
Warner's Tippecanoe Bitters	Clasped Hands
Warner's Safe Bitters	Shoo-fly
Wishart's Pine Tree Cordial	Picnic
C. W. Merchant, Lockport, N. Y.	
Clarissy's White Oil Liniment	
Shilo's Cough Cure	
John Roach Bitters	
Stimson and Hebblewhite Blacking	
C. B. Woodworth, Rochester, N. Y.	
(Many shapes: boots, slippers, etc.)	
Summerville Horse Medium, Buffalo, N. Y.	
(Shape of a horse's hoof)	
Monitor Inks	
Barrel shaped	
Flora Temple	

Quite a long list; and yet we may doubt that it is complete, as my informants had only memory to rely upon, the accounts and books of the old company having been destroyed some years ago. The above list, however, is of items positively identified.

THE SCROLL FLASK

It is of great interest to have a maker of the *Scroll* flask known in addition to the Louisville Glass Works. The *Scroll* flask of Figure 1 was positively named as being of the type that had been made at Lancaster at some time in the past. Neither of my informants could remember the *Scroll* molds being put to use during the period of their experience, but both recall having seen these molds in the storage room.

THE URN-CORNUCOPIA FLASK

The most familiar marked flask from the Lancaster works is the *Urn-Cornucopia* type, marked *Lancaster Glass Works, N. Y.* The exact date of its production could not be determined, as this occurred previous to the memory of my friends. This fact seems to confine the period of manufacture of the *Urn-Cornucopia* type within the dates 1850–1860. Flasks of this type are frequently found blown of the coarsest glass, filled with bubbles, or "seeds," as the glassmaker terms them. Lancaster seems to have been notorious for this characteristic of its glass. One of the old-timers recalls a Buffalo liquor dealer who jokingly told him that the filled flasks on his shelves were leaking. The mold for the *Urn-Cornucopia* flask is reported to have been made in the factory machine shop by the company's moldmaker, Thomas Leary. One glassmaker told me that it was cut in plaster of Paris, and that the shallow

modeling is due to this circumstance, as well as to the fact that shallow cutting facilitated removal of the blown vessel from the mold. This flask seems to occur in as many variations of color as any we have. It is found in two sizes: one pint (*Fig. 2*) and one-half pint (*Fig. 3*). The one-half pint size has not been found marked; and not all of the one pint sizes are found marked (*Fig. 4*).

THE PIKES PEAK FLASK

The *Pikes Peak* flask was identified only in general without reference to specific detail of design. What was known to the concern as a *Traveller Flask* was also made. This was evidently the type which shows the "Weary Willie," but without the inscription.

THE RAILROAD FLASK

A most thrilling piece of information was the description of a *Railroad* flask carrying the locomotive across the flask, with a spread eagle on the reverse. I have not seen this flask, but I understand that specimens have come to the hands of more fortunate collectors.

THE FLORA TEMPLE

The *Flora Temple* has been found in several colors, and in two sizes, with and without handle. Its inscriptions vary slightly, the date *Oct. 15, 1859* being omitted in some cases.

VARIOUS SPECIMENS

The *Clasped Hands, Picnic, Shoo-fly,* and bitters bottles mentioned are all too well known to collectors to warrant extended description.

Many articles other than bottles, made in Lancaster, have been found in the homes of the former glass blowers and their friends. These consist of the usual objects made offhand as gifts: canes, pipes, hats, water hammers, flowers, cigar and cigarette holders, doorstops in the form of turtles, and paper weights.

The majority of such objects occur in brown glass, of the same metal that was used in the bitters bottles. Some clear glass pieces are also found; but in canes, hats, and pipes the brown predominates. The most interesting of these articles are the paper weights and turtle doorstops. The weights come in many colors: clear glass, smoky glass, aquamarine bottle glass, and deep sapphire blue. Their contents varied apparently with the materials at hand, and consist of all of the above colors of broken glass, while one is at hand that has a sprinkling of pot clay over the broken colored glass. The turtles are frequently found in mixtures of many colors fused together.

In all, I feel that The Lancaster Glass Works is one of the most interesting of the later bottle houses of what was once the Middle West, and I am confident that, when further data are forth-coming, some of our rarer types of flasks may be found to have been made there.

SUMMARY OF COMPANY NAMES

Reed, Allen, Cox and Company	1849– ——
Reed, Shinn and Company	—— –1863
James, Gatchell and Company	1863–1866
James and Gatchell	1866– ——
James Glass Works	—— –1881
Lancaster Coöperative Glass Works, Ltd.	1881–1890

One of the first serious students of early American craftsmanship was Dr. Walter Hough, former Head Curator of Anthropology in the United States National Museum. An ethnologist, he extended the limits of his field to include the folkways of our own civilization. The result was to enrich the Museum's collections of useful objects from the American past and to preserve many specimens of interest to present-day antiquarians.

Among his acquisitions for the Museum is a group of ceramics and glass from the Monongahela Valley, which he collected in the 1890's. The ceramics are products of the Thompsons' Morgantown, West Virginia, pottery, and of the Vance-Boughner pottery in nearby Greensboro, Pennsylvania. These were described in a monograph in the Appendix of the Annual Report of the Smithsonian Institution for 1899. The glass, which was obtained in 1898, has not been published until now.

Dr. Hough was a native of Morgantown, which is a few miles south of Greensboro. Greensboro, it will be remembered, is across the river from New Geneva, the site of the glassworks founded in 1797 by Albert Gallatin's company and a band of former Amelung employees from New Bremen. Greensboro itself was the site of a second glassworks established by substantially the same group in 1804.

The potteries were still running during Dr. Hough's youth and the last manufacture of glass had ended only

Blown candlestick of deep sea-green glass. Made about 1812 in the New Geneva Glass Works. Height 8 inches.

Aquamarine glass bottle, blown by Adolph Eberhart, Sr. in a 24-rib dip mold at Albert Gallatin's New Geneva (Pennsylvania) Glass Works between 1803 and 1806. Height 7¾ inches. Diameter 4½ inches.

Photographs courtesy of the Smithsonian Institution.

Some New Geneva and Greensboro glass

BY C. MALCOLM WATKINS

Engraved clear-glass flip. Made at Albert Gallatin's Greenboro, Pennsylvania, factory. Height, 5⅞ inches. Diameter of base, 3⅜ inches.

doubt the authenticity of the legend, however, since it would have been kept alive by three generations of Eberharts who worked at New Geneva and Greensboro.

One can also point out that several pieces attributed to New Geneva, including one of indisputable origin, were blown in a 24-rib mold, as this was. There is nothing in the character of the glass or its workmanship that would preclude its having been made at the Gallatin factory.

The candlestick was presented to Dr. Hough by Mrs. Dorcas Haymond, daughter of John W. Thompson of the Morgantown pottery. She inherited it from her mother, who, the accession papers state, was born late in the eighteenth century. The date of the candlestick is given as "about 1812," and the place of manufacture as "Albert Gallatin's factory at New Geneva." Here we have typical Amelung workmanship combined with the rich, deep green metal found in both Amelung and New Geneva fragments as well as in some of the more ambitious New Geneva pieces. The large hollow knops are reminiscent of the Amelung pokals. One detail, however, seems to tie it to New Geneva. This is the molded base of the nozzle where it is joined to the top of the stem. This base is a superimposed gather of glass shaped in a 16-rib mold by a primitive sort of pillar-mold technique. This was probably accomplished by blowing the extra gather against the bottom part of the same 16-rib dip mold which has survived among the descendants of Christian Kramer, one of the early New Geneva glassblowers. The mold is illustrated in *American Glass*, Plate 46, #8.

The clear engraved flip glass, like the candlestick an affectionately restored victim of an ancient and forgotten accident, is perhaps a unique specimen. Not in any of the glass ascribed to Stiegel or Amelung, or yet to Pittsburgh, do we find such a free-flowing, vine-like type of copper-wheel engraving as this. Executed with no great skill, it still has naive charm and individuality. The metal is thin soda-lime glass with a slight greenish-blue tint visible in the thicker portions, while the bottom is noticeably domed. According to Mrs. Haymond, from whom this also was acquired, it was made at "the Albert Gallatin Glass Works at Greensboro, Pa." There is a clear distinction here from the older New Geneva factory. Although Miss Evelyn Abraham ("The Glass of New Geneva and Greensboro," *The Antiquarian*, August 1931) found nothing but pale green fragments at Greensboro, the McKearins, quoting the Gallatin papers (*Two Hundred Years of American Blown Glass*, p. 47), show that clear glass was listed in the account books. Moreover, instead of a tumbler resembling the products of some other factory, we have here a clear-glass specimen with no known counterpart, ascribed in 1898 to Greensboro by the same person who attributed the green glass candlestick to New Geneva. Such a distinction must indicate a definite association of each piece with its source.

All three of these specimens, with their comparatively reliable documentation, are of interest to students and collectors of American glass. The fact that local recollection of them was recorded fifty-four years ago by a trained scientist brought up in the vicinity of their use gives them a special significance.

(Published by permission of the Secretary of the Smithsonian Institution)

a few years before he was born in 1859. In Morgantown, where he made his home until the 'nineties, he knew the Thompson family, while in Greensboro he was acquainted with the Boughners, whose handsome stoneware represented the last flowering of the rural potter's art in western Pennsylvania. Interestingly enough, it was from members of the potters' families that Dr. Hough acquired the glass described here. This is not surprising, for preservation of the glass by the potters was to be expected in the appreciation and pride that one group of local craftsmen would have felt for the kindred work of another. The potters, also, more than ordinary laymen, would have cherished the traditions that went with the glass, so that credence can justifiably be given the information passed on to Dr. Hough.

The aquamarine ribbed bottle illustrated here was obtained from the Reverend Claude Boughner of Greensboro. According to the Museum's records, Mr. Boughner provided the following statement: "This bottle was made at the Albert Gallatin glass factory on George's Creek near New Geneva, Pennsylvania, about 1803 to 1806 and was blown by Adolph Eberhart, Sr., who was one of the soldiers who carried LaFayette off the battlefield at Brandywine in the year 1777. Mr. Eberhart was the great-grandfather of the famous Robert J. Burdette."

Eberhart was one of the former Amelung workmen who comprised the first New Geneva group. His glass-making career has been described by Rhea Mansfield Knittle in *Rex Absolutus of the Monongahela* (ANTIQUES, April 1928), as well as by the McKearins. He stands today as a well-known figure in the history of American glassmaking. But to Mr. Boughner in 1898 his reputation must have been mainly that of a local patriot and ancestor of a contemporary humorist, while the bottle was an interesting associational relic. There is little reason to

The Midwest became early, and remains today, one of the most important glassmaking centers in the country. Ohio was making blown glass as early as 1814, and developed distinctive pattern-molded types that have long been beloved of collectors. Blown glass was made in Michigan by 1835. Later in the century pressed glass was produced in all the six states that once made up the Northwest Territory, and so were various types of art glass before and after 1900.

The earlier pieces shown here represent types that have been attributed to Ohio and Michigan glasshouses; the later ones have been identified by marks or by documentary evidence.

Glass

The old Northwest Territory

Ohio glass, blown and pattern molded, 1815-1850.

Bottle, deep amber, free blown. *Baugh.* Miniature bottle, probably Zanesville. Pattern molded, 16 rib; green. *OHS.* Bottle, probably Zanesville. Pattern molded, 30 rib; aquamarine. Height 11¾ inches. *HFM.* Jug, probably Zanesville. Pattern molded, 24 broken rib; deep amber. *DIA.*

Blown and pattern-molded glass made by the Mantua Glass Works, Mantua, Ohio, 1821-1829.

Salt, pattern molded, 16 rib; light green. *Simmons.* Sugar bowl. Pattern molded, 16 rib; amethyst. *HFM.* Pan. Pattern molded, 16 rib; moonstone. *OHS.* Mug, free blown, threaded neck, applied handle; olive green. Height 4⅛ inches. Ex coll. *Harry Hall White. DIA.*

Pattern-molded glass, 24 rib, deep amber, attributed to Zanesville, Ohio, 1815-1835.

Bowl with drawn foot. *DIA.* Covered sugar bowl with drawn foot. Height 7½ inches. *Elsholz.* Cream pitcher with applied handle. *Baugh.*

Pattern-molded glass in ten-diamond design, attributed to the White Glass Works, Zanesville, Ohio, 1815-1835.

Chestnut bottle, deep amber. *OHS.* Compote, deep amber. *HFM.* Inkwell, aquamarine. *Baugh.* Sugar bowl, light green. Height 6¾ inches. Ex coll. *W. T. H. Howe. CAM.*

Free-blown glass by Hall & Grovier, Mount Clemens, Michigan, 1835-1843.

Milk pan, aquamarine. Diameter 10¾ inches. *HFM.* Jar, aquamarine. *DIA.* Vase, aquamarine. *DIA.*

Pressed glass made by the Indiana Tumbler and Goblet Company, Greentown, Indiana, 1894-1903.

Dolphin, opaque nile green. *Brunner.* Compote, caramel (originally called chocolate), cactus pattern. Height 8⅜ inches. *Luedders.* Cream pitcher, holly amber (originally, golden agate). *Elsholz.*

Onyx glass, made by Dalzell, Gilmore and Leighton Company, Findlay, Ohio, patented 1889.

Covered butter dish, raspberry with white decoration. Mustard jar, cream with apricot decoration; pewter top. Water pitcher, white with silver decoration. Height 7¾ inches. *Brunner.*

Whimseys and novelties.

Paperweight, black glass in the form of a turtle. Chase Glass Works, Bay View (Milwaukee), Wisconsin, c. 1900. *MPM.* Flower, pale aquamarine, Milwaukee Glass Company, c. 1905. *MPM.* Whimsey in form of a hat, pale aquamarine, Milwaukee Glass Company, c. 1900. *MPM.* Amberina cream pitcher, Libbey Glass Company, Toledo, Ohio, c. 1888. Printed paper label, *Libbey Made in U. S. A.* Height 4½ inches. *OHS.* Iridescent vase, Imperial Glass Company, Bellaire, Ohio, c. 1910. Mark *Nuart* molded on edge of base. Height 6 1/16 inches. *Simmons.*

EARLY NINETEENTH-CENTURY GLASSMAKING IN OHIO

By HELEN McKEARIN

ONLY A LITTLE OVER TWENTY YEARS AGO collectors of American glass never had read of the early nineteenth-century glasshouses of Ohio and of the Monongahela-Ohio River districts, of which the Pittsburgh section was the apex — an area now defined as "midwestern" in the glass collector's lexicon. If they realized that any glass originated in this region they probably thought of the panes in their windows or the tablewares of A. H. Heisey and Company. Unwittingly, they might have owned a few pieces, but catalogued as "Stiegel." Today the expertly fashioned early midwestern glass, particularly the individual pieces blown and usually pattern-molded from the brillant metal produced in the many bottle and window glasshouses, is as highly prized as the Stiegel and South Jersey types. And it should be: it is truly American. Many of the finest examples were blown in small Ohio houses of the 1815-1835 period.

So far as we know today it was in 1814 that the first Ohio company was formed for the purpose of establishing a glassworks, and in 1815 that the first glass was blown. By the end of another year four companies in all had been organized and their furnaces built. One wonders a little at the optimism of the investors for in spite of appearances conditions were not propitious for business ventures. True, even in 1815 the rush to promote the "infant industries" fathered by the War of 1812 had not been checked completely. And only the first ripples of the economic débâcle touched off by the ratification of the Treaty of Ghent were appearing on the stream of business; ripples so soon to become tidal waves of financial disaster, in no small part due to England's imposing drastic trade restric-

tion and flooding our markets with her dammed-up wares.

While the Ohio glassmakers may have had a slight hope of capturing some of the trade outside their state, they undoubtedly counted on an eager demand at home. For the potential customers were increasing rapidly in numbers and wealth — the population had risen from a little over 41,000 when statehood was granted in 1803 to over 230,000 in 1810. But the majority of Ohioans lived in the burgeoning towns and settlements along the arteries of trade, the main rivers and pioneer roads. Thus the most profitable local markets were readily accessible to and already well supplied by the ever-multiplying glasshouses of the Monongahela-Ohio River areas which made wares for every possible need, taste, and pocketbook. Regardless of any other considerations, in the face of such competition even one glass furnace in Ohio producing even one bottle would seem, to the cautious, like carrying coals to Newcastle.

The first Ohio glasshouse was built by the Cincinnati Glass Manufacturing Company promoted by Major Isaac Craig who, with General James O'Hara, initiated the industry in Pittsburgh in 1797. It was located in Cincinnati, Hamilton County, in a section near the Ohio River, far down from Pittsburgh, a fact doubtless counted upon by the owners. Shortly afterward a group of Cincinnati businessmen financed a small furnace at Moscow, thirty miles away. Neither house proved to be an Eldorado. Each was short-lived in spite of the transfusions given by new ownerships which achieved only an ephemeral prosperity.

A few stark facts reported in the United States 1820 census summarize the conditions of a Hamilton County glassworks, probably that in Cincinnati, then operated by Pugh & Teeter. The firm reported a capital of $25,000, a yearly output of window glass, hollow ware, chemical and philosophical apparatus valued at $19,000, and produced by *ten* blowers. Their total employees numbered "twenty-one men" and "ten boys and girls." Certainly not a large outfit; certainly not handicapped by a forty-hour week. The proprietors' estimate of their own and, one suspects, their country's plight is disclosed in their statement that "the establishment is rather languishing for want of encouragement owing 'to the supply overrunning the

FIG. 1 (*above*) — ZANESVILLE BRILLIANT SAPPHIRE-BLUE BOWL AND CREAMER. Typical nineteenth-century bowl with galleried rim but resting on an unusual eighteenth-century type of base or foot composed of "petals" flaring slightly from very short straight-sided stem — a combination not used in eastern glasshouses of the same period. Patterned in the 10-diamond mold attributed to Zanesville; flasks, a few dishes, jugs, salts, and small compotes, as well as the rare sugar bowls and creamers with and without foot, were patterned in same mold. Overall height of sugar bowl, 6⅝ inches; of pitcher, 4 15/16 inches. The only matched blue set of which we know at this time. *From the collection of George S. McKearin.*

FIG. 2 — ZANESVILLE SEA-GREEN SUGAR BOWL AND SAUCER. Typical nineteenth century form, the midwestern variety having sharper shoulder and wider spread of sides than eastern. All known bowls of this shape and these proportions with same type of double-domed cover either have had a Zanesville history or were found in that locality. A similar body form, usually with comparatively short straight-sided cylindrical neck, is characteristic of midwestern pitchers ranging from creamer size to a quart and more in capacity. Height, with saucer, approximately 6¾ inches.

FIG. 3 (*right*)—PLAIN DEEP AMBER SALT, attributed to Zanesville. Characteristic midwestern type, with narrow flaring flange on an ogee salt form of eighteenth-century, and Stiegel, type. Other midwestern variations of the ogee shape were achieved by a change in usual proportions, the lower section being very narrow, the upper wide and with sides either nearly vertical or contracted below a narrow rim. Height, 3½ inches. *Photographs of this and Figures 2, 4, 5, 6, courtesy of Earl J. Knittle.*

FIG. 4 (*far right*)—SMALL PLAIN DEEP AMBER COMPOTE attributed to Zanesville. Typical midwestern form and size; found occasionally with deep saucerlike bowl and sometimes with narrow folded flaring rim, also pattern-molded in ribbed and diamond designs. Height 3¾ inches; top diameter 6 inches.

demand in consequence of large foreign importations." Nor by foreign did they mean Pittsburgh. They were plugging hard for the policy of protective tariffs and internal improvements which Henry Clay dubbed "the American System."

In 1822 Lot Pugh and Henry Teeter offered the Cincinnati works for rent and took over the Moscow furnace. That they kept up with swiftly moving national events and political trends as well as the fashion in whiskey flasks is revealed by an advertisement in a Cincinnati newspaper. On June 11, 1824, they informed the public that they had for sale "ribbed Lafayette, Clay and Jackson flasks." Two months *before* Lafayette landed at Castle Garden! Also mentioned were one-half, one- and two-gallon claret and porter bottles, jars, pitchers, and the always irritating "etc."

The other two houses of this first period were erected at Zanesville, Muskingum County, which, from a commercial point of view, was strategically situated on the National Road and the banks of the Muskingum River, a tributary of the Ohio. Neither had any degree of success until about 1823. Both passed through several ownerships but unlike the Cincinnati works survived that repeated operation and ran almost continuously for over thirty years. Though as early as 1923 a few collectors knew about Zanesville's fine glass, detailed information about the works was first published in 1924 and 1932 in ANTIQUES, and in 1927 in *Early American Glass*, by Rhea Mansfield Knittle. Characteristic examples of the fine free-blown and pattern-molded types attributed to Zanesville, principally to the so-called White Glass Works, are shown in Figures 1-5. The shape of the sugar bowls including the type of double-domed cover appears to be peculiar to Zanesville. Every one of which we have known has either had a Zanesville history or was found in that locality. It is also generally ac-

cepted as fact that a 24-rib mold and a 10-diamond-above-flutes were used there.

Marked flasks prove that the first two Zanesville houses made flasks, blown in full-size molds, in the purely American-historical and pictorial category. The White Glass Works during its operation by J. Shepard & Company (*1823-1838*) produced a pint flask having Farmers Arms (agricultural emblems) within a Masonic arch on one side; on the other, *Zanesville* above an American eagle perched on an oval framing *Ohio,* and below the oval, *J. Shepard & Co.* (McKearin No. 249 G. IV-32; Van Rensselaer No. 4 D2:G.IV). The same firm probably made the half-pint flask with the American eagle above an oval framing *Zanesville* on the obverse, and on the reverse, the filled cornucopia, symbol of plenty (McKearin No. 140 G.II-18). The second Zanesville glassworks, after it was taken over by Thomas Murdock and Joseph Cassel in 1832, made a flask like the pint Shepard & Co. except for the inscription *Murdock & Cassel* in place of *J. Shepard & Co.* (McKearin No. 250 G. IV-33; Van Rensselaer No. 5 D2: G. IV). They made also an interesting pint flask in a geometric design of a band of diagonal ribbing above one of vertical, and below inscriptions—*Murdock & Cassel* on one side, *Zanesville Ohio* on the other (McKearin No. 381 G. X-14; Van Rennsselaer No. 112 G. VI). The pint Shepard is common; the others are rare.

With the return of good times in the early 1820's, especially after the passage in 1824 of the protective tariff, which was almost notoriously favorable to the glass industry, capital again flowed freely into manufacturing enterprises. In the years from 1820 through 1830 at least seven glasshouses were erected in eastern Ohio, not one of which lasted more than ten years. For one reason, they still could not compete with the well-rooted industry in the Monongahela-Ohio River areas.

FIG. 5 (*far left*)—CITRON-COLORED "SPHERICAL"-BODIED BAR BOTTLE. Ribbing expanded and swirled to left after being patterned in a 24-rib dip mold. This type with this number of ribs is accepted as having been made at Zanesville. Capacity, two quarts.

FIG. 6 (*left*)—BRILLANT AMBER "GRANDFATHER" FLASK, attributed to Zanesville. Largest size of chestnut flask characteristic of the output of Ohio and other midwestern bottle works; pattern-molded and expanded in vertical ribbing. Capacity, one quart.

FIG. 7 (*right*) — BRILLANT AMBER HANDLED JUG. Patterned in a 24-rib dip mold and given a rather tight broken-swirl design; narrow flange instead of usual collared lip. Midwestern jugs have been found, as yet, only in greens and amber, usually in ribbed, rarely in diamond designs. Height 5½ inches; capacity, about 1½ pints. *Collection of George S. McKearin.*

FIG. 8 (*below*) — MANTUA AQUAMARINE BOWL. Patterned in a 16-rib dip mold and given a widely expanded broken-swirl design. Mr. White proved from quantities of excavated fragments that a 32-rib dip mold, a 15-diamond part-size piece mold, and a full size three-piece mold in the geometric pattern (McKearin G.II-33) also were used at Mantua. *Formerly in the Harry Hall White Collection.*

west. Many crafts were well represented by artisans with whom, inevitably, went the traditions and techniques followed in the eastern shops and glasshouses.

Perhaps at this point a warning should be parenthesized. It must be kept in mind that, with a few exceptions, in describing Ohio glass one is simply localizing midwestern types. For hardly anyone doubts that most of the bottles and individual pieces of Ohio were similar to those made in earlier and contemporary glassworks of the Monongahela-Ohio River areas. Also one can scarcely argue that Zanesville, Kent, and Mantua had patents on the number of ribs or diamonds used in their molds. However, if a piece bears the number of ribs or diamonds known to have been used in one of these houses, is found within a reasonable radius of the house, and has a family history of having been blown there, it would not seem exactly hasty in judgment to accept the attribution.

It is almost axiomatic that the bottle, from medicine vial to demijohn, was the principal article of production, with those for hard liquor leading the ranks. The popular usage of the whiskey bottles is high-lighted by observations in a biographical sketch of Marvin Kent, one of the founders of the first Ravenna glass factory about 1850, and son of Zenas who was associated briefly with the first works in the village of Kent. The writer remarks quite casually, "The customs of the day respecting the use of whiskey are well known. The beverage was free as water, and every visitor [to Zenas Kent's Ravenna store] whether entering for the purpose of trade or chat was expected to 'help himself.'" When at the ripe age of nine Marvin went to work in his father's store "his first and chief duty" was "to see that the whiskey bottle was kept full."

In Ohio's bottle and window glasshouses the custom was followed of making household utensils and tablewares for family, friends, and to meet the local need, especially in those com-

Although the decade, because of high import duties, was one of expansion in the manufacture of fine flint (lead) glass wares, it would appear that only one of the new Ohio houses attempted to specialize in this lucrative branch of glassmaking; that probably was the very short-lived Zanesville White Flint Glass Manufacturing Company of Edmonds, Bingham & Company. At any rate, it seems likely that this was the Zanesville firm which in the 1820 national census reported having one furnace, employing ten adults, and making "cut flint" worth $2,200 a year — a gross return of less than a dollar a day for each employee! No wonder it was "declining for want of funds and legislative aid." Doubtless the well-to-do ladies preferred to remark on their imported — at the very nearest from Pittsburgh — tablewares.

At present there is exact information about the history and products of only three of the glasshouses built in this decade: those located in Portage County at Mantua in 1821 and Kent in 1823 and 1824. The main facts, results of the late Harry Hall White's researches, excavations, and the scientific analysis of his findings in connection with the sites, were published in ANTIQUES. Besides giving evidence of the forms and patterns, the excavated fragments proved that Mantua used 16- and 32-rib molds and a 15-diamond mold; Kent a 20-rib mold; both, a full-size three-piece mold in a geometric pattern. Of course, as in the case of many Zanesville pieces, family history and "place found" have played their familiar rôles in the attributions of specific pieces to the Portage County works. Typical examples are illustrated in Figures 8–11; the *extremely* rare Mantua Jackson-Masonic flask in Figure 12.

In connection with Mantua it is interesting to note that the Jonathan Tinker associated with David Ladd, the founder, was a glassblower who had emigrated from Vernon, New York, and may have been employed at the Mt. Vernon Glass Works. In all likelihood Tinker was one of the thousands who during the hungry days of the postwar depression left the stricken east, and, anticipating Horace Greeley, tried their luck in the

FIG. 9 (*above*) — BRILLANT AMETHYST SUGAR BOWL. Patterned in a 16-rib mold and expanded in vertical ribbing on the cover, swirled to left on the bowl; applied foot with 14 petals or scallops, an unusual number. Thoroughly eighteenth-century in form but blown in the nineteenth, probably at Mantua in the 1820's. Overall height 7⅞ inches. *This and Figure 10, collection of George S. McKearin.*

FIG. 10 (*right*) — MANTUA PALE YELLOW-GREEN SUGAR BOWL. Patterned in the 15-diamond piece mold and expanded. A perfect example of the persistence of the sugar bowl forms of Stiegel's period well into the nineteenth century. Overall height 5¾ inches. Cover patterned with 16 vertical ribs.

54

FIG. 11—TWO BLOWN-THREE-MOLD DECANTERS. *Left*, Kent clear-green blown-three-mold decanter. In *geometric* pattern (McKearin G. II-6) and with original stopper. Bar bottles, deep bowls, pitchers and a few individual vases are also found in this Kent pattern. Besides the use of the full-size three-piece mold in this pattern, Harry Hall White established the fact that a 20-rib dip mold also was used at the Kent house of Parks, Edmunds & Parks. *Right*, Mantua brillant-green blown-three-mold decanter. In the *geometric* pattern (McKearin G.II-33); one of three recorded pieces from the particular mold in this pattern used at Mantua. Height, approximately 8⅜ inches. *From the collection of George S. McKearin.*

munities more or less isolated from the large centers of trade. It is likely too that many of the citizens could not afford more expensive glass, if any. But there is the familar roster of household and tavern articles—flasks and bottles, flips and mugs, deep and shallow bowls and dishes, pitchers from small creamers to water pitchers holding a quart or more, sugar bowls and salts, small compotes, and an occasional vase. Among these pieces one finds no absolutely identical twins. Even among the bottles, each seems a distinct individual.

The majority of pieces are fashioned from a single gather of fine-quality bottle glass, generally blown in a small dip or a part-size mold for pattern and expanded, quite in the Stiegel tradition. The molded designs are few but rather fascinating in effect—vertical (*Fig. 6*), swirled (*Fig. 5*), and broken-swirl ribbings (*Figs. 7, 8*), all-over diamonds (*Fig. 10*) and diamonds-above-flutes (*Fig. 1*). As a rule the metal, principally a soda-lime composition, has great brilliancy which is intensified by the thinness of the glass and the broken surface caused by the molded pattern. This is markedly true of the broken-swirl which is formed by double molding, a vertical ribbing molded upon one which has been swirled or spiraled after the first molding. By the degree of expansion the blower could, and did, praise be, achieve an unprecedented variety of effects in this pattern. At its greatest expansion it frequently resembles a diapering of lightly drawn diamonds-on-the-diagonal, sometime called "feathered"; when but little expanded, tight ranks of popcorn kernels. As a matter of fact, the broken-swirl effects on a single gather of glass are a mid-western variation of pattern-molded design and, we believe, peculiarly American.

The colors, as one might expect, are predominantly shades

and tints of green and amber. The exceptionally beautiful and clear ambers are found in nearly every tone from rich deep brown to golden or honey, sometimes almost a true yellow. The greens are even more varied, running from the palest aquamarine to deep olive, frequently in unusual tones of olive-yellow and citron. Of course the only colors in window glass are the pale green tints and aquamarines. Blues and amethysts, more expensive to make, were used, but sparingly. The blues are chiefly sapphire, cobalt, and a delicate cornflower hue; the rarer amethysts, light to dark, often uneven and streaky, doubtless due to under-cooking the batch. Very rarely purple is found, and occasionally clear glass and a lovely cloudy crystal resembling a polished moonstone.

Outstanding among American bottles and flasks are those of Ohio, the typically midwestern chestnut flasks from miniature in size up to the "grandfather" of a quart or more in capacity (*Fig. 6*), and the globular and cylindrical bar bottles. The flasks when closely like the chestnut in shape and the bar bottles having the precisely shaped "spherical" bodies seem to be peculiar to the midwest (*Fig. 5*). The chestnut flasks are found in all the known pattern-molded designs; bottles, only in the ribbed. To this group should be added the scarce and handsome jugs (*Fig. 7*) made by slight alteration of the normal globular-bodied bar bottle—a short collared neck and small neat handle.

Like the bottles, the plain free-blown and pattern-molded individual pieces, articles for home and table, seem rather fragile and very expertly formed, more so than those pieces in the South Jersey tradition fashioned in the eastern bottle and window glasshouses. While contemporary styles were followed by their creators to some extent, often much that was fine of the old was retained and frequently something new was added that was different and American, as is pointed out in the captions to Figures 1-10. Many of the differences which add so much to the character of the glass probably resulted from the fact that the blowers were more or less free to exercise their fancy and ingenuity as they would not have been in a commercial factory such as Bakewell's in Pittsburgh, or under the New England Glass Company in East Cambridge, and certainly not in the Ohio glass factories which grew up during the last half of the nineteenth century.

The mechanization of glass production, the discovery of natural gas (a cheap fuel for glass furnaces), and the developments of the railroad were important factors contributing to the growth of a successful and large industry in Ohio. Toward the end of the century it became one of the most important glass centers in the country. But except perhaps for some of the early pressed pattern glass, the products of that success have little attraction for collectors today. They seek and treasure most the handiwork of the unknown artist-craftsmen who were the blowers in the glasshouses built so hopefully before 1835.

FIG. 12 — MANTUA'S CONTRIBUTION to historical flasks — the Jackson-Masonic in aquamarine. Harry Hall White found fragments in sufficient quantity to constitute evidence of manufacture, though this type is very rare. Andrew Jackson and Masonry were logical subjects for an Ohio glassmaker to choose as motifs; both had ardent adherents in that state. (McKearin No. 70, G.I-70). *From the collection of William Wilson Wood III.*

The Story of the Mantua Glass Works

Part I. Quest and Quarry

By HARRY HALL WHITE

Nothing comes fairer to light than that which
has lang been hidden. — *Old Scottish Proverb*

IN MY studies of the early manufacture of glass in Ohio, I several times crossed and recrossed the trail that eventually led me to the Mantua Glass Works. Little did I suspect that my collector's curiosity would carry me as far as it did, in spare moments, over a period of ten years. One discovery followed another until I find that I have written the first and most complete story of the products made by a frontier glasshouse during that obscure and virtually uninvestigated period in American glassmaking between 1820 and 1830.

I had been collecting in that part of northern Ohio known as the Western Reserve, and had occasionally found bottles of calabash shape, in light green glass. However, as old flasks of the historical or patriotic type were of greater interest to me, I had paid little attention to these calabash items except as I encountered one that was ribbed. Then I recalled a visit with the late Howard Davis of Kent, Ohio, who happened to mention these examples as "Mantua bottles," adding that he thought certain of them were made at an old-time glassworks in Mantua Township.

Mantua Township lies in Portage County, a thoroughly rural section; but such a statement from a man of Mr. Davis' standing was significant, especially when supported by a personal experience gained through more than fifty years of active collecting and dealing in antiques. After examining the bottles in question, I decided to investigate.

Mantua Township, I learned, embraces the three villages of Mantua Station, Mantua Corners, and Mantua Center. In search of further information I visited the library of the Western Reserve Historical Society in Cleveland, where the Director, Doctor W. H. Cathcart, with the capable assistance of his librarian and staff, made a wealth of material available to me.

In the *History of Portage County, Ohio*, published by Warner, Beers and Company (*1885*), the following brief statement occurs:

In 1821 David Ladd built a brick kiln; but in the fall he secured a glassblower named Jonathan Tinker, rented his brother Daniel's tannery (built in 1812) and began the manufacture of bottle-glass December 1st 1821 under the title of the Mantua Glass Company, continued here until 1823 when he moved the plant to Kent, Ohio (then Franklin Mills), where he built a factory.

Searching further to learn whether the location of the old factory

Note. The following article recounts the search for the remains of the quite forgotten glassworks at Mantua, Portage County, Ohio, the successive steps whereby the long-buried foundations of the works were located and uncovered, and the patient research devoted to gathering and piecing together scattered scraps of historical and biographical data until a clear and convincing pattern finally emerged. In subsequent issues of ANTIQUES Mr. White will describe and analyze his finds of glass fragments on the old Mantua site and will present his conclusions as to the types of glass produced at the factory. His text will be amply supported by pictures. Entirely aside from their value to the glass collector desirous of identifying his specimens, these articles constitute an exemplar of methodical investigation and judicious presentation in the field of American industrial archæology that deserves the highest admiration and praise. Almost anyone, be he layman or glass enthusiast, will be absorbingly interested in the first instalment. Succeeding chapters, while more technical, will reveal the same processes of detective work as they slowly build up an irrefutable case.
— *The Editor.*

grist mill on the Cuyahoga, where the diagonal road from "the brick tavern" to Garrettsville crosses the river. But their dam flowed water back on to the lands of Rufas Edwards, who prosecuted it as a nuisance. The Grand Jury returned an indictment against it, and on the trial Edwards swore he had "seen a scum on the waters of the pond, so thick a goose could walk across on it and not wet her feet." This settled the matter, and the court ordered the dam to be prostrated as a nuisance. In 1820–21 Ezekiel Ladd and others erected a glass manufactury *on the diagonal road from "the brick tavern" to Skinners Mill.* It was occupied for several years, but David Ladd, one of the proprietors, moved to Franklin and became engaged in business there, when the Mantua Glass Company stopped business, and it merged into the Franklin Company.

Here was further evidence that a glassworks had operated at Mantua. With the location so specifically given, it seemed but a simple matter to identify the old site. The old brick tavern, which stands today, though used as a residence, is a familiar and interesting landmark on the north-and-south road between Mantua Corners and Mantua Station (*Fig. 1*). Concerning the history of this structure I also found an interesting note:

In the spring of 1816 Jotham Atwater erected a log cabin at the intersection of

might be recorded, I finally brought to light copies of *The Portage County Democrat.* In the issue of this paper for Wednesday, June 9, 1858, a local historian, writer, and jurist of considerable prominence, General Lucien V. Bierce, contributed to a column known as *Home Reminiscences, from the Unpublished History of the Western Reserve.* I quote a paragraph from the General's article:

In 1822–3 William and Joseph Skinner erected a dam, and built a

the roads from Ravenna to Chardon and Garrettsville to Aurora for the purpose of a tavern and on the fourth of July opened his tavern under the image of a plow hoisted about twenty feet in the air on the end of a pole with *J. ATWATER'S INN* inscribed on the side of the beam. The first tavern kept in Mantua, log until 1825, when brick tavern erected, the second brick building in Mantua. . . . Atwater continues till his death in 1828, others up to date. [*1866*]

The "diagonal road to Garrettsville" passes the tavern, and, about a half mile farther east, crosses the Cuyahoga River. It was on this stream and near this crossing that the Skinners built the mill referred to by Bierce in his *Reminiscences.* It was locally called the

Fig. 1 — MAP OF PART OF MANTUA AND HIRAM TOWNSHIPS
Showing location of the Mantua Glass House Site, the brick tavern, and "Mud Mill."
Garrettsville (Ohio) Quadrangle, U. S. Geological Survey, Edition of 1907, reprinted 1926

"mud mill," because supported on piles rather than a stone foundation.

But it was not until the fall of 1921 that I had opportunity to test my various clues. I had no difficulty in locating the particular division of the road, along the river, and the "mud mill." So far, so good, except that the sinking of numerous test pits in the place where the old furnace should have been revealed nothing beyond what is usually found on turning over the turf of old pasture land. Accordingly, I sank more pits in undisturbed strata, but with equally negative results. Either the record was faulty or the precise spot had eluded the spade. At subsequent intervals I spent many days along that diagonal road on the banks of the Cuyahoga River near the "mud mill" site, and even on such hillsides as seemed a possible location for such glassworks. All without avail. It seemed impossible that a site used at one time both for a tannery and a glasshouse could have been lost without trace. Eventually I decided that the old records must be incorrect, and sought other means of enlightenment.

Directions offered by local residents served only to confuse the situation until, one day, a woman who was crossing the field where I was working enquired regarding my search. Evidently she was in doubt as to whether something had been lost or a lunatic had just escaped from a sanitarium. After my explanations the woman suggested that an aged aunt of hers might be able to tell me more accurately where to look.

Fig. 2 — THE SITE OF THE MANTUA WORKS IN OCTOBER 1921

Fig. 2a — THE SITE OF THE MANTUA WORKS IN 1931

A later day found me again at Mantua, equipped with the usual tools, but with new directions supplied by the elderly aunt. "Take the *left fork* on the diagonal road," she had said, "cross the creek, let down the bars to the pasture on the right side of the road, and there you will find the foundations of the old glassworks." Surprising, this, for the place was nearly a quarter of a mile from the locations I had been investigating.

I found the pasture, but apparently the foundations were gone. As innocent-looking a green slope as ever existed lay before me, extending from the willows, along what I later learned was Mud Brook, to the hilltop, with here and there a few trees and clumps of thorn (*Fig. 2*). I began sinking pits, fairly high up, along the east bank of Mud Brook, just above the line where the hillside joined the marshy land bordering the stream. Imagine, if possible, my intense excitement and satisfaction, when, after sinking hardly a dozen pits, I was uncovering burned bricks and a few fragments of opalescently coated light green glass whose color closely resembled, if it did not actually duplicate, that of the so-called "Mantua bottles." The site of the works of the Mantua Glass Company

— after long and sometimes arduous labors — had been found at last.

The treasure-trove of my first digging consisted of large numbers of old handmade bricks, some soft and friable, some burned and glazed in the furnace; and, in addition, half a bushel of glass fragments, all of them green or light green. Most of them revealed the same opalescent coating of oxide resulting from one hundred years' repose in damp earth. With the care that would have been exercised had green diamonds been uncovered, I conveyed my hoard to Cleveland.

The land in the triangle is part of a pasture now belonging to E. J. Hamill of Mantua Station, who is also the owner of the old tavern. I had proved the falsity of the historical record and had established the fact that the glass works had been located near Mud Brook rather than the Cuyahoga River, and on the *left* fork of the diagonal road instead of on the *right* (*Fig. 1*). It was now an exciting and stimulating endeavor to read, from the excavated material, the story of this old glasshouse — forgotten for a century; and to catalogue its products.

History

At the close of the Revolution, the territory now comprised within the limits of Ohio, then a part of what was known as the "Old Northwest," was claimed by both Virginia and Connecticut. These rival claims were finally adjusted. Virginia accepted "The Virginia Military Tract" between the Scioto and the Little Miami Rivers in southern Ohio; while Connecticut took as her allotment a reservation of about four million acres along Lake Erie, known as "The Western Reserve," or "The Connecticut Western Reserve."

The adjustment between the states was a simple accomplishment compared with the difficulties encountered by the settlers from the east when they attempted to locate and occupy the lands that they had purchased, or were theirs from military service. Various treaties made with the Indians had not achieved the results anticipated. The Indians did not fully understand treaties. They were reluctant to give up their beloved valleys, particularly those of the Cuyahoga and the Tuscarawas Rivers. They became extremely unpleasant neighbors for the white frontiersmen. Periodically and without formality they went to war, killed outlying settlers, carried families into captivity, destroyed crops and improvements, and drove stock to their own corrals.

Such great risk to life and insecurity of property prevented more than a trickle of eastern immigration from reaching Mantua during the first ten years of the nineteenth century. The first settlement in Portage County was made here in 1798 — just a log cabin in a small clearing with a hastily prepared seeding of wheat. The planter did not remain, and it was in the next year that the owner came and harvested the crop. Such was the precarious and diffident beginning of Mantua, which thereafter grew year by year. But it was not until after the War of 1812, in fact beginning with the memorable Battle of Tippecanoe, in 1811, that, with the support of England gone, the rebellious spirit of the Indian subsided. The final removal of Indian title to the lands occasioned a greater feeling of security, and settlers began to pour into the Western Reserve. Log cabins in the clearings became more numerous, and even frame buildings began to appear. The established settler was now encouraged to enlarge his possessions and pay attention to industries other than those of home manufacture. An era of peace and prosperity had fairly opened.

First came a hand gristmill, then a small tannery, whose importance is attested by the establishment of a new and larger undertaking of the same kind by Daniel Ladd, in 1812. Along with these enterprises came William Russell with his distillery. Bierce, evidently an early dry, in his *Reminiscences* remarks, "The distillery, then, like the gallows a constant attendant on civilization, furnished mash to feed forty hogs per day and liquor for forty others." Russell's whiskey was long remembered in the community as one of the features of sheep-washing and barn-raising days.

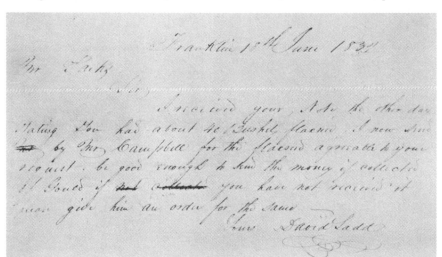

Fig. 3 — Note and Signature of David Ladd

As the primal industries of this frontier community changed hands or were reëstablished, or new ones were started, the sawmill came, also the brick kiln. Finally the glass factory made its appearance, through the industry of David Ladd and his glassblower, Jonathan Tinker.

Both the Ladd and Tinker families figure prominently in American history. Every library that makes any pretense of genealogical reference has some works covering their ancestry. But from these sources I did not obtain answers to the many questions that arose in my mind about the particular Ladd and Tinker who were chief figures in the industrial picture I was trying to restore. From the records at the County Court House in Ravenna, Ohio, I learned just what land the pair purchased, when and where, and occasionally what they paid for it. The civil, probate, and criminal records yielded not another word of useful data.

When I came to the records of the County Engineer in the office of the Road Commissioner, I wished to determine whether or not the "left fork road" had been cut through at a time when the glassworks were in blast. Information on this point might explain the confusion over the location of the glasshouse site. Fortunately the records were extremely well preserved. They made it evident that the "left fork road" and "the diagonal road to Garrettsville" had been laid out at the same time, in 1812. No confusion here was responsible for the discrepancies in the historical statements concerning the glasshouse site. The engineer's survey of the "diagonal road" very clearly indicates "Ladd's Tan Yard," where his survey line crossed Mud Brook.

The second record of the "left fork road" occurs in an 1818 petition to the County Road Commissioner for its repair. This document not only states that the road from the Tavern to Deacon Ladd's is much used, but mentions another prominent early family, the Harmons. The latter circumstance gave me a very fortunate lead, since reference to that name brought two bundles of letters and manuscripts from Orrin Harmon for my inspection in the Department of Documents at the Western Reserve Historical Society. This material had been gathered many years before by Doctor Cathcart. Among these documents I made an amazing discovery: a 162-page manuscript written by Orrin Harmon in 1866 and affording many hitherto unpublished details of Mantua history. These begin on page 148 under the heading: "Items

of Facts appertaining to the History of Mantua after 1814 which may be of use in writing a history of the Township," and end on page 162 with the closing statement: "The foregoing history of Mantua is copied by my son Julian C. Harmon from my original manuscript on detached sheets and compared with them by him and myself. Therefore I adopt it as the original Manuscript History. Ravenna, O, July 4 1870. Orrin Harmon."

Orrin Harmon was the son of Judge Elias Harmon, the fourth settler in Mantua, a man of leadership who during his lifetime held many offices of trust. Like his father, Orrin was associated with civic affairs in the County; for a long time was county surveyor, and continued his father's business of representing the original eastern owners of lands in the Western Reserve. This I mention in evidence of his sound knowledge of early Mantua events. I could hardly ask for a more complete story than that recorded in "Item 5" on page 150 of his manuscript:

David and Jeduthan Ladd sons of Daniel Ladd Seignor came into Mantua the Summer of 1816 with their families. Jeduthan was a house joiner and carpenter by trade. He continued his residence in Mantua about four years then he removed to Kirtland, Lake Co., O. David Ladd was bred a clerk in a store in the city of Hartford, Connecticut. When he came to Mantua he brought with him a small lot of dry goods which he apparently lived on whilst they lasted. He resided for about a year after he came into Mantua in Samuel Moore's log cabin built by him on his farm in anticipation of some day having a wife. A country life in a new country appeared to be a strange element for him. But he was a Yankee. In the fall of 1817 he built for a residence what would be called a double log cabin on the N.E. Corner at Mantua Corners on land then owned by his brother Ezekiel and moved into it. In the spring of 1818 he purchased about twenty cows and by renting pasture of Wm Skinner and on what was then known as the Jas Nooney farm on the E end of Lot 22. He carried on a dairy the summer of 1818. In the fall of that year he built a boat on the Cuyahoga River at the Rapids in the township of Hiram by taking a large canoe and splitting it lengthwise with a saw and widening it by putting in boards or planks so as to give it the wished for dimentions. He loaded his cheese aboard his boat and passed down the Cuyahoga River carrying by land his boat and it's load around the falls in Franklin (now called Kent). At the then location of Wetmores Mill in the Township of Stowe he left the Cuyahoga River taking his boat and it's load by land to New Portage on the Tuscarawas River. He then went down the Tuscarawas into the Muskingum continuing his course down stream till he found an acceptable market for his boat and its load. Report at that time said that he made the trip a paying speculation. In the Spring of 1820 when Ezekiel Ladd sold his farm to Thomas Merryfield the sale included the then residence of David Ladd. Between this time and the time David Ladd left Mantua he resided in several places where he found chances to rent. The Summer of 1821 David Ladd put up a large brick kiln near the Cuyahoga River on what was then known as the Russell farm at that time in the possession of his brother Ezekiel. The Manufacture of so large an amount of brick at that time in Mantua was considerable of a mystery to the inhabitants as the market for brick was very limited. But the fall of 1821 David Ladd procured the building erected by his brother Daniel in 1812 for a tannery and erected the necessary additions and fixtures thereto for manufacturing glass. This solved the mystery as to his brick speculation. Jonathan Tinker a glass blower by trade and also a son in law of Oliver Lewis who came into Mantua with his family in the Spring of 1818 from Vernon Oneida County, N. Y., superintended the work etc of preparing David Ladd's glass manufactory for business. David Ladd commenced making glass about December 1st 1821 and he continued the business in Mantua till the summer of 1823 when he left Mantua and went to Franklin now called Kent and built a new glass manufactory enlarging his business and continuing in the business there several years. The glass manufactory erected in Mantua by David Ladd was what is called a bottle manufactory.

What a remarkable and vivid picture Harmon has drawn of the man David Ladd and of his activities in the frontier Mantua! Ladd's trip down the river to New Portage reveals the source of his inspiration to undertake the manufacture of glass. New Portage, at that time, was the Eldorado of the west, the new boom town of the 'twenties. The community had sprung up at the south end of the famous trail, the Portage Path, the highway of the Indian before the coming of the white man, the connecting link in the traveled route from the Great Lakes to the Ohio River. This town, by reason of the keel- and flatboat traffic, such as that of Ladd's venture, was a seaport at the head of navigation on the Tuscarawas River! From here cargoes were shipped to New Orleans without breaking bulk; time, four to six weeks.

Ladd must have made more than one trip to New Portage. The Harmons state that the speculation paid, and Ladd was a Yankee. Besides, he purchased land in the vicinity of New Portage. To do this he must have become acquainted with Colonel Ambrose Palmer, who surveyed and laid out the plat for New Portage in 1818, and, with others, held the majority of the local real estate. Soon after the settlement of New Portage, Colonel Palmer

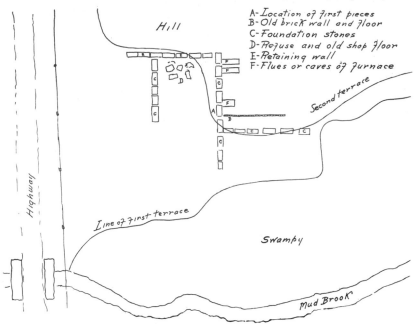

Fig. 4 — Sketch Showing Foundations and Site of the Mantua Works

A-*Location of first pieces*
B-*Old brick wall and floor*
C-*Foundation stones*
D-*Refuse and old shop floor*
E-*Retaining wall*
F-*Flues or caves of furnace*

proceeded with other activities, which are well detailed in *The History of Summit County, with an Outline Sketch of Ohio*, edited by William Henry Perrin and published by Baskin and Battey, 186 Dearborn Street, Chicago, Illinois, in 1881.

Chapter XX, Coventry Township, (page 528): Shortly after starting this new industry [building flatboats for navigation of the Tuscarawas River to New Orleans by William W. Laird, 1818] and the opening of New Portage as a port, one Ambrose Palmer and a Dr Clark settled in what they considered the future metropolis and started a glass factory, the site of which is in that part of New Portage located in Norton Township. It was in operation for several years and turned out considerable quantity of glass ware. . . . The glass is a good article but has a yellowish green cast.

Here was an example not to be overlooked by a venturesome young man whose brother had a suitable building heavy on his hands as the result of an unfortunate business deal.

Harmon's Manuscript History of America, (page 134): In 1811 there came into Mantua Daniel Ladd Junior and family. . . . Summer of 1812 Dan Ladd lived in the school house N. W. ¼ of Lot 24. He was a tanner and shoemaker. Bought of Phineas Pond 50 acres E ½ Lot 29 in the fall of 1812 erected a frame building 30 x 40 two stories arranged and constructed so he occupied the lower story for a tannery and the upper story as a temporary dwelling house. . . . In 1816 Dan Ladd Jun leased the tannery to Ephraham Gloyd and devoted his attention to the manufacture of boots and shoes and by reason of the laziness and dishonesty of Gloyd about 1819 the tannery suspended for want of patronage. In the fall of 1821 Daniel Ladd Jun leased or sold the tannery building to his brother David Ladd for a glass Manufactory.

The Western Reserve Chronicle was established about 1815, in good time to leave a few references to Ladd's glass factory. It was published weekly at two dollars per annum by Hapgood and Thompson from their offices at Warren, Trumbull County, Ohio. The issue for Saturday morning, December 29, 1821 (page 4, third column) carries this brief note, without doubt the very first mention of the glasshouse:

Mr. David Ladd is erecting a glass manufactory in Mantua, Portage County.

Considering the fact that the new enterprise carried no advertisement in the *Chronicle*, that sheet was generous with its publicity. Possibly news items were scarce; at any rate, in the issue for January 26, 1822, I found that the

New glass works now in operation in Mantua and promise to do well. The glass is said to be superior for it's clearness.

Ladd let no opinion as to the quality of his glass go by hearsay. The editor asked for a demonstration, and received it promptly, for in the *Chronicle* issued two weeks later, February 9, 1822, he states:

We have lately received, as a present, from the proprietors of the Glass Works in Mantua, a very clear well shaped, decanter and elegent sweetmeat, as a specimen of their skill in the important manufacture in which they are engaged. Both of these articles are ample proofs of the ability of the enterprising and meritorious owners of this establishment, to serve the public in their line of business. We hope they will receive all the encouragement necessary for the support and prosperity of their highly useful undertaking.

From the above it is evident that the editor was well pleased with Ladd's donation. In 1823, Ladd disposed of his ownership in the Mantua Glass Company and moved to Carthage, Portage County, Ohio, where, in company with Benjamin F. Hopkins, he became interested in another glasshouse. Ladd and Hopkins purchased this property from Joshua Woodard and Frederick Heymaker for $3,000. The date of the recorded deed is June 20, 1826, nearly three years after Ladd's departure from Mantua. As the description of the property in the deed contains reference to a "flattening house" and speaks of the plot as "the glasshouse lot," it is certain that a plant had been erected before the sale was made. Ladd and Hopkins may previously have operated the property under a lease. Some accounts even state that Ladd, Woodard, and Heymaker were associated in the inauguration of this plant as early as 1822.

By 1826 Ladd was well established in a home on a half-acre fenced lot opposite the glass factory. He was in partnership with another promoter of the time, Zenas Kent. Together they purchased five or six hundred acres of land about Carthage and Franklin Mills, including the waterpower rights of the Cuyahoga River at that point. Kent was the father of Marvin Kent, a distinguished citizen in whose favor the town names of Carthage and Franklin Mills were changed.

By fortunate chance I discovered among the small folded papers in an old leather wallet from an attic in Geauga County, Ohio, a short note written by David Ladd (*Fig. 3*), when he was interested in an oil mill and tannery in addition to the glasshouse. It is easy to recognize a trained hand in this finely written and carefully worded note.

Franklin 18th June 1832

Mr. Parks
    Sir
    I received your Note the other day stating you had about 40 Bushels flaxseed. I now send by Mr. Campbell for the flaxseed agreeable to your request. be good enough to send the money if collected of Gould if you have not received it please give him an order for the same —

Yours
David Ladd

About 1833 Ladd disposed of his holdings in Franklin Mills, most of which were purchased by Zenas Kent. In the deeds, the conveyor's wife appears as Abby Ladd. After Ladd's departure, Kent secured John Brown, later of Ossawatomie fame, to carry on the tannery. Ladd meanwhile had moved to Maumee, Lucas County, Ohio, a thriving town rivaling Toledo in its development and a contestant for the site of the County Court House. From his correspondence preserved among the

Whittlesy Papers, at the Western Reserve Historical Society, I find that Ladd actively participated in the politics and in the business expansion of Maumee and Perrysburg, Ohio. Here I am content to leave him, the vital promoting spirit behind the glasshouses of Mantua and Carthage.

Of Ladd's superintendent and glassmaker, Jonathan Tinker, "Item 5" of Harmon's *Manuscript History of Mantua* affords startling though satisfying revelations. The fact that Tinker came with his father-in-law, Oliver Lewis, from Vernon, Oneida County, New York, tells me where the man had worked and possibly where he had served his apprenticeship. I am familiar with Vernon, New York, where the Mount Vernon Glass Works were at one time located. The story of my excavations on that old site is to be found in ANTIQUES for September and November 1929, *New York State Glasshouses*, Parts II and III.

Reviewing the records consulted during my study of the Mount Vernon Glass House, I found no mention of Jonathan Tinker. On the other hand, I learned that in 1810 Oliver Lewis was one of the original nine petitioners to the New York State Legislature for the patent to incorporate the Mount Vernon venture.

As then known, Oliver Lewis was a builder, an expert millwright and bridge builder. The Harmon manuscript tells something of his family, two boys and three daughters who reached Mantua in 1814, one year later than their father, and speaks also of Lewis' value in the pioneer community as a joiner and carpenter. Hence it seems quite certain that he did not actively participate in the operation of the Mantua furnace. Of the two men, Jonathan Tinker was the practical glassmaker.

Concerning his operation of the Mantua furnace there are no detailed records available. I must derive my inferences chiefly from the material excavated on the site of the old works. There is, too, a statement in a letter from Joseph Skinner to Orrin Harmon, dated at Leavittsburg, Trumbull County, Ohio, May 24, 1864, in which the writer, replying to a series of numbered questions from Harmon, states:

David Ladd commenced making glass in the winter of 1822–3. The first grist I ground on starting the mill consisted of burned clay for making glass pots.

This was hardly to be expected. Almost anyone familiar with the pioneer glasshouses would have at least surmised that Ladd secured his glass pots either from the east, or from the Zanesville-Pittsburgh area. However, this is a very clear assertion from a man who later was interested in the same business himself.

Skinner's replies to Harmon's seventh and eighth questions raised many doubts in my mind until I found the *Manuscript History*. "We commenced making glass in the winter of 1824." "Continued two winters." From these notations, one may fairly assume that the Skinners continued to operate Ladd's factory. But there is too much assumed glasshouse history, as it is. Harmon, however, meets the situation in his *Manuscript History (page 127)*:

William Skinner came to Mantua in 1806 from Middlefield, Massachusetts, bought Lot 17 built on the S. E. part and resided until his demise October 31 1852. Somewhat unstable of mind and discontent to continuously farm . . . in the fall of 1823 Joseph Skinner in company with Joel Scovill and William Skinner and others purchased the building and location which had been occupied about two years previous by David Ladd as a glass Manufactory and made sundry improvements and additions to it and commenced a glass bottle manufactury. Manufactured considerable flint glass as well as common glass. The business was continued at that Location till the spring of 1829. There was many changes in the ownership of the establishment during that time and at times it was in dispute who were the partners in the business. The winters of 1828–29 the business was nominally carried on by Oliver Lewis and his son Oliver H and his son-in-law Horatio Terril.

This solves most of my problems except that of the fate of Jonathan Tinker, glassmaker. Deeds in the Court House at Ravenna, Ohio, reveal that Tinker purchased land farther up the "left fork road" near the rapids, where David Ladd launched his flatboat, and that he sold property near Mantua Station as late as 1837. Another transfer, of 1827, names his wife Lucinda, who according to Harmon was Lucinda Lewis before her marriage. Harmon also observes that Tinker purchased a house and moved it to a location convenient to the glass factory, which suggests that he held rather a substantial position as superintendent of the works (*page 153*):

In the fall of 1822 he [Vergil Moore] built a frame house. . . . He occupied his house for a short time and sold the building to Jonathan Tinker who moved it to near where the glass factory was in successful operation.

After long search, these meagre scraps of Tinker's past are all that I have been able to retrieve. I do not know where this glassworker received his training, except by inference and by observing some slight hints in his methods. Yet every serious student of American glassware will immediately recognize him as a skilful operator of his period.

Nearly every generation of Tinkers has had its Jonathans; but this particular one of the name, a plain mechanic and glassmaker, is overshadowed by teachers, lawyers, town clerks, missionaries, and surgeons. If genealogical mention of him was ever made it can have been only of "the one who went west." But I know Jonathan Tinker to have been of that restless, ever-shifting, pioneer group who made American glassware both useful and beautiful, glassware which in this age is almost priceless.

Excavation

As already stated, the Mantua glasshouse stood at the foot of the hill joining the low land bordering Mud Brook. I found that its remains were covered with from two to three inches of heavy sod, to all appearances undisturbed during recent years. Under this sod, and beneath from six to twenty-four inches of loam, I uncovered the old foundations, and what, for lack of better name, I called the shop floor, the refuse of the dismantled furnace. The heavy overlay of earth had been carried up by freshets from Mud Brook, and washed down from the hill by storms for approximately one hundred years.

The shop floor was distinguished by a thin gray line of ashes above the yellow clay subsoil. In general, it was filled with quantities of broken glass. On the shop floor lay rocks and dressed foundation stones from the retaining wall against the hill as well as from the old building foundations. At some time in the past these stones must have served as target rests on which small boys set pieces of glass for smashing, for between them I found quantities of fragments.

The sketch in Figure 4 gives a general idea of the plan of the old foundations, and indicates where some of the glass specimens were found. Only a fraction of the foundations remains, the greater part having been taken to furnish material for rebuilding the abutments of the bridge over Mud Brook. At the same time, it is said, not a little filling for use back of these abutments was taken from the refuse of the old glasshouse.

From this excavation I took about four bushels of glass fragments. When digging permitted, the earth was passed through a screen of one-half-inch mesh. Otherwise, it was spread on a tarpaulin to facilitate careful searching. Virtually all of the excavation was by the trench method.

(*An analysis and pictorial record of Mr. White's finds will appear in a later issue of* ANTIQUES.)

Fig. 5 — MATCHED FRAGMENTS OF A MANTUA GLASS POT

The Story of the Mantua Glass Works

Part II. Remains and Reconstructions

By HARRY HALL WHITE

Note. Part I of this series of articles dealt with the author's search for the long-lost site of the glassworks in Mantua, Ohio. This establishment was founded in 1821 by David Ladd, who transformed his brother's tannery to accommodate the furnaces and other apparatus essential to glassmaking. After less than two years of operation in Mantua, Ladd transferred his factory to other hands and departed to a more favorably situated locality. His successors continued the business until 1829. In the present article Mr. White describes his finds among the ruins of the old factory and particularly stresses such features of the exhumed glass fragments as may assist in identifying whatever unshattered specimens of the Mantua product still survive. Unless otherwise noted, illustrations are from the author's collection. — *The Editor*.

THE significant material excavated at Mantua now calls for consideration.

A. Handmade bricks, the product of David Ladd's kiln, were unearthed in quantities. They were not particularly well burned, and, near the edge of the low ground, at the margin of the first terrace, offered little resistance to the spade. Others, which had been set in the lining of the furnace, were beautifully glazed and vitrified. It appears that no great quantity of fire brick was used; for I was able to account for that serving for the seat of the pots, the siege, and the shaped pieces framing the working opening, or glory hole. If other fire bricks were employed they must have been removed when the old furnace was dismantled, and thereafter transferred to some other furnace. This seems doubtful.

The average size of these red, handmade bricks was 2 by 4 by 8 inches, although many were found that measured 1 ⅜ by 3 ⅞ by

7 ½ inches and a few 2 ¼ by 4 by 8 inches. These measurements were taken from whole bricks neither distorted in burning nor glazed in the glass furnace.

B. Glass-pot fragments were saved during the excavation in sufficient number to permit reconstruction of pots to the point of determining the approximate size of the melting vessels made by Jonathan Tinker. At least two sizes were used: a large pot for aquamarine and green glass, and a pot of the same diameter but of less height and thickness for the various shades of amber.

Figure 5 shows the assembling of a group of fragments from bottom to top edge. This pot was about 20 inches high, had a bottom thickness of 2 ½ inches, and was about 1 to 1 ½ inches thick at the top edge. The interior form was intended to be circular; but the exterior was polygonal in section. A layer of aquamarine glass about 2 ½ inches thick adheres to the bottom. Between fragments 2 and 3 (see plan of assembling) the wall of the pot is deeply corroded, and in one spot eaten almost through. Such decay was a frequent cause of pot failure, and of all the colors then made aquamarine metal was the most corrosive.

While the Harmon manuscript states that, in the later period of operations at Mantua, flint glass was produced, I was unable to find among these shards any evidence of the typical covered flint-glass pot. Whatever flint glass was made at Mantua came from open pots.

C. Fragments of glass. The material secured consisted of what I would roughly term "worked glass" and "cullet," or refuse glass. The fragments range in character and magnitude from the bottom of a large calabash bottle or small demijohn to the smallest piece capable of revealing a single letter or ornamental motive. With one exception I recovered only fragments; but I did find unbroken stoppers for decanters and druggists' bottles.

The neophyte, I am sure, would be hopelessly confused if introduced to several bushels of broken glass and told to determine accurately the form of the original objects from which they had come. Nevertheless, it is surprising what may be accomplished by patience and observation. In fact, these fragments lent themselves readily to classification. After the original grouping that I have mentioned,

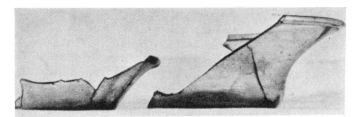

Fig. 6 — MANTUA BOWL (*left*) COMPARED TO THE MORE COMMON TYPE (*right*)
Fragments built up to show characteristic profiles

Fig. 7 (*above*) — MANTUA PLAIN BOWL IN AMETHYST GLASS
Found three miles from the Mantua site, where fragments of a similar bowl were excavated. *Size*, 5 ½ by 2 inches

Fig. 7a (*right*) — FRAGMENTS OF MANTUA PLAIN BOWLS
In aquamarine, amber, and a few in amethyst and cloudy-white glass

the "worked glass" was carefully sorted into the following divisions: offhand blown, pattern-mold blown, mold blown, manipulated.

A careful re-examination of the pieces constituting the first three of these main divisions resulted in their further resolution into many smaller groups, each of which represented the remains of some particular object made at the old glasshouse. In one case this procedure permitted an actual reconstruction that was almost complete. In others an accurate conception of both form and ornamentation of the original article was obtained.

In a way this seemed to bring me face to face with the living glass-blowers. In fact, before me, in the fragments of their handiwork, lay the indelible record of their ability. In translating this story I found several helpful guides. In matching and organizing my fragments into various object groups, several factors had to be considered:

First, the color or shade had to be the same, governed largely by the thickness; *second*, the thickness had, of course, to check; *third*, lines of fracture had to be exact, and fit perfectly; *fourth*, the glass of joined fragments had to have the same imperfections, such as bubbles, striæ, and unmelted sand; *fifth*, the surface appearance of the glass was helpful where all the fragments had been subjected to the same amount of moisture and consequent oxidation. This, however, was not always the case. Where similar fragments, or adjoining fragments, were equally oxidized, their appearance was similar as to opalescence. If deeply corroded, the adjoining pieces showed the same "grain" or striation of the glass itself.

Such imperfections, so frequently present in primitive glass, were my aids in reconstructing certain articles. Of these I could identify numerous objects in worked glass — offhand blown, pattern-mold blown, mold blown, and manipulated — aside from cullet and refuse. A tabulation of these identifications will be found on page 77.

Operation

Rather than indulge in the popular pastime of speculation and surmise regarding the methods followed at this glasshouse, I believe the description of a contemporary factory that was written about fifty years ago by a man fully competent to set down faithfully the facts as told to him by eye-witnesses will suffice. M. Louis Shook, at the time a resident of Norton Center, Chatham Township, Medina County, Ohio, by profession a painter and artist, by avocation town clerk and post-master, wrote the description of the glassworks of Colonel Ambrose

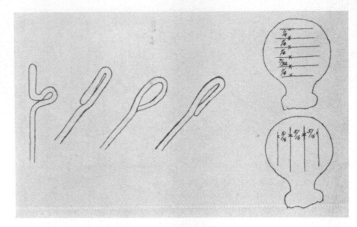

Fig. 8 — MANTUA RIM SECTIONS AND DECANTER STOPPERS
Decanter stopper illustrates variation in the spacing of horizontal ribbing. Vertical ribbing on the reverse uniformly spaced

frame sprang up and soon a thriving town stood where a few years before, there were nothing but woods to be seen. A glass-house was started by Palmer soon after, in a large barn like structure, with stack or furnace in the center. His pots and molds were brought from Zanesville, Ohio. Sand was produced by pounding sand stone in a huge trough, the pounding or crushing being done by means of a spring pole and pestle. Black salt was used as a flux. This was abundant as black salt was made at many places thro the new country where ashes were plenty from log heaps that were burned by thousands in all directions. Wood was used as fuel for smelting the sand and the consequence was that much of the glass was smoky and could not be used for window glass, when it was made into hollow ware such as tumblers, goblets, drinking glasses, bottles and many other articles useful and ornamental. At first six blowers were employed, but, afterward the shop was enlarged and eight blowers were employed. Sand of good quality was found in the marshes of Coventry about the time of the enlargement and it was used from this time on. But the business proved a failure and Palmer joined the Mormons and went west.

This is as early a non-technical account of the Midwest glasshouse as I have been able to find. I have at hand more or less technical descrip-

Fig. 9 (left) — MANTUA 16-RIB BOWL IN AMBER GLASS
Size, 5 by 2 inches.
From the Follansbee collection

Fig. 9a (right) — MANTUA 16-RIB BOWL IN AQUAMARINE GLASS
Size, 5 ¼ by 2 ¼ inches.
From the Follansbee collection

Palmer at New Portage, Ohio. This is the town I have mentioned before, and this is the glasshouse that inspired David Ladd to venture the Mantua project.

Shook wrote for the *History of Summit County with an Outline Sketch of Ohio* referred to in Part I of this study. In Chapter xxv on Norton Township (*p. 587*), I find this valuable contribution to our slowly accumulating hoard of industrial knowledge:

New Portage was part of the first village laid out either wholly or in part in the township. It was laid out in 1818 by Ambrose Palmer — or at least that part which belonged to Norton Township. Buildings both log and

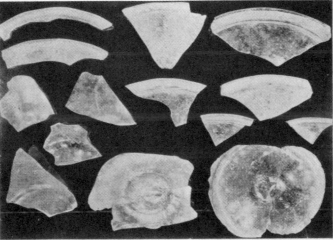

tions and instructions for the building of furnaces, both for green and flint glass, for pot kilns and annealing arches or lears. One book in particular, published at Washington, Pennsylvania, in 1824, is the *Arcana of Arts and Sciences or Farmers' & Mechanics' Manual*. This volume, published on subscription by Dr. M. Parker and printed by J. Grayson, gives elaborate and detailed specifications, listing the size and number

Fig. 9b — FRAGMENTS OF 16-RIB BOWLS IN AQUAMARINE
Note the terminal ring of rib pattern clearly surrounding the pontil mark on the middle piece, bottom row

Fig. 10 — Mantua 16-Broken-Rib Bowl in Aquamarine
Size, 7 ½ by 3 ½ inches.
From the Follansbee collection

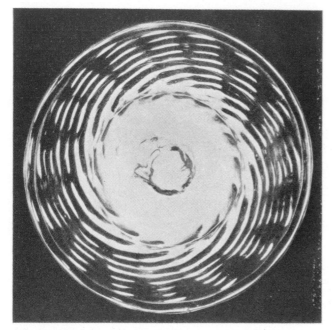

Fig. 10a — Mantua 16-Broken-Rib Bowl
Photographed with special lighting to emphasize individual ribs

Fig. 10b — Mantua 16-Broken-Rib Bowl in Aquamarine Glass
Size, 5 ⅛ by 1 ⅜ inches.
From the collection of Mrs. Grace Black

of each brick in every course of the furnace and of each arch. All this, however, is too remote from our interest to be useful here.

It will be remembered from the statement of Skinner in his letter to Harmon, that the Mantua people at least started to make their own pots instead of importing them from Zanesville as did Colonel Palmer. From Dr. Parker's *Arcana* I learn that a good grade of fire clay was available from the vicinity of Pittsburgh and

Zanesville. The clays from the Pittsburgh area originated at Sewickley, and are mentioned as Sewickley clay. From Beaver on the Ohio River came what was known as Beaver clay. Of the Beaver clay, Parker observes (*p. 245*):

Beaver clay, if it could be procured in sizable lumps, is the purest and most refractory clay of any yet found in America, and comes nearest in quality to the Stourbridge clay; but as it is only got in small lumps about the size of a walnut, and sometimes a little larger, it must be wet and made into cakes for burning, which is afterwards ground and mixed with raw clay. There are great varieties of refractory clay in America, but it depends more upon accident than experiment to form a concise judgement of their goodness.

The Zanesville clay answers very well for brick, but it cannot be relied upon for pots, though there are instances where pots have stood some time.

Such detailed information appearing in book form at this early date might at first seem surprising. But it will be recalled that the Pittsburgh area had been thoroughly prospected for clays in response to the offer of Peter Eichbaum, superintendent of the first glasshouse in Pittsburgh. In May 1802 Eichbaum advertised "to give $100.00 for the discovery of clay fit for their melting pots if found within one hundred miles of Pittsburgh and within ten miles of the Allegheny or Monongahela Rivers." (ANTIQUES, November 1926, *pages 363-368: Early Pittsburgh Glasshouses*.)

The paragraph from Dr. Parker's *Arcana* also gives a clearer explanation and added light on the statement Skinner made in his letter to Harmon: "The first grist I ground on starting the mill consisted of burned clay for making glass pots." There is no indication as to the source of the silica used at Mantua. Colonel Palmer crushed sandstone for his use at New Portage; Tinker had recourse to several near-by lakes which afforded good beach sand, and also to accessible limestone openings. Later the glasshouses of Kent and Ravenna were to rely on these sources.

The furnace and foundations revealed by my excavation were too far disintegrated to sustain any useful conclusions as to the size and type of the furnace or the number of its pots. Only the bottoms of two or three of the flues or caves were in position. These measured approximately 18 inches across. The upper portion, nearest the eye of the furnace, was beautifully glazed in blue and green. These glazed bricks and the bricks in the flues were red clay, not fire clay.

Thus from Shooks' written account of the New Portage glasshouse, at New Portage, Ohio, with a few details added from the Harmon manuscript, and Dr. Parker's *Arcana*, it is possible to obtain a fair picture of this early industry, and to judge to what extent the frontier glassmaker was dependent on the "outside" for his materials.

Mantua Products

Bowls. I use the general term "bowl" to cover the several objects of hollowware such as basins, pans, and pots, because it is the designation commonly used in the trade. Such hollowware was an important part of the Mantua product. In fact, bowls were about as useful to the pioneer housewife as anything made at the glasshouse. Indeed, they were so necessary that many womenfolk were glad to have even those made of the very heavy and clumsy salt-glazed stoneware or of red clay.

The majority of Mantua bowls exhibit one quite specific characteristic: that may, in fact, eventually prove to be an inclusive means of identification, at least for Ohio and possibly for the early Midwest. Many bowls and pans from other districts are quite like inverted hats, have a definite crown and a flaring, widened brim or rim. Mantua bowls, on the contrary, do not rise so sharply from the base or exhibit so strongly convex a profile. Instead the sides spread at a wider and more uniformly constant angle. The characteristic profile of the Mantua, Ohio, bowl may be compared with the more usual form in the partial reconstruction shown in Figure 6. The larger,

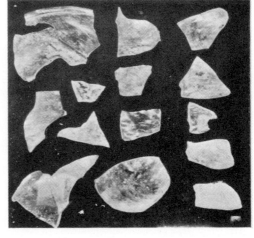

Fig. 10c — Fragments of Mantua 16-Broken-Rib Bowls in Aquamarine and Deep-Amber Glass

hat-shaped bowl at the right is from plain fragment, while the smaller
Mantua, Ohio, bowl at the left is from aquamarine ribbed fragments.

Mantua bowls were made in many sizes from a small sauce dish, say
of 3-inch diameter, to a large and relatively more shallow milkpan of 18
inches in diameter. At Mantua the 6, 8, 8 ¼, and 9 inch sizes seem to
have been most in demand. Judging from the quantity of fragments, the
production of patterned pieces far exceeded that of the plain types.

The plain bowls were made in several colors and shades: green,
aquamarine, amber, and amethyst (*Fig. 7*). The amethyst bowl pictured
has none of the ever-present tradition to testify to its origin. It was
found in the unromantic summer kitchen of a farmhouse about three
miles from the Mantua site. I gladly emptied it of its cargo of stewed
onions and added it to my hoard. From the old Mantua site I excavated
fragments which check closely with this specimen.

The majority of Mantua bowl rims were folded; *i.e.*, the lip was
finished by being folded over like the hem of a sheet. On plain pieces
this rim was turned outside. Two general forms prevail: the flattened
form and that of ovoid section (*Fig. 8*).

To date there had been no concerted attempt to apply accurately
chosen descriptive designations to blown patterned glass. For immediate convenience I shall venture the following: ribbed (*Figs. 9, 9a*);
broken rib (*Fig. 10*); swirled (*Fig. 11*); corrugated (*Fig. 13*); fifteen
diamond (*Fig. 14*); three mold (*Fig. 15*).

At Mantua all of these patterns were blown in shades of green, aquamarine, and amber, aquamarine predominating. A few were blown in
amethyst. Reversing the rim turning on the plain pieces, the majority
of the patterned pieces have the rim folded *inside* when finished. There
are two exceptions: fifteen-diamond pattern, and three mold.

Thus far among students, the source ascription of pattern mold-
blown pieces has been based on tradition, the memory of an owner —
generally a person of advanced years and receding memory — or the
memory of what someone heard someone say, years ago. At best this is
a very questionable practice, and hardly permissible despite the in-
ordinate demand by collectors to know origins. The study of this excavated material has given me a clue which, I believe, though at present
somewhat faint, will eventually allow a few attributions to be made
with considerable certainty.

To those who are not entirely familiar with the process of blowing a
pattern mold or even expanded mold-blown glass, I suggest reference to
ANTIQUES for August 1930, pages 141–143, where these processes are
made very clear. With this information in mind, it is obvious that
successive pieces patterned in the same mold will invariably have the
same number of ribs, whether the finished article is dish, comport, wine
glass, or bottle. Likewise, the same number of ribs will occur in all of the
patterns, ribbed, swirled, corrugated, or broken rib.

On examining the patterned pieces made in Mantua — in this case
the base fragments of bottles and dishes — I find that this factory employed two types of molds: one with 16 ribs, and the other with 32 ribs.
The majority of the aquamarine and green patterned pieces were from
the *16-rib mold*. A few aquamarine and green, as well as most of the

Fig. 11 — MANTUA 16-RIB SWIRLED BOWL IN AQUAMARINE GLASS
Size, 10 ½ by 3 inches

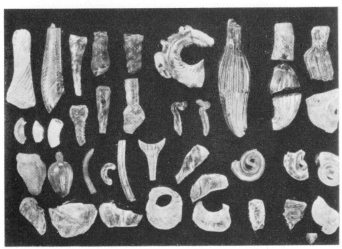

Fig. 12 — NECKS OF PATTERNED GATHERS, CANES, TWISTS, ALL FROM THE
16-RIB MOLD
Handles ornamented with rigaree work. Fragments of scent bottles in right
upper corner, ornamental spirals below

Fig. 13 — FRAGMENTS OF MANTUA CORRUGATED BOWL IN AQUAMARINE AND
DEEP-AMBER GLASS
(No complete specimen available)

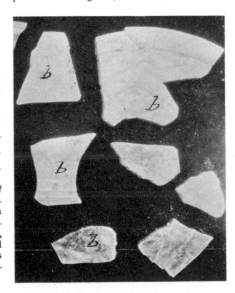

Fig. 14 (*extreme right*)
— MANTUA 15-DIA-
MOND PATTERN BOWL
IN AMBER GLASS
Size, 5 ½ by 1 ¾
inches. *From the Fol-
lansbee collection*
Figs. 14a, 14b (*above and
right*) — DIAMOND-
PATTERN FRAGMENTS
a. One half of tube connecting pipe to parison,
showing 15-diamond
pattern. *b.* Fragments
of bowls in aquama-
rine and amber

Fig. 15 — MANTUA THREE-PART-MOLD BOWL IN AQUAMARINE GLASS
A heavy bowl patterned in the Mantua three-part decanter mold. (A partial reconstruction from fragments excavated at Mantua.) *Diameter*, 7 inches

amber pieces produced at Mantua, were patterned in the *32-rib mold*.

Some time ago I began a survey of pattern-mold pieces, keeping a record of the type of object, size, color, and number of ribs in the pattern. So far I have recorded molds with the following number of ribs: 8, 10, 11, 12, 13, 14, 15, 16, 18, 20, 24, 25, 26, and 32. From these were made a wide range of articles in shades of aquamarine, green, amber, sapphire, amethyst, and clear glass.

The 16-rib designation for Mantua is supported not only by the bottoms of bottles and dishes, but by the necks of gathers, ornamental twists, canes, and manipulated fragments as small as ⅛ inch in diameter (*Fig. 12*).

It follows, likewise, that a study of the half-post, or so-called "Pitkin type" of pocket bottle will be of similar value. I found so few fragments of this type in the Mantua excavation that I am unable to tell exactly the number of ribs in the pattern-mold. However, if in this particular instance I allow myself to be guided by bottles of like color found in the vicinity, I should say that the mold had 16 ribs. This half-post I shall discuss later.

From the bottles of this general type in my collection and the fragments taken from excavations of other factories, in the East, I can see that all may readily be segregated in typical groups.

The discovery of the 15-diamond pattern and the three-mold bowl among Mantua products was indeed a surprise. The diamond is very distinct in design. Fragments in the upper right-hand corner of Figure 14*b* show it quite well. These occur in both aquamarine and deep amber. The bowl of Figure 14 is a rare and splendid specimen. It shows 15 diamonds in the row next to the rim, and the same number in each row in its circumference. This is also true of the bottle to be shown in Figure 37*a*, which was patterned in this same mold. It is a 15-diamond pattern bottle in aquamarine glass. I will also show the bottom and an enlarged view of the neck which will afford a better idea of its quality.

Returning now to the bowl of Figure 14, its rim was turned inside when folded or reamed, thus making an exception to the usual rule at Mantua for this pattern. Rims of three separate bowls or dishes among the fragments were turned outside.

The three-mold bowl shape recovered and assembled from the

fragments represents a distinct departure from the more usual milkpan type (*Fig. 15*). Its ornamentation was achieved by patterning in the same mold used for the decanter of Figure 15*a*. This decanter's band of diamonds (full three diamonds in width), between bands of vertical ribbing, is dimly perceptible in the bowl.

This bowl has a rim diameter of 7 inches, and evidently stood about 6 ½ or 7 inches high. In the process of reconstruction I was unable to find fragments for the base, which may have been pushed up like the base of a calabash bottle, or have consisted of a blown or cast-on foot. A footed base would seem more suitable for such a noble vessel. Both of the base types mentioned are to be found among these fragments (*Fig. 16*). But such heavy three-mold bowls as the one illustrated are very much the exception in Ohio and are to be viewed as an important discovery. Indeed, the fragmentary example of Figure 15 is the first of its kind in the three-mold category to be accorded a positive source identification. I found fragments of such bowls in both aquamarine and amber — a very light amber. In some of the rim fragments, which did not belong to this particular bowl, the turning of the folded rim outside had caused the viscid glass to leave small tails adhering to the top of each rib, an unusual and attractive effect, as will be seen in the fragments in the centre of the lower row (*Fig. 47*).

Fig. 15a — MANTUA THREE-MOLD DECANTER IN GREEN GLASS
From the Follansbee collection

Colors

I have tried to be accurate in naming the colors of the different objects or fragments of Mantua glass, while at the same time avoiding all effort to be excessively precise. To summarize the whole matter of Mantua colors, let me add a few sentences. The majority of the material excavated is in a strong aquamarine, which, in the thicker portions, becomes a deep green. Colors and shades are not very uniform, for Tinker had no such complete control of his materials as has the modern glassmaker. Varying shades of amber also occur in progression from a very light topaz to the deep reddish amber so long associated with Zanesville products. Signs of experiment with other tints may be detected among the remains: such as the olive amber of the usual New England and eastern New York type. But of this not much is in evidence. I found also a few fragments of dishes in amethyst and in a cloudy, milky white that is somewhat streaked. Trials of clear glass, evidently flint glass, likewise left their traces in the ruins.

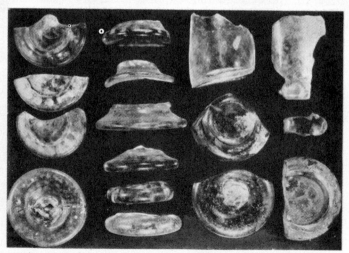

Fig. 16 — FRAGMENTS OF MANTUA FOOTED GLASS
Both blown and cast feet, in aquamarine and amber

(*Part III of Mr. White's article will appear in an early issue.*)

Fig. 17 — Fragments of Sweetmeat Covers, with Two Types of Edges, Folded and Expanded
Upper left corner, finials. *Patterns:* Ribbed, corrugated, broken-rib, and swirled. *Colors:* Aquamarine, green, and amber

Fig. 18 — Fragments of Mantua Plain and Swirled Pitchers in Aquamarine and Amber
Amber shades, very light to deep in tone.
Illustrations, unless otherwise noted, from the author's collection

The Story of the Mantua Glass Works

Part III. Further Remains and Reconstructions

By Harry Hall White

IT IS by no means easy to distinguish between the fragments of a calabash-shaped bottle and the bowl of a comport, with foot or without, patterned or plain. In the case of very small fragments, differentiation is, in fact, impossible. So it is that fragments from the sides and bottoms of calabash-shaped bottles will convey a correct impression of the appearance of fragments from comport bowls, both patterned and plain, with pushed-up bottoms (*Figs. 30, 32, and 33*). Fragments from footed comports will be like those shown in Figure 16 (Part II, ANTIQUES for February 1935). Fragments of covers and rims offer no serious problem, for here a characteristic shape guides identification. The very short reverse curve, or ogee, of a cover is easily distinguished from the curve of a small bowl, particularly when the cover thickens rapidly for the attachment of a knob or finial.

Fragments of covers excavated at Mantua are shown in Figure 17. Mantua covers are of two general descriptions: *1.* Those which contact the bowl rim with a folded flange. *2.* Those which contact the bowl with an expanded flange. Bowl fragments show two types of rims or edges: *1.* Plain and vertical for first type cover. *2.* Flanged and recessed for second type cover. Bowls were made with pushed-up bottoms, or with a supporting foot.

I have purposely omitted pictures of complete sweetmeats or comports, as examples at my disposal could be attributed to Mantua only by tradition and not as a result of comparison with available fragments. In general, the shapes and patterns of such items may be visualized by reference to ANTIQUES for December 1931 (*American Glass Sugar Bowls*, by Rhea Mansfield Knittle, *Figures 7, 8, and 10*, in plain, ribbed, and broken rib).

However, at Mantua, the broken-rib patterns were *not* achieved by employing a mold "horizontally ribbed and vertically fluted." Mantua patterns of this kind were produced by two applications of the gather to the mold (the same mold, or at least a mold with the same number of ribs). Thus, the gather, or parison, having been vertically ribbed by one contact with the mold, was then given a half twist before a second insertion in the same receptacle. This process has hitherto been a complete mystery to collectors and students of old glass. Only by the continual saving of all types of gathers and material cracked off from the pipes of these glassblowers and arranging them for careful study have I been able to unravel the tangle of opinions regarding it.

Pitchers

Pitchers, apparently an important part of the Mantua product, were made in many sizes. This statement is supported mainly by the evidence afforded by pitcher handles; for, as with calabash bottles and comports, the bulbous body of a pitcher declines to yield identifiable fragments. Handles and rim fragments will have to tell most of their story. In the lower row of Figure 18 the various finishes of the lower end of Mantua pitcher handles are exhibited. Since no hollow handles were found, it is safe to conclude that large pitchers were not produced. Pitchers above five and six inches tall called for hollow handles which would expand and contract with temperature fluctuations at the same rate as the body of the vessel.

The fragments indicate three types of finish above the neck: (*1*) corrugations made with a tool parallel with the edge of the rim; (*2*) applied threads of glass; and (*3*) a plain edge, slightly thickened. If there were any departures from the usual blown pitcher form found in Ohio — though infrequently — I have been unable to discover them (*Fig. 22*). The glass employed was in aquamarine, green, and amber — of course in many shades. The tint of one pitcher of which I have been able to secure numerous fragments, including the handle, is amber approaching a light topaz hue. The piece is ribbed, swirled, and very thin. In several places oxidation has progressed to the point of perforating the material. All of the amber-glass fragments at Mantua were

Fig. 19 — Mantua 16-Rib Pitcher in Yellowish Amber Glass
Size, 3 ⅝ inches.
From the Ralph G. Jones collection

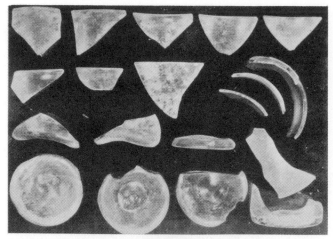

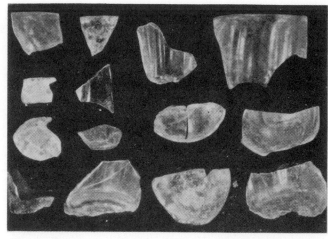

Fig. 20 — FRAGMENTS OF PLAIN TUMBLERS IN AQUAMARINE
Two upper rows, rims; *bottom rows*, bases

Fig. 21 — FRAGMENTS OF RIBBED AND SWIRLED TUMBLERS, AQUAMARINE AND AMBER

much more oxidized than those in aquamarine and green tints. Due to inability to distinguish bottoms of pitchers from bottoms of bottles, I cannot be certain whether patterned pitchers displayed 16 or 32 ribs. Nevertheless, the closeness of the ribs on the fragments available suggests that the mold normally used for patterned pitchers had 32 ribs.

Tumblers

In comparison to other objects made at Mantua the percentage of tumblers was large. The glass used was aquamarine and amber, while the fragments are ribbed, swirled, and plain (*Fig. 20*). The plain tumbler was made in sizes ranging from a small whisky glass to glasses of a diameter sufficient for a flip (*Fig. 23*).

The ribbed examples are very striking, and were made in quantity (*Fig. 21*). The bottoms reveal an unmistakable pattern. The fragment on the top row at the left of Figure 24 is from a swirled amber tumbler of 16 ribs. It shows quite distinctly the termination of the ribs against a ring or ridge encircling the pontil mark. This treatment is characteristic of Mantua 16-rib patterned tumblers.

A tumbler size that, to judge from the number of fragments, must have been highly popular, had a base diameter of 2 1/4 inches, and a rim diameter of 2 13/16 inches. The largest rim diameter that I was able to recover, from a fragment large enough to be reliable, is 3 1/2 inches. The household breakage of all such articles was large, and few intact specimens are to be found in the countryside today.

Stemware, Goblets, and Wine Glasses

Stemmed wine glasses, natural adjuncts of the decanter, and, perhaps for that reason, classic examples of the glassblower's art, were made at Mantua in the varying shades of green and amber. The diameter of some of the foot fragments of stemware suggests the likelihood that goblets were also produced, though it is true that a large foot may be a relic of a salt cup. Concerning Mantua wine glasses I am certain, since I have some of their bowl fragments (*Fig. 25*). The edge of the foot in every instance is plain,

Fig. 22 — A PITCHER COMPARISON, MANTUA TYPE IN CENTRE
Right, Geneva Glass Works, Geneva, Ontario County, New York; deep amber; *height*, 8 3/4 inches. *Centre*, Mantua type, aquamarine; *height*, 6 inches; *courtesy of Mrs. Prochaska*. *Left*, generally attributed to South Jersey; deep sapphire; *height*, 5 1/2 inches

Fig. 23 — MANTUA-TYPE SWIRLED FLIP GLASS IN GREENISH AMBER
Height, 4 3/4 inches.
From the Follansbee collection

never folded, and the stems of these pieces are invariably straight.

Certain salt cups and goblets have deep amber feet that show a fine beading where the stem joins the foot. This beading was patterned in an eighteen-rib mold, a mold not used for aquamarine and green pieces. In my opinion the amber pieces were made during the latter part of the operation of the glasshouse, at the time when flint glass was attempted. Some of the fragments have sufficient tension and resonance to indicate that flint glass was actually made at Mantua.

In the course of the excavation I found a sapphire fragment of a salt cup. I believe this to be a stray piece, possibly used as a model. It has eleven ribs in both bowl and beading. On account of the small quantity of sapphire glass taken from the site, I hesitate to attribute the sapphire cup to Mantua. In every case, I have withheld my decision until I found enough cullet and broken glass showing the scale or oxide from the blower's pipe definitely to indicate that the glassblowers had worked in the particular shade or color in question.

I am very fortunate to have the opportunity, through the courtesy of Ralph G. Jones, to show the amber Mantua 16-rib swirled salt cup (*Fig. 26*). This cup and likewise the 16-rib pitcher (*Fig. 19*) came from Mr. Jones' family homestead at Warren, Ohio, approximately twenty-five miles from Mantua, which, at the time when the glasshouse was in blast, was the nearest metropolis.

Footed Glasses

The term "footed glasses" I apply very generally to cover a considerable number of articles of which I have only the base and a short vertical piece without further evidence as to what the shape and final finish at the rim may have been. These feet are appropriate to vessels variously known as measures or Hogarth glasses, as well as to sweetmeat jars and bowls. But without a vast quantity of additional fragments it is impossible to determine the precise nature of the footed vessels of Mantua.

Foot fragments may be divided into two

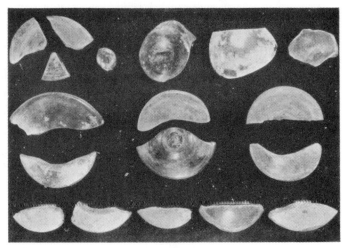

Fig. 24 — MANTUA BOTTOM PATTERNS
Upper row, left to right, 16-rib swirled tumbler, amber; 16-rib blown foot, aquamarine; 16-rib swirled inkwell, aquamarine. *Lower row, left to right*, three-mold decanter, showing concentric rings and 33 ribs on the bottom, aquamarine; 16-rib bowl, showing termination of ribs in ring concentric with the pontil mark, aquamarine; 16-rib chestnut-shaped pocket bottle with termination of ribs at ellipse about pontil mark, aquamarine

Fig. 25 — FRAGMENTS OF WINE GLASSES AND SALT CUPS, AQUAMARINE AND AMBER

Fig. 26 (*left*) — MANTUA 16-RIB SWIRLED SALT CUP, GREENISH AMBER
Height, 2 7/16 inches.
From the Ralph G. Jones collection

classes (*Fig. 16, Part II*): *1.* Those of convex section approximating a semicircle and extending as a foot beyond the point of attachment to the body of the article. None of these are pattern molded. *2.* Those of concave or ogee section sufficiently flaring to extend beyond the body of the object. Fragments show that feet of this type were blown both plain and pattern molded.

The diameters of the feet that I have reconstructed are: *First type*, average 2 ½ inches; *second type*, patterned, 2 ¼, 2 ⅛, and 2 ⅜ inches; *second type*, plain, 2, 2 13/16, 2 ½, and 3 inches.

A foot of the second type, plain but of suitable diameter, possibly three or three and one half inches, would be proper for the three-mold bowl of Figure 15. In fact, I have found this type and such a size at a contemporary glasshouse site near Kent, Ohio. Feet of type one, and of type two patterned, were blown in the same piece as the vessel. Plain feet of the second type were added gatherings of metal shaped by a manipulation similar to that employed in forming a wine-glass foot. These pieces are proof of the ability of Jonathan Tinker and his workmen.

Bottles

First of all the Mantua bottles, I shall describe the calabash type

(*Fig. 27*). My most reliable points of identification for these plain Mantua pieces, a difficult matter at best, is the neck finish and the surface of the glass.

The ring, or reënforcing collar, applied to the aqua, green, and amber pieces is generally well formed and fairly heavy (*top row, Figure 28 for aqua; Fig. 29 for amber*). Occasionally the collar will betray a pair of dents or depressions made by the points of the finisher's tools. These depressions are visible in the fragment pictured at the end of the top row (*Fig. 28*). I have found several bottles with such dented collars from the countryside in Portage County.

The bottom cavity of larger and heavier calabash bottles was produced by pushing in the glass with the points of the procellas rather than with the punty, *i.e.*, before attaching the punty. This method, I believe, reduced the chances of making such an extensive heavy contact between bottle and punty as to cause breakage of the latter when it was snapped off from the rod. The pontil mark on many of the best of the smaller bottles, approximately quart size, is no more than a narrow ring marking the outside circumference of the punty. A flanged finish was also used on both aqua and amber plain calabash bottles (*Fig. 29*).

The surface of these bottles and of their fragments shows pronounced

Fig. 27 — MANTUA CALABASH-TYPE PLAIN BOTTLES IN AQUAMARINE

Fig. 28 — FRAGMENTS OF AQUAMARINE CALABASH BOTTLES

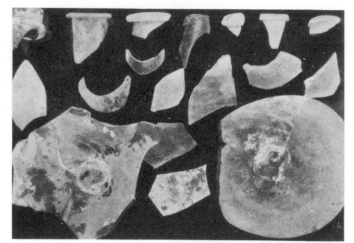

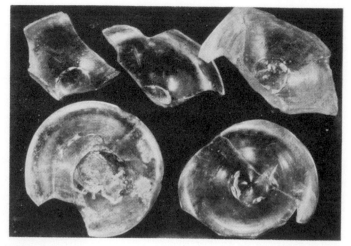

Fig. 29 — FRAGMENTS OF AMBER CALABASH BOTTLES

Fig. 31 (right) — MANTUA 16-RIB CALABASH-TYPE
BOTTLE IN AQUAMARINE
    Height, 6 inches; *capacity,* approximately ½ pint

Fig. 30 — BASES OF AQUAMARINE CALABASH BOTTLES
    Lower right fragment shows bottom pushed up by
    tool before applying punty — an attempt to
    minimize breakage

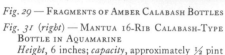

striations and strings or veins. These occur so frequently as to suggest that the glassmaker had trouble in maintaining a sufficiently high furnace temperature. Aquamarine glass, it may be observed, requires a great heat to fine it. Bottoms with pontil marks and striated surfaces accentuated by oxidation are shown in Figure 30. The amber fragments are invariably more corroded than those in aquamarine or green (*Fig. 29*).

The ribbed and swirled bottles of calabash shape never fail to arouse the admiration of those who see them (*Fig. 31*). Mantua examples were made in aquamarine, green, and the various shades of amber, with 16 and 32 ribs.

Among the aquamarine fragments, in Figure 32, those on the left are from 32-rib molds, while those on the right show the wider spacing of the 16-rib mold. In the lower right corner are two 16-rib base fragments. It is difficult to determine whether a base fragment should qualify in the group of calabash bottles, or in that of chestnut bottles and comports. However, I have tried to take a middle path as similar molds were used to pattern all of these articles.

At Mantua amber plain and ribbed bottles were less common, if we

may judge from the infrequent occurrence of their fragments. As the latter were found in an area quite separate from that in which the majority of aquamarine and green pieces were turned up, I surmise that they are souvenirs of the Skinners or the Lewises during the latter part of the operation of the works. Intact examples would be fine in pattern, form, and color.

Both light and dark amber bottles of 16 and 32 ribs contribute to the group in Figure 33. Here the lower right corner reveals quite well a ribbed bottom built up from fragments assembled for the purpose of counting the ribs, in this case 32 in number. This group demonstrates, on the left, the wide spacing of the 16-rib fragments; on the right, the closer spacing of the 32-rib fragments. In the upper right corner the fragment of a tightly twisted neck may be observed. These fragments, especially the darker ones, are in the deep amber shades hitherto attributed solely to Zanesville, Ohio. It is unfortunate that the old glasshouse sites at Zanesville are inaccessible. Investigation would solve many mysteries.

(*The concluding chapter of Mr. White's story of the Mantua Glass Works will appear in an early issue.*)

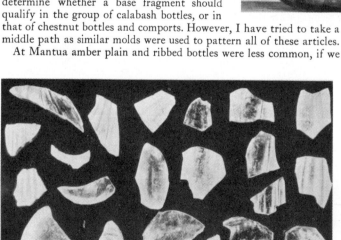

Fig. 32 — FRAGMENTS OF 16- AND 32-RIB CALABASH-TYPE BOTTLES, AQUA-
MARINE

Fig. 33 — FRAGMENTS OF 16- AND 32-RIB SWIRLED CALABASH BOTTLES IN
AMBER

The Story of the Mantua Glass Works

Part IV. Reconstructions, and Conclusion

By Harry Hall White

Fig. 34 — Mantua Plain Chestnut
Pocket Bottle in Aquamarine
Height, 6 ½ inches; *capacity,* about 1
pint

Fig. 36 — Mantua 16-Rib Swirled
Chestnut Pocket Bottle in Aquamarine

Fig. 36a — Fragments of 16-Rib Swirled Chestnut Pocket Bottles in
Aquamarine

Chestnut or Pocket Bottles

THE interesting Western bottles of pocket size surely eclipse their drab Eastern cousins made at Manchester, Keene, Coventry, and Vernon. The Western versions, however, appear not to have had a collar, either ringed or flanged. If they did, the feature was the exception. On the other hand, the Eastern plain chestnut pocket bottle without a flanged neck is almost entirely unknown.

Graceful and delightful in form and pattern, these pocket bottles will always give the finder great satisfaction. In Mantua fragments of these vessels every local color and shade is represented as well as the various patterns. But, strange to state, the plain chestnut form is the most uncommon of all (*Fig. 34*). Nearly all the fragments of the chestnut bottle taken from this excavation are ribbed, swirled, or of the splendid broken-rib pattern. A very few represent diamond and Pitkin types.

The broken-rib pattern most closely resembles the Pitkin type, but it is not the same thing. The pattern was obtained by means of two insertions in a ribbed mold, but only the original "post" or gather was used, and was heated between the two patterning operations. No second gathering or "half post" was employed as in the Pitkin type, so long and erroneously called the "inserted neck." Which are the handsomer, the ribbed chestnuts (*Fig. 35*) or the swirled (*Fig. 36*), is a subject for debate. Both specimens pictured are aquamarine.

Two good examples of the broken-rib ornamentation are shown in Figures 37 and 38. One is twisted a half turn to the right, the other a half turn to the left. Like the calabash bottles, this type was patterned either in 16- or in 32-rib molds. In the 16-rib examples the ribs terminate at a ring or ridge concentric with the pontil mark. In the 32-rib examples, the ribs diverge from a common point under, or near, the pontil mark. Fragments of a broken-rib pocket bottle are shown in Figure 39.

When fragments of the fifteen-diamond pattern appeared among my captures, my attitude was that which my reader may quite naturally assume — that of scepticism. After so many years of ascribing diamond items exclusively to Manheim, it was indeed quite shocking to realize that some of the Stiegel-type diamond-pattern dishes and pocket bottles,

and even diamond chain salts, might have been made fifty years later in Ohio. Accordingly, I proceeded with extreme caution.

I was rewarded by finding definite evidence in the single fragment of Figure 14a (ANTIQUES for February 1935, p. 67). This is one half of a gather or of the tube connecting a parison to the blowpipe, showing the direct impression of the pattern received from the mold. Figure 40 presents an excellent example of aquamarine bottle in the fifteen-diamond pattern as produced at Mantua. I have recently seen an amber chestnut pint pocket bottle from the same Mantua mold. By way of giving a clearer idea of just how this diamond pattern was produced, I am reproducing an enlargement of several of the diamonds at the neck of the aquamarine item already referred to (*Fig. 40a*). This shows just how the diamonds opened into full bloom as blowing expanded the body of the bottle. The diamonds in a piece of this kind may be counted at any place in the circumference, though I generally take the neck or the base. Figure 40b shows the base of this particular specimen with arrows to indicate the fifteen points of wear, which are actually the ridges outlining the diamonds as they pass the ridge forming the base.

The two so-called half-post or Pitkin-type bottles of Figure 41 are respectively of one half and one pint capacity, and of aquamarine glass. They are much heavier than the typical greenish-amber bottles so common in the East, where like bottles in aquamarine are uncommon.

I found at Mantua fragments shown in Figure 41a, both in aquamarine and in amber; but the amber was the golden amber of Ohio. To ensure against error, I magnified the edges of two fragments, one in aquamarine and one in amber, where the oxidation was sufficiently deep to show the actual "grain" or crystalline structure of the metal itself (*Fig. 41b*). In the upper, larger amber fragment, the junction of the two layers of glass is clearly marked by a line of minute bubbles imprisoned at the time of the second gather. However, in the lower fragment edge, which is of aquamarine, the overlay or second gather may be more clearly identified by the wavy lines over the book-edge laminations of the original or first gather on the pipe. It is interesting to observe that both in these fragments, and in

Fig. 35 — Mantua 16-Rib Chestnut
Pocket Bottle in Aquamarine
*Illustrations, unless otherwise noted,
from the author's collection*

Fig. 37 — Mantua 16-Broken-Rib
Chestnut Pocket Bottle in
Aquamarine
From the Follansbee collection

wares approximated our modern drug emporium.

Mantua supplied several sizes of medicine phials. I have taken boxes of similar delightfully frail bubbles from under the counters of old stores in the Western Reserve. No one could tell definitely where they were made, but the Mantua phials are of the same type and color and virtually of the same size. Offhand blowing entails a considerable variation in this respect (*Figs. 42, 47*). Fragments of such vessels at Mantua were always green or aquamarine.

The druggist's bottles with flanged neck had an average diameter of approximately 2 ¼ inches. From the fragments I was unable to determine the height. Other sizes were made, of course; but this particular size was evidently produced

Fig. 40a — Neck of 15-Diamond Mantua Bottle, to Demonstrate the Development of the Pattern
The numbers assist in tracing the graduated expansion from the narrow grooves at the narrow diameter of the neck to the full diamonds on the body of the bottle

the two bottles, the "twist" of the pattern on the second gather may occur either to the left or to the right.

Druggist's Bottles

No frontier glasshouse could miss the opportunity to cater to all requirements of the early Midwest settlement. Sooner or later came a physician, with his own stock of drugs if there was yet no general store; for in such communities the general store long served as apothecary shop, or rather, in the variety of its

Fig. 39 — Fragments of 16-Broken-Rib Chestnut Pocket Bottles in Aquamarine

in quantity, as I found many fragments. They were exclusively offhand, plain, no mold being used to ensure a uniform diameter. Figure 47 in the second row pictures the fragments and their flanged necks.

Ink Bottles

As might be expected, Mantua did not neglect the lowly inkwell. In fact, it glorified some of these simple utensils with pattern molding. Both conical and cylindrical forms were turned out, in

Fig. 38 — Mantua 16-Broken-Rib Chestnut Pocket Bottle in Light Greenish Amber
Shows half-turn twist to left

plain, swirled, and broken-rib patterning (*Fig. 43*). These fragments indicate fine work and ornamentation. I have not seen any of these in intact examples, but eventually some fortunate collector will find them. The fragments of a conical well appear at the left side of Figure 43. This shows the broken-rib pattern. The glass is aquamarine and very light amber. The other four vertical rows of fragments are of the cylindrical type in the broken-rib and corrugated patterns. These are also in aquamarine and green glass.

Three-Mold Decanter

Fairly early in the excavation I realized that I was bringing to light what seemed to be fragments of a molded decanter or bottle. Many of the pieces were quite large and some very heavy.

Fig. 40b — Bottom of Mantua 15-Diamond-Pattern Bottle
The arrows indicate the ridges between the indentations of the pattern where they have become worn into small facets

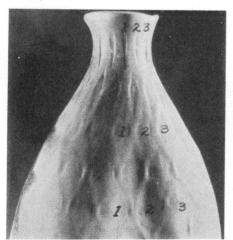

Fig. 40 — Mantua 15-Diamond-Pattern Bottle in Aquamarine Glass
Height, 7 ¾ inches.
From the collection of Mrs. Grace Black

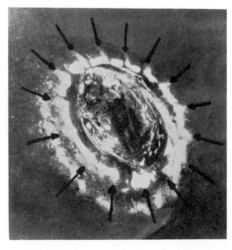

Fig. 41 (left and right)—Swirled Double-Patterned Overlay Mantua Pocket Bottles
Patterns obtained by this process are variously known as "corncob," "half-post," "inserted neck," and "Pitkin type." Both specimens in strong aquamarine. *Note:* Swirling turns both to right and to left

Fig. 41a (below, left) — Fragments from Overlay-Type Bottles
All of these pieces show the extent of the second gather or dipping. Unless they are selected in this manner it is very difficult, perhaps impossible, to tell them from the broken-rib fragment. Both aquamarine and amber

Fig. 41b (below, right) — Edge of Two Fragments Magnified
Oxidation has advanced sufficiently to show the grain or striations of the metal structure. Triangular area lettered *ABC* is the overlay. The laminated or "book edge" appearance of the glass below *AB* is the original gather. Upper specimen in amber, lower in aquamarine

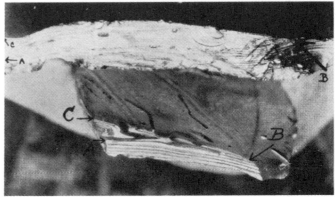

Then one day my associate noisily announced the amazing discovery of a stopper, a whole one, evidently pressed in some manner (*Fig. 44*). True enough, it seemed to match the design and general spirit of the decanter pattern which I had succeeded in translating from the fragments (*Fig. 45*) to paper (*Fig. 45a*).

I had never found such a decanter intact, and none of the collectors or dealers in the locality recalled having seen one. Of the decanters referred to me by collectors and correspondents, some were very like the Mantua article, but they invariably carried their diamond-patterned areas above and below a band of vertical ribbing such as we find in three-mold decanters made at a factory near Kent, Ohio.

When I had my material sufficiently well in hand to give others an intelligent view of the case, I took counsel with one of the most consistent collectors of antiques among my acquaintance, Mrs. George E. Follansbee, of Cleveland, Ohio, who has graciously permitted me to obtain several of my illustrations from her comprehensive collections. During my discussions with her, Mrs. Follansbee recognized the decanter that I had sketched from my Mantua fragments, and, to my surprise and delight, brought from her cabinet an actual specimen (see Fig. 15a, p. 68, Antiques for February 1935). The peculiar markings on the bottom show quite clearly in the lower right fragment of Figure 45. There are 33 diverging ribs along the edge. Within are two concentric circles. The lower band of ribbing, on the decanter body,

consists of 39 ribs. In the band of diamond ornamentation, just above this, there are 36 diamonds in the circumference of one row. The ribbed area above the diamond band comprises, as does the lower ribbing, 39 ribs. These features, I believe, definitely identify the Mantua three-mold decanter. All fragments that I have found were aquamarine and green, though I did excavate a broken stopper in light amber. Mantua stoppers may be identified by the lack of uniformity in the spacing of the bars (see Fig. 8, *p. 65*, Antiques for February 1935).

The Mantua decanter here described is *the first three-mold decanter to be indubitably identified with a specific glasshouse.* If the date of its manufacture be accepted as approximately 1825, we at once have a safe starting point for judging the period of three-mold decanters produced at some of the glass factories located in the East.

Jackson-Masonic Flask

Having uncovered fragments of the three-mold decanter early in the course of my excavations, I surmise that I may at the same time have taken out many pieces of flasks without recognizing their significance. Never did my highest hopes comprehend the pioneer discovery of an important early historical flask. However, one evening the revelation came when, as I was washing a bit of my treasure trove, I suddenly uncovered on the familiar Masonic emblem of the Holy Bible, the square, and the compasses. I have seldom undergone a more intensely dramatic experience than my subsequent search for additional fragments,

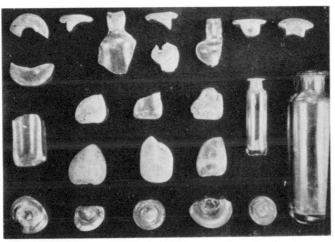

Fig. 42 — Druggist's "Phials" and Fragments in Aquamarine

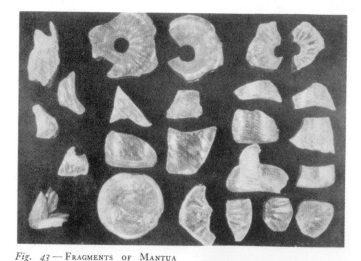

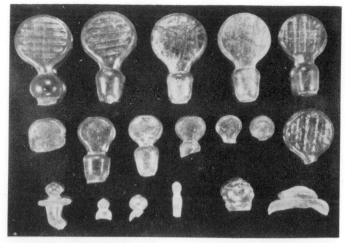

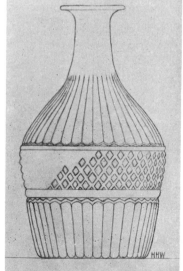

Fig. 43 — FRAGMENTS OF MANTUA INKWELLS IN AQUAMARINE, VERY LIGHT AMBER, AND GREEN

Fig. 45 (right) — FRAGMENTS OF MANTUA THREE-MOLD DECANTER
Bottom fragment at lower right clearly shows the peculiarity of the mold marking on the base. Two concentric circles and 33 ribs of the pattern extending over the edge of the base and terminating in the third ring

Fig. 44 — MANTUA STOPPERS
Top row, three-mold decanter in aquamarine and green. Centre row, druggist; last fragment at right an amber stopper for three-mold decanter. Bottom row, at left, stoppers for cruets and scent bottles; at right, parts of knobs and finials for sweetmeat-jar covers

Fig. 45a — DRAWING OF THREE-MOLD MANTUA DECANTER AS RECONSTRUCT-ED FROM FRAGMENTS PRIOR TO FIND-ING AN ACTUAL DECANTER
An actual three-mold Mantua decanter was illustrated as Figure 15a, in the second part of this article (see ANTIQUES for February 1935, p. 68)

and, as these were found, the piece-by-piece reconstruction of the Jackson-Masonic flask. When the work was complete I had retrieved from oblivion a flask of splendid proportions and of exceptional historical value. It bears the simple, eloquent legend: A JACKSON/OHIO. Above the arc of Jackson's name are the initials J T, standing for Jonathan Tinker, glassblower and co-founder of the Works.

The reverse is ornamented with more Masonic symbols than I have ever seen used before — the spade, the coffin, and a sprig of acacia. Above the usual beehive, and at the right of the pillars, appears the triangular form of seven lighted tapers. For the rest, the design follows precedent.

To the present time of writing I have not seen a single unbroken specimen of this flask. I have excavated enough bases to account for a dozen dropped among the Mantua ruins. In relation to the quantity of material excavated this number justifies the belief that the flask must have been produced in commercial quantities.

Events may prove that my drawing of this flask is somewhat out of proportion in respect to height, for in measuring from piece to piece some errors will accumulate. This I found to be the case when I compared my drawing of the three-mold decanter with the actual specimen.

The lettering A JACKSON evidently was not the original inscription cut in this mold. Either some patching was done, or some kind of alteration was made in the lettering, for traces of other letters unrelated to the present inscription are faintly perceptible. Thus far, however, I have been unable to decipher them all.

The flask fragments occurred in green and aquamarine (Figs. 46 and 46a). Apparently the vessels themselves were not so heavily blown as the Masonic flasks of Keene and the New England Glass Company, but more closely approximated the weight of Coventry and Stoddard flasks. The neck fragments are quite thin, but have a generous diameter. These necks also have a tendency to be short, that is, they are finished rather close to the shoulder (Fig. 47, top row, right). In addition to the corrugated edges and the two lines of beading carried below the neck, much in the design of this flask suggests the Coventry Masonic series. In Figure 47 among the neck finishes in the lower rows are some interesting flanged, folded, and threaded necks usually associated with "Ohio Stiegel."

Conclusion

In closing this study of the Mantua Glass Works I wish to emphasize that the material on which it is based has been obtained from an examination of original sources. I deplore the tendency to accept at face value what is so often merely surmise as to the provenance of glassware. The lamented "Baron" Stiegel, despite his expansive temperament, would blush to know the number of articles glibly attributed to his Manheim factory. While it must be admitted that the identification of American glass is attended with great difficulty, I can find in that circumstance no excuse for loose and unsubstantiated ascriptions. Hunger for information has too largely been satisfied with supposition and the warmed-over statements of imaginative fabulists and purveyors of old wives' tales. No matter how honest their intent, such offerings should be viewed with suspicion until their validity has been subjected to the most rigorous tests. It will be noted, for example, that in this discussion I have not even suggested that the Mantua glassworks were the first to be established in the Western Reserve, though obviously they must have been among the earliest. It has, however, been demonstrated that the products of this establishment were neither very large in quantity nor greatly varied in character. Surviving

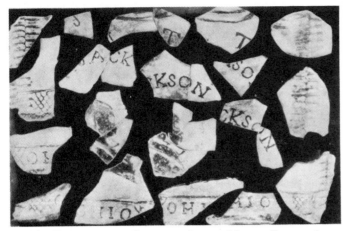

Fig. 46 — Fragments from Obverse of Jackson-Masonic Flask in Aquamarine

Fig. 46a — Fragments from Reverse of Aquamarine Jackson-Masonic Flask

examples are, therefore, bound to be excessively rare and of high desirability to the collector.

In my opinion, the outstanding single discovery made during this research was that of the hitherto unknown Jackson-Masonic flask. At present only a few fragments rescued from the earthwork of Mantua are at hand to testify that such a flask was ever made. But it is well within the range of possibility that somewhere an intact specimen awaits a lucky finder.

Of nearly equal importance, I believe, is the linking of the Mantua three-mold decanter with a particular decade of glass history, thus erecting another guidepost for the study of a type of glass about which very little is known.

The establishing of indices for the closer identification of hitherto doubtfully ascribed pieces of early blown and molded glass will, I trust, prove increasingly helpful to studious collectors. However that may be, if all in all I have been so fortunate as to add to the sum of our knowledge of early American glassware, I am content.

Lastly I wish to express my appreciation of the sympathetic interest in my work shown by E. J. Hamill, owner of the property in the Mantua triangle. I also owe a debt of gratitude to my friend and

Fig. 46b — Drawing of Mantua Jackson-Masonic One-Pint Flask as Reconstructed from Fragments Excavated

colleague, Doctor Frederic Wade Hitchings, whose association I have enjoyed through the ten years' study of the Mantua glasshouse. His help and encouragement eased many a difficult task. In the matter of information concerning the processes of glassmaking I wish to thank Frederick Carder, of the Steuben branch of the Corning Glass Works. I gratefully acknowledge the assistance of the Cleveland Museum of Art, through I. T. Frary and Edd A. Ruggles, who with great liberality assisted me in the difficult matter of color photography. Without the cooperation of Director Cathcart and his competent library staff at the Western Reserve Historical Society, the historical background of this report would have been much less complete. One of the most important aids was the attitude of my friends among collectors and dealers, who placed no limit on time and patience while I searched and studied their collections. The fact that I cannot name them all in no wise diminishes my appreciation of their manifold helpfulness.

Fig. 47 — Various Neck Finishes used at Mantua

Fig. 48 — Various Types of Rims as Finished at Mantua
Left vertical row, inward folded rim of ribbed bowls. *Second vertical row*, outward folded rim of plain bowls. *Right half*, rims of pitchers, covers for sweetmeat jars, and, *lower centre*, part of the rim of a very large three-mold bowl

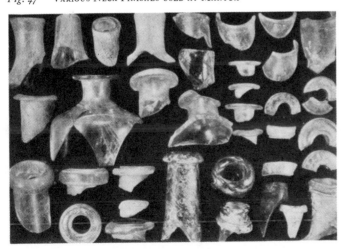

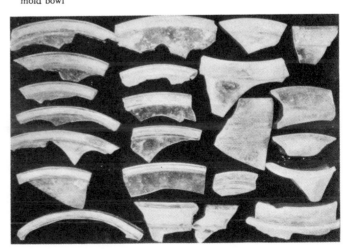

THE MANTUA JACKSON-MASONIC FLASK

By HARRY HALL WHITE

THERE IT STOOD in full tradition on a timber in an old barn. It was only a few miles from Mantua, in a lake-shore village in the Western Reserve — the first specimen of the Mantua Jackson-Masonic flask to be found intact. Doubtless it had stood there for years, awaiting the fortunate discoverer.

It was in The Magazine ANTIQUES for November 1935, where I completed my account of the glassworks at Mantua, Ohio, that I had told what I knew of the Jackson-Masonic flask made there. This exceptionally interesting bottle had been hitherto unknown, and I considered it the outstanding single discovery made during my research in connection with that glassworks. All I had ever found, however, was fragments, and from them I had made a piece-by-piece reconstruction of the flask's form and design (*Fig. 1*). From the number of fragments found I concluded that this flask must have been

produced in commercial quantities, but no single unbroken specimen had I found.

When I first learned, recently, that a complete specimen had made its appearance, I was impressed not so much by the fact that it had been found — I suppose I had always thought that sooner or later that was inevitable — as by the considerable length of time, since publication of my reconstruction, required to bring it to light. This to me is a pretty accurate gauge of rarity. Through the characteristic graciousness of Neil C. Gest, prominent Ohio collector, this first specimen was made available for my study (*Fig. 3*).

The flask bears on one side a bust profile identified by the legend *A Jackson*. Above the arc of this name are the initials *J T*, of Jonathan Tinker, glassblower and co-founder of the Mantua works. Below the portrait is the word *Ohio*. On the reverse is an extraordinarily diverse aggregation of

304

ANTIQUES

Fig. 1 (*left*) — Drawing of Mantua Jackson-Masonic One-Pint Flask as Reconstructed from Fragments (see Antiques, November 1935, pp. 201-203).

Fig. 2 — Sketch of Inscription on Flask. Dotted lines show remaining letters of original cutting.

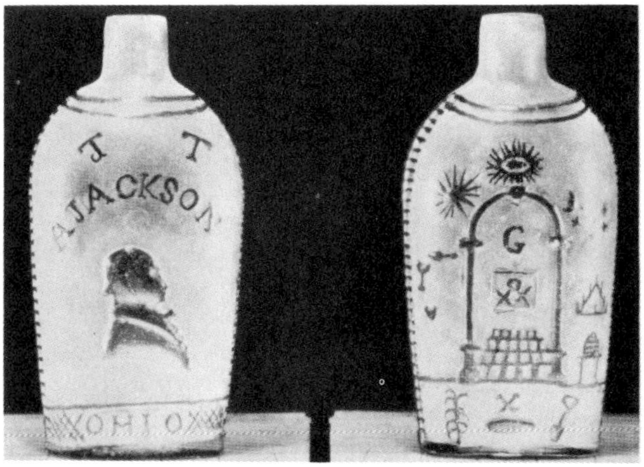

Fig. 3 — One-Pint Light-Green Mantua Jackson-Masonic Flask. Height, 7¾ inches; width, 3¾ inches; 2½ inches at thickest part. *Privately owned; photograph by courtesy of Neil C. Gest.*

flask seems to have poor detail, but, upon comparison with the fragments, I found it to be full-blown and faithful to detail. The rather crude appearance is due simply to the fact that the mold was not deeply incised.

In my original story of this Mantua flask I mentioned that there seemed to have been some alteration in the inscription *A Jackson*; traces of other letters, presumably the original inscription, were faintly perceptible (*Fig. 2*). I suspected that these might be traces of a double impression due to rotation in the mold. Now with the flask at hand for detailed study, I have arrived at a more reasonable explanation. First I considered the possibility that the mold had been used to commemorate some other contemporary hero or popular favorite, and lined up all the possible candidates. None of the names fitted the few scattered letters that I had segregated.

Masonic symbols. All this corresponds exactly with my reconstruction.

At first glance, however, I was surprised by the form of this flask. It is proportionately taller than I had visualized it from the fragments, though, as I wrote at the time, I based my drawing on the ornamental details and might easily have made an error in proportion. Moreover, I was influenced by the shapes of the other members of the Masonic series, while this form is much more like that of the earlier Connecticut flasks from Manchester and possibly Keene. In fact, it has several factors in common with Connecticut examples, such as the corrugated edge, slender form, and particularly the use of the artisan's name or initials in the general ornamental design.

The color is distinctly Mantua green — but who can describe a color? This queer shade of light green, sometimes loosely called aquamarine, is notably difficult to photograph in black and white, for irregularities in glass thickness fail to appear in the negative.

The distribution of glass in this specimen is very similar to that in the fragments: quite thin in the upper part and much thicker in the base. Jonathan Tinker may have been a skillful offhand worker in glass, but from this bottle and also the fragments it seems that his preparation of the gather for bottle-blowing was not the best. When I first studied the fragments it seemed probable that this poor distribution was responsible for the breakage of the flasks in the group of fragments I had excavated. It now appears that they were fragments of normal flasks as blown at Mantua.

There may have been some slight elongation after removal from the mold, but the surface of this flask shows only enough warming or flashing at the furnace to round or smooth the raw edges of the cracked-off neck. In fact, the neck seems about the original pipe diameter, and apparently was not opened or slightly flared or funnel-shaped by the use of a tool. This is mentioned only because of the flask's unusual capacity. The storekeeper who weekly replenished grandpap's flask, if he filled it up to the neck, would unknowingly contribute two and one-half ounces over the normal pint.

In checking the surface appearance of the glass to make sure that there was a minimum of distortion I was also careful to get a true record of the inscription. Superficially, the

Then I hit upon the possible solution. Names ending in *I* are rare in English, but the letters *I* and *J* were often interchanged in inscriptions of the period. So I considered the last two letters as *AJ* instead of *AI* and the answer was easy when I arranged Jackson as Noskcaj.

Molds are cut intaglio and *in reverse*. Whoever first cut this mold forgot that, and cut the name Jackson from left to right, so he had to correct his mistake. Evidently the initial *A* was not included in the original inscription as the arc is balanced without it, but it was easy to add, using the final upright of *N* as one leg of the letter *A*.

A like mistake in the peculiarly symmetrical word *Ohio* was more easily corrected. Likewise the strange wide bar and the small hook on the *J* in Jonathan's first initial testify to a similar error in the initials *J T*.

The majority of profile bas-relief cuttings on flasks face to the left, and here again the moldcutter may have made a mistake, though one that did not require correction. My guess is, however, that he followed the contemporary style of facing right which is exemplified in the flasks of Coventry and the Mt. Vernon Glass Works.

Regarding the use of Masonic ornaments on the reverse little need be said. It departs from the conventional arrangement and several symbols are added.

Thus far this is the only known flask of New England type of the 1820-1830 period made in what was then the west. Pittsburgh and Zanesville flasks were influenced by the mold fashions of eastern Pennsylvania and southern New Jersey. It is also the only known specimen of its type, but it is hoped that a more thorough search for flasks of the most interesting Ohio era may bring other examples to light.

The Kentucky Glass Works

By Harry Hall White

Except as noted, illustrations are by the author from his own collection.

HISTORY

THE earliest available history of Louisville is contained in *Sketches of Louisville and Environs*, by H. McMurtrie, M.D. This is a report, published in 1819, describing the local industries of the time in considerable detail and with great thoroughness. Since no mention of a glass works occurs in the book, we are justified in assuming that, in 1819, no glass was being produced in Louisville.

The next writer to record early Louisville industries is Ben Casseday. In his *The History of Louisville from its Earliest Settlement until 1852*, Casseday clearly follows McMurtrie and adds little material concerning the early period. Concerning the later years, he records that the census of 1840 assigns to Louisville "one glass cutting works"; also the establishment of a second glass cutting works in 1845.

This refers to the establishment of H. and T. Hunter. This pioneer concern made a comprehensive line of cut glass on blanks secured from Pittsburgh. In their advertisements they specify cut glass for brooches, cut bottles for table sets, and feature the matching and replacement of broken bottles. They also made crystals for miniatures; but it is probable that the bulk of their product consisted of engraved clear and colored glass panels for the windows and doors of steamship cabins. Their handiwork was to be found in a large proportion of the early steamboats on western waters. Evidences of the Hunter activities are found almost continuously in the Louisville *Directory* from 1844 to 1870. The Louisville *Directory* for 1836–38–39 carries no mention of glassmakers. Directories searched up to 1849 show no glass factories.

The *Seventh Federal Census* for 1850, however, credits Louisville with a factory in operation, employing fifty hands, twenty-one of whom were glassblowers. In my search for information concerning early Louisville glassmakers, this census note proved encouraging, until I learned that the Louisville *Directory* for 1850 was not available. Fortunately the *Directory* for 1851–52 by John B. Jegli was to be had, and here I found the record of the men associated in this first glass factory, but no record of the factory's date of establishment.

Then I turned to a careful search of contemporary Louisville newspapers. Here I was amply rewarded. Crowded in a long narrow column of *The Louisville Morning Courier* for August 12, 1850, sandwiched in among announcements of the arrival of Madam Smith, who, upon the arrangement of suitable appointments, was prepared to give readings of the past, present and future, the advertisement of a gunsmith who recommended a particular type of pepper-box pistol, bids for the prospective gold seeker and offers to purchase gold dust, I found the following, to me, notable advertisement, which I am reproducing in *facsimile:*

KENTUCKY GLASS WORKS.

TAYLOR, STANGER, RAMSEY & CO., Manufacturers of Vials, Demijohns, Porter and other Bottles, of every description, are now in full operation and ready to receive orders, at their establishment on Clay, near Washington st., Louisville. Orders left at Casseday & Hopkins' store, on Main, near Third street, will be promptly attended to.

☞ Particular attention paid to private Moulds.
au12 d1y

In those feverish days, to be located on one of the main highways of travel, to witness the excitement of the gold rush, and the swelling traffic toward "Pike's Peak or bust," to read daily the newspaper letters from gold miners and from travelers at Panama — and yet to remain at home and invest money in a glass factory must have called for great confidence and determination on the part of the men who made the choice. Theirs was the initial attempt at actual glassmaking in Louisville, the Kentucky Glass Works.

As was the case in a great number of such pioneer works, the company consisted of a group of practical men, real glassblowers, without doubt men who had received their training at Pittsburgh, Wheeling, or possibly at Zanesville. The following list is taken from one of the current Louisville directories:

William Doyle	Glass blower
John Stanger	" "
Gottlieb Leopold	" "
Joseph Ramsey, Jr.	" "
Theodore Greiner	" "
Frederick Mowrey	
Adam Bedenburg	Pot maker
John Reilly	Laborer
H. Adernechter	"

Following almost without variation the fortunes of the average pioneer works possessing a similar type of organization, in a few months the company needed assistance. Whether financial aid was wanted, or the experience of an executive capable of securing an outlet for the factory's product, we do not know. Whatever the cause may have been, the fact is that, in November of the year of founding, the partnership was dissolved and a reorganization occurred, in which a part of the original company was strengthened by the affiliation of George L. Douglass, a Louisville planter. The original factory name, *Kentucky Glass Works*, was retained; but the company name was changed to that of *Douglass and Taylor*. The text of the concern's advertisement, in *The Louisville Morning Courier* for Thursday, November 28, 1850, is interesting.

KENTUCKY GLASS WORKS

Geo. L. Douglass and James Taylor having purchased the above works, have formed a partnership, under the name and style of Douglass and Taylor.

They have a good stock of ware on hand, and will fill promptly orders for all description of green and black glassware, consisting of fancy and plain vials of every description; Packing, Porter, Mineral and Wine Bottles, Pickle and other Jars, Flasks and Demijohns.

☞ Particular attention paid to private moulds.

Orders by mail, or left at Casseday and Hopkins store on Main near Third Street or at the Works on Clay Street near Main will receive prompt attention.

The next bit of positive information regarding this company comes in the form of the following advertisement found in *The Louisville Directory and Annual Business Advertiser* for the years 1855–56, published by W. Lee White & Co.:

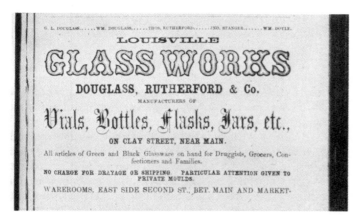

This advertisement shows changes in the firm name, and offers the first instance in which I have found the works referred to as the *Louisville Glass Works*. A few of the original company remain, John Stanger and William Doyle, the two practical men. Possibly Stanger was a descendant of the runaway apprentice boy for whom Richard Wistar offered a reward, the "German servant lad," who, with his brother, founded the first works at Glassboro, New Jersey. The name seems to have been spelled both ways.*

However that may be, these two glassmakers, strengthened by the finance and business management of their associates — Douglass, the planter, and Rutherford, evidently a relative of John M. Rutherford then a member of The Exchange Banking Office — continued their busi-

*Barber, *American Glassware*, p. 44.

ness with apparent success, sufficient at least to attract a man, who, later, was to become prominent in the business and civil circles of Louisville, John A. Krack, M.D. In 1856 Dr. Krack purchased a half interest in the concern, and the Louisville Ky. Glass Works was then operated by the new firm of *Krack, Stanger & Co.*

The earliest directory at hand to show this company's advertisement is that for the years 1859–60. It contains a most interesting woodcut of the glass works (*Fig. 1*). The warerooms were now located at the works, which were still at their original location, the southeast corner of Clay and Franklin streets.

The following ten years were probably the era of the company's greatest prosperity. A wide line of wares other than flasks was advertised. Coal oil lamps, trimmings and tumblers were added to an already comprehensive list of goods for grocers, druggists and confectioners. Evidences of the company's decline begin to show about 1869, the firm name having previously been changed to that of

Fig. 1 — ANOTHER ADVERTISEMENT
From *The Louisville Directory and Annual Business Advertiser* for 1859–60, compiled by Henry Tanner. Cut taken from front of title page.

J. A. Krack & Co. Stanger had withdrawn, and no trace can be found of his subsequent movements. In 1869 Krack was joined by Leander S. Reed and William D. Reed, and the concern changed its name to that of *Krack, Reed & Co.* Two years later Krack withdrew, leaving Reed in the company with his brother. The operating company then became known as *L. S. Reed & Brother.*

The slump in the company's affairs was now rapid. Reed soon relinquished his interests and joined Krack, who was now city assessor, as assistant assessor.

Fig. 2 — SCROLL FLASKS
Scroll flask, quart, pint and half pint. Such flasks are known to have been made both at Louisville, Kentucky and at Lancaster, New York. They were probably made at the majority of Southern and Central States glass works. Obverse and reverse of these flasks are virtually the same.

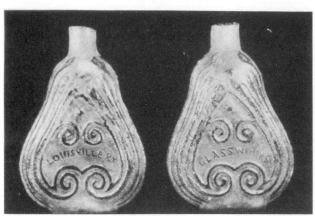

Fig. 3 — MARKED SCROLL FLASK
Pint size, aquamarine. Obverse and reverse.

These scroll flasks are generally found in three sizes, viz.: quart, pint and half pint (*Fig. 2*). Those marked *Louisville Ky. Glass Works* are generally the pint size (*Fig. 3*). I have not seen a quart flask so marked, but one has been reported. These flasks come in the widest range of colors, including all the varying shades of aquamarine to deep green. Unmarked specimens are found in clear glass, olive amber, amber, brown and sapphire blue. They occur in every combination of finish at the neck, and with scarred, plain and hollow bases. Besides the curious scroll motif used in their decoration, different combinations and placings of stars are used. The stars vary in the number of their points as well as in size. In the three capacities, quart, pint and half pint, I have found better than three dozen variations in these decorations. The subject of this type of flask with its variations and different decorations is, indeed, too broad for this article, and will be discussed separately at another time.

The ribbed or fluted type flask (*Fig. 4*) is characteristically a Louisville product. No specimens marked by other glass-houses have been found. It was made in the same three sizes as the scroll flask, and has been found in the usual variations of aquamarine and amber. It is a beautiful flask in any shade. It is considerably more rare than the scroll flask, occurring but occasionally. Not all the examples are marked. Where the inscription occurs, it reads *Louisville Ky. Glass Works Louisville Ky.* Unmarked ribbed flasks of a slightly different shape, but with a similar shaped area provided for a label, are frequently found about this locality and may be safely attributed to the Louisville works (*Fig. 5*).

The competition of Pittsburgh and of the newly opened glass factories in the natural gas belts to the north had proved more than could be met. But by this time the manufacture of glassware had passed beyond the point of present interest to collectors.

PRODUCTS

First of all it is evident that the Kentucky Glass Works and its successors marked only a very small portion of their wares. To my knowledge *no* specimens from the Kentucky Glass Works, so marked, have been found. Whether or not any of the product was marked, time may tell.*

Many specimens of Louisville, Kentucky glass are in the hands of our collectors. Two of the most characteristic types made there are the *scroll flask* and the *ribbed*, or *fluted flask*. Both are particularly attractive, and either would be sufficient to popularize the Louisville works, even if they had made no other patterns.

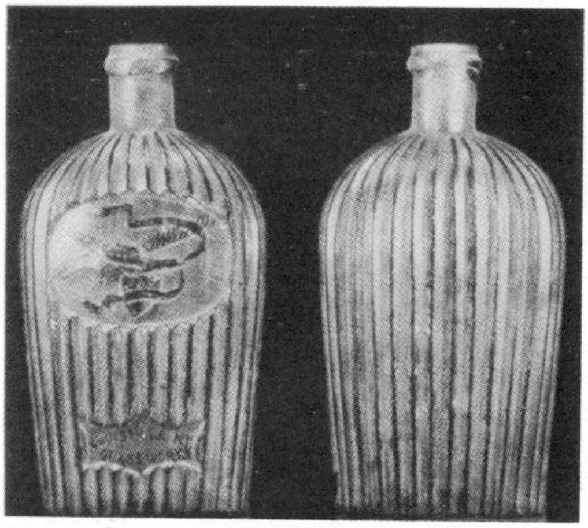

The scroll flask (*Fig. 2*) sometimes, for no apparent reason called a *fiddle bottle*, seems to have been one of our best-known western and southern flasks. Investigation among the early inhabitants shows that it was the flask most commonly in use seventy-five or eighty years ago, and the universal *camphor bottle*. The collector may truly give thanks for the widespread and continued use of spirits of camphor. A high percentage of our flasks were thus preserved.

The same general type of scroll flask was made at many glass-houses. Indeed, it is possible that nearly every western window glass-house had one or more molds of this type and kept them busy, especially when glass was "off color," or "too seedy" for making window glass.

We are certain, however, of two factories which made such bottles — the works at Louisville, Kentucky, and those at Lancaster, New York.

Fig. 4 — LOUISVILLE KY. GLASS WORKS FLASK
Ribbed or fluted type. Obverse and reverse.

Another marked flask from the Louisville works is the *double eagle flask* (*Fig. 6*). This is a fairly late product. The mold was made by the moldmaker employed by such Pittsburgh firms as Cunningham & Co., Berry & Co., William McCully and William Frank & Son. With the exception of the flasks marked with the company names, the products of these concerns were "alike as two peas."

The Louisville double eagle flask is marked in the oval area reserved for that purpose.

A few specimens have been found of marked pickle bottles, of

Fig. 5 — LOUISVILLE KY. GLASS WORKS FLASKS
Ribbed or fluted type.

*A possible exception occurs in a recently found flask, marked on the bottom, *Ky. G. W. Co.* But this specimen may be a product of the period subsequent to that with which these notes are concerned. Hence it may as well be left out of present consideration.

Fig. 6 (above) — LOUISVILLE KY. GLASS WORKS FLASKS

    a. Obverse of repeated eagle flask; quart, amber.
    b. Obverse of repeated eagle flask, ribbed; pint, aquamarine.
    c. Obverse of ribbed flask; same type as Figure 6, but in quart size, aquamarine.
    d. Obverse of ribbed flask; different type, pint, aquamarine.
    From the collection of W. E. Russell.

Fig. 7 (below) — REVERSE OF FLASKS SHOWN IN FIGURE 6

which I have no record. The large, hexagonal pickle bottles are reported to have been made at Louisville, but I have not seen a marked specimen from that city.

In the neighborhood of the old works, in days past, evidences of the glassblowers' spare moments were found; of course, in the usual form — glass hats, pipes, paper weights and rolling-pins, for friends, sweethearts and admirers. The old works are gone and the site has been occupied successively by a sand company and a lumber concern. Nothing at the southeast corner of Clay and Franklin streets today even suggests a glass-house or the maturity of seventy-five years of occupation. However, the persistent investigator will find just beyond the site of the old works a dark group of brick terraced houses that were used by the Works' foreman and some workmen. To their present occupants there remain no reminders of the old glass-house save a few iridescent bits of glass to be found in garden and flower bed.

EARLY KENTUCKY GLASS

By JANE KELLER CALDWELL

THE EDITOR of a volume printed early in the nineteenth century writes in vexation: "Our American publications are so deficient in point of dates, and the circumstances of the settlement and activities of our country, that it is likely many of our beginnings are as well known in London or Paris as by ourselves." He then proceeds to dangle as tantalizing a statement as any of his confreres — that in the summer of 1814 a number of new enterprises were begun in the town of Louisville (pop. 4,000), among which was a glasshouse. There is also confirmatory mention of this glassworks in a newspaper advertisement of wares offered by a merchant, and in a contemporary volume of *Early Western Travels*, though no firm name is given. A description of the Kentucky town of Maysville also states that glassworks were then in operation there.

A guide to the navigation of the Monongahela, Allegheny, Ohio, and Mississippi rivers, with a description of their towns, published biennially beginning about 1801 and called *The Navigator*, contains quaint river maps and carefully listed additions, from year to year, to the business and cultural activities in the communities touched by the streams. In several editions around 1814 the editor mentioned the existence of a glasshouse in Louisville, and the prospect of one in Frankfort, and legends of both persist. In the latter, they are strengthened by the digging up of a box containing a number of flasks on the bank of the Kentucky River near Frankfort close to the site mentioned in *The Navigator*. The bottles were plain and undecorated, with sloping shoulders and mold and pontil marks showing. Also I am told that the sale of stock in a glass company planned in Frankfort about 1909 met with a cold reception "because a local glasshouse failed a hundred years ago."

If the Louisville date of 1814 is correct, it marks a far earlier enterprise than that of 1840 when the census first lists a glass-cutting works, the firm of H. & T. Hunter, who produced a line of cut glass on blanks imported from Pittsburgh. In their newspaper advertisements they specified "Cut bottles for table sets, clear and colored panels for entrance doors and steamboat cabins, and [I am pained to add] cut glass for brooches."

In the City Directory of 1850–1851, the names of stockholders in the Louisville, Kentucky, Glassworks appear and a contemporary business roster gives the concern 50 workers, many of them expert blowers, and an annual business of $50,000. It is here that the name Stanger, familiar in American glass history, makes its interesting appearance in Louisville. In the year 1770, Caspar Wistar, in the columns of *The Pennsylvania Chronicle and Universal Advertiser*, offered a reward for the return

of two runaway apprentices — one, Jacob Stanger, described as "of a thin, long visage," the other, Adrian Brust, who could be identified from his enchanting habit of wearing his shirt "with the bosom part behind."

The runaway Stanger established himself successfully in Jersey, where he and his brother founded a glassworks which continued in operation for many years. It is perfectly possible that the Stanger so closely associated with Louisville glass was a wandering member of the clan. Among blown pieces which have come down in families of artisans here there is often a charm of proportion and line and a reminiscent feeling of glass of an earlier day, and we cannot fail to wonder if an apprentice son of Wistarburg or Manheim was somewhere in the picture.

Over a period of a quarter of a century in Louisville, glassmaking changed its management with bewildering frequency, as evidenced by the directories and advertisements of the day, and additions to the list of commodities were constantly made. In production were "vials, bottles, jars, flasks, lamps and lamp chimneys, tumblers and window glass," as well as the heavy blown glass with characteristic applied ribs, and well balanced to prevent tipping, made for the "water palaces of the Ohio and Mississippi," and locally called "steamboat glass." The familiar scroll or "violin" flasks, found in a range of sizes and colors, are only one of several types of bottles marked with the name or initials of the Louisville or Kentucky Glass Works. As it was the firm's boast that there was "especial attention paid to private molds," we also find a number of items of odd shapes and sizes such as the "pig bottle" (in several variations), the bottle marked *Garrison, Bullitt Street*, and the other vials and bottles in the accompanying illustrations.

The elusive history of the glass industry in Louisville is as fragmentary as a box of bits and pieces from one of its old factories. The growth of Louisville has been great, and the sites of early buildings repeatedly changed by floods as well as by progress. It is tantalizing to go about the old neighborhoods and find no traces or records of the industry, but continuing research may unearth new information.

LOUISVILLE GLASS. (*above*) Two black medicine vials with original red seals; three heavy blown balls, amber, brown; brown pig bottle, marked. (*left*) Pint and quart scroll flasks, small aqua flask, heavy blown lamp chimney, dark brown snuff bottle. *Chimney and bottles from the collection of M. K. Archibald.*

An enthusiastic collector of Kentucky and other American glass, Mrs. Caldwell, a resident of Anchorage near Louisville, here makes a significant addition to the history of the Kentucky Glass Works (1850–c. 1879) recorded by Harry Hall White in ANTIQUES for February 1926.

CLEAR BLOWN GLASS, made by the Louisville glass blowers.

"STEAMBOAT GLASS." Two clear "petticoat" bottles, used without glass stoppers; deep amethyst cruet; two large, clear compotes. Used on steamboats of the Ohio and Mississippi Rivers.

LOUISVILLE GLASS. Aqua and green vials and bottles, marked with names or initials of purchasers. *Flat flask from collection of M. K. Archibald.*

Except as noted, illustrations are from the author's collection.

AMERICAN GLASS

AMERICAN GLASS

From the Pages of *Antiques*

II. Pressed and Cut

EDITED, WITH AN INTRODUCTION, BY
ROBERT E. DiBARTOLOMEO

Contents

CUT AND ENGRAVED GLASS

Introduction

Of all the varieties of glass produced from ancient times to the present, the type which is peculiarly American is pressed glass. That it may have been made earlier elsewhere on a limited basis does nothing to diminish that statement. No other nineteenth-century glassmakers turned out the quantity of ware or approached the quality achieved by pressed glass manufacturers in the United States.

A view of the glass industry in this country from 1830 to 1900 seems to present a panoply of better methods of pressing glass, improved molds and presses and more economical techniques of production resulting in more items being made more cheaply. These advances, more than any other improvements in glass technology, enabled American makers to control a major proportion of the domestic market and even export large amounts of ware. Lowell Innes, in an article reprinted in this collection entitled "Pittsburgh Pressed Glass, Part I," points out that "the whole country imported about $38,000.00 worth of pressed glass, while Pittsburgh alone in 1878 was exporting over $860,000.00 worth." This to him is ample evidence that American pressed glass production was "tremendous."*

In the late 1820s and early 1830s when pressing first began in the United States, all of this was in the future. It was the economic climate that made it essential to develop a new form of mass production in glass. The Wars of Independence and 1812 were behind us. Tariffs were low or non-existent, and many American industrialists must have been discouraged as their candidate, Henry Clay, was defeated again and again. Economic stability was decades away and the home market had to be shared with foreign producers when the first drawer knobs, lamp bases, and lacy cup plates were pressed. It was essential that an inexpensive product be developed so that our glassmakers could compete. Eastern factories near the centers of population had been established, and the resources of the eastern part of the Middle West, especially the area's huge coal fields in places like Pittsburgh and Wheeling, were beginning to be tapped. Cheap fuel, improving transportation facilities, an influx of skilled workers and growing population would soon enable Midwestern glassmakers to compete not only with their Eastern counterparts but also with European manufacturers.

During this period glasshouse owners had to struggle simply to survive. Each minor downturn in the American economy was apt to be a crisis. Many companies were undercapitalized and totally dependent on this week's profits to pay last week's bills. Before 1865, with a few notable exceptions, glass companies came and went rapidly, leaving little behind as proof of their existence. Large companies like the Central Glass Company of Wheeling, W. Va., pressing a multitude of pieces a year, did not begin to operate on this scale until well after 1870. Gigantic combines like the United States Glass Company were not even thought of.

*All of the articles quoted in this introduction have been reprinted in this collection.

Writers of introductions are expected to bring forth revelations which pull the material they are discussing together. Such revelations usually take on the form of generalities which are intoned with such strength that they appear to be rules. Unfortunately glass does not lend itself to such treatment, because for every "rule" stated there are a host of exceptions. The reader would be wise, then, not to consider the next few paragraphs as dogma, but rather as "a general putting together of material."

Most glass students agree that the first pressed glass items produced were small: drawer knobs, lamp bases, cup plates and salt cellars to name a few. Many of the early patterns, lacy or otherwise, were geometric in nature and/or imitated cut flint glass. During the height of the lacy period much of the surface of the pieces was covered with designs in order to conceal manufacturing flaws, but the stippling utilized to accomplish this added new qualities to the material. For the interplay of light amidst the tiny facets or points of the stippling imparted a brilliance to the glass unknown before in any ware.

After 1850, when the lacy product had run its course, the patterns remained geometric and were in some cases still imitations of cut ware, but a slight element of naturalism began to creep in. The dolphins on those candlesticks could not be mistaken for anything else. The "Bellflower" and "Ribbed Palm" patterns of McKee and Brothers were made up of stylized geometric elements, but in combination there was a hint of realism.

Natural patterns grew in popularity and no buyer could doubt what Hobbs Brockunier and Company's "Blackberry" or "Grape Frieze," or the Central Glass Company's "Cabbage Rose," all issued in 1870, were meant to portray. As the manufacturers continued to stress realistic patterns it must have seemed as if the country's tables were being submerged in an endless stream of fruits, birds, and animals, human or otherwise, on goblets, compotes, covered dishes, celeries, spoonholders and nappies. Some of these patterns covered most of the surface of a vessel, but other motifs were sparse, so that even in this era of increasing mass production, glass could be personalized, by the copper-wheel engraver or the acid etcher, with initials or monograms.

Geometric patterns never really disappeared and by the mid 1880s they became popular again. This was the era of "Daisy and Button" and its many variants. But, as time passed, competition among pressed glass manufacturers grew more intense. Price cutting occurred, and one producer attempted to outdo the other, offering more colors and more eccentric designs. In many cases the quality of both the glass and the patterns on it declined. Styles became more decadent, as, in their search for novelty, the glassmakers imitated one another. Pressed glass was even made to seem like material it wasn't. The early twentieth century was the period of carnival glass, and a piling of one motif upon the other, or of imitating the cut glass of the Brilliant Period. It was only a matter of time until a reaction set in, and patterns in pressed glass reverted to simpler themes.

During the lacy period relatively few pieces of colored glass were made, and of course they are much sought after. In the 1870s opal (milk) glass was popular, and eventually a rainbow of colors was introduced for the Victorian housewife. When single shades were not enough, bi-colored wares like amberina or the arsenic, bone ash opalescents were issued. Whatever other trends in pressed glass may be identified, one of which we can be certain is the ever-increasing use of a variety of hues.

Neither the colors nor the patterns existed in a vacuum. Styles in architecture and furniture were mirrored in pressed glass. Many lacy cup plates are rococo in design. From style classique furniture came the dolphin and the caryatid. Those "Cathedral" sugar bowls from New England contain gothic elements, and "Daisy and Button's" intricacy is symbolic of the Victorian's attachment to detail and ostentation.

If progress from the simple to the complex were the only criterion of judgment, it would be easy to conclude that cut and pressed glass followed parallel lines of development. However, cut wares often set the standards for pressed glass, and in almost every instance the designs on cut pieces were executed with much more restraint.

Largely this is due to the state of the material when it receives its motifs. Cutting is an extrinsic form of decoration. Only so many things can be done to a cold piece of glass with a stone wheel and sand. Its general shape has already been formed. In contrast, glass in its molten state about to be pressed is an empty pliable surface, capable of accepting almost any design. The only limitations are the imagination of the mold maker and some technological consideration. For example, is the design such that it can be pressed into the glass and the piece removed from the mold intact?

Cut glass manufactured in the first half of the nineteenth century owed much to Anglo-Irish cut ware. The motifs used were simple geometric ones like panels, flutes, fans and mitre-cut diamonds. One factory's production resembled another's because design elements were limited. Between 1860 and 1880 the same decorative devices were being used, but in greater combination upon a single piece. Strawberry diamonds might be combined with fans, panels, flutes and ovals. This complexity of design continued, culminating in the cut glass of the Brilliant Period with its pinwheels, hobstars and intricate sunbursts. Still the individual elements making up these complex designs were those of the earlier decade merely presented in new sets of combinations. If the period from 1830 to 1860 was cut glass's sedate youth, then the era from 1890 to the First World War was its matronly middle age. The entire surface of vessels was covered and every set contained large, thick-walled pieces. The glass cut was still the more expensive lead flint with its astounding clarity, rather than the lime glass used in pressed ware after 1864. Cut glass's place was primarily at the table of the affluent. If pressed glass belonged to every man, then cut flint was the ware of the well-to-do.

The articles reprinted in this book are not only a history of a number of aspects of the glass industry, but they also are a record of the phenomenal growth of a hobby— pressed glass collecting. The articles fall into several categories: histories of glass companies and their owners, stylistic influences, methods of manufacture, and how to attribute and identify individual patterns. Before this book's publication this information was available only to those who had access to a full file of *Antiques* and its indices. Now it has been collected in one volume and access to it simplified.

As a chronicle of glass collecting these articles underline how authors may popularize a hobby and even set its standards of taste. A debt is owed to those who came first. Writers like Lura Woodside Watkins, Rhea Mansfield Knittle, Ruth Webb Lee and Harry Hall White provided the foundations on which other research was done. On their heels came a second wave of researchers who almost immediately refined and enlarged existing information. Helen McKearin made collectors aware of the New England Glass Company and its products, and James Rose and Lowell Innes enlarged the horizon of those interested in glass to include the products of Pittsburgh and other Midwestern factories. In the decades that followed others have written, refining the subject matter even more, but their task was made easier by those who came before.

It is not difficult to isolate the trends in collecting which these authors consciously or unconsciously promulgated. For instance, it is obvious that initially many writers were interested in the products of the Boston and Sandwich Glass Company and in all lacy pressed produced anywhere. Authors ardently championed the cause of their favorite factory, describing its ware in glowing terms while denigrating the production of other houses in other regions. Some of the authors became enmeshed in the virtually insoluble problem of who pressed what, where, first.

If Sandwich and other eastern glass was discovered first, it was not long before the supporters of Midwestern factories made their presence felt. The editors of *Antiques* may well have started this trend with an article printed in 1927 entitled "By No Means Sandwich" in which the products of McKee and Brothers were discussed. Ruth Webb Lee wrote pieces which she entitled "Pittsburgh vs. Sandwich." In one of them she declared, " 'When in doubt, say Sandwich!' has been the one collecting commandment heeded. 'When in doubt, don't call it Sandwich!' is far wiser counsel."

The articles on earlier pressed glass in this collection far outnumber the ones on late nineteenth-century pattern glass and cut and engraved wares from any period. One has to suspect that in the case of the late pattern glass it was simply too close to the writers in time to be fully accepted. However, the lack of articles on cut and engraved items needs to be discussed in more detail.

As was noted earlier it is difficult to differentiate between the products of early nineteenth-century cut glass manufacturers. To attribute such ware and write incisively, a handle is needed—glass owned by the descendants of workers, family histories or other documentary material. Those descendants are difficult to find, and once discovered they often know little about their ancestors, or they own no glass. Documentary evidence on pre-1865 cut ware is rarely found, so the articles simply weren't written. During the Brilliant Period some pieces were marked but there were many which were not, so the situation was not improved that much. What appears in this collection is virtually all of the articles on nineteenth-century cut and engraved ware which appeared in *Antiques* from the late 1920s until 1972. It is apparent, then, why articles like Katherine Hait Dorflinger Manchee's three-part series on Dorflinger glass are so valuable to collectors and scholars alike.

The nineteenth-century copper-wheel engraver was not so handicapped by a limited number of motifs as the glass cutter. With his tools he could do many of the things which an artist does with his brush. It is still difficult, however, to tell one man's work from another and little has been done to classify it. Cutters and engravers may have held a privileged position among glassworkers in a factory, but outside of that circle they worked anonymously, and this does not facilitate research. As in the case of the Dorflinger series, articles like Carl Fauster's on Louis Vaupel are welcome.

The desire to make attributions motivates many collectors, museum curators and authors. Whenever anything appears which makes that task easier, it is greeted warmly. Therefore, when immense amounts of glass fragments were unearthed on the site of the Boston and Sandwich Glass Company, the discovery was heralded as extremely important. Over and over, writers claimed these shards as definite proof of point of manufacture. For a time, any fragment said to come from those cullet piles was automatically attributed to the Sandwich Company. Confusion resulted with the addition of evidence showing that some of the items unearthed were not of Sandwich origin. The lack of precise archaeological techniques in their exhumation has been cited as compounding the problem.

Still the shards were there and the non-Sandwich fragments had to be explained. Some companies in New England probably purchased cullet elsewhere. Glassmakers often acquired competitors' ware in order to copy it. In the later periods much Midwestern glass was sold in New England. For a time there was a brisk trade in Sandwich Glass cullet, so it may be that Grandmother's Midwestern compote had more value as bogus Sandwich glass shards than it did intact. Obviously much of the material found in the Sandwich cullet piles is valid, but we are still left with fragments which aren't. How they got there will probably never be known, and as the years pass researchers will continue to praise or damn collections of Sandwich shards as they have done in the past.

Since attribution is taken seriously, it may be helpful to cite some of the advice given to collectors by the authors who have been included in this book. Harry Hall White suggests, in the second part of his series "New Views of Old Glass," that collectors base their "judgments of old glass—or anything else for that matter—not on a single indication or a sign but upon a careful study of many indices, and an appraisal of their relative importance." Ruth Webb Lee, in one of her "Pittsburgh vs. Sandwich" articles, warns us that attribution can become a "mania . . . responsible for much misinformation" because collectors "avail themselves of any peg on which to hang theories that automatically become facts through the magic of speech plus wish." One can't help adding also, "through the power of the printed page."

Attributions are constantly being revised as new information becomes available. Take the case of *The Maid of the Mist* cup plate, a humble little thing made well after lacy styles had passed their peak. Initially it was attributed to a New England factory and it was said to be a view of *The Maid of the Mist*, a boat which traveled back and forth below Niagara Falls. Alice Van Leer Carrick, in "Historical Glass Cup-Plates," clings to the Niagara Falls interpretation, but attributes the piece to an un-named New York factory. A number of years later James Rose published new material which laid the earlier versions to rest. He stated that the cup plate, indeed, had nothing to do with Niagara Falls, but was made by a Wheeling glasshouse to commemorate the completion of the Wheeling Suspension Bridge, then the longest in the country. The view was not of Niagara Falls, but of a scene on the Ohio River at Wheeling, Virginia, now West Virginia. The maker, however, is still unknown.

Ruth Webb Lee, in "Rarities in Pattern Glass," outlines an intriguing thesis that pressed glass kept interest in antiques alive during the Depression. What she and the other writers who published then leave unsaid is the effect of their work on what collectors bought. Their articles on the "ten best" or the "hundred best" instantly affected prices. If the authorities said it was desirable then it surely was worthwhile to acquire.

At its peak, pressed glass collecting seemed to deal more in quantity than in quality. It became fashionable not to collect one of something but to own dozens of pieces in a pattern—the ultimate being to possess several of every piece in every color in a large set of pressed tableware. Articles praised collectors for owning 400 pieces of "Moon and Star," or any other pattern for that matter. Those who were mentioned must have felt that they had arrived in the world of collecting.

If the hobby has declined in recent years it may be because of this tendency to build large collections. During the Depression, when dealers were interested in low-priced volume items, it was necessary to cultivate the buyer who wanted to complete that set of a dozen pressed goblets. But as affluence returned, stocking higher-priced items became the order of the day. After all, a piece of art glass occupied the same space and brought more money. A fine piece of eighteenth-century furniture occupied more space but the potential for profit was even larger. Queries to several dealers about pressed glass in stock brought me this reply, "I have a little but it's too much bother to specialize in it."

Pressed glass collecting has always been a relatively controversial subject. It has had its ardent group of supporters as well as its detractors. Lura Woodside Watkins considered some Sandwich glass to be the "handsomest pressed glass ever made." Miss Flora Jarves, Deming Jarves' granddaughter, declared that "It is useless to describe this silly fad for Sandwich glass which is trash." In her opinion, pressed Sandwich was inferior to the factory's other wares, which proved too expensive to make, so "they began this pressed stuff much to the disgust of my father (James Jackson Jarves)."

Yet, despite its detractors, pressed glass collecting continues today. The ware is more difficult to find, and much more expensive than when many of these articles were written. Perhaps the interest in it remains high because, as Mary E. Bakewell wrote in her article on "The Bakewell Glass Factory":

> There will always remain an element of the marvelous about glass, a substance resulting from the fusion of a combination of silica with various bases. . . . This beautiful translucent thing which we call glass awakens in us more than response to beauty. For here we are near such transformation as urges our thoughts beyond the confines of a factory.

April, 1974

Robert E. DiBartolomeo
Director, Mansion Museum
Oglebay Institute
Oglebay Park
Wheeling, W. Va.

New Views of Old Glass

Intended Primarily for the Neophyte Collector
I. Pressed-Glass Compotes

By HARRY HALL WHITE

BY WAY of starting things, let me ask a favor. Will every owner of a pressed-glass compote who can tell, without looking, whether his specimen was pressed in one piece, or in two pieces, please raise the right hand? Not many hands. There might be still fewer if I were to ask what conclusion should be drawn from the evidence that a piece had been assembled instead of formed as a complete unit. Here is a simple point that apparently has escaped some collectors. I know that it has escaped not a few dealers. It is made clear in the accompanying illustrations.

The four compotes pictured in Figure I illustrate the highly popular pattern variously known as *thumbprint* or *thumb mold:* one of the earlier pressed designs, which came on the market about 1850 and went out of style about the time of the Centennial Exhibition. These dates are, of course, only approximate, but are based on trustworthy evidence and are generally accepted.

From a note in ANTIQUES for April 1927 we learn that the *thumbprint* pattern is pictured in the 1868 catalogue of M'Kee & Brothers of Pittsburgh, where it bears the name *Argus*, in deference to the hundred-eyed Greek demigod whose visual apparatus was eventually used by Juno for embroidering the tail of her favorite bird, the peacock. Ruth Webb Lee, in her *Early American Pressed Glass*, illustrates the same pattern, under the same name, from an undated catalogue of Bakewell, Pears & Company, also of Pittsburgh. No doubt *Argus* glass was produced by other manufacturers, though apparently not at Cambridge or Sandwich.

Mrs. Lura Woodside Watkins illustrates in *Cambridge Glass* (p. 105) some pressed bowls with a decoration resembling the *Argus* pattern, but differing from it in that the "eyes" are circular instead of oval in outline. The Cambridge factory name for this pattern was *punty*. Again, in the list of Sandwich molds quoted by Mr. Chipman in his *Romance of Old Sandwich Glass*, I find *punty* mentioned on page 69. We may, I think, accept this circular *punty* motive, now generally known as *mirror*, as the Yankee analogue of the Pittsburgh oval *Argus*, or *thumbprint*. Sometimes confused with the latter are the shallow faceted patterns originally christened *New York* and *Vernon*, but now

Fig. 1 — COMPOTES: THUMBPRINT PATTERN (*c. 1850*)

In the terminology of the glass catalogues of the 1860's the taller objects here would be known as bowls; the footed dish as a "nappy" with foot; and the covered dish as a sweetmeat. Apparently, however, a footed nappy was usually classed among the sweetmeats. If it attained a considerable diameter and corresponding depth it became a bowl

Fig. 2 — DETAIL OF COMPOTES

These pieces were pressed in two separate parts, which were assembled and joined by means of a wafer of molten glass. The wafer here has been painted black to increase its visibility. Note what Mrs. Watkins has to say about this method of making candlesticks (p. 106 of *Cambridge Glass*)

classified under the head of *honeycomb*. Thus on page 75 of *The Romance of Old Sandwich Glass*, several pieces of *honeycomb* (*New York* and *Vernon*) are pictured as *thumbprint* — a matter of no serious importance except that, since Ruth Webb Lee has so competently done for glass what Adam and Eve did for the animal kingdom, there seems no adequate reason for upsetting her nomenclature. On page 74, however, of Mr. Chipman's volume both terminology and description are quite confusing.

But to return to the structural consideration. The earliest, and perhaps most desirable, of compotes will, on close examination, be found to consist of two distinct parts — the bowl and the foot, which were separately pressed and then fused together with soft adhesive wafers of molten glass. This method was necessitated by the limited capacity and power of the early pressing machines. In Figure 2 this wafer has been blackened so as to show clearly. Later compotes, on the contrary, including the majority of those in so-called pattern glass, will be found to have been pressed in a single piece.

Besides the evident line where bowl and base meet, assembled pieces may also exhibit traces of the pontil used to support the parts at the time of their joining. These traces are additional evidence of early workmanship. All such indices of age must, of course, be employed with discretion. At most they can only point to a method of manufacture; they are by no means a guarantee of date. Many an early process was, and for that matter, still is, continued in certain localities long after its general abandonment by progressive manufacturers.

Except for the device just described, I know of few, if any, technical signs by which the relative age of pressed glass items may be judged. Design, however, affords us a few hints, though they are singularly vague. We are, for example, fairly justified in placing fine lacy patterns between 1830 and 1850. It is, indeed, possible that very little lacy glass was made in this country after 1845. From 1850 to 1870 occur geometric patterns. After 1870 the more or less naturalistic compositions which are designated by the term "pattern glass" attain precedence. Thus the age of a piece may be roughly estimated.

New Views of Old Glass

II. *Surface Lines and Rounded Edges on Pressed Glass*

By HARRY HALL WHITE

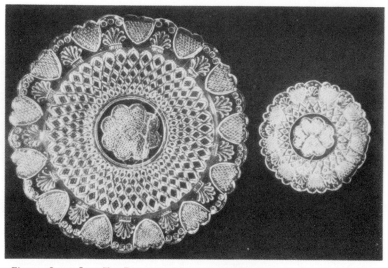

Fig. 1 — SEVEN-INCH TEA PLATE AND MATCHING CUP PLATE
Here christened *heart and honeysuckle*. What appear to be scratches on the larger piece are ruptures in the surface of the glass due to uneven cooling

PLATES of various sizes, from cup plates to bread platters, have long been collected, and much has been written about them; but to Rose Lohr Ayer, I find, belongs the credit for the first article devoted to glass tea plates (see ANTIQUES for July 1931, p. 34). The specimen here pictured is larger than any in the six-inch group shown in Mrs. Ayer's article: to be exact, it measures seven inches. Recently brought to me for examination by a collector, it seemed so evidently of early period that it was placed in comparison with the cup-plate collection, where, as expected, a smaller edition was found measuring three and seven sixteenths inches. While, to my knowledge, this cup plate is as yet unnamed and hitherto unpublished, it may be identified as *Marble*, Number 176. Since the ornaments interspaced between the hearts of the border are presumably stylized honeysuckles (anthemia), we may properly christen the pattern *heart and honeysuckle*. Large plate and small show many similarities besides those of design. Among the features common to both, there is one in particular whose explanation my enquiring collector was anxious to learn: namely, the peculiar network of lines, or shallow grooves, observable on the upper surface of each piece — a somewhat fascinating blemish.

These lines have been variously accounted for, though seldom in terms corresponding to the actualities of glassmaking. Their revelation is of certain difficulties in the operation of pressing glass, which the pioneer glassmakers were not able quite to overcome. In short, these hairlike cracks are surface ruptures, shallow fissures that were opened as the face of the glass cooled and shrank more rapidly than the still viscous interior, until, like a too tight garment, it had to yield somewhere to the strain. Such strains might have been avoided if mold and plunger could have been kept at a uniform temperature so as to prevent the occurrence of prematurely cooling areas. But that was something more easily talked about than accomplished.

The reason why the cracks appear most frequently on the plunger side of the glass is that the plunger was generally devoid of pattern, thus allowing a slight slipping under pressure, while the side bearing the design would be quite securely anchored in the mold. Of course, when the mold temperatures were

Fig. 2 — DETAIL OF PLATE IN FIGURE 1
Taken at an angle so that reflected light will reveal the surface ruptures. Such ruptures are among the evidences of age in pressed glass

pervasively unequal, ruptures would appear on both plain and corrugated faces. The bottoms of the fissures on the pattern side of the glass are usually rough, while those on the face are more smooth and rounded.

Pressed articles were withdrawn from the mold while they were still in what may be called a rather limp condition, and were placed in forms calculated to support them during their stay in the annealing oven.

These curious surface fissures are almost unfailing attributes of the earliest pressed glass, and were largely eliminated as technical methods improved. Yet their presence in a piece of glass is not in itself an infallible sign of age. In truth, glassmakers today encounter troubles of the same kind. Now, as of old, when production is hurried, or the water-cooling of a plunger is excessive, uneven shrinkage becomes manifest in an outbreak of lines. Look for them within the mechanically formed white-glass ointment or cold-cream jars of the "beauty table."

It is the old story: we must base our judgments of glass — or of anything else, for that matter — not on a single indication or sign, but upon the careful study of many indices, and an appraisal of their relative importance.

A chipped or crumbled rim on an early pressed-glass plate constitutes a blemish; an incompleted rim, if smooth or rounded, may be regarded as an asset. The two are easily differentiated. Chipping will show the characteristic shell-like fracture with sharp edge. An incomplete rounded edge, on the other hand, indicates that the mold was not entirely filled with metal, an overcautious or excessively thrifty gatherer preferring to mold a piece scant than to have it too thick. As more precise methods of measuring quantities were devised, and molds were no longer either underfed or overfed, pressed pieces became more perfect from the mechanical standpoint. Yet to me those which fail of complete exactitude are the more attractive. Both of the plates here illustrated exhibit what may be called partially atrophied edges; but the fact makes them no less desirable.

Broadly speaking, if the pattern corroborates other evidences, the presence of the defects described is fair guarantee that a specimen of pressed glass is of collectible age. Since imitations of old patterns are common, this is worth remembering.

Fig. 3 — DETAIL OF RIM (*greatly enlarged*)
Contrasting incomplete, or atrophied, portions and full-pressed portions. This unevenness, due to unequal and insufficient distribution of glass in the mold, is a desirable evidence of somewhat primitive technique

Early Glass Pressing at Cambridge and Sandwich

Part I

By Lura Woodside Watkins

THE longer one studies early pressed glass and the first methods of pressing, the more is one amazed at what seems to be a sudden transition from breath and hand shaping to a complete mechanical technique. In the early 'twenties of the last century the greater part of American glass was blown or molded. By 1827 pressing had become a regular practice in half a dozen factories that we know of, and, probably, in a number of others about which we are uninformed. At the beginning of the next decade virtually every glasshouse was acquainted with the process, and Deming Jarves was already turning out the handsomest pressed glass ever made.

Undoubtedly the shift to machine methods took place less abruptly than it seems to have done. English goblets, bowls, candlesticks, and castor bottles with square, pressed feet were on the market in the late eighteenth century (it is said that feet of this type did not appear before 1775), and advertisements show that the New England Glass Company was making tableware in the same manner before 1820. Jarves imported pressed salts from Holland and other glass of the kind while he was a member of the Henshaw & Jarves firm (*1815–1818*). The squared feet required cutting or polishing to smooth rough edges, as the first pressing apparatus could not finish the work as one operation.

For a long time persons interested in glass research have speculated as to which factory made the first pressed glass as we know it today. The answer should probably be: they all did. Deming Jarves has usually been given the credit for the invention. If his own story can be depended upon, he was certainly the first glass man to press an article like a tumbler. He doubtless showed the way to the use of hinged molds — perhaps by adapting a plunger to a mold intended for blowing. This I have discussed in a previous article (ANTIQUES, October 1931).

The activities of other factories in the direction of mechanical molding have remained in a haze of doubt which a survey of patents could not dispel. Unfortunately, important information was lost when the early Patent Office records were destroyed in a disastrous fire. Nevertheless, there are still enough data to show that Jarves was not the sole originator of the pressing process. Door and furniture knobs were the products of the first attempts at pressing; and several of the earliest patents were for such knobs. One, taken out by J. P. Bakewell of Pittsburgh, September 9, 1825, covered an "improvement in making glass furniture knobs." Another, patenting "glass knobs for doors," was secured by Henry Whitney and Enoch Robinson of Cambridge, November 4, 1826. A third, for "glass knobs pressed in one operation," was granted to John Robinson of Pittsburgh, November 14, 1827.

With no information beyond the names of these patents, it has been impossible to determine whether all were for methods of pressing knobs or merely for knob hardware. A paragraph in a volume entitled *The World of Science, Art, and Industry, illustrated from Examples in the New-York Exhibition, 1853–54*, edited by Professor B. Silliman,

Fig. 1 — Sandwich Knob with Glass Screw Stamped *Patent*

Fig. 2 — Sandwich Lacy Pitcher Handle pressed in one with body

Jr., and C. R. Goodrich, throws some light on the matter. The value of this evidence may be judged from the authoritative background of the work, and from the fact that Joseph N. Howe, Jr., was an employee at Cambridge as early as 1822 and could give first-hand information.

We have taken some pains to ascertain the history of this branch of glass making in the United States, and have been obligingly furnished with some facts relating to it by Mr. Jos. N. Howe, the Agent of the New England Company. It appears that moulded glass has been made in a certain rude form, but that in 1826 Mr. Enoch Robinson, then in the employ of the New England Company, took out letters patent for the invention of a process by which furniture knobs, door handles, &c., were made of pressed glass. The validity and originality of this patent was fully tested by a closely contested lawsuit in Philadelphia, carried on against powerful parties in Pittsburgh. In 1827 Mr. Robinson, against the ridicule of the craft, succeeded in moulding a salt stand, and various other articles for table use, and from that time the invention, as one of general applicability, may be considered as established. In 1832 about £100 sterling in value of the Boston pressed ware was taken to London by Mr. Ryan, an Englishman, where the articles in question excited much curiosity and sold profitably. But it was only so late as 1837 that a thin vessel like a drinking glass was fashioned by the pressing process, which branch of the manufacture has since steadily increased.

The Jersey City Glass Company was also early in the field. A patent for a glass-pressing mold secured by P. C. Dummer of Jersey City, October 16, 1827, is evidence of that company's progress in the use of mechanical methods. All of the above-mentioned patents antedate Jarves' first claims by more than a year, although we know that Sandwich was making cup plates in 1827.

In his patent papers of December 1, 1828, Jarves claimed a method of "pressing melted glass into moulds." His next device was a furniture knob, which he describes as a "glass knob with a glass screw or shank." One of these knobs, with the word *Patent* stamped on the bottom of the screw, may be seen in Figure 1. Its identity as a Sandwich knob is established by comparison with a sapphire-blue specimen that now reposes in the Harrison Gray Otis House, Boston, in the collection of Sandwich fragments assembled by Doctor Irving P. Lyon. It exemplifies Jarves' ingenuity in turning out an object by mechanical means without waste of time in finishing; for the knob, after being pressed in a two-part mold, was complete and required no metal attachment whatever. Its practicability seems doubtful. The necessity for boring a hole in the wood large enough to accommodate a glass screw and the wear occasioned by this sharp-threaded member must have wrought havoc with drawer fronts.

It has been assumed, since so much pressed glass of an early type is known to have emanated from the works at Sandwich, that Jarves was the first glass man to capitalize the sales possibilities of the new process. A comparison of Sandwich glass made in the 'thirties with that pressed at other glasshouses leads to the conclusion that the assumption is sound. Jarves' 1830 patent, perfecting his earlier experiments, secured to him the sole right to press glass by

Fig. 3 — Authenticated New England Glass Company Early Pressed Plates *a*, Clear light green, full of grit and bubbles; *b*, light green opalescent, good quality

the same fundamental method that has been in use ever since. His claim reads as follows:

The improvement claimed is the forming of a handle or handles or other similar projections on glass cups, by pressure at one operation, instead of attaching them to the cup after it has been blown, in the way heretofore practised.

The mould is to be made in the usual manner of brass or other suitable metal, excavations being provided for the formation of the handles. The plug or piston which is to form the inside of the cup is made to fit exactly into a rim which forms the top of the mould, so that when it is pressed down none of the fluid glass which has been put into the mould can escape at the top, but will by the pressure be forced into the cavities described. The claim is to the forming of the mould in the manner above indicated.

This patent was in force for fourteen years. Thus until 1844 no factory other than the works at Sandwich had the right to press pitchers or mugs with handles integral with the body. That attempts were made to infringe on Jarves' patent seems unlikely. It is noteworthy that lace-glass pitchers of known Sandwich origin are pressed in this manner, while one of the few pressed jugs of the period from Pittsburgh was made without the benefit of this invention. A glance at the photographs of a stippled pitcher bearing the mark *R. B. Curling & Sons Fort Pitt* (AN-TIQUES, December 1933, *p. 207*) will show that its handle was pressed separately and was then applied.

There is so little general knowledge of the appearance and operation of a pressing mold that it may be well to pause here and examine the diagram of such an apparatus (*Fig. 5*). It may easily be seen that the removable rim or cap plate prevented excess glass from running over at the top. It did not regulate the thickness of the glass. The matter of thickness was controlled by the workman who dropped the glass into the mold. Several writers have stated that molten glass was poured into the mold from a ladle. Any practical glass man will contradict this assertion; and pictures of workmen operating a press show quite a different method of procedure. Two men worked together at a press. One brought a sufficient gathering from the furnace on the end of a punty, from which the second workman cut off the correct portion with his shears. The glass thus released dropped into the mold, which was then pushed into place on the table of the press beneath the plunger. A strong pull on the lever arm finished the operation. The mold was then tipped upside down, and the ejected article carried to the annealing oven on a wooden tray or shovel, or on a pronged stick.

For many years, glass collectors have been puzzled by the so-called "scratch" or "straw" mark that appears almost invariably on early Sandwich glass. The explanation of this defect is simple. In cutting or shearing the gathering of glass from the punty, the presser inevitably pulled a portion of it out to a thin wisp. One can picture this easily by recalling the effect of cutting soft molasses candy. The slight ridge thus occasioned in the lump was bound to show as a line or apparent scratch after the glass had hardened. Skilled workmen were usually able to give the ball of molten glass a twist as it fell into the mold, thus allowing the cut wisp to melt into the inner portion of the gathering. Accordingly, the "shear" mark, as glassmakers call it, is found sometimes inside, sometimes outside the finished piece. Sometimes it is entirely eliminated.

The process just described was essentially that followed by Jarves as early as 1830. It is obvious that other concerns must have stumbled on the idea of the confining ring without infringing on his patent.

Bearing in mind the method of its production, we may more easily appraise early pressed glass. Just how good was it? The answer is that the virtue of Sandwich lacy glass lies wholly in its clearly defined technique and in the nature of its patterns. It is absurd to say that the glass was of excellent quality. It wasn't. It was full of bubbles, grit, and lumps of quartz. Much of it was off-color. That these irregularities endear it to the collector does not alter the facts. Furthermore, early Sandwich is not to be admired for any subtlety of finish. The glass was slapped into the mold, pressed as quickly as possible, and hurried off to the annealing oven without any sort of hand finishing. The result would have been unbearable had not Jarves or his clever moldmakers retrieved the appearance of their mechanically contrived wares by pressing them in patterns more nearly suitable for the process than any since devised. Where or how the designers in a little country town obtained the idea of lacy glass we may never know. To them, at any rate, goes the credit for a new and beautiful product, and to Jarves the credit for perfecting a means of pressing that made possible the use of such molds.

Early glass in lacy pattern and in designs of similar character from other factories seems to be less brilliant than the ware from Sandwich. This inferiority is due partly to the quality of the glass itself, and partly to lack of skill in pressing. Well-cut molds, however, rather than any inherent quality of the Sandwich metal, produced the sparkle and silvery glitter that is so much admired and often attributed to the addition of barytes. I have seen pressed glass from the New England Glass Company, where barytes was not used, that would be quite as brilliant as anything from Sandwich had it been pressed in a mold of lacy pattern. By such means Jarves developed pressing to a point whence it could progress no further in the direction he had given it. For by mechanical methods alone he had achieved a product whose unique beauty was derived from the special fitness of its designs.

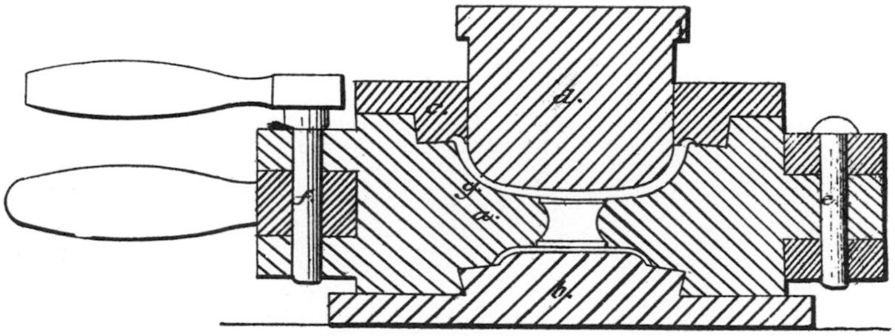

Editorial Note. The second part of Mrs. Watkins' discussion of glass pressing at the New England Glass Company and at the Sandwich Glass Works will be published in an early issue. Part II will be a consideration of fire polishing as it was practised in the two glasshouses in the mid-nineteenth century. The glass pictured in the present article is from the author's collection.

Fig. 4 — THE PRESSING MACHINE
With shears in his right hand, the presser detaches a portion of glass (*B*) from the assistant's punty. His left holds aloft the arm (*D*) which operates the plunger (*C*).
From "Curiosities of Glass-making," Apsley Pellatt, 1849. By courtesy of the Massachusetts Historical Society

Fig. 5 — CROSS-SECTION OF HINGED MOLD FOR PRESSING A FOOTED BOWL
a, body of mold; *b*, core-plate of base; *c*, removable rim, ring, or cap plate; *d*, plunger; *e*, hinge-pin; *f*, bolt-pin; *g*, matrix (which gives the shape of article to be formed). Worth noting is the large volume of metal constituting the mold in relation to the free space into which the molten glass was to be forced by the plunger.
From an 1869 patent specification

Early Glass Pressing at Cambridge and Sandwich

Part II

By Lura Woodside Watkins

JARVES in his lacy glass had brought the pressing process to a point where it could go no farther in the direction he had given it; he had attained unique designs by purely mechanical means. But other glassmakers were dissatisfied with the rough surfaces and raw edges of the lacy ware, for it must be understood that fire polishing played no part in the making of lacy glass. The heat incidental to that process would have melted the delicate stippling beyond recognition. In England little attention was paid to early mechanical methods because of these seemingly inevitable crudities. It was not until 1837 that Richardson of Stourbridge began to press glass. With the English adoption of pressing, careful fire polishing became a general practice. Thus, almost as soon as the Sandwich project was launched, we find other glassmakers working toward an entirely different goal.

The object of fire polishing was to give pressed glass a surface and texture like that of blown glass. It was accomplished by attaching a punty rod to the pressed object and reheating the latter slightly before the open flame of the furnace. The smooth scar of a ground-off pontil mark is to be seen on pieces thus treated, and by this scar they may be dated before the invention of the snap holder in the late 'sixties. By 1840 Jarves himself was finding his lacy glass impracticable and unprofitable. An inventory of that year shows that he too was fire polishing his shank ware.

A review of pressing in the 'forties as carried on at the New England Glass Company will show that the preservation of the lustrous appearance of blown glass was the prime desideratum. As early as 1840 pressed patterns were being changed from dainty feathery and lacy designs to motives imitating early cutting. Four patterns of the 'forties made at both Cambridge and Sandwich were the *Washington, Huber, diamond point* or *sharp diamond,* and the *New York* or *honeycomb.* All of these had previously been known in cut ware. The *Ashburton,* or large thumbprint, seems to have been turned out at Cambridge over a period of thirty years. It was made at Sandwich, too, but not to so great an extent; patents at Cambridge may have discouraged competition.

Some time in the early 'forties, Joseph Magoun became foreman of the pressing department at East Cambridge. Born in 1811, he had gone to work at the New England Glass Company when still a very young man. As a figure in glass history he is notable for a series of patented inventions perfected in the course of many years, by which he succeeded in eliminating mold marks. He seems to have been obsessed by the idea,

eventually developing it so that pressed glass might exhibit no visible mold marks whatsoever.

As a first step in this direction, he secured, September 25, 1847, two patents for molds — one a mold for a fluted goblet and the other for a lamp body. The full text of these patents is worth reading as throwing light on the methods of pressing at this date. Magoun explains in his papers that, previously, it had been customary to make goblets in a two-part mold, contriving that the seams of the mold, which left their telltale ridges, should come at the angles of the flutes or other form of ornamental treatment. He says, "Whenever these mold marks appear in any plane or curved or cylindrical surface, they materially injure the beauty of the article and thereby affect its marketable value." It was, for example, almost impossible to present the upper surface of a goblet foot to the action of the furnace flame in such a manner as to remove these blemishes by fire polishing. Accordingly Magoun invented a mold in which the foot was pressed as a hollow cylinder. In this shape, it could be held to the fire, the joint marks thus eliminated, and the foot worked up to a flat disc with the aid of the glassmaker's tools. Furthermore, the body of the goblet was so formed that the upper part of the mold could be made without seams. Thus, when the lower hinged section had been opened, it was possible to remove the whole goblet by pushing it upward by means of a contrivance devised for the purpose.

The other patent aimed at eliminating the marks on the plain upper surface of a lamp reservoir (*Fig. 1*). The body section of the mold was made in two or more parts, but the plain part was in one section. After the lamp bowl was pressed, the upper part of the mold could be lifted to allow the removal of the article. The plain cylindrical portion, quite free from marks, was then drawn together into its domical shape by hand manipulation.

This second patent is particularly significant. Its term of fourteen years covers precisely the period when whale-oil and fluid lamps enjoyed their greatest popularity. This circumstance indicates that a pressed lamp reservoir whose curved shoulder shows absolutely no sign of mold marks is an East Cambridge product. It does not follow that goblets without visible marks were made exclusively at the New England Glass Company, unless one happens to be certain that they were pressed during the period 1847–1861. The same principle was applied in the pressing of toilet bottles, which were pressed, so to speak, wrong side up, that is, from the base end, and the plain cylindrical portion subsequently

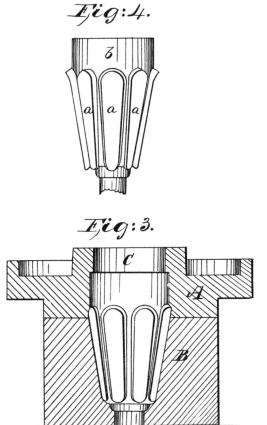

Fig. 1 — Mold Diagram of 1847. Magoun's Patent

Fig: 3 pictures a section of the mold for pressing a lamp bowl without visible mold marks. *A* represents the seamless ring, which may be lifted after the article is pressed; *B* is the hinged body section of mold; *C,* the plunger.

Fig: 4 shows the lamp bowl after removal from the mold. *b* is the seamless cylindrical section to be drawn together by hand manipulation into the neck of the lamp

flattened and drawn together to a small nub in the centre of the bottom (*Fig. 2*).

In 1848 Magoun concentrated his inventive powers upon accomplishing the same result with the *Ashburton* pattern. He produced a mold with a series of retracting pistons or cams that shaped the thumbprints. After the plunger had done its work, a handle was turned, withdrawing the little cams from their contact with the glass. The tumbler could then be removed without any opening of the mold.

Many years later — in 1867 — Joseph Magoun carried his ideas to their logical conclusion in a very complicated device that made it possible to press goblets and glasses of many kinds in molds without joints. It is said that the New England Glass Company reaped a goodly profit from the invention, which legally belonged to them, although the patent had been taken out in Magoun's name. Feeling that he deserved a bonus for his invention, he sued the company for part of the profits. His action was fruitless, and he left the company soon afterwards, a broken-hearted man.

Magoun is also to be remembered for having made, in 1845, a pressing machine to which any mold could be adjusted. To quote his description: "Heretofore it has been necessary to have a press or a series of springs and rods applied to each mold used; but now I am enabled to make use of but one press and one series of springs and rods for numerous molds, thus saving much expense."

Aside from the labor of polishing away mold marks, there was so much hand work required in making the heavy early glass that the ware might almost as well have been shaped entirely by blowing. This is exemplified by the pitcher in Figure 3. This piece was first pressed in a straight-sided mold. The pitcher form was then developed by hand. After attaching a punty to the base of the piece, the glassmaker pinched the body in, cut the lip with his shears, and manipulated it into shape. He then fire polished the vessel and applied a handmade handle. When, after all this treatment, the piece had cooled, the pontil mark was ground away. The result is a pitcher whose slight element of pressing does not prevent its having the character of a blown piece. The glass itself is beautifully clear and white, and its texture has a velvety smoothness not usually associated with pressed glass.

During the past year I have examined many pieces of fire-polished pressed ware easily identified as of East Cambridge origin because of their likeness to the series of excellent line drawings in a catalogue printed in 1869. Some of these patterns were in vogue throughout a period of many years and recur in glass ranging in date from the 'forties to the 'seventies. The mugs illustrated in Figure 4 were finished by hand manipulation, as the ground-off pontil marks on their bases testify. The high standard of their metal and finish we shall probably never see equaled. Glass today is fire polished by gas flame while still in the mold, thus entirely eliminating the personal equation. Moreover, flint metal is rarely used at the present time for ordinary tableware.

It must not be assumed that the New England Glass Company was the only concern that so carefully made pressed glass. In the early period similar methods were in use at Wheeling, and doubtless in other glasshouses. But the fact that Cambridge processes were patented made it impossible for competitors to attain quite the same perfection of finish. In the pursuit of pattern glass it would be well for the collector to ask himself whether he is acquiring, at no little expense, glass manufactured without benefit of human handling and of a quality below that of the modern five-and-ten, or whether he is saving for posterity the product of an era before speed and cheapness in production were the all-essential considerations.

Note. Magoun's invention of a pressing machine adjustable to a diversity of molds not only reduced the quantity of apparatus required for making different patterns, but cut time and labor costs by enabling three or four men working at one press quickly to substitute a reheated and refilled mold for one that had just served its purpose and had to be prepared to receive its next molten morsel. By this new though simple process, the output must have been greatly increased and the even quality of the product assured.

Fig. 2 (left) — BASE OF NEW ENGLAND GLASS COMPANY TOILET BOTTLE
Pressed from bottom end, and drawn in by hand, with resulting nub in the centre

Fig. 3 (right) — NEW ENGLAND GLASS COMPANY FIRE-POLISHED PITCHER, "ASHBURTON" PATTERN

Fig. 4 — FIRE-POLISHED MUGS
Left: Honeycomb pattern from New England Glass Company; handmade handle. *Right: Huber* pattern from Boston and Sandwich Glass Company; handle pressed with body in one operation. Both have ground pontil marks

Pressed Glass a Debtor to Staffordshire?

An Editorial Note

THE collector of early pressed glass will have observed two divergent tendencies in the decorative motives employed during the 1830's. On the one hand, he will encounter pieces whose elaboration reveals a careful adherence to the cut designs of their day. On the other, he will find ornamental devices that would have defied the capabilities of the cutter's wheel. Among the latter is the stippled background which serves so helpfully in giving cohesion to a poorly articulated design in whatsoever medium executed. Stippling imparted brilliance to the early pressed glass; but we may reasonably doubt that the achievement of such an effect was anticipated by the mold maker who first punched tiny dots to fill the voids in a cup-plate border.

The procedure was but an imitation of a method become familiar to the artisan through long communion with the printed Staffordshire tableware on which his daily bread was served. From a like experience, also, he may have derived the idea of giving a pictorial flavor to cup plates, and of wreathing the border of larger plates and dishes with acanthus scrolls and, at times, with floral garlands. The theory that many patterns of American early pressed glass owed at least something to printed Staffordshire tableware may easily be pushed too far. Nevertheless, the accompanying illustrations will suffice to suggest its fundamental validity. It is, of course, unlikely that the mold cutter's imitation of an earthenware technique was often conscious. Visual impressions may be most casually received. They are likely to repose latent and forgotten in the mind until evoked by creative necessity. Then they emerge in the guise of original ideas.

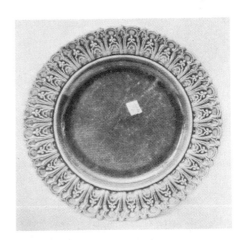

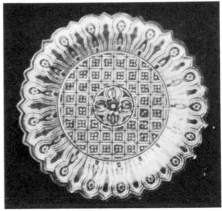

Fig. 3 — GREEN-GLAZED ENGLISH EARTHENWARE PLATE, GOTHIC BORDER: "HAIRPIN" BORDER IN PRESSED GLASS
From the collection of Julia D. S. Snow

Fig. 1 — DETAIL OF STAFFORDSHIRE STIPPLED BORDER BY WOOD: GLASS CUP PLATE, SCROLLED BORDER

Fig. 2 (*left*) — STAFFORDSHIRE OAK-LEAF BORDER BY R. STEVENSON AND WILLIAMS: PRESSED-GLASS FLORAL BORDER

Fig. 4 (*right*) — WEDGWOOD PRINTED DISH EARLY PRESSED-GLASS PLATE
Note the background figure of the Wedgwood plate, also the resemblance between major motives in the two items

An ANTIQUES survey:

Stylistic influences on
nineteenth-century American glass

BY MILLARD F. ROGERS JR., *Assistant to the director, Toledo Museum of Art*

AMERICAN GLASS FROM 1800 TO 1900, like its European counterpart, illustrates the whole trend of nineteenth-century taste, as clearly as does furniture, architecture, painting, or any other of the fine and decorative arts of the time. We can see in glass forms and decorations the classic, Gothic, rococo, and Renaissance revivals, and even the combination of two or more styles in the eclectic spirit of the late 1800's. This wide range of styles also reflects the American glassmaker's ability to digest European influences and adapt them to native products. His talent for improvisation resulted in a good deal of individuality in designs and patterns. He revived old techniques as well as styles, sometimes adapting them in such a way as to produce pieces quite different from their prototypes.

This photographic survey of style relationships in nineteenth-century glass is based on examples from the collections of the Toledo Museum of Art. That this museum should be associated with the art and history of glass is not surprising, since its founder was Edward Drummond Libbey (1854-1925), an outstanding figure in American glass manufacturing who directed the operations of one of the nation's largest glasshouses. No American or European glass was owned or exhibited in the museum until twelve years after its founding. Then, in 1916, Mr. Libbey acquired Edwin A. Barber's collection, and donated it to the museum as the beginning of what has become one of the most extensive collections in the world.

Neoclassic. Cut-glass decanter, c. 1827-1830. Height 13 inches. Clear glass.

In the first decades of the nineteenth century, classical formalism in glass decoration and form remained supreme. The influence of contemporary English and Irish models on form and decoration is apparent here, but the design of tulips and fine crosshatching in shallow relief shows the labor-saving simplification of American cut-glass design in this period. The restrained fluting at the shoulder of the decanter is a reaction against florid Continental embellishments.

Neoclassic. Blown and engraved urn with cover, c. 1830-1840. Height 12¾ inches. Clear glass.

Sir William Hamilton's archeological efforts and Josiah Wedgwood's reliance on classical forms and motifs for pottery influenced England and, in turn, America via immigrant glassworkers and imported English and Irish ware. On this covered urn the wheel-engraved oak leaves and narrow wreath on the neck are simplified classical forms occurring frequently in English ware. The relationship to the classical Greek amphora shape, so admired and copied in the late eighteenth century, is also seen in this decorative footed piece.

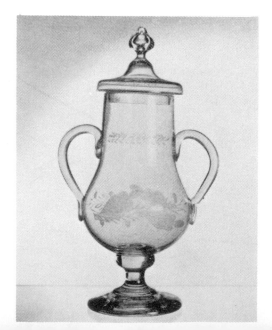

Neoclassic. Pressed-glass salt cellar, c. 1840. Height 2 inches, length 3 inches. Clear glass.

A piece produced when the Greek revival style in architecture was gaining popularity. Grecian forms were easily adapted to the decoration of glass. The Ionic columns at the corners of the salt cellar suggest in miniature the main elements of this order; even the fluting is reproduced. A frieze of oak leaves beneath the top edge is classic in its simplicity, but does not copy the Greek motif literally.

Baroque revival. Blown-three-mold decanter and cream pitcher, c. 1825-1830. Height of decanter, 11 inches; of pitcher, 4¾. Clear glass.

The flowing and rhythmical line, the full form give its baroque character to this scarce decanter (McKearin, GV-16) and pitcher (GV-8). Soft, rounded edges of shell and gadrooning on the pitcher produce reliefs not unlike those on European seventeenth-century stucco panels and silver. However, the term baroque serves more to distinguish designs of this kind from geometrical and other patterns than to suggest a derivation from the seventeenth-century style, and this blown-three-mold ware was actually made in imitation of English and Irish cut glass. The same technique was employed to produce designs that might be classed as Gothic revival and classic revival.

Gothic revival. Pressed-glass sugar bowl with cover, c. 1840. Height 5¼ inches. Peacock blue glass. Pressed-glass salt cellar, c. 1840. Height 1⅝ inches; length 2¾ inches. Clear glass.

The American gift for capturing the essential elements of a style was never better demonstrated than in pressed glass in the Gothic revival style. This Gothic arch motif was borrowed from architectural examples appearing first about 1830 and representing the innovations of Alexander Jackson Davis, Ithiel Town, and others. The pointed arch was the most familiar decorative symbol of this revival; it is found in pattern books and engravings, and in the design and decoration of furniture, silver, ceramics, textiles, cast iron, as well as in architecture.

Rococo revival. Pressed glass salt cellar, c. 1840. Height 2 inches, length 3. Clear glass.

The rococo was a popular style because it characterized elegance, and in glass the elaborate ornamentation made possible by improvements in the technique of pressing became synonymous with the term. The style of American salt cellars went rapidly from simplicity to the profuse decoration of the 1850's. This fairly common example, its surface crowded with rosettes, baskets of flowers, and scrolls, illustrates the mid-century's choice of motifs and the stippled background characteristic of lacy glass enhances the rococo effect. A kinship with furniture is apparent in the shape, suggesting Victorian black walnut sofas.

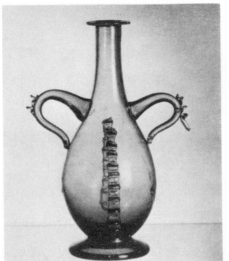

Neo-Venetian. Blown vase, c. 1825. Height 8¼ inches. Light blue glass.

Rigaree trailing on handles and body of this simply shaped vase suggest the *façon de Venise* of the sixteenth to eighteenth centuries, though the decoration of this piece is crude in comparison with most European examples.

Neo-Venetian. Bellows bottle, c. 1885. Height 19⅞ inches. Body of rose with opaque white loops; clear glass base and applied trailing and rigaree.

John Liddell of the Mount Washington Glass Company created this bellows bottle as an exhibition piece or keepsake, using the form of similar bottles produced in the first half of the nineteenth century. The looped bands of rose and white in the body of the piece are reminiscent of South Jersey swirling reintroduced by 1830, but applied rigaree and quilling were patterned after Venetian handling of decorative pinched-glass trailing seen on many seventeenth-century examples.

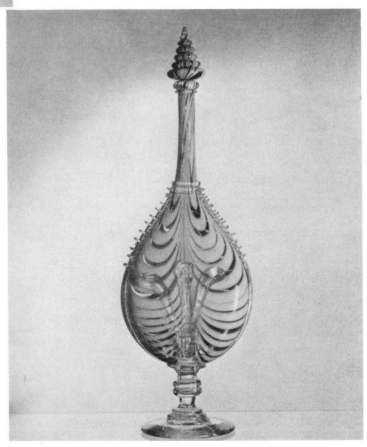

Medieval revival. Tumbler or beaker, c. 1850-1860. Height 6 inches. Dark ruby overlay on clear glass, with gilding.

This drinking glass harks back to medieval prototypes in shape. The early mid-European glasses its resembles, however, were not cut and decorated in this manner. The type is often called Bohemian glass, a term loosely used to describe all ruby glass with cut or engraved decoration.

Naturalistic. Cameo-glass vase, c. 1885. Height 9 inches. Light ruby glass with pattern carved in overlay of opaque white.

The style of this vase foreshadows the *art nouveau* of the end of the century, but it was executed in a medium developed by the ancient Romans and revived by English glassmakers in the last third of the nineteenth century. Joseph Locke (1846-1936), who came to the New England Glass Company in 1883 from Stourbridge, brought the technique to America but it flourished here only briefly. In ANTIQUES, June 1954 (p. 474), Geoffrey Beard said that he knew of the whereabouts of only one example of Locke's work. This vase can now be added to the record.

Fig. 1 — "VIEW OF SANDWICH GLASS WORKS" (*from a wood cut*)
The above entitlement appears on a wood cut owned by Mrs. P. W. Whittemore. It bears the further entitlement *Glass Manufacture in the United States*. The source of this work of art is, however, not divulged.

The Boston and Sandwich Glass Company

By PRISCILLA C. CRANE

NOTE — The following article is based on information gleaned, for the most part, on a trip to Sandwich in May, 1924. In spite of diligent search, I have been unable to locate any manuscript records concerning the Company beyond the old account book now for the first time discussed. The material here compiled is derived chiefly from personal interviews. A list of the persons seen, together with a bibliography, is appended—P. C. C.

Beginnings

IN 1825 Deming Jarves, born 1791,* a resident of Boston, living near the corner of Boylston and Tremont Streets† and interested in the New England Glass Company at Cambridge, Massachusetts, started a glass factory at Sandwich, Massachusetts, called The Sandwich Manufacturing Company.

Ground was broken in April, dwellings for the workmen built, and manufactory completed, and on the 4th day of July, 1825, they

commenced blowing glass, three months from first breaking ground. In the following year it was purchased of the proprietor, a company formed, and incorporated under the title of the Boston and Sandwich Glass Company.*

The Act of Incorporation may be found in Chapter 99, Acts of 1825, *Private and Special Statutes of the Commonwealth of Massachusetts*, and reads as follows:—

Sect. 1

Be it enacted, etc. That Deming Jarves, Henry Rice, Andrew T. Hall, and Edmund Monroe and such persons as may become associated with them and their successors and assigns be and hereby are made a corporation by the name of the Boston and Sandwich Glass Company for the purpose of manu-

Fig. 2 — THE GLORY THAT WAS GLASS
Ruins of the Cape Cod Glass Factory, from the north. The Cape Cod Glass Company was founded in 1858 by Jarves after his withdrawal from the Boston and Sandwich concern.

---

*Deming Jarves is said to have been born in Boston, but he is not listed on the city records.
†Charles F. Dalton, old glassworker, born 1845.

*Reminiscences of Glass Making, Deming Jarves, Boston, 1865.

Fig. 3 — SANDWICH GLASS
Three characteristic examples of glass are shown on this page. It would probably be impossible to fix accurate dates for these pieces. *Owned by Mrs. P. W. Whittemore.*

facturing glass in the city of Boston and town of Sandwich in the county of Barnstable and for that purpose shall have all the powers and privileges and shall be subject to all the duties, requirements and disabilities prescribed and contained in an act defining the general powers and duties of manufacturing corporations and the several acts in addition thereto.

Sect. 2

Be it further enacted that the said corporation in their corporate capacity shall and may lawfully hold and possess such real estate not exceeding $100,000 and personal estate not exceeding $200,000, as may be necessary and convenient for carrying on the manufacture of glass in the places aforesaid. As of February 22, 1826.

In so far as I can learn, most of the invested capital came from Boston and not from Sandwich.* The factory was located in Sandwich for two reasons: *first*, the abundance of local fuel; and *second*, easy transportation. At this time the New England glass factories burned wood, and easy access to timber was a chief reason for settling on Cape Cod. At Sandwich, too, there is a tidal creek which reaches back from the ocean for about a mile, and which is navigable for small boats. From Sandwich to Boston by water is approximately fifty miles:—easy transportation was thus assured. The factory was built on the edge of the creek, which was later widened to permit boats to come directly to the plant.†

There is no foundation for the statement that Jarves picked his site at Sandwich on account of the sand to be found in that neighborhood. In fact, the sand at Sandwich contains too much iron, and is too coarse for making fine glass. All of this product used at the factory was imported from Morris River, New Jersey, and from the Berkshires

*William E. Kern, old glassworker, born 1830, started to work in factory as boy of thirteen. See contrary statement by Walter A. Dyer in ANTIQUES for February, 1922 (Vol. 1, p. 58).
†John Jones, old glassworker, born 1850.

in western Massachusetts. It came at first by boat, and later by train.

Fact and Tradition

It has been said that, from 1825 to 1858, the factory output was "transported by boat to Boston in the sloop *Polly*, which was able at high tide to come up the creek almost to the doors of the factory."* There seems to be no local record of this boat, and the evidence concerning the creek and the transportation of the glass is quite varied. I was told by one man† that the creek was dredged and water gates were built, and that, when the boat had been loaded, these gates were opened so that the force of the water rushing out carried the boat through the creek. Entrance was only possible at high tide.

Still another man‡ told me that all the glass was loaded on flat-bottomed scows, and poled down the creek on high tide to the boats waiting outside. Supplies of coal, sand, etc., were brought up in the same way. He also said that there was a small railroad, or "bogey," built about 1827,§ to carry the glass across the marsh—approximately a mile—to the shore. This is said to have been one of the earliest railroads of its kind in America.

Fig. 4 — SANDWICH GLASS

The merchants of the town had a sloop, the *Osceola*, which was used to carry freight and passengers to and from Boston, and no doubt it carried glass also. The creek now shows no signs of having once been dredged; at low tide it is merely a mud flat.

Early Organization

The Boston and Sandwich Glass Company owned over 20,000 acres of forest land, from which the wood for firing the furnaces was procured. This fuel was cut chiefly by farmers living in the hills back of Sandwich, and was brought by ox team down into the village,—a matter of six

*Walter A. Dyer in ANTIQUES as before.
†Thomas Montagu, old glassworker, born 1848.
‡William E. Kern.
§See contrary statement by Dyer as before.

Fig. 5 — SANDWICH GLASS

or seven miles. Fifty cents a cord was the pay for cutting and hauling the wood. It is said that most of the town taxes of these early farmers were paid with the money thus received. The old roads through the woods near Forestdale (part of Sandwich township) are still deeply rutted, and show signs of the wear and tear of the heavy hauls which formerly passed over them.*

The men who tended the furnaces were called "shearers"; and the operation was known as "shearing the furnace." In the old account, or sloar†, book of the factory‡ there are listed, "2 shearers $12"; but no information occurs as to whether this is a weekly or a fortnightly rate. I am inclined to believe it to be the former, as the wages in all glass factories were remarkably high for the period.

In this same account book, the first date in which is Ju'y 9, 1825, the following glass-workers and their wages are listed:

John Snowdon	17
Jos. Crosby	14
Samuel Kern	8
2 boys	6
	45
Benj. Haynes	17
Benj. Tewkes	14
Alford Green	6
2 boys	6
	43

---

*John Jones and others.

†Sloar is a familiar word in glass phraseology. May it not be a corruption of *slore:* to grasp?

‡Now in the possession of William E. Kern and very kindly loaned to me for reference purposes.

Fig. 6 — SANDWICH CANDLESTICK
A piece whose massive outline and heavy base seems to suggest a fairly early date in Sandwich history. Unusually handsome for its type. *Owned by Mrs. P. W. Whittemore.*

John Doyle	16
John Scott	14
Isaac Fesenden	7
2 boys	6
	43
M. Doyle (Michael)	16
Arratt	10
Wm. Lapham	5
2 boys	6
	37
Thomas Lloyd	16
Samuel do	14
C. Lapham	5
2 boys	6
	41

2 shearers $12, 2 shear men $12, 2 W. Dryers 12		36
1 pot-maker 9, 2 assistants 6–12		21
2 packers 12, 2 stoppers 12, 1 boy 2		26
Doudy (?) Drake 0.50, 2 laborers 12	24	50
Blacksmith		8
		324.50

Deming Jarves was manager of the factory until 1858. Captain William Stetson was his assistant until 1830, when he was succeeded by Theodore Kern, who subsequently served as superintendent for some thirty-six years. George Lafayette Fessenden, or "Lafe" as he was almost universally called, became manager on Jarves' retirement (1858). The former's brother, Sewall H. Fessenden, was agent in Boston for many years. George Lafayette Fessenden was succeeded by Henry V. Spurr in 1882.

First Products

The factory, in 1825, consisted of an eight-pot furnace, each pot holding eight

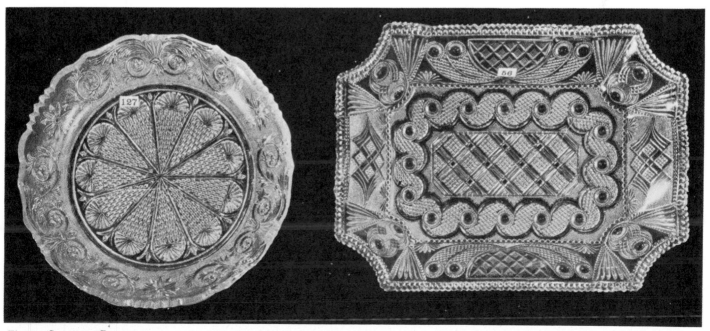

Fig. 7 — SANDWICH PLATES
The peacock feather and the bull's scroll of the second example suggest certain French glass patterns of the 1830's. It is worth noting, further, that this same design occurs in the Pittsburgh eagle cup-plates attributed to the decade of the '30's. Compare Figures 3 and 5. The first example appears to be considerably later in date. *Owned by Mrs. P. W. Whittemore.*

Fig. 8 — Sandwich Glass in Miniature

Sparkling to the eye and imparting a pleasant sound when struck, such specimens of children's glass possess certain cheerful qualities which, though hardly appealing to the higher aesthetic sensibilities, are admittedly attractive. *Owned by Mrs. P. W. Whittemore.*

hundred pounds. The weekly melts did not exceed seven thousand pounds. The yearly product was valued at $75,000. From sixty to seventy hands were employed.*

The pots in which the glass was annealed were all made directly on the grounds in a special building. In order that the clay of which they were made should be very fine, it was trodden by a man and a boy. As one old worker† said, "I got in a trough and danced all day."

There was one glass house at first with five "shops," as the individual crews were called. In 1849 a second house was built, the two being known as the *upper* and the *lower* house. Each had a ten pot furnace.‡

First Products

The first products of the factory were tumblers, cruet stoppers, moulded hats, toy decanters, twisted cruets, common salts, pint pocket bottles, ½-pint mold jugs, 5-inch mould patty pans, star and ball stoppers.§

The first piece produced at the factory was blown July 4, 1825, by Charles W. Lapham.¶ Chamber and "high blown stem lamps," "lamps on foot," and "peg lamps" were first made on July 30, 1825. "Six-inch round dishes, heavy plain ink, 5-inch molded patty pans, button stem short lamps, common pungeons,‖ flint champaigns, molded salts for cutting, molded mustards, Liverpool lamp glasses, small and large rose foot lamps, oval moulded, 9-inch dishes, fount inks, tulip lamp glasses, cylinder lamp glasses, flint

Reminiscences of Glass Making, as before.
†Hugh Brady, born 1830.
‡William E. Kern.
§Account book.
¶William E. Kern.
‖This word is found spelt in many different ways: pungeonts, pungeens, pungrants, etc. May it not be a corruption of the word *puncheon*—slang for a bowl? Bowls would undoubtedly have been among the first products of the factory, but there are few entries of them, while *pungeons* are numerous.

licquieurs, cologne bottles, centers dishes, 38-pound bowls, 21½-pound bowls and bird boxes" are among the entries of the first three months in the account book.

Invention of Pressed Glass

It has been said that the modern method of pressing glass was invented at the Sandwich works. Joseph D. Weeks, writing in 1880* says:

The invention of the American press (for glass) is ascribed to a Massachusetts carpenter in the town of Sandwich about 1827 who, wanting an article of glassware made for some purpose, went to Mr. Deming Jarves and asked him if he could make the article desired. Mr. Jarves told him it would be impossible to make such an article. The carpenter asked if a machine could not be made to press glass into any shape. The idea was scouted at first, but, on second thought, Mr. Jarves and the carpenter fashioned a rude press and made the experiment. This machine was intended to make tumblers, and when the hot molten glass was poured into the mold which was to determine whether glass could be pressed, the experiment was witnessed by many glassmakers of that time. They were nearly all of the opinion that the experiment would come to naught and were greatly amazed when the result demonstrated that it was possible to press glass. The first tumbler that was manufactured in the rough, improvised press remained in Mr. Jarves' possession for many years and then passed into the hands of John A. Dobson, a well-known glass dealer of Baltimore and was exhibited at the Centennial Exhibition by Hobbs, Brockumier & Co., where it was accidentally broken by Mr. John H. Hobbs.†

Mrs. Williams, in *Sandwich Glass*‡ states that the pressing mould for glass was invented in 1827 at the New England Glass Company. In all of this the evidence is purely of the hearsay variety. But the oldest surviving worker§

Report on the Manufacture of Glass, by Joseph D. Weeks, in Department of Interior, *Report on Manufactures in United States in tenth census.*
†In the Philadelphia U. S. International Exhibition, 1876, *Official Catalogue*, J. H. Hobbs, Brockumier & Co. are listed from Wheeling, West Virginia, as exhibiting "soda lime glassware."
‡*Sandwich Glass*, by Leonore Wheeler Williams, N. Y., 1922.
§William E. Kern.

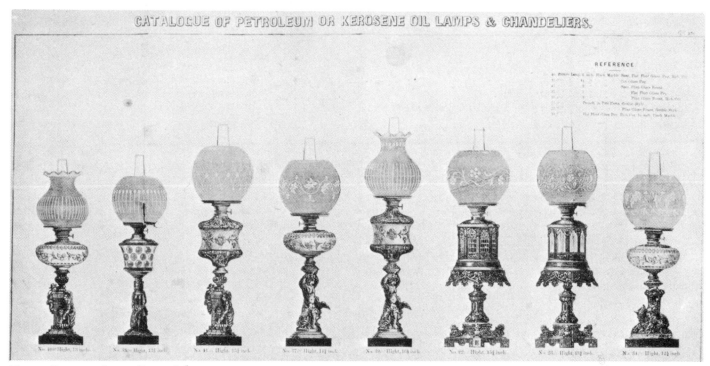

Fig. 9 — SANDWICH LAMPS (*late period*)
The extensive use of petroleum for illuminating purposes is a phenomenon of the last quarter of the nineteenth century. The illustrations here are from the leaf advertisements issued by the Boston and Sandwich Glass Company. They probably belong to the decade 1875–1885. *Reproduced from sheets owned by H. S. Dowden.*

of the Sandwich plant gives credit for the pressing mould to the New England Glass Company. The date appears to have been earlier than 1827, however, since the process seems to have been known to Jarves previous to his establishing of the Sandwich factory.

Hiram Dillaway, an Englishman, was long the head mould maker at the Sandwich factory, and designed most of its patterns.* Without doubt, he and Jarves improved the process of pressing glass, which Jarves had perhaps known at the New England Glass Company.† If such is the case, the story told by Weeks may be the correct one, with merely the change of location to Cambridge, and the date to before 1825. That Jarves was constantly interested in improving the process of pressing glass is without question. On May 28, 1830, for example, he took out a patent for an improvement in glassmakers moulds:‡—

The improvement claimed is the forming of a handle or handles or other similar projections on glass cups, by pressure at one operation, instead of attaching them to the cup after it has been blown, in the way heretofore practised.

The mould is to be made in the unusual manner of brass or other suitable metal, excavations being provided for the formation of the handles. The plug or piston which is to form the inside of the cup is made to fit exactly into a rim which forms the top of the mould, so that when it is pressed down none of the fluid glass which has been put into the mould can escape at top, but will by the pressure be forced into the cavities described. The claim is to the forming of the mould in the manner above indicated.§

---

*Frank Ellis.

†On December 1, 1828, from Boston, Jarves obtained a patent for a method of "pressing melted glass into moulds." Moore, *Old Glass, European and American*, New York, 1924, p. 339.

‡*Repertory of Patent Inventories*, London, 1831, Vol. XI, p. 239, American Patents.

§Deming Jarves had taken out patents for a machine for opening glass blowers' moulds, February, 1821. In June, 1829, and October, 1830, he took out patents for "glass knobs." Moore, *Old Glass European and American*, p. 339.

The moulds employed for pressing glass were for the most part made of brass. For large articles the presses worked with a screw instead of a lever. The designs were cut on the plunger and pressed upside down and the article, while very hot, turned into a receiver of the same shape as the mould.*

Early Cut Glass

That glass was made for cutting in 1825 is indicated by several entries in the account book, but no statement occurs as to whether the cutting was done at Sandwich or elsewhere.

Octagon dishes, sugar bowls, decanters, cruets, 10-inch oval dishes, 7, 8 and 9-inch octagon dishes, ship tumblers, etc., were common articles of manufacture, besides the ones already mentioned. Some of these were doubtless cut.

First Record of Familiar Items

On September 23, 1826, occurs the record† of "310 Dolphin tall pungeants $18.10." On November 4, 1826, are first listed "34 Lafayette Chamber Cylinder Lamps $5.66" and "56 Lafayette lamps $14." Petticoat lamps are noted as first having been made on December 23, 1826: "211 petticoat lamps $25.22." The first entry of cup-plates is on April 20, 1827, and is as follows:

132 No. 1 cup plates	$7.92
305 No. 2 cup plates	15.25
77 No. 3 cup plates	2.98

There is no explanation as to what the difference in the numbering of the cup-plates means. It will be observed that they are listed at six, five and four cents each, but whether these figures represent cost of manufacture or

---

*William E. Kern.
†Account Book.

selling price is not clear. It would seem to be the selling price.

On March 9, 1827, are listed "7 Lafayette Salts $1.16", I should imagine that these are the same as the salt reproduced some time since in ANTIQUES.* It is interesting to note that one salt was worth 16½ cents.

Various Forms and Colors

What is known as *lace* glass must have been turned out quite early in the history of the factory, for it was presumably not made after 1840.† *Colored* glass was first made in the thirties, but its great improvement and extension of manufacture did not occur until after the Civil War.‡ *Snakeskin* glass is supposed to have been made about 1860;§ *hobnail* somewhere in the ten years following the Civil War; *cable* glass at the time of laying the French cable (*1867*); *opaque* after the Civil War.

Fig. 10 — WOOD PATTERNS FROM SANDWICH
Metal moulds used for glass pressing were cast from wooden patterns. The pattern at the left is evidently that of a lamp base. The one at the right is unidentified. *Owned by Frank Lloyd.*

**ANTIQUES for April, 1922 (Vol. I, p. 152).
†John Chipman, who was told by an old glassworker, now dead. Rather long-range evidence, to be sure.
‡John Jones, and receipt book, dated 1868, in possession of Frank Lloyd.
§This and the other dates were given to Mr. Chipman by the old glassworker, who identified the pieces for him.*

The *diamond* pattern was first cut by "Gaffer"*Cook, who is said to have designed the pattern.† What is known as the *Grant* pattern, i.e., a pattern in which the diamonds are quite fine, was made at the time of Grant's candidacy for president (*1868*). *Alabaster* glass is the bluish white glass, similar in aspect to china ware, which is so often found used in lamp bases.‡

Opal glass, it is said, was first introduced in America by the Boston and Sandwich Glass Company, which sent to England for a man, Rice Harris, who came to this country for six months and taught the process of making it. He received for his services $5000 and expenses.§

Factory Methods

Beginning in 1843 and continuing until 1867, the workmen in the factory were divided into four shifts, or "turns." The first turn was from one A. M. until six. The second turn was from seven until noon; the third from noon until

**"Gaffer" means the head man of a shop.
†Ella Silsby, corroborated by others.
‡Hugh Brady.
§William E. Kern*

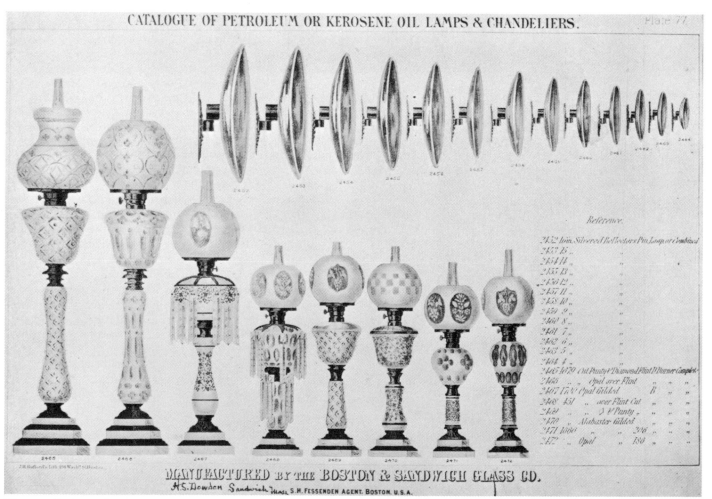

Fig. 11 — SANDWICH LAMPS
The influence of mid-century Bohemian types of glass is apparent in these lamps. They probably date from 1870–1885. *Reproduced from sheets owned by H. S. Dowden.*

six P. M. The same men who had served on the first turn came in for the third. The last turn was from six until midnight, with the second turn men on.

This meant that the factory worked night and day and thus required only four working days a week, leaving a holiday for the men from Friday morning at six until the following Monday.

The boys worked tending the glory holes and getting in wood. Every Fourth of July these boys were presented with fifty cents each to spend on fireworks. They were likewise allowed to gather and work the glass in their spare time, and were encouraged to learn the glassmakers' trade.*

Treatment of Employees

The Company, as was perhaps natural in a small town, looked after its workers in every way. The employees began to work while mere lads, and continued in service until they were old men. If they were unable to make good in one job, another would be found for them. At Christmas time the Company made presents of flour, coal, etc., to the widows of men who had been in their employ.

The Company likewise built workmen's houses and established near the factory a small village, which is still standing.† The houses could be bought on the instalment plan.

Many are the stories told of the kindness of the Company to its employees, and of "Lafe's" personal kindness to individuals. As one old man said, "It was the best place any man ever worked. 'Want for nothing' was Lafe's common saying."‡ Sewall H. Fessenden, the Boston agent, whose offices were at 26 Federal Street for many years, was the hero of all the small boys of Sandwich. He used to visit the works once a month, and the tale goes that on each occasion he wore a new suit of clothes!§

When the Railroad Came

After the railroad came to Sandwich, in 1848, much of the factory's supplies and products was transported by rail. Several years after it had reached Sandwich, however, the Old Colony Railroad raised its rates, to the disgust of the Boston and Sandwich Glass Company. Accordingly, in 1853, the steamer *Acorn* was built. It was at this time that the channel was probably dredged to admit of her entrance.

For several years this vessel carried all supplies, and was also used as an excursion boat, the trip to Boston and back costing one dollar.¶ The railroad soon came to terms with the Company, which then built a wharf at Cohasset Narrows, now Buzzards Bay, where coal, brought up the bay, was landed and was transported nine miles by rail to Sandwich, thus saving the long and hazardous trip around Cape Cod.‖

Shifts and Changes

Much glass was exported to South America, Rio de Janeiro being a port often appearing on the books of the Company.* February 18, 1853, the capital stock of the Company was increased $200,000, making a total of $500,000.† February 26, 1859, this was reduced to $400,000, par value of shares $80.‡

The Cape Cod Glass Company

In 1858 Deming Jarves resigned from the Boston and Sandwich Glass Company, and, together with James D. Lloyd,§ built the Cape Cod Glass Company works at Sandwich, about half a mile from the old factory. Mr. Jarves built this plant for his son, John, who, however, died a few years later. The works were opened with much ceremony, every person in the town of Sandwich receiving an engraved invitation to a clambake and an inspection of the new factory.

The Cape Cod Glass Company commanded all the modern improvements then known to glass manufacturing,¶ and paid ninepence more a day to its workers than did its rival. William E. Kern became superintendent, earning $35 a week as superintendent, and $12 a day as workman.‖

Jarves imported men from England to teach special methods. Among others were Nehemiah Packwood and John Jones from the Stourbridge district in Worcestershire, where there were many glass factories. Packwood worked for the Cape Cod Glass Company for about six months, and then went over to the Boston and Sandwich concern. He was a designer of cut glass, and under his direction the first chandeliers made at the Boston and Sandwich works were cut.**

Troubled Days at Sandwich

During the Civil War John Jarves died, and many of the Sandwich men went to fight. Deming Jarves, too, was growing old. The Cape Cod Glass Company never succeeded in becoming a successful competitor of the Boston and Sandwich Company.

Deming Jarves died in Boston April 15, 1869, aged 78, after a long illness.†† The Cape Cod Glass Company was disposed of by the Jarves family and remained unused for a period of years, until taken over by one Dr. Flower, who experimented with a glass which he called "vassa murrhina." It was, however, never commercially successful.

In 1882 the factory was bought by Charles W. Spurr and was used for a veneering plant. This venture was short lived. The factory has since slowly fallen to pieces. Only the stack and part of the building now remain standing. The workmen scattered, some to New Bedford, some to Philadelphia, and some to Brooklyn. Not a few went west, where glass factories were everywhere springing up.

---

*William E. Kern.

†This village was contemptuously referred to by the old inhabitants of Sandwich as "below the tracks," and one's social standing was gauged by whether one lived "above or below the tracks."

‡Hugh Brady.

§Charles F. Dalton.

¶Charles F. Dalton.

‖The Cape Cod Canal has since been cut through—its northern entrance is about a mile from the old factory.

*Charles F. Dalton, who remembers, as a child, looking at the names in the record books, and hunting them up on the map in his geography book.

†Acts of 1853, Chapter 12, Commonwealth of Massachusetts.

‡Acts of 1859, Chapter 65.

§Frank Lloyd, son of James D. Lloyd.

¶See account of Delano patent feeder, a new invention, used in the Cape Cod Glass Company, in Jarves' *Reminiscences of Glass Making* appendix.

‖William E. Kern and Thomas Montagu.

**John Jones.

††Mr. Kern says that, on the night of April 15, he had, after seeing that the fires were all right, just left the Cape Cod works when some boys called after him, "Up he goes" referring to the smoke from the fire. It was not until the next day that he learned that Jarves had died. The fires that Mr. Kern stoked that night were never relighted.

Last Years of the Boston and Sandwich

The later years of the Boston and Sandwich Glass Company may be quickly summarized. In 1870 the Company had offices at 26 Federal Street, Boston, 20 Murray Street, New York, 419 Commerce Street, Philadelphia, 246 West Baltimore Street, Baltimore. They did little advertising and had few travelling salesmen. The factory was run continuously—good times or bad—and the stock, as made, was stored in the old railroad round-house until wanted.

The factory was one of the best known glass houses in the country and its better products were much in demand. Most of its later work was in cut and etched glass, although it still continued to make cheaper pressed glass, together with lamps with metal bases, which last were imported from England.

In the Philadelphia 1876 Exhibition the Company exhibited "Cut crystal chandeliers, rich cut glassware of every description, including the 'Daniel Webster Punch Bowl.'"*

In 1882, George Lafayette Fessenden was succeeded by Henry V. Spurr, who had long been head salesman in the Boston warehouse, and who had originally entered the Company's employ in 1849. The agent still continued to be Sewall H. Fessenden.

Competition from the West

Competition in the glass industry became much keener after the Civil War, the western factories having the advantage over those in the east owing to their use of natural gas for fuel, and to their proximity to coal, sand, etc. The profits of the Boston and Sandwich Glass Company began to dwindle. For several years the works were run with no profit whatever. In 1887, however, a crisis occurred. The men had formed a union, at the instigation of a western "agitator." They presented demands for many new rules. The Company explained that it could not continue its business if these were put into force, and called attention to the good it had done and was doing for the inhabitants of Sandwich. Eventually it issued an ultimatum to the effect that, "If the fires are allowed to go out they will never be re-lighted."

The Finish

The men, unable to believe that the Company meant what it said, struck. The furnaces were allowed to die. On January 2, 1888, the works were closed, never to reopen. The Company's charter was dissolved March 6, 1894, after the books had been destroyed. Cases of glass were dumped in heaps outside the factory, and many of the cheaper kinds of glass were sold to a chain of five-and-ten-cent stores. Then the population of Sandwich began to shrink. In 1857 it numbered 4800; today there are scarcely 1500.

It is said that, during the height of its prosperity, the Company cleared as much as fifty per cent a year for several years; and that, during the sixty-three years of its existence, it produced about $30,000,000 worth of glass.

After the closing in 1888, many attempts were made to start the old works again, but none were successful. Among others came Cardenio King, who bought the factory and remelted the *cullet*, or imperfect glass, producing a brown and unattractive output. This, too, proved a failure. Since then the factory buildings have fallen to pieces. What remained was torn down in 1920, except for one building used as a fish freezing plant, and a new building erected for a bark factory.

The ruins have been pretty well searched over for pieces of glass, some of which have been mounted into jewelry by a Sandwich woman.* The town has no industry now, and the younger people are gone, leaving a sleepy Cape Cod village with but memories of the industrial city that might have been.

***

LIST OF PERSONS INTERVIEWED

In *Sandwich*, Massachusetts.
John Jones, old glassworker.
Thomas Montagu, old glassworker.
Hugh Brady, old glassworker.
Frank Lloyd, son of James D. Lloyd, glassworker in Boston and Sandwich and Cape Cod Companies.
Frank Ellis.
William Nye, president Sandwich Historical Society.
John Chipman.
Frank Howland, town clerk of Sandwich.
Fletcher Clark, old inhabitant of Sandwich.
Mrs. Bertrand C. French, maker of jewelry from glass.
Miss Eliza Wing, daughter of Paul Wing, Sandwich school teacher.
Miss Caroline Nye, whose father worked in factory.
Mrs. Ambrose Pratt, family inhabitants of Sandwich since founding.
Mrs. Benjamin Webber, East Sandwich.

In *Sagamore*, Massachusetts.
Miss Ella Silsby, much interested in Sandwich glass history.

In *New Bedford*, Massachusetts.
William E. Kern, former superintendent of Cape Cod Glass Company.

In *Boston*, Massachusetts.
Russell Spurr, son of Henry V. Spurr, manager for Boston and Sandwich Company.
Charles F. Dalton, old glassworker.
Mrs. Robert T. Swan, whose father, Joshua Crane (my great grandfather) was, according to tradition, president or one of the main directors of the Boston and Sandwich Company between the years 1839–1846.

BIBLIOGRAPHY OF BOOKS ON SANDWICH, OR RELATING TO GLASS, CONSULTED

Encyclopedia Americana, New York, 1910, under "Glass Manufactures in America."
Reminiscences of Glass Making, Deming Jarves, Boston, 1865.
Account Book of Boston and Sandwich Glass Company, owned by William E. Kern.
Report on the Manufacturer of Glass, Joseph D. Weeks, in Department of Interior, Report on Manufactures in United States in tenth census.
Official Catalogue, Philadelphia U. S. International Exhibition, 1876.
Sandwich Glass, Leonore Wheeler Williams, New York, 1922.
Repertory of Patent Inventories, London, 1831, Vol. XI., p. 239, American Patents.
American Glassware, Edwin A. Barber, Philadelphia, 1900.
Curiosities of Glass Making, Apsley Pellatt, London, 1849.
Private and Special Statutes of the Commonwealth of Massachusetts, Acts of 1825, 1853, 1859, 1894, 1895, 1904, 1907, and *Files* at office of Commissioner of Corporations, State House, Boston.
Reminiscences of the Boston and Sandwich Glass Company, William E. Kern, paper read before American Association of Flint and Lime Glass Manufacturers, July 20, 1906.
Yarmouth Register, August 18, 1906.
Boston Herald, March 23, 1907.
Boston Evening Transcript, September 4, 1920.
ANTIQUES, Vol. I, p. 58; Vol. I, p. 61; Vol. I, p. 152.
Old Glass, European and American, N. Hudson Moore, New York, 1924.

*In *Official Catalogue* 1876 Exhibition as before. The punch bowl seems to have disappeared; several of the older workers remember that three or four big bowls were sent to the Exhibition, but no one had heard of the Daniel Webster bowl.

*Mrs. Bertrand C. French.

Deming Jarves and His Glass-Factory Village

By MABEL M. SWAN

NO ONE had ever heard of a glass-factory village when as a boy Deming Jarves went to Sandwich, Massachusetts. Nor, imaginative though he was, did the lad dream of the many brick buildings and the rows of little gray houses which he was later to build on the meadows bordering the creek. The *Dictionary of American Biography* today characterizes Jarves as "chemist, inventor, organizer." True enough; but to me the word "gentleman," as he was called in his father's will of 1823, is his most appropriate designation. He stemmed from the Gervaise family, French Huguenots, who, finding refuge in England, accepted the name of Jarves and became prominent not only because of their wealth but for their staunch Whig principles.

Urged by his republican views, John Jackson Jarves, Deming's father, came to America in 1787, established himself in business as a cabinetmaker in Boston, and advertised:

Jarves
Cabinet, Chair, & Clock Case Maker from London
No 76 Newbury Street, Boston
Respectfully informs Gentlemen and Ladies that he makes the following Mahogany Furniture on reasonable Terms, viz: Library Book Cases, Desks & Book Cases, Chests & Book Cases, Double Chest of Drawers with Desk Drawers, single Chest of Drawers, Desks, Gentlemen's Portable Writing Desks, Counting House Desks, Ladies Commode Dressing Tables with furniture Drawers, Library Tables, Dining Tables in sets, round & square Card Tables, Pembrook, Claw, China, Chamber, Toilet & Night Tables, convenient Stools, China Shelves & Brackets, Balance, Pole, Face, and Hand Fire Screens, Side Boards, Cellerets, Butler's Treys, Knife Treys, Oval Tea Treys, Tea Chests & Cadys, Sconce & Swing Glass Frames, Ladies Urn Stands, Gentlemen's Wardrobes, Sophas, Easy Chairs, carved & plain, Chairs, Four post, Field Bureau & Common Bedsteds, Weight & Spring Clock Cases, Watch Cases, & all kinds of Picture Frames (*Massachusetts Historical Society clipping.*)

This extensive cabinetmaking business, occupying several buildings on Newbury Street and later at 6 Beach Street, was very successful if one may judge from the will of "John Jarves, gentleman deceas'd," administered in September 1823. The late cabinetmaker left $25,000, in addition to six buildings, to his widow and two children, Deming and Sally Jarves Hastings, the bulk of the estate going to Deming. The family's comfortable circumstances are further indicated by the inventory item, "Pleasure Boat & Sails $50."

Deming Jarves' mother was Mrs. Hannah Deming, widowed daughter of the celebrated Samuel Seabury (*1729–1796*), who, when the politically prejudiced Church of England refused to consecrate bishops for America in 1783, moved to Scotland, there received the coveted recognition, and became the first American Episcopal bishop.

Jarves was born abroad, where his parents were traveling, and was baptized in the New South Church, Boston, December 9, 1790. He is first listed in the Boston directory of 1813 as in "dry goods 11 Cornhill." In 1815 and 1816 he is listed as a member of the firm of Henshaw & Jarves, dealers in crockery ware; and, in 1818, as a glass factor on Belknap Street. In 1815 he was married to Anna Smith Stutson (often spelled Stetson), a daughter of Captain Levi Stutson, Revolutionary soldier. Nine children were born to the couple: John W., George, Deming, Jr., James Jackson, Anna Maria, Isabella, Mary, and two sons who died in infancy.

In November 1817, the Boston Porcelain & Glass Company in East Cambridge, of which Jarves was the clerk, disposed of its property at public auction. This event projected Jarves into the first of his five glass organizations. With several associates, soon to be incorporated as the New England Glass Company, he purchased the Boston Company's works.

From the first it appears to have been his policy to keep his business ventures largely in the family's hands. His father's will records a note to the New England Glass Company for $1,900. Daniel Hastings, Boston merchant and importer and one of the directors, was the nephew of Deming Jarves' sister. Edmund Munroe, also a director, was a wealthy relative of Jarves' wife. The first superintendent of the Boston & Sandwich Glass Company was Deming's brother-in-law, William Stutson. The Southacks also were relatives on his wife's side. A strong family loyalty governed the Jarves family, all of whose members seem to have been at one in their admiration for the young glass organizer.

Well they might be proud of his ability: for his initial attempt to discover a formula for making red lead, the secret of which had long been held by English glass manufacturers, was successful. Thereafter his new company was able to supply native glasshouses with this essential ingredient. Such creative genius as his could not long be content with merely turning out apothecary and chemical wares, electrical apparatus, entry lamps, globes, decanters, and similar merchandise such as the company advertised. In 1821 he obtained his first patent, covering a machine for opening glassblowers' molds. The following year he took out a patent for an improvement in the tubes for glass lamps.

Encouraged by his success, and rendered financially independent by the death of his father in 1823, Deming Jarves the next year made an extended visit to Pittsburgh. Here he saw many superior methods of glassmaking in operation, for the Bakewell & Page flint glassworks of Pittsburgh was one of the most advanced in the country. Many years later Jarves in his *Reminiscences of Glassmaking* wrote of Mr. Bakewell: "He truly merits the *artium magister* so often bestowed on those less worthy of its dignity and honor."

On his return to Boston, he severed his connection with the New England Glass Company and undertook the organization of a new concern. The move was in no wise due to any misunderstandings with his directors, but, almost certainly, to Jarves' desire to experiment independently and without the restrictions imposed by the normal schedules of a large factory.

Though living in Boston, Deming knew Sandwich. There game abounded, and he knew well the extent of the pine forests. He also realized that so remote a spot would offer no urban lure to his workmen, that transportation by water was at hand, and that in the quiet little town he might in many ways reduce sundry manufacturing costs. So he called a meeting of the Sandwich citizens and told them, among other things, that workers in the Pittsburgh factories were making from $2 to $2.50 a day in an employment neither arduous nor dangerous, and that if sufficient interest was manifest he would build a glassworks in the town. (His wage estimate seems to have been optimistic.)

Ground was broken in April 1825, and the

Fig. 1 — "ALABASTER" VASE, CREDITED TO JAMES D. LLOYD

first building erected with a small furnace of eight pots. On July 4 the first piece of glass was blown. The new enterprise was called the Sandwich Manufacturing Company until April 3, 1826, when the capital stock was increased and the concern incorporated as the Boston & Sandwich Glass Company by Deming Jarves, Henry Rice, Andrew T. Hall, and Edmund Munroe.

One week before this reorganization, Deming Jarves and Edmund Munroe established the New England Glass Bottle Company "for the purpose of manufacturing black and green glass wares in the city of Boston and the town of Cambridge." This, the second of Jarves' five glass companies, continued in operation until 1842.

For his first superintendent at Sandwich, Jarves chose his brother-in-law, William Stutson, a young man as forceful and vigorous as Jarves himself. At the age of nineteen Stutson had been in full command of a ship, and during the War of 1812 commanded a privateer, which was captured by the British, who landed the young captain in Dartmoor to remain until the end of the war.

Fig. 2 — Cut-Glass Crystal Flashed with Ruby, Credited to James D. Lloyd

Charles C. P. Waterman, the first clerk and paymaster, was born in Wareham, Massachusetts, and remained in the Boston & Sandwich Company until 1858, when Jarves left to organize the Cape Cod Factory. Waterman went with his employer and remained with him until his chief's death in 1869.

Some of the glassmakers of the New England Glass Company followed Jarves to Sandwich. Others were obtained from South Boston; many others were imported from England. Later Ireland, Belgium, and France contributed to the working force. Wherever he could find the most skilled workmen, Jarves gathered them in, exhibiting a distinct flair for picking good material.

Among the first expert glassblowers whom he obtained from England were Benjamin and Edward Haines, who came from Dudley, England, in 1825. Other English workers of the same period were James McDonald, William Teasdale, Alfred Greene, and George W. Scobie. Subsequently Jarves laid out lots and built houses for his employees in what became known, far and wide, as Glass Factory Village. Some interesting documents in the Sandwich Town Hall record mortgages granted by Jarves, and even by some of the glassblowers, who appear to have had plenty of ready money. The borrowers were mechanics and other laborers, who, giving their furniture as security, paid one dollar a week in liquidation of their debts. During the hard times of 1840 the Company charged no rent to its tenant workmen and at all times recognized the value of good wages and consideration for all classes of help.

One of Jarves' most valuable aids was Hiram Dillaway (*1813–1887*), a master mechanic to whose skill much of the success attending the manufacture of pressed glass was due. Dillaway drew designs, made patterns, and was the chief moldmaker even after Jarves left the Boston & Sandwich Company in 1858. Dillaway came to Sandwich early in 1828 after serving a year's apprenticeship with E. M. Bartholomew, moldmaker in South Boston. His notebook, now in the possession of his grandson Charles Lloyd of Sandwich, records the receipt of $50 in payment for the first year under Bartholomew. He abandoned the glowing prospect of a second year at $55 to join forces with Deming Jarves. Dillaways seem to have been plentiful in South Boston. Enoch Dillaway, and later, Enoch Junior, were both moldmakers in South Boston. In 1853 Enoch is listed as a moldmaker at 51 Federal Street, sales headquarters for the Sandwich Company.

Deming Jarves organized the Boston & Sandwich Glass Company at a time when experimentation by glass manufacturers throughout the country was in progress. The Bakewells of Pittsburgh, Henry Whitney and Enoch Robinson of Cambridge, John Robinson of Pittsburgh, the Dummers of Jersey City, all crowded forward with patents for improvements in glassmaking. In 1828 Jarves himself was granted his third patent: for an improvement in the mode of pressing melted glass into molds. This was presently followed by two others, and, in later years, by many more. As his son James Jackson said, Deming both made and lost fortunes in his many experiments. Hiram Dillaway's inventions brought this maker ten patents and a sufficient sum in royalties to permit the accumulation of $200,000. He was with the Boston & Sandwich firm until his death in 1887.

Another standby of Deming Jarves was James D. Lloyd (*1836–1920*), son-in-law of Hiram Dillaway. His father, Thomas, and his uncle, Samuel Lloyd, came to Sandwich from Birmingham, England, where they had been expert glassmakers. James began work in the Sandwich factory as a busboy at the age of eight. He later became the color expert for the Company as well as of the Cape Cod, Mount Washington, and New Bedford Companies. His notebook, now in possession of his son Charles Lloyd, contains such receipts as *Best flint Wm. Kern's recipe; Common flint James D. Lloyd; Flint G. L. F [George L. Fessenden]; Badger's recipe for wine metal; French recipes March 15, 1874; French green for cutting; Best white enamel Hummaberg's; Pluk Glyn recipe for Chinese Glass.*

These and other recorded formulas give not only quantities of the ingredients but explicit directions for making ruby, flint for etching, flint for cutting, flint for coating with ruby, green for hocks, "very good alabaster," best blue, Victoria blue, blue for casing, best white enamel, bottle glass, crown glass, alabaster as used by the old Company, opal in all its various colors — pearl gray, lilac, rose, turquoise, alabaster blue, iris, pale green, lemon, dove, "Imporatria," purple, and many others.

Lloyd developed alabaster, and during his experiments Jarves sent him to England to obtain information and recipes. While there he went on to Ireland and brought home some very lovely pieces of Belleek from the Belleek china factory, which he thought appropriate for model . Lloyd's notebook records certain sources of materials, thus:

Fluorspar you can buy in New York as well as in England. If you get it from England the best house is Hall & Co., Marble Works, Derby. Their price is .75 for 112 pounds but what is bought in France is as good. In Europe the best man for felspar is Monsieur Jouket, Beauvoir, par Lalizolle, Allier, France.

Uranium you can get the best from Poulenc Wittman, rue Neuve, St Mary, Paris. Price $5. It is better than the English. Sulphate of copper get anywhere in Boston. Pick out pieces which have no yellow stains in them.

Jarves evidently insisted upon obtaining the best of everything, whether glassmakers, ingredients, color recipes, or patterns. Never quite satisfied, he experimented with sand from New Jersey, Plymouth beach, Sandwich, Berkshire, Massachusetts, and even obtained supplies from France and South America.

When in 1858 he left the Boston & Sandwich Company and organized the Cape Cod Factory, less than half a mile from the old works, he hoped to interest his son John W. Jarves in the glass industry. Lloyd went with him. John, however, died in 1863, and thereafter his father showed little interest in a business which, for forty-five years, had completely absorbed his time and thought. Jarves was doomed to disappointment in his efforts to launch his sons as glassmakers. Much earlier he had organized the Mount Washington Glass Works in South Boston in behalf of his son George, then in his twenties. But George was not interested in glass, and the new company was conducted for two years by Captain Luther Russell. It then reverted to George, who for a short time had a Mr. Labree as partner. The 1846 Boston directory lists the concern as Labree & Jarves, brass lamps and chandeliers, 71 Summer Street — which was the home address of Deming Jarves. In 1850 Labree was succeeded by Henry Cormerais of Dedham. Operating under the name of Jarves & Cormerais, the new partnership enlarged its business by adding furnaces. Later purchased by W. L. Libbey, in 1869 the enterprise was transferred to New Bedford.

Deming Jarves, Jr., though inheriting his father's versatility and business ability, showed no inclination to pursue glassmaking. At the age of eighteen his chief ambition, that of becoming a professional sailor, was diverted by the wisdom of his father, who gave him a trip around the world, starting him out as the only passenger in one of McKay's clipper ships. After rounding the Cape of Good Hope in the dead of winter, encountering a typhoon in the China Sea, arriving in Calcutta at the height of the Indian Mutiny, he returned to Boston on the *Niagara*, a Cunard paddle-wheel steamer. His ambition for a life at sea had quite evaporated.

For a short time he served as clerk in his father's glass headquarters at 51 Federal Street, Boston, but at the beginning of the Civil War he enlisted, and served throughout the war. From 1866 he sold Sandwich glass and the products of other glass factories in New York, until he was ready to start in business for himself. Organizing a boneblack factory in Michigan, he made a fortune manufacturing commercial fertilizer as a by-product. In 1880 he bought an old farm on the River Rouge, increased the capital of his company, and built three different factories, one for producing boneblack, one for fertilizer, and the third — strange to relate — for making glass. Following his retirement from active affairs, he spent his remaining years in France, where his estate, *Val Fleuri*, at Dinard was filled with choice antiques. In October 1919 he was decorated by the French government with the order of Chevalier of the Legion of Honor for war work.

James Jackson Jarves, another son well known for his interest in art, was permitted to travel abroad when illness and impaired eyesight compelled him to abandon his intention of entering Harvard. From California, Mexico, Central and South America, James went to

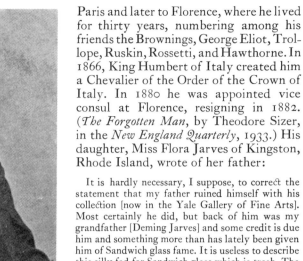

Fig. 3 — DEMING JARVES
From a photograph taken about 1863

Paris and later to Florence, where he lived for thirty years, numbering among his friends the Brownings, George Eliot, Trollope, Ruskin, Rossetti, and Hawthorne. In 1866, King Humbert of Italy created him a Chevalier of the Order of the Crown of Italy. In 1880 he was appointed vice consul at Florence, resigning in 1882. (*The Forgotten Man*, by Theodore Sizer, in the *New England Quarterly*, 1933.) His daughter, Miss Flora Jarves of Kingston, Rhode Island, wrote of her father:

It is hardly necessary, I suppose, to correct the statement that my father ruined himself with his collection [now in the Yale Gallery of Fine Arts]. Most certainly he did, but back of him was my grandfather [Deming Jarves] and some credit is due him and something more than has lately been given him of Sandwich glass fame. It is useless to describe this silly fad for Sandwich glass which is trash. The real Sandwich glass is seldom seen and very rare. I have the real pieces and the bad ones. My father tried to bring the art of Venice into the works because of the fine sand there, but there was not enough of it nor could they make it fine enough — so when they gave up the Sandwich glass proper they began this pressed stuff, much to the disgust of my father, but when it sold for twice as much as the real, "cui bono?"

Although Sandwich is over sixty miles from Boston and there was no railroad in the early days of the glass manufacture, Deming Jarves kept his residence in Boston, living first at 47 Hancock Street, then at 71 Summer, and finally at 64 Boylston Street. He spent his summers at the old Stutson place in Swampscott. The Jarves house, still standing in Sandwich and often thought to have been the home of Deming, was built for the son John when the Cape Cod factory was started and Deming was still hopeful of interesting the young man in glassmaking. An interesting note of the family's visit to Sandwich is recorded in the log book of the sloop *Henry Clay* in the Sandwich Historical Society:

"Capt. Gibbs — From Boston to Sandwich July 17, 1830: Deming Jarves & family — state room — Fare $8.75;

[and on July 23, 1830]

Capt. Stetson & wife — 2 passages — $2.50"

The expansion of Glass Factory Village or Jarves Village, as the section of the town adjoining the factory buildings was called, was in no sense a mushroom growth, but reflected the careful planning of Deming Jarves. The tall elms which he planted in the little park in front of the factory are still standing. The typical Cape Cod houses which he built for his workmen are still in good condition although gray and weatherbeaten. The company store, a large brick building, now provides quarters for several families. The bakehouse, bakery, and shoe shop formerly provided for the glassworkers are gone. On a recent visit to the old factory I found children on a platform of one of the factory buildings. They were selling fragments of Sandwich glass which they had dug

Fig. 4 — SANDWICH MOLD FOR LACY-GLASS PLATE
Of cast iron. On the back is a mark probably indicating where the mold was attached to the pressing machine. *Diameter, 5 inches.*
From the collection of Mrs. Isabelle Murray

Fig. 5 — CAMEO-GLASS CIGAR HOLDER (*c. 1880*)
Broken white pattern on blue ground. Produced during the régime of
James D. Lloyd.
From the collection of Mrs. Charles Lloyd

up from old cullet heaps — broken curtain pulls, bits of broken lamps, inkwells, and salt cellars.

Deming Jarves' tax bill for 1829 from the town of Sandwich recorded "½ homestead (Davis estate) ½ house valued at $1500, lot of land and shop $200, 2 tenements & lot $800, block & tenements $600, carpenter & wheelwright's shop $300, 177 acres of land $1200." By 1858 some of the additional items were: "Store, bake house, bake shop, shoe shop, hammer & pattern shop, planing, saw, and grist mills, Spring Hill stave mill, building and water privileges at Upper Mill, North Sandwich, ice house" — all assessed at

$26,405. In the following year he had built the new Cape Cod glass factory, pot house, machine and blacksmith shop, which were appraised at $15,000.

In 1860 he had added still more: "the Herring River Iron Works upper and lower, $6500, lumber yard and planing mill $3000, stone mill at Spring Hill $1500, pine grove at Cohasset, cutting shop for the new Cape Cod Factory, a cooper shop and new storehouse" — all valued at $40,000.

He made it possible for a glassworker to furnish his home by paying one dollar a week, giving the furniture as security. On moving to another locality the man was little burdened with worldly goods.

It will be remembered that, following labor troubles in 1887, which really started with the advent of the Glass Union in Sandwich in 1879, the old Boston & Sandwich Company closed its plant. At the time Jarves' former lieutenant, Lloyd, was approached by Nathaniel J. Bradlee, president of the Company. In the event of the re-opening of the Sandwich works would Lloyd assume the position of manager? Lloyd's answer, here in part quoted, is interesting. Under the date of September 1888 he wrote to Bradlee:

It is very desirable to have a smart energetic man there with much ability for designing and that will insist upon good work from the men. Mr. E. J. Donovan has applied for the position. But this matter can be deferred until we know if the factory is to start. . . .

As I view the situation the factory must be brought to a paying basis and I should not advise starting it until all these things are agreed to by the men. Every point where it is probable there might be disagreement should be understood and settled now, and I think it would be proper for you to frame from these suggestions what you expect from the men and wish your manager to carry out. Then I would suggest calling the men together and having it read and agreed to by them. It seems to me Mr. Seaver is just the man to do it.

Now concerning what I want by means of salary I don't think the situation warrants such pay as you have been giving and I am willing to work for $1500 a year if I should accept the position of manager. But as I have said before if you can find another man to occupy this place I will willingly by suggestion wherever needed help all in my power freely. . . .

Nathaniel Bradlee died shortly after this and, as we know, the old factory was never restored to its former status.

Deming Jarves' will, administered April 8, 1869, recognized what he had done for his children by the clause, "Having in mind all I have done for my children." He left a modest fortune, $200,000, to his wife. His lifelong ambition seems to have been to perfect a glass which would be equal to that of Venice. But his efforts in importing the best workmen, seeking the best ingredients wherever they were to be found, sending his men far and near to learn new methods or receipts, seeking suggestions as to forms from his son in Florence — all availed little. Today his reputation rests on the product that he viewed as potboiler stuff — pressed glass. His granddaughter wrote, "The real Sandwich glass is seldom seen and very rare." We may wonder to just what she refers.

Fig. 6 — SANDWICH RUBY TUMBLER (*c. 1840*)
Given by Deming Jarves to his granddaughter, Flora Jarves, who was extremely fond of horses.
From the Sandwich Library

Fig. 7 (right) — SANDWICH GLASS ORNAMENT
Not improbably a souvenir of the early days of the factory. Evidently an off-hand piece, and of exceptional interest.
From the collection of Mrs. Charles Lloyd

Acknowledgment. In preparing the foregoing article I have been greatly assisted by Mrs. Charles Lloyd, Miss Flora Jarves, Miss Elizabeth Driscoll, and George S. Burbank, of whose kindly aid I am glad to express my very keen sense of appreciation. — *M. M. S.*

Notes. To the finding of fresh fragments of information on any subject there is apparently no end, however thorough may have been the previous siftings of material. In an early paragraph of this article, I stated that Deming Jarves was born abroad. I may now add, more specifically, that the "blessed event" occurred in London.

To students of glass who enjoy delving, I suggest search for evidence regarding the scope of E. Dillaway's activities. Dillaway was moldmaker for Jarves, with

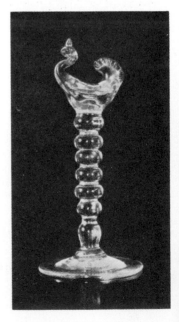

In compliance with your request . . . I give you in my opinion the best methods of running your factory. . . . The following would be my way of conducting the business if the gains or loss were to be my own. . . . First — In running the Blowers Department I desire a capable man to assist me. . . . I would prefer to have Mr. Kern. Then I wish it distinctly understood by the men that we want work made in the best possible way and that no poor work will be paid for; no orders to be made in the factory not ordered except by permission; and should the factory be run nights those who work on the night run are expected to be in place promptly as day men — to see that the boys also are on hand promptly to do good work.

Then I should like to say I don't think any factory can be made to pay unless run nights — neither can men stand around outside the factory or elsewhere in working hours as they have in the past. . . .

In regard to the Cutting Shop, in other places it is run by the day. Men going in at 7 o'clock in the morning and working till 6 at night with exception of one hour at dinner, and it seems a fair way to me. Here in the past they have worked by the piece. There are advantages both ways, should wish to consult with you and the directors before deciding about that.

headquarters at the Boston office. I suspect that he served several other manufacturers in a similar capacity. If my surmise should prove correct, it would solve not a few problems. In 1879 many factories were producing virtually identical articles, whose output volume was, however, in each instance regulated by the Glass Union. The purpose of the restriction seems to have been that of preventing any one factory from monopolizing the advantages accruing from its own creative ingenuity. An illuminating story might be written concerning the development of this early union and the resultant effect on the glassmaking industry in New England. — *M. M. S.*

Fig. 1 — TOUCHSTONES FOR DATING
Eagle, *1831*; Queen Victoria, *1837*; Victoria and Albert, *1840*; President Harrison, *1841*

Sandwich Lacy Glass

By HOMER EATON KEYES

THE more one sees of American glass of the nineteenth century, the more his respect increases for the ware generally known among collectors as "lacy Sandwich." Nor is such meed of admiration due solely to the facts that the metal itself is of high excellence, and that its transformation into useful and ornamental forms was accomplished by mechanisms that owed their origin to Yankee ingenuity and commercial alertness. Rather may it be ascribed chiefly to the realization that lacy glass is not, as generally assumed, a slavish imitation of cut glass, but is, on the contrary, a virtually independent substitute for the more expensive ware. Hence, in its way, this product deserves consideration in a class by itself, just as do the early patterned papers that took the place of tapestries and other expensive fabrics as a covering for walls.

The makers of lacy glass were, to be sure, desirous of equaling, or surpassing, the enticing brilliance of cut glass; but they accomplished their end by technical devices virtually impossible to the cutting wheel. In place of the geometrical, finely crosshatched faceting of cut glass, they employed stippling. With this they combined ornamental motives that are, in aspect, somewhere between cut

Fig. 2 — "PENNSYLVANIA STEAMBOAT," *6 ½ in.*
The palmette or anthemion ornaments of the border thoroughly neo-classic in type, and so strongly reminiscent of the late 1820's as to argue for placing this plate in the very early 1830's

designs and those more skilfully wrought decorations usually associated with the art of the glass engraver. And because the press permitted them to produce intricate patterns in a metal too hard to submit readily to the older methods of hand decoration, they achieved effects of non-prismatic gleam and sparkle beyond anything previously known to ornamental glass.

The labor involved in making the molds for such glass must have been prodigious, and in time, as wages increased, so costly as to forbid its profitable employment by the manufacturer. Hence it is safe to say that the shift from lacy patterns to bolder and simpler designs was compelled less by a change in popular taste than by the relentless force of economic necessity.

Precisely when that shift occurred we have no certain means of knowing, although documents upon which to base some fairly reliable guesswork are at hand in the form of several cup plates that either carry an imprinted date or, because of the nature of their decoration, may be assigned to a specific year. These cup plates are the so-called *1831 Eagle*; the *Queen Victoria*, without doubt issued as a souvenir of the young monarch's coronation in 1837; the *Victoria and Albert*, celebrating the royal marriage in 1840;

Fig. 3 — "ROSE," *6 ½ in.*
The struggle between Victorian naturalism and the neo-classic tradition is here apparent. No doubt contemporary with Fig. 2

Fig. 4 — "CONSTITUTION," *6 ½ in.*
Allied with Figures 2 and 3. The frigate *Constitution*, though condemned to destruction in 1830, was rehabilitated in 1833. This plate may date between those two years, perhaps slightly later than Figures 2 and 3

41

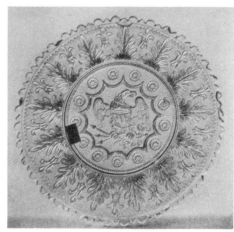

Fig. 5 (left) — "FLOWER BASKET AND GRAPES," 7 ⅝ in.
In this exceptionally fine plate we encounter motives dear to McIntire in the early 1800's. One of the most refined and logical of Sandwich designs, 1830–1833

Fig. 6 (centre) — MEDALLIONS, 6 ½ in.
Here the more classic motives have yielded to adaptations of French Regency details. A lush design, extremely well executed and but little later than the preceding

Fig. 7 (right) — "EAGLE," 6 in.
Difficult to place, but maintaining a delicacy of pattern and justness of scale that, aside from the classic anthemions of the border, point to the early 1830's (Fig. 2)

and the *President Harrison*, bearing the date *1841*. With this final item must be associated the *Bunker Hill* plate, inscribed *Finished by the Ladies 1841*.

We have but to compare the two last-named plates with the preceding three to perceive how quickly simplicity of decoration has supervened upon ornateness. Some slight stippling is discoverable in the border swags surrounding the Harrison profile, but it is reduced to a minimum. The *Ringgold* plate *(1846)* displays no stippling whatsoever, while the various members of the log-cabin series, likewise of the 1840's, are either quite unadorned as to their rims, or carry merely a straggling vine or detached flower sprays.

Similarly, the host of conventional cup plates may be quite sharply divided into two classes: the first usually signalized by an astonishingly detailed richness of quite exquisitely handled motives set off against a stippled background; the second characterized by the virtual absence of stippling and by the employment of bold, large-scale, and often rather coarsely commonplace motives in place of the refined elements for which the first class is notable. If we are justified in believing that the year 1840 establishes the line of demarcation between the gener-ously enriched historicals on the one hand, and the relatively plain ones on the other, we are equally justified in placing the first class of conventionals prior to that year, and the second, subsequent thereto. What is true of cup plates should be true of the larger plates and dishes. We may not say that all pieces of the kind which prominently display stippling were made before 1840. In fact, the 1860's and 1870's witnessed a considerable revival of that device. Nevertheless, we may confidently insist that all notably brilliant items that liberally employ fine stippling as a background for traceries of exceptional refinement in both form and scale are, without much question, a product of the 1830 decade.

Whether or not it is possible to determine to which half of that decade a particular example should be assigned is another question. No two mold cutters were equally gifted in judgment and skill. The constant demand for new patterns must, at times, have taxed the most lively invention. Not a few experiments, too, were made in the direct imitation of English cut patterns. Considerations such as these must give pause to dogmatic assurance. Yet, in spite of them, it is impossible to resist the temptation to arrange a few of the old patterns on the basis of certain significant attributes of design, and thus to infer a probable chronology.

The accompanying illustrations present such an arrangement. Their captions indicate certain reasons for the position of each item in the sequence. The examples

Fig. 8 (left) — PALMETTE AND SCROLLS, 7 ¼ in.
Far less delicate than any of the preceding and less well considered as a composition, but placed early because of the predominance of classic or semiclassic motives

Fig. 9 (centre) — STAR AND LOZENGE, 6 ½ in.
Very difficult to place on the basis of its pattern, which, on examination, resolves itself into a thing of shreds and patches, most of which would seem rather nondescript except for the brilliance of the glass

Fig. 10 (right) — CORNUCOPIAS, 5 ¼ x 8 ¼ in.
A favorite early motive associated with others of a somewhat neutral variety. Unless the work of an inferior designer and mold maker, this and Figure 9 might qualify for a rating in the late 1830's

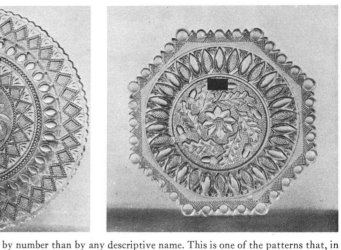

Fig. 11 (left) — SHELL AND BULL'S-EYE, *7 ½ in.*
　　Obviously indebted to Figure 6 for its inspiration, but not so logically de-
signed or so fine either in scale or in mold cutting. Either somewhat later than
Figure 6 or by an inferior artisan

Fig. 12 (centre) — "STAR, FLOWERS, AND LOZENGES," *8 in.*
　　This name, like all the others, is purely arbitrary, and is intended merely to
emphasize some feature or features of the pattern. Cup plates, plates, and
dishes in lacy glass, particularly if conventional in pattern, are better known

by number than by any descriptive name. This is one of the patterns that, in
many respects, follows the geometrical design of cut types. There is no sign
of neo-classic influence. Though the workmanship is excellent and the scale
beyond criticism, the whorl of flower forms in the centre points forward toward
the 1840's rather than back toward the 1820's. Perhaps, therefore, about 1835

Fig. 13 (right) — "STAR, OAK, AND LANCE HEAD," *5 ½ in.*
　　The geometrical character of the rim and the whorl of naturalistic leaves
about a starlike centre associate this in type and probably in date with 12

selected are from a carefully picked collection, and, with one or
two exceptions, have not hitherto been published. All are rare
and well worthy of study regardless of the relative correctness or
incorrectness of their date ascriptions.

Conclusions

The reader will no doubt already have remarked that this
brief study has stressed peculiarities of pattern and has not even
mentioned indications afforded by the character of the glass
itself. In general, it may be noted that the metal of all the pieces
here considered is of the same high quality. Its handling, however, is not uniformly competent. Some of the examples illustrated are of almost double thickness, usually considered a sign
of early period. Some clearly betray the curious surface lines
　　　　　　　　　　　　　　　　　　explained by Harry
　　　　　　　　　　　　　　　　　　Hall White in AN-
　　　　　　　　　　　　　　　　　　TIQUES for April

1933, page 146. Since these lines, or fissures, are due primarily to
unequal heating of the mold, they, too, are widely accepted as
significant of crude methods and hence of relative antiquity.
Bubbles in the body of the glass are similarly viewed.

　　These various signs and symbols should not be overlooked,
or their great importance denied. Yet it may be possible to
emphasize unduly their value in determining whether a given
piece in which some of them may be discovered is of earlier date
than another, in the same general class, which chances to be free
from alluring flaws. Between the years 1830 and 1840 the technique of glass pressing as a mechanical process was far from
achieving perfection, albeit the artistry of pressed-glass design
reached its zenith during that period. Hence we may not rely
solely on the inperfections in a single piece of one pattern to
reveal the date of
the pattern itself.
The lone specimen

Fig. 14 (left) — "VICTORIA CORONATION," *6 ½ in.*
　　The year 1837, that in which Victoria was crowned queen, may be accepted as
dating this plate. Rose, thistle, and shamrock, signifying England, Scotland,
and Ireland, are entwined in the wreath of the rim. The design would be
better were the likeness larger and in profile, but, as a whole, the plate is a
fine piece of work

Fig. 15 (centre) — PANELED DISH, *6 ⅛ x 8 ¼ in.*
　　This is the first piece in the group whose rim is clearly divided into separate
panels. The fanciful centre and the motives of the long sides of the rim are
obviously derived from Louis XVI designs; the thistle corners recall the
Victoria and Albert cup plate of 1840, the first of the paneled cup plates. The

leaf and anthemion are evidently the selection of desperation. The workmanship is better than the somewhat mixed design. Date of this dish, probably
1839-1840

Fig. 16 (right) — PANELED DISH, *9 ⅜ in.*
　　The paneling here is unmistakably similar to the Victoria and Albert wedding
cup plate of 1840. The handling of the motives is quite distinctive; first, for
the large size of each element, and the considerable but well-disposed areas
of clear glass; second, for a new quality of modeling specially observable in
the petals of the dahlia-like centre flower. There is here a curious quality in the
detail, as of stamped metal, such as we have not hitherto encountered. Date,
about 1840

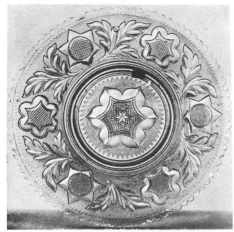

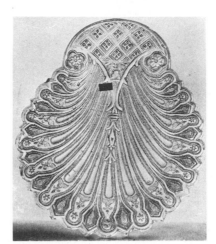

Fig. 17 (left) — "STAR AND MEDALLION" PLATE, *9 ½ in.*
Here again we find large clear surfaces rather subtly modeled instead of being outlined with a ridgy border such as bounds a considerable proportion of the previous examples. The technique is so similar to that of Figure 16 (compare the central motives, and the use of clear glass in the design) that we must ascribe both to virtually the same year, 1840

Fig. 18 (centre) — BONBON OR CARD DISH, *8 x 9 ½ in.*
More or less in a class by itself, though the so-called hairpin motive occurs in cup plates, plates, and dishes. Judged by the weight of glass and the fineness

of workmanship, fairly early in the 1830's — perhaps 1835; but affording few if any stylistic clues. Perhaps based on a silver design. An excellent piece of workmanship

Fig. 19 (right) — "BUTTERFLY, FLEUR-DE-LIS, AND FAN" DISH, *7 ¼ x 10 in.*
Another very puzzling item. So brilliant in quality that when seen in the original it is likely to blind the observer to its imperfections in design, which consists of a rather heterogeneous accumulation of unrelated motives. Again the product of a quite unimaginative shop designer despite its neat workmanship. Date perhaps about 1840

may be heavy in body, bubbly, covered with surface fissures, badly atrophied about the edge. But, unless we can find several more from the same mold, all exhibiting like peculiarities, we shall lack the evidence essential to any really valid conclusion. The possibility that the piece before us is a "second," representing a minor accident rather than pervasive inexpertness on the maker's part, must be recognized and taken fully into account.

At the same time, it must be admitted that attempts to determine dates, in the jumbled eclecticism of the nineteenth century, exclusively on the basis of pattern are fraught with no little peril. They are worth while primarily because they compel con-

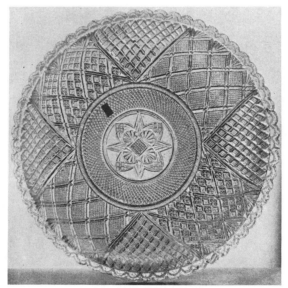

mental design and workmanship in the mold. Their results will be indicative rather than definitive, and must, therefore, be checked and counterchecked against the testimony borne by the fabric of the glass itself.

Of one thing, however, our study may leave us reasonably certain. Most of the brilliant, finely stippled American pressed glass, the so-called lacy glass, is a product of the 1830–1840 decade. For reasons that need not be rehearsed it may be credited to the factory at Sandwich. While in quality of metal it varies but slightly, in quality of design it betrays wide divergencies. But, whatever its occasional deficiencies, it is to be recognized as a distinctive and distinguished contribution to our industrial art.

Fig. 20 — THREE LARGE DISHES, *11 and 12 in.*
Arranged in probable order of date from about 1830 to 1840. All three are palpable imitations of English or Irish cut glass. The second, which borrows motives common in early nineteenth-century cut decanters and tumblers, is handsomest

sideration of individual decorative motives and their probable bearing, and, even more important, because they involve the temporary ignoring of merely superficial glitter, and necessitate concentration upon quality of funda-

MUSEUM EXAMPLES OF SANDWICH GLASS

An Editorial Note

IN NOT a few museums of the United States today one may encounter somewhat heterogeneous, often nondescript, and frequently mislabeled accumulations of pressed glass. In so far as we are aware, however, the Metropolitan Museum of Art in New York is the first to place on display a cabinet of selected examples of the pressed glass made under the supervision of Deming Jarves at his factory in Sandwich, Massachusetts, apparently between the years 1828 and 1842. Though these examples are a loan from the collection of Mrs. Charles W. Green of New York City, they were, we understand, chosen by Curator Joseph Downs, to whom, further, must be credited their excellent arrangement in a large alcove cabinet adjacent to the entrance to the American Wing.

In view of the care exercised by all concerned in preparing and

placing this display, we see no reason to question the ascription to Sandwich of all the items shown. Nevertheless, the more critically one examines this group of glass, the more astonishing will he find its variety of forms, ornamental patterns, and colors. And the more readily will he admit that the early pressed glass of Sandwich deserves recognition as an important and worth-while contribution to American art-industrial history.

If the mechanically produced glass manufactured by Jarves and his coworkers had been no more than a cheap and imitative substitute for the cut and engraved wares of its period, it would merit little if any attention. Occasionally it descends to such a relatively low level. In the main, however, it owes little or nothing to wheel technique and, unlike the variously produced output of a later generation, nothing to the influence of cast iron. On the contrary,

it stands as a really quite new and independent type of glass, often quite original in form, and in general exhibiting a style of decoration exceptionally well adapted to enhance the brilliance of the material in ways feasible for the pressing machine but quite beyond the capabilities of the cutter or the engraver. Such glass could have been turned out only under the favorable conditions created by relatively low labor costs and exceptionally resourceful and progressive management — such conditions as, in its heyday, the Sandwich factory enjoyed and utilized to the full.

While various considerations preclude picturing all the specimens of this glass exhibited at the Metropolitan, we believe that our readers will be glad to examine portrayals of representative specimens from a group considered worthy of a place in an outstandingly great American museum of art. Thanks to the courtesy of the authorities, who went to no little trouble in taking special photographs, we are able to illustrate a number of pieces from the Green collection, accompanied by brief descriptive notes. Most of the pieces illustrated in ANTIQUES for August 1933 are included in the loan to the Metropolitan Museum. One or two of them are republished in the present group of illustrations.

According to Doctor Charles W. Green, specimens of lacy Sandwich glass are most frequently found in New England, the

FIG. 3 — COVERED DISH (*10 ½ by 8 ½ inches; overall height, 5 inches*)
Clear glass, with fluting, stippling, and mingled floral and abstract forms. It was no small undertaking to press these large pieces of irregular shape and to ensure satisfactory fitting of cover to dish. This may account for the scarcity of covered examples in comparison with those made and marketed without covers

FIGURE 4

FIG. 4 — CREAMERS (*all approximately 4 ¼ inches high*)
These patterns, usually occurring in clear glass, are here respectively pressed in sapphire, fiery opalescent, and brilliant but rich blue. Gothic patterns of surbase of *a* and *b* virtually identical. In this couple reversion to a form akin to the much earlier helmet shape is interesting. From the standpoint of design these creamers might properly be rated in the order of their photographic presentation

FIGURE 5

FIG. 5 — BOWLS: ALL BUT ONE COVERED
(*Overall height of covered items, from 5 ¼ to 6 inches*)
Covered bowls, whether blown or pressed, with cover fitting into a galleried rim, are specifically of the nineteenth century. If, as we believe, fine delicacy of detail is indicative of relative age in pressed glass, *b* would be the latest in this interesting quartet. Colors: *a*, sapphire; *b*, exists in *claire de lune*, deep blue-black, and green; *c*, deep blue, oval form; pattern an ingenious combination of bull's-eyes surmounted by scalloped scalelike motives interspersed with thistles; ends show pineapple. As usual, brilliance is enhanced and unification achieved by stippling the ground. *d*, clear butter bowl, circular

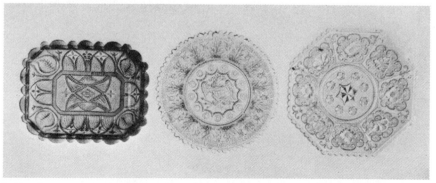

FIGURE 6

FIG. 6 — PLATE AND DISHES
a, Sapphire-blue oblong dish with chamfered corners; gothic design with leaves in corners; not uncommon pattern in clear glass, but rare in color. *b*, Six-inch clear plate with serrate edge, acanthus or palmette with *fleur-de-lis* border and eagle centre; a highly refined and consistent design, probably of the 1830's. *c*, Octagonal 6 ½-inch dish with border of rococo implications and six-pointed star centre surrounded by a ring of shells

Hudson River Valley, and eastern Pennsylvania. The last-named locality appears to have been partial to the colored glass. Miniature specimens of lacy glass are now believed to have been made, not as samples, but as a tribute to juvenile interest. The variety of patterns in lacy Sandwich glass defies enumeration. Hitherto unknown examples are constantly turning up. Goblets, tumblers, compotes, a large diversity of plates and dishes, egg cups, small cups and saucers, sugar bowls, creamers, sand shakers were turned out in lacy patterns. So, too, were candlesticks and lamp standards. It seems fair to surmise that Jarves'

FIG. 7 — DISHES (*approximate diameters, 7 in.*)

a, Clear glass, twelve sided; border motives capable of sundry interpretations. *b*, Clear glass with irregular-shaped edge, pressed from an unusually well-designed and cut mold. *c*, Circular dish with pearl or bull's-eye and finely designed oak wreath in centre; for octagonal variant, see ANTIQUES for August 1933 (*p. 60*). *d*, Octagonal; clear glass with well-conceived and executed grape border and flower-basket centre

the 1820's and 1830's, was being imported in vast quantities into the United States. In some instances, at least, it would seem that Sandwich patterns owe their inspiration more to Staffordshire designs than to contemporary ornamental glass. But the point should not be overstressed. As already observed, the early lacy Sandwich is virtually peculiar to itself, and though it was produced in an era when excessive decorative elaboration was the rule, it almost invariably represents a just sense of the inherent quality of glass as a material, and a remarkably sound taste in adjusting patterns at once to the capabilities of the ma-

intention was to compete not only with more expensive glass tableware, but also with Staffordshire earthenware, which, during chine and to the nature of the substance employed. Later, and in other localities, this rule was less carefully observed.

FIG. 8 — DISHES OR DEEP PLATES, ALL IN CLEAR GLASS

The meticulous elaboration of fine detail in *a*, *b*, and *c* contrasts decisively with the larger handling of the motives in *d*, and hence may point to a somewhat earlier date for the first three items. It should be unnecessary to call attention to the almost constant employment of stippled grounds in the various examples illustrated. See ANTIQUES for August 1933 (*p. 58*), where is published an article on Sandwich lacy glass which attempts to establish some basis for dating certain patterns

FIG. 9 — PLATES AND DISHES

a, Shallow dish, clear glass, 9 ¼ inches, scroll and sunburst border, double-fan centre. Rare. *b*, Brilliant clear-glass *beehive* dish, 9 ¾ in. Examples vary greatly in degree of brilliance. *c*, Soup plate in clear glass with amber border; while the pattern itself is of not infrequent occurrence, this combination of clear glass with amber is exceptionally handsome and, in so far as known, unique. *d*, Flat plate similar in pattern to *c* but in clear glass

NEW ENGLAND GLASS COMPANY INVOICES

Part I

By HELEN McKEARIN

Discovery of the invoices here discussed is an exciting event for students of early American glass, and ANTIQUES is proud to be able to reproduce them here with Helen McKearin's scholarly analysis. She interprets the often cryptic notations and elucidates their significance for glass collectors. The documents, except for one which is private.y owned, were formerly in the Archives of the Maryland Collection at the Enoch Pratt Library, and are now owned by the Maryland Historical Society. They were discovered by Richard Wood of Baltimore, who was able to track down in the Baltimore city directories all but one of the dealers mentioned on the invoices; his identifications are given in the captions. This study will be continued in ANTIQUES next month.

— THE EDITOR

A PROMISING LODE of information as to the early products and business procedures of the New England Glass Company has been discovered by Richard Wood of Baltimore. He has located a bill of lading and four invoices of consignments, sent by water, between September 13, 1828, and 19, 1829, to William E. Mayhew & Company, commission merchants of Baltimore. Heretofore as Lura Woodside Watkins states in her authoritative *Cambridge Glass*, contemporary newspaper advertisements have been the source of nearly all our knowledge of the wares made before 1830. Information so obtained has been general — largely as to genus and species. These newly discovered documents are a little more specific, confirm some old conjectures, and contain evidence for new, tentative if not positive, attributions.

The study of these papers, the ferreting out of factual and implicit information from prices (f.o.b. factory) and somewhat cryptic wording, has been more engrossing than a double acrostic. But the conclusions are not so capable of proof. Since nearly every line has been re-phrased and interpreted in the light of personal experience and research it is not unlikely that, as in the case of many translations, the exact meaning of the original text and idiom may have been missed. So, as a check and balance, the text of the privately owned 1828 invoice is given here as Figure 1 and of the four 1829 invoices now owned by the Maryland Historical Society the three dated January 3, April 18, and May 2 are illustrated as Figures 2, 3, and 4. Each line and column has been numbered so that the entries, as they are discussed, can be identified by L. (line) and C. (column) with the corresponding numbers. Also, an arbitrary division of the material into three parts has been made. Part I is devoted to drinking vessels and tableware.

Decanters and drinking vessels almost invariably led the glassware lists in the innumerable contemporary advertisements of merchants and auction houses. So, as one would expect, a large proportion of these comparatively small shipments consisted of these objects. In all there were 231½ dozen glasses — wines, clarets, champagnes, and tumblers. Of these 16 dozen were plain stem wines at 3/ (equivalent to 50¢) a dozen: 8 dozen entered on Line 2, Column 1 (*Fig. 3*) and 8 on Line 9, Column 1 (*Fig. 4*). It is a fair assumption that they were free-blown with an applied, unadorned stem and the flat circular foot of the period. As to the bowl, who knows?

It is probable that another and one of the most common of the free-blown forms is indicated by the "taper" wines — 3 dozen tale at 3/ (*L.5, C.2, Fig. 3*) and 3 dozen common at 3/ (*L.24, C.1, Fig. 4*). These were wines similar to Figure 5 with drawn bowl and stem.

Tale, which characterized other items also, indicated a quality of glass. Whenever it was impossible to secure pure ingredients for glass a scumlike substance, sandgall, was formed on top of the batch by the impurities carried upward by the bubbling of the cooking metal. While this was removed as completely as possible, the metal at the top was usually inferior to that below. Wares made from the best metal were the fine glass, for instance that used for extrinsic decoration. Those made from the top were considered inferior as a rule and were called tale. I suspect the term is of English origin because weight of glass and excise taxes went hand in hand for so very long in England. And "tale," which according to Funk & Wagnalls may be a "numbering as distinguished from a weighing," "a valuing by tale and not by weight," might have seemed a logical term for the cheaper glass.

In the 1828 shipment (*L. 7 and L. 8, Fig. 1*) there were 12 dozen "Flint flute & wing" wines. That descriptive phrase, no reference to molding, the high price — 2.25 a dozen as compared with 50¢ a dozen for taper wines — point to free-blown wines fashioned from fine lead glass (called flint from the days of the Englishman, Ravenscroft) and with wheel-cut decoration. This was a field of manufacture which the New England Glass Company cultivated almost from its inception in the spring of 1818. Its patterns, like its heritage of technical and decorative practices, undoubtedly were as British as the shillings and pence which peppered its invoices. Flute was, and is, a common British cut-glass term, apparently first used in the eighteenth century to designate a vertical decorative element resembling half a flute or reed divided lengthwise. Eventually, it embraced all similar motifs — convex or concave, long or short, shallow or deep, broad or narrow, tapering or even horizontal. Often a differentiating adjective such as flat or fan was

FIG. 1 — COPY OF ITEMS on the earliest of the New England Glass Company invoices of glass shipped to Wm. E. Mayhew & Co., commission merchants at 22 South Charles, Baltimore. As the document itself is privately owned and not available for reproduction, Richard Wood has supplied the transcript.

		Sept. 13th 1828	
1. 6 pr 3 sq foot cyl-lamps plated caps	13/6		13.50
2. ½ Doz 9 in Straw◇fruit dishes on feet			7.50
3. 4 " Tale champaigns	10/6		7.00
4. 3 pr. Qt flute & flute Dects	12/		6.00
5. 12 pr. 3 Pt Dble flute carofts cut rings		3.50	42.00
6. 12 Doz Flint flute & wing Tum		2.75	33.00
7. 3 " " " " " Wines		2.25	6.75
8. 9 " " " " " "		2.25	20.25
9. 6 " " " " " Clarets		2.75	10.50
10. 6 " " Fluted champaigns		3.50	21.00

FIG. 2 — JANUARY 3, 1829, INVOICE of apothecaries' wares and blanks for cut glass, the latter for a Mr. Tingh, probably one of the many independent glasscutters who were located in our cities, especially along the seaboard, some even prior to '76. Mr. Wood was unable to locate Tingh in the directories, but he did find a Baltimore Steam Glass Cutting establishment. *This and Figures 3 and 4, courtesy of the Maryland Historical Society.*

FIG. 3 — APRIL 25 COPY of the April 18, 1829, invoice of glass consigned to Wm. E. Mayhew & Co. for the accounts of Albert Koster, china, glass, and queensware merchant at South Calvert, and Thomas Sutliff, owner of a furniture store at 60 West Lexington, both of Baltimore. Across the face of the invoice is a notation enough of which can be read to learn that "this invoice by the Marshall Ney did not come to hand . . . having been lost on her passage . . ." *Fig. 2 above, Fig. 3 below, facing page.*

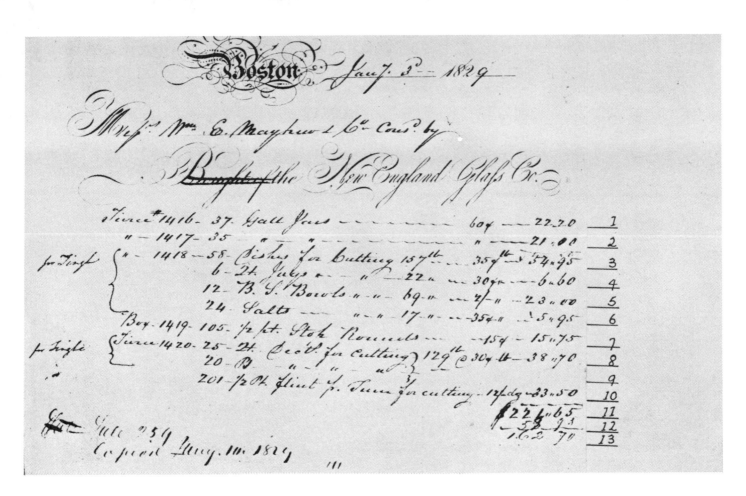

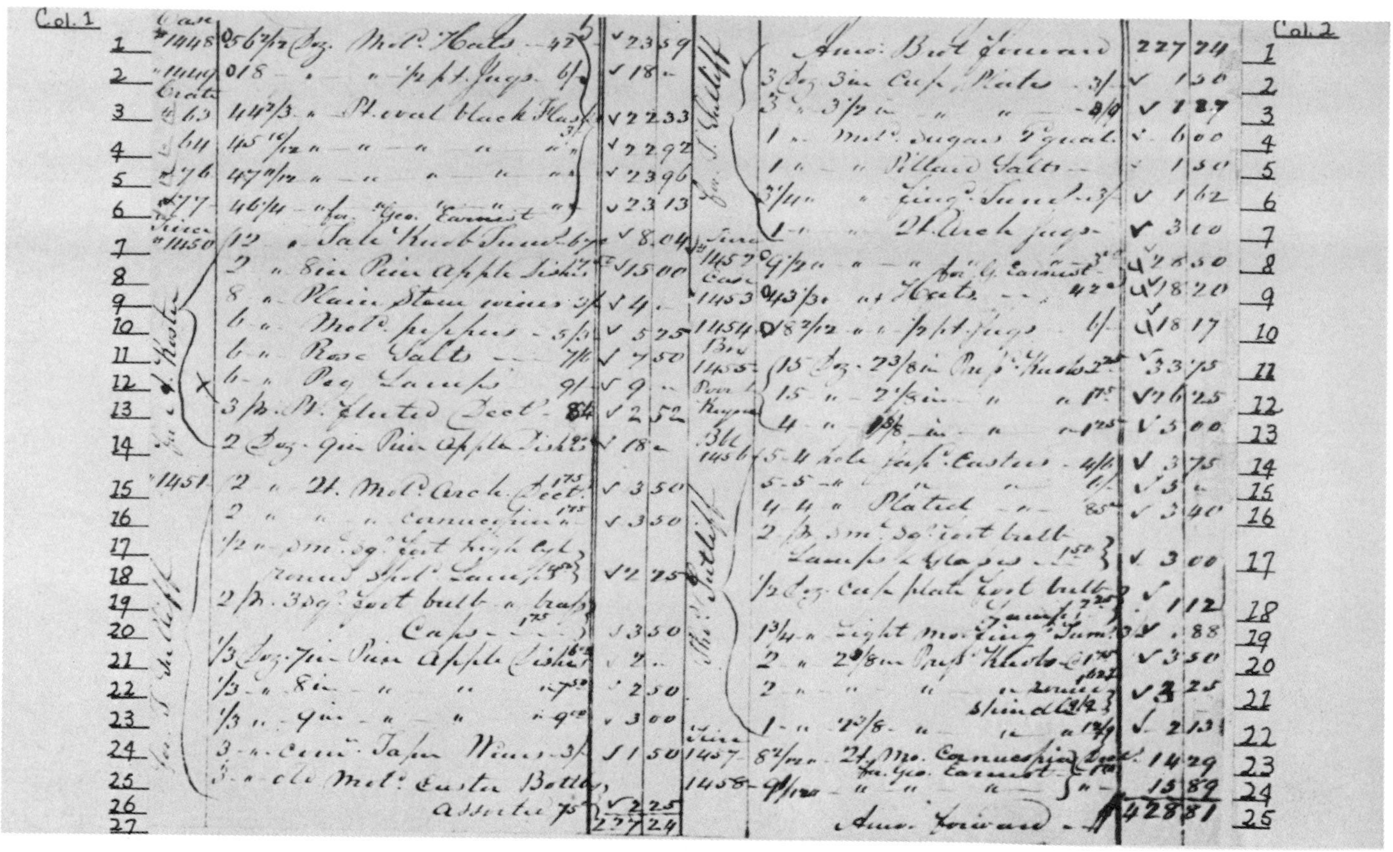

Col 3

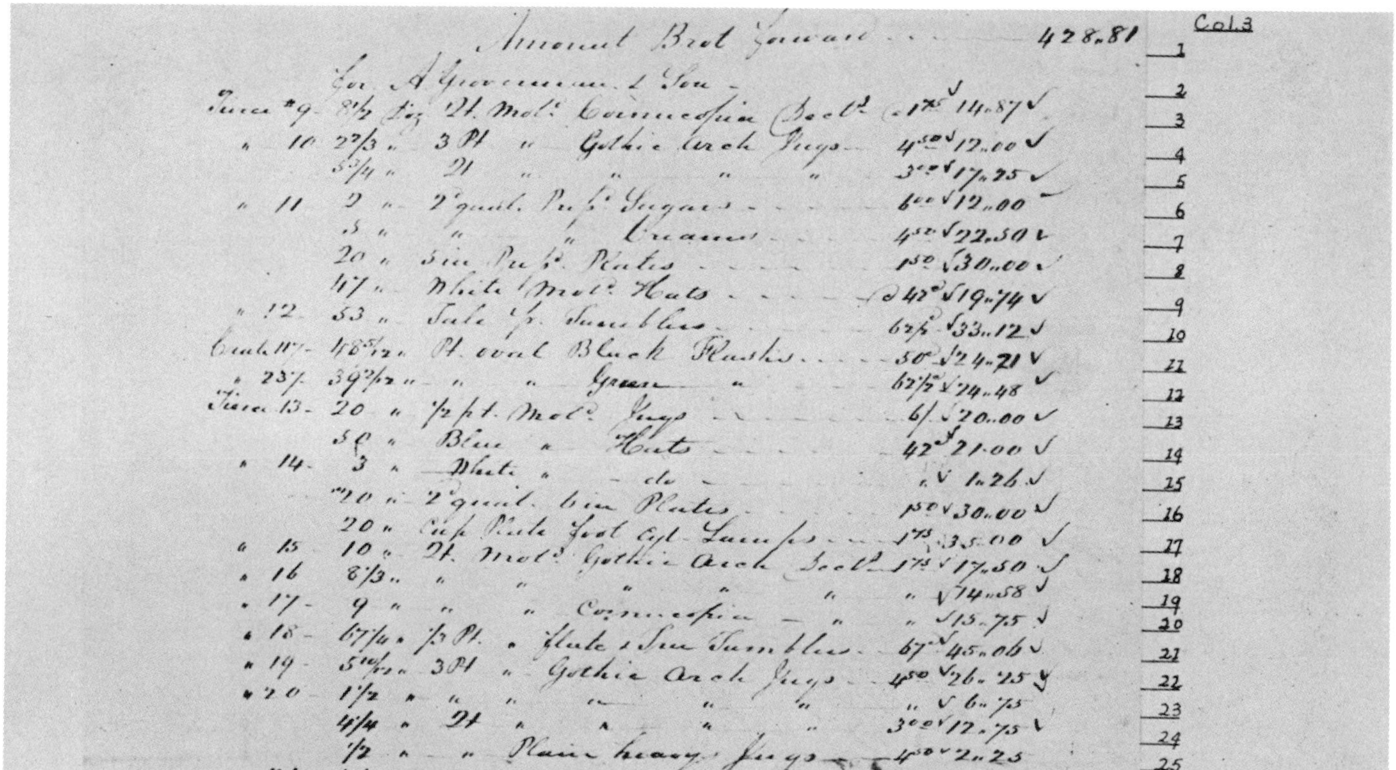

added. Sometimes very fine flutes were called finger flutes; fine and slanting, blazes. And the broad, convex vertical flutes — ribs to us — introduced by Irish designers after 1790 were known as pillar flutes, or just pillars. These flute and wing wines might be described as having fine flutes in winglike formation above a band of vertical flutes around the lower part of the bowl.

The same suppositions may be held, regarding the 6 dozen "Flint flute & wing" clarets (*L.9, Fig. 1*), billed at 2.75 a dozen and totaled at 10.50! The arithmetical error is especially irritating since the price might provide a clue as to whether the clarets were larger or smaller than the wines. Obviously they were unlike in some respect. In fact, for centuries the claret glass appears to have had an identity of its own: it occurs in English lists far back in the seventeenth century. But so far I have been unable to identify one. Since, however, this *claré* French wine was light-bodied and usually taken with meals it seems likely that it was served in glasses having more capacious bowls than those used for a heavier and headier wine. Jerome Strauss, an outstanding student and collector of drinking vessels, concurs in this opinion. It is not impossible, of course, that the shape was similar to that of the *Ashburton* so-called claret, the much later pressed form resembling a stubby and chubby parfait glass. Whatever its shape, one thing seems certain, if the claret was larger than the wine a dozen would have been 2.75; if smaller, 1.75.

During the prosperous 1820's and '30's another French wine, champagne, long a favorite of the wealthy, appeared with increasing frequency in the daily newspaper notices of wines and spirits for sale. An immediate corollary was the more regular inclusion of champagne glasses in the listings of cut glass for sale. So it is not surprising to find them on the 1828 invoice of the Cambridge firm — 4 dozen tale at 10/6 a dozen (*L.3*), and 6 dozen flint fluted at 3.50 a dozen (*L.10, Fig. 1*). It can be inferred that both types were free-blown; the first, probably plain; the second with simple cut flutes probably rather flat and extending only part way up the bowl. Their shape is a matter of conjecture. One probability is the French "flute" like that in Figure 6 which from the seventeenth century had been used for this sparkling wine. Another is the Victorian champagne or "coupe" which supposedly came in vogue about 1830 and had a shallow "saucer" bowl with foot or very tall stem. A third is a glass with a large tulip-shaped bowl which André L. Simon maintains in his *Champaign* was the proper form.

The tumblers, 181¼ dozen in all, outnumber all other drinking vessels. Two descriptions, I believe, admit of easy translation — 12 dozen flint flute and wing at 2.75 a dozen (*L.6, Fig. 1*), and 67¼ dozen ⅓-pint flute and tree at 67¢ a dozen (*L. 21, C.3, Fig. 4*). The first presumably were free-blown lead glass and matched the cut wines and clarets in pattern. The second, I believe, were blown-three-mold in the *arch* pattern G.IV-2 (as classified by McKearin, *American Glass*), or possibly G. IV-3 (*Fig. 7*). Two tumbler molds have been determined in G.IV-2. One, because of tumbler fragments unearthed at Sandwich, has been attributed to that factory. The other mold and the rare pieces from it have never been associated with any glasshouse. Nor has the one determined mold in G.IV-3, a tumbler mold.

The knob tumblers at 67¢ a dozen (12 dozen, *L.1, C.1, Fig. 3* and 12 dozen, *L.7,*

C.1, Fig. 4) are as yet an unsolved puzzle. Diligent search through many books on drinking vessels has been unrewarding. Newspaper research has revealed only their popularity in the 1820's and '30's. Cask upon cask of English knob tumblers were imported, many in 1825 by George Dummer & Company of New York City, founders in 1824 of the Jersey Glass Company. The Brooklyn Flint Glass Works of John L. Gilliland & Company as well as Cambridge made them, and in quart, pint, and ½-pint sizes.

The remaining type of tumbler which, if I have translated the abbreviations correctly, was named "fingered," presents one of the most intriguing problems in these documents. A careful scrutiny of the letter before *Tum* (*L.10, Fig. 2*) and the beginning of the word after *Mold* (*L.16, C.2, Fig. 3*) leaves no doubt in my mind that in the former invoice the tumblers for cutting (blanks) at 12/ a dozen, were also "fingered." Nowhere in the many illustrations I have surveyed have I found a tumbler or other article so labeled. Nor have I found any certainty as to its meaning among the students I have consulted. One suggestion, which would fit the molded glasses but not the blanks which were free-blown, was a band of finger flutes. Another suggestion, quite likely the correct one, I feel, comes from Frederick Carder, noted glassman and founder of the Steuben Glass Works. He writes, "These must be what were called thummers and had deep depressions, pushed in while hot, in the lower part so that when one had too much to drink he could at least hold onto the glass." Mr. Strauss is of the same opinion. Such a shape could be formed in a mold as well as by hand. Whatever they were, the molded variety was in popular demand and was cheap, 50¢ and 62½¢ a dozen. The total number destined for the Baltimore dealers was 61¼ dozen (*L.16, C.2, Fig. 3; L.6 and L.19, C.2, and L.10, C.3, Fig. 4*).

Three other articles might be·mentioned briefly: flasks, jars, and stopper rounds. In the April shipments there were 295 11/12 dozen oval black flasks at 3/ a dozen (*L.9–15, C.1, Fig. 3*); in the May, 233 1/12 dozen of the black at 3/ or 50¢, and 39 2/12 dozen oval green flasks at 62½¢ a dozen (*L.3–6, C.1 and L.11, 12, C.3, Fig. 4*). These undoubtedly were plain blown or molded flasks from the affiliated New England Bottle Glass Company. The 72 gallon jars and 105 half-pint stopper rounds (*L.1, 2, 7, Fig. 2*) were probably on their way to apothecaries. I have found stopper rounds — wide mouth containers with meticulously fitted stoppers — advertised under the heading *Apothecary Wares*. The New England Glass Company like most of its competitors produced quantities of such goods. It may be that the method of glass stoppering described by Apsley Pellatt in his *Curiosities of Glass Making* was used at Cambridge.

Other articles of tableware included vessels for serving wine, spirits, and water; castors and peppers; plates and hats. Only the carafes and three pairs of decanters were in the September 1828 shipment; the others were all sent in 1829. The consignments of decanters, carafes, and pitchers were even larger than those of their boon companions, the drinking vessels already discussed. In all there were 120 11/12 dozen pitchers, 12 pairs of carafes, and 70½ dozen decanters. The last, as I interpret the entries, were of three species — blanks, cut glass, and blown-three-mold.

Of the two tierces of blanks sent on January 3 for a Mr. Tingh, one contained 25

FIG. 5 — CLEAR WINE GLASS with drawn bowl and stem, one of the commonest forms, and probably that of the taper wines entered on line 5, column 2 of the April invoice (*Fig. 3*), and line 24, column 1 of that of May 2 (*Fig. 4*).

FIG. 6 — CHAMPAGNE GLASS (*early nineteenth century*). So-called French flute (shape) with simple flute cutting around the lower half of the bowl. Possibly the form, and decoration of the New England Glass Company's "Fluted champaigns," line 10, Figure 1.

FIG. 7 — BLOWN-THREE-MOLD TUMBLERS in the arch patterns (McK. G.IV-2 and G.IV-3) which might be described as flute and tree. That having the single motif springing from the spandrels of the Roman arches of G.IV-2 is perhaps the more tree-like so more likely to exemplify the "flute and tree" of the tumblers entered on line 21, column 3, Figure 4 than the one having two sprig-like motifs from the spandrels of the Gothic arches of G.IV-3. *Collection of George S. McKearin.*

quart and 20 pint decanters "for cutting" (*L.8, 9, Fig. 2*). Blanks, heavy free-blown forms usually of the finest quality of lead glass, were to the glasscutter as sheets of silver to the silversmith, a raw material and the medium for displaying his art and skill. As a rule they sold by the pound, not by the dozen as did the tumblers. And, as a comparison of prices shows, they were far more costly than finished molded glass. Even at the average weight of nearly 2¾ pounds one of these American-made decanter blanks cost nearly twice as much as a pair of molded quart decanters. Undoubtedly foreign rather than domestic imports were the most favored blanks with Mr. Tingh as with the majority of our independent glasscutters and firms prior to 1824. That year marked the passage of a truly protective tariff which included the imposition of a duty of 2¢ a pound plus 30 per cent ad valorem upon the glass including blanks. The American System began to function and the New England Glass Company as well as other producers of fine glass got a nice slice of the melon.

The Company's own cut-glass wares would have shown the influence of currently fashionable European styles — if it wished to sell them. Among them were designs of simple flute cutting. In one of the May consignments there were three pairs of pint *fluted* decanters at 84¢ a pair (*L.13, C.1, Fig. 4*); in that of April 18, three of pint *flute and flute* at 1.50 a pair, (*L.8, C.1, Fig. 3*); and in the September 13, three of quart *flute and flute* at 12/ ($2.00) a pair, (*L.4, Fig. 1*). The exact form of the flutes is a matter of surmise. But judging from known examples of the period, one might assume that the *fluted* had merely a band around the lower part of the body. A simple and not expensive cutting seems indicated by the price which was much lower than that of the pint *flute and flute* decanters. The latter doubtless had two bands, probably one around the lower part of the body and one running from the shoulder to the base of or into the neck. There may have been only one type of flute motif, as on the decanter in Figure 2; or two types, for example, a narrow shallow flute at the bottom and a broad tapering one at the top.

Whereas, even at wholesale, the presumably cut decanters were sold by pairs, the much cheaper — about 30¢ a pair — molded decanters sold by the dozen, and, as would be expected, in much larger quantities. The invoices included 65 ⅔ dozen molded quart decanters at 1.75 a dozen which, I believe, belonged in what we call today the blown-three-mold category. In the first place the full-size piece mold was used almost universally for both shape

and pattern at this period. In the second, the Company's descriptive *Arch flute*, *Arch*, *Gothic Arch*, and *Cornucopia* immediately call to mind recorded blown-three-mold patterns, not one of which has been associated heretofore with any specific glasshouse.

The first three would fall in the *arch* group. As pattern G.IV-5 (*Fig. 9*), has an arch over a broad pillar flute or rib, need we look further for the design of the 2 dozen quart molded *Arch flute* decanters of the April shipment (*L.22, C.1, Fig. 3*). At present I have a record of only two molds in this pattern, each of three pieces, one for a quart and one for a pint decanter. Though it is quite possible that the 2 dozen quart *Arch* decanters (*L.15, C.1, Fig. 4*) were in an unfamiliar pattern I suspect they were molded in G. IV-5 and "flute" was omitted because of cramped space. The 20 dozen quart molded *Gothic Arch* decanters, (*L.18, 19, 28, C.3, Fig. 4*), I believe, were in the pattern G. IV-6 like the pitcher in Figure 10. A three-piece mold in each of three decanter sizes — quart, pint, and half-pint — has been determined in this blown-three-mold pattern. Incidentally, neither Mrs. Watkins nor I found any pieces in either of these *arch* patterns among the Sandwich fragments we examined. Nor does Mrs. Lee mention having identified any.

This is true also of the decanters in the so-called *horn o' plenty* pattern (*Fig. 11*). It seems far more than a possibility that this *baroque* pattern G. V-17, of which only one mold has as yet been determined, was the *Cornucopia* of the New England Glass Company. That it was popular, perhaps a new design, is attested by the 41¼ dozen sent to Baltimore — 2 dozen (*L.25, C.1, Fig. 3*) in the lost April shipment and the others in May (*L.16, C.1; L.23, 24, C.2; L.3, 20, 27, C.3; Fig. 4*).

In the September 13 lot of glassware were "3 Pt Dble flute carofts" with "cut rings" (neck rings or collars) at 3.50 a pair (*L.5, Fig. 1*). Caroft, without doubt, was a corruption of carafe, still in 1829 a very young English word for water bottle. Its liquid capacity and, surely, a wider neck were probably the features distinguishing this member of the bottle family from normal decanters. Apparently these items went in pairs even though not intended for wine or spirits. It is possible that *double flute*, because of the short entry line, was a contraction of *flute and flute*. Quite likely it meant two bands as on the decanter in Figure 8. At any rate it may be assumed that the carofts were free-blown and wheel cut, because of their price, the phrase "Dble flute," and because of their cut rings.

"Jug" rarely calls up any image other than that of a bottle-like vessel with a very short narrow neck with or without a flange and pouring lip, and a small handle. Merely by widening the neck, flaring a rim, forming a lip, and perhaps enlarging the handle a bit, a jug could be transformed into a "pitcher." Perhaps some such evolution, plus the fact that most molded pitchers prior to mechanical pressing were patterned in bottle or decanter molds, explains in part the persistence of the old name though, except in Britain where jug is still in common usage, it was used here from the 1830's on about as seldom as pitcher was in the eighteenth. During that period, when tea with cream was a dictate of fashion, the small vessels for serving cream were called cream jugs no matter from what substance they were made. Even Steigel listed cream jugs and cream pots among his products. In these invoices the old-fashioned "jug" was used for large pitchers, the nineteenth-century "creams" for the half-pint size.

Surprisingly, jugs and creams far outnumber the decanters. In the total of about 120 dozen, three methods of fabrication were represented: free-blown, molded, and mechanically pressed. Of the free-blown there were 6 "Qt. Jugs for Cutting" averaging 1.10 each (*L.4, Fig. 2*) and, presumably, the 4¾ dozen quart plain heavy jugs at 37½¢ each (*L.25, 26, C.3, Fig. 4*). Except for the pressed creams the remainder was the cheaper molded glass. The half-pint molded creams at 1.00 a dozen — 15 dozen on the April invoice (*L.16, C.1, Fig. 3*) and on the May, 56 2/12 dozen (*L.2, C.1; L.10, C.2; L.13, C.3, Fig. 4*) — might have been pattern-molded. But it is more likely they were blown in a full-size piece mold since that method required less hand work.

Evidently pitchers as well as decanters were popular in the *arch* patterns already discussed in connection with the decanters. And doubtless, as was customary, they were patterned in the same molds. Although I have never seen a pitcher of any size in G.IV-5 (*Fig. 9*), I have expected to do so. For in my experience, decanters and pitchers in the same blown-three-mold patterns are as inevitable as death and taxes. There were 10 dozen quart and 10 dozen three-pint *Gothic Arch* pitchers (*Fig. 10*) on the May invoice (*L.4, 5, 22, 23, 24, C.3, Fig. 4*); 8½ dozen *Arch flute* on that of April 18 (*L.22, 23, 26, C.1, Fig. 3*); 10½ dozen *Arch* on that of May 2 (*L.7, 8, C.2, Fig. 4*). That these pitchers should cost 25¢ each and their decanter companions in pattern about 15¢ is quite understandable, a matter of time and labor. To finish a decanter blown in a full-size mold required only forming a flange and, after annealing, fitting a stopper which, no matter how it was formed, cost little. That of a pitcher necessitated widening the neck, forming rim and lip, attaching and forming a handle, operations not only involving more manipulation but three or more re-heatings at the furnace to maintain the metal's plastic state.

Molded hats at 42¢ a dozen, 3½¢ apiece, were more numerous than any other article except the pint flasks. In the April shipments there were 49½ dozen molded hats (*L.17, C.1, Fig. 3*); in the May 99½ dozen of unidentified color, 50 dozen blue, and 50 dozen white (*L.1, C.1; L.9, C.2; L.14, 9, 15, C.3, Fig. 4*). It is safe to assume that those without color designation were clear glass. But while white in a glassman's language often meant colorless, Mrs. Watkins states in *Cambridge Glass* that when used by the New England Glass Company it invariably meant milk-white glass. The period was one, of course, when fine quality milk-white glass was being produced almost everywhere. As to the design, one cannot go beyond the assumption that, like the known blown-three-mold hats of the period, they resembled the popular beaver hat. It is probable too that they were blown in full-size three-piece molds.

Other molded articles on the April and May invoices which probably would fall in the blown-three-mold category were peppers and castor bottles — 12 dozen peppers at 5/3 a dozen (*L.3, C.1, Fig. 3; L.10, C.1, Fig. 4*); and 3 dozen old molded castor bottles at 75¢ a dozen (*L. 25, C.1, Fig. 4*). While "old molded" may be open to more than one interpretation, my own guess is that it referred to discontinued patterns, especially as at least 46 patterns in 75 different molds are known today. It is of interest that the glass manufacturers supplied the castors for the bottles. In the May consignments there were a few 4- and 5-hole japanned castors and 4-hole plated (probably silver) castors (*L.14–16, C.2, Fig. 4*).

The indisputable evidence that early pressed 5″ and 6″ plates and 3″ and 3½″ cup plates were produced by the New England Glass Company is most gratifying to those of us who for years have maintained stoutly that they just *must* have been. In the April shipment were 3 dozen 3″ cup plates at 3/ a dozen (*L.9, C.2, Fig. 3*), and 3 dozen 3½″ at 3/9 a dozen (*L.10, C.2, Fig. 3*). They were duplicated in one of the May consignments (*L.2, 3, C.2, Fig. 4*). The May shipment carried also the 5″ and 6″, second quality, pressed plates, 20 dozen of each (*L.8, 16, C.3, Fig. 4*) at 1.50 a dozen — or 12½¢ apiece. The factory prices were surprising to me — a second quality 6″ pressed plate only about 3¢ less than a quart molded decanter, a 3½″ cup plate more than a molded hat! But then, pressed glass was still "new" in 1829 and molds for it were intricate and expensive as compared with piece and dip molds.

(*To be continued*)

Illustrations below, left to right:

Fig. 8 — Clear Glass Decanter, typical of the early nineteenth century, with simple decoration of cut flutes, possibly the type used on the New England Glass Company's flute and flute decanters or double flute carafes, line 8, column 1, Figure 3, and lines 4 and 5, Figure 1. *Collection of the Connecticut Valley Historical Society.*

Fig. 9 — Rare Quart Blown-Three-Mold Decanter in *arch* pattern (McK. G.IV-5), which, having a broad vertical rib or pillar flute under an arch, easily fits the New England Glass Company's descriptive "Arch flute" of the decanters and pitchers of the April invoice (*Fig. 3*), and probably also those of the May consignments described as "Arch" (*Fig. 4*). Heretofore there has never been any kind of evidence for even a tentative attribution to any glasshouse. *Collection of George S. McKearin.*

Fig. 10   Blown-Three-Mold Pitcher in *arch* pattern (McK. G.IV-6), probably the pattern in which the "Gothic Arch" pitchers and decanters of the May shipment (*Fig. 4*) were molded. The only articles recorded in this pattern to date are the scarce pitchers and decanters which were molded in the same three molds of quart, pint, and half-pint sizes. The three-pint pitchers undoubtedly were patterned in the quart decanter mold. Until now there has been no inkling as to their possible source. *Collection of George S. McKearin.*

Fig. 11 — Blown-Three-Mold Quart Decanter in the *baroque*, so-called *horn o' plenty* pattern (McK. G.V-17), with original stopper. Probably the *Cornucopia* of the New England Glass Company's decanters (*Fig. 4*). As in the case of the *arch* patterns G.V-17 has never been associated with any glasshouse. *Collection of G. S. McKearin.*

NEW ENGLAND GLASS COMPANY INVOICES

Part II

By

HELEN McKEARIN

THE DISCOVERY *by Richard Wood of Baltimore of several invoices of the New England Glass Company dated in 1828 and 1829 has furnished new and important documentary material regarding the products of this firm. The documents themselves were illustrated through the courtesy of the Maryland Historical Society in Part I of this article, which appeared in September 1947. There the author discussed the drinking vessels, jugs, pitchers, decanters, hats, peppers, castor bottles, and cup plates listed in the bills. Her analysis is continued here, and will be completed in our December issue. References to the bills are given here by date, and, as in Part I, L. means Line, C. means Column. The view on this page is a detail taken from a view reproduced on the invoices discussed here.* — THE EDITOR

A SIGNIFICANT CONTRIBUTION made to the history of American glass by these New England Glass Company invoices is that they bear witness to the fact that the Company was well launched in the field of mechanical pressing before 1830. I know of no earlier documentary, specific evidence of the long-accepted conclusion that many articles besides knobs and salts were pressed at Cambridge before that date. Plates of cupplate size and of five-inch and six-inch diameter have been mentioned in Part I. We now turn to other articles in this category, even more exciting, particularly sugar bowls and creamers. Unfortunately there is no clue as to the shape and decorative patterns of the pressed creams at 4.50 a dozen and sugars at 6.00 a dozen, both second quality (*L. 7, 6, C. 3, May 2*). However, Mrs. Watkins believes, and many of us will agree with her, that there is a strong possibility they were similar to, if not exactly like, the very early pressed examples in Figures 1 and 2. One would expect 1829 designs to be simple, and the forms to be reminiscent of other bowls of the period and also to lend themselves readily to mechanical pressing.

The April 18 shipment contained one dozen "new molded" sugars (*L. 11, C. 2*). "New molded" is a somewhat puzzling phrase open to many interpretations, such as new pattern, new method, or both. Since the presumably blown-three-mold quart pitchers were 3.00 a dozen and as, I figure, the time and labor needed for fashioning a cover would not double the expense of production,

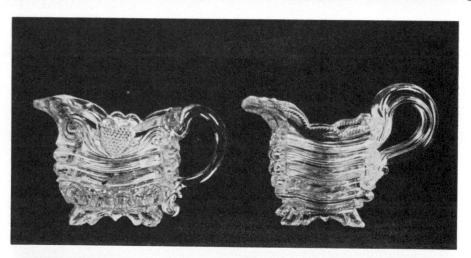

FIG. 1 — (*two views of each*) TWO EXTREMELY RARE and early creamers pressed in simple designs and forms reminiscent of many Staffordshire creamers of the 1820's. Unusual applied handles formed by free-blown techniques. While there is no way of knowing what the creams entered on line 7, column 3 of the May invoice (*Fig. 4, Part I*) may have been like, it is far from impossible that they were similar to these. In fact it is probable. The heart on the creamer at the left is a pressed-glass motif long associated with the New England Glass Company and one of the designs mentioned in the 1826 patent for pressing knobs. *Collection of Lura Woodside Watkins.*

FIG. 2 — *(two views)* EXTREMELY RARE and early pressed sugar bowl. The bold, simple, but effective design is similar to those of the creams in Figure 1, probably typical of such pieces made by mechanical pressing prior to 1830. The shape carries on a popular rectangular Staffordshire form and is similar to that of the heavy bowl blown-molded in the earlier 1820's, presumably by the New England Glass Company (*see* ANTIQUES, *August 1939, page 69*). Probably the pressed creams of the May invoice and "new molded" sugars of the April and May were similar in shape and pattern, perhaps even the same. *Collection of Grace Lyman Stammers.*

it seems unlikely that these sugars were blown in full-size piece molds or, for that matter, in pattern molds. There were two outstanding "new" methods of molding at the time, mechanical pressing and pillar molding, either of which would have been more expensive than the others. Still, since these particular sugars, like those entered as pressed, were *second quality* and *6.00 a dozen* I am inclined to believe they too were pressed, not pillar molded.

Incidentally, two facts about these pressed, and presumably pressed, sugars and creams are arresting. One is the smallness of the lots; the other that they were all second quality. The implication might be that the type of ware was still in its infancy and practice had not yet made it perfect, for either or both of which reasons the public had not taken it wholeheartedly to its tables.

Another fascinating description is the "½ Doz 9 in Strawberry diamond [symbol used for diamond] fruit dishes on feet" at 15.00 a dozen (*L. 2*), on the September 1828 invoice. Obviously they were distinguished by strawberry diamonds, either in a diaper or as the pattern's dominating feature. This diamond, one of the most ubiquitous cut-glass diamond motifs of the period, was exceedingly popular with the composers of our early pressed patterns, many of which boldly aped cut glass. However, inasmuch as a quart pitcher blank was 1.10 and a B. S. bowl nearly 2.00, the price of 1.25 each for these footed dishes seems much too low for cut glass. And their price seems equally high for molded glass since a quart molded *gothic arch* pitcher could be sold for only 25¢. I think the logical conclusion is that they were pressed glass.

Equally thrilling entries were those for "Pine Apple" dishes which were made in three sizes. The 7-inch size sold at the factory price of 6.00 a dozen or 50¢ each, (*L. 2, C. 2, April* and *L. 21, C. 1, May*); the 8-inch, at 7.50 a dozen or 62½¢ apiece,) *L. 5, C. 1; L. 3, C. 2, April* and *L. 8, 22, C. 1, May*); the 9-inch, at 9.00 or 75¢ each (*L. 6, C. 1; L. 4, C. 2, April* and *L. 14, 23, C. 1, May*). The descriptive phrase "Pine Apple" may have had reference to design or function or both. The pineapple, a favorite motif of that period with artisans in many crafts, was incorporated into more than one pressed glass design. If, in this case, the words signified a design, or the characterizing motif of one, the dishes may have been the same as or

similar to that in Figure 3. And, of course, there were precedents galore for christening a dish or any vessel for something to drink or eat. The times were ripe for one to be used in serving pineapples. They were a West Indian delicacy sufficiently newsworthy to be listed among imports even when brought into the country in very small quantities. As to whether or not the method of production was pressing, even if there were no other considerations, price again seems to indicate an affirmative answer.

The "B. S." of the 12 bowls for cutting (*L. 5*) of the January 3 invoice is an intriguing abbreviation. If the article were a wine any glass student, without a second's hesitation, would say "baluster stem." Perhaps it was just that. Such compotes were made. Perhaps Mr. Tingh ordered compotes intending to embellish them with cut strawberry diamonds. Another possibility is that it stood for "Big Salad." Salad bowls were advertised by the New England Glass Company before 1829 and, in contemporary newspapers, they appear often in the cut-glass invoices given in auction announcements. (At this time by far the majority of advertisements of glass for sale were those of auction houses, not of manufacturers or independent merchants.) But whatever its form, the B.S. bowl was a comparatively large object; the average weight was 5¾ pounds, 2 pounds more than that of the quart jug blanks and quite a bit more than the average of the "58 Dishes for Cutting" entered on line 3 of the invoice. That there is no clue to the shape and sizes of these dishes and bowls is regrettable. Perhaps they were assorted.

Like the pitchers, the salts in these consignments presumably were free-blown, pressed, and blown-molded. The free-blown were the 24 blanks (*L. 6, Jan. 3*), remarkable for an average weight of nearly ¾ pound each and costing 35¢ apiece. The "Rose" and the price of the 6 dozen salts (*L. 4, C. 1*) of the lost April shipment, an order duplicated in that of May (*L. 11, C. 1*), leads to the inference that they probably were pressed in one of the New England Glass Company

FIG. 3 — HEAVY EARLY PRESSED GLASS dish having a pineapple motif in each corner of the base and, on the sides, a Gothic arch, another popular motif of the day of these invoices. Possibly similar in design and shape to the New England Glass Company's "Pine Apple" dishes in the April and May 1829 shipments. *Privately owned.*

276

FIG. 4 — EARLY PRESSED GLASS salt marked on the bottom in four lines *N E Glass Company Boston;* on sides, a well-modeled version of the popular basket-of-flowers motif, and on the ends, a rose from which perhaps the Rose salts in the May shipments took their name. While there are at least three other similar Basket of Flowers-Rose salts, one also marked *N E Glass Company Boston*, this rose differs widely from its fellows. *Privately owned.*

salt patterns having a rose on each end, one of which is shown in Figure 4. The inference is bolstered by the fact that, according to Joseph Howe, Jr., who became the Company's agent in 1822, pressed salts were produced in 1827. If only he had mentioned their design! In connection with these Rose salts it should be noted that they were 1.25 a dozen whereas the pillar molded salts (*L. 13, C. 2, April*) were 1.50. This is the only instance in the scale of costs in which, according to my interpretation, pressed glass was less than blown-molded.

The pillar molded salts sent in April and the molded pillared salts, in May (*L. 5, C. 2*) also at 1.50 a dozen, give rise to considerable speculation. The paramount question is whether the May lot was a replacement of the April and the words reversed in making the entry or whether two distinct types were meant. Only one thing seems absolutely certain: regardless of the method of molding, the design contained vertical ribs, or, in English-Irish terminology, pillars or pillar flutes. If molded pillared or pillar molded meant only design without reference to method there is a possibility, to my way of thinking a very, very slight one, that the salts were the same as or similar to that illustrated in ANTIQUES for August 1939 (Fig. 1, lower A, p. 68). As the method of molding this type of salt (described in the article referred to) required little, if any, more time and labor than a blown-three-mold salt, I doubt very much if it would have sold for as much as 12½¢ apiece. If a molded hat, probably blown-three-mold, was 3½¢, a salt would hardly have been more than 5¢.

If on the other hand, pillar molded was the proper phrase and can be taken literally — as I believe it can — the question as to how the salts were made is easily answered and the high price reasonable. About this time pillar molding, a method known and practiced by the Romans, was "re-discovered" by an English glassman and hailed as a great modern improvement. Two gathers of glass were used. After allowing the first to cool to a greater degree of hardness than was customary, a second was made over the first, and, while it was as hot as possible, the whole was rammed into a small fluted dip (pattern) mold. Because of this procedure pronounced ribs or pillars projected on the outside while the inside remained smooth. After the gather had been impressed a piece was fashioned by free-blown techniques.

In this case the fact that neither I nor anyone whom I have consulted has seen an identifiable pillar-molded salt fails to shake my belief that they were made at

Cambridge and some of them sent to Baltimore in April and May 1829. There are other reasons for such a conclusion besides the use of the words in the invoices and the existence of such a method. For one thing, Apsley Pellatt, who gives a lucid and detailed account of the method in his *Curiosities of Glass Making*, mentions salt cellars among the articles for which it was "used advantageously." Moreover, there is evidence that at this time there was a demand here for such wares. For instance, "half pint pillar molded tumblers," "pillar stem champaigns," and "pillar molded sets" were imported in quantities from England. Bowls, pitchers, and vases, many attributed to the Pittsburgh district, are known which have the earmarks of having been molded in this fashion. So why should not the progressive New England Glass Company have used it? Even the price might be positive evidence if the Rose salts at 1.25 a dozen were indeed pressed. Pellatt, speaking of "American pressed glass," states that while its effect was not so good as pillar molding it was less expensive. If that was true in England, it probably would also have been true at Cambridge.

Inasmuch as since November 1826 the Company had had control of the second United States patent for pressing glass knobs it would be a disappointment not to find these articles on the invoices. They are there. The knobs in Figure 5 could have been made at Cambridge; they bear the physical signs of having been pressed in the type of mold called for by the patent specifications. Apparently, if one can judge from the prices, each size of knob had its number by which it could be identified. In the April shipment there were 15 dozen #1 pressed furniture knobs at 2.25 a dozen (*L. 18, 19, C. 1*); 15 of #2 at 1.75 (*L. 20, C. 1*), and 4 of #3 at 1.25 (*L. 21, C. 1*). In May there were the same quantities of the 2.25 and 1.25 knobs but entered respectively as 2⅜ inches (*L. 11, C. 2*) and 1⅜ inches (*L. 13, C. 2*). At 1.75 there were 17 dozen 2⅛ inch knobs (*L. 12, 22, C. 2*). In addition there were a dozen 2⅜ inch and 2 dozen 2⅛ inch knobs with round spindles at 12/9 (2.13) and 9/9 (1.62½) a dozen. It might be startling to know what designs the faces of these knobs wore, if they were listed in the patent specification: ". . . circles, rings, hearts, roses, fruit, animals or any other fancy or ornamental shape that has been or may be used in brass or other ornaments . . ."

To be Concluded

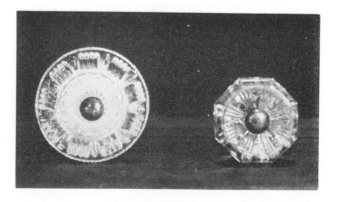

FIG. 5 — TWO GLASS furniture knobs which were pressed in a mold the same as or similar to that described in the patent of 1826 obtained by the New England Glass Company. Simple geometrical pattern. *George S. McKearin.*

NEW ENGLAND GLASS COMPANY INVOICES

Part III

By

HELEN McKEARIN

The discovery by Richard Wood of Baltimore of several invoices of the New England Glass Company dated in 1828 and 1829 has furnished new and important documentary material regarding the products of this firm. The documents themselves were illustrated through the courtesy of the Maryland Historical Society in Part I of this article, which appeared in September 1947. There the author discussed the drinking vessels, jugs, pitchers, decanters, hats, peppers, castor bottles, and cup plates listed in the bills. Her analysis was continued in October 1947 and is completed here. References to the bills are given here by date, and, as in Part I, L. means Line, C. means Column. — THE EDITOR

ONLY TWO ARTICLES remain to be considered in this final part of the discussion of the New England Glass Company documents. But these last, the lamps and enameled deep plates, are far from the least important and interesting. They are further evidence of the fact that when our tariff-sired production of fine glassware was beginning to ride the 1820's wave of industrial expansion, the company was quick to counter competition at home and from abroad and alert to the possibilities in developing new and old types.

Glass lamps which, before many decades, were to form one of the vertebrae in the backbone of the glass industry were among the "lines" steadily increasing in popularity. In the many 1827–1829 newspaper advertisements of imported or domestic lamps which I have found, glass ones — cut and plain, sometimes even painted and enameled — appeared frequently, whereas a few years earlier they seldom were included. And advertising is a fair yardstick by which to measure a growing demand. The presence

FIG. 1 — ONE OF THE earliest types of glass lamp with pressed base made by the New England Glass Company. Free-blown font, probably one styled "cylindrical" by the Company, attached by heavily ringed knop to square three-step base or foot. Quite likely the design of "3 sq foot cyl lamps plated caps," Line 1 of the September 13, 1828, invoice. *Photograph courtesy of Lura Woodside Watkins.*

in the Baltimore shipments of six, or eight, apparently distinct designs representing two methods of production, added to the evidence of its own and its agent's advertisements, testifies to the New England Glass Company's enlargement of its line of lamps.

Among the articles "lost" in April 1829 when the *Marshall Ney* of the Union Dispatch Line went aground on Handkerchief Shoal and "sunk in 6 fathom water" were six dozen "½ arch ribed" peg lamps, one half dozen "cyl" lamps with square foot and round shoulder, and two pairs of "bulb" lamps with three-square foot and brass caps (Part I, *Fig. 3, C.1, L.7; C.2, L.7 & 8, 14 & 15*). Since Parts I and II of this discussion have been written I have found that the possibility of raising the brig noted on the May invoice by the agent, Mr. Whitney, became a certainty, and also that about $1000 worth of merchandise had been washed ashore. On May 1 the brig was drawn by two schooners into Chatham harbor where she remained in five fathom of water until suitable tackle could be procured by Captain Howes whose services had been retained to raise her. Six months later she was once more plying between Boston and Baltimore. So it is not impossible that the company recovered its wares — fit for cullet if not for customers. In any event it is unlikely that the firm suffered any financial loss since there was $7000 insurance. As for Wm. E. Mayhew & Co., the consignment of lamps appears to have been replaced in the May shipment (Part I, *Fig. 4, C.1, L.12, 17, 19*).

The "½ arch ribed" immediately calls to mind a well-known dip-molded decoration of an arch, more commonly called a panel, usually formed by an almost hair-like rib. On small articles, such as peg lamps, the arch extended about halfway up the body or, in this case, the font. Many articles besides peg lamps were so ornamented. It is probable the "arch rib ⅓ pint tumblers" which were listed in an 1820 advertisement of the New England Glass Company were made by the same method and bore the same type of arch or paneled decoration as the peg lamps.

Around the other lamps itemized in the invoices of September 1828, April and May 1829, an elaborate fabric of conjecture can be woven. The entries, grouped according to foot or base, are listed and numbered for reference as follows:

No. 1 — 6 pr. 3 sqr foot cyl lamps, plated caps (Part I, Fig. 1, L.1.)	13/6	13.50
No. 2 — 2 pr. 3 sqr.foot bulb lamps, brass caps (Part I, Fig. 3, C.2, L.14 & 15; Fig. 4, C.1, L.19 & 20)	10/6	3.50
No. 3 — ½ doz. sml sqr foot cyl lamps round shoulder (Part I, Fig. 3, C.2, L.7 & 8)	4.50	2.25
No. 4 — ½ doz. sml sqr foot high cyl round shold. lamps (Part I, Fig. 4, C.1, L.17 & 18)	4.50	2.25
No. 5 — 2 pr. sml sqr foot bulb lamps and glasses (Part I, Fig. 4, C.2, L.17)	1.50	3.00
No. 6 — ½ doz. cup plate foot bulb lamps (Part I, Fig. 4, C.2, L.18)	2.25	1.12
No. 7 — 20 doz. cup plate foot cyl lamps (Part 1, Fig. 2, C.3, L.17)	1.75	35.00

In the fabrication of all these lamps it may be inferred, I believe, that the company was combining the ancient and the modern in lamps having free-blown fonts and pressed bases. Undoubtedly "cyl" and "bulb" referred to the fonts, the part of

Fig. 2 — Clear Glass Lamp with large free-blown pear-shaped font and cup-plate foot pressed in one of the sheaf-of wheat patterns. Possibly the "cup plate foot bulb lamps" in the May shipment were of this type — or of that shown in Figure 4. *From the collection of George S. McKearin.*

There are so many known different square pressed bases that it would be silly to speculate as to which one supported the fonts of Nos. 3, 4, and 5. Because the cylindrical lamps with round shoulders and square base, Nos. 3 and 4, were being sold by the dozen and at a comparatively low figure, I feel there is a strong probability that "small" modified the whole lamp as well as the base or foot. On the other hand, I have never seen or heard of one of these early lamps shorter than that shown in Figure 1 which was equipped with glasses. Therefore, though recognizing the possibility of short lamps being so fitted, I should conclude that "small" as applied to No. 5 probably referred to the foot only.

Of the dozen or more cup plates which show outward and visible signs of having been used as feet or bases, the best known is one of the common so-called sheaf-of-wheat (version of the classical palmette) patterns like that of the lamps in Figures 2, 3, 4. Tradition long ago attributed this design to the New England Glass Company; though it never, to my knowledge, has been confirmed. It is quite likely that the "cyl" lamps I have listed as No. 7, which were only 25¢ more a dozen than the peg lamps, were like that in Figure 3.

As far as description goes, the bulb cup plate foot lamps, No. 6, could have been like either Figure 2 or Figure 4. Probably either would have been about 50¢ more a dozen than the cylindrical: one has a much larger font; the other a knop stem the making of which required more metal, minutes, and movements. In the past, cup plate foot lamps have been attributed to Sandwich and to Cambridge, as was quite reasonable and logical. In my mind there is no doubt that other makers of fine wares produced them likewise. Still, insofar as I know, the only *documentary proof* of an origin is contained in the May 2, 1829, invoice of the Cambridge firm.

Two kinds of caps are mentioned, plated and brass. The plating was probably silver; the brass is news. Mrs. Watkins tells me that

the lamp which held the lighting fluid. From a rather wide survey of glass lamps and illustrations of them the opinion seems tenable that the cylindrical fonts were those with straight sides, whether vertical or tapering from a flat or slightly rounded shoulder to a narrow base as in the lamps of Figures 1 and 3; and that the bulb fonts were the various types with rounded sides such as the round or spherical font of the lamp in Figure 4, the pear-shaped in that in Figure 2, or one resembling the modern electric light bulb. All of the vertically straight-sided cylindrical fonts I have seen have been quite small. In size and oil capacity they would compare to the font in Figure 1 as the round in Figure 4 would to the pear-shaped in Figure 2. If a tall lamp was desired the height was achieved by joining the font to the base or foot by a shaft fashioned by free-blown techniques. The forming of a straight-sided font with either vertical or tapering sides would require a little more of those cost-increasing factors, time and labor, than a bulb. A bulb, after all, would be the more natural result of just inflating a gather of metal. This may account in part at least for the fact that, with the exception of the cup-plate foot bulb lamps (No. 6), the lamps with cylindrical fonts were more expensive than those with bulb fonts — 2.25 a pair for No. 1 and 75¢ for Nos. 3 and 4 as against 1.75 a pair for No. 2 and 1.50 for No. 5 which included the cost of a pair of glasses or globes. Probably a third or more of the cost of the last can be attributed to their being fitted with globes. I find no clue as to which type, or types, of "bulb" were used.

It is a fair assumption that the three types of base — three square foot, Nos. 1 and 2; (small) square foot, Nos. 3, 4, and 5; and cup plate foot, Nos. 6 and 7, — were pressed. The time and the price were right for them. As it seems likely that the mold for many of the known pressed square bases would have been neither more costly nor more complicated than that for a knob, probably lamps with such bases were made by, if not before, 1826. That was the year in which the Whitney-Robinson patent for pressing knobs was obtained. The "three square foot" doubtless was like or identical with that shown in Figure 1, a square base with three steps. In fact, lamps Nos. 1 and 2 might well have been counterparts of that shown in Figure 1, of which Lura Woodside Watkins writes, "This lamp was one of the earliest types made at Cambridge."

Fig. 3 (*below, left*) — Clear Glass Lamp with "cylindrical" free-blown font and cup-plate foot pressed in a sheaf-of-wheat pattern. Possibly the "cup plate foot cyl lamps" of the May shipment were of this type, and also fitted with the cork and tin disc burner. *This and Fig. 4, courtesy of Lura Woodside Watkins.*

Fig. 4 — Clear Glass Lamp with round spherical bulb font, applied knop stem, and pressed cup-plate foot in a sheaf-of-wheat pattern.

the general belief has been that the cork disc burner was used until about 1830, to be followed by pewter fittings. The cup plate foot lamps undoubtedly had cork disc burners like those shown in Figures 3 and 4.

The last article to titillate the glass student's imagination is the enameled deep plate. The bill of lading, dated September 19, 1829, for the tantalizingly described package of 25 dozen is shown in Figure 5. No one whom I have consulted has seen a deep plate of any kind or color with enameled decoration. Nor have I. Yet, putting together bits of information gleaned from many sources, I believe they were just that.

The period was one when many facets of fashion reflected French styles. In tablewares richly colorful and gaily bedecked china, made chiefly in France itself, was enjoying a tremendous vogue here as well as in Europe. The newspapers abounded in announcements of its arrival. Such phrases as "elegant sets of French gold band Festoon," "light blue and gold embossed," "painted and gold," and "every description of French china gold burnished and lustered" called attention to this ware which was a luxury in reach of the few. One dealer quoted dinner sets from $75 to $500. So glassmen in England, Ireland, France, and Germany, scenting profit in simulating fine china in their less costly medium, had created a line generally called enameled or porcelain ware. In England, perhaps elsewhere, it had been done before, in the mid-eighteenth century, when Chinese porcelains had captured Occidental fancy.

A large proportion of the nineteenth-century wares, as of the eighteenth, were of opaque white glass often but not always bearing enameled decoration plus gold embellishment. Included in the same category was enameled and gold-decorated clear and transparent colored glass. Mr. Frederick Carder tells me the decoration was done "in impasto or paste applied by brush or spatula and fired in the muffle." He says also that in this period "the French did some very fine work in this manner as well as two English firms." In Germany the term enameled glass seems to have been as inclusive as elsewhere, except Ireland where it was reserved for the opaque white glass with and without decoration.

If enameled glassware was made in Europe, why not in the United States? Is it improbable that an enterprising firm like the New England Glass Company should have entered the lists? While the price of $2.75 for a dozen deep plates may seem very low for a fancy glass, it must be remembered that the decoration would not have been costly since at that time women could be hired at about $1.00 a week to paint and gild glass. Moreover, two very important items of information tip the scales definitely toward an affirmative answer, in my opinion. Mrs. Watkins found an early recipe for white enamel in Thomas Leighton's recipe book of compositions used at Cambridge. And the following from the *New England Palladium* for June 23, 1829, four months before the shipment, speaks eloquently: "New Articles: The New-England Glass Company has, within a few weeks, commenced the manufacture of ENAMELLED GLASS WARE, which resembles the finest Porcelean and Pearl and, surpassing what has been done in Europe, has extended it to the making of dishes, plates, nappies, cups, saucers, jelly, custard and egg cups, salts, knobs, etc. They are most beautiful articles — attract general attention — and so strike and interest the public taste, that already large

orders have been given for them./A rich assortment may be seen at the Company's extensive Warehouse, South Row,/ Washington-street, Boston."

Perhaps a wide bias in favor of home industries led the editor of the *Palladium* to place this bit of news at the head of column one on page one of his paper but it hardly seems likely that a plain piece of transparent or opaque glass would have aroused so enthusiastic a report. (Incidentally I found not one New England Glass Company advertisement in that paper during the entire year.) Also the same item, omitting only the final sentence, was published in *The Hartford Times* for June 29. In July it appeared without the reference to the Boston warehouse, in the Baltimore *Weekly Register* of Hezekiah Niles, intensely loyal and vocal advocate of the American System. The news was obviously considered important by those interested in domestic manufactures.

Questions immediately arise as to what happened to the nappies, the salts, deep plates and the "etc." of the announcement. Perhaps the whole line was not so eagerly received by the buying public as other types which have survived in quantity, or else was so popular that constant usage has left no specimens for posterity. On the other hand, it is possible that known enameled pieces have not been recognized as belonging in this period, for instance the *Remember Me* mugs. My own experience with glass which would fall in this category is too limited for me to do more than speculate on the question. Maybe someday one of us will find and recognize a deep enameled plate. In the meantime if anyone has light to shed upon these plates or any other article listed in the invoices, let him not hide it under a bushel.

(Conclusion)

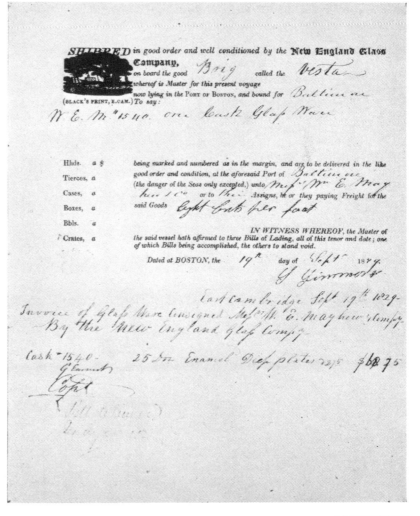

FIG. 5 — REPRODUCTION of Bill of Lading of shipment sent by the New England Glass Company to Messrs. Wm. E Mayhew & Co. of Baltimore, September 19, 1829.

448

New England Glass in Toledo

BY DOROTHY DANIEL

TO SPEAK OF THE "development" of American glass as though it were a gradual climb from primitive to aesthetic values is scarcely accurate. Glass progresses or declines in design and fabric in direct relation to the tastes, habits, and purses of the people with whom it enjoys a common environment.

This is clearly seen in the products of the New England Glass Company of Cambridge, Massachusetts, for this glass works kept close pace with the trends and tastes of American society in the nineteenth century. Some of these trends are well illustrated in a collection of Cambridge glass at the Toledo Museum of Art.

The museum was founded by Edward Drummond Libbey, who in 1888 moved the New England Glass Company from Cambridge to Toledo, Ohio, where it eventually became the Libbey Glass Division of the present-day Owens-Illinois Glass Company. On its fiftieth birthday in 1951, the Toledo Museum received as a present from the Libbey company its own collection of New England glass, along with a number of technically interesting Libbey pieces, as an addition to its permanent American glass exhibit. For the birthday celebration, Miss Nell Jaffe of the museum staff was able to augment the permanent gift with loans from the families of former New England Glass Company workmen and officials who migrated to Toledo with Edward Libbey in 1888.

From the earliest lead glass produced in Cambridge to the twentieth-century Libbey glass, each example was identified by family or company records. The pieces selected for illustration here show the scope of the New England Glass Company's output, and also reflect the times in which they were made.

Editor's Note—The New England Glass Company was founded in 1818, with Deming Jarves serving as manager until 1825. Our knowledge of the early products is scanty, based for the most part on advertisements. We do know, however, that "the company was well launched in the field of mechanical pressing before 1830" (Helen McKearin in an article on New England Glass Company Invoices, ANTIQUES, October 1947).

The cut and engraved glass was of the greatest richness and delicacy. According to Lura Woodside Watkins, author of the pioneer work on this firm, *Cambridge Glass*, the cut-glass department at one time employed as many as a hundred men. The early cutting was simple, frequently combined with engraving; later designs, in the taste of the times, covered practically the whole object. "In the closing years of the factory," Mrs. Watkins writes, "the fashion changed from heavy substantial glass to ware of almost paper-like delicacy." Colored glass was produced in a wide range of shades, with various types of art novelty wares.

The New England Glass Company maintained a consistently high standard of fine quality lead glass, even in the face of the almost overwhelming competition provided by the introduction of lime glass in 1864. The financial problems which began in the 1860's grew acute in the 1870's. In 1878 the works were leased to William L. Libbey, with his son, Edward D., as partner, the latter becoming head of the firm at his father's death in 1883. Five years later, beset by strikes and other difficulties, Libbey moved the company to Toledo, and continued the business there under the name of the Libbey Glass Company.

Summing up the company's achievements, George S. and Helen McKearin have this to say in their comprehensive volume, *American Glass:* "From the very beginning, and throughout its long career, the New England Glass Company produced glass which in quality and purity was not excelled by any other manufacturer in America, or for that matter in any country."

Pressed glass *(c. 1870). Left to right:* waffle and bull's eye compote; New England pineapple cream pitcher; Huber compote; Ashburton sugar bowl; Ashburton compote. *All except the Huber compote, from the collection of Mrs. E. M. Belknap.*

Covered urn. Gold ruby flashing over clear glass (c. 1845). Fine example of partitioned cutting. Overall height, 29¾ inches.

Milk glass (c. 1870). *Left*, covered dish, sawtooth pattern with acorn finial. *Right*, bowl, thumbprint pattern. *From the Belknap collection.*

Mid-nineteenth-century engraving. *Left*, cased glass, ruby over clear. *Right*, clear glass with stained panels.

Early decanter with panel cutting. Fine lead metal of good color. Note unusual flat rings. *From the collection of Mr. and Mrs. P. R. Hughes.*

Photographs, courtesy of the Toledo Museum of Art. Except as noted, all examples are in the Museum's permanent collection.

Tumbler engraved by Henry Fillerbrown at the New England Glass Company *(1875-1880)*.

Pressed glass salt cellars. *Right,* opalescent glass, basket of fruit on sides, rose at each end. Marked on base *N. E. Glass Company Boston. Below,* base of an example in same design in clear glass.

Clear glass decanter engraved with inscription *New England Glass Co. Boston Mass. Genl. Head Qrs.* Made for the Centennial Exhibition in Philadelphia in 1876. Probably not original stopper. Height, 10⅝ inches.

Crystal and gold ruby goblet (*probably c. 1850*). Pressed and cut.

Fig. 1. Latticinio glass. Goblets; white and clear with band of red at rim, c. 1840; height 6 inches. *Henry Ford Museum.* Decanter, white and clear, height 10 15/16 inches; and vase, white and clear with applied ruby prunt, height 8 1/4 inches. Both c. 1860-1870. *Collection of Marion H. Pike.*

The New England Glass Company:
some discoveries

BY MILLARD F. ROGERS JR., *Assistant curator, Toledo Museum of Art*

CONSIDERABLE INTEREST in American glass has been generated lately by archeological excavations of such glasshouse sites as those at Jamestown; New Bremen (Frederick), Maryland; and Glastonbury, Connecticut. However, museum exhibitions and their resultant catalogues remain invaluable tools for any study of American glass. The New England Glass Company, perhaps America's most important nineteenth-century glass factory, has been the subject of an important book by Lura W. Watkins *(Cambridge Glass 1818 to 1888)* and of many articles in ANTIQUES and other magazines, but the first major exhibition devoted to this company's glass was that held at the Toledo Museum of Art from November 8 to December 15, 1963. Two hundred and seventy-three objects chosen from over one thousand illustrating this important phase of American glass history were studied during the exhibition, and its monograph-catalogue incorporates past scholarship, recent studies, and newly discovered material.

The most impressive glass made by the company was the free-blown ware of 1818 to 1850, which was generally of clear lead metal. Until 1850, Anglo-Irish design influences were strong. Colored glass was produced in quantity as the century progressed. Cut and engraved glass was a company mainstay between 1818 and 1888, reaching its zenith from 1855 to 1860 under Louis Vaupel and Henry Fillebrown, when the Bohemian style became fashionable and wheel-engraved decoration was superlative.

Mechanically pressed glass, introduced by the ingenious Deming Jarves, had a revolutionary effect on the market and on glassblowing operations. The company's pressed glass, which ranged from early lacy products to Victorian pattern glass, shows an especially conservative choice of design motifs. It is thought that mold-blown ware, intended as an imitation of cut glass, was never produced here in great quantity although several articles in this technique have been attributed.

New England Glass Company lamps, pattern glass, and paperweights had not been surveyed thoroughly until this recent study accumulated new evidence on the company's activity in these fields. Two other areas of importance received special study as well: glass formulas used by the company, and examples of marked glass indicating company provenance. The *Journal* of Thomas Gaffield, an important Boston diarist of the New England glass industry, also yielded many interesting items about the company (the four volumes of this *Journal*, covering the years from 1858 to 1894, are now in the library of the Massachusetts Institute of Technology).

Such an exhibition and study could not fail to provide discoveries and interesting reappraisals. Those that are perhaps most meaningful are included in the following discussion.

Latticinio glass (Fig. 1). The quality of the New England Glass Company's rare latticinio glass is excellent, and it has a sophistication not often seen in nineteenth-century American glass. It is not known whether the company workers acquired this technique by contact with Venetian glassmen or whether it came to Massachusetts from England, where it had been known for some time. Apparently this "filigree" glass was not produced in any quantity, nor was it ever marketed.

Ruby and Bohemian-style glass (Figs. 2, 3). What John Leighton called a "simple solution of gold" gave the company's ruby glass its color. The earliest formula for it in the Leighton recipe books is dated about 1848, but it is known that the company made it practically throughout its entire existence. Gaffield saw "ruby ware" made at the factory in 1875, and a year earlier he had watched company workmen making ruby plated glass for cutting purposes.

Bohemian-style glass, which began arriving here from abroad at least by 1820, was a popular product of the company by mid-century. A writer in *Gleason's Pictorial* stated in 1852 that: "We were repeatedly struck by the fact, new to us, that most of the exquisite, highly colored and decorated glassware, which is so much admired under the name of Bohemian glass, is manufactured at these works." The writer noted, too, that the company's Bohemian glass had an orange tint in comparison with true Bohemian pieces. It often involved gold enamel decoration combined with cut designs, and this technique occasionally was used with green glass instead of ruby. The company must also have explored the less expensive staining technique, since in 1827 the Franklin Institute of Philadelphia awarded it an honorary mention for stained glass.

Flasks (Fig. 4). Several flasks, because of the letters impressed in their sides, are identified with the New England Glass Company. The McKearins, in their book *American Glass,* tentatively attributed the flasks illustrated here and one more, Masonic flask GIV-15,

which is marked N. G. Co., to the Marlboro Street glass-house in Keene, New Hampshire, but added that GIV-27 might have been made there for the New England Glass Company. It is here suggested that the marks on all four of these refer to the New England Glass Company and that they were all made by the company or by the New England Bottle Glass Company, also of East Cambridge, which was organized in 1826 by Deming Jarves and Edmund Monroe for the sole purpose of making bottles. This latter company ceased operations in 1845; a price list dated November 1, 1829, listed "flask bottles" in half-pint, pint, and quart sizes in "black and green ware." The New England Glass Company listed "oval black flasks" and "oval green flasks" on an invoice. It should be noted that in neither instance is there any proof that the seller was also the manufacturer of these flasks.

Astral lamps (Figs. 5-7). Astral lamps of classical design made by the New England Glass Company are among the few objects marked with the company's initials and business location: N. E. GLASS Co./BOSTON. Lamp shades for this type of lighting device were advertised on January 15, 1825, in the *Boston Evening Gazette.* When the company began blowing astral lamp stems is not known. Those in black glass are simply tooled in baluster shape, and some stems in clear glass were cut in broad fluted and faceted patterns. An interesting variation of the black-stem astral lamp is a composite of an astral lamp stem (about 1825-1850) with a kerosene font which must have been made about 1865, after kerosene became popular as a lighting fuel. The metal fittings for the astral lamps probably were made in the company's trimming shop, where, in 1855, fifty men were employed.

Fig. 2. Ruby glass. Vase in so-called Chinese form, c. 1865; height 11 15/16 inches. *Brooklyn Museum.* Vase on clear foot, c. 1865; height 13 1/4 inches. *Collection of Dorothy-Lee Jones.*

Fig. 3. Bohemian-style ruby glass cased with clear; gold decoration. Three-piece toilet set; height of bottles, 9 3/4 inches. C. 1860-1870. *Pike collection.*

Fig. 4. Flasks. McKearin GIV-26: Masonic flask, half-pint size; marked NEG. *Collection of Charles B. Gardner.* McKearin GIV-27: Masonic flask, pint size; marked NEG/Co. *Gardner collection.* McKearin GII-77: concentric ring eagle flask, quart size; marked NG/Co. *Collection of George Austin.*

Fig. 5. Astral lamp, height 16⅝ inches; c. 1825-1850. Marked on metal plate near burner N.E. GLASS Co./BOSTON. *Collection of William J. Elsholz.*

Fig. 6. Pair of blown, pressed, and cut lamps, c. 1825-1850; height 16⅝ inches. *Jones collection.*

Fig. 7. Lamp with blown, clear and frosted shade engraved in grape design; height 18⅝ inches; c. 1865. *Collection of Dorothy Donovan Farrell.*

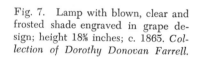

Fig. 8. Three-piece toilet set made for Eliza Leighton, wife of Thomas Leighton Jr. Opaque white glass with transfer printing and gold enamel decoration; c. 1860-1870. Height of bottles, 9¾ inches; of jar, 4 inches. Each piece inscribed *Eliza* in gold. *Collection of Mr. and Mrs. Stephen H. Sampson.*

Decoration (Fig. 8). Enameling, painting, and transfer-printing with decalcomanias on glass were company decorating techniques at various times during its seventy-year existence. As early as June 23, 1829, according to an advertisement in the *New England Palladium* noted by Helen McKearin (ANTIQUES, December 1947, p. 448) enameled glassware resembling porcelain was offered for sale by the company. Hand-painted decoration is common on company glass, usually on opaque white examples.

The most interesting new discovery regarding decorated glass was found in the Gaffield *Journal*, where it is recorded by the diarist that when he visited the company on March 17, 1873, to see William L. Libbey, the agent, he saw "nice painting on lamp shades . . . transferred." Bound into this *Journal* are two examples of paper transfers of birds, probably samples given to Gaffield by Libbey during this meeting. Gaffield also saw artists painting directly on glass.

1876 Centennial glass (Figs. 9, 10). The New England Glass Company first sponsored an exhibition of its products at a world's fair at New York City in 1853, a fair patterned after the Great Exhibition of 1851 at the Crystal Palace in London. At the 1876 Centennial Exposition in Philadelphia the company was one of forty-five entrants representing the manufacture of glass; it was awarded an honorary mention for its fluted tableware and decorative pieces. Photographs record sections of the company's lavish array of goblets, decanters, epergnes, and chandeliers elaborately cut and decorated. Thomas Gaffield learned from William L. Libbey (*Journal*, June 19, 1875) that the large and impressive display was suggested by the glass cutters themselves: "It seems that the idea of a display arose in the minds of some English workmen in the cutting shop, a committee of whom waited upon Mr. Libbey only a few days before the 17th and told him that in trade processions in London, they had seen the finest show made by the glassworkers, and they guaranteed a similar success here." The men worked night and day building a furnace on wheels to be drawn by horses in a parade opening the exposition; glass was actually blown during the parade's progress.

Volume III of Gaffield's *Scrapbook* gives a detailed description of the company's glass displayed in the Centennial Exposition, a valuable record of company design and decoration at this date.

Art glass (Fig. 11). The popular glass associated with the company in its last years was art glass of exotic and ornamental nature (see ANTIQUES, June 1964, p. 671). Amberina, Agata, Pomona, Wild Rose, and Maize art glass were all made in the five-year period between 1883 and 1888, and several patents testify to the company's need for legal control of these products. The observant Thomas Gaffield wrote in his *Journal*, July 20, 1883, that the "new" art glass, Amberina, already enjoyed a large sale; it was not patented, however, until July 24, 1883, when its inventor, Joseph Locke, assigned it to William L. and Edward Drummond Libbey.

After William L. Libbey died, his son operated the business. Art glass production continued. Edward Drummond Libbey showed Gaffield, according to the *Journal* entry of January 7, 1884, new types of colored and etched glass to be marketed soon. In spite of Gaffield's concluding note, "The Amberina has had quite a successful run," the company lost between five and six thousand dollars in 1883 because the works were closed in deference to a ruling of the Glass Manufacturers Association after the market became glutted.

Because of the amount of Amberina in private and public collections, and because it was produced at least a year before other types of company art glass, it is better known than the other art glass objects attributed to the New England Glass Company.

In an undated entry in Gaffield's second *Journal*, about 1864-1874, he records a visit to the company where he saw mechanical etching and cutting operations. This etched glass was the immediate forebear of Pomona, first produced in 1885. Gaffield records a day at the company, February 23, 1885, as follows: "We saw in the decorating rooms a new kind of glass, called Cremona [sic] glass. It is etched by acid and the upper portions stained so as to give a gilt and an iridescent effect also. The glass has not yet been introduced into the market and will not until Mr. Libbey has manufactured a considerable amount of stock to meet the first demand." In a later entry Gaffield noted that this glass was properly called Pomona.

Fig. 9. Goblet cut in hobnail-diamond pattern, c. 1876; height 6¼ inches. *Brooklyn Museum.*

Fig. 10. Wineglass, c. 1876; height 4 7/16 inches. Engraved on bowl *New Engld. / Glass Co. / Boston,* and *Mass. Centl. / Head Qrs. Corning Museum of Glass.* Decanter, c. 1876; height 10 5/8 inches. Engraved *New Engld./Glass Co./ Boston,* with *Mass. Centl. / Head Qrs.* on reverse. *Toledo Museum of Art.*

Fig. 11. Amberina, c. 1883-1888. Mug cut in Russian pattern, height 5 11/16 inches. *Toledo Museum of Art.* Twenty-six rib pattern-molded decanter, height 9 7/8 inches. *Corning Museum of Glass.* Pattern-molded jar with cover, diamond pattern; height 8 1/8 inches. *Metropolitan Museum of Art.*

New England Glass Company marks

BY MILLARD F. ROGERS JR., *Assistant curator, Toledo Museum of Art*

THE NEW ENGLAND GLASS COMPANY of East Cambridge, Massachusetts, founded in 1818 and a prominent American factory for the next seventy years, marked its glass in several ways: by cutting, engraving, metal stamping, etching, and molding, and by affixing printed labels to bases. At least eighteen different company marks came to light in an exhibition of products made by the New England Glass Company held at the Toledo Museum of Art in 1963. In addition, there are a number of presentation pieces directly associated with the firm by engraved inscriptions that do not, however, include the company's title or an abbreviation of it. A large presentation goblet made for Thomas Leighton on the occasion of his retirement from the company was the superlative in this class. Its inscription did not identify the firm by name or initials; instead, the silhouette of the factory complex on the Charles River in East Cambridge was depicted on one side, and on the other was an engraved tribute: *Thomas Leighton/east Cambridge/August 1843/—a token of great remembrance.* Unfortunately, this rare object has disappeared; it was last shown in 1935 at the Fourth Exhibition of the National Early American Glass Club, when it was owned by Mary Leighton.

While eighteen New England Glass Company marks on glass are now known, some have never before been recorded, and few were listed in Lura Woodside Watkins' definitive history of the company (*Cambridge Glass*, Boston, 1930). Practically the entire seventy-year span of production at East Cambridge is represented by these marks. The earliest was applied about 1825; the latest identified certain art-glass creations of about 1887. There appears to have been no particular reason for marking some pieces and not others. Items produced in quantity, such as pressed saltcellars, were marked, as well as astral lamps, which are quite rare today. Some positive dating of marks may be made by means of actual dates incorporated in the mark itself, and other dates are based on stylistic analysis of the marked object.

The New England Glass Company's cutting and engraving reached its zenith in its display at the Philadelphia Centennial Exposition of 1876; a spectator there, Thomas Gaffield, recorded that most of the glass it showed belonged in one or both of these categories. This decanter and goblet were part of a set made specifically for the exposition. *New Engl^d/Glass C^o./Boston* is engraved in script on one side of each piece, and on the reverse is inscribed *Mass. Cent^l./Head Q^{rs}*. See Millard F. Rogers Jr., *The New England Glass Company 1818-1888*, catalogue of the Toledo Museum of Art 1963 exhibition: Nos. 62, 63.

The following marks were used by
the New England Glass Company
between 1818 and 1888:

1. NEG/C° in serif letters in relief within beaded oval. Illus. A, detail of mold-blown flask, c. 1826-1850. Height of letters, ⅜ inch (9 mm.); George and Helen McKearin, *American Glass* (New York, 1948), pp. 556-557, GIV-27, and Rogers, No. 79. Any bottles marketed by the New England Glass Company probably were manufactured by the New England Glass Bottle Company in East Cambridge, a firm incorporated on February 15, 1826, by Deming Jarves and Edmund Monroe, and operated until 1845. Only this one flask exactly abbreviates the parent company's title, avoiding the contraction of the name appearing on other flasks (on most specimens the o is almost indiscernible). According to McKearin, fragments were found by Harry Hall White at the site of the Marlboro Street Glass Works in Keene, New Hampshire. As the New England Glass Bottle Company was closed after 1845, perhaps the Keene factory made such marked containers to fill flask requirements for the New England Glass Company between 1845 and 1850, when it too went out of business.

2. NEG in serif letters in relief. Illus. B, from a mold-blown flask, c. 1826-1850. Height of letters, ⅜ inch (9 mm.); McKearin, pp. 556-557, GIV-26, and Rogers, No. 78. Masonic and American eagle motifs appear on three of the flasks marked with company letters. Flasks with this mark may have been made by either the New England Glass Bottle Company or the Marlboro Street Glass Works.

3. N.G. C°. in serif letters in relief. Illus. C, detail of mold-blown flask, c. 1826-1850. Height of letters, ½ inch (13 mm.); McKearin, pp. 554-555, GIV-15. "Flask bottles" in "black and green ware" were made by the New England Glass Bottle Company in half-pint, pint, and quart sizes. The firm for which these bottles presumably were made, the New England Glass Company, listed "oval black flasks" and "oval green flasks" on an invoice, and these entries may refer to such marked bottles. An invoice, however, records only the shipper—not the manufacturer.

4. NG/C°. in serif letters in relief. Illus. D, detail of mold-blown flask, c. 1826-1850. Height of letters, ⅝ inch (16 mm.); McKearin, pp. 548-549, GII-77, and Rogers, No. 80. A rare quart flask with concentric-ring ribbing, bearing the abbreviation here associated with the company, which may have been made at the Marlboro Street Glass Works.

5. N.E./GLASS/COMPANY/BOSTON in serif letters raised in relief, within inverted-keyhole cartouche. Illus. E, pressed glass saltcellar, c. 1825-1850. Height of cartouche, 1 3/16 inches (3 cm.). Rogers, No. 118; and L. W. and D. B. Neal, *Pressed Glass Salt Dishes of the Lacy Period, 1825-1850* (Philadelphia, 1962), NE 3; see NE 1, NE 2, and NE 4 for variations. The most common company mark, this is frequently encountered on clear glass salts though opalescent and opaque-white examples are also marked in this way. Generally the keyhole cartouche is surrounded by a garland of flowers, but on this scarce salt (NE 3) the garland is missing. The word *Boston* appears on other objects as well as the salts but these are of slightly later date.

6. NE/GLASS/COMPANY/BOSTON in serif letters raised in relief, within inverted-keyhole cartouche surrounded by garlands. On pressed saltcellar, c. 1825-1850. Height of cartouche, 1 3/16 inches (3 cm.); *cf.* Neal, NE 1a. (Not illustrated.) This pressed mark, perhaps the earliest one employed by the company, is rare. It duplicates the mark on other saltcellars, except for the periods after the N and E. It may be a poor or late pressing from the same mold. There were examples in the George McKearin and Louis Lyons collections, according to L. W. Neal. Mr. McKearin felt that his salt was a good pressing and had never had periods on the die.

7. N. E. GLASS CO/BOSTON. in serif letters stamped in relief on metal plate. Illus. F, detail of lamp fixture, c. 1825-1850. Height of plate, 3/8 inch (9 mm.), length 7/8 inch (2.2 cm.); Rogers, No. 196. Small metal plates carrying this mark were attached to tubular fixtures just below the fuel reservoir of Argand lamps. Such a large factory as the New England Glass Company had several non-glassmaking operations subsidiary to the manufacturing and marketing of glass; its own metal and trimming shop probably made these plates.

8. N.E.G.Co/E.R:S.R. in serif letters in relief. Illus. G, on pressed opaque white glass lamp base, c. 1825-1845. Diameter 7/8 inch (2.3 cm.); Rogers, No. 104. Certain whale-oil lamps with pressed square plinths decorated with lions' heads and flower baskets are attributed to the company's great competitor, the Boston and Sandwich Glass Company, when they do not carry this mark. The mark is pressed within a circular depression located inside the hollow plinth. Clear glass, light blue, and opalescent white lamps are known in this pattern. Half of the enigmatic second line of the mark may represent the initials of Enoch Robinson, the company employee who secured a patent for pressed-glass knobs in 1826.

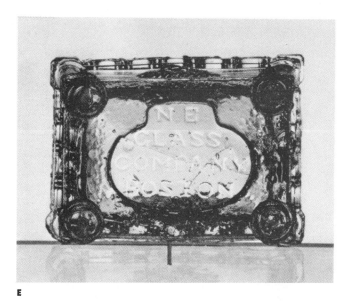

E

F

G

9. NEG Cᵒ. in serif letters. Illus. H, from glass plug in base of "mercury glass" vase; c. 1850-1860. Diameter 15/16 inch (2.4 cm.); Rogers, No. 28. Small glass vessels lined with silver nitrate had clear, circular plugs in the base marked on the reverse in the glass, or on a piece of metal or foil which was then applied to the plug. The company first exhibited silver, or mercury, glass in 1850 at the Twentieth Exhibition of the Franklin Institute, Philadelphia. Glass plugs for silvered objects were carefully ground to fit the opening in the base. Base and plug were numbered with a diamond point to avoid confusion during assembly operations.

10. PATENT APPLIED FOR N. E. GLASS CO. in serif letters. Illus. I, stamped in crescent on base of railroad lantern, c. 1854. Height of letters, 1/8 inch (3 mm.); Rogers, No. 201. Railroad lanterns were produced by the company in 1854 and later. The locking bases for these were first produced about 1854, the date of their patent, but this rare mark on the underside of the base indicates a production date prior to the granting of the patent. Lantern assemblies may have been made in East Cambridge, in the company's own metal shop.

11. N.E. GLASS CO. PATENTED OCT. 24. 1854 stamped in serif letters. Illus. J, from base of railroad lantern; 1854. Height of letters, 1/8 inch (3 mm.); Rogers, No. 202. The date refers to the official recorded date of the patent for the snap base of these lanterns. Occasionally a lantern bears the railroad's initials cut into its glass globe.

12. N.E. GLASS CO. in serif letters. Stamped in crescent on base of railroad lantern; c. 1854. Height of letters, 1/8 inch (3 mm.). (Not illustrated.) This mark occurs on the base of a railroad lantern at the Henry Ford Museum. It bears no patent date but is otherwise similar to the more complete marks on other lanterns. Cornucopia, circle, and five-pointed star motifs pierced in the metal of this lantern and in others without marks suggest that the company's metal shop produced lanterns for other firms. All marked New England Glass Company lanterns I have seen have cornucopias only on the top assembly.

13. N.E. GLASS CO. PATENT OCT. 24, 1854 EXTENDED OCT. 24, 1868. in serif letters. Stamped in crescent on base of railroad lantern; c. 1868. Height of letters, 1/8 inch (3 mm.). (Not illustrated.) This mark occurs on a lantern in the Walter Simmons collection. The success of the patented snap base on railroad lanterns produced by the company no doubt warranted the extended patent protection.

14. N.E. GLASS Cᵒ. PATENTED JAN. 16, 1855 in serif letters. Stamped or engraved on pewter shank of mercury glass curtain knob; 1855. Length of inscription, 2 inches (5.1 cm.); Rogers, No. 95. (Not illustrated.) Mold-blown curtain knobs of mercury, or silver, glass were marked on the pewter shank. The patent may have been for an improvement in the molding and related to Enoch Robinson's earlier patent of 1826.

H

I

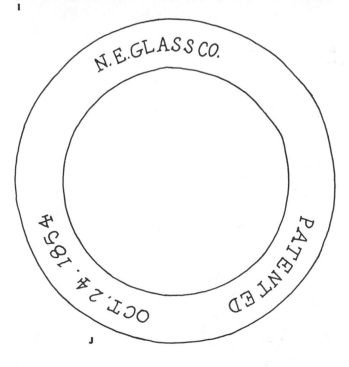

J

15. NEGW/AMBERINA/PAT^d/JULY 24, 1883. Illus. K, oval paper label, red ink on buff, on a covered jar; 1883-1888. Height of letters, ¼ inch (6 mm.), length ½ inch (1.3 cm.); Rogers, No. 255. During the company's last five years in East Cambridge, printed labels pasted to the bases and pontils of art-glass objects gave the trade name of the glass as well as that of the manufacturer. Simple and economical, this new type of mark was unfortunately subject to loss by washing. The Amberina mark used for the first time the company's changed name (New England Glass *Works*), adopted in 1880; subsequent paper labels all carried the initials NEGW. There were other patents for Amberina glass (November 13, 1883; July 29, 1884; June 15, 1886), and these may have had separate paper labels, although no examples are known.

16. NEGW/POMONA/PAT^d/APRIL 28, 1885. NEGW/POMONA/PAT^d/JUNE 15, 1886 (?). 1885-1886 (?). (Not illustrated.) The second paper label to be used on company glass was applied to the base of Pomona pieces. Although this glass did not enjoy great success during the company's history, it was produced in some quantity before formal introduction into the market. Thomas Gaffield witnessed extensive production on February 23, 1885, when he visited the factory and noted it in his diary as "Cremona." Two patents were awarded Pomona, the second referring to an easier method of decoration than the original for the amber, blue, and rose-color stained ware. The first of the two patent dates has been seen on Pomona objects (McKearin, p. 420, and R. W. Lee, *Nineteenth Century Art Glass*, p. 53), but I have not seen an example. If the second date was used on a label, it has not been recorded.

17. NEGW/WILD ROSE/PAT^d/MARCH 2, 1886, on a diamond-shape paper label, red ink on buff, 1886-1888. Height of label, ½ inch (1.2 cm.), length 1 1/16 inches (2.7 cm.); Rogers, No. 269. (Not illustrated.) This example is from a vase in the ware known today as New England Peachblow, which was patented under the name Wild Rose and produced for only two years, from 1886 to 1888. An early mention of this label occurs in a note by R. W. Lee (ANTIQUES, August 1934, p. 59) who mistakenly called it "a triangular mark." J. Stanley Brothers (ANTIQUES, April 1935, p. 129) recalled seeing "a label on the bottom of a vase, which read, *N.E.G.W./ Peach Bloom/W.L. Libbey & Son*—a mark which may well have been related to this one.

18. NEGW/AGATA/PAT^d/MARCH 2, 1886 (?), or JAN. 18, 1887 (?), on round label, printed in red ink on buff. Illus. L, label on Agata vase in the Bennington Museum; diameter of label, 7/16 inch (1.1 cm.). The latest of the four paper labels used by the company, employed only one year before it moved from East Cambridge to Toledo, captures the character of the *art nouveau* movement in the exotic type face used for the name of the ware. The date on the lower edge of the illustrated label, the only known example, is illegible except for the last two digits and the first letter of the date line. The month of March or May is indicated by the first letter of the date line, and the last two digits appear to be 86. The official patent date granted to Agata was January 18, 1887; March 2, 1886, is the patent date for the company's Wild Rose art glass. Is the date on this Agata label a printer's error?

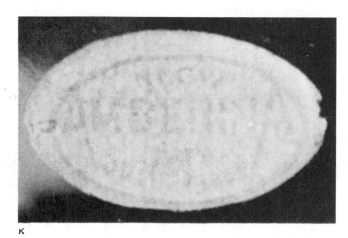

K

L

In addition to the well-authenticated marks
catalogued above at least three have appeared which
for one reason or another seem to be questionable.
All have been found on pieces acquired in the
vicinity of Newburyport, Massachusetts.
They are described and illustrated below.

M

N.E.G.CO. in serif letters engraved or stamped on brass
fixture. Illus. M, detail of lamp, c. 1865 (?). Height of
letters, 1/8 inch (3 mm.); Rogers, No. 200; No. 196 is
similar. This mark appears on the brass fixture joining
the glass stem of a lamp to its font. The tooled stem is
similar to those dating forty years earlier, yet the font
is a kerosene type, c. 1865; it may be assumed that the
lamp is a composed piece. Lamps marked with the
metal plate shown in Illus. F do not bear an additional
marking of this type, as far as is known. The mark illustrated here may be a later addition to the lamp.

N. E. GLASS CO. in sans-serif letters etched or engraved
in a rectangle. Illus. N, detail of base of cologne bottle,
c. 1865-1870 (?). Height of rectangle, 3/16 inch (5 mm.),
length 5/8 inch (1.6 cm.); Rogers, No. 210. The
cologne bottle on which this mark appears was illustrated
in an 1869 catalogue of New England Glass Company
pressed glass. This mark may be a later addition.

N

O

New England Glass Co in script, etched or engraved
within a circle. Illus. O, detail of base of overlay bowl,
possibly Czechoslovakian in origin; c. 1865-1870 (?).
Diameter of mark, 9/16 inch (1.4 cm.). This mark occurs
on the polished pontil of a few pieces attributed to the
company; there is no mention of it or of that shown in
Illus. N in the company's books or papers. The vase bearing this mark which was exhibited in the Toledo Museum
of Art show in 1963 (Rogers, No. 37) may be a modern
piece by the H. C. Fry Glass Company of Rochester, New
York.

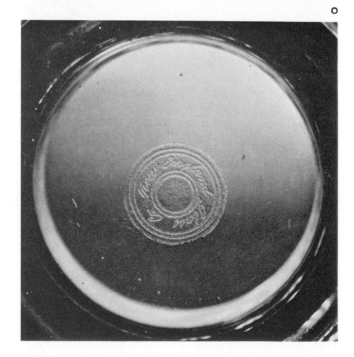

For assistance in obtaining photographs of the objects, and
for helpful suggestions, I am grateful to George Bird and
C. W. Brown of the Henry Ford Museum, Dorothy-Lee Jones,
Richard C. Barret of the Bennington Museum, Paul Perrot
and Kenneth M. Wilson of the Corning Museum of Glass,
A. Christian Revi, L. W. and D. B. Neal, and Paul V. Gardner
of the Smithsonian Institution.

GLASSMAKING IN SOUTH BOSTON

The first part of this article appeared in *Antiques* for September 1945, pages 140-142.
It covers blown wares made at South Boston.

By LURA WOODSIDE WATKINS

THE PHOENIX GLASS WORKS. Patrick F. Slane, who took over the old South Boston glasshouse in 1848, was the first lessee to establish a thriving business there. Something of his work is told in Part I of this article. Slane, William A. Hayes, and Reuben H. Ober were incorporated as the American Glass Company, April 28, 1854. After 1848 the city directories list this company's agency at 13 Doane Street, Boston; from 1854 to 1857 they were at 15 Kilby Street, and a year later back at 17 Doane. Thereafter the firm name disappears, presumably shortly after Slane went out of business. In 1880 a corner of the old Boston Glass Manufactory was still standing, but part of the land had been sold to the railroad.

The fortunes of Thomas Cains ran a smoother course than did those of other South Boston glassmakers. In 1817 he had purchased from Edmund Munroe two lots of land on B Street running down to low-water mark. He had built a house on Second Street and there he continued to live even after he had put up his brick factory in front of it (*Fig. 11*). Later he acquired virtually all the land between B and C Streets from the waterfront to Broadway. Cains's glasshouse was comparatively small, employing only fifteen men, but as business grew he enlarged his building and superseded his first furnace with a ten-pot structure.

According to his son William, Thomas Cains was invited to positions in Sandwich, in Richmond, Virginia, and in New York before he embarked upon his independent career. His decision to run a glasshouse of his own was a wise one. The Phoenix Glass Works, as he called it, naming it perhaps after the Phoenix works in Bristol, where he may have received his training, was able to operate continuously and successfully until 1870. Cains became one of the wealthiest citizens of South Boston. In the mansion house that he later built near the crossing of B and Bolton Streets, he entertained lavishly and enjoyed the fruits of his labor.

William Cains, who was born in South Boston June 24, 1814, went to work in the glasshouse in 1832 and became his father's right-hand man in the enterprise (*Fig. 10*). Also associated with the business and with the family was William Johnston, who married Cains' daughter Susan. He and young Cains ran the factory for about three years after the father retired in 1852. But when Johnston died in 1855, Thomas Cains returned to his furnace and managed the works again until he, too, passed away ten years later. William Cains kept the fires going for five more years. At the time of his retirement his affairs were somewhat involved, and it is evident that the father was the more capable businessman. William Cains lived on for some thirty-five years. He was known as the "grand old man" of South Boston, and, indeed, by virtue of having seen the district grow from a village to a city, he

FIG. 10—WILLIAM CAINS, son of Thomas Cains.

was thoroughly identified with its development.

Recently I acquired a batch of papers — letters, memoranda, circulars, and inventories — relating to the closing of the works. From these I have been able to glean some interesting material as to how the glasshouse was run, and, better still, a fair knowledge of its products at that time.

The Phoenix works ran one ten-pot furnace, each pot of 2,000 pounds capacity, and employed about thirty men and boys (*Fig. 12*). The organization of workers was the usual one — three men and two boys to a shop: the gaffer or blower, one servitor, one footmaker, a "sticker-up" boy, and a "taker-in." There were five of these crews, which, however, required the services of only two footmakers. The other employees were firemen, "slower" men, packers, laborers, a pot-maker.

The principal materials were New Jersey sand at $7.00 a ton, lead, and soda ash. St. Louis clay was used for the pots, which cost about forty dollars each to manufacture. Ten tons of this clay lasted for one year to a year and a half. An estimate of the materials consumed in one week includes coal — 18 to 20 tons; sand — about one ton; soda ash — 450 pounds; lead — 600 pounds; cullet — one and one half to two tons; packing hay — one quarter ton. The expense for labor in the same period was between $350 and $400.

To the glass students the most important item in this list is cullet, for it offers definite proof that glasshouses of this period *bought* cullet. The Phoenix Glass Works spent about $300 a month for it. With this fact in mind, we should view with some reserve the evidence of fragments excavated at Sandwich or elsewhere as proof of manufacture there.

Several grades of glass were mixed. Men-

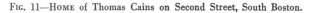

FIG. 11—HOME of Thomas Cains on Second Street, South Boston.

tion is made of "best batch" for the wine shop, soda batch, lime batch. Flint glass was used for lamp chimneys, an important part of the output. A circular published in February, 1870, reads:

A general complaint from housekeepers of the trouble and expense caused by the brittleness of the glass, has induced us to recommence the manufacture of chimneys.

Our chimneys are made of a superior quality of flint glass.

Each chimney will have Mr. Cains' name pasted on it, and a paper in it, showing that the responsibility for the higher prices asked, rests with the manufacturer and not with the dealer.

We claim that they are less liable to crack than those now in common use.

Sun and *lip* chimneys were produced in large quantities, while *bulb, star, Argand, Ashley,* and *petticoat* were other designations. One type was called the *15th Amendment* chimney. Globes for gas and kerosene lamps, some of them roughed or cut, also appear in the inventory. *Egg blown* and patent *Jenny Lind* lantern globes, the latter with two rings, and saucer, tulip-shaped, or conical shades were other lighting equipment. Three kinds of glass lamps are mentioned: the *Boston Beauty* hand lamp, the *Tom Thumb,* and ring handle.

The blown ware for cutting and decorating seems to have been limited in these closing days of the factory to stem ware, tumblers, lemonade mugs, and nappies. Among these glasses were goblets, wines, champagnes, clarets, and cordials. They were made in shapes such as *Astor, Mitchell, bell, band,* and *straw stem* — terms employed by all glassmakers of the period. Usually they were cut, although engraved leaf goblets are mentioned. Nappies and mugs had star-cut bases.

More easily identified by the average collector is the pressed glass, itemized in a number of familiar patterns. There were complete sets — creamer, covered sugar bowl, spoonholder, and covered butter dish — in the *diamond, grape, leaf,* and *reed and lily* patterns. These sets sold at wholesale for $4.50 to $5.00 per dozen — about ten cents for each piece. The *diamond* pattern also included goblets, salts, and three-inch cup plates. The manufacture of cup plates at this late date may seem strange, but early styles were frequently carried over a long period of years. In the *leaf* pattern, goblets, egg cups, and four-inch nappies (sauce dishes) appear.

A mold known as *split diamond* was utilized for six-inch plates, four- and six-inch nappies, and seven-inch nappies on foot (compotes), with and without covers, for individual salts, and for three-inch cup plates. Four-inch nappies were also made in the *cable* pattern or were sometimes plain with frosted finish.

Various patterns are listed in one form only. The greatest variety is in goblets, which were made in *plaid, huber, crescent, punty and flute,* and *mirror* design, as well as in other simple patterns for bar-room use. Ice cream tumblers are also mentioned. Table salts, salts on foot, and individual salts appear in this list: the first in *punty* pattern; the salts on foot in *diamond, diamond and star,* and *diamond and bead* designs; and the individual containers in *diamond, split diamond, cog wheel, punty,* and *diamond and bead.*

Of the earlier products of Cains's glasshouse we have little information. An advertisement in the *New York Journal of Commerce* in the early spring of 1829 gives a list of glass for sale by "Johnson & Neilson, 46 South Street, Agents of the South Boston Glass Works." Since the old South Boston flint works was unoccupied in 1829, this notice was probably inserted by Cains, and "Johnson" may have been William Johnston, whose name is frequently misprinted with that spelling. The advertisement reads: "Glassware — A complete assortment, consisting of Decanters, Wines, Tumblers, Lamps of various patterns, Salts, Cruets, Castor Bottles, Moulded plates and platters, Specie Jars, Stopper Rounds, Salt Mouths,

FIG. 12—PHOENIX GLASS WORKS.

Jewelers Globes, Retorts, Funnels, Breast Pipes, Nipple Shells, Frosting, etc., etc."

THE BOSTON GLASS BOTTLE MANUFACTORY. From the files of the *Boston Commercial Gazette* we learn that there was also a bottle works in South Boston in the early period. The concern was incorporated June 20, 1826 by Charles Wade, Thomas Haskins, and William Underwood "for the purpose of manufacturing bottles and other glass ware." Wade was the owner of a "porter cellar" at 12 Merchant's Row; Haskins was a distiller of cordials on Front Street; and Underwood had a mustard factory on Broadway, South Boston. Bottles evidently played a large part in their vocations. The company advertised its wares as follows September 21, 1826:

Wine and Porter Bottles, Demijohns, Carboys, &c.
For sale, 100 gross Wine Bottles — 100 do. Porter and Cider do. The public are respectfully informed that the South Boston Glass Bottle Manufactory is now in full operation, where they may be supplied with Wine, Porter and Cider Bottles — Demijohns — Carboys, from one to ten gallons. Also, all kinds of Ware, made of black or green glass. Samples of the Bottles and other Glass ware may be seen at Store No. 2, Union-street, where orders will be received.
Cash paid for empty Hampers, Crates, and Broken Bottles.

An advertisement in the *Boston Commercial Gazette,* March 15, 1827, gives a more itemized list of bottles. The flasks mentioned may well have been of the historical variety whose attribution is so often a puzzle to collectors.

BOTTLES

The Boston Glass Bottle Manufactoring Company offer for sale at their Ware House, No. 5 Battery-March-street

    350 groce Porter
    450 do Wine
    150 do Pint Porter
     50 do Pint Wine
     50 do Quart
     50 do Ink
     15 do Gallon
     10 do 2 Gallon
     10 do 3 Gallon
     10 do half gallon salt mouth do
      8 do quart salt mouth do
     50 do pint Flasks
     25 do half do
      5 do ½ gallon salt mouth, ground stoppers
     12 do ½ pound Snuff Bottles
      1 do Case Bottles
    260 do 5, 7, and 9 gallon Carboys

FIG. 13—SUFFOLK GLASS WORKS.

At their works, South Boston, they now manufacture all kinds of black Glass Bottles, with any stamp or device required, of a quality equal to Bristol Bottles.

Cash paid for hampers and black glass. Orders addressed to John Stimpson, Agt., will receive due attention.

THE MOUNT WASHINGTON GLASS COMPANY. It is well known that the Mount Washington Glass Company had its beginnings in South Boston, that it was built by Deming Jarves and managed by Luther Russell. "Capt." Russell, whose transition from a wharfinger to a glassman seems to have occurred overnight, was first engaged in running a small glassworks near the old South Boston company. The management of this venture appears to have been in the hands of one William Eayrs, whose history defies research, except that he was probably the same William Eayrs who was placed in charge of the short-lived Providence glasshouse. When Jarves in 1837 put up this new factory on the waterfront next door to the Boston company, Eayrs was out of the picture and Russell became Jarves' superintendent.

The Mount Washington Glass Company was organized for the benefit of young George D. Jarves, who was not actively concerned in its operation except perhaps in the salesroom. In 1846 he had joined with John D. Labree under the style *Labree & Jarves*. Labree died very soon after the association was formed. Thereafter, until 1860, Henry D. Cormerais was the other member of the firm.

The history of the Mount Washington company merits more space than can here be given it. It has continued under different firms until the present day. Known until recently as the *Pairpoint Manufacturing Company*, the concern still makes fine glass in New Bedford, Massachusetts.

SUFFOLK GLASS WORKS. The Suffolk Glass Works was in existence for thirty-three years *(Fig. 13)*. The Boston Directory first mentions it in 1852 in the list of glass manufactories, with the address "Second Street." Whether the factory building at that time was actually on Second Street or whether the office is indicated is uncertain. The business is usually mentioned in connection with its proprietor, Joshua Jenkins. Throughout the 1850's, however, he is listed as a painter. Not until 1859 does he appear for the first time as the proprietor of the Suffolk Works with offices at 13 Liberty Square, Boston. It is possible that someone else owned or managed the establishment during its initial period; it may even have started in the small glasshouse on Second Street once operated by Luther Russell and William Eayrs. Later on, the factory stood near the foot of Mercer Street, at some distance from the other glasshouses. A description of the glasshouse in 1885 says that it was a large brick structure with "2 cones of 7 pots each."

Joshua Jenkins ran the Suffolk Works without interruption until 1880, when he retired and moved to Scituate. For five years thereafter it was carried on by S. B. Lowland, who had been agent for a time under Jenkins. The buildings, after remaining idle for many years, were burned in 1900.

Jenkins made a general line of ware. In the *Boston Directory* of 1862 he advertised as a manufacturer of "all kinds of Flint-Glass Ware, Blown, Pressed, and Cut. Kerosene and Gas Shades. Rich Cut Table Ware. N. B. Particular attention paid to Kerosene Lamps and Chimneys; also, Druggists' and Chemists' Ware." This advertisement shows a cut of Jenkins's "Tubulated" lamp fount *(Fig. 14)*. By his patent, dated September 18, 1860, he secured the rights for blowing a lamp reservoir in such a way that two openings could be made in it, one for the wicks and the other for receiving oil. This was done in one operation.

FRANKLIN GLASS COMPANY. A bill in the possession of Warren C. Lane, dated November 17, 1859, reveals that the Franklin Glass Company manufactured "Plain, Molded, Colored, & Cut Flint Glass-Ware in all its Varieties." As this concern appears only in the 1859 and 1860 directories, it is probable that it represents a brief attempt at revival of the former American Flint Glass Works after Slane's departure.

TREMONT GLASS WORKS. All that we know about the Tremont Glass Works is contained in an advertisement in the Boston Directory of 1860. From this we learn that the factory was at 70 Second Street, South Boston, and that J. M. Cook was the proprietor. He made "Plain, Cut, Pressed and Colored Flint Glass, Gas, Kerosene and Solar Shades, Plain and Rough Chimneys, Homoepathic and Chemical Glass Ware of every description." These articles were for sale by Horace Farrington, Commission merchant, at 87 Kilby Street.

In conclusion it may be of interest to note a few facts gleaned from the *Statistics relating to certain branches of Industry in Massachusetts*, which were published at ten-year intervals. In 1845 there were but two glasshouses in operation in South Boston. Ten years later, when Slane's American Flint Glass Works was in full swing, we see what happened during a business boom. Five hundred and eighty-six men were employed in the three glasshouses, making in one year glass worth $1,190,000. The South Boston glasshouses were actually producing nearly twice as much glass as was being turned out either by the combined New England and Bay State Works in Cambridge or by the two companies at Sandwich. Nine Boston Glass manufactories were in operation in 1865 (all those of which account has been given and four others), but only 332 hands were at work in all of them, with a glass production worth $611,600 annually. After that period the production dwindled. At Cambridge it had increased, giving employment to 653 men and women. The situation at Sandwich, also, had improved, with 590 employees in the two glasshouses.

FIG. 14—ADVERTISEMENT from the *Boston Directory*, 1862, showing Jenkins' patented lamp. Illustrations from *History of South Boston* by John J. Toomey and Edward P. B. Rankin.

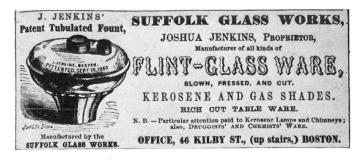

The Portland Glass Works

By Martha York Jones

MAINE now qualifies as a member of the family of states known to have possessed old glass works. The Portland Glass Company's pressed tableware may today be collected in authenticated patterns. This will be pleasant news, particularly to the many persons of Maine birth or ancestry who visit New England during the summer and like, when possible, to carry back to their adopted homes worthwhile souvenirs of the Pine Tree State.

Not so early in its inception as the New England works at Cambridge, or the famous Boston and Sandwich Glass factory on Cape Cod, the Portland Glass Works ceased operations in 1873, about fifteen years before the closing of either of the Massachusetts plants. Hence Portland's final products are antecedent to the New England, or Sandwich, or Pittsburgh-district wares of the last half of the 'seventies or the early 'eighties. For instance, they are a little earlier than the patterns brought out for the centennial, of which the *liberty bell*, the *three face*, and the popular *Westward ho* are examples. They are quite a bit older than the New England *amberina*, *pomona*, *agata*, and *peachblow*, and precede the blown, colored, threaded glass made at Sandwich in the early 'eighties.

According to the Portland directory for the year 1869, the Portland Glass Company received its charter in 1863, and, with a capital of $150,000, began making glass in 1864. For nine years it ran at full factory capacity, turning out lamp chimneys as well as pressed-glass tableware in sets, both clear and colored. In 1865, its output is said to have totaled 105,300 pieces. The Company was no less valiant than its rivals in claiming high excellence for its products, thus: "Portland Glass is not inferior to any made in the country and is, indeed, superior to most." Portland patterns, all of which were locally designed, won favor in the principal markets. The sole reason for closing the factory in 1873 was the impossibility of meeting the price competition of glassworks more favorably situated for obtaining fuel supplies and for shipping their output to inland localities.

John B. Brown was the Company's first president, J. S. Palmer its treasurer, and W. C. Davis its superintendent. Its directors were J. B. Brown, Rensellea Cram, Charles E. Jose, George Brock, and Joseph Walker. The works occupied a fine brick building on what is now Commercial Street, very near the old Boston and Maine station at the foot of State Street. It was equipped with the best facilities, and its staff workers originated the designs for the molds, which they made themselves. When the Company discovered that its special designs were being copied, it took measures to secure patents. That a patent was secured, in at least one instance, we know from *tree of life* goblets, spoonholders, and compotes, the bottoms of whose feet are marked *P. G. Co.* with the word *Patented* below. I possess a goblet thus marked. Two unmarked colored pieces of the same pattern I have recently found. One is a six and a half inch plate in light amber; the other, a deep blue finger bowl. I have also seen a green egg cup in *tree of life*, and a light blue dish. There is a yellow color, too; but I have encountered no one who has seen a piece of Portland glass of any type in any shade of red. Let me say in passing that the patent mark on Portland glass is not readily seen against the elaborate interlacings of the *tree of life* pattern. It is more quickly revealed to touch than to sight.

Both the *tree of life* goblet and the finger bowl have a band of plain, clear, undecorated glass, about three-eighths of an inch wide, around the top. Except for this, the glass is covered with a raised pattern consisting of small, irregular facetings resembling uncut crystals, though perhaps intended to suggest foliage, tucked into the spaces between the endlessly twining branches of the *tree of life*. These branches bear a delicate tracery simulating the bark of a tree. By the casual observer the crystalline elements of the decoration might be mistaken for snakeskin glass. But true snakeskin is really quite different, and is achieved by an entirely distinct process. An undecorated piece of glass, while still hot, is rolled in finely ground particles of glass, which adhere to the soft metal and give a curiously variegated surface. *Tree of life*, on the contrary, received its entire ornament from a mold in which the pattern had been cut.

It may be remarked that the *tree of life* pattern was slightly rearranged after the design had been patented. In order to make room for the patent mark, such of the decoration as had formerly been impressed on the bottom of the base of footed pieces was transferred to the upper side, thus leaving a free surface for an imprint beneath the foot. I recently examined a green egg cup whose decoration appeared on the outside of the bowl and on the under side of the foot, a circumstance that permits classification of the item among the pre-patented pieces. A small, clear-glass berry or honey saucer carries the design on the outside. The patent mark, almost indistinguishable, is in the interior centre.

Other seemingly well-authenticated patterns claimed for the Portland factory are those belonging to the *loop and dart* group. Ruth Webb Lee, in Chapter XVII of her book *Early American Pressed Glass*, remarks: "It would seem that one factory must have had a monopoly of this design; but just why so many similar variants were made is a question." She further remarks that these designs are suggestive of the late 'sixties. This observation accords rather well with the dates of our Portland factory, and with other links in the chain of evidence binding the *loop and dart* to the Maine establishment. Other Portland patterns are the *Roman rosette*, sometimes called *pinwheel*; the *grape, leaves, and buckle*; the *horseshoe*; the *melon*; the *shell and tassel*; and the *shell and jewel*. The *shell and jewel* pattern comes in a fine, very brilliant deep blue, as well as in clear glass. I have seen water sets consisting of a large pitcher and tumblers of this pattern — both in clear glass and in blue. The *shell and jewel* is a very well-authenticated Portland product.

Collectors who wish to see Portland glass will have opportunity to do so at the glass show in Sandwich — if they were not at Plymouth. They will also welcome the information that a good collection of this glass, the gift of Miss M. H. Jewell, is on permanent display at the Harrison Grey Otis House, Cambridge Street, Boston.

Fig. 1 (right) — TREE OF LIFE: PORTLAND GLASS OF THE 1860's Sometimes marked *P. G. Co./ Patented*. Probably the earliest and, in many respects, the best of Portland designs

Fig. 2 (below) — LOOP AND DART BOWL, AND ROMAN ROSETTE PITCHER: HERE ASCRIBED TO PORTLAND
The *loop and dart* pattern has many variants. The handle of the rosette pitcher is of later type than the off-hand shaped, crimped handle of the *tree of life* pitcher

Fig. 3 (below, at left) — SHELL AND JEWEL PITCHER: HERE ASCRIBED TO PORTLAND

Fig. 4 (below, at right) — SHELL AND TASSEL COMPOTE: HERE ASCRIBED TO PORTLAND
Quadrilateral, with rounded corners. Another version of this pattern occurs, in which the items are circular in horizontal section. The treatment of the shells recalls the *tree of life* design

The items illustrated are from the collection of the author

Fig. 1 — PITTSBURGH GLASS (*1868*)
Sprig Pattern.
This and other illustrations are from the Catalogue of M'Kee and Brothers of Pittsburgh, and are facsimiles of the original cuts, errors included.

By No Means Sandwich

Some Examples of Late Pittsburgh Glass

By THE EDITOR

VALUABLE information as to the source and approximate date of manufacture of certain types of pressed glass which, under the general entitlement of *Sandwich*, have been popular with a number of collectors, is discernible in a little brochure which Harold Rugg of Hanover, New Hampshire, has very thoughtfully loaned to ANTIQUES for examination. This brochure is a price list of glassware issued by M'Kee and Brothers, "flint glass manufacturers," of 17 Wood Street, "corner of Wood and First," Pittsburgh, under date of April first, 1868. The work consists of thirty-two pages of woodcut illustrations, and sixteen pages of itemized prices. It was printed by W. S. Haven, whose press was conveniently located at Wood and Third Streets. One "Seymour," whoever he may have been, is credited with the adequate but totally uninspired "engravings."

Besides the usual run of household and hotel glassware, M'Kee and Brothers produced "carbon oil lamps," candlesticks, lanterns for burning either oil or candles, sundries such as toys, shoemakers' globes, butter prints, soap slabs, hyacinth glasses, and apothecaries' shop furniture, including jars, funnels, mortars and pestles, and show globes of various sizes. These last are advertised and pictured as *cone or globe shape, pear shape,* and *French style.* They run from two to four stories, or sections, in height, and the large specimens in the French style, when engraved, are priced at $18.00 each.

The price list closes with a note as to terms of sale, which are "net cash, less (blank to be written in) per cent discount, to be paid within ten days from date of invoice." The customer is "at the same time assured" that "there is nothing elegant or extra in Flint Glass Ware, made or furnished in this vicinity, but we make and supply." This is followed by a disclaimer of responsibility for breakage (comforting word) of glass in transit except when special insurance has previously been arranged.

Round Ind. Salt.

Fillmore Salt.

Mason Salt.

Rope Salt.

Tomato Salt.

Imperial Salt.

Fig. 2 — PITTSBURGH GLASS (*1868*)

Vine C. O. Lamp, 5 in. Base.   Stedman C. O. Lamp 5 in. Base.   Prism Lamp, C. O 5 in. Base.   Vine Footed C. O. Lamp.   Shell Footed C. O. Lam

Fig. 3 — PITTSBURGH LAMPS (*1868*)
   C.O. stands for *coal oil*.

The most interesting aspect of this catalogue, however, is its pages of pictures with entitlements of the different patterns illustrated. There is, for example, the *sprig* pattern, in dishes, goblets, bowls, "sweetmeats,"* pitchers, "nappies," and so forth. The sprig consists of a somewhat ungainly anthemion, or palmette, displayed against vertical ribbing. One design, in imitation of faceted cut-glass, is given the name *New York*; another, quite similar, is entitled *Cincinnati*. Certain goblets decorated with a kind of bull's-eye pattern are called *mirror* goblets, others, quite appropriately, *argus* goblets. That widely popular pattern which many persons have hitherto inclined to believe might have been derived from a peacock's feather is listed as *comet*; though a typographical error in the catalogue confuses it with the *leaf* pattern.

Collectors who have assiduously gathered items of glass in the well-known *bellflower* design, for table use, will be more or less pleased to learn that this pattern, too, is listed among the multifarious products of M'Kee and Brothers,

in 1868. But in the catalogue it is not identified by the pretty and now popular name of *bellflower*, but by the mysterious initials *R. L.*, the meaning of which has thus far eluded discovery. The letters may, of course, stand for *ribbed leaf*.

In 1868, M'Kee and Brothers were likewise advertising two types of candlesticks which enthusiastic amateurs of glass now look upon as highly valuable members of the Sandwich tribe. These are the *Boston* candlestick, whose name suggests frank borrowing from a Massachusetts source, and the dolphin candlestick, which, though we must all agree that it had no right to be manufactured some hundreds of miles from the seaboard, is here so pictured and labeled as to establish its Pittsburgh affiliations beyond peradventure.

There were, most certainly, other dolphins in other crystal seas than those owned and operated by the enterprising brothers from Pittsburgh. The M'Kee cetacean, it may be remarked, displays one peculiarity which differentiates it from others of the general school. In its extraordinary act of balancing, wherein it emulates Old Father William's feat of posing an eel on the end of his nose, it plants its chin firmly upon a *circular* base instead of upon a *square* one.

---

*Sweetmeats appear to be *covered* bowls of six-inch diameter on a high foot. Items of the same form and size, or smaller, with or without covers, and without foot, are *nappies*. When a sweetmeat adds one or two inches to its diameter, it is listed in the M'Kee catalogue as a *bowl*.

6 in. Comet Sweetmeat and Cover.   6 in. Comet Nappy and Cover.   in. Leaf Nappy and Cover.   7 in. Leaf Sweetmeat and Cover.

Fig. 4 — PITTSBURGH GLASS (*1868*)
   Obviously the labels of the first item and the last have been mistakenly transposed. This *comet* pattern is sometimes known as *peacock tail*.

½ gall. R. L. Pitcher.   Qt. R. L. Pitcher.   Qt. Ribbed Pitcher.   ½ pt. Plain Cream.

Fig. 5—PITTSBURGH GLASS (*1868*)
The first two pitchers exhibit the so-called bellflower pattern, here designated by the letters *R. L.*

Dolphin and Boston holders, as they are pictured in the Catalogue, are both here reproduced. The prices quoted for them, in 1868, were: for Boston candlesticks, $7.50 per dozen; for dolphins, $6.75 per dozen.

On the same page with the Boston candlestick and the dolphin, appear, among other things, a glass butter print, a three-inch plate — *not indicated as a cup plate* — and a bird bath. On another page — here in part reproduced — appear a number of glass salts of a type which many persons have esteemed as possessing a greater antiquity than inclusion in this catalogue would appear to indicate.

Over the M'Kee line of tumblers, goblets, ale glasses, and beer mugs, it is perhaps well to draw a veil. All the items of glass specifically dedicated to the dispensing of enlivening beverages are, virtually without exception, of a form and pattern which — though extremely simple — yet seem artfully calculated to turn mortal mind to thoughts of thirst. Their comfortable contours invite the clasping hand; the wide circle of their rims suggests potations generously broad as well as comfortingly deep.

The purpose of these notes, however, is not to review in detail the glass of M'Kee and Brothers, of Pittsburgh, but to point to one or two fairly obvious deductions to be drawn from a study of the catalogue issued by these gentlemen. In the first place, we may rest satisfied that many so-called *Sandwich* patterns, if produced in the Cape Cod establishments at all, were certainly not an exclusive specialty of Jarves and his associates. On the whole, it seems probable that, at various times, the same, or similar, patterns were turned out by a number of unrelated and widely scattered concerns, which either copied each other's successful designs, or else purchased their molds from mold-makers who impartially supplied all their clients with the same thing.

Again, the actual age of the various patterns pictured may not fairly be judged by the fact of their publication in an 1868 catalogue. Some of these patterns were, no doubt, novelties which made their début among the iron-clad engravings of Seymour. Others may have been in use for a generation or more — indeed from the beginning of the pressed glass period in the 1830's; for, whatever of antiquity the firm of M'Kee may have boasted, there were probably luckless predecessors from whom the concern inherited many varieties of both patterns and molds.

The vagaries of design in glass hollow-ware have always been such as to render hazardous any attempt to determine dates of individual pieces on the sole basis of stylistic peculiarity. What in earlier times was confusion develops into sheer chaos during the mid-nineteenth century. Hence we are safe in assuming only that the designs pictured in the M'Kee catalogue under consideration were more or less popular as late as the year 1868. As to their previous status and subsequent fate, no present means of knowing is available.

Boston Candlestick.   Butter Print.   3 in. Diamond Plate.   Bird Bath.   Dolphin Candlestick.

Fig. 6 — PITTSBURGH GLASS (*1868*)
Here are two familiar candlesticks to prove the wide prevalence of Sandwich types.

PITTSBURGH PRESSED GLASS, I

By LOWELL INNES

In ANTIQUES *for December and January Mr. Innes, honorary curator of glass at Carnegie Museum in Pittsburgh, published articles based on the first large exhibition of Pittsburgh glass ever held, which he had organized for the Historical Society of Western Pennsylvania in 1947. This year he has staged a far more comprehensive exhibition of the locally made glass at Carnegie Museum. Opened in April, it is being kept on view, by popular demand, until November. For the excellent catalogue of this exhibition* ANTIQUES *released some material by Mr. Innes which was already in manuscript in our files. This manuscript, with new additions, is now presented here, and illustrated by courtesy of Carnegie Museum with pieces shown in the exhibition. We shall publish shortly a further article by Mr. Innes, on the pattern glass of the Pittsburgh district.*

—THE EDITOR

WHEN THE COMPLETE STORY of American pressed glass is written, we shall undoubtedly read that the factories of Pittsburgh produced contemporaneously the cycles of pressed glass hitherto attributed only to the eastern seaboard. For instance, John P. Bakewell, Jr., actually held the first American patent for pressing of glass knobs, 1825. Several indentures of the early 1830's support the evidence. One in particular shows the interweaving of glass families in the trade. An indenture of Robert Bryce, aged fifteen years, eight months, and twelve days, to Benjamin, Thomas, and J. P. Bakewell, Jr., and John Palmer Pears states that young Bryce will be taught in the best manner they can "the art and mystery of a Glass Blower and Presser." That document, dated December 26, 1836, indicates that pressing glass in Pittsburgh had been well under way in the early thirties. Wheeling also, at the southern boundary of the Pittsburgh district, in the same decade had several firms advertising pressed glass: Ritchie and Wilson, Plunkett and Miller, and the Sweeneys. So the tri-state district formed an attractive center for experienced glassmen.

Although marked Pittsburgh pieces like the J. & T. Robinson plates and boat-shaped salts and the Curling creamer and Fort Pitt eagle cup plates advertise the district, most convincing evidence of its supremacy lay in the presence of many flourishing moldmakers' establishments. In 1860 the capital value of five metal mold works was $285,000, the value of raw material alone was $105,211, and these works employed 334 male workers. Not all of these were skilled mold designers and cutters. The Joseph D. Weeks' 1880 *Report on Glass Manufacture* numbers moldmakers at 120 with daily pay running from $1.50 to $6.00. Factories like Bakewell's or Lorenz and Wightman contained their own moldmaking establishments within their plants. Besides, there were always itinerant journeymen moldmakers.

Washington (Wash) Beck, to whom Mrs. Knittle paid tribute in *Early American Glass,* was the most famous and enterprising of all the moldmakers, known at home and abroad. For twenty years his factory, possibly the largest establishment of its kind in the United States, flourished and prospered. Other men also deserve notice. Andrew Thompson, born in Ireland in 1818, took over the A. J. Miller & Co. machine shop in 1849, two years after it had been founded. By 1880 his building at 90 Eighth Street, South Side, compared favorably in size and equipment with Beck's. It was said to be "the first establishment in Pittsburgh devoted to the manufacture of flint and green glass molds, presses, and light machinery and mechanical appliances for the production of glassware." Certainly one 12-horse-power engine was not to be sneered at even in 1880. Robert M. Jones, who worked a number of years as pattern-maker at the Fort Pitt Works, went into patterns for castings and models of every description. The Birmingham Foundry and Machine Shop of George Fisher and Peter Wentzel advertised in *Industries of Pennsylvania* (Richard Edwards, Ed. & Pub., 1879): "They take

FIG. 1—EARLY PRESSED COMPOTES with blown bases, and cobalt dish. Stars, ribs, and diamonds were favorite early geometric patterns.

FIG. 2—MIDWESTERN LACY, showing characteristic patterns of the Pittsburgh district.

special pride in their ability for turning out machinery and castings adapted for glass works." Their annual $30,000 business even in depression years when low prices were prevalent employed eighteen skilled workers. *And the product was bought almost entirely in Pittsburgh!*

Molds and statistics seem much less exciting and alive than a well-designed, sparkling piece of early pressed glass. We should remember, however, that pressing by mechanical means in metal molds is largely an American invention, and that the improvements between 1870 and 1880 enabled manufacturers to turn out a finished product which would belie the faults of the early mold. New pieces could be fire-polished, could be designed with sharp angles like cut glass, could be removed from the mold with spring snaps, could have the mold marks almost obliterated. When one recalls that the whole country imported about $38,000 worth of pressed glass, while Pittsburgh alone in 1878 was exporting over $860,000 worth, he will realize that production was tremendous. Weeks' *Report* of 1880 tabulates Pennsylvania as leading all the other states in production of pressed ware (called in his catalogue "glassware") at 51% of the total. New York is second with 12.10% and Massachusetts a weak seventh with 7.3%. Of producing localities Allegheny County (Pittsburgh) was out in front with 26.79%. Certainly in quantity Pittsburgh led the field.

As to quality the debate is still raging. It is pleasant now, however, to have a friend return from California with two handsome goblets purchased at twice our local price. "Why did you pay so much?" we asked. She said that she had demurred but that when she had actually complained the dealer announced triumphantly, "Oh, but these are Pittsburgh!"

Midwestern Lacy

Any showing or discussion of lacy glass is provocative because the origins are still in doubt. Today most students can recognize the sophistication, the classic designs, the clarity and brilliance, and the redundance of Baccarat decoration. American collectors still argue bitterly as to whether most of our lacy is Sandwich or midwestern. It is too bad everyone interested cannot see two authentic Sandwich pieces set amidst thirty-odd midwestern lacy pieces, all showing well against a background of dark green velvet. The general differences between the two types of American lacy are these: the Sandwich product is more brilliant, the stippling finer, the metal clearer, the designs more sophisticated. Yet those generalizations often break down.

In addition to the four pieces illustrated in Figure 2 there were three bowls (two *princess feather* with lifeless stippling) and one of soda-lime metal such as appears in McKearin's Plate 144, Figure 2. The small open compote in our Figure 2, with arrowhead design and the circled rim, one of a pair, was originally presented to a minister of the German Lutheran church on the South Side of Pittsburgh in the early fifties. Possibly these pieces were made at the Bakewell factory after it moved from the early location in the city proper following the fire of 1845. The plate beside it in Figure 2 was duplicated except that the outer rim on the second plate carried no circles, only the ordinary scalloped edge. The plate at far right in Figure 2, also one of a pair, exemplifies well the early combination of simple geometric patterns with an unadorned arch. The rim is a popular one on larger plates and compotes of our locality.

Easily the finest workmanship and most brilliant stippling were revealed by a rare *eagle* toddy plate resting on extended acanthus leaves, illustrated in Figure 3 on the following page (lower left), and also by McKearin (Plate 142, Figure 3). It seems so much more vital than the other pieces in sparkle and so much more elaborately designed that one immediately thinks of lacy Sandwich. With little chance of documentary authentication the student asks two questions: If the *eagle* plate is midwestern, as Mr. McKearin thinks, can it be that Pittsburgh paralleled Sandwich in the production of lacy? If it is midwestern, can it be that only a limited amount of first-quality lacy was made here? Mr. McKearin has owned this *eagle* plate in all three sizes, he tells me, but considers the 7-inch octagonal one the most important and characteristically midwestern.

About two weeks before the exhibition opened, the plate shown at upper right of this same illustration was discovered. Though the pattern has not yet been identified, the center design and rays are reminiscent of Pittsburgh-district cup plates. The border scroll, the circular edge, and the eight circles at the corners, each impressed on the under side with a star, mark the new find as typical of the midwest. The

FIG. 3.—MIDWESTERN LACY GLASS. (*Upper right*), brilliant octagonal plate in an unknown pattern, recently discovered; (*lower left*), *eagle* plate, illustrated by McKearin; other examples of unknown origin, showing coarse stippling and bold design.

metal is unusually heavy and clear and though the stippling may seem coarse, the piece has a great deal of brilliance. The specimen in the same figure, upper left, furnishes an admirable contrast—a much later piece with obviously bold circles and arches and decadent design. Like many midwestern plates it rests on a series of dots (eight in this case). But the metal, undoubtedly with the lead content decreased, is dull compared to that of the one on the right. The illustration makes a nice comparison between two pieces typical of one area yet of different times.

Certainly the sound generalizations made by James H. Rose and George S. McKearin are borne out by the examples illustrated: coarser and smoother stippling, sometimes even to the point of dullness; bold and coarse designs, the frequent use of circles in the body of the piece, in the rim, and even as

supporting feet; rather stiff conventionalized scrolls and figures such as the acanthus; serrations on the rims (Figures 2 and 3 give a good idea of adequately usual types); metal that was often heavy with the lead content steadily decreasing. The very weaknesses of midwestern lacy, however, give it a virility and individuality which bespeak pioneer life and clearly remove us from Baccarat (French) influence, often confusing to collectors of lacy Sandwich.

Cup Plates

Through the scholarly work of James H. Rose and Mrs. Ruth Webb Lee in their *American Glass Cup Plates*, it is apparent that Pittsburgh and the midwest produced generously. Nevertheless, probably neither Mr. Rose nor Mr. Marble, who compiled the first list of cup plates, would unequivocally name more than fifteen plates that could be assigned with certainty to Pittsburgh itself. For the exhibition we were content to display those that characterized the district, and in general mirrored the designs and patterns popular in midwestern glass.

Naturally two variations of the *Fort Pitt eagle* were shown: one with the smooth rim decorated with the twenty-four bull's eyes, the other with the attractive ridges running toward the border and with serrated edges minimizing the

FIG. 4—SUGAR BOWLS. (*Left to right*), cobalt pressed; opaque white Ihmsen (*1851*); blown, deep pink lined with opaque white.

170

ANTIQUES

FIG. 5—A GROUP OF PIECES. (*Left to right*), covered sweetmeat dish, early McKee pattern; pressed fiery opal and clear compote marked *B. P. & Co. Pat. Sept. 29, 1874* (Bakewell, Pears & Co.); *excelsior* candlestick, McKee & Bros.; *thistle* candlestick, Bakewell, Pears & Co.

prises from 1807 to his death in 1828. Christian took over his father's interests then, had his own factory by 1850, and in 1851 conceived the idea of trying papier-mâché and wooden molds. Not being certain of success, he planned an advertising venture: a sugar bowl that would illustrate in the design of its side panels forms and patterns produced by the Ihmsens. Thus we know that the Ihmsens made *excelsior* as did McKee; made *flute* and *Ashburton* as did Bakewell. The inside of the lid has smaller figures impressed: an *excelsior* footed tumbler with a handle, a champagne and a goblet in *flute,* and odd pieces of *excelsior.* (See ANTIQUES, August 1938.)

importance of the eyes. These well-known plates were manufactured by R. B. Curling & Sons in the 1830's. Other eagles were Rose #670, 675A, and 677. Allied to this group the popular *liberty torch* (Rose #158) and the octagonal *steamboat* (Rose #612A) seems to strike a pioneering note. Though much later, the *anchor* (Rose #693) belongs to the same decorative scheme.

The emotion of recognition is stirred pleasantly in looking at most of the cup plates. The conventionals with wide scallops, point serration, shells, and circles, making use of the stiff scroll designs, employed the same devices incorporated in larger pieces. Most of them have what Mr. Rose calls "a clothlike stippling." His #124A, 136, 150, 165, 183B, 253, and 262 give a true picture of what the west liked and was making. Yet #203 assigned by Mr. Rose to Pittsburgh might be called a Sandwich piece by many dealers and new collectors. A problematical plate (#341), the clear seven-sided one, cannot be attributed on the basis of either distribution or manufacture. An intriguing theory that Bakewell made it is based on its likeness to a famous large plate divided into twelve looped and arched sections very similar to those on the cup plate. It is amazing to anyone studying Mrs. Lee's and Mr. Rose's new book to realize how important and prolific the midwest and Pittsburgh really were in cup-plate production.

Marked Pieces

No American glass district has furnished many marked pieces except the nineteenth-century historical and decorated flasks. From Pittsburgh, two marked plates and a cobalt blue boat-shaped salt dish by J. & T. Robinson are shown. Strictly speaking, the magnificent milk-glass Ihmsen sugar bowl is not a marked piece, but it is as good as marked, since it was devised as a means of factory advertisement and identification. Charles Ihmsen, the father of Christian, had worked in Pittsburgh glass enter-

Another striking bowl is the low open compote of two colors, fiery opal and clear (*Fig. 5*). Under the apron at the base is printed: *B. P. & Co. Pat. Sept. 29, 1874* (Bakewell Pears & Co.). This patent number 155,403 drawn by Bakewell & Kerr, attorneys, was issued to Benjamin Bakewell, Jr., who claimed the following: "As an improvement in the method of forming glass articles of two or more colors, pressing one color upon another successively by means of interchangeable plungers and rings or molds, substantially as and for the purpose specified." In the diagram from the U. S. Patent Office the article pictured is a footed tumbler called *double bouquet.* Apparently, however, the process was not too easy to carry out or else the style did not appeal to the public, for such specimens seem exceedingly rare. An obvious technical difficulty was to have the welding heat for all the subsequent operations constant. A two-part mold was used. George McKearin owns a two-color goblet which he attributes to Ihmsen (McKearin, Plate 58, Figure 2). In the Pittsburgh exhibition two goblets of milk white and clear are shown.

Rather coincidentally, two milk-white marked Atterbury ducks also exemplify the use of double color: one has a blue head and neck; the other has amethyst. These large ducks, often called Sandwich in the east, were patented on March 15, 1887, by Thomas Bakewell Atterbury, president of the Atterbury Glass Company at Carson and Tenth Streets, South Side. It was called *Design for a Dish, Patent No. 17,192* and represents another very popular piece of old Pittsburgh glass.

To be Concluded

FIG. 6—MILK GLASS ITEMS, including rare boar's-head covered dish and two Atterbury ducks with amethyst and blue heads.

PITTSBURGH PRESSED GLASS, II

By LOWELL INNES

In this discussion of the pattern glass of Pittsburgh Mr. Innes concludes his series of articles (December 1948, January, and September 1949). The exhibition at Carnegie Museum, from which many of the illustrations were drawn, has been extended by popular demand to January 1. This exhibition, staged by Mr. Innes as honorary curator of glass, has focussed attention as never before on the glassmaking activities of Pittsburgh.

THE PRESENT large and comprehensive exhibition at Carnegie Museum emphasizes Pittsburgh's contribution to American pattern glass. Though only 450 of the 890 specimens in the exhibition are pressed, it would be a simple matter to fill the Museum. One local collector, for instance, has over four hundred pieces of *Argus* (Bakewell's *thumbprint*); another has several hundred pitchers of different pressed designs. The amount of pressed ware is evidenced not only in statistics from *Weeks' Report on Glass Manufacture in the United States 1880* but also in the concentration of factories in the Pittsburgh area. Between 1830 and 1870 at least fourteen pressed-glass establishments were operating, with a yearly average of three thousand workmen, the capital value of all being better than one million and a half. Annually, from 1848 to 1872, thirty-two thousand tons of pressed tableware at Pittsburgh would be a conservative average. More than 50 per cent of the output was packaged west, the remainder going east to compete directly with the wares of some of the famous-name factories.

Not long after Sandwich and the New England Glass Company had closed their doors, the United States Glass Company formed the greatest combine in glass manufacturing history. In 1891 it joined twelve factories from the Pittsburgh-Wheeling district to six from Ohio. The shifting of the center of influence from east to west had definitely taken place before the merger. The pioneering spirit which encouraged research in a project like Leighton's lime-soda formula of 1864 is shown by the fact that John Adams of Adams, Macklin & Company, Pittsburgh, had been experimenting along the same lines in the 1850's. Though Leighton at Wheeling deserves the final credit

ARGUS, OR THUMBPRINT, by Bakewell, Pears and Company (*1836-1882*), noted in a family catalogue by Thomas Pears as one of the earliest and most popular patterns. On view in the case is a bill of sale: Pittsburgh, 1863, from Henry Higbee, Importer and Dealer in China & Glass and Queensware, 122 Wood St., to Calvin Adams for a 7-inch *Argus* footed saucer at 45 cents. The popularity of *thumbprint* with its adaptations (*diamond, almond, Victoria*, and the New England rival, *punty*) continued through the 1870's. A late edition put out by the United States Glass Company after 1891 has smaller "prints" and decidedly inferior metal.

for having perfected the formula, Pittsburgh men had been trying contemporaneously with a degree of success.

Besides the appeal of experiment and innovation, manufacturers found the proximity of basic materials and cheap fuels desirable. Western labor also was inclined to be more reasonable. Finally, rail and river transportation could effect any market distribution needed on a sound competitive basis. These hidden factors appear in the number of pieces and patterns and in the variety of wares in this show.

The line of demarcation between eastern and western pressed glass can never be clearly drawn. The best example of the interdependence of glassworkers and companies is the case of William O. Davis, an experienced foreman in the employ of J. B. Lyon and Company at the O'Hara factory in Pittsburgh. In 1854 he was credited with a patent for a press for molding glass. Nine years later he patented another improvement in glass presses. In 1868 he was put in complete charge of the newly formed glass company at Portland, Maine. While Davis was directing this enterprise, he designed the popular *tree of life* pattern, working his own name into the tree and branches. Sandwich soon adopted this pattern. In 1873, after the Portland enterprise folded and Davis returned to Pittsburgh, George Duncan and Sons, later the Duncan Miller enterprise of Washington, Pennsylvania, produced *tree of life* and *shell and tassel*, another popular pattern of the Portland Glass Company. Admittedly, the Duncan *tree of life* is heavier than that of either Sandwich or

BELLFLOWER. Established as a Pittsburgh pattern by a Bryce, McKee catalogue of 1868, but the design probably originated at Sandwich in the 1830's. Among variations acquired over the years are fine or coarse ribs, single or double vines, scalloped, beaded, or plain rims, ribbing extended to the edge or stopped by a plain band, plain or knobbed stems of hollow pieces, and differences in base patterns.

SAWTOOTH. Several pieces are pictured in a McKee catalogue of 1868, but the pattern can be assigned to no single factory. That it is an early one was evidenced a few years ago when a pair of wines was found with the pontil ground out. It was made at several eastern factories as well as in Pittsburgh.

Portland, yet the pattern is similar enough to confuse the inexperienced. One authority believes that the McKees also made *tree of life*.

A series of comparison pieces in the exhibition included *tree of life* from Portland, Sandwich, and Pittsburgh; *sawtooth* in the fine diamonds of the New England Glass Company, the medium-sized and coarse ones from Sandwich and Pittsburgh; *plume* from Sandwich and from Adams and Company of Pittsburgh; *bellflower* in the coarser ribbing often attributed to McKee as well as the conventional Sandwich; and even such identical patterns as *loop* (Sandwich) and *leaf* (McKee, Pittsburgh). The adaptation of patterns and the close relationship brought on by competition are typical of our American system.

A point of great interest to students of pressed glass, in addition to the relationship of patterns, is the popularity of certain design forms. Glass mirrored taste. The earliest patterns of the thirties and forties (*Argus, colonial, Ashburton*) were spare in ornament and followed the simplest geometric figures. Though Sandwich temporarily loosed the Baccarat lacy influence, most of its ornateness persisted in cup plates and tea plates rather than in pattern glass, *princess feather (Rochelle)* being one of the few lacy patterns which lasted. *Horn of plenty* and *arabesque* represent more practical adaptations of the lacy, for the intricacies and the costliness of molds forbade too frequent change. Therefore, except for commemorative patterns, design went from plain geometric figures to ornamented ones representing a combination like *tulip and sawtooth*.

Then a new lime-soda formula effected a cheapness of production and a lowering of quality in resonance, weight, and brilliance. It allowed more money to be spent on molds and increased the number of patterns. To offset limitations of poor quality, Pittsburgh went in for naturalistic motifs.

About the time George Duncan took

THOUSAND EYE. In the 1870's and 1880's this was made in quantity by Adams and Company of Pittsburgh in two varieties, plain with knobbed finials or stems, and with the fan; and by Richards and Hartley of Tarentum, with scalloped edges. Colors include amber, canary, blue, and apple green.

over Ripley and Company in 1874 the idea of incorporating a woman's face in the stem of pressed ware resulted in the selection of Elizabeth Blair of Steubenville, Ohio, as a model. Miss Blair (Mrs. Ernest Miller, 1847-1943) stated that she posed when twenty-eight. Rumor has held that *three face* won a prize at the Centennial Exhibition in 1876, but facts cloud the picture. The Free Library of Philadelphia, in studying the *International Exhibition, 1876, Reports and Awards* (J. B. Lippincott & Co., 1878) found no specific mention of *three face* among the Duncan wares, nor was this pattern registered at the patent office until 1878.

This phase of decoration called into play other devices: frosting, engraving, and the wide use of color. *Wildflower* exemplifies well the popular colors used. Often a simple pattern like Bakewell's *prism* would be elaborated by engraving. The final period of western, or should we say American, design was marked by a return to the classical figures—*plume, thousand eye, ribbon candy*—a return made decadent by heaviness and over-ornamentation as in *moon and star (palace)*. A disturbing fact is that there are few large sets of the plain and early patterns in private collections, yet sets in the naturalistic and decadent patterns are numerous. A weakness in American taste may be repeating itself today.

Obviously the Pittsburgh district produced so many patterns that no exhibition could show them all. Each of the patterns illustrated here, and discussed in the accompanying captions, is given a whole case, and so also are *wildflower, three face, deer and pine,* and *shell and tassel*.

No Pittsburgh exhibit would be complete without *wildflower*, largely because the midwest promoted naturalistic designs. The pleasant blue pieces in our display are a credit to the business acumen of John Adams, who had worked for Bakewell, Pears & Company in the forties and formed the first partnership in 1851 with Macklin. By 1861, when this firm became Adams & Company, the plant covered two acres

PRESSED PITCHERS in popular Pittsburgh patterns. (*Top row*), *Rochelle* (*princess feather*), Bakewell, Pears and Company; *tree of life*, George Duncan and Sons; *tulip*, Bryce, Richards; *cherry*, Bakewell, Pears and Company. (*Bottom row*), *Ashburton*, several firms; *ribbed palm*, McKee; *Stedman*, McKee; *almond thumbprint*, Bakewell, Pears and Company.

and had all the necessary machinery and appliances for huge-scale operations. It achieved a weekly payroll of better than $2,000, a yearly volume of better than $200,000, and markets in Cuba and South America, too. Probably because Adams himself had been one of the pioneers in helping to develop the lime-soda formula, the firm's glass retained an attractive clarity even through the late years of the century. In addition to tableware, Adams & Company made lamps, chimneys, and bottles. Finally it was absorbed by the United States Glass Company. *Baltimore pear,* another naturalistic Adams pattern, runs a good second to *wildflower* in popularity.

We planned two small cases of pitchers and one of miscellaneous pieces. Old-favorite pitchers like *Stedman* (McKee), *almond thumbprint* (Bakewell), *Jacob's ladder* (Bryce), *stippled grape and festoon* (Doyle), *maple leaf vaseline* (Gillinder), *Baltimore pear* (Adams), and *wheat and barley*

(Bryce, Walker) covered a range of time and taste. Among the odd pieces a few that stood out were *excelsior* candlesticks, *Rebecca at the well* frosted compotes, *pillar* variant pieces and bowls in *loop* (or *leaf,* to use the Pittsburgh name), a good amethyst paneled salt, a *honeycomb* celery worthy of New York state, *colonial* and *Ashburton* tumblers, and a McKee *colonial* covered sweetmeat in cobalt.

It seems anticlimatic to close a discussion of Pittsburgh glass with miscellaneous pieces and the decadent patterns of the nineties. The only way for any student or collector to gain a rounded picture of the variety of products, the skill of workmanship, and the soundness of design is to visit the exhibition at Carnegie Museum. No other American glass center can equal the continuous time of operation from 1797 to the present and the amount of glass produced, or can show greater versatility in its craftsmanship and wares.

PLUME, by Adams and Company (*1874-1890*). Often used as premiums by merchandising firms. This pattern, like its fellow *moon and star,* was continued by the United States Glass Company. *Moon and star,* more widely known, possessed a dignified heaviness of design, useful as a table set and appealing enough to modern collectors to be reproduced.

Pittsburgh white and clear
and the Bakewell patent

BY LOWELL INNES

THE USE OF WHITE AND CLEAR glass together may be traced throughout the history of glassmaking. Loops, dragging, marvering of white in a matrix of another color were techniques popular in earliest times around the Mediterranean. The combination has long appealed to glassmakers as dramatic, and the Venetians particularly employed it widely and successfully.

All the glass made by these early techniques was, of course, free blown and hand manipulated. American examples in the white and clear group include blown clear glass pieces with white loopings, as well as cased articles such as the blown sugar bowl of about 1835 in Figure 1 and the mid-century pillar-molded vase in Figure 2. Figure 3 shows another type, a pressed white vase on a clear blown foot; and Figure 4 still another, a clear goblet blown into a pressed base.

It remained for Benjamin Bakewell Jr., of the famous Pittsburgh glass firm which bore the Bakewell name from 1808 until 1882, to devise and patent a mechanical technique of pressing together glass of two different colors. In this process neither layer envelops the other, as in cased glass; the two colors join only at the contact surfaces. (Apsley Pellat in his *Curiosities of Glassmaking* describes clearly the steps in casing glass. The gaffer blows a bubble of the lining color; at the same time his assistant prepares one of the next color layer, opening the end of his bubble, or parison, and widening it almost like a bowl. To steady and to shape it, the assistant may insert it into a metal shell or he may merely rest it on the shell. Now the gaffer blows his lining bubble into the bowl-like aperture, and the two layers of glass adhere. Perfect fusion is accomplished by reheating in the glory hole, and the cased bubble is then worked into its final form. This process can be repeated for three or more colors.)

To quote from the patent itself (it was applied for on July 18, 1874, and is dated September 29 of the same year):

My invention consists in the manufacture of glass articles by pressing glass of different colors, one upon or above another, in a mold or molds, so as to form an article made up of two or more colors . . . by means of interchangeable plungers and rings or molds . . .

The patent drawing shown here (Fig. 5) does more to clarify the process, perhaps, than the long and involved description contained in the patent application itself.

At the close of this technical description Bakewell adds: "I am aware that bas-relief glass-work has been united to the outer surface of blown glassware by first pressing articles of bas-relief, and then blowing a glass article so as to unite therewith, and do not claim such a

Fig. 1. Free-blown sugar bowl, milk-white with clear casing; Pittsburgh type, c. 1835; over-all height, 7½ inches. *Except as noted, illustrations are from the author's collection.*

Fig. 2. Pittsburgh pillar-molded vase in white with clear casing, on clear blown base; c. 1850; height 10⅝ inches.

process"—a remark which sheds an interesting light on a well-known piece of white and clear glass, the Ihmsen goblet now at the Corning Museum of Glass (Fig. 4, here, and Plate 68, McKearin, *Two Hundred Years of American Blown Glass*). Frederick Carder, the noted glass technologist and founder of the original Steuben Glass Works, says that the Ihmsen goblet was produced in exactly this way; the process described, he says, is one that he himself used over many years.

In spite of the ingenuity of Bakewell's new method, the very scarcity of surviving specimens in double glass, as the pressed white and clear was called, shows that the new product did not "catch on." In the Bakewell and Pears catalogue of 1876 only four pieces are pictured, on page 47: three fruit bowls identical in design but of different sizes (Fig. 8, here, and Revi, *Nineteenth Century*

Glass, p. 154) and the footed tumbler (Fig. 6) which the catalogue calls a Boquet and which is also shown on the patent drawing. Only one other piece, the goblet with swirled stem shown in Figure 7, is known. The white portions of these five pieces of double glass are all formed of a definitely fiery opal except for that of Figure 7, which is of opaque white with only the faintest of opal shadings on the edge of the bottom rim.

Whether the fiery opal texture, which had appeared intermittently in American glassmaking without ever paying its way, made the cost of the new glass prohibitive I would not venture to guess. We do know, however, that until the formula for cheap "milk" glass was developed toward the end of the century, fiery opal never became a major product of one factory or swept the market as a separate fashion.

The few surviving pieces made by the Bakewell patent of 1874 have an undoubted charm of their own, but to anyone with a knowledge of other forms of white and clear glass it is plain that the artistic possibilities of this combination were better realized by craftsmen of the old world and by individual artisans in the new than they could ever have been by Mr. Bakewell's "new and useful Improvement."

Fig. 3. Pittsburgh vase with fiery opal pressed top and clear blown base, c. 1850; height 8⅜ inches.

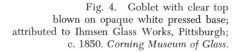

Fig. 4. Goblet with clear top blown on opaque white pressed base; attributed to Ihmsen Glass Works, Pittsburgh; c. 1850. *Corning Museum of Glass.*

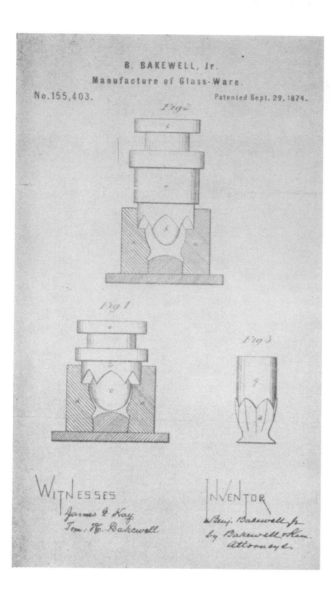

Fig. 5. Diagrams forming part of the Letters Patent of Benjamin Bakewell Jr. dated Sept. 29, 1874: "Figure 1 is a vertical section of the mold and the plunger and ring first used therewith. Fig. 2 is a like view of the mold with the second plunger and ring used therewith, and Fig. 3 is a view of the article formed by the mold and plungers shown."

Fig. 6. Double glass "Boquet" tumb clear on fiery opal pressed glass; Bakewell, c. 1875; height 4½ inches.

Fig. 7. "Double glass" gob clear and opaque white pressed gl Bakewell, c. 1875; height 6 inch

Fig. 8. Double glass open fruit or salad bowl of clear and fiery opal pressed glass; marked *B.P. & Co. Pat. Sept. 29th 1874;* height 3⅝ inches.

THE BAKEWELL GLASS FACTORY

By MARY E. BAKEWELL

BENJAMIN BAKEWELL by James R. Lambdin. *Courtesy of Mrs. T. H. B. McKnight.*

This article was written by the great-granddaughter of Benjamin Bakewell, the pioneer glassmaker of the Pittsburgh area. It was first published in Carnegie Magazine, *Pittsburgh, for July 1947, and is here reprinted by special permission. Lack of space prevents inclusion of Mrs. Bakewell's recollections of a childhood visit to the glasshouse — "a Crystal Abode of the Fairies."*

A DAMNING adjective was applied to Pittsburgh by the recent writer who spoke of "the disconsolate Monongahela." One must admit that the term might be deserved for certain aspects of the city: begrimed, incomplete, really inchoate — begun, but not yet finished and realized.

Yet some hundred and thirty years ago, to a newcome young Englishman, it doubtless seemed all of Utopia. For here were green hills, full-flowing rivers, a new settlement with opportunity at every hand; here he found the stuff of which life weaves good patterns.

Benjamin Bakewell was born at Derby, England, in 1767, the son of Joseph and Sarah Woodhouse Bakewell. Married in young manhood to Anne White, for support of her and their future family he became an importer of French goods. Through his constant expeditions across the Channel young Bakewell received a wide education, not only in another language but in another history, another culture than his own — in architecture, beautiful objects in church, museum, shops, in men and women different from those he knew and yet much the same. Furthermore, since he was to become a Liberal in outlook, it is interesting to note that he was a spectator of the French Revolution. Thereafter came the grim chapter of war between France and England — and the business of importation was ended.

In 1794 Benjamin Bakewell with his wife and children set sail for that new and promising country of the United States of America, to which many English eyes had turned. He established his family in New York City and started his old business of importing, but with little success, for the French and English war had effect even upon this far land, and when President Thomas Jefferson laid a stern embargo upon all foreign trade, importation died.

Why or how my great-grandfather's attention was drawn to glass manufacture has not been ascertained. England had known glass since the end of the first century A.D. With his intelligence and esthetic sense well developed it is reasonable to think that he may have mulled over certain ideas. Practically considered, Pittsburgh, ideally situated on navigable rivers, was in strategic position for any manufacturing. The art of glassmaking was older than history; a factory was at hand. Mr. Bakewell was an astute business man and grasped the possibilities. More than that, he had appreciation of beautiful things. Why not produce glass, then, in this new country just emerged from the wilderness? Records are few, but we have the information that, in 1808, a small glass plant in Pittsburgh, Pennsylvania, was purchased by Benjamin Bakewell from the firm of Robinson and Ensell, unsuccessful operators. The factory was located at the foot of Grant Street on the bank of the Monongahela River.

Over those almost impassable mountains, then, came his wife and children, the loyal housekeeper, and the "bound boy," the long journey made in what must have been a variety of the Conestoga wagon. After life in London — think of it, so to settle on the frontier. Pittsburgh had been a lonely outpost against a savage wilderness, a collection of rude log cabins surrounded by a stockade. In 1794 the little town had barely one hundred and fifty houses and, though by 1808 these had become frame or brick, even so, civilization was not far advanced.

Difficulties abounded for the mother of the family, not only in household supplies but in the matter of watching the children with the fear of Indians not yet driven from her mind. There were difficulties for the man in charge of family and business. Construction of the factory was poor; each glasshouse must have specially built furnaces to receive the melting pots of fire clay, in which was placed the combined ingredients — the sand, the potash, oxide of lead, sometimes saltpeter, and so on — to be fused in the ovens; materials were poor and costly and had to be transported by long distance on wagons or barges — pearl ash and red lead might come from Philadelphia, pot clay from New Jersey, white sand from Missouri; skilled workmen had to be brought in from considerable distance. The occasion was "piled with difficulty." For Benjamin Bakewell, it was to rise to the occasion.

Pittsburgh, however, grew with amazing speed. Not only were houses multiplied, but many of them became mansions whose architects were rightly proud. Niceties of existence began to be evident. The little town could boast of a post office, a canal, a stagecoach route providing a mere four days' trip to Philadelphia. Trade and commerce began to flourish.

For the Bakewell glasshouse the difficulties were gradually

PAIR OF PRESSED-GLASS COMPOTES with *Rebecca at the well* base. One is owned by Mrs. Douglas Stewart and the other by Henry King Siebeneck. COVERED SUGAR BOWL pressed in *Argus* pattern now known as *thumbprint*.

surmounted, by intelligence and persistence overcome, and the first successful flint-glass factory in this country became a reality. To the West Indies, Mexico, Bermuda, Buenos Aires, Lima, eventually were shipped crates filled with tons of glass — white, clear-metaled, beautiful. A reputation was made.

Though to modern ears it sounds a small affair, consider the time, the very early nineteenth century. A typical year was 1825 — the year, by the way, when the Sandwich glass began its career. In the Bakewell factory were sixty-one hands, exclusive of designers and engravers, sixty-one workmen trained in and brought from England, Belgium, and France. For these workmen was all consideration, the firm taking utmost interest in the men's welfare. With the living quarters nearby, the close association made for friendliness and high morale. Games and contests were staged, swimming, skating, and racing enjoyed. The sick or injured, widows and orphans were all cared for.

In this year $45,000 worth of glass was sold and shipped. Apothecary sundries, bottles, tumblers, épergnes, decanters, perfume holders, bureau knobs, and so on, had already gone down to Rio. Bakewell glass, furthermore, was on the shelves of the White House, President James Monroe in 1817 having ordered, in the words of the Pittsburgh *Mercury*, "a splendid equipage" of wineglasses, decanters, and tumblers of double flint, each bearing the engraved coat of arms of the United States. President Andrew Jackson, too, in 1832 ordered a set of Bakewell glass for his own use.

For nearly fifty years Bakewell's was a showplace in Pittsburgh, given loud acclaim from a never-ending stream of visitors. Elias Pym Fordham in his *Personal Narrative of Travel* in 1817 wrote, "Mr. Bakewell's works are admirable . . . His cut glass equals the best I have seen in England."

The following year Henry Bradshaw Fearon in his *Sketches of America*, published in London, wrote: "Witness such perfection on this side of the Atlantic, and especially in that part of America which a New Yorker supposes to be at the farther end of the world . . . It is well to bear in mind that the demand for these articles of elegant luxury lies in the western states! the inhabitants of Eastern America being still importers from the Old Country."

In 1825 Bakewell glass won the silver medal of the Franklin Institute for the best specimen of cut glass, in a competition that included the whole country.

Mrs. Anne Royall, who visited Pittsburgh in 1828 and published *Mrs. Royall's Pennsylvania, etc.* in Washington the following year, exclaimed, "Bakewell's is the place! . . . This establishment is entirely devoted to the manufacture of white or flint glass, and has succeeded in producing the best specimens of this article ever made in the United States . . . There is scarcely a stranger visits Pittsburgh who is not desirous of taking a peep at Bakewell's Glass House . . . The quality, variety, beauty, and brilliance of the endless piles of glass at Bakewell's is the greatest show I ever saw."

It is significant that Deming Jarves, thoroughly familiar with the flint-glass industry in the eastern states, and also proprietor of the Sandwich glassworks, writes in *Reminiscences of Glass-Making* in 1865: "We may well consider Mr. Bakewell as the father of the flint-glass business in this country; for he commenced the work in 1808, and by untiring efforts and industry brought it to a successful issue."

The pioneer position of Bakewell's in the history of American glassmaking was later substantiated by Joseph D. Weeks' *Report on Glass* in the Census of 1880, an exhaustive study of the whole subject. This concludes, "There can be no doubt that Mr. Bakewell is entitled to the honor of erecting and operating the first successful flint-glass house in the United States."

Magazines and newspapers of the time tell the story of Lafayette's visit to Pittsburgh in 1825. It was a flower-strewn, flag-waving, drum-resounding occasion for the city, and an occasion for Bakewell's as well: workmen pulling the forelock, "making a leg," grinning, and bashful; the owners, pleased, and all of graciousness; the General and his escort proving most admiring guests.

At the glasshouse of Bakewell, Page and Bakewell, as it was then known, were presented to General Lafayette two cut-glass, double-flint vases, beautiful in quality and design. These vases were lent by Lafayette's granddaughter to the World's Fair in Chicago in 1893. The letter of acknowledgment, written by the distinguished visitor, is a treasure in the Bakewell family:

> Gentlemen:
> The gratification I have felt at the sight of your beautiful manufacture is still enhanced by the friendly reception I have met from you and by the most acceptable present you are pleased to offer me. Accept my affectionate thanks, good wishes, and regards.
>
> Lafayette

Benjamin Bakewell died in 1844. The glass firm continued under management of the two sons, Thomas and John Palmer, also a nephew, John Palmer Pears. Benjamin Bakewell and Benjamin Bakewell Campbell, both grandsons, and Benjamin Page Bakewell, grand-nephew, later joined the firm, and still later, more distant relatives, Thomas, Benjamin, and Harry Pears.

Through success and vicissitudes the factory wrought on. In the great fire of 1845 it was totally destroyed, with what loss one can guess. It was rebuilt immediately on the same location, however, and in 1854 moved to the south side of Pittsburgh. In 1881 the business dissolved.

There will always remain an element of the marvelous about glass, a substance resulting from fusion of a combination of silica with various bases. That such diverse constituents as sand, lime, lead, even bone, iron filings, cobalt, can be fused into this beautiful, transparent, translucent thing we call glass awakens in us more than response to beauty. For here we are near such transformation of matter as urges our thought beyond confines of a factory.

SPOONHOLDER, CREAMER, SUGAR BOWL, and BUTTER DISH, pressed in sawtooth pattern. *Collection of Mr. and Mrs. Donald Campbell Bakewell.*

PRESSED GLASS DECANTER in honeycomb pattern. BLOWN CELERY GLASS and WATER GOBLET. *Collection of Mrs. Charles Wharton, Jr.*

Fig. 1 — GLASS BY BAKEWELL OF PITTSBURGH
The two bell goblets are of blown glass, and appear to be of the early period. The "patent" shell dish and the dolphin-footed dishes are of pressed glass, and belong to the mid-nineteenth century or somewhat later. This dolphin design was popular with many different factories.
Owned by Miss Mary E. Bakewell

The First Successful Flint Glass Factory in America

Bakewell, Pears & Co. (1808-1882)

By THOMAS C. PEARS, JR.

Illustrations furnished by Mrs. T. H. B. McKnight, from collections as noted in the text

WHEN the Marquis de Lafayette visited Pittsburgh on his famous tour in the year 1825, he expressed a wish, according to the account of Levasseur, his secretary, to see

some of the ingenious establishments which constitute the glory and prosperity of that manufacturing city, which, for the variety and excellence of its products deserves to be compared to our own Saint-Etienne or to Manchester in England. He was struck by the excellence and perfection of the processes employed in the various workshops which he examined; but that which interested him above all was the manufacture of glass, some patterns of which were presented to him, that, for their clearness and transparency might have been admired even by the side of the glass of Baccarat.*

These patterns consisted of two beautiful vases of cut-glass, on one of which, engraved in a medallion, is shown a view of the chateau at La Grange, the salon of which the pieces were to adorn, and on the other, the American eagle, likewise in a medallion. These vases were loaned by a granddaughter of Lafayette to the French Commission and exhibited at the World's Fair at Chicago in 1893. Miss Mary E. Bakewell of Sewickley, Pennsylvania, is in possession of the original autographed letter in which Lafayette expresses his thanks for these handsome specimens of early American glass. It reads as follows:

*A. Levasseur, Lafayette in America in 1824 and 1825. Philadelphia, Carey and Lea, 1829, Vol. II., page 183.

Pittsburgh, May 31, 1825.

Gentlemen,
The patriotic gratification I have felt at the sight of your beautiful manufacture is still enhanced by the friendly reception I have met from you and by the most acceptable present you are pleased to offer me. Accept my affectionate thanks, good wishes and regards.
LAFAYETTE.
Messrs. Bakewell, Page and Bakewell.

In the same year the proprietors of this establishment were awarded the silver medal by the Franklin Institute, for the best specimen of cut-glass. Several years previously, 1817, they had made a service of glass to President Monroe's order, which is described in part in a contemporary editorial in the Pittsburgh *Mercury*, as

a splendid equipage of glass . . . consisting of a full set of Decanters, Wine Glasses and Tumblers of various sizes and different models, exhibiting a brilliant specimen of double flint, engraved and cut by Jardelle, in which this able artist has displayed his best manner, and the arms of the United States on each piece have a fine effect. The glass itself must either have been selected with great care, or the spirited proprietors must have made considerable progress in their art, for we have seldom seen any samples so perfectly pellucid and free from tinct. Upon the whole we think the present service equal, if not superior to the elegant Decanters presented to the President when he passed through Pittsburgh last year.*

Again, a few years later, 1832, another President of the United States, the redoubtable Andrew Jackson, ordered from this same firm:

*Pittsburgh *Mercury*. November 10, 1818.

Fig. 2 — Glass by Bakewell of Pittsburgh
Two *prism* pattern footed dishes, a cake or fruit dish, *Rebecca at the Well,* a blown and engraved decanter showing an interesting development of the earlier *Chestnut* bottles, and a six-inch pressed plate in *Saxon* pattern. Of the group, the decanter is perhaps the earliest. The *Rebecca* probably belongs not far from the Centennial period. The cover of the first dish should be omitted.
Owned by Mrs. T. H. B. McKnight.

a set of glass for his own use, consisting of large and splendid bowls, with and without stands, celery glasses, pitchers, quart and pint decanters, tumblers, wine and champaign glasses, salts, etc., all executed in the very best style of workmanship. The glass is as pellucid as crystal; and the beautiful cuttings give a brillancy of effect not easily described. We understand the order is valued at about $1500.*

These examples will suffice to indicate that the old Bakewell, Pears & Co. glasshouse enjoyed an unusual reputation in the early days of the last century; hence it is not surprising to find that it is the one establishment in the city that is always mentioned by name and described in detail by all the early travelers who passed through the Gateway of the West.

When Alexander Wilson, the famous ornithologist, visited Pittsburgh in 1810, he wrote a letter wherein he remarked particularly on the various glass works, and stated that,

Mr. Bakewell, the proprietor of the best, shewed . . . yesterday a chandelier of his manufacture highly ornamented . . . for which he received 300 dollars. It would ornament the . . . in Philada. . . . and is perfectly transparent.†

Fordham in his *Personal Narrative,* 1817, says:

Mr. Bakewell's works are admirable. He has excellent artists, both French and English. His cut glass equals the best I have seen in England.‡

Fig. 3 — Glass by Bakewell of Pittsburgh
Blown and cut flint decanter.
Owned by Mrs. Charles Wharton.

And Fearon in his *Sketches of America,* 1818, remarks his astonishment

to witness such perfection on this side of the Atlantic, and especially in that part of America which a New Yorker supposes to be at the farther end of the world. At Messrs. Page & Bakewell's glass warehouse I saw chandeliers and numerous articles in cut glass of a very splendid description; among the latter was a pair of decanters, cut from a London pattern, the price of which will be 8 guineas. It is well to bear in mind that the demand for these articles of elegant luxury lies in the western states! the inhabitants of Eastern America being still importers from the Old Country.*

This same note of astonishment appears in *A Journal of Travel into the Arkansas Territory (1818)* in which Thomas Nuttall writes:

The day after my arrival (in Pittsburgh) I went through the flint-glass works of Mr. Bakewell, and was surprised to see the beauty of this manufacture, in the interior of the United States, in which the expensive decorations of cutting and engraving (amidst every discouragement incident to a want of taste and wealth) were carried to such perfection. The productions of this manufacture find their way to New Orleans, and even to some of the islands of the West Indies. The President, Monroe, as a liberal encourager of domestic manufactures, had on his visit to those works given orders for a service of glass, which might indeed be exhibited as a superb specimen of this elegant art.†

And so the testimony goes, all of it

*John Newton Boucher, *A Century and a Half of Pittsburgh and Her People.* The Lewis Publishing Company, 1908, Vol. I, page 236.
†Letter to Alexander Lawson. Quoted from Francis Hobart Herrick, *Audubon the Naturalist.* New York, D. Appleton and Company, 1917, Vol. I, pages 205 and 206.
‡Elias Pym Fordham, *Personal Narrative of Travel,*

Cleveland, The Arthur H. Clarke Company, 1906, pages 75 and 76.
*Henry Bradshaw Fearon, *A Narrative of a Journey,* London, printed for Longman, Hurst, Reese, Orme, and Brown, 1818, pages 206 and 207.
†Thomas Nuttall, *Early Western Travels,* Vol. XII, page 45.

bearing out the judgment of the eccentric Mrs. Royall, who visited Pittsburgh in 1828, that "Bakewell's is the place!" And indeed it was for fifty years or more the show place of Pittsburgh. Mrs. Royall's description is too long to quote in full, so we shall content ourselves with one or two brief extracts. She writes:

This establishment is entirely devoted to the manufacture of white or flint glass, and has succeeded in producing the best specimens of this article ever made in the United States. The admiration of this glass is not confined merely to home observers, but the great amount of it which has been exported testifies the reputation it enjoys abroad; and there is scarcely a stranger visits Pittsburgh, who is not desirous of taking a peep at Bakewell's Glass House. . . . The quality, variety, beauty and brilliancy of the endless piles of glass at Bakewell's is the greatest show I ever saw. Everything made of glass is found here, — and I would say, the patterns and clearness of the pieces, is equal, if not superior, to the Boston glass. It cannot be exceeded. . . . In the manufacture of this article Pittsburgh and the surrounding country enjoys an extensive reputation. . . . The glass of Pittsburgh, and the parts adjacent, is known and sold from Maine to New Orleans. Even in Mexico they quaff their beverage from the beautiful white flint of Messrs. Bakewell, Page and Bakewell.*

Fig. 4 — GLASS BY BAKEWELL OF PITTSBURGH
Blown and cut decanter, and a celery holder. Of the two, the decanter seems much the older. The type suggests the earliest period of the factory.
Owned by Mrs. George I. Holdship.

on page 86 of his *Report on Glass*, Census of 1880, says, "There can be no doubt that Mr. Bakewell is entitled to the honor of erecting and operating the first successful flint-glass house in the United States." In a letter dated December 17, 1836, and reproduced in Lyford's *Western Directory* (page 103), Mr. Bakewell himself states that his establishment for the manufacture of flint glass "is the oldest of the kind now extant in the United States." And Deming Jarves, who was thoroughly familiar with the flint glass industry in the Eastern States, and was the proprietor of the Sandwich Glass Works, writes in his *Reminiscences of Glass-Making* (page 71):

We may well consider Mr. Bakewell as the father of the flint-glass business in this country; for he commenced the work in 1808, and by untiring efforts and industry brought it to a successful issue. For the skill, judgment, labor and perseverance devoted by him to the progress of the art, he truly merits the *Artium Magister* so often bestowed on those least worthy of its dignity and honor.

It is not within the scope of this article to write the history of Bakewell, Pears and Co., interesting as that history is, and important in the development of the American glass industry. The concern was always a family affair, and,

These rather extended notices will prepare the reader for the statement that the old glasshouse of Bakewell, Pears & Co., founded in the year 1808, and continuing in uninterrupted operation for nearly three-quarters of a century, or until the year 1882, was the first successful flint glass factory in America, a claim for which there is abundant testimony which it would be entirely outside the purpose of this article to cite. We shall, however, record the deliberate judgment of three competent authorities.

Joseph D. Weeks

Mrs. Anne Royall, Mrs. Royall's Pennsylvania, etc., Washington, 1829, Vol. II, pages 110, 113, and 125.

under the successive management of Benjamin Bakewell, the founder, Thomas Bakewell, his son, and John Palmer Pears, who, on his death in 1874, is spoken of as "the oldest person in this country engaged in the business," it spanned the entire period of that development from the very beginning which it inaugurated, up to the point where the making of flint glass had become one of the most important branches of manufacturing in

Fig. 5 — GLASS BY BAKEWELL OF PITTSBURGH
Two engraved tumblers in the Bohemian style; and a pressed goblet.
Owned by the author.

the country.* When the fires were finally allowed to go out, in the year 1882, it had indeed an honorable record to show from the day when, in Albert Gallatin's *Report on Manufactures (1810)*, the recently established works at Pittsburgh were cited as the only works of the kind in the United States, and were described as, even then, making "decanters, tumblers, and every other description of flint-glass of a superior quality."

The recent death of my own father, Thomas C. Pears, of Pittsburgh, removed the last surviving member of the firm. It was "a famous institution in its day, but now numbered among the things of a forgotten past." It seems strange to the writer that it is referred to only in a brief note in Mrs. N. Hudson Moore's excellent work, *Old Glass*.

In concluding this article let us glance at some of the patterns made at the old Pittsburgh Flint Glass Works. A number of fine specimens are still in existence, and are cherished by various members of the family and by other fortunate possessors. We have already described the glass made for Presidents Monroe and Jackson and for the Marquis de Lafayette. There is mention also in the family correspondence of a Clinton tumbler, made in the year 1826.

Mrs. Sicard has pointed out that the pattern described by Mrs. Royall, on her visit to Pittsburgh this same year, is identical with that of the hound tumbler shown in Figure 221 of *Old Glass*, and attributed to the Kensington Works. Indeed I strongly suspect that there are other specimens of Bakewell-Pears glass that are described as unknown or are wrongly attributed.

For instance, in a little handbook, *Sandwich Glass*, 1922, by Lenore Wheeler Williams, is to be found a section on *The Dolphin Group*. The Dolphin pattern is described, and several illustrations are given. On page 73, the author says:

Illustration 8, page 68, is a very remarkably clear white Dolphin dish on standard. It measures 9 by 10½ inches. There is a full size Dolphin, early type, with hollow head supporting a balanced shell. The piece is unique.

Not quite so unique as it appears. The writer of the present article possesses one

*J. Leander Bishop, *A History of American Manufacture*, Philadelphia, Edward Young and Company, 1864, Vol. II, p. 156.

Fig. 6 — GLASS BY BAKEWELL OF PITTSBURGH
Heavy pressed decanter finished by cutting and engraving.
Owned by the author.

duplicate specimen, and another belongs to Miss Mary E. Bakewell. It is not a Sandwich, but a Bakewell-Pears product. The specimens referred to have been in the family from the day they were brought from the old factory. In fact my father was manager of the factory at the time they were made, and an old catalogue shows several cuts, one in opal glass. There is likewise a very beautiful and graceful *Pony Dolphin* champagne.

The illustrations which accompany this article include, in addition, from the collection of Miss Bakewell, a shell dish which was made in various sizes and styles of glass; two very old bell goblets; and another dolphin supporting a dish of a pattern designed by Thomas C. Pears, and used to good effect in other articles, especially in a set consisting of tray, water pitcher, and goblets (*Fig. 1*).

The specimens from the collection of Mrs. T. H. B. McKnight of Sewickley, consist of a six-inch plate in the *Saxon* pattern; a fine old whisky decanter; a bowl and cover, and a comport, both of the *prism* pattern. The comport should not have a cover on it as in the illustration. This has evidently been supplied from another piece. The gem of Mrs. McKnight's collection, however, is the *Rebecca at the Well* supporting a dish of the pattern above referred to (*Fig. 2*). The *Rebecca at the Well* was also used as a candlestick. Mrs. McKnight has the punch bowl which was exhibited by Bakewell, Pears & Co. at the Centennial at Philadelphia in 1876 and the medal which was awarded for it. The piece was designed by her father, Benjamin Bakewell, Jr.

I would likewise call attention to the decanters and the bell goblet owned by Mrs. Charles Wharton and Mrs. George I. Holdship. They are very old, and the cutting is excellent. From my own collection I have shown illustrations of two engraved tumblers, and a goblet of the *diamond* pattern, called, by the layman, *pineapple*. The two carafes are cut, and are engraved with the family initial. The cake plate is likewise good (*Figs. 5, 6, 7*). It is of very heavy flint, and of great brilliance. It was purchased by my grandmother, Mrs. Sarah

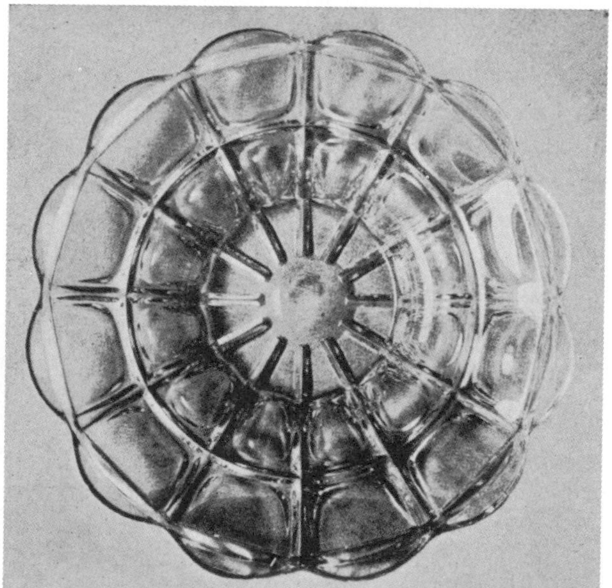

Fig. 7 — GLASS BY BAKEWELL OF PITTSBURGH
Cake plate of heavy flint glass. Purchased in 1853.
Owned by Mrs. Thomas C. Pears.

Fahnestock, at the old factory, in 1853. I have noted the origin and ownership of these various specimens as evidence of their authenticity.

Two other very interesting specimens remain to be described. One of them appears as an illustration of this article. It is a communion cup presented by Benjamin Bakewell to the Unitarian Church in Meadville, Pennsylvania, where it is still in use. One of the handles has been broken off and has been replaced.

For the information concerning my final specimen, I am indebted to W. J. Holland, Director Emeritus of the Carnegie Museum, Pittsburgh. In the Museum is a glass prism that is truly famous. It was made from a piece of flint glass, part of a large mass found in the ruins of Bakewell, Pears & Co.'s glasshouse after the disastrous fire, which, on April tenth, 1845, nearly destroyed the city of Pittsburgh. The prism was cut by Dr.

Fig. 8 — GLASS BY BAKEWELL OF PITTSBURGH

A fine old communion cup presented by Benjamin Bakewell to the Unitarian Church in Meadville, Pennsylvania, where the piece is still in use. One of the handles is a restoration. On the other side of the cup appear the words *This Do In—*.

David Alter, of Freeport, Pennsylvania, "a physician of inquiring and ingenious mind, who was early in life attracted to the study of electricity and chemistry, having as a boy read the story of Franklin, and who, quite independently, and yet in fact before the discovery of Morse, invented a crude system of telegraphing." It was by the use of this prism of Bakewell-Pears glass that the doctor made the experiments which entitle him to be known as the first discoverer of spectrum analysis.

Among the many patterns used again and again in various articles turned out by the old glass works may be mentioned the following: *argus, thistle, prism, flute, flute and mitre, arabesque, cherry, lace, heart, Rochelle, Etruscan, Saxon,* and so on. How many of them I used to see on the shelves of our pantry when I was a boy, and how comparatively few of them have survived the hazards of subsequent years!

Concerning William Peter Eichbaum and Bakewell's

By RHEA MANSFIELD KNITTLE

"STRIKE the drums!" shouts the Comte d'Oyat. Dr. Guillotine's knife descends; blood spurts; and the head of Louis XVI rolls from the block. Grotesque shadows of Marat, Danton, Paine, seem to draw the curtains, but the act is not done. At the palace, a scintillant chandelier of crystal crashes to the floor, a shattered mass; and the heart of William Peter Eichbaum, glass cutter to the King of France, bleeds as he hears the ill-omened tidings.

Ever to America from the trouble spots of Europe, come the emigrés — staggering now from the cataclysm of the French Revolution. It is 1793, and they are docking at the wharves of the City of Brotherly Love, where the persecuted of many lands have found a haven. A year passes, and William Peter Eichbaum is now superintendent of a small glasshouse on the Schuylkill River, above Philadelphia.*

Two more years elapse, and we find this man, who has fashioned exquisite glass buttons for the little Dauphin's

blue velvet coat, joining his fortunes with those of the irrepressible Irish-American James O'Hara, and plodding over the Alleghenies to the garrison town of Pittsburgh, where O'Hara and Isaac Craig are about to erect a glasshouse. Eichbaum directs the building of the works, where, in 1797, the first bottle is blown. Eichbaum is recognized as the best glass expert of the district.

But for a time he cherishes ambitions in another direction, for we read the following in the Pittsburgh *Gazette* of September 12, 1800:

WILLIAM EICHBAUM

Begs leave to inform the public that he has opened a house of Entertainment at the Sign of the INDIAN QUEEN, on Front Street, near Market street, where he shall use his utmost endeavors to give satisfaction to travellers and others who may please to call upon him.

Pittsburgh May 15, 1800:

N.B. He wishes to acquaint the public that he follows the glazing business and cutting of glass to any pattern.

Again, from *The Tree of Liberty*, a new name for the *Gazette*, under the date of February 12, 1803, this self-explanatory notice appears:

---

*Eichbaum was born in Attenbach, Saxony; migrated to Burgundy; was recognized by the Court of France. He came to America to escape the Revolution. He came to be recognized as a leading citizen of Pittsburgh, where he died in 1866.

Eleven years go by after Eichbaum has come to the fast-growing little town. And then we find him engaged by two young Englishmen, Benjamin Page and Benjamin Bakewell, who have taken over an unsuccessful glasshouse from Robinson and Ensell. Bakewell is an arrival from Derby, England, in 1808. So the famous house of Bakewell's starts on its way. Eichbaum is its leading glass cutter. In 1810 he cuts the first crystal chandelier in America, six lights and shower upon shower of rainbow-casting prisms.

* * *

Early chronicles state that Ensell owned an interest in the works for about a year, or until 1809, and then withdrew, and that Thomas Kinder had a share in the new management. The house was represented in New York by another member of the Kinder family, Robert, who handled the trade along the coast and acted as commission merchant for foreign exportations. Bakewell's was, from the start, a glasshouse of pretensions, with shipments from the Manhattan port, and, by the water-ways of the Ohio and the Mississippi rivers, to the Gulf.

This southern artery, afforded by the navigable river system, gave the early Pittsburgh houses a far-reaching channel of commerce; for, loaded on flat boats — and later, on steamers — at the point where the Allegheny and the Monongahela conjoin, boxes and boxes of glass started on their way to Mexico City, Bermuda, Rio de Janeiro, and around the Cape to Buenos Aires and Lima. And today, a Yankee in almost any Latin port may gaze upon some glittering lighting fixture "ravishingly beautiful" (as Mark Twain described those later lights on the Mississippi River boats), believing them products of English, Irish, French, or Spanish glasshouses; whereas, truth to tell, they are more than likely to be Bakewell products from the magic hand of Eichbaum.

The early output of the firm was surprisingly large. To note a few at random: vases, decanters, pitchers, bottles, flasks, cruets, candelabra, tumblers, wines, sweet-meats. In 1828, the Pittsburgh *Mercury* carried the following advertisement, which speaks for itself:

BAKEWELL, PAGE & BAKEWELL
Flint Glass Manufacturers
Have for Sale, an Assortment of
ASTRAL, OR SINUMBRAL LAMPS
On Pedestals and for Suspension.
Also, Tuscan, Vase, Mantel and
Chamber Lamps
Which, in addition to their usual stock of
Plain and Cut
FLINT GLASS
Patent Moulded, Plain
and Cut
Bureau Mountings (etc. etc.)
Will be disposed of on the lowest terms.
Pittsburgh, November 20

To go back to the year 1811, Bakewell and Page moved from the old Monongahela works to more commodious buildings on Water Street, corner of Grant, with a warehouse on Wood Street, near Second. Theirs was recognized thus early as the largest flint glasshouse in the Western Hemisphere. Distance had no more terrors for a Bakewell than for a Ledyard, a Crowninshield, or a Perkins. All roads led to and from their glasshouse. Their saltpeter, until 1825, was brought from the caves of Kentucky, and then, for a time, from Calcutta, India. Holland clay was used. The world gave; they assembled and produced; the world assimilated.

During the red letter year of 1825, sixty-one hands were employed, exclusive of twelve engravers and ornamenters; $45,000 worth of goods was turned out; and the plant consumed 30,000 bushels of coal in its furnaces. For a period of ten years one employee alone blew six hundred tumblers daily. The firm took great pride and interest in their workmen, who are said to have excelled both in quantity and quality of production. The living quarters of the men, adjacent to the works, developed a friendliness of intercourse and a high morale which might well turn a modern welfare worker green with envy. Games and contests of all kinds were staged; skating, swimming, and boating races were engaged in; and the injured, the sick, the widow and the orphan were never forgotten. It was, in a manner, an ideal condition, similar in many ways to that which made for satisfaction at Sandwich. Pity that neither could endure!

They made opal curtain holdbacks, mirror and bureau knobs which cannot be distinguished from those of Sandwich, and turned out all manner of river-boat equipment, which, at that period, was elaborate to the last degree. The finest grade of bar goods also came from their furnaces, and much glass which now is catalogued as "Baltimore" is also Bakewell. From compotes to cup plates the list continues. The popular bellflower and dewdrop came from Bakewell's firm as they did from every other flint glass factory of the period.

A diversified list, not at all inclusive, taken from one month's production, gives us an idea of the versatility of the concern:

Apothecary sundries.	Perfume and unguent bottles.
Confectionary jars.	Bottles, vials, flasks.
Decanters.	Glass canteens.
Carafes.	Table glass.
Lighting devices.	Bar goods for river boats.
Bureau knobs in amber.	Lantern glasses.
Mirror knobs — ditto.	Colored glasses for ships.
Holdbacks — ditto.	Toothpick holders.

Tons of glass, tons of beautiful, clear-metaled glass: in a line, this sums up the accomplishment of this house. Yet the collector in general knows little about it.

In 1836, John P. Pears entered the firm, and remained with it until his death, in 1874. During this period the house was generally known as *Bakewell's & Co.* — Benjamin, Thomas, and John Bakewell being the other members of the firm at the time of Pears' joining. Harry C. Pears entered the business in 1878, and, I believe, all the later owners of this well-known establishment were descended from the original founders. The plant ceased operation in 1881-2.

THE FORT PITT GLASS WORKS

By JOHN RAMSAY

FIG. 1 — "FORT PITT" EAGLE CUP PLATE. Made at the Fort Pitt Glass Works, Pittsburgh. Occurs likewise with plain edge and with alternating large and small scallops

FIG. 2 — FROM THE PITTSBURGH AND ALLEGHENY DIRECTORY, 1856–1857

THE first glasshouse in Pittsburgh was that built by O'Hara & Craig in 1797. These men were not glassmakers, but promoters, who played a large part in the development of the city. They brought William Peter Eichbaum, a German glasscutter, from the Schuylkill Glass Works in Philadelphia to manage their plant. In December 1798, they leased it to Eichbaum, Wendt & Company, a firm made up of employees, but as this arrangement proved unsuccessful, the owners regained control in 1801. Eichbaum left, to start a tavern and later a glasscutting establishment, and William Price, an Englishman, became manager of the reorganized firm.

The plant had been making green window glass and bottles, but Price evidently understood the making of flint glass, and the owners decided to enter this field. A letter from Craig to O'Hara states that he "offered to show a specimen of his abilities without charge." The flint-glass furnace was built in 1802. In the same year the equipment of the unsuccessful Ohio Glass Company, organized by General James Wilkinson, Hugh Scott, Ebenezer Denny, Anthony Beelen, and others, was bought by O'Hara and Craig. They likewise engaged that company's superintendent, J. B. LaFleur, a Frenchman. He may have managed the factory's green glass production, but no record of him after 1802 has been found. According to

Cramer's *Almanac*, however, the factory was in 1804 turning out cut and blue flint glass, and was still making "flint glass tumblers, decanters, wine glasses" in 1810.

Price was the first of a number of Englishmen who entered the glass industry in Pittsburgh. He was followed by Bakewell & Ensell (the firm later became Bakewell, Page & Bakewell), who built a flint glasshouse in 1807 and were so immediately successful that they drove the earlier establishment from the field. They attracted other English glassmen to the town. One Robert B. Curling is listed as a "pot-maker" at Bakewell's in the Pittsburgh directory of 1815. Price does not appear in this or other directories of the period, but in 1827 William Price, Robert B. Curling, and his sons, William and Alfred B., built the Fort Pitt Glass Works at Washington and Franklin (later Fourth) Streets, in the downtown section of Pittsburgh proper. This is Price's first reappearance in available records since 1802. A year later, in September 1828, Price left the firm, which became R. B. Curling & Company, made up of the three Curlings and Henry Higbee (also spelled Higby). The latter, a merchant, was in charge of the sales end of the business.

FIG. 3 — LACY PRESSED-GLASS PITCHER. Base marked *R. B. Curling & Sons Fort Pitt*. Probably made between 1828 and 1834

The Fort Pitt Glass Works is listed in the directories of the period as making flint glass, and later describes its wares with the familiar term, "Cut, Moulded and Plain." In accordance with the custom of the times, the firm probably made a variety of tableware, and anything else in flint glass that it found salable. But the Curlings were obviously alive to new developments in glassmaking. A pressed-glass pitcher (*Fig. 3*) shows that they were quick to adopt the new method of pressing glass developed at Cambridge and Sandwich. The piece also shows that they copied with considerable fidelity the delicate "lacy" designs so closely identified with the latter factory. In my opinion the inscription on the base, *R. B. Curling & Sons Fort Pitt*, dates the pitcher between 1828, when Price left the company, and 1834. For on July 13 of the latter year, Higbee retired from the firm and it became Curling, Robertson & Company. It may be noted in passing that Higbee, after a period of dealing in imported and presumably domestic "China, Glass, and Queensware," re-entered the glass manufacturing business in 1847 as a partner of Higby & Gallagher.

Robert B. Curling remained as head of the Company, but apparently retired before 1839. He is listed in the directory of that year as "gent," not "glass mfr.," invoking the old definition of gentleman as a man with no visible means of support. William Curling remained a member of the firm until about 1840, Alfred until 1856. Morgan Robertson and Henry A. Ringwalt represented the new interest. In 1856 another partnership, Curling, Ringwalt & Company maintained what was probably a sales office or warehouse on Penn Avenue opposite the Pennsylvania Railroad Station.

The manufacturers continued to produce the same "line," though there is little evidence regarding it beyond their advertisements. The fairly common Fort Pitt eagle cup plate (*Fig. 1*) was undoubtedly made at this glasshouse, but it cannot be dated accurately, since the name Fort Pitt was used throughout the life of the factory. It is probable, too, that the Curlings, with two or three other Pittsburgh firms, made lacy glass, although in most cases exact identification is impossible and even tentative attribution is dangerous.

But one or two lacy cup plates, in addition to the *Fort Pitt*, can be traced to Pittsburgh factories. And those shallow bowls, from three and a half to eight inches in diameter, bearing a design of shields with three stars — the "Washington arms" — on a stippled ground may be Pittsburgh products; likewise bowls, up to eleven inches in diameter, with a design of acanthus scrolls and fine stippling. For one thing, they seem to be found more commonly in the middle west than in the east. Moreover, they frequently show poor pressing and poor metal, in clear glass as well as in aquamarine, green, and pinkish shades. And it is worth noting that the marked Curling creamer shows crude workmanship, both in the glass itself and in the making of the mold with its "off-center" motives and incomplete band of serrations. The *Fort Pitt* cup plate has been found with the pinkish tinge that is due to the use of too much manganese dioxide as a "decolorizer" — a characteristic of other early Pittsburgh flint glass — and in a rather unsuccessful light amethyst. It is usually, however, sharply pressed in sparkling clear glass, and also occurs in beautiful shades of deep amethyst and sapphire blue. Hence the Fort Pitt glasshouse could, on occasion, turn out first-class ware.

The Pittsburgh directory of 1856–1857 contains a full-page advertisement of the Fort Pitt Glass Works (*Fig. 2*). This shows, in addition to a number of examples of tableware in heavy pressed designs similar to those made by other Pittsburgh houses, a lacy-glass covered sugar bowl. The artist has sketched the pattern crudely, but accurately enough to indicate the octagonal paneled shape and delicate detail. Among the pieces of pattern glass that are portrayed appear two new patterns, exemplified by two covered sugar bowls. Since neither is shown in Ruth Webb Lee's *Early American Pressed Glass*, they may be considered rare.

Of the other pieces shown, the decanter and goblet at the top

of the page are in the pattern classified by Mrs. Lee as *waffle and thumbprint* and credited to the New England Glass Company, with the notation that it was copied by other houses. The Fort Pitt decanter lacks the "patent stopper" of the New England original. *Waffle and thumbprint* occurs again in what appear to be a wineglass and cordial illustrated in the group on the right-hand side of the page. The other pieces at the top are a small bitters bottle in unusual shape with square base, and a wineglass in the pattern called *colonial* by Mrs. Lee. Other pieces in apparently the same pattern, though with hexagonal base and slenderer proportions, are shown on the right: a footed tumbler, a wine, and a cordial. A tall slim *colonial* goblet with plain base, matching the piece at the top, is illustrated in the left-hand group.

The same group includes a hexagonal paneled tumbler. This type was made by many of the midwestern flint glasshouses and is found in a wide variety of colors, as well as in a number of design variations. This example has an applied handle, but that fact should not encourage attribution of all such handled tumblers to the Fort Pitt Glass Works. The tall flared tumbler in the same illustration is also a common type; in fact, the pattern continued to be made until very recent times. But the footed tumbler on the other end of the row is unusual.

Finally, the advertisement adds, in the old tradition, "Also Window Glass of Every Description. Also Druggists' Ware, Demijohns, and Black Bottles." Possibly the factory actually made these; possibly they were bought from green glasshouses and carried in stock at the warehouse which, at 17 Wood Street, was some distance from the plant.

The firm of Curling, Robertson & Company was dissolved in 1857. Edward Dithridge, who is named as a partner in the advertisement, was a glassblower in the factory in 1839, and is so listed again in the directory of 1850. By 1856 he had been admitted to the firm. In 1863 his name appears in directories as owner of the business. The introduction of kerosene and of chimneys for oil lamps had created a great demand for lighting glassware, and Dithridge entered this field, abandoning the manufacture of tableware. He was highly successful and made some fine engraved and etched lamps and globes. The firm continued in business until the turn of the century.

SOUTH GERMAN SAMPLER (*1737*). No motive enjoyed greater favor among makers of samplers — German, English, French, or American — than did flowers. These are unusually realistic. *From the Boston Museum of Fine Arts*

THE IHMSEN FAMILY:
PIONEER PITTSBURGH GLASSMAKERS

By JESSIE and DELPHINE McCREADY

THE more one studies the subject, the more completely one agrees with Rhea Mansfield Knittle's statement, "The various members of the Ihmsen family became associated with so many glass-making endeavors that it is next to impossible accurately to chronicle their undertakings" (*Early American Glass*). However, thanks to acquaintance with a member of the Ihmsen family, we think that we may throw considerable light on a hitherto obscure chapter of personal history. At any rate, we have established the relationships of the various Ihmsens engaged in glassmaking in this country. The following genealogical table, though lacking some dates, presents the case in compact form:

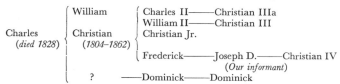

Charles Ihmsen was born in Steinbach, Westphalia, Germany. For over two hundred years his ancestors had been glassmakers, the business always descending to the eldest son in each generation. Charles came to America about 1795 and settled at Frederick, Maryland, where he was doubtless in the employ of Amelung's glass factory at the time of its collapse in 1798. We find him next, in 1807, after the embargo had been imposed against English goods, stopping at Friendship Hill, to confer with Albert Gallatin. Advised by that extraordinary person to undertake glassmaking in Pittsburgh, Ihmsen trekked westward to the smoky city. He was by no means penniless, for we find him almost immediately in partnership with Ensell, Wendt & Company. Theirs was the fourth glasshouse to be established west of the Allegheny Mountains, and the second to produce window glass. The factory, located in the Birmingham district of Pittsburgh, also turned out bottles and vials. We are sure that this pioneer Ihmsen was Charles, and not Christian, as Mrs. Knittle states in *Early American Glass*, because Christian was not born until 1804, at least nine years after Charles had begun his career in this country.

From this time on Charles Ihmsen seems to have been connected with several different concerns. We may suspect that the associations were concurrent rather than consecutive, since the dates available curiously overlap. Ensell, Wendt & Company became Ihmsen, Wendt & Company. In 1812 we find the name Impson, instead of Ihmsen, among the owners of the concern to be known as Beltzhoover, Wendt & Company, whose articles of copartnership have come to our attention. The latter document, inscribed on parchment, is the property of H. J. Cochran of Aliquippa, Pennsylvania, whose maternal great-great-grandfather was Frederick Wendt. Thanks to Mr. Cochran's courtesy we are able to summarize the contents of this valuable piece of historical evidence.

The agreement, dated January 17, 1812, names George Sutton and John K. McNickle and Daniel Beltzhoover, who on the one hand were to supply the necessary capital to start the venture, and Frederick Wendt, Charles Impson, Peter Hane, Daniel Tucker, and Edward Ensel Jr. (glassblower), who were to receive wages and varying shares in the hoped-for profits in return for their services. It would appear that the working partners of the concern were at the time in the employ of James O'Hara, since the agreement states that they are to join forces with the new concern "as

soon as their present contract or engagement" with that individual expires. The paper was never signed. Mr. Cochran believes it to be a duplicate of a fully completed contract. Mention of the firm of Beltzhoover, Wendt & Company will be found in George Thurston's *Allegheny County One Hundred Years Ago.*

During subsequent years the corporate name underwent several changes. In 1822, according to Thurston, we encounter Sutton, Wendt & Company, in which figure Daniel Beltzhoover, George Sutton, John McNickle, Edward Ensell Sr. and his son, Frederick Wendt, Charles Ihmsen, and Peter Hane. About this time we find Charles Ihmsen's son William entering the glass business near Williamsport, now Monongahela City, where in 1826 he established a factory.

In 1828 Charles Ihmsen died and his interests were taken over by his second son, Christian, an enterprising businessman. He was associated at various times with Thomas I. Whitehead, William Phillips, and Frank Plunkett, and apparently prospered. In 1850 he was operating as C. Ihmsen (Knittle); in 1855 as C. Ihmsen & Company. In 1862, the year of his death, Christian took two of his sons, Charles and William, into the firm. But the younger men lacked their father's ability and failed within a few years. In 1865 we find another member of the family, Dominick, entering the glass business in company with Wilson Cunningham, under the name of Cunningham & Ihmsen. According to Mrs. Knittle, Dominick's interests were later disposed of and Dominick himself disappears from the record.

We now come to the third generation of the Ihmsen family in America. In 1885 Christian Jr. opened a glassblowing house on the site of the old Beltzhoover, Wendt & Company factory. Called the Ihmsen Glass Company, this enterprise lasted only ten years. With its demise the Ihmsens went out of the glass business forever.

Concerning the profitable business conducted by Christian, which in the 1830's had an annual glass production worth $100,000 to $120,000, Mrs. Knittle observes, "Almost nothing has appeared in print concerning this very large establishment — a glass-works which was turning out as much flint-goods as any house in the United States. What did it make? We ought to know as much about its 1836 production as we do concerning that of Sandwich, the New England Glass Co., or Bakewell's."

Though we are unable to give a specific answer to Mrs. Knittle's question regarding the products of this factory in 1836, we do possess information concerning a few of the items turned out in 1851. Fifteen years· was, of course, a long time as measured by the vicissitudes of the glassmaking industry in that period and by frequent changes not only in personnel but in the character of the goods produced. While we know that patterns in pressed glass which proved popular were continued over a term of years, it seems probable that those produced in 1851 were recently introduced novelties rather than repetitions of those devised when pressed glass was first coming into vogue. The 1850 decade, it may be recalled, was one of newly awakened activity and wide competition in the manufacture of glass.

The sugar bowl of which three views are here pictured is not only an 1851 product of the Ihmsen factory; it also furnishes evidence regarding the character of other products of the establishment. Until recently acquired by us, it had been cherished by an old lady, now eighty-four years of age, residing on 12 Street near Sarah Street, two squares from the site of the old glass factory

SUGAR BOWL: THREE VIEWS (*c. 1851*)

Reliably ascribed to the Pittsburgh-district factory operated by Christian Ihmsen. Said to be the product of experiments with new methods of moldmaking, the bowl was evidently intended to advertise the sundry articles and diverse patterns of glass tableware produced by the Ihmsen concern. The three views pictured exhibit in the order given a variety of items, framed in arched panels. *Diameter:* 5 inches; *overall height:* 5 ½ inches.

From the authors' collection

A: bowl — *Ashburton* decanter; *flute* goblet; spillholder in *star* or *sunburst* pattern; cover — *excelsior* compote; *flute* champagne; *flute* goblet

B: bowl — *excelsior* ale glass; hexagonal six-banded candlestick; *excelsior* spillholder; cover — *excelsior* footed tumbler with handle; bitters bottle; *excelsior* tumbler

at 14 and Bingham Streets, Birmingham, Southside, Pittsburgh, then operating under the name of C. Ihmsen and Company (*1851*).

The late owner's elder brother was an employee of the Ihmsen factory. By him she remembers having been told that, about 1851, a series of experiments was undertaken to improve upon the wooden molds then in use, which soon became charred and worn and hence incapable of producing a distinct impression. To remedy this defect an attempt was made, she said, to utilize pasteboard (probably *papier-mâché*); but in what manner she was unable to recall.

Whatever the method attempted, it proved to be a failure, since the process was not only time-consuming but expensive because of breakage of the article upon removal from the mold. An article that escaped such destruction is the sugar bowl here illustrated. Though this piece shows several fractures on the base, near the bottom, they are interior and do not involve either surface. They may have resulted from temperature changes subsequent to manufacture. A number of tiny nicks and chips on the approximating rims of base and cover affords evidence of considerable use.

Aside from the more or less reliable tradition attaching to it, and to its portrayal of contemporary styles in Ihmsen pressed glass, the bowl appeals on other grounds. It appears to be a unique medium for advertising the products of a glass factory. The former owner stated that, had the experiments proved successful, it was intended to utilize the sugar bowls for advertising other items. The bowl itself is fairly heavy, while the lid is thinner and lighter in weight. The glass is quite clear, and bubbles and heat checks are comparatively few. Resonance of the base is somewhat im-

C: bowl — *excelsior* covered sugar bowl; *excelsior* decanter; *excelsior* champagne; cover — what appears to be a hexagonal salt above an inkwell; *flute* champagne; *excelsior* footed tumbler

paired by cracks, but the lid responds to the lightest touch with a clear bell tone. The design, which occurs on the outer surface of the bowl and the inner surface of the lid, is well defined.

Ruth Webb Lee does not mention the Ihmsens as the makers of any of the patterns described in her *Early American Pressed Glass*. She attributes the *excelsior* pattern to McKee Brothers and reproduces a page of items in that pattern from that firm's 1868 catalogue. She remarks, however, that this pattern also appeared in an earlier list of about 1859. *Excelsior* would seem to have been a favorite with the Ihmsen factory, to judge by the relative number of items in that pattern found on the sugar bowl.

Of *Ashburton*, Mrs. Lee observes: "It has been definitely established that this pattern was made in three factories, though doubtless it was produced at others as well." She names the New England Glass Company and Bakewell, Pears and Company as among the firms producing it.

The *flute* pattern was probably made at numerous factories, among which Mrs. Lee mentions the Sandwich works and Bakewell, Pears and Company. The Ihmsen factory may now be added to the number of those to which it may safely be attributed.

NOTES

1. The confusion of baptismal names among the Ihmsens is due to the fact that members of the family were prone to indicate their first name only by an initial. Our informant, Joseph D. Ihmsen, tells us that his son follows the same custom, always signing himself C. Ihmsen instead of Christian Ihmsen IV.

2. Frederick Wendt's daughter, Charlotte, married John McKee, a brother of Samuel McKee of the firm of S. McKee and Company, one of the largest concerns in its field. The unsigned contract referred to was found in an old McKee family Bible.

Fig. 1 — Cover of George Duncan & Sons Catalogue (*c. 1875*)

The Duncan Trio

By Ruth Webb Lee

IT IS generally conceded, at least by dealers, that, at the moment, collectors of American things are more interested in early pattern glass than in other kinds of antiques. The sales prove it. Naturally, the desire for fresh historical information has been intensified by the increased demand for the material. Knowledge, or at any rate the ability to talk learnedly about their prizes, has always been sought by owners of antiques. According to Edwin Lefevre, no deaf mute can be a collector: no talk, no use collecting. Q. E. D.

From the beginning of the interest in American pressed glass there has been much speculation as to the date, origin, and meaning of the trio of countenances in the pattern known as *three face*. Many legends, all apocryphal, circulated for years. For example, there was the tale of the beautiful member of a well-known Philadelphia family who ordered a portrait from a distinguished artist, but was told that her extraordinary beauty could be captured only by three likenesses — full face, profile, and fifty-fifty. Getting three commissions instead of one was not only high art but high finance.

Classical students called the ware the *three Graces*. However, Aglaia has exactly the same face as Euphrosyne, and Thalia is a dead ringer for her

sisters. None of the three looks like either father or mother. Other stories circulated. Many well-meaning souls contended that *three face* was a Sandwich product, though without any corroborative evidence other than the desire to call everything in pressed glass Sandwich. No collector knew even approximately the date when this pattern was made, or where it was made.

It is, therefore, gratifying to find, in an old trunk, a catalogue issued by George Duncan & Sons of Pittsburgh, Pennsylvania, in which several pages are devoted to *three face*, known simply to the trade in those days as *Pattern No. 400*. It is to be doubted that *three face* was made at any other factory, for no variants of any of its forms have been found. When a factory copied a pattern that had been originated by some

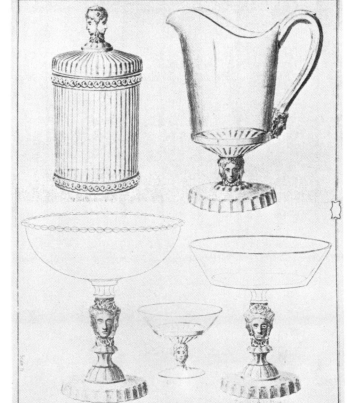

Fig. 2 — Page from Duncan's Catalogue Showing "Pattern no. 400"

This pattern, now known as *three face*, shows, reading left to right: half-gallon biscuit jar (rare); half-gallon pitcher; 8-inch bowl, round (the same bowl occurs also in 7- and 9-inch diameter, with and without cover, and in 10-inch without cover); 4 ½-inch comport (occurs also in 4-inch size); 7-inch bowl (the same bowl occurs in 8- and 9-inch diameter with and without cover, and in 10-inch without cover)

Fig. 3 —
LAMPS
PLAIN AND
ENGRAVED
Each type
of lamp
was pro-
curable in
three sizes

Fig. 4 —
ROUND
BOWL
COVERED
This bowl
is shown
without
cover in
Figure 2

rival concern and had proved popular enough to be plagiarized profitably, slight differences or variations were introduced, either because they could not be avoided or because they were considered a safeguard against accusations of infringement. In the case of *three face*, no variations have been found to indicate that more than one master model was used for any of its different items as produced by George Duncan & Sons.

Collectors always wish to know when and by whom a particular pattern was made, as well as to have a full list of its various items, in order to know when the "series" is complete. It is also desirable to know the original trade name, though we are all agreed that only confusion would ensue were collectors to substitute long-forgotten pattern names for familiar descriptive titles now in use.

For most pattern glass it is obviously impossible to establish the date of manufacture, the reason being that, as a rule, the old catalogues are not only scarce but undated. Nobody deemed trade lists worthy of preservation for the benefit of collectors yet unborn. Moreover, the memory of glass blowers and salesmen is untrustworthy. It is too much to ask the average man to recall

exactly the first making of an article, which may have been one of dozens that he sold year after year four decades ago. The only way to judge the age of glass is by ascertaining its period, which, in turn, is determined by the character of the pattern and the number and variety of articles made in the particular design.

In the earliest days of pressing, very few pieces were considered necessary to complete a set. A "set," for instance, consisted of sugar bowl, creamer, butter dish, and spoon holder. Goblets were made in the same pattern but were not inevitably sold with the set. The changes in fashion between 1870 and 1885 afford the most reliable guide to the age of certain forms. It was between these years that many of the combined frosted and clear effects were produced, as, for example, *three face, lion, Westward-Ho, polar bear*, and so on. For years Eastern collectors have credited many of these to Sandwich; but we now know that they were made in the Pittsburgh district. Incidentally, *camphor glass*, used to designate a frosted finish, was a term unknown to the old glassmakers, who always referred to it as *satin finish*.

The trade name of *three face* in the Duncan catalogue is *Pattern No. 400*; but among the Duncan workmen it was known as *the*

Fig. 5 — BUTTER DISH, CREAMER, SPOONER, SUGAR BOWL

Fig. 6 (extreme left) — GOBLET
Likewise obtainable in plain form. Three smaller sizes of same form were known respectively as *wine*, *claret*, and *champagne*

Fig. 7 (left and right) — CELERY GLASSES OF TWO TYPES

Fig. 8 (extreme right) — PICKLE JAR
Hardly of the pattern; but none the less a pickle jar

Fig. 10 (bottom of page) — SAUCER CHAMPAGNE
Probably very few were made, since the demand would have been limited

three sisters. One old glass blower assured me that he recalled making it at the Duncan factory in 1872. Though he was very aged, his memory was apparently as reliable as human memory ever is. It should be borne in mind that much pressed glass was made in 1874 and 1875 in expectation of an active demand from the souvenir-loving public that was planning to attend the Philadelphia Centennial Exposition in 1876. Many novelties were manufactured then, some at Sandwich, some at the old Pittsburgh glasshouses.

Parts of the pages illustrating the *three face* pattern are here reproduced from the George Duncan & Sons' catalogue. I also present a list of the articles in this design illustrated in the catalogues of the 'seventies. It is a pleasure to settle the dispute about the piece in this pattern which was originally intended for a butter dish (*Fig. 5*). For years, collectors have insisted that the covered dish on high standard, now proved to be a butter dish, was really a sweetmeat dish, similar vessels in earlier patterns being so designated by the makers. They undoubtedly based their argument on the fact that in the 'fifties all butter dishes were without standards. The salt shaker was called *salt bottle.*

Everyone knows that in the *three face* pattern, the bowls of the dishes are found both clear and engraved. The factory sold them "plain or engraved." The design for the engraving was selected by the purchaser from a pictorial list submitted by the salesman, and

Fig. 9 — "SALVER" (*This form came in 9-, 10-, and 11-inch diameters*)

the work was done to order. The cracker jar listed in my book *Early American Pressed Glass* is shown in Figure 2. It is listed in the catalogue as "half gallon biscuit jar." I know of but one of these jars that has been found in recent years. The saucer champagnes are so scarce that we may safely assume that very few of them were made (*Fig. 10*). A slight demand yesterday means collectors' heartaches today.

The *pickle jar* (*Fig. 8*), apparently intended for use with *three face* ware, is so unlike its associates that the reason for including it in the series is not apparent. The little salts, which many dealers and collectors have called *celery dips*, are listed as *individual salts*. It is interesting to note that compotes were made with both rounded and flat-bottomed bowls, and were either open or covered in all but the largest size.

LIST OF ARTICLES MADE BY GEORGE DUNCAN & SONS IN PATTERN NO. 400, NOW KNOWN AS "THREE FACE"

Butter dish; sugar bowl; creamer; spoon holder; goblet; champagne (deep bowl); saucer champagne; claret; wine; comport (footed sauce) 4″, 4½″; half-gallon water pitcher; biscuit jar; pickle jar (not really matching); salt and pepper shaker; individual salt; celery (scalloped edge); celery (plain edge); salver (cake plate on standard) 9″, 10″, 11″; lamp (3 sizes) plain bowl; lamp (3 sizes) fancy bowl; round bowl (compote) covered and uncovered 7″, 8″, 9″, uncovered 10″; bowl (compote with angular profile) covered and uncovered 7″, 8″, 9″, uncovered 10″.

Pittsburgh *versus* Sandwich

Adams & Company

By RUTH WEBB LEE

THE mania for attributions is as old as collecting. It is responsible for much misinformation, for even conscientious students avail themselves of any peg on which to hang theories that automatically become facts through the magic of speech plus wish. During the past thirty years the line of least resistance has led not only dealers but collectors of American pressed glass in the direction of the Cape. "When in doubt, say Sandwich!" has been the one collecting commandment heeded. "When in doubt, don't call it Sandwich!" is far wiser counsel.

For some time, nevertheless, it has been widely recognized that certain patterns of glass were made by more than one factory in the Pittsburgh district, and elsewhere; but accurate information was not easy to obtain. Moreover, the name "Sandwich" was too good a selling point to be willingly abandoned. Shrewd buyers cheerfully pay for misattributed ware, and proudly help to spread the error. This misuse and abuse of the Sandwich name is particularly true of the later patterns — those, say, which date from the 'seventies.

Almost all the old Pittsburgh houses made what dealers and collectors, east and west, still call "genuine Sandwich." They began before 1850, and some of them have kept at it. Adams & Company were among the leaders after 1850.

In an old account book of Bakewell, Pears & Company for 1846 appears the name of John Adams, a presser, who "made $1 per turn." He earned as little as $16.50 during February of 1846, and as much as $38.33 in July of the same year. For the six months he made $116 in all. And yet, in 1851 this same Adams established the firm of Adams, Macklin & Company, which started its first glass factory at the corner of Ross and Second Streets. It is easy to visualize here an American industrial romance; but imaginative tales are not for these pages. It was this same John Adams who, in that same factory, succeeded in making the first lime glass, which became a substitute for the heavier and costlier lead glass previously produced by American manufacturers of tableware. To this substitution, and to the improvement in the pressers, is due the rise of the manufacture

Fig. 1 — ADAMS & COMPANY, PITTSBURGH. "NO. 140 PATTERN"; KNOWN TO COLLECTORS AS "WILDFLOWER" (*c. 1870*)

of pressed glass to a commanding place among the important industries of the United States.

From the very start the concern made pressed, figured tumblers and tableware. In 1860, the firm name was changed to Adams & Company. The works were then on South Tenth and Washington Streets, Pittsburgh, according to accounts in old numbers of the *National Glass Budget.*

During the decade beginning in 1850, the development of the pressed-glass industry did not show the rapid progress that was later manifest. Pennsylvanians, of course, declare that the chief reason for this was the lack of an adequate protective duty on pressed ware. At all events, when the Civil War broke out and the government needed money, a twenty-five per cent duty did the trick, and an amazingly rapid development of the industry followed. To be sure, in addition to the twenty-five per cent duty, many improvements were made in the molds and appliances used in the production of pressed ware. Handy levers on presses, the mold oven, the interior cooling of plungers with water, the eccentric key in place of the old lock, and the use of a cold blast around molds and plungers, all contributed to a much larger and more economical production. According to an anonymous article in an old trade paper, Pittsburgh, in 1856, boasted thirty-two factories, of which fourteen were window-glass houses, eight made flint-glass tableware, eight turned out vials and drug ware, and two produced black bottles. In that year, the Pittsburgh factories fabricated 6,340 tons of flint glassware, valued at $1,147,540. I am certain that in all that output were many "Sandwich" pieces. Ten years later the tonnage of Pittsburgh pressed tableware was 4,200 tons. I am equally certain that many of these 1866 Pittsburgh patterns are still called "Sandwich."

This statement implies no slur on Sandwich glass. On the contrary. In an old and, unfortunately, undated catalogue of Adams & Company, I found one of the best-known of the more popular patterns collected today. We now call it *wildflower*. In the Adams & Company lists it is called *No. 140 Pattern*. Scarcely a day passes that my mail does not bring one or more enquiries

Fig. 2 — ADAMS & COMPANY, PITTSBURGH. "GIPSY PATTERN," PREVIOUSLY "FIG"; KNOWN TO COLLECTORS AS "BALTIMORE PEAR" (*1888*)

about "the *wildflower* pattern of Sandwich glass." Apparently there are hundreds and perhaps thousands of pressed-glass buyers who either wish to know whether *wildflower* was made at Sandwich, or else assert that it was. As a matter of fact, it was made and sold by Adams & Company. An old moldmaker who worked at the latter factory told me that it was made and sold by them in the 'seventies. Its popularity lasted during two decades; and, as a matter of fact, it still sells — as an antique! (See *Fig. 1.*)

We find this ware in crystal, amber, blue, canary, and apple green. Certain forms, or pieces, which did not sell freely were discontinued from time to time; but, as a whole, the pattern had strong sales vitality. I hazard the personal opinion, for reasons that I consider adequate, that *wildflower* was never made at Sandwich. Moreover, I believe it to have

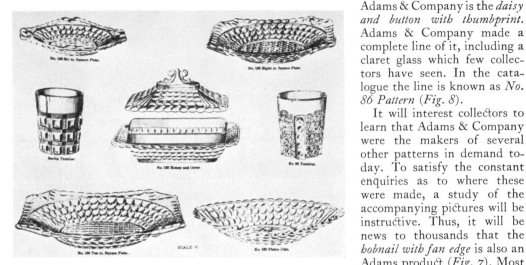

Fig. 3 — ADAMS & COMPANY, PITTSBURGH. "No. 130"; KNOWN TO COLLECTORS AS "THOUSAND EYE" (*1870's*)
The tumblers are of a different pattern

been exclusively an Adams product. Incidentally, I would ask those critics of what has been accepted as the standard nomenclature, to consider whether this pattern should be known as *wildflower*, the name given to it by modern collectors and dealers, or as *Adams No. 140*, which was its official designation. In the matter of rechristened patterns, what is true of *wildflower* is true of scores of others that originally were known merely by catalogue numbers or trade names, forgotten years ago. Better a recognizable alias than a meaningless birth certificate!

Certain persons, anxious to cater to collectors' demands or prejudices, have assured buyers that the pattern known today as *moon and star* was made at Sandwich. This ascription has found its way even into books on Sandwich glass. In Adams & Company's catalogue the pattern appears under the name of *palace*. An old glassblower, who worked at the factory, assured me that the design was first brought out in the late 'eighties. I found it in a catalogue printed after the Sandwich Company went out of business. It was listed in my book as *moon and star* because it had gone by that name for years. Nobody would have recognized it as *palace*. In any event, it never was Sandwich. Other Pittsburgh houses may possibly have made it, but I am sure of only Adams & Company (*Fig. 4*).

Another question that I am asked almost daily concerns a pattern that I did not include in my book because I confined myself to patterns collectible in sets; and, at the time of going to press, I had not come across examples other than goblets. As usual, my correspondents wish to know whether or not this is Sandwich. In an old Adams & Company catalogue it appears under the name of *plume*. It is probably an earlier pattern than *palace*, though I find both in a trade list of the 'eighties. As the *plume* pattern was not

illustrated in my book, collectors may now find it in a goblet shown in Figure 5.

Another so-called "Sandwich" pattern that was made by Adams & Company is the *daisy and button with thumbprint*. Adams & Company made a complete line of it, including a claret glass which few collectors have seen. In the catalogue the line is known as *No. 86 Pattern* (*Fig. 8*).

It will interest collectors to learn that Adams & Company were the makers of several other patterns in demand today. To satisfy the constant enquiries as to where these were made, a study of the accompanying pictures will be instructive. Thus, it will be news to thousands that the *hobnail with fan edge* is also an Adams product (*Fig. 7*). Most of its items were sauce dishes and bowls. Among its forms not included in my book are six-inch, seven-inch, and ten-inch berry bowls and a five-inch sauce dish. Individual salts and a flanged butter dish, without the fan edge, are shown with this group in the catalogue. A toy set in *hobnail* with thumbprint base, made by Adams, included an individual sugar, creamer, spoonholder, and butter dish. A puff box to match is an odd item.

Some of the ten goblets shown in Figure 5 are of patterns familiar to collectors. With the exception of the *Nevada*, complete sets were made. Incidentally, the catalogue spelling followed the English fashion, "sett." When did "setts" become "sets" in the glass trade? I surmise, in the early 'nineties.

No end of dealers and collectors have asserted that what we now know as *Baltimore pear* (called in certain localities *twin pear* and *Maryland pear*) was made by a glasshouse in Maryland. As a matter of fact, it was first made in 1888 by Adams & Company. In the beginning it was known as the *fig* line. Later, the name was changed to *gipsy*. Today collectors and dealers call it *Baltimore pear*, even though it is neither Baltimore nor pear. In Figure 6 is pictured the *Hidalgo* pattern, which is not included in my book. This line was made to be sold either plain or engraved and included many interesting forms. Among other patterns made by Adams & Company, which likewise are not illustrated in my book, though they are collectible in sets, are the *crystal wedding*, plain and engraved, *art*, and *Apollo*, samples of which may be seen in Figure 5.

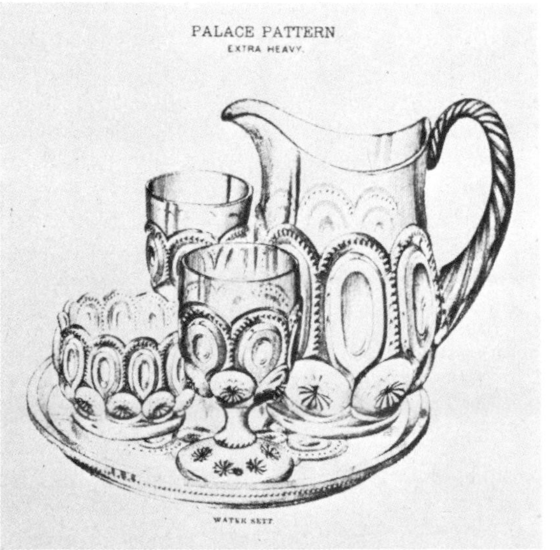

It will interest collectors to learn that the very popular pattern known as *thousand eye* was made by Adams & Company, who called it *No. 130* (*Fig. 3*). It came on the market in the 'seventies, and for many years was a good seller. The firm produced the square plates in three sizes and the unusual oblong covered dish, listed as a "honey and cover." Two distinct

PALACE PATTERN
EXTRA HEAVY.

WATER SETT

Fig. 4—ADAMS & COMPANY, PITTSBURGH. "PALACE PATTERN";
KNOWN TO COLLECTORS AS "MOON AND STAR" (*late 1880's*)

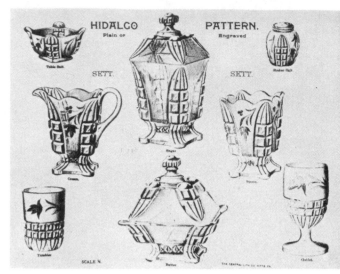

Fig. 5 — ADAMS & COMPANY, PITTSBURGH. VARIOUS GOBLETS
From left to right, first row: *No. 329, Apollo, Cottage, Nevada, Gipsy (Baltimore pear)*. Second row: *No. 65, Palace (moon and star), Plume, Crystal Wedding, Art.* With the exception of *Nevada*, all of these patterns were made in sets

Fig. 6 — ADAMS & COMPANY, PITTSBURGH. "HIDALGO PATTERN"; BOTH PLAIN AND ENGRAVED

styles of this glass are found, one having three round knobs forming the handle of the cover for covered dishes, and also adorning the stems of compotes, and so on; and a second style, produced by Richards & Hartley of Tarentum, Pennsylvania (another old factory of the Pittsburgh district) and widely advertised by them during the 'eighties (*Fig. 9*). This latter style is referred to by its makers as *No. 103 Pattern*.

The same firm made a wide variety of shapes in crystal,

Fig. 7 — ADAMS & COMPANY, PITTSBURGH. "No. 150 PATTERN"; KNOWN TO COLLECTORS AS "HOBNAIL WITH FAN EDGE"

amber, blue, canary, and crystal-opalescent. All the Richards & Hartley pieces are scalloped at the top and base, except those which obviously could not be so made, like the twine holder and salt and pepper shakers. "Crystal-opalescent" was a combination of opal and a decided blue tone. That the Tarentum output of "Pattern No. 103" was inconsiderable may be assumed from its marked scarcity today. Collectors eagerly seek it, doubtless because of its attractive color and its rarity. The Adams pieces can be identified by the three knobs noted in the preceding paragraph.

Fig. 8 — ADAMS & COMPANY, PITTSBURGH. "No. 86 PATTERN"; KNOWN TO COLLECTORS AS "DAISY AND BUTTON WITH THUMBPRINT"

Fig. 9 — RICHARDS & HARTLEY, TARENTUM, PENNSYLVANIA. "No. 103 PATTERN"; KNOWN TO COLLECTORS AS "THOUSAND EYE" (*decade of 1880*)

Fig. 1 — FROM RICHARDS & HARTLEY'S CATALOGUE (*1888*)
"No. 544 Pattern." The bowl occurs in 7- and 8-inch diameters, and the
"comport" in diameters of 4, 7, and 8 inches

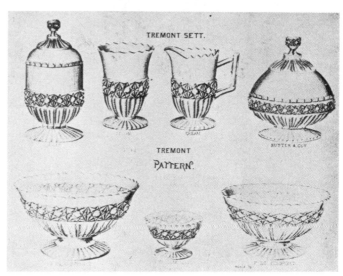

Fig. 2 — FROM RICHARDS & HARTLEY'S CATALOGUE (*1888*)
"Tremont Pattern." "Comports" occur in 4-, 7-, and 8-inch diameters.
Specimens of this pattern are relatively scarce.

Pittsburgh *versus* Sandwich

Richards & Hartley

By RUTH WEBB LEE

ONE is brought to a constant realization of the difficulties besetting the glass historian by the exasperating dearth of documentary evidence — and even of trade gossip — concerning well-known firms that were active not in the comparatively remote era of James Buchanan, but as late as the presidency of Grover Cleveland. For example, after a diligent search of directories and price lists, and a careful examination of scrapbooks assembled by glass men with a fondness for trade history and anecdote, nothing more could be definitely ascertained about the Richards & Hartley Company than that, having organized in 1866, it built its glassworks during the same year at the corner of Pride and Marion Streets in Pittsburgh, Pennsylvania, and that, some years later, in order to secure better railroad facilities, it moved its manufacturing plant to Tarentum, Pennsylvania. The firm remained in business until the end of 1891. From three large trunks full of old trade catalogues, I obtained one Richards & Hartley volume, dated *1888*, and an incomplete copy of an earlier edition. Incidentally, it may be recorded here that, in 1892, the principal American manufacturers of glassware operated in the states of Pennsylvania, Ohio, and New York.

To collectors of pattern glass, Richards & Hartley are

Fig. 3 — FROM RICHARDS & HARTLEY'S CATALOGUE (*1888*)
"Clover Pattern." A variant of what is now known as *daisy and button*

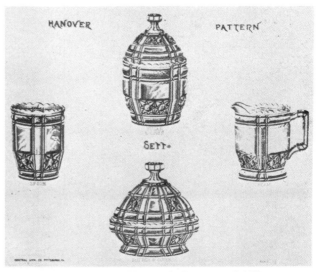

Fig. 4 — FROM RICHARDS & HARTLEY'S CATALOGUE (*1888*)
"Hanover Pattern"

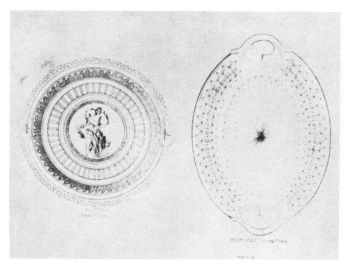

Fig. 5 — From Richards & Hartley's Catalogue (*1888*)
Bread plate in pattern "No. 500," known as *Cupid & Venus;* also called
Cupid and Psyche. Another in "Peerless" pattern

Fig. 6 — From Richards & Hartley's Catalogue (*1888*)
"No. 900 Pattern." Nappies occur in 4-, 6-, and 8-inch sizes; bowls, 7 and
8 inches; goblets in water and wine sizes

important chiefly because they produced so many of the patterns in popular demand today. For example, the *lion, Cupid & Venus, thousand eye, three panel,* and several varieties of the *daisy and button* were all specialties of this concern. In the company's 1888 catalogue the *lion* is called the "No. 525" pattern. *Thousand eye* is "No. 103"; *three panel,* "No. 25." The *daisy and button with crossbar* appears as "No. 99 Pattern" and also as the "Mikado." The Richards & Hartley "Clover" pattern, another *daisy and button* variant, is today found in antique shops in three-petaled sauces and preserve dishes (*Fig. 3*). Another variant, little known to collectors, appears in the catalogue as the "Tremont Sett." It is safe to assume, from the present scarcity of this particular pattern, that it did not prove commercially successful and was discontinued before a large quantity was issued.

In glass, as in politics and every other human interest, truth is not only stranger than fiction, but far more difficult to obtain. Where a demand exists, some kind of supply is sure to be forthcoming. We may not blame collectors for wishing to know everything that bears on their individual specialties, nor be surprised that every meeting of glass enthusiasts inspires sometimes extraordinary accounts of the origin and *raison d'être* of sundry patterns. In default of facts, ingenious fairy stories are eagerly absorbed. The publication of reliable evidence contradicting such tales does not put an end to them. Collectors continue to welcome fictitious accounts of how such patterns as *three face, Westward-ho, peachblow,* and others came into being.

The *lion* pattern has gathered more than its share of legend. It has been attributed to Sandwich, the almost inevitable fate of Pittsburgh designs. There is no valid reason for doubting that *lion* belongs to that group of frosted and clear glass known to have been made just prior to the Centennial Exposition in 1876, perhaps for display during that event. The fact that the *lion* bread plate appears in a catalogue as late as 1888 merely indicates that its particular popularity was maintained

over a long period and survived the decreased demand for other forms. Several variations of the *lion* exist, one made by James Gillinder & Sons. They are differentiated by the lid knobs of the covered pieces. But which of the unidentified variants came from Richards & Hartley works it is impossible to tell, because no covered dishes are shown in their available catalogues.

The picturing of the *Cupid & Venus* plate, without accompanying items, in the 1888 catalogue implies that the demand for plates in this pattern also persisted beyond that for other forms. Incidentally, the firm's prosaic name for this design was "No. 500" pattern — a circumstance that should end controversy as to whether the relief was intended to portray Cupid and Psyche or a guardian angel, as some collectors still believe.

Several patterns made by Richards & Hartley were not included in the first edition of *Early American Pressed Glass.* Among them are the "Richmond," or "Pattern No. 190"; "Peerless," often mistaken for *Hamilton,* particularly in the six-inch plates; "Hanover Pattern"; and patterns "No. 544" and "900," illustrated here for the first time, from the original catalogue. The *leaf and dart* pattern, resembling the *loop and dart* and others of that group, was made by Richards & Hartley. Similarity in design is a dangerous basis for the attribution of patterns to any one factory. The manufacturers cheerfully entered into gentlemen's agreements not to plagiarize from one another, and they kept scant faith by making slight changes. The variants, therefore, may have been turned out by different glasshouses. The exceedingly popular *thousand eye,* made by Richards & Hartley, was fully described on page 67 of ANTIQUES for August 1933.

Of all the patterns produced by the firm, the most important is the *three panel.* In quality of glass and in design it is one of the best of our later commercial colored patterns. I believe it to be one of the earliest designs of colored ware to be made in complete sets. The color range covers only amber, blue, yellow, and crystal. Amethyst was not included because it did not become popular until later. But the reason for

Fig. 7 — From Richards & Hartley's Catalogue
(*1888*)
"Etched" bread plate, "No. 525," popularly known
as *lion* pattern

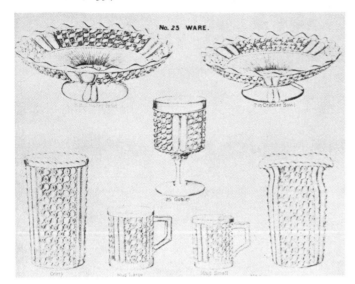

Fig. 8 — FROM RICHARDS & HARTLEY'S CATALOGUE (*1888*)
"No. 25 Ware," now called *three panel*. So-called cracker bowls in 7- and 8-inch diameters, and two sizes of mugs, are shown in the catalogue. In design, and in quality of glass, this is the firm's most important pattern

Fig. 9 — FROM RICHARDS & HARTLEY'S CATALOGUE (*1888*)
"'Mikado,' No. 99 Pattern," now called *daisy and button with crossbar*. Besides tray, pitcher, finger bowls, and goblets, a tumbler, wine glass, and mugs of two sizes appear in the catalogue. Crystal, amber, blue, and canary

excluding green is difficult to surmise. No plates in this pattern were made, and only one size of footed sauce dish. It should be noted that the low, footed compotes with flaring bowls were listed as "cracker bowls," while bowls with straight sides, like the goblets, were called "comports." Both were made in two sizes, as were also the water pitchers. The *three panel* pattern has much to recommend it to collectors.

The *daisy and button with crossbar*, or "Mikado," pattern was obviously a favorite, for it is extensively illustrated in the catalogue. The color range is the same as for the *three panel*. Incidentally, goblets in *oval panel* were also made at Tarentum.

To the novelties, so popular today, for holding matches and cigarettes, is devoted one catalogue page. Clearly, Richards & Hartley did not go in for these so extensively as many other factories in the "old Pittsburgh glass district." The page in question is dedicated chiefly to odd salts; but it portrays several toothpick holders usually attributed to Sandwich, such as the attractive rabbit with a large container strapped to its back;

the kitten, in amber, blue, or canary, reclining on a cushion and supporting the same container found in the *daisy and button* pattern. Still another curious "tooth-pick" consists of a monkey's head. It looks more like a salt, and is appropriately listed as the "Darwin." A "gem horse radish" is an odd dish, displaying a horse head as cover knob; and a bird salt is clumsier and much less attractive than the one with the cherry in its beak generally ascribed to Sandwich.

Richards & Hartley could not have been in business for much more than twenty-five years; but they contributed their share of items that are sought by present-day collectors. First in importance is the six-inch "Peerless" plate, now universally used as a substitute by *Hamilton* collectors, because, so far, no credible evidence has been adduced that any size of *Hamilton* plate was ever made. The mere sight of a single specimen would bring joy to the hearts of those *Hamilton* hunters who accept "Peerless" *faute de mieux*. We have heard the assertion of its existence. Where is the plate?

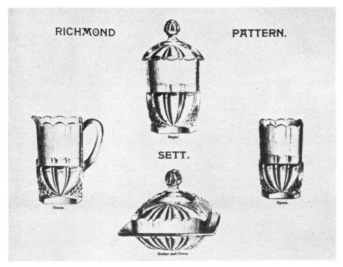

Fig. 10 — FROM RICHARDS & HARTLEY'S CATALOGUE (*1888*)
"Richmond Pattern," also listed by the manufacturers as "Pattern No. 190"

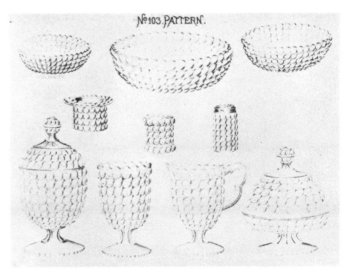

Fig. 11 — FROM RICHARDS & HARTLEY'S CATALOGUE (*1888*)
"No. 103 Pattern," known today as *thousand eye*. Nappies in 5-, 6-, and 8-inch sizes. Colors: crystal, amber, blue, and canary

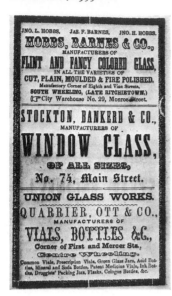

Glassmaking in Wheeling, West Virginia

By RHEA MANSFIELD KNITTLE

ALL is not Sandwich, Cambridge, or Pittsburgh pressed glass that glitters, or, for that matter, that loops the jewel, or that hails the comet. Bellflowers blow in the breeze as gracefully in West Virginia as in Massachusetts. Hearts and flowers, hearts and stars, fade not, falter not along the old Ohio. For in Wheeling-Martin's Ferry pressed glass was extensively made. Not that Wheeling manufactured lacy glass and the later types of pressed tableware to the exclusion of blown, molded, and cut-flint varieties, or cylinder and bottle glass. All of these were made. Almost from the day of its settlement, Wheeling made glass. Between the years 1845 and 1870, the local output of clear glass overshadowed that of any other centre of the industry in America, with the exception of Pittsburgh. The glassworks responsible for this industrial triumph were operated by the finest technicians, trained in the Cambridge, Sandwich, and Pittsburgh flint furnaces. Yet they have never received adequate recognition from the historian.

It is out of the question even briefly to describe the flint-glass factories of Wheeling in this note, or more than to mention some of the green-glass or bottle works. The earliest Wheeling furnace on record was built near a good-sized coal hill at the edge of the little town, one hundred and thirteen years ago. Similar happy solutions of the fuel problem were the chief influence in establishing glasshouses in this district. Coal in hitherto undreamed-of abundance was to be had from the sides of the Monongahela-Ohio hills.

George Carothers built the first furnace, and his little factory was referred to as "an elegant establishment." Its output was advertised as "fine flint." Undoubtedly it was. It was too fine, in fact, for the times and the locality. Forced to abandon his notions of quality, Carothers transformed his furnace into a green-bottle glasshouse. Within a few years these "Virginia Works" (West Virginia had not been created) were taken over by Knox & McKee of Pittsburgh, who retained Carothers as superintendent. The new owners enlarged the plant, and were soon turning out large quantities of window glass and bottles. Later they altered it into a clear-flint hollow-ware factory under the trade name of Wheat, Price & Company. The output was shipped "to Boston and all ports of New England," to New Orleans and New Mexico. During one period it was known as the Fairview Glass Works.

In 1829 the first cut-flint-glass factory in the district was established by John and Craig Ritchie.

The production also included blown tableware, molded ware, apothecaries' supplies, vials, flasks, and "household necessities." Michael and R. H. Sweeney built their first furnace in 1835. Eusell & Wilson, S. G. Robinson, R. C. Knowles, Plunket & Miller, and House & Taylor were manufacturing glass in Wheeling prior to 1850. Ownership of these various plants changed frequently, but nothing is to be gained by listing all of the firm and trade names.

John L. Hobbs, James Barnes, and their sons, John H. Hobbs and James F. Barnes, all expert operators from Massachusetts, came to Wheeling, and, in 1845, erected works patterned after those at Cambridge. In 1854 the furnace capacity was greatly enlarged, and the concern developed into one of the finest flint-glass factories in the land. Many of its forms and designs were similar to or identical with the molded and pressed patterns turned out at Cambridge, Sandwich, and Pittsburgh. It would be folly to award to any one glasshouse between 1845 and 1875 priority in the invention and production of more than a few pressed designs. I have met three men, each of whom asserts that his grandfather positively brought the secret of ruby-colored glass to the United States from Europe.

Hobbs, Barnes & Company built another furnace of good size directly across the Ohio River at Martin's Ferry, Ohio. In 1863 the firm name became Hobbs, Brockunier & Company. For a number of years the mass tonnage of this house exceeded that of Cambridge, of Sandwich, and of several among the Pittsburgh plants. The quality of the metal was excellent. Production included almost everything from large chandeliers with many prisms to small cup plates. This firm also introduced sundry improvements and took out patents for several significant inventions. They did more to better the wage scale than any other house in their district.

Three of the advertisements here reproduced are from the directory of the City of Wheeling & Ohio County, compiled by Oliver I. Taylor and printed at the office of the Wheeling *Daily Gazette*, in 1851. Accompanying statistics show that, next to iron (bar, sheet, and nails), glass was the chief local output. In 1850 the flint glasshouses employed 500 hands, paid in wages $187,200, and produced glass to the amount of $568,456. The green glassworks employed 348 hands, paid in wages $105,866, and produced glass to the amount of $300,000. The hollow-ware houses listed in this directory are: *flint glass*, Sweeneys & Bell, Hobbs, Barnes & Company, D. H. Southwick & Company; *green glass*, Quarrier, Ott & Company. I am quite sure that, at this time, two other bottle houses were operating in the vicinity.

Sweeneys & Bell were capitalized at $75,000, with $12,000 in miscellaneous materials. The

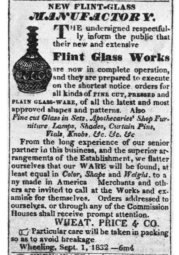

Figs. 1, 2, and 3 (top and centre of page) — WHEELING GLASSHOUSE ADVERTISERS OF 1851
From the directory of the City of Wheeling & Ohio County
Fig. 4 (right) — WHEELING NEWSPAPER ADVERTISEMENT OF 1832

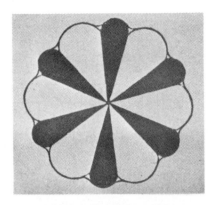

Figs. 1 and 2 (above, and centre, top) — Woodcut of the First Pressed Tumbler, Made by Deming Jarves
See Antiques for October 1931, page 220

Figs. 3 and 4 (above, and centre, bottom) — Two Views of Tumbler in the Pennypacker Collection
Probably one of the original group produced by Jarves

employees numbered 131, and wages totaled $30,796. In commenting upon Sweeneys & Bell, the directory remarks:

The quality of their glass is unsurpassed in all respects, and especially in transparency and beauty. They have succeeded in making the largest vessels, composed entirely of solid cut glass, which have, perhaps, ever been produced. Their three magnificent vases, one of which is in the possession of the Hon. Henry Clay, and another of which has for some time been on exhibition at Washington City, have been objects of universal admiration and wonder. The largest one is 4 feet 10 inches high, holds 21 gallons and weighs 225 pounds.

They have received gold and silver medals from the Franklin Institute, Philadelphia, and the American Institute, New York, for the best cut glass designs and finish to be exhibited at these institutions.

The outstanding achievements of both Sweeneys & Bell, and Hobbs, Barnes & Company, were blown, molded, and pressed tableware; and river-boat, hotel, and barroom flint-glass supplies. Wheeling became the centre of the glass-lamp industry, just as Steubenville did of the tumbler, and as Sandwich had been of the glass candlestick, and Pittsburgh of the cup plate.

It would be much simpler to list the articles of glassware that were not manufactured at Wheeling, than to record those that were.

Exhibitions and Sales

IN Antiques for October 1931, Lura Woodside Watkins presented the history of the first glass tumbler pressed by Deming Jarves at Sandwich, Massachusetts, in 1827, and therewithal a woodcut picture of this important vessel, evidently based on a crude pen and ink drawing. In the course of her article Mrs. Watkins remarked, "It is not outside the bounds of possibility that other examples from the same mold may still be in existence and will some day come to light."

Happily, A. J. Pennypacker is a consistent reader of Antiques. Just at the time when Mrs. Watkins' note appeared in the magazine, he was busily engaged in packing and sorting his stock of old glass for transfer to a newly opened branch shop at Colmar, on Bethlehem Pike, Pennsylvania. With the picture of the old Jarves tumbler in mind, he was peering at the jumbled contents of a dusty top shelf when his astonished eye encountered an actual tumbler, apparently twin brother of the woodcut portrayal in Antiques. Forgotten and neglected during some ten years, this crude bit of glass suddenly assumed an extraordinary importance. Today it is one of Mr. Pennypacker's proudest possessions.

Not long after the epochal discovery, I made a special pilgrimage to Colmar, where Mrs. Emilie W. B. Hennings, who is in charge of the shop in that community, permitted me to examine the historic tumbler. The piece stands 3 1/4 inches high and tapers slightly to a top diameter of approximately 2 7/8 inches. The bottom shows a pontil scar. The pattern, strongly marked on the outside of the tumbler, presents corresponding ridges and depressions on the interior surface, fair evidence that the tumbler's shaping was not accomplished solely with the aid of a close-fitting plunger. Faint mold marks about the rim indicate the employment of a sectional mold.

In all important particulars this tumbler conforms to the woodcut rescued from oblivion. It has fewer swags below the bull's-eye, and the twelve rays of its sunburst base are of equal rather than unequal size. On the whole, I think it fair to assume that the woodcut was taken from a preliminary sketch from which, in behalf of simplicity, depar-

tures were made in the preparation of the actual mold. Hence I have no hesitation in accepting Mr. Pennypacker's find as, without reasonable doubt, a member of the first group of articles shaped in Deming Jarves' improved press of 1827, to the consternation of the glassblowers whose threats against his life compelled him to go into hiding for six weeks.

Figure 1

A Glance at Glass Knobs

By Letitia Hart Alexander

Illustrations from the author's collection

DESPITE the present furor over early American glass, I have come upon little or nothing in print concerning the glass knobs used on old furniture. It may be that knobs have been exhaustively discussed, and that the fact has yet escaped me, though I have, in a lazy way, long been looking for something authoritative on the subject. In so far as I know, therefore, while many writers make a cursory allusion to glass knobs, few seem to think that these charming bits of glass are of any importance.

Looking back, I think my interest in knobs began with my admiration for a set attached to the toilet table of an ancestress. The table had been bought in Philadelphia, in 1832, and shipped by sea to New Orleans, where the ancestress commenced her married life. Later it came, *via* the Mississippi and Ohio Rivers, to Kentucky. It was a veritable aristocrat among furniture, this much traveled toilet table. The knobs were of clear glass, shaped like melons, and their brass bolts passed through little washers of mother-of-pearl. In the eventual division of the possessions of my ancestress, the toilet table and its alluring knobs passed to a descendant in another branch of the family. Nevertheless, my childish admiration for those gleaming attachments of an early day continued, and I never could resist acquiring a stray specimen, even though *one* was of no use. I have found almost as many patterns as Solomon had wives, so I take it for granted that all factories made them.

N. Hudson Moore, on page 339 of *Old Glass*, says that Deming Jarves, June 13, 1829, and October 19, 1830, took out patents for glass knobs; though what style of knobs these may have been she has been unable to determine. Alice Van Leer Carrick, in an article describing a visit to the Sandwich Factory, observes that an old lady had, among other treasures of glass, "pressed glass knobs on her bureau that were things to dream about." These two statements indicate that at least a fair proportion of knobs must have been produced at Sandwich.

I have always been curious to know what was the nature of Deming Jarves' patents. But, in my prowlings, I have found only one knob that bears a name. If you rest your eye for a moment on Figure 1 *h*, you will notice a specimen bearing cable rim and an old pewter headed screw. On the round base of this knob a square projection, about one eighth of an inch thick, is superimposed. This projection fits into a mortise on the front of the drawer and prevents the knob from twisting, as time and use loosen the grip of the screw.

Around the screw hole of this knob appears the inscription *Bakewell's Patent*, the two words separated by a five pointed star. N. Hudson Moore, in her list of American glass factories, under *Bakewell and Page*, notes that this firm began business in Pittsburgh, in 1808. The firm name was Bakewell and Anderson in 1820; Bakewell and Company in 1824. From 1845 until 1880 the concern operated under the name of Bakewell, Pears and Company. The device described was a happy thought on Bakewell's part, for, as I have said, it held the knob firm and kept the drawer from being abraded by its movement.

After finding this knob, I discovered another exemplifying much the same idea, though there was no name to indicate whose brain had produced the improvement. If you care to look at Figure 2 *f* you will observe this specimen. On either side of the screw hole, at the back, appear two spikes of glass each about one eighth of an inch long. These fitted into holes in the drawer front and thus steadied the knob.

Speaking of knobs that are out of the usual, I would mention the find of a whole set which came to me nearly twenty years ago. I was walking on a mean street, when, through the door of a little shop dealing in secondhand pianos, I saw a twin of the ancestral toilet table! It did not take me long to secure the treasure, though the "song" asked for it approached the price of the warblings of a prima donna. The table had to be done over, but, as it boasted no handles, I let it board with the cabinetmaker, asking his good offices in securing me glass knobs that would not shame my lovely find. Hope was almost dead when my cabinetmaker friend invited me to inspect a set of knobs that had come into his hands. He had just purchased a bed and a sideboard from a broken down wagon, the driver of which told a story of having bought in the pieces at a country auction. After the furniture had been disposed of, the driver pulled out a dirty buckskin bag from which rolled a set of unusual knobs, quite good enough to satisfy my fondest dreams. You will see one of them in Figure 1 *l*.

These examples have about the diameter of a silver half dollar and are beautifully fluted on top and flank. But, instead of being pierced with a *metal screw* through the centre, they carry a heavy *glass screw* molded in one with the knob. This screw is so heavy that it is in no danger of breaking when turned into the wood. These knobs show three-mold seams. After years of daily use, they remain as firm as a stone wall.

The more knobs one examines, the greater become both knowledge and interest. The first knowledge gained is that hunting glass knobs is like hunting brass candlesticks. Secure a single one, and, however conventional its design, you seem never able to match it *exactly*. You may think

Figure 2

it easy to find a mate; but try it. When you joyfully bring home a stick that you are certain will complete a pair, and set it beside the one you had in mind, it will show so many small differences that you register a vow never to try again—but you do. Matching glass knobs is much the same kind of sport. It matters not how clearly a junk shop find seems to resemble one of your home collection, when you compare it with its presumptive twin, the identity of pattern vanishes.

I think that I have seen all the varieties of knobs which N. Hudson Moore quotes from the advertisement of M. Nisbit, 77 South Front Street, Philadelphia: "plain, fluted, fine twisted, molded, and sunflower." This advertisement also offers "same as the above in deep blue, turquoise, opal, pearl, agate." The only colored knobs I recall are those commonly called "opal." "Deep blue, turquoise, pearl, and agate" knobs I have never met with.

I have shown in Figure 1 *d* a pair of opal knobs. They are not larger than a silver dime and carry circular fluting on the top, much like that of the large knob below. When held to a strong light, they show the colors of a real fire opal. I have always wondered whether these fairy knobs were made for a doll's chest of the eighteen hundreds. I shall use them on a fragile Sheraton dressing stand.

I have found, not only a variety of designs in knobs, but a variety of technical methods in manufacture: knobs showing no seams, molded knobs showing seams, and blown knobs of various patterns. The blown knobs, as I suppose the hollow ones to be, are generally plain, resembling a squat vial, with a

hole for the screw; though some display elaborate patterns. *All* the cut glass knobs that I have seen are hollow, the greater number of them cut in simple diamonds; though now and then an intricate cutting turns up, such as that shown in Figure 2 *c*. Another point is that all the cut knobs are of fine, clear glass, with no bubbles or imperfections.

Molded knobs are liable to be coarser than the cut specimens: sometimes their glass shows a purplish or greenish tinge. Frequently the heavy, common knobs look as if their molds had been used until the outline of the design had become blurred. I have four heavy, large ones, that, except for the screw holes, might be taken for salt cellars. Hoping to complete the half dozen, I succeeded in finding one more of the same queer style, but when I compared it with the four, it agreed in pattern but not in size. Another was found, but alas! though a duplicate in design, it was not of the same dimensions as any of the others.

I once discovered a black walnut chest, of graceful Sheraton lines, bearing a full set of knobs showing well designed whorls that extended around the neck of the knobs. The chest may have been of domestic origin, for, on many large farms in Virginia and Kentucky, it was the custom to apprentice a bright slave to a cabinetmaker for a sufficient time to give him at least an elementary knowledge of the trade. I have seen one or two pieces of furniture made by such slave cabinetmakers. Of course, the hardware and trimmings for such pieces were probably purchased in the near-by town.

Now I come to the last of my knobs. These are the three *a*, *b*, and *c* in Figure 1. The centre one was picked up in a junk shop many years ago. The other two boast the same origin, but were acquired much later. They are of clear glass, artistically cut, and are sunk in brass cups, to which the screws are attached. The glass seems to be backed with silver foil, as is the case in mock jewels. I have never been able to place this pair. The first knob in the row was already impaling its present oak nut when I found it in a junk shop. I have often pondered what the pieces looked like that bore such expensive fixtures and where such fixtures were manufactured.

I once saw at an auction a clumsy elephant of a walnut bureau, whose knobs were bits of mirror surrounded by tiny frames of wood, about the thickness of a straw. They were unique in my experience. I am yet waiting to see the "deep blue, turquoise, pearl, and agate" mentioned in M. Nisbit's advertisement quoted by Mrs. Moore. M. Nisbit states that his glass is "from the Jersey Glass Company." George and P. C. Dummer? I am hopeful, too, that someone will tell us what Deming Jarves patented in the way of knobs and will, if possible, show the pattern of those articles. Meanwhile, I trust that my pictured bits of glass will interest some collectors who have hitherto neglected such "small deer." I can assure them that knobs, besides exercising something of the fascination of jewels, are not expensive, and that they occupy but little space.

THE CASE OF THE
PRESSED GLASS KNOBS

By HELEN McKEARIN

FIG. 1—PRESSED GLASS KNOB marked *Bakewell's Patent (three views)*. Probably pressed under John P. Bakewell's patent of 1825. *From the McKearin collection.*

Helen McKearin, a long-time contributor to ANTIQUES *and the co-author of those indispensable books* American Glass *and* Two Hundred Years of American Blown Glass, *has recently catalogued the antique items in the Museum of Glass opened by the Corning Glass Company in May. In this article she presents new documentary evidence that the pressing of glass by machine was first developed in America.*

THE TERM "PRESSED GLASS," today reserved for glass produced by mechanical pressing, applies to any molded glass forced into a plain or decorated form, not by blowing but by pressure exerted upon the metal. Whether the instrument of pressure be a hand-operated mold or tonglike device or a mechanically controlled pressing machine matters not. But whereas "hand pressing" dates from the early Christian era, mechanical pressing is generally conceded to be an innovation of the 1820's. Where and by whose ingenuity the hand-operated molds evolved into the mechanized are topics of a perennial debate.

Deming Jarves' 1865 remarks on pressing glass have become standard quotes as evidence in this debate. He mentions there English candlesticks and bowls with ". . . square feet, rudely made, somewhat after the present mode of molding glass" and Holland "salts made by being pressed in metallic moulds." These are always cited in evidence against American responsibility for the mechanization of glassmaking. But unless Jarves was using "pressed" in its broad sense rather than in the particular sense of machine-pressing, he had executed a neat about-face sometime during the eleven years between the editions of his *Reminiscences.* In 1854 he had written: "soon after the introduction of the business (flint or lead glass) into this country a very great improvement in the mode of manufacture was introduced . . . Pellat in his admirable work on glass alludes to the American invention in only a few words and passes it by as but of slight importance, but it has brought about a very great change, and is destined to exert a still greater; in fact it has revolutionized the whole system of flint glass manufacture simply by mold machines for the purpose of pressing glass into any form." This seemed nearly clinching evidence that mechanical pressing was a Yankee invention, until the case of the pressed glass knobs cast doubts from another direction.

Apparently mechanical pressing finally hatched from glass knobs, not from "square feet" or "Holland salts." And success in even the most rudimentary stage of the process inevitably led to experimentation by glassmen tumbling to its inherent possibilities. Between September of 1825 and June of 1829 no less than four patents pertaining to making glass knobs were granted—the first to John P. Bakewell of Pittsburgh's Bakewells, for a *method;* the second to Henry Whitney, agent, and Enoch Robinson, mechanician, of Cambridge's New England Glass Company, for a *new and useful improvement;* the third to John Robinson of Pittsburgh's Stourbridge Flint Glass Works, for *pressing in one action;* the fourth to Deming Jarves of the Boston and Sandwich Glass Works, for pressing *glass knobs and screws.*

So far as we know, no glass has been identified with the Robinson patent. The knob marked *Bakewell's Patent (Fig. 1),* probably pressed under John's patent, is a poor thing necessitating disfiguring cutouts wherever it was attached. The Jarves knob proclaims itself as one of doubtful popularity *(Fig. 2).* Glass screws making more than half-inch holes in faces of bureau drawers! The Bakewell and Jarves knobs must have been weak competitors of the type produced by the New England Glass Company. That *type (Fig. 3)* has been determined from the patent specifications, an exact *copy* of which was appended to the Whitney-Robinson Bill of Complaint sworn to on April 25, 1829, and, on May 2, filed by their lawyer, John Cadwalader, with the Philadelphia Circuit Court of Equity.

In that bill Whitney and Robinson of the New England Glass Company swore that their "new and useful improvement" was of much greater use than any mode before known or invented, for "such knobs were manufactured more easily, expeditiously and neatly and by fewer hands than for any former mode." They were "more solid and better adapted to their ordinary purposes . . . more readily made to correspond exactly in size, shape and appearance one with another." Too, they required "less finishing after their form was given them in the first instance" and were "more readily accommodated to the reception of a spindle of the shape best calculated to secure them to the article." During the brief period (about two years) in which the patentees enjoyed exclusive benefit of their improvement, 300,000 knobs or trimmings worth $5000 had been produced and shipped to the principal markets of the United States, including "Boston, Providence, New York, Philadelphia, Baltimore, Washington, Richmond, Charleston, Louisville and New Orleans." To some competitors aware of this new industrial plum mere rumors of such production, sales, and markets could but be an irresistible temptation to bypass the rugged road of experimentation for the shorter one of infringement. All of which happened . . . so a Philadelphia jury decided.

"The validity and originality of this patent was fully tested by a closely contested lawsuit in Philadelphia carried on against powerful parties in Pittsburgh." Thus in 1854 Professor Benjamin Silliman quoted Joseph N. Howe, Jr., of the New England Glass Company (Industry of All Nations). Was the Fort Pitt Glass Works, origin of some eagle cup plates and the Curling creamer, involved? Probably not. No glass was made there until May 1828, and even in 1830 only cut and plain flint glass were being advertised. Were J. Robinson and Son guilty? Were the "300 sets of Patent Glass Knobs" on hand and for sale at reduced prices at their Cincinnati Pittsburgh Glass Warehouse in June 1830 made under John Robinson's patent or not? Or were the culprits Bakewell, Page and Bakewells? They were the most famed makers of fine glassware in the Pittsburgh area and, even though "Patent Moulded Knobs" apparently were not advertised until November 1827, John did hold the 1825 patent. Those Pittsburgh "powerful parties" have been puzzled over for some years.

Now light cast by legal documents and records reveals only the Union Glass Company of Kensington, Philadelphia, *provably* caught in the act. Still, there was no doubt in the minds of Whitney *et al.* that the Union Glass Company in the persons of Emmett *et al.* were not alone guilty; they were "combining with divers persons at present unknown," whose names when discovered should be added to the list of defendants. And events following the trial did point a finger toward Pittsburgh. If they gave no real substance to the charge, they certainly strengthened any suspicion that the Union Glass Company was the scapegoat of a conspiracy. They undoubtedly were the cause of Howe's categorical

statement which was made about ten years later.

As nearly as can be determined from the Court records still extant, the alleged infringement began in the fall of 1828. Possibly the deed was uncovered and reported to the home office by William M. Muzzy, then the comparatively new Philadelphia agent of the Cambridge firm. In any event, Whitney and Robinson deposed that, prior to October 1828, they as well as their agents had asked Emmett *et al.* to forswear making or selling knobs, and they were asked to render an account of those made and the money procured by their sale since the patent date. It was also asked that they be ordered to hand over the total receipts and to deliver up or destroy any knobs on hand. If the charges were disputed or the conditions rejected by the accused, then a trial on the law side of the Court was demanded. William Muzzy gave surety for costs. Thereupon the Court of Equity granted an injunction whereby Emmett *et al.* were "informed and commanded under penalty of $400.00 each to desist from making knobs" until they had fully answered the Bill of Complaint.

This they did within five days. On May 7 C. T. Ingersoll, attorney for Emmett *et al.*, filed their confident denial of nearly all allegations and a demand of their own. Let the complainants be required to prove they had sold upwards of 300,000 knobs for $5000, "which from the respondents knowledge of the subject would be difficult for them to do." As for the alleged warning, they had never even heard about the patent until three weeks previous when William Muzzy spoke to Charles B. Austin. If anyone had been informed about it prior to that time, he must have been William Granville. *He* was named in the Bill of Complaint, to be sure, but not only had he been an ex-member of the company for over a year but one with whom no member had had any correspondence whatever about knobs. In fact, all Emmett *et al.* knew of the patent was the copy affixed to the Bill of Complaint and there was nothing startlingly new about that. (It seems odd indeed that not one of them had read the description of it in the March 1828 issue of the Franklin Institute's magazine.) The Union Glass Company in the persons of William Emmett (once with the New England Glass Company), William Bennett, Joseph Capewell, Richard Synar, James Venables, and Charles B. Austin, had made no knobs until about October 20, 1828. Of about 650 dozen produced, 300 dozen were still unsold. On the others, sold at $1.75 to $2.00 a dozen with 5% to 15% discount, the profit was inconsiderable owing to the expenses "attending an experimental undertaking not yet carried far enough to be profitable."

The crux of the reply for us is the disposition concerning

FIG. 2—PRESSED GLASS KNOB marked *Patent*. Pressed under Deming Jarves' patent of 1829 (*two views*). *Collection of Lura Woodside Watkins.*

FIG. 3—PRESSED GLASS KNOB of the type made under the patent of the New England Glass Company in 1827. *From the McKearin collection.*

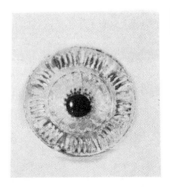

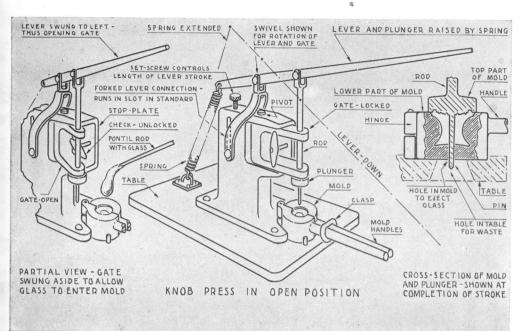

FIG. 4—RECONSTRUCTION of a press for making glass knobs, drawn from descriptions of the machine patented by the New England Glass Company in 1826. The description given in the *Journal* of the Franklin Institute is slightly less complete than that attached to the *Bill of Complaint*, which is the only known surviving copy in the original wording, since the records of the Patent Office were destroyed by fire in the 1830's. The exact forms of the parts shown here are theoretical only, and do not necessarily reflect the machine design practices of the early nineteenth century. *Drawing by James L. McCreery.*

the pressing. They asserted that the method and equipment of Whitney and Robinson in no way inspired their own. William Bennett, an Englishman brought up in the glass business in England, had introduced them. Bennett declared Whitney and Robinson were "wrong in supposing themselves to be either the first or the true inventors and discoverers thereof . . . or that anyone ever enjoyed sole right to or use of the improvement" before or since the alleged patent. Before he came to the United States in 1822 he was perfectly familiar with the method. In fact, while he was employed by Wm. Smith & Company in Cork, Ireland, the glass cutters Graham & Brown brought in a mold just like the mold described and "in all respects as to the machine, application, object and results, precisely the same . . ." Bennett himself had used it to make knobs for Graham & Bell. The defendants had no objection to a trial.

From this point on the records are meager. There is little or no evidence of the actions leading to the few maddeningly skeletal entries in the dockets of the law and the equity sides of the Court. Not until May 21 was it recorded that Whitney and Robinson were to institute action on the law side of the Court. At the same time, the injunction was dissolved, but, until further notice, the defendants were ordered to keep account of all glass knobs made and sold by them. About three months later, August 28, Mr. Muzzy gave surety for cost of a trial. Even so it was October 12 before all the defendants were served with subpoenae. And thus ended the first year of the case of the pressed glass knobs.

On April 6, 1830, the case reopened. By the 18th Whitney *et al.* had asked that a commissioner be sent to Cork, Ireland--obviously to investigate Bennett's claim. For some unmentioned reason the chosen Nathaniel Staniford was unacceptable to Emmett *et al.* On an affidavit from Charles B. Austin the Court ruled on May 29 that Whitney *et al.* show cause why another should not be appointed. Seemingly they were unable to defend their man, or did not care who went: they were given three months in which to name another who, as far as the record goes, is nameless. A single entry on August 19 reads, "Exit commissioner to Cork"; on October 6 another, "Exit commissioner to Boston." Thus we know that the rival claims were assessed, presumably by impartial experts, and on physical evidence. Whatever their content, the reports apparently disturbed the assurance of neither party. Far from being intimidated by them Emmett *et al.* pleaded "not guilty" on December 7. The Court ruled for a trial.

On April 6, 1831, just one year after the case had gone over to the law side of the Court, a jury was called. The trial was short and sweet for Whitney *et al.* On May 7 the jury returned a verdict which gave them a moral victory though, in the light of their demands, hardly a financial one. They had charged that "on September 1, 1828 and divers other days to commencement of action October 1, 1828 and afterward . . ." Emmett *et al.* had "unlawfully made 500,000 infringing knobs and sold 100,000," thereby damaging Whitney *et al.* to the extent of $10,000. Therefore $30,000, a sum three times the alleged loss, should be recovered. The jury awarded damages of $500 plus 6/100 for cost; judgment for $1500 plus 6/100 was handed down. Within two days Ingersoll filed for a retrial. About seven months later, on December 12, the judgment was sustained. But not until April 12, 1832, did Henry Baldwin, the judge in the Court of Equity, sign the final judgment whereby the "defendants were perpetually enjoined and prohibited from making or causing to be made or selling" the knobs. On March 18, 1833, the epitaph of the case was entered in the docket: "Costs paid."

In the meantime there had been an aftermath to that judgment; one which undoubtedly called forth louder hallelujahs in the offices of the New England Glass Company than any $30,000. It was probably in Howe's mind when he spoke of "powerful parties in Pittsburgh." Our evidence of it is the following advertisement in the Pittsburgh *Statesman:*

Pressed Glass Knobs

The subscribers, having purchased from the New England Glass Company the exclusive right to make Patent Pressed Knobs west of the Allegheny mountains, hereby caution all persons against making, buying, or selling the same, except such as are manufactured by the patentees, or *Bakewell, Page & Bakewells.* May 9, 1832.

Historical Glass Cup-Plates

By Alice Van Leer Carrick

[EDITOR'S NOTE — The following discussion is based upon Miss Carrick's own remarkably comprehensive collection of cup-plates. Additional material has, however, been derived through the generous co-operation of Mr. John Overholtzer, of Norristown, Pa., and Mrs. E. C. Hoyt, of Stamford, Conn. Most of the plates mentioned are common to the collections of all three. Notable exceptions are the scalloped Fort Pitt Eagle, belonging to Miss Carrick; the acorn-bordered Log Cabin; the shell-bordered Bee Hive; the crude Sun-burst Eagle and the smooth-edged Fort Pitt Eagle, belonging to Mrs. Hoyt; the pseudo Henry Clay, belonging to Mr. Overholtzer. Illustrations are from all three collections, but, in the main, from a superior series of photographs loaned by Mrs. Hoyt.]

CUP-PLATES

Our Forbears, whom they call polite,
And used to good society quite,
Would without straining any rule
In saucer pour their tea to cool.
Quaffing from which (as they would fain
The tablecloth protect from stain),

They placed their cups which might be wet
In "cup-plates" for the purpose set.
Some of the small glass plates portray
The visage mild of Henry Clay,
On others, through the workman's craft,
Stands Bunker Hill's Memorial shaft.

Advancing taste set up a wail,
That such a fashion should prevail.
The plates were thrown aside forlorn,
Treated with carelessness and scorn,
Thus added value do they gain,
As coveted, but few remain.
MARY SALTONSTALL PARKER.

PRESSED GLASS was first made in the United States by Deming Jarves, a Boston merchant, in 1825; and Sandwich, Massachusetts, a quaint and still charming little town on Cape Cod, was selected as the place where the works were to be built. To quote from Deming Jarves's *Reminiscences of Glass Making*, a slender volume, which modestly tells you all too little of his own successful venture, "Ground was broke in April, 1825, dwellings for the workmen built and manufactory completed; and on the 4th day of July, three months from first breaking ground, commenced blowing glass." Equally important, and to my knowledge never before quoted, is the first advertisement of the glassworks published in the *Columbian Centinel*, November 9, 1825.

FLINT GLASS

The subscriber informs his friends and the public that his Flint Glass Manufactory in Sandwich is now in full operation, and is ready to receive and execute orders for any article in that line—particularly Apothecaries, Chemical and Table Wares. Also, Chandeliers for Churches and Halls, Vase and Mantel Lamps, Lamp Glasses, and all other articles usually made in similar establishments, and on as favorable terms.

Orders directed to Sandwich, Mass., will receive prompt attention. DEMING JARVES.

It is a pity that the old pattern-books of the factory are not to be found; so many disputed points might be proved by them. I have heard them discussed at Sandwich, and have talked with several of the people who remember to have seen them in their childhood, but no search, so far, has revealed them. It is certain, however, that the Sandwich glassworks were started in imitation of and competition with those already established in England, where pressed glass had been made for some years. Deming Jarves imported English workmen experienced in this trade, probably as foremen and expert glass-blowers only, since, in 1832, of the two hundred men and boys employed at the factories, two-thirds were American.

I was so fortunate on a visit to Sandwich as to meet the son of one of these Englishmen, old Mr. Lloyd, who, as a lad, had worked pressing cup-plates after school hours. That was in the early forties, and he told me that the price was then about thirty-five cents a dozen, and that a man and a boy working together could turn out sixteen hundred a day. He also told me that he remembered pressing Bunker Hills, Log Cabins, one or two Eagles, and some of the heads — from his description I judge the smaller heads of Henry Clay. He insisted, too, that the Heart designs were made "out West" (by which I suppose he meant Pittsburgh, where there have been flourishing glass-factories since the last decade of the eighteenth century).

I have seen an English cup-plate made in Birmingham, and dated 1862. Suppose, then, that our first cup-plates were stamped in 1825, the Sandwich glassworks' initial year. That gives them over thirty years of continuous making, though, of course, the English piece was pressed on especial order, since it bore the owner's name, and may, therefore, reflect only an individual whim. But, certainly, we may not date our latest American cup-plate *The Maid of the Mist*, sometimes called the *Niagara*, earlier than 1855, for the Suspension Bridge was not built until that year. Oddly enough, then, a ship begins and a ship ends the list, for, to my thinking, the *Cadmus* design was the first used.

I base this statement upon two things; first, that Lafayette's visit to the United States was one of the great events of its time; next, that I have what I believe to be one of the first pieces of glass to be pressed at the Sandwich works. It seems, even, experimental as well as commemorative, for this round salt-cellar is not only stamped alternately with the eagle and the *Cadmus* (the ship that brought Lafayette to this country in 1824), but it has a crude aspect and is straw-colored rather than white, as if the process of its making had not yet been perfected. But the *Cadmus* is so frequently met with that I can but suppose the design to have been popular enough to continue long after 1825. It is the only other pattern besides the small Henry Clay that I have ever found in half-dozens, a sure proof of its vogue.

But the list of commemoration glass cup-plates includes more than ships. Here is my classification of them:

THE SHIP CADMUS (*Fig. 1*) — A plate three and a half inches in diameter, with a scalloped edge consisting of alternating scallops and points; the outer border shows scrolls and formalized acanthus leaves spaced with four stars; the inner border very

Fig. 1 — The Cadmus

Figs. 2 and 3 — The Chancellor Livingston

Fig. 4—The Benjamin Franklin

Fig. 5 — The Constitution

Fig. 6 — The Robert Fulton

Fig. 7 — The Maid of the Mist

GLASS CUP-PLATES

much the same except that there are two shields and two stars. The central design measures about an inch, is set in tiny dots, and shows a ship, the *Cadmus*, under full sail. A variant shows a large scallop and two small ones, repeated to form the edge.*

THE CHANCELLOR LIVINGSTON (*Figs. 2 and 3*) — A plate three and a half inches in diameter, even scalloped edge; outer stippled border of scrolls, stars, shields, and hearts. There are three variants of this plate. All are side-paddled steamboats (the rigging is accounted for by the fact that, in those early days of steam, sails still had to be depended upon). In all of the plates the ships face to the right. The slight difference between these examples is that in one plate the ropes are indicated by straight lines, in the other by twisted lines. Both show waves indicated by dots. In the third example, the ship is faintly printed, the flag hardly shows, waves are indicated by lines instead of dots, and the hearts in the border are clear glass, not stippled. In all three plates *Chancellor* is impressed above the ship, *Livingston* below. The ship was one of the first steamboats—certainly as early as 1827—plying between New York and Providence. It was named for Robert Livingston, the patron of Fulton, and one of the five drafters of the Constitution.

THE BENJAMIN FRANKLIN (*Fig. 4*) — A companion plate, the same size. The stippled border has scrolls, anchors, large and small stars, and at the top the American Eagle, shield on breast. *Benjamin Franklin* is printed in a semi-circle over the top of the ship, which faces toward the left. The ropes are twisted, not straight lines, the waves indicated by short, curved lines, and the ship flies three flags: one marked B. F., a pennant, and the Stars and Stripes. F. is marked on the paddle-box also. The name, of course, needs no explanation, and the *Franklin* took the same route as the *Livingston*.

THE FRIGATE CONSTITUTION (*Fig. 5*) — One of the three octagonal plates; the size is a full three and a half inches. The edge shows small scallops, the outer clear glass border has a slight decoration of stars and formalized sprays; the inner rim is stippled and spaced by stars and a conventional motif. Around the center of clear glass is a circle of large raised dots almost like small knobs; the waves are clearer and more natural than in the

other plates, and the ship design is a frigate under full sail. It is commemorative, of course, of *Old Ironsides*, the fighting frigate of 1812, vanquisher of the *Guerriere*, and commanded by Captain Isaac Hull. The plate is rare and valuable.

THE FULTON STEAMBOAT (*Fig. 6*) — A companion piece, octagonal also, with the same scallops and outer edge. The inner border, however, is different; lined, not stippled, and adorned with scrolls and shields. The plate lacks the large glass dots; the central circle is stippled, and the boat is shown as a real steamboat, not with sails, which may indicate that the design was taken from a later drawing. A pennant and the Stars and Stripes are displayed, a star marks the paddle-box, and the waves are flowing and clearly indicated. A very rare and desirable piece.

THE MAID OF THE MIST, OR NIAGARA (*Fig. 7*) — A very crude and ugly piece of glass, made evidently when the worker's art had degenerated, since it could not have been stamped before 1855, the date of the completion of the Suspension Bridge. (The *Maid of the Mist* we know from Prescott's letter to have been already running some years in 1851, and in 1850 Frederika Bremer mentions a Suspension Bridge as well.) This plate, probably, symbolizes the larger, and, perhaps, more imposing structure. The rim is plain, the border has a design of pressed circles, and the central design shows the Suspension Bridge, a part of the Falls, the *Maid of the Mist*, and a most primitive sun. An unbeautiful cup-plate, but valuable on account of its rarity. It is certainly *not* a Sandwich piece — it is a popular fallacy to ascribe any and all pressed glass, it matters not what date or design, to Deming Jarves's factories — but was probably made at some New York State glassworks. Barber does not mention any in his "History of American Glass," but I have seen early nineteenth-century advertisements of factories both at Bristol and at Albany.†

HENRY CLAY (*Figs. 8, 9, 10, 11*) — The three and a half inch cup-plate stamped with the small head of Henry Clay is one of the most frequently found designs. There are six variants of this pattern, the least rare having a scalloped rim precisely like the *Cadmus* variant, a border of cornucopias, and a double-topped shield that resembles nothing so much as an opened umbrella. The elements of this border are common to all Henry Clay cup-plates, but are not equally well handled. Sometimes two, sometimes four, of the shields occur, — an inner circle of sprawling sprays and flowers, and a cameo-like bust of Henry Clay within a

---

*Not illustrated.

†Van Rensselaer: *Early American Bottles and Flasks*, p. 107, notes the Van Rensselaer Glassworks at Albany, started 1807; Albany Glassworks; Allenville, N. Y., glassworks, about 1847; Lancaster, N. Y., glassworks, about 1840.

Figs. 8 and 9 — Henry Clay   *Fig. 13 — George Washington*   *Figs. 10 and 11 — Henry Clay*

GLASS CUP-PLATES

circle an inch and an eighth wide. A star is impressed directly below the bust. A variant shows scallops of different sizes on the rim. An extremely interesting variant of this, and the handsomest of the series, exhibits a rim of large and small scallops; the cornucopias and umbrellas, or double shields, appearing twice, only, in the border and supported by flowing acanthus scrolls. The inner rim is decorated with a somewhat snaky design, within whose convolutions two stars appear. The "N" in Henry is turned about, thus, "И." Yet another variation has a border of regularly recurring scallops. The next commonest has the name omitted and no star. Otherwise the plate is standard. Another,

Fig. 12 — Pseudo Henry Clay

which is rare, has an alternately rounded and pointed edge, a slightly different inner rim — flowing lines rather than any direct pattern — and five stars.* A very interesting comparison of this cup-plate border can be made with the one on the Victoria cup-plate, which is, of course, an English piece. It closely resembles the Clay, the only difference being the heads. The time of Clay's great popularity was, I believe, in 1844, when he was the Whig nominee and ran for the Presidency against Polk. This was some seven years later than Victoria's coronation, but an English plate would naturally have an earlier pattern. English workmen, as we know, were brought over to Sandwich by Deming Jarves; they may have carried with them the design, or it might have been copied from imported glass.

THE LARGE HEAD OF HENRY CLAY (*Fig. 12*) — One of the rarest and most desirable of glass cup-plates, ranking second only to the octagonal Washington. It is three and three-eighths inches in diameter, and the head itself is five-eighths of an inch high and half an inch wide. It has a stippled border with conventionalized fleur-de-lis. The inner circle has Henry Clay printed at the top; underneath sprays of laurel at the right, oak and acorns at the left, tied with a bowknot.† The head is really lifelike; evidently an attempted portrait with ambrosial locks, stock and cravat of the period. The coat sleeves, even, show the gathered-in effect of the early forties. Apart from any rarity and historical interest it is a beautiful piece of glass.

THE OCTAGONAL WASHINGTON (*Fig. 13*) — The desired cup-plate of all collectors. It is the same size as the Fulton steamboat and the frigate *Constitution*; the edge is scalloped, and the head is really magnificent, profiled as it is against a sunburst set in a stippled circle. Next there is an encircling wreath of laurel leaves, and a conventionalized scroll and flower border just inside the scalloped edge. The rarest of all historical cup-plates, probably,

*Not illustrated.

†This plate must be wrongly labeled. The old warrior represented has not the faintest resemblance to Clay. The suggestion is that of Zachary Taylor. Examples of mislabeling are common in blue Staffordshire; why not in glass? This plate is reproduced in larger scale to facilitate comparison of the portrait. May it not be of English manufacture?

‡Variant edge has scallops and points.

because in the particular time that it was made, the sweeping popularity of Washington had lessened, perhaps since no direct political significance then attached to him. Beautiful as the design is it can never have been much in demand, or the plates would not now be so rare.

RINGOLD—PALO ALTO (*Fig. 14*) — The third rarest of the heads. A crude plate three and three-eighths inches across, with an edge of large and small scallops; of clear glass and with no stippling at all.‡ The head, however, is a very finely modeled bust nearly an inch and three-quarters in height, and so carefully depicted that the hair, stock, military collar and epaulets are plainly discernible. On the left side of the bust is the word Ringold; on the right, Palo Alto. This is a commemorative cup-plate made in 1846, the date of Major Samuel Ringold's death on the field of Palo Alto. This battle was the opening wedge in the Mexican War, and, for a brief time, Ringold was a national hero. He soon dropped out of remembrance, however, which, perhaps, accounts for the rarity of the plate.

This piece has none of the Sandwich characteristics, and, in view of the fact that Ringold was a Marylander, I have no doubt that the cup-plates *may* have been stamped at the Baltimore Glass Works, though there is also a chance that the Dyottville Glass Works of Kensington, Philadelphia, may have pressed the Ringold plate, for this firm is known to have made the Taylor and Ringold bottles. I have seen but four of these plates, and all were picked up in Philadelphia, which scores another point for Dyottville.

HARRISON (*Figs. 15 and 16*) — Moderately rare; three and a half inches in diameter, and with an edge composed of small scallops. The draped border resembles the one used on one of the Bunker Hill cup-plates. At the top, set in a dotted space, is the word Harrison, with a star on either side and a star as a period; below is the date of his presidency, 1841. The inner circle shows a rim of stars with the bust in the center and the words Maj. Gen. W. H. Harrison above, born Feb. 9, 1773, below. It is interesting to compare this cup-plate with the political medal of the same date, for both, of course, mark the spirited and picturesque Log Cabin Campaign. Allowing for the natural differences of material and size, the copper and glass heads are almost precisely similar. The coin may easily have been used as a model. A rarer variant of this plate has the word President and the date 1841 omitted, undoubtedly the fault of some mould; unless the unmarked example was sold during the campaign preceding the election.

LOG CABIN WITH CIDER BARREL, FLAG AND TREE (*Figs. 17 and 18*) — One of the smaller cup-plates, three and a quarter inches in diameter. It has a small scalloped edge, a border of sprays and flowers, and a central design of a Log Cabin with a Flag, a Tree and a Cider Barrel; symbols, of course, of the Hard Cider Campaign of Tippecanoe, and resembling very closely the design on the reverse side of the Harrison medal. A variant, very rare in-

Fig. 14 — General Ringold

Figs. 15 and 16 — General Harrison

 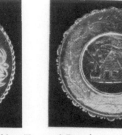

Figs. 17 and 18 — Log Cabin—Tree and Barrel

Fig. 19 — Fort Meigs Cabin

Fig. 20 — Cabin with Flag

Fig. 21 — Chimney Cabin

GLASS CUP-PLATES

deed, has an acorn border, which may prove that this Log Cabin was made at Sandwich, for there is an interestingly traditional little story of Deming Jarves's controversy with the captain of the vessel who carried his wares to Boston; of his threatening to build a ship of his own, and of the captain's retort, "The acorn isn't yet planted which will grow the oak that is to build your ship." And of Deming Jarves's answer to the taunt in the naming of the ship, which he immediately built, *The Acorn.* This idea, naturally, would apply to all acorn designs, and is pure conjecture.

Figs. 22 and 23 — Bee Hive

FORT MEIGS LOG CABIN (*Fig. 19*) — About as rare as the first Log Cabin. It is larger, a trifle over three and a half inches. The edge is scalloped, the border a wreathing of acorns, and the central design a log cabin, heavier and lower in construction than the one on the Cider Barrel and Flag Cabin. On the border, at the top, is the word "Tippecanoe" (Harrison was so called from his victory over Tecumseh), below "Wm. H. Harrison"; while just above the log cabin are the words "Fort Meigs," in memory of the first skirmish of the War of 1812.

LOG CABIN WITH FLAG (*Fig. 20*) — Very rare, and one of the smallest of all cup-plates, measuring just a fraction over three inches. The edge is a plain, small scallop, the border has two encircling lines, and the ground on which the Log Cabin stands is indicated very much as the waves in the ship cup-plates are.

LOG CABIN WITH CIDER BARREL AND OUTER CHIMNEY (*Fig. 21*) — Three and a quarter inches, very heavy and crude, with a rare twisted scalloped edge, and a large, heavy log cabin occupying the center of the plate. This design more resembles the Fort Meigs than the two others, but it is bigger, shows a wide front view, a side displaying a wide, substantial chimney, and an ample cider barrel rolled under the window. It is by far the rarest of all the Log Cabins.

THE BEE HIVE (*Figs. 22 and 23*) — One of the smaller three-inch cup-plates, and decidedly one of the prettiest of all the historical ones. It has a plain scalloped edge, a graceful border of laurel leaves and a lacy stippled inner circle adorned with a bee hive outlined with nine bees. There is a variant, a heavier plate,

crude and smaller, with a border that shows a shell pattern. I have heard that there are other types, too, and since the Bee Hive is a typical Harrison symbol, fashioned into appropriate and useful ink bottles by the firm of Whitney Brothers of Glassboro, and woven into 1841 table linen, I have no doubt of this statement, although I have never seen them.

THE 1831 EAGLE (*Fig. 24*) — Three and a half inches in diameter, with a scalloped edge, a charming stippled border, ornamented with flower sprays and fleur-de-lis, and, at the bottom, what may be interpreted as four pine trees. In a way, these trees may be symbolic of the event the plate commemorates, the settlement of the boundary line between the United States and Canada. The inner circle is stippled and decorated with arabesques and four stars. This encloses the eagle with head to the right and shield on breast. Below the eagle the date, 1831, is marked. Fairly common.

PLAIN EDGED EAGLE (*Fig. 25*) — Size three and three-eighths inches. A stippled edge decorated with arabesques and a large eagle, head turned to right, is set in a stippled center. There is no shield on the breast, but the eagle appropriately grasps arrows and an olive branch. Probably dedicated — as most of these eagles were—to the jingoistic "spread-eagleism" of the time. About as rare as the Dated Eagle.

SMALL EAGLE WITH DOTTED EDGE (*Fig. 26*) — The width is three inches, perhaps a shade more. The edge is scalloped, with dots in each scallop. The glass is plain, and the central eagle, facing the right, has a shield on breast and holds arrows and the olive branch. Also, scattered around, are thirteen stars, symbolizing, of course, the Thirteen States. A very rare plate.

THE GRAPEVINE EAGLE (*Fig. 27*) — One of the prettiest of the eagle plates, and rare. The edge is alternate points and rounds; stars, scrolls, and a fleur-de-lis-like motif — all in clear glass — adorn the stippled border. The central eagle (still with olive branch and arrows) is very tiny, three-quarters of an inch perhaps. It is set in a small dotted circle, and the outer rim is quite charmingly decorated with a grapevine.

THE FLEUR-DE-LIS EAGLE (*Fig. 28*) — An equally desirable

Fig. 24 — Eagle, 1831

Fig. 25 — Plain Edged Eagle

Fig. 26 — Eagle with Dotted Border

Fig. 27 — Grapevine Eagle

Fig. 28 — Fleur-de-Lis Eagle

Fig. 29 — Eagle with Thirteen Stars

Figs. 30 and 31 — Eagle with Thirteen Stars in Sun-burst

GLASS CUP-PLATES

plate, measuring three and three-eighths inches. The edge is plain scalloped, the border stippled and adorned with leaves and formal flowers of bright (clear) glass. The eagle is a trifle larger than the Grapevine Eagle, and this time the enclosing ring is stippled glass. The eagle has a shield, arrows and olive branch, and the outer rim (which gives the plate its name) is composed of fleur-de-lis and little starlike flowers.

EAGLE WITH THIRTEEN STARS (*Fig. 29*) — A rare cup-plate, which measures three and a quarter inches. The edge is scalloped; the border is made up of a conventional design made of pineapples, acroteria and rosettes, the latter resembling daisies. The eagle is large; head turned to right; shield, arrows, and olive branch. In a semi-circle above the eagle are stamped thirteen stars.

EAGLE WITH THIRTEEN STARS IN SUN-BURST (*Figs. 30 and 31*) — This cup-plate measures three and three-eighths inches, and the edge is scalloped with alternate points and rounds, and the rounds are dotted. The border is stippled and embellished with "fine fingering"; the eagle is a little smaller than the one just described, but shows the conventional shield, arrows and olive branch; and thirteen large stars set in a stippled border form a circle around it. A crude variant shows crowded borders and a close-clipped scalloped edge. At the Essex Institute in Salem there is another interesting variant of this plate, in which, the edge is plain, the scallops being omitted. A rare type.

THE FORT PITT EAGLE (*Figs. 32 and 33*) — The most beautiful of all the eagles and the second rarest. It is large, measuring three and three-quarters inches; the edge is scalloped, and the border that beautiful peacock design found on English plates. The eagle is medium-sized, but very finely done; there is more of an attempt at plumage than in the others. There are twenty-four stars,— a fact which dates the plate subsequent to the admission to statehood of Missouri, in 1821, and previous to that of Arkansas, in 1836; for Missouri was the twenty-fourth state. I date it Pittsburgh, 1835. It looks like a memorial to commercial progress, of whose further exemplification a collecting friend of mine has a steamboat cup-plate marked Pittsburgh Glassworks, 1836. It is more than probable, since this eagle plate represents Fort Pitt — the first name of Pittsburgh — that it should have been stamped in that city and at those works. The details are

very fine; the shield, arrows, and olive branch very clearly impressed, the sparkle of the glass, white and radiant. The words Fort Pitt are printed on a scroll that the eagle carries in his beak. A variant of this plate, the plain-edged type, is sometimes found, but it seems hardly so fine.

THE HOP-VINE (BLACKBERRY-VINE) EAGLE (*Fig. 34*) — In my experience, rarer than any other eagle. It is three and one-quarter inches in diameter, as heavy as the Ringold and very nearly as crude in texture. The edge is plain, the border an interesting and very graceful vine. The very small eagle is encircled by a dotted ring; the rest of the center by concentric circles. The glass is very full of bubbles showing improper "cooking," and the plate bears none of the Sandwich aspect. I am inclined to attribute it to some New York State glassworks.

BUNKER HILL (*Figs. 35, 36, 37 and 38*)—There are four Bunker Hill variants, all very well known. All have scalloped edges; two have braided, two draped borders. The largest is three and five-eighths inches. This is the Bunker Hill with the Braided Border, indicating the stonework of the monument. There are stars at the crossings of the braids and thirteen stars around the monument in the center. In the outer circle is printed, "Bunker Hill Battle Fought June 17th, 1775."

The second Braided Border is a little smaller, three and a half inches; the monument shows no stones, only twelve stars are displayed, and the plate is rather crude. There are two circles of printing, "Bunker Hill Battle Fought June 17, 1775," and "From the Fair to the Brave." The more usual Draped Border has an outside rim of printing, "Cornerstone Laid by Lafayette June 17, 1825. Finished by the Ladies"; otherwise the printing is the same as on the second Braided Border plate. This monument has stones, but lacks the stars. The second Draped Border is precisely the same except that it has twelve stars impressed around the monument. I think that there is no doubt whatever that these Bunker Hill plates were made at Sandwich. They are a distinctly Massachusetts design, of course. "From the Fair to the Brave" and "Finished by the Ladies" mean that the money for completing the monument was given by Massachusetts women, and a quaint little legend, handed down to me by an old lady of seventy, who in her turn had heard it from a woman forty years older, says that one way the women raised their necessary funds was

Figs. 32 and 33 — Fort Pitt Eagle, Scalloped and Plain

Fig. 34 — Hop-Vine Eagle

Figs. 35 and 36 — Bunker Hill—Braided Border

Figs. 37 and 38 — Bunker Hill—Draped Border

GLASS CUP-PLATES

by selling these cup-plates. I merely give this for what it is worth.

* * *

And so ends my tale of historical glass cup-plates. May I add a few "Don'ts"?

Don't call all pressed glass Sandwich. That's as bad as all eighteenth-century glass being labeled *Stiegel* and all eighteenth-century furniture *Chippendale*. Deming Jarves happened to be the first in the field, and you must remember that all successful enterprises have their imitators.

Don't confuse cup-plates with butter plates. Butter plates have no flattened surface on which to rest the cup.

Don't let dealers sell you the *Cadmus*, and insist it is the *Mayflower*.

Don't forget to look carefully at the borders and edges, for that is where the difference in variants is most likely to occur.

Don't — having bought cup-plates — pile them one on top of the other, for that way is sure to nick the edges. Better to follow my plan and put them in a cabinet drawer against black velvet. This keeps them safe, and accentuates their lustre.

Don't forget that cup-plates are still to be found on distant farmhouse shelves, perhaps up in the attic at your grandmother's.

Last of all, don't forget that cup-plates offer one of the most beguiling of all possible quests for the collector.

"WESTERN VIEW OF SANDWICH (Central Part)" in 1839

This woodcut, reproduced from John Warner Barber's *Historical Collections*, "shows two Congregational churches, town house, and in the distance some of the buildings connected with the glassworks." It will be observed that the artist makes up for the diminishment of the factories, due to the requirements of perspective, by depicting smoke emerging from their chimneys in volume sufficient to cover the upper heavens, — sure indication of successful activity.

Notes on Historical Glass Cup-Plates

By Alice Van Leer Carrick & The Editor

[*Illustrations from the collections of Mrs. R. C. Taylor, Mrs. C. S. Bull, Mr. A. H. Scott, Mrs. L. G. Verrill, Mrs. A. E. Folsom, Mrs. M. B. Cookerow, Mrs. C. A. Brouwer, the Peabody Museum, the George Shepley library, and the Essex Insitute. The generous co-operation of these interested owners is appreciatively acknowledged* — Ed.]

IT is now nearly a year since my original study of historical cup-plates was published in Antiques. The purpose of this study was to offer a check list of known plates. It carried with it the obligation of endeavoring to identify the various designs shown and, where possible, to explain their significance.

As the check list was printed, it inevitably contained some errors. There were also, of course, many omissions, for hardly a day passes without the discovery of a new design. In several instances, further, the identifications and attributions have aroused differences of opinion. Out of these various circumstances and the forces which they set in motion has emerged a considerable amount of new material, very uneven in both quality and quantity; but, in general, of sufficient interest and value to be worth placing before readers of Antiques as informal notes, which, in turn, may well serve as a body of reference in case the check list is eventually published in concise and reasonably well balanced book form, in which chief emphasis would be placed on conclusions rather on the reasons back of them.

These notes concern two topics: 1, new light on the already well known plates; 2, newly encountered plates. They can not well be separated. I shall take up the well-known plates which call for discussion in the same order as that in which they appear in Antiques for February, 1922 (Volume I, p. 61), shall give them the same numbering, and, where it seems advisable, shall repeat the old illustrations.

The Cadmus

In case of newly encountered plates I shall either apply new numbers to new examples or shall use an old class number with a letter to indicate a sub-class.

I. Cadmus vs. Constitution

Cadmus, No. 1. Constitution, No. 5
(Both described in Antiques, February, 1922)

Some question has arisen as to whether the *Cadmus* and the *Constitution* plates were really intended to represent different ships or should properly be designated merely as the *large* Constitution and the *small* one. Some persons, it is understood, now use that designation.

The evidence is as follows: A water-color drawing by Anton Roux (*1765–1835*), in the Peabody Museum at Salem shows us the *Cadmus*. No frigate in the American navy ever bore this name. In the present instance the high bulwark, the painted port holes and the general shape of the vessel indicate that she was a merchantman. The *Cadmus*, by the way, was built in 1816 by Thatcher Magoun at Medford, Mass.

Likewise in the Peabody Museum occurs a five-foot model of the *Constitution*, which, in 1813, was given to the Salem East India Marine Society, by Captain Isaac Hull. It is the only accurate contemporary model known and was followed by the United States naval authorities when the *Constitution* was restored in 1907. The actual frigate was built in Boston in 1797.

The ordinary landlubber might well be forgiven if he should fail to perceive any very clear marks of difference between the two ships depicted, the one in water color, the

The Constitution

THE SHIP CADMUS
From a water color by Anton Roux in the Peabody Museum, Salem.

THE FRIGATE CONSTITUTION
From a model in the Peabody Museum, Salem.

other in the rounded wood. When two such similar forms are reduced to the dimensions and material of cup-plate decoration, it
seems absurd to try to distinguish between them on the basis of
appearance.

At this point tradition appears to offer the safest guide. Tradition calls the small vessel the *Cadmus*, the large one the *Constitution*. It finds verification in the case of the second vessel in such
marks as the angle of the bowsprit, the shape of the stern, and
the placing of the row of portholes.

Granting, then, that the large plate represents the *Constitution*,
probability would yet favor a plate depicting the *Cadmus*. Lafayette's visit to America bulked very large in the events of the
day and was signalized by the newly established Sandwich
works.* To represent the *Chancellor Livingston*, and to omit
representation of the ship which bore the hero himself to this
friendly shore would have been an oversight of which Deming
Jarves would hardly have been guilty.

What may be the *Cadmus* appears likewise on a crude early
salt here pictured. The color of the glass and the general aspect
of the dish seem to imply early manufacture at Sandwich.

The following quotation from a contemporary newspaper will
serve to show how important was Lafayette's visit:

"General La Fayette, accompanied by his son, George Washington La Fayette, Mr. Auguste La Vasseur, a companion, and
one servant, arrived here yesterday morning in the Ship *Cadmus*,
captain Allyn, after a pleasant passage of thirty-one days from
Havre. The fact of his arrival was made known by the Telegraph
at an early hour, and it spread through the city with electrical
rapidity. Broadway was soon thronged, and the Battery crowded
with people." . . . He landed at Staten Island. . . . "The news of
the General's arrival had spread through the surrounding country with the rapidity of lightening; and from the dawn of day
until noon, the roads and ferry boats were thronged with people
who were hastening to the city to participate in the fete."

The Committee of Welcome chartered the steamship, *Robert
Fulton*, and the steamboats, *Chancellor Livingston*, *Oliver Ellsworth*, *Henry Eckford*, *Connecticut*, *Olive Branch*, and *Nautilus*,
which were used as an escort. They were ranged as an aquatic
guard between the south part of the Battery and Governor's
Island, and thence proceeded in order to Governor's Island. The
West Point Band played during the ceremony *See, the Conquer-
ing Hero Comes*, *Hail Columbia*, and the *Marsellaise*.

*See the B & S salt illustrated in ANTIQUES for April, 1922.

STEAM SHIP BENJAMIN FRANKLIN.

CAPT. R. S. BUNKER, will leave Providence
on FRIDAY next, 12 o'clock, M. Passengers by leaving their names at the Marlboro' Hotel,
or at A. J. ALLEN'S, No. 72, State-street, will be
provided with Coaches.   March 11

COPY OF THE BENJAMIN FRANKLIN ADVERTISEMENT
  For some reason the masts and rigging are omitted. But otherwise note close
  similarity to cup-plate.

EARLY SANDWICH SALT
  Shows alternate ship and eagle medallions.

II. BENJAMIN FRANKLIN, *No. 4*.

The study of this plate has been complicated by the appearance of an imitation, which is illustrated and discussed in
ANTIQUES for December, 1922 (Volume II, p. 252). There seems
good reason for believing that this plate was pressed at Sandwich; for the steamship *Franklin* occasioned great excitement in
and around Boston. The *Columbian Centinel* of September 10,
1828, quotes at length from the *Commercial Advertiser* a description of this new vessel:

"She has been several times put upon trial, and answered the
most sanguine expectations of owners, is now ready for service,
and, we understand, will depart hence tomorrow afternoon for
Providence, and thence on an excursion of pleasure for Boston.
She has been built according to the plans, and under the superin-
tendence of the veteran Captain E. S. Bunker by whom she is to
be commanded. In addition to her two engines of great strength
and power, she is ship-rigged, having three masts;† the length is
144 feet; breadth of beam 32 feet; breadth of guards 21 feet; making her extreme breadth 53 feet. Depth of hold ten feet. Her model
is of a graceful cast. The stern combines neatness, taste, and
beauty. In the centre is an excellent bust of the great philosopher
whose name she bears, on the left of which is the figure of Fame,
with her trumpet in her left hand, and, in her right, an olive
branch with which she is in the act of crowning the patriotic
sage. On the right is the Muse of History with her scroll to record
the deeds and the lessons of wisdom which fall from his lips. And
there are other emblems carved in relief upon the stern: such as,
books, a globe, mathematical instruments, and implements of
husbandry, with leaves of oak gilded, etc. She sits upon the water
like a swan, and is indeed a noble and stately ship.

"The interior of the ship has been finished with an eye solely
to neatness, plainness, comfort, and convenience. The ship was
built by Brown and Bell under the direction of Captain Bunker
himself. The engines were constructed by Ezra R. Dod of the
Sterling Works. The joinery, which is
finished in the very best manner, by
J. Wells and S. B. Macy.

"The design of the interior of the
ship, which is in all arrangements
most complete, has been taken without essential change or alteration
from those of Captain Bunker, upon
which the old *Experience* packets

†Omitted, perhaps for reasons of space, in
the advertising column.

LANDING OF
LAFAYETTE
Cover of snuff box

The Robert Fulton

Pittsburgh Steamboat

which formerly plied between Hudson and New York, were constructed in 1807, nearly twenty-two years ago. The *Experiment* was the first vessel built in the United States with the express design of conveying passengers only, and we think it no mean compliment to Captain Bunker that for twenty-two years, while so many able and accomplished artists have been engaged in constructing steam and other packets of every size and variety of form and beauty, for convenience of arrangement, beauty of design, and comfort of construction, the last was built upon the model of the first, as the *ne plus ultra* of this department of marine architecture.

"But enough for one day. The *Benjamin Franklin* will be put upon service tomorrow, and if she proves, as we believe she will, the *crack boat* of the Sound, we may write a letter to ourselves upon the subject from Boston." (Taken from the pages of the *Commercial Advertiser* "on Monday last.")

Here is part of a description of an excursion to Salem that took place September 17, 1828. It is the immense excitement in Massachusetts about the boat that makes its cup-plate seem to me a Sandwich piece. "This excellent steamer made an excursion to Salem on Saturday, and took from thence even 600 passengers and after skirting the shores of Marblehead, Nahant, and Lynn, passed over to Cape Ann shore, and returned after a long run to Salem." The tickets seem to have been fifty cents for the round trip.

Probably the first advertisement of regular passage was October 4, 1828. It is reproduced on page 21.

III. THE ROBERT FULTON, *No. 6.*

Here is the story of the *Fulton's* part in the welcoming of Lafayette:

"The appearance of the *Robert Fulton* as she came down the East River from the Navy Yard, escorted by the *Connecticut* and *Oliver Ellsworth*, all superbly decorated, was rich beyond description. The yards were manned to the round tops with about two hundred seamen from the *Constitution*, who made an elegant appearance. Directly in the rear of the *Chancellor* was the *Robert Fulton*, whose lofty masts and widespread arms, which literally swarmed with men, towered proudly above her less pretending, but not less gay and beautiful consorts.

"It was the *Chancellor Livingston*, however, which was honored by the presence of the Committee, and Lafayette went on board of her under a triumphal arch, and over richly carpeted steps.

"The Battery was crowded with respectable people of both sexes, Castle Garden was filled; every boat that arrived to take its station was completely crowded with elegantly dressed ladies and gentlemen."—From the New York *Spectator*, Aug. 20, 1824.

A contemporary engraving presents this scene. It was used by Clews for a blue china pattern, and appears likewise on a snuff box belonging to Mrs. L. G. Verrill of Rochester, N. H. The

latter is here reproduced. Mrs. Hudson Moore, in the *Old China Book*, affirms the inaccuracy of this picture, since, as she states, the *Robert Fulton* had but one mast instead of three. This is, in turn, at variance with the implications of the description of the Lafayette reception. But the existence of three masts, or of one, might appear to vitiate my earlier identification of this cup-plate as the *Robert Fulton*, for the glass representation displays no mast whatsoever. Yet this is not necessarily the case. The cup-plate in question has the appearance of Sandwich glass, its border is very similar in pattern to that of the *Chancellor Livingston*, which facts imply a relationship between the plates. That its shape is octagonal like that of the *Constitution* cup-plate, may here also imply some relationship, for on the gala day the *Fulton* was manned in part by seamen from the *Constitution*. There is no certainty in all of this. Each student of the subject will draw such conclusions as he sees fit. But if he is unduly troubled by the absence of masts on the cup-plate, he is referred to the advertisement of the *Benjamin Franklin*, which represents that vessel as innocent of masts as a diving bell.

There remains the possibility that this nondescript craft to which so much attention is here devoted is, in reality, nothing better nor worse than a river steamer such as that pictured on the razor illustrated in ANTIQUES for December (Vol. II, p. 267). Yet it seems to me rather a possibility than a probability. I am inclined to view the 1836 Pittsburgh cup-plate, noted below, as a conscious reversion to the earlier Sandwich type exemplified in the *Robert Fulton*.

IV. THE PITTSBURGH STEAMBOAT, *No. 7a.*

"Union Glass Works, Pittsburgh, 1836." This is the legend on this plate. It is three and one-half inches in diameter, octagonal, and rather crude in effect. The border is scalloped and patterned with little ovals; at each octagonal point is a larger figure; around the inner border are conventional figures, two small eagles, and the numbers from one to eight. The central design (enclosed by the words quoted above) is a small side-paddle steamboat an inch and one-half long, flying the Stars and Stripes, and with a very realistic curl of smoke, the kind that children draw. The boat I have not been able to identify; I searched through the lists published in Hall's *The West*, in vain. Out of the hundred and seventy-three steamboats built at Pittsburgh none was dated 1836.

Nor are contemporary pictures helpful; the closest resemblance I found in the steamboat printed on a *Reward of Merit* card which admonished the receiver to remember his Creator in the days of his glad, glad youth. Such illustrations, I believe, were intended to give children a knowledge of mechanical contrivances, and of the busy world outside. Still, Ohio River commerce was so justly important in the early nineteenth century that the cup-plate really needs no explanation. An Ohio River steamboat was an object of great consequence. To quote from an enthusiast of those beginning days, "It was all that the Western country needed; and the name of Fulton should be cherished with that of Washington; if the one conducted us to liberty, the other has given us prosperity—the one broke the chain which bound us to a foreign country; the other has extended the channels of intercourse, and multiplied the ties which bind us to each other."

Henry Clay, *8 and 9*

George Washington

Henry Clay, *10 and 11*

V. Henry Clay and Pseudo Henry Clay or Henry Clay turned to right.

Henry Clay has suffered at the hands of the imitator, but it is the *Henry Clay*, Nos. 8, 9, 10, 11, that has, or have, a grievance on this score. Concerning the extremely rare *Henry Clay* turned to the right, it was suggested in An-tiques for February, 1922, that the head shown on that plate was more likely to be that of General Zachary Taylor, mistakenly used and hence wrongly labeled. Curious confirmation of this theory has recently come to light. One of Mrs. Verrill's snuff boxes depicts the rough and ready general. Forehead, nose, mouth, and chin are quite those of the individual of the cup-plate. With due allowances for trans-lation into glass this would seem to be the man. The sharp-featured, straight-haired Clay bears no resemblance whatever to the plate.

If further confirmation were needed it might come from the study of a large lithograph, belonging to Dr. J. Milton Coburn of South Norwalk, Conn. In its delineation of the general this lithograph is almost identical with the engraving on the snuff box. It bears, however, this legend, "Entered according to the act of Congress in the year 1847 by Edw. Clay and F. Mitchelin." Is it not reasonable to suppose that Edward Clay, the publisher, was hastily accepted as the subject of a lithograph used as a basis for a cup-plate designed in honor of Henry Clay, the statesman, and that the error was not discovered until some few plates had been made and mar-keted? The extreme scarcity of the plate would thus be accounted for.

VI. Octagonal Washington, *No. 13.*

The enormous adoration of Washington had per-ceptibly lessened two decades after his death, but the feeling was once more at high tide with the second visit of Lafayette. The blue Staffordshire china bearing the likenesses of both Washington and Lafayette, Lafayette at Washington's Tomb,

Washington Seal
Illustration from Cloquet's Recollections of Lafayette

etc., are evidences of this. I am inclined to place the Washington cup-plate as one more Lafayette link. In a book, published in France the year after Lafayette's death, 1835, *The Recollections of the Private Life of General Lafayette*, by M. Jules Cloquet, M.D., it is stated that, in the library of Lagrange Lafayette, is "a seal habitu-ally used by him, and given to him by Mr. Barnet, consul for the United States in Paris. It represents the head of Washington surrounded with rays." This is an inter-esting coincidence even if it is nothing more.

VII. Major Ringold, *No. 14.*

Ringold appears to be somewhat more common than was indi-cated in my previous discussion of this plate. There is a variant of the plate as shown. It displays scallops and points.

VIII. General Harrison, *Nos. 15 and 16.*

In previous discussions of this plate I spoke of the political medal of the time as being closely like it. A reproduction of this medal, taken from one in my possession, is illustrated on page 24.

IX. Log Cabins, *Nos. 17 and 18.*

The close relation between campaign medal designs and cup-plates finds further exemplification in the resemblance between the small metal and enamel Harrison Campaign medal and the log cabin, tree, and barrel cup-plate illustrated.

X. Log Cabin with Liberty Cap, *No. 21a.*

To the log cabin series must now be added the *Log Cabin with Liberty Cap* which, as probably the rarest of log cabins, deprives No. 21 of that emi-

Major Ringold

Zachary Taylor
Cover of snuff box.

Pseudo Henry Clay

Henry Clay
From an old lithograph.

Log Cabin with Liberty Cap

Log Cabin—Tree and Barrel.

The Plow.

nence. It is three and three-quarter inches in diameter; and of rough glass somewhat similar in touch to *No. 20.* The edge consists of large and small scallops. The plate displays cider barrel, bench, and tree, and, in addition, a flag pole surmounted by a liberty cap.

While Harrison emblems are under discussion, it is worth while to point to an interesting log cabin tea plate in which the Harrisonian log cabin is further embellished with an equally Harrisonian plow—likewise, no doubt, generally indicative of agriculture, just as the ship is indicative of commerce. Manufacture is probably symbolized in the glass factory.

What this factory represents is left to the judgment of the student. It has been called the Dyott works, but comparison with an old print belonging to Mr. Arthur H. Scott of Media, Pa., does not entirely support the attribution. In a case of this kind, so small a matter as the presence or absence of chimney caps may be of vital importance in the process of identification. The crude wood block of Sandwich published in ANTIQUES for February, 1922, shows the glass works pouring forth smoke from two capped chimneys. The careful capping of the stacks on this tea-plate is, therefore, not to be ignored.

Strict adherence to the lit-

General Harrison

LOG CABIN TEA PLATE
Bears emblems of agriculture, commerce and manufacture. The last is signalized by a glass factory.

eral presentation of various apparently minor details, and indifference to what an artist would consider basic exactitudes, is characteristic of the untrained or partially trained delineator. This is a fact not to be overlooked in studying resemblances in the field of the minor arts.

The care with which the makers of moulds for souvenir pressed glass followed copy will be shown by a comparison of the *Chancellor Livingston* cup-plate with the contemporary lithograph, from which it may, quite possibly, have been derived.*

XI. THE PLOW, *No. 22b.*

Probably dedicated to rural thrift and agricultural activity and hence produced in honor of Harrison, occurs this very attractive cup-plate. It is so rare as to be, perhaps, unique.

Within the year a number of hitherto unpublished eagles have come to light. These will presently be shown and discussed in ANTIQUES. Meanwhile additional material on the subject of cup-plates— whether in the form of substantiation, well-founded doubt or new discovery— will be very welcome.

*See frontispiece.

DYOTT GLASS WORKS
From a lithograph.

HARRISON CAMPAIGN MEDAL AND TOKEN
Note the similarity of the head to that on the cup-plate.

CUP PLATES OF THE PHILADELPHIA AREA

By HELEN McKEARIN and JAMES H. ROSE

FOR SOME TIME a few students have believed that cup plates were produced in the Philadelphia area. The theory advanced in *American Glass* (pp. 350, 352) that the Ringgolds, running-vine cabins, and other cup plates with identical serration patterns (*Fig. 2*) were made in the Philadelphia area was based on circumstantial evidence. In our experience a good seventy-five per cent of the known specimens of these plates have turned up in the region around Philadelphia, and the character and treatment of their designs differ in many respects from both New England and Midwestern practice. Besides, in the case of the Ringgolds it seemed a reasonable point of origin since Major Ringgold was more a local than a national hero, with his greatest popularity in the Philadelphia-Baltimore area. And if we attribute the Ringgold plates to that locality, we may also attribute the related items.

To the layman the number of varieties in each series might seem to indicate production in several factories, and for his benefit we explain briefly that all of these particular plates were pressed in molds having the serration pattern on the surface die and the design on the plunger. Since the measurements correspond, it is evident that the design could be varied at will simply by changing the part of the die attached to the plunger, while a change in the serration pattern meant nothing more difficult than changing the surface die. Thus with one die for each design (the two varieties of Ringgolds, the log cabin, and each of the three conventionals) plus four surface dies each with a different serration pattern, a factory could make twenty-four varieties of cup plates. Such a method was, of course, very economical, especially for a firm which bought its molds from an independent moldmaker. Not only could any number of made-to-order design parts be purchased separately, but also relatively few of the less expensive surface dies, which could be, and were, used over long periods of time, would be needed. It is interesting to note that twenty of these twenty-four possible varieties have been numbered by Albert C. Marble, and a twenty-first, a cabin with even serrations, is in the collection of Mrs. Palmer Graham. We are confident that the other three will turn up, for instance, a variant of 826-661 with even scallops as on 412.

The most likely date of the Ringgolds is 1846, the year of the major's death. But we do not believe that all the plates shown in Figure 2 are as late as that. The running-vine cabins, for example, are surely mementoes of the Harrison campaign and so date from 1839, or, at the latest, 1840. The three conventional groups cannot be precisely dated but might be said to record three steps in the decadence of design. The 826-661 series which is at the peak of the lacy type probably dates from about 1835. While the 81-80 series may be considered a more effective and consistent design than that of the 84-85 series, both are on the downgrade to Victorian coarseness. So it seems likely that they were pressed in the 1840's, the 81-80 series slightly antedating the 84-85. Thus these plates in Figure 2 represent a recognizable output over a period of about ten years (roughly from 1835 to the fall of 1846).

While all this evidence seemed conclusive we realized the danger of creating a new ghost like that of the Stoddard-three-mold fiasco,

FIG. 1—"A VIEW OF PART OF THE UNION GLASS COMPANY'S WORKS KENSINGTON NEAR PHILADª."

a ghost that might prove ubiquitous and hard to lay if new facts turned up to discredit our assumption. Yet we felt very strongly that collectors should be turned from their far too facile faith that all pressed glass of the lacy period originated either in Massachusetts or the Pittsburgh-Monongahela district. And so we were much gratified by the receipt of an important piece of further evidence in its support from Mrs. Claude N. Campbell, great-great-granddaughter of Charles B. Austin, one-time proprietor of the Union Glass Works, Kensington, Philadelphia. In Mrs. Campbell's family there are four Ringgold cup plates like 634, with a strong family tradition of their having been made at this Union Glass Works. According to Mrs. Campbell, these Ringgolds came to her mother from a cousin who had been employed at the Excelsior Glass Works at Kaighn's Point, in New Jersey. Mrs. Campbell's mother also received from the same cousin a conventional cup plate like 421.

The history of the Union Glass Works is still somewhat obscure, though there is nothing in what we now know to indicate that glass was not pressed there; on the contrary, there is some evidence that it was. Jarves in his *Reminiscences* says that in 1820 a group of workmen left the New England Glass Company "to embark on their own account their savings of many years in the doubtful enterprise of establishing flint glass works in Kensington, Philadelphia under the title of the Union Flint Glass Company." An uncharitable undertone of "I told you so," if not of scorn for mere workmen attempting to turn entrepreneur, seeps through his brief account of their tragic failure. "The works passed into other hands," whose or when he does not say. The year in which the remnants of these New England glassworkers lost their financial interest was probably 1826. Thomas Porter, writing in the 1831 edition of Mease's *Picture of Philadelphia,* under the heading *Union Glass Works,* states that the Union Cut and Flint Glass Works was established in 1826 "by a company formed for the purpose." The company was probably that of Charles B. Austin and Company, a firm which met with considerable success under the guidance of its founder, Charles Baldrey Austin.

Until recently we have had only a few additional facts regarding the Union Glass Works and Charles B. Austin & Company. Briefly they are: specimens of their cut glass were shown in the exhibitions of the Franklin Institute in 1827 and 1831; various wares were exhibited in 1841 and 1842, in the latter year the colored glass receiving special mention; the company maintained warehouses at 10 Minor Street and 23 Dock Street in Philadelphia; Charles Austin was the agent; and by 1848 the works were operated by the firm of Lancaster & Hartwell. The picture has been filled in a little more by information from Mrs. Campbell and by evidence from directories.

Charles Austin, who was born in England September 9, 1787, was probably connected with the glass industry and was one of the many skilled artisans who escaped the hard times resulting from the Napoleonic wars by coming to the United States. He and his family sailed November 2, 1818, and landed in New York City, January 13, 1819. Since a Charles Austin was listed as a glasscutter at 7 Park in the New York City directories from 1821 through 1824,

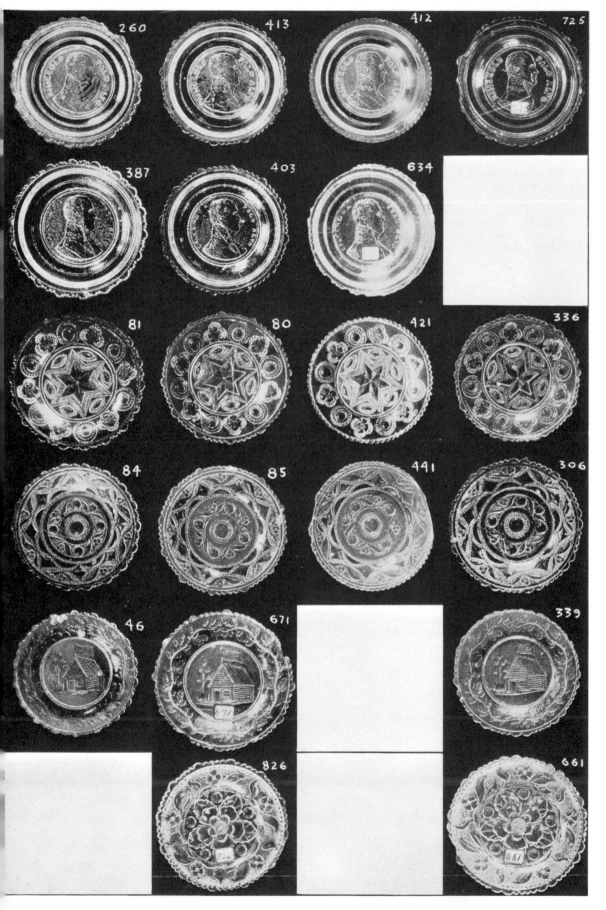

Fig. 2 — Cup Plates of the Late Period *(c.1835-1846)*. Attributed to the Philadelphia area. Numbers 81, 80, 826, 421, 336, and 661 occur in dirty apple-green as well as in clear glass. It seems likely that a Ringgold or log cabin in green may turn up. *Cup plate numbers used in text and illustrations are those of Marble's check list.*

and no other glasscutting firm is listed at that address, it is likely that he established his own shop there.

Just when he left for Philadelphia or who was associated with him in forming Charles B. Austin & Company we do not know. But by 1837 William Bennett and John Capewell, family connections and both capable glass men, were associated with the works. When Austin died in October 1840, William Bennett assumed management of the works. That within a short time the affairs of the company became involved is indicated by a lawsuit of "Ann Austin Administratrix of Charles B. Austin deceased Vs. William Bennett, Maria Capewell Bennett, Joseph Capewell, and Sarah Synar." In 1844 the firm was dissolved and it would seem that the works were idle until 1847. In October of that year the Union Glass Works exhibited at the Franklin Institute. Hartwell & Lancaster, who are listed in 1848 as the proprietors, probably took over in 1847.

In the meantime John Capewell, possibly during the period of the lawsuit, left the works and in 1842 with his brother James established the Excelsior Glass Works across the river at Kaighn's Point, South Camden, New Jersey. Here they made a high grade of glassware, specializing in cut and engraved. Undoubtedly they did pressing too. It is possible that the Capewells may have taken with them some of the molds from the Union Glass Works, including the surface dies for cup plates. These they might have used in conjunction with new design dies which they would have had made for the Ringgolds and perhaps also for the late conventionals of the 81-80 series. Thus there would be a continuity from the Union Glass Works, and the theory of origin for the entire series in the Philadelphia area would still hold.

Even if the Union Glass Works did not make the Ringgolds and the late conventionals, we still feel that they produced the earlier cup plates in the group, for the company was in operation during the period of early pressed and lacy glass manufacture. By 1826, the year the works began to prosper, at least two firms, the Bakewells of Pittsburgh and the New England Glass Company of Cambridge, Massachusetts, had been experimenting in the new art of mechanical pressing and had obtained patents in 1825 and 1826. In the following year the Jersey Glass Company secured a patent on an advanced method. Since this new money- and labor-saving method of production was adopted by virtually all manufacturers of tableware in the country it would be almost a miracle if the Union Glass Company failed to follow suit. In fact, it is not at all unlikely that the John McGann of Kensington who in November 1830 took out a patent on a pressing process far more complicated and advanced than any other on record at the time was associated with the company. (The only other glass factory in Kensington at that time of which we have record was the Philadelphia and Kensington Glass Works of Doctor Dyott, in 1833 christened the Dyottville Factory, which was a bottle and vial factory and did not make tableware until the 1840's when it changed ownership.) Moreover, the very intricacy of the McGann patent indicates that simpler pressing had been previously practiced at Kensington.

We have belabored the idea of the relative earliness of pressing at the Union Glass Works because we are convinced that many less subtle patterns preceded even the comparatively early 826-661 group. If this be true then there should be in existence cup plates which are peculiar to the Philadelphia area and of a cruder, hence earlier, type than those shown in Figure 2. Such plates, to fit ideally into our theory, should show characteristics in design and technique exclusive to the region, although traces of New England practice might be expected since it is likely that pressed ware of the New England Glass Company and the Boston and Sandwich Glass Company was popular in Philadelphia before the Union Glass Company began pressing. In the cup plates of Figure 3 these conditions are nicely realized.

We believe the plates in this group antedate 1830, excepting possibly 76 which is very Victorian in design. At first glance one might be tempted to assign 785 to the New England district. The large scallops of its rim are traditionally associated with New England and even, perhaps erroneously, with the New England Glass Company, as is also the sheaf-of-wheat pattern of its shoulder. A basket of flowers appears on the earliest salts of New England origin as well as on lacy salts and the so-called Providence sugar bowl. These New England manifestations of the motif are not, however, nearly so well conceived or modeled as that in 785. To the best of our knowledge but two examples of 785 are known to collectors and both of these turned up in the Philadelphia area.

Again in 462 (*Fig. 3*) we find the large New England scallop and the sheaf of wheat, both by the way indicative of early manufacture, but combined with a center pattern that from the New England point of view is unorthodox. Note the six-pointed star that reappears in the much later 81-80 series, and especially the acorn which gradually became one of the outstanding motifs of the

Philadelphia district. Although we know of three specimens of 462, we have been able to trace but two of them and these came from dealers in eastern Pennsylvania.

Still with the big New England scallops but lacking any other recognizable Massachusetts characteristic, we find 76 (*Fig. 3*), whose incidence in the Philadelphia region is truly remarkable. Although it is a very rare plate, we have owned fully a dozen examples that have been traced to eastern Pennsylvania. Moreover, we have seen a few toddy plates identical in pattern, all found in the area. Finally, 76 has a frosty upper surface like that found on 785 and 462. In fact, the incidence of a frosty or "sick" upper surface in these three plates is extraordinarily high. While we do not consider this conclusive evidence of a common origin it is so unusual to find "sick" cup plates that it is not unimportant.

Another early plate, possibly the earliest of all those we are considering, is 153 (*Fig. 3*). This shows no direct stylistic affiliations with any particular section but does demonstrate the widespread early habit of basing patterns on cut-glass designs. All, or virtually all, the specimens of both this plate and its variant, 759, of which we know have turned up around Philadelphia.

The last of these very early plates is 767 (*Fig. 3*). Besides a typical New England scallop it has the shoulder heart and the heavy stippled band in the center that are ordinarily associated with early Sandwich and New England Glass Company design, but the spacing and its center cross are completely unlike anything encountered from these factories. The distribution of this plate is confusing, to say the least. All the specimens known to us have been found either in western Pennsylvania or Ohio but it differs so radically in design and technique from accepted Midwestern practice that it seems incredible that it was made there. So, *tentatively*, we lean toward a Kensington attribution.

Thus far in this group we have been considering plates that we think antedate 1830. We believe this is unquestionably true in the case of 785 and 153, and probably true in the case of 462 and 767, but 76 is a stumbling block. It has the early type of scallop, it is often rather thick and heavy, and it frequently shows the sickness of 785 and 462; but the design shows a Victorian fussiness. It may or may not have been made before 1830. It should be noted, however, that the plates in Figure 3 were made without benefit of the cap ring, a gadget that, on the basis of its history in the Patent Office, we believe was in rather common use by that time.

Next in chronological order we come to the plates shown in Figure 4, which we place about 1830. 291 has one New England feature in the concentric bands, including the strawberry diamond, in its center, and perhaps another, much modified, in the alternating simple motifs on its shoulder. This plate and its variant, 816, which are scarce but not rare, are found much more often in eastern Pennsylvania than elsewhere. In the metal (we were about to say in the flesh), 296 seems at first glance to be an earlier plate than 291. It is heavier and cruder but its design is more mature and disciplined. Possibly more conclusive, it was made with a cap ring while 291 was not. The chances are that 296 postdates 1830, but by very little. So far as we know it is seldom found outside the Philadelphia area.

All the plates in Figure 5 we believe were made after 1830. While one of them is an eagle and the others conventional they are related through a running-vine motif which they have in common, an approach to naturalism characteristic of the period. All of these plates but 386 turn up largely if not always in the Philadelphia

FIG. 3 — CUP PLATES OF THE EARLIEST PERIOD *(before 1830)*. Clear glass.

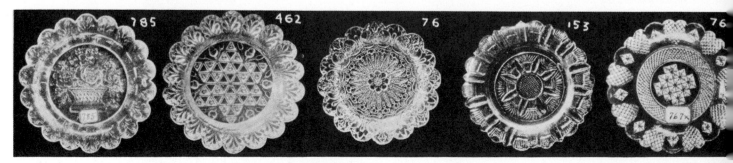

district. The latter is quite common and is often found as far afield as Ohio although even there its highest incidence is along the old National Road (now U. S. Route 40), in the early days the best road from the East. The unusual and artistically absurd practice of having a pattern on the top as well as the bottom of the plate as in 19 and 386 may derive from the very rare eagle of New England provenance, 504. Note the reappearance of the acorn motif in 141, 386, and 552, as well as the vague resemblance to the jewel-like drops of 76 in the beads pendent below the bellflowers of these three plates.

In conclusion we call attention to the astonishingly high incidence of a peculiar green, somewhat like a slightly dirty apple-green, in these plates as noted in the captions. The occurrence of this same color in plates which we have good reason to believe were made at different times would seem to indicate the use of a particular recipe over a long period of time, especially since the shade is a very unattractive one and seldom met with in other areas. Note, too, that 552 has been found in a very beautiful shade of amethyst. 386, 296, and 421 are encountered quite commonly in faint but still definite tints of green and amethyst, as though the melting pot had been used just previously for a mix either of green or amethyst and had not been thoroughly cleaned. While these tints could have been caused by too much or too little black oxide of manganese, we feel they have significance considered with the other evidence. In fact, we feel strongly that our theory as to the origin of all these plates is much enhanced by the evidence of color.

Not wanting to spoil collectors' fun in further speculation on the other possible patterns from the Philadelphia area (and they undoubtedly were many), we will content ourselves with pointing to a certain similarity between 76 and 151-346 and add that the apparent connection is enhanced by the

occasional occurrence of lavender specimens of 151. For the collector of larger pieces of lacy glass who is usually far more firmly wedded to Sandwich attributions, we call attention to Lee's *Sandwich Glass*, Plate 101, lower left, which matches our 153, as well as to the already noted toddy plates matching 76. We have little doubt that many large pieces of hollowware stem from this area, but we leave further speculation to specialists in that field. Further research and comparative study, we feel sure, will vastly increase the meager number of patterns here attributed to the Philadelphia area and probably made at the Union Glass Works.

EDITOR'S NOTE: In the past ANTIQUES has published several articles on the general subject of cup plates. We are listing these below for the benefit of our readers.

Historical Glass Cup Plates, by Alice Van Leer Carrick, February 1922 (pp. 61-66).

Notes on Historical Glass Cup Plates, by Alice Van Leer Carrick and Homer Eaton Keyes, January 1923 (pp. 22-26).

A Check List of Colored Cup Plates, by James H. Rose, August 1933 (pp. 63-64).

Early Glass Pressing at Cambridge and Sandwich, by Lura Woodside Watkins. Part 1, October 1935 (pp. 151-152). Part II, December 1935 (pp. 242-243).

Rims and Reasons, by James H. Rose, August 1936 (pp. 68-69).

Pressed Glass a Debtor to Staffordshire? Editorial Note, August 1937 (p. 78).

Fresh Reflections on American Glass, Editorial Note, February 1938 (pp. 82-83).

Cup-Plate Fragments Excavated at Sandwich, by Lura Woodside Watkins, September 1938 (pp. 132-133).

A Question in Cup Plates, by Mildred K. Pike, January 1939 (pp. 16-18).

The Fort Pitt Glass Works, by John Ramsay, April 1940 (pp. 190-191).

FIG. 4 — CUP PLATES OF THE EARLY-MIDDLE OR TRANSITION PERIOD (c.1830). 291, faint green tint. 296, faint green tint and faint amethyst tint.

FIG. 5 (above, left) — CUP PLATES OF THE MIDDLE PERIOD (c.1830-1835). 19 occurs in green, also in faint green tint and faint amethyst tint. 386, faint green tint and faint amethyst tint. 141, green. 552, green, also amethyst.

FIG. 6 (above, right) — CUP PLATE (c.1835). A plate not discussed in the text since its design shows no stylistic affinities to other plates of the area as they are now known. It is found nowhere, however, but in the Philadelphia region, and the authors are convinced that it was made there.

FIG. 7 (below) — NEW ENGLAND CUP PLATES. Compare with plates here attributed to Philadelphia area. 468 and 180 exemplify the running vine. 176, early New England type of scallop; compare also shoulder heart with 767. 101, scallop and stippled band. 124, big scallop and strawberry diamond; compare with Figures 3 and 5.

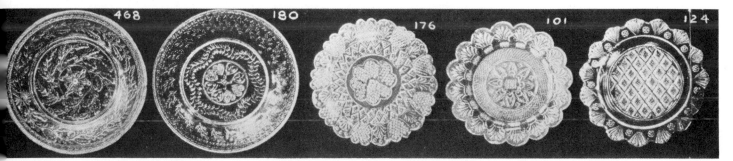

MIDWESTERN CUP-PLATE DESIGNS

By JAMES H. ROSE

FOR NEARLY twenty years the glass specialists and the better informed collectors have quite generally agreed that a not inconsiderable fraction of our collectible early glass had its origin in obscure factories west of the mountains. As they became more familiar with types and techniques they discovered that they could distinguish between examples made on the seaboard and those hailing from the hinterland, and gradually specific characteristics became recognized clues to regional origins.

Thus, in the cup-plate field, there is a tacit and virtually unanimous consent that six peculiarities in design are, beyond any reasonable doubt, indications of midwestern manufacture. If, however, the expert is goaded by the skeptic into extending his critical faculties beyond these too few basic symbols, he inevitably falls back upon the old cliché about "feel." Actually, there is no such thing. "Feel" is only the piling up in the subconscious of many bits of evidence, and it remains intangible, a mysterious sixth sense, only until someone takes the trouble to analyze, arrange, and catalogue these bits of evidence.

So if we can segregate certain hitherto unidentified mannerisms of design that appear very frequently in conjunction with the six universally accepted midwestern motifs, we shall have measurably increased the tangible evidence and, let us hope, limited the use of the vague generalities in which we are now forced to take refuge. Moreover, we shall have substantially bolstered the force of our six axioms.

For the benefit of the beginner as well as for convenience and clarity in our future argument, let us first consider the six fundamental traits of midwestern design. They are, in what would seem to be the probable order of their introduction (numbers given refer to Marble's classification of cup plates):

(A) The use of a large, plain (in the sense of having no stippling or other pattern) type of serration. It should be noted that while these serrations are deeply indented, there is still a considerable margin between the deepest indentation and the beginning of the shoulder pattern. Since plates having this feature are always fairly crude and are rare, they seem to represent very early midwestern practice, at least the earliest we can at the moment rec-

ognize. This serration is shown in plates 658, 456, 451, 351, etc.
(B) The use of a peculiar cloth-like stippling. Here again we seem to be dealing with a very early technique. Note that it appears in the plates mentioned above and also that it seems to have persisted into somewhat later manifestations as, for instance, in 299, 416, and 279.
(C) The use of an exaggeratedly high foot or table-rest — in fact the use of a foot at all — as shown in its extreme form on such plates as 451 (coupled with A type serrations and cloth-like stippling), in 658 and 351 (again with our A and B motifs), in 299 and 416 with B, and so on.
(D) The use of a type of scallop-and-point serration which is related to our A type but which appears to be slightly later in origin and almost certainly was simply a further development, a refinement, of the A type. Here again, it should be noted that it is the relative plainness, not the form, that indicates midwestern manufacture. The scallop and point were used in both east and west, but only in the west do we find this wide gap between the rim of the plate and the beginning of the shoulder pattern. See 429, 503, 410, and especially 713. In this last plate we again encounter our C device, the table-rest.
(E) The use of the bull's-eye and bull's-eye-and-point type of serrations. (It is true that Sandwich, or some eastern factory, used a variation of this but only, so far as I know, on one piece — a large plate; see Lee, *Sandwich Glass*, Plate 122, top. But this in no way resembles the midwestern type of bull's-eye which is best exemplified by 284 and 487.) No eastern cup plate known to us today has anything remotely resembling a bull's-eye border. For typical midwestern uses of these two motifs see 416, 55, 249, 73, and so on; note that many of these show other midwestern characteristics already discussed.
(F) And, finally, the use west of the mountains of a coarser stippling than is generally encountered on eastern plates. Here we are on rather dangerous ground for, while this is the midwestern characteristic most often cited, it is not always true and must be considerably modified lest it become a dangerous tool in the hands of the amateur. Look, for example, at those indubitably eastern

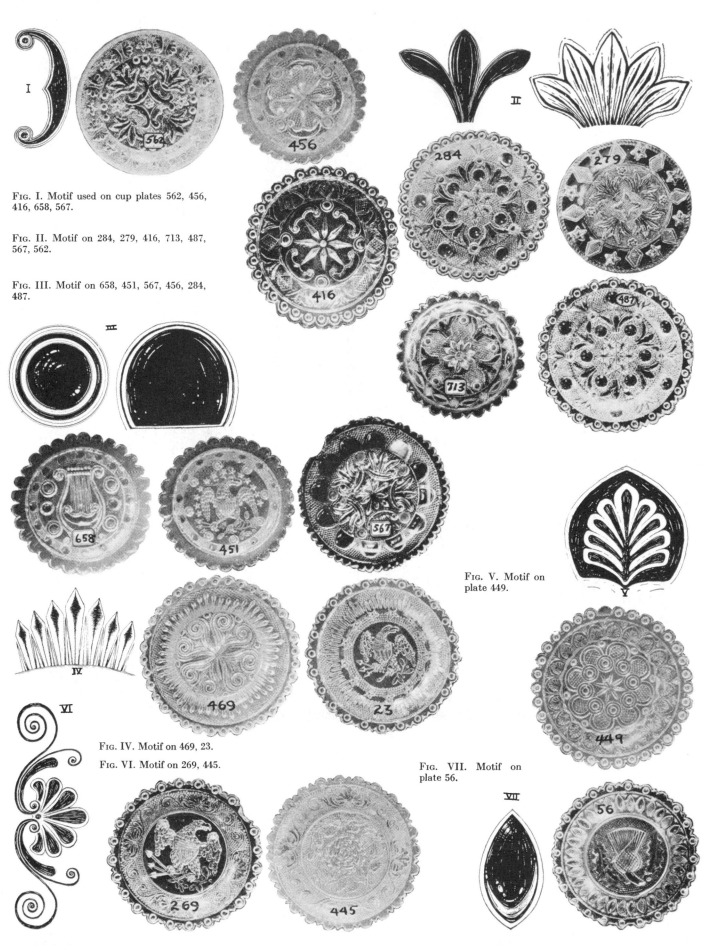

Fig. I. Motif used on cup plates 562, 456, 416, 658, 567.

Fig. II. Motif on 284, 279, 416, 713, 487, 567, 562.

Fig. III. Motif on 658, 451, 567, 456, 284, 487.

Fig. V. Motif on plate 449.

Fig. IV. Motif on 469, 23.

Fig. VI. Motif on 269, 445.

Fig. VII. Motif on plate 56.

plates, 105, 132, 295, etc., where the stippling is even coarser than we commonly find on midwestern plates. Our proposition should be stated conversely, *i.e.*, that no truly fine stippling (as fine, let us say, as that on 1) is found on midwestern plates. Thus, coarse stippling means nothing unless coupled with other known midwestern motifs, but *really fine stippling always indicates eastern origin.*

These six characteristics are quite generally accepted as typically midwestern. We can even go so far as to say that no one of them appears on any known eastern plate. Let us now go still further and see whether we can discover additional motifs occurring commonly in conjunction with these first six and, of course, never appearing on known eastern plates.

(I) The earliest of these new motifs to appear seems to be the peculiar form of lunette or C-scroll found in 658, in combination, with A, B, and C characteristics; in 456 again with A, B, and C; in 416 with B, C, and E; in 575 with C and E; in 567 with C; in 562 where the C-motifs form a four-sided figure; and so on.

(II) Further examination of typical plates shows us a peculiar leaf form that occurs in a truly astonishing number of plates. In cup plates this motif assumes two guises: trefoil as, for example, in 284, and cinquefoil as in 279. Tying it in with our midwestern axiomatic techniques we find it in trefoil form in 284 along with a bull's-eye serration pattern, while in 487 it is coupled with the bull's-eye and point type. Its incidence in that extremely interesting series, 456, 465, 299, 546, and 416, permits us to hazard a guess that, relatively speaking, it is a device that did not come into use in the earliest period. It is missing in 456, where we find the most primitive type of serration in conjunction with very crude cloth-type stippling, and in 465, again with this same stippling. With the further development of this series and the further refinement of its stippling, the trefoil comes into its own. Plate 279, in which the motif assumes its cinquefoil shape, has been authenticated as a Pittsburgh product (see ANTIQUES, August 1937, pp. 90, 92). This leaf form was very popular in the midwest, and we will not belabor the point beyond directing attention to such plates as 562, 73, 673, and 713.

(III) Still further inspection reveals the frequent occurrence of what, for want of a better term, we may call the porthole device. In its most archaic form this is merely a series of plain circular or semicircular reserves in a stippled band on the shoulder of a plate, as in 451, 658, 456. Gradually, it was modified into such forms as we find on 284, 567. Of course, the east as well as the west understood the dramatic value of relatively large plain surfaces framed in stippling, but the practice in the east seems to have been to tie these plain surfaces into the pattern. This was difficult if not impossible on a small surface and the device was used on no eastern cup plate, but is rather commonly encountered there in larger pieces. This, of course, ties in with the rather broad generality that the east was committed to the use of a more delicate scale than the west. Finally, it should be emphasized that our consideration of this particular motif is limited strictly to its appearance on the curve of the shoulder.

(IV) We now come to the widespread use in the midwest of a sort of rayed or sunburst effect on the shoulders of cup plates, as in the eagles, 22 and 23, and the conventionals, 423, 469, 352, etc. It is true that this motif was used at a considerably later date on plates that are very probably of eastern and perhaps Sandwich origin, such as plates 187, 218, 220, etc. So far, however, as its early use is concerned, it was confined to the west. It would be unwise to assume that the east pirated this motif from the west, since it seems more than probable that both sections stole it from the French where it was extremely popular in all branches of design.

(V) Another shoulder pattern frequently used in the west was a leaf form or palmette enclosed in a crude gothic arch. See 449 (note the feet or table-rests in an undeveloped form), 359.

(VI) Another palmette device that appears on midwestern plates is the anthemion with streamers or scrolls, as in the eagle, 269, and in the conventional, 445. This same motif occurs also on larger plates (see Lee, Plates 156, 157).

(VII) Finally, we come to the use of a conventionalized leaf motif, pointed at both ends, as a shoulder decoration. This is another characteristic midwestern device, appearing on such typically western cup plates as 56.

The motifs here enumerated and illustrated are specific and may be readily identified. Thus, by careful examination of a cup plate and analysis of its design, we may go far toward crystallizing the definite components of "feel." We may, too, distinguish readily and accurately between many of the cup plates produced in the east and those of the midwestern glassmaking area.

LACY GLASS WINDOW PANES

Their Use, Process, and Origin

By JAMES H. ROSE

THE LITERATURE ON LACY GLASS WINDOW PANES that I have been able to discover is limited to brief discussions in ANTIQUES for February and December 1938. It may be summarized as follows: A Bakewell, Page and Bakewell advertisement of 1836 mentioning "Pressed panes for steamboats," quoted by Rhea M. Knittle in *Early American Glass* (New York, 1927), was the basis for attribution of the few panes then known to that famous Pittsburgh glassworks. A certain waviness of surface readily observable on the blank sides of these panes led to the theory, first, that they were not pressed in the ordinary fashion but on the contrary were rolled, and, later, that they were simple castings.

When these articles were written, the mechanics of early pressing was imperfectly understood. It was then reported that two patterns of lacy panes had been discovered, though it now appears that the examples found were all of the same pattern. In the intervening eight years at least three new patterns have turned up and a thorough investigation has been made of early pressing techniques so that a reexamination of the pioneer conclusions is advisable. Such an inquiry should cover three specific problems: 1. *Use.* Were these panes in-

tended for use exclusively on steamboats? 2. *Process.* Were they cast, rolled, or pressed in the normal fashion? 3. *Origin.* Who made them?

Use. The pane in Figure 1 came from the door of a corner cupboard found near Lisbon, Ohio. Like all the others it measures, roughly, 5 by 6⅞ inches and is about ¼ inch thick. Since most cupboard doors of the period had much larger panes this is most likely a very rare or perhaps even a unique use. It can even be argued that the cabinetmaker built his cupboard, so to speak, around some available panes. Judged by design this pane was made between 1835 and 1840.

Panes of the pattern shown in Figure 2 are from the sidelights of the doorway of a house built about 1850 in Franklin County, Indiana. Half the panes were clear glass and half were amethyst and these were set alternately. The design here seems to be the earliest of all the four known patterns, dating probably about 1835.

A correction can now be made of the note in ANTIQUES for December 1938 which told of panes from a house built in Oxford, Ohio, in 1851, and described them as of a design "different in detail" from those of the Indiana house recorded in the February 1938 issue. Actually all the panes are of the same pattern and came from the Indiana house. Though the house was not built until about fifteen years after the date ascribed to the panes on the basis of their design, information provided by Mrs. G. V. Chapin of Oxford, Ohio, tends to substantiate this dating. The original owner of the house was Doctor William Ashton, who settled in Franklin County in 1834 and first lived in a loghouse, building his brick house about 1850. According to his grandson, the panes were stored in a box in the original dwelling and later placed around the doorway of the new home.

The panes of the type shown in Figure 3 came from door panels, not sidelights, in the old Schenley residence in Pittsburgh. In feeling their design is very close to that of the Lisbon cupboard pane and this suggests a date of 1835 or 1840. According to data furnished by George Wisecarver and George E. Born, the so-called Schenley mansion was built in two sections. Dates for the first structure are given

FIG. 1 *(above, left)*—LACY GLASS PANE from the door of a corner cupboard found near Lisbon, Ohio. 5 by 6⅞ inches. This pane is unique. *Collection of George C. Cannon.*

FIG. 2 *(above, right)* — LACY GLASS PANE in amethyst from Franklin County, Indiana. 5 by 6⅞ inches. Clear and amethyst examples of the pattern are owned by Doctor Parke G. Smith (see ANTIQUES, February 1938, p. 81). *Collection of Doctor Grace O. Doane.*

FIG. 3 *(right)* — LACY GLASS PANE from the old Schenley mansion, Pittsburgh, Pennsylvania. 5 by 6⅞ inches. *Collection of George E. Born.*

FIG. 4 *(far right)* — LACY GLASS PANE marked with maker's name. 5 by 6⅞ inches. Said to have come from a hall lantern in Wheeling, West Virginia. This pane is unique. *Collection of George C. Cannon.*

variously as 1825 or "the 1830's," while the addition is said to have been built in 1840 or 1845.

The pane in Figure 4 came from southeastern Ohio with a history of having been used in a hall lantern in Wheeling. The design is of extraordinary importance and interest for several reasons. It bears the imprint of Curlings and Robertson, proprietors of the Fort Pitt Glass Works, and is a pirating of the well-known Eastern (Sandwich?) tray. According to the McKearins, Morgan Robertson entered the Curling firm in 1834, but this pane was made much later, probably after 1840. Its stippling is of the irregular variety characteristic of the '40's and '50's.

Thus of the four known patterns of panes not one is directly traceable to steamboat use but this by no means proves the panes were not so used. River boats of so early a date have long since been dismantled and it is improbable, to say the least, that any direct proof of this use of such panes will now be found. Indeed, is any needed? The Bakewell advertisement seems sufficient. The available evidence does prove, however, that cabinetmakers, manufacturers of lighting devices, and especially builders and glaziers found them convenient and used them wherever their size was suitable.

Process. Glass *can* be cast, it is true, but not into intricate or delicate patterns because of its great surface tension. Considerable pressure would be necessary to force it into the tiny depressions constituting the designs found here. Those who wish to explore this casting process further should consult C. J. Phillips' excellent book, *Glass, The Miracle Maker* (New York, 1941, p. 173 ff.).

Theoretically it would have been possible to cut any of these patterns into a metal roller which would then have been rolled across a gather of glass that had been dropped into a dam-type mold, but the difficulties of such a procedure are tremendous. Consider the problem of centering the design on a 5 by 6⅞-inch blank. Made in this fashion easily ninety per cent of the output would have been imperfect.

Both the "cast" and "rolled" theories seem to be based on misconceptions about the causes of the uneven surfaces found on early pressed glass. A gather of glass begins to cool, particularly on its surface, the minute it is removed from the pot. It is carried to the pressing machine and held over the mold while a workman shears off the amount of glass he considers correct to produce the article to be pressed. Now this sheared gather drops into the mold in a shape resembling a tadpole which drops *tail first*, not, as is commonly pictured, head first. This thin string or tail of glass — remember it is preceding the body of the gather into the mold — has cooled to a temperature dangerously near the setting point before it even touches the mold. Perhaps depending upon the steadiness of hand of the workman, such a string normally takes one of two forms in the mold: a "coiled snake" effect that on pressing produces more or less faint circular or spiral waves; or, more rarely, an accordion pattern that shows up after pressing as lateral waves.

At this point it becomes evident that the advocates of the "cast" and "rolled" theories picture these panes as having been made with their plain surfaces up. On the contrary practically all flat pieces were pressed plain side down or, in other words, with their designs on the plunger. This is a dogmatic statement and space does not permit its full discussion but a study of Figures 5 and 6 should convince the skeptical. Figure 5 represents a cross section of one of these panes with dotted lines indicating vestigial fins. Such fins appear where the parts of a mold join and there is no denying their evidence. Figure 6 shows a schematic cross section of a mold made by extending these fins and joining the extensions. The plunger, *P*, comes down, forces the gather of glass out along the base mold, *BM*, to the walls of the cap ring, *CR*, and impresses the design on

FIG. 5 — CROSS SECTION of typical pane with draw angles exaggerated. The dotted lines are extensions of fins or mold marks.

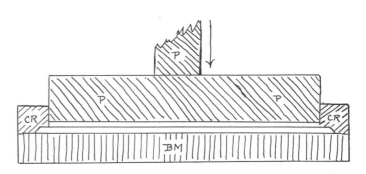

FIG. 6 — SCHEMATIC CROSS SECTION of mold based on the fin locations shown in Figure 5. A gather of glass is dropped into the receptacle formed by the base mold (BM) and cap ring (CR) and the plunger (P) is brought down forcing the glass into the *shape* formed by the base mold and cap ring and into the *pattern* cut on the face of the plunger.

the surface. The glass sets almost at once and the plunger is withdrawn. The cap ring, *CR,* is then lifted (note that its draw-angle must permit this); the mold is inverted and the finished pane falls out and is taken to the annealing furnace.

Origin. All of the known panes are of the same size, 5 by 6⅞ inches, which may indicate that but one base die and one cap ring were used with interchangeable design plungers. The fact that one design die carries the Curlings and Robertson imprint could lead to the conclusion that this firm made all of the four known patterns. There is some supporting evidence for this theory. According to Mr. Born, the Schenley residence was built by James O'Hara for his daughter, Mary, who married William Croghan. Mary Croghan, their daughter, married Major Schenley. Now James O'Hara with his partner, Isaac Craig, started the Pittsburgh Glass Works in 1797. In 1800 the superintendent of this glass works was William Price, the same Price who in 1827 with Robert Curling started the Fort Pitt Glass Works, predecessor of Curlings and Robertson. It is possible that O'Hara kept in touch with his former workman and, needing panes for the new house, secured them from this firm.

This hypothesis, however, seems too flimsy to warrant so positive an attribution. Probably 5 by 6⅞ was a standard structural size of the period and so Bakewell as well as the Fort Pitt Works would have pressed the same size. Both firms advertised such panes; both firms must have made them. It is also not unlikely that similar panes were pressed by other factories in the Pittsburgh-Wheeling glassfield but, since there is no recorded instance of lacy panes turning up east of the mountains, they are probably a purely Midwestern product.

So far, with but four finds, such panes may be classed among the great rarities in early pressed glass. The chances are that part of this seeming rarity is due to pickers' not understanding their importance if, indeed, they recognize them at all. As more people become familiar with them it can be safely predicted that additional patterns will be found.

Wheeling lacy glass

BY JAMES H. ROSE

STEAMBOAT PANE; 5-1/6 inches by 7. This is the first marked piece of Wheeling lacy glass to be recorded. A similar pane in the Grossman collection measures 5 by 7. It may, or may not, be significant that both panes are one-eighth inch longer than any of the other known (i.e., Pittsburgh) lacy panes. Each element in its design should be compared with analogous motifs in the other illustrations. *The Corning Museum of Glass.*

WE HAVE KNOWN FOR YEARS that glass was pressed in Wheeling as early as 1829, but although pressed glass of that period had to be lacy and good lacy at that, the few pieces we have attributed to Wheeling have been relatively coarse and comparatively late. All attractive mid-western lacy has been called "Pittsburgh"—too hastily, it turns out, if the lacy pane shown here is a fair example of Wheeling work. Without its inscription it would be assigned with no hesitation to Pittsburgh. It has everything—the shell, the rose, the sidewheel river boat—formerly considered evidence of Pittsburgh origin.

But J. & C. Ritchie (I follow here the account given by Josephine Jefferson in *Wheeling Glass*) were Wheeling glassmakers. The factory was founded in 1829 by John Ritchie and Jesse Wheat and did business under the name of Ritchie & Wheat until 1831, when Wheat left to start Wheat, Price & Company. John Ritchie tried it alone for a while and then, in 1833, sold a half-interest to his brother, Craig Ritchie, and the firm's name became J. & C. Ritchie. It was in this year that they made the lacy pane, as George Wilson bought into the company in 1834 and its name then became Ritchie & Wilson.

The pane's discovery calls for a re-examination of the two plates related to it stylistically, the rose and the steamboat shown here, and also of a larger group of plates allied to these two by cap-ring analogy that includes the *Constitution,* the eagle, the basket of flowers, a unique strawberry diamond, a late sunburst and, most important, the acorn, illustrated here in compote form.

These acorn compotes were purchased by Mrs. John J. Grossman many years ago in a Pittsburgh second-hand store. With them came a history that they were the first pieces pressed in a glass factory that had just moved to Pittsburgh's South Side and that, no doubt because of the coincidence, they had been presented to a Rev. H. Reck who had just started a new church, also on the South Side. Through a nice piece of research John Grossman has established the date of Bakewell's move to the South Side as 1853; he has also discovered that the Rev. H. Reck founded the Grace English Evangelical Church on the South Side in 1852, and that the "present" (as of 1889) church was built in 1853. Since the dates of the founding of both church and glasshouse are the same, the Bakewell origin of the compotes is confirmed—and so too, by extension, is that of the whole series of related plates.

But how are we to explain the resemblance of a Wheeling pane to a group of Pittsburgh plates? The range of possibilities is large but four solutions seem more plausi-

ROSE PLATE; about 6½ niches in diameter. This rose design occurs in circular as well as octagonal form and in several sizes, including cup plates. Its shoulder shells, or anthemia, have streamers but are otherwise remarkably like that on the pane. Its rose is not as well modeled.

Collection of Mrs. John J. Grossman.

STEAMBOAT PLATE; about 6½ inches in diameter. Recorded only in octagonal form and in this size. Again the shoulder anthemia resemble the shell on the pane as does, superficially, the sidewheel river boat. Cup plates with similar steamboats but with a varying shoulder pattern exist.

Collection of Mrs. Grossman.

ble than the others. First, there is the possibility that all these dies are the work of one free-lance moldmaker. Inasmuch as Pittsburgh was the larger town and probably had more artisans, this talented man's habitat is more likely to have been there than in Wheeling. On the other hand, he could have started in Wheeling and been lured away by the fleshpots of Pittsburgh. Either way, he did better work for Ritchie than he did for Bakewell; but this might be explained by the Ritchies' telling him to spare no efforts on their advertising pane while Bakewell's instructions to him were to keep costs down.

Or the problem may be one of simple piracy, the deliberate copying of one factory's wares by another. If such was the case, there is no clue as to which of our glassmakers was the pirate.

Third, it is not impossible that Bakewell bought Ritchie's molds when the latter failed about 1840. If the date of that failure had coincided with the Pittsburgh fire of 1845, in which it seems likely that Bakewell's molds suffered some damage, this would be an attractive theory. The five-year gap in dates is not fatal, however, since Bakewell could have bought the molds on the earlier date. In that case, both factories made these plates, Ritchie before Bakewell.

Finally, the resemblance of pane to plates may be pure coincidence, no more than might be expected from two moldmakers working in the idiom of their region and their period.

In spite of the fact that the pane's discovery has not so far led to the recognition of other pieces of Wheeling lacy, we may be sure that no small amount of it was made there and that, in all probability, it looks much like that which was made contemporaneously in Pittsburgh. Until we have further evidence, it is safer to call unmarked pieces from the area "Midwestern" than to label them "Pittsburgh."

ACORN COMPOTE; 7¼ inches by 4. This compote, one of a pair, has a history of having been pressed at Bakewell's South Side factory in Pittsburgh in either 1852 or 1853, an astonishingly late use of an earlier mold. Found more commonly in plate form, it is related by base mold (cap-ring and surface die) analogy to a long series of Midwestern plates, including the rose and steamboat plates shown here.

Collection of Mrs. Grossman.

Mr. Rose, a frequent contributor to ANTIQUES, is an authority on American glass. He organized the Corning Museum's 1954 exhibition *American Pressed Glass of the Lacy Period* and wrote its catalogue; and he is co-author, with Ruth Webb Lee, of *American Glass Cup Plates.*

Unrecorded rarities in lacy glass

BY JAMES H. ROSE

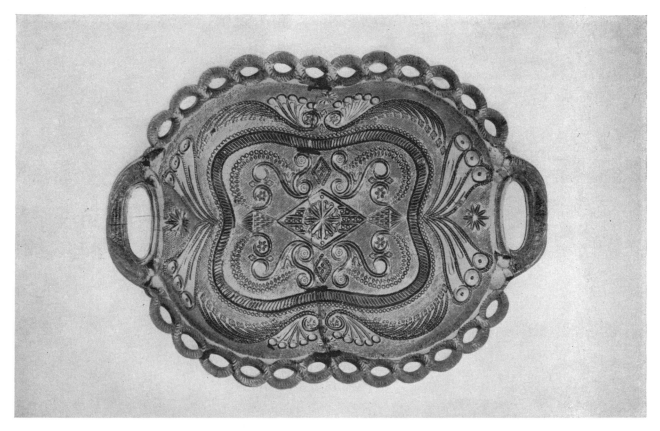

Variant chain-border tray. 11 9/16 x 8⅛ x 1¾. *Collection of William J. Elsholz.* The tray shown here has a star at each side between the chain border and the leaf scrolls. These stars are lacking on the recorded variety which, however, shows a curious and perhaps significant change in stippling at this spot as if something (the stars?) had been erased and the background restippled. More important, on this unlisted tray the border links are stippled on both top and bottom, while the standard type has stippling on the backs of the links only. Even in the known type a few examples have turned up with incompletely filled links or handles due to failure of the glass to flow. The roughness of stippled surfaces would obviously impede easy flow and, since fins show that these trays were pressed upside down, the obvious correction would be to buff the stippling off the tops of the links (the bottom in pressing) to facilitate flow. This would seem to indicate that the variant tray shown is the earlier, experimental version. On the other hand there

seems to be some evidence that in these chain-border trays we are dealing with the output of more than just two molds. The garden variety of tray in Mr. Elsholz's collection measures 11¾ x 8¾ x 1½. The McKearins in *American Glass* give the size as 11¾ x 8½, while Mrs. Lee in *Sandwich Glass* records 11½ x 8. While in pieces as large as these we can expect some diversity of size due to warping, annealing sag, or some similar factor, the disparity recorded seems excessive. Jarves mentions brass as well as iron molds, but a brass mold with its melting point lower than the working temperature of glass would have had a very short life. The assumption has been that it was used only for special-order work or for a very elaborate or intricate mold where the relative softness and workability of brass would ease the moldmaker's labors and reduce costs. Since no mold was more difficult to cut than that of the chain-border tray, it is not impossible that the diversity of size noted above is due to the use of several short-lived brass molds.

Tray. 7 13/16 x 5⅝. *Collection of George C. Cannon.* This is a midwestern pressing related through the lancet leaves of its cavetto to the well-known series of round and octagonal "acorn" plates. Oddly enough, the familiar Sandwich casket exactly fits this piece, suggesting that some similar piece of hollow ware may have originally accompanied this tray. Only two of these trays are known, the other in the collection of Mrs. John J. Grossman. This great rarity may be due to the irregularity of outline. A mold of such shape would be particularly liable to damage, as would be the trays made from it.

In recent years the intense interest in lacy glass has brought out of hiding many hitherto unknown pieces, many more than can be shown here. Since selection from among these riches has been arbitrary some account of the process seems necessary.

Cup plates and salts were never considered. Each is a highly specialized field with a literature and a reporting system of its own. Toddy plates and sauce dishes were also disregarded but for opposite reasons. Practically nothing is known of the range of pattern in either field so that almost any toddy or sauce is likely to be unpublished, although it by no means follows that it is rare.

This left some forty pieces for consideration. Of these a remarkable sugar bowl was excluded because neither of the two known examples has a cover. It seemed best to defer publication until a complete specimen is found. Six superb compotes were eliminated since the patterns of all their bowls are on record in either plate or dish form. Several lamps and a candlestick were discarded on similar grounds; they were unrecorded combinations of recorded parts.

The remainder was judged on the basis of earliness, design, and size. No one of these factors predominated. If an eight-inch dish had a pattern less interesting than a seven- or even a six-inch one, it was cast aside albeit with reluctance. Conversely, if two pieces had equally interesting designs, the larger was chosen. This boils down to what is called "importance." But this term is not an absolute, and in the many borderline cases other judges might have made different decisions.

Some attempt has been made in the following notes to suggest reasons for the great rarity. This is pure speculation and should be so regarded. It is arguable that rarity is due to a lack of commercial appeal so that few examples of a specific item got into circulation, or that such pieces as were sold were broken due to large size or awkward shape, or that a mold was technically unsatisfactory and was soon discarded, or—and this last is probably the most likely—that a mold cracked or was otherwise damaged before many pieces were made in it. But to assign any one of these in a specific case is very risky indeed.

Finally I must disclaim any omniscience. Beyond doubt other equally large, attractive, and early pieces exist unknown to me. I will be grateful if collectors and dealers will call them to my attention.

Oval dish. 8¼ x 5½ x 1¾. *Elsholz collection.* The strawberry diamonds in the triangles at sides and ends are generally considered proof of early work. The radial lines just inside the serrations are seldom seen but occur again in the deep bowl from the Innes collection shown on the following page and, since that bowl is unquestionably eastern and probably Sandwich, this dish is probably from the same source. The most striking feature of the design is the use of the curious and, I think, unique diagonal checkered bands. Mr. Elsholz's dish is the only known specimen and its rarity may perhaps be accounted for by the difficulty of getting glass to flow over the extraordinarily rough surface.

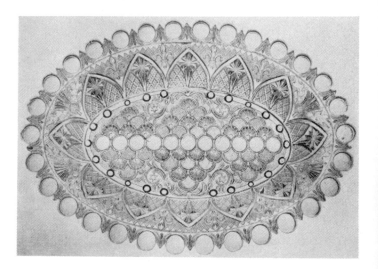

Oval vegetable dish. 9⅞ x 6 15/16 x 1⅜. *Collection of Lowell Innes.* A midwestern piece with regionally characteristic big bull's-eye and point serrations. But two of these magnificent dishes are known. The other is the property of the Historical Society of Western Pennsylvania. Unless it lies in the vulnerability of the serrations, no reason for this great scarcity is apparent.

Large, shallow bowl. 12 x 1¾. *Collection of Mrs. Paul Esterly.* The cross pattern is a well-known eastern device in the early days of pressing and points to an origin in that area, probably at Sandwich or the New England Glass Works. The most astonishing thing about this piece is that while Mrs. Esterly's is the only one known in this tremendous size, two others slightly smaller (11 inches) exist. One is in the Elsholz collection, the other in the collection of Mrs. Oscar R. Haase. The large size, hard to make and easy to break, may account for the rarity.

Deep bowl. 9 3/16 x 3¾. *Innes collection.* The wide band in plaid pattern and the treatment of the trefoil tulips point to an eastern and probably Sandwich origin. The radial flutes near the rim resemble those of the oval dish from the Elsholz collection illustrated on the previous page. This bowl is unique in form as well as pattern. In fact, it is not unlikely that its rarity is due to its shape, which tended to sag if taken from the mold a second too soon or if exposed to a bit too much heat during annealing. Most deep pieces from the early period, where thick, heavy metal was the rule, are straight-sided to avoid such buckling.

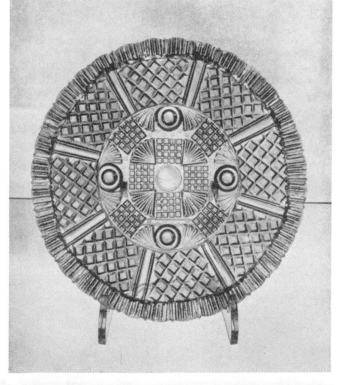

Large bowl. 9⅛ x 2⅜. *Elsholz collection.* This, the only known specimen, shows some stylistic affinity (the cross pattern) to Mrs. Esterly's large bowl, and to the Elsholz oval dish in its extreme use of the strawberry diamond. It seems certainly to be very early and of eastern manufacture. It has still another claim to distinction in four small ball feet, which are unique.

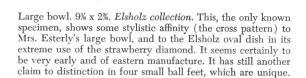

Covered sweetmeat. 7¼ to top of finial, 6½ across. *Elsholz collection.* The typical midwestern hairpin foot shows the origin beyond doubt. Only one other example is on record, in the Cannon collection. The mold with its turned-over rim and the die for the terraced cover (the standard was pressed separately and attached by a wafer) was a complicated one and must have been quite expensive. But this cannot account for the extreme rarity, which must be due to breakage of the finished product or, more likely, to damage to the mold before many of these pieces were made.

Covered butter dish. 4⅝ to top of finial, 4⅞ across. *Elsholz collection.* While several of these little dishes are known lidless, this seems to be the only complete one on record. The plain finial is unusual but is very like one on a sugar bowl that is generally credited to Sandwich and may be a clue to origin. There is no apparent reason for its scarcity.

Large plate. 9⅜. *Collection of Dr. Grace O. Doane.* The bull's-eye rim stamps this unique piece midwestern. The flat shoulder and the stylized shells are, in cup plates, considered to be marks of Curling's practices at his Ft. Pitt Glass Works. The rarity is probably due to the large size.

Small octagonal plate. 5⅛ side to side, 5⅝ point to point. *Esterly collection.* An unrecorded, possibly the earliest, member of the midwestern plate series which includes the *Constitution-Union,* the steamboat, the basket of flowers, the rose or chrysanthemum, and the acorn. No other example known.

A lacy glass rarity

Illustrated in James H. Rose's article, *Unrecorded rarities in lacy glass* (ANTIQUES for March 1954), was a lacy glass tray, measuring seven and thirteen-sixteenths by five and three-eighths inches, of which only two examples were then known. (Another has since been reported.) "A midwestern pressing," as Mr. Rose described it, the tray is "related through the lancet leaves of its cavetto to the well-known series of round and octagonal 'acorn' plates." He went on to point out that the tray exactly fits one of the known Sandwich caskets and suggested that "some similar piece of hollow ware" originally accompanied it.

His surmise was confirmed when the glass casket illustrated here came to light. Now part of the collection of George S. McKearin, Hoosick Falls, New York, this apparently unique specimen was on view with the matching tray described above in the recent exhibition *Pressed Glass of the Lacy Period* at the Corning Museum of Glass, Corning, New York. A midwestern product of the early period, c. 1830-1835, it is noteworthy for its elaborate design—which, as Mr. Rose suggests, may be one reason this and certain other rarities in pressed glass either were not made in quantity or have survived in few examples.

Enormous bowl: 14 by 3 inches. The design is familiar to all collectors and, in its smaller manifestations, is one of the most frequently seen of all lacy patterns; in this tremendous size, however, it is unique. Furthermore, it is the largest known piece of lacy glass. Its origin is probably New England in the 1840's. *Henry Francis du Pont Winterthur Museum.*

Unrecorded rarities

in American glass

35TH
ANNIVERSARY
ARTICLE

Lamp: 12 inches high, its base 4¼ inches in diameter. While this imposing lamp has ringed knopping that resembles New England practice it rests on a Western toddy-plate base (an unrecorded, plain-rim version of No. 800-A in Lee and Rose, *American Glass Cup Plates*) and so unquestionably was made west of the mountains about 1835 or 1840. The wonder is that it has lasted as long as it has with so unstable a form. It is the only Western lamp recorded on a toddy-plate base. *Duckworth collection; photograph by Ben Lawrence.*

More lacy items

THE PIECES OF LACY GLASS pictured here have been chosen as worthy additions to the group shown in ANTIQUES for March 1954 (pages 224-227). None has been published; none was chosen on the basis of color; only the Winterthur bowl, the largest known piece of lacy, was selected because of size; yet each is in its own way truly exceptional. —JAMES H. ROSE

Lacy candlestick: 5¼ inches high, its base 3¾ inches square. Only one other piece, a lamp with its font in the blown-three-mold Horn of Plenty pattern, is known with this handled, lacy base. This rarity is probably due to the difficulty of getting glass worked at the low temperature characteristic of the period to flow through the handle mold: as the illustration shows, the glass forming the handle congealed before its two sections met. *Collection of Harold G. Duckworth; Lawrence photograph.*

Opaque white lamp: 6¾ inches high, base 3½ inches in diameter. The base is pressed in a small waffle pattern and at first glance seems to be an unrecorded cup plate—but is not, since it has a domed center. As this lamp, one of a pair, appears to be the only known example of the use of this foot, it is likely that something happened to the mold before many were made. The origin is New England, probably before the year 1830. Right, lamp with lacy foot: 10½ inches high, its base 4½ inches in diameter. The lacy foot is one that is seen fairly frequently. The lamp owes its distinction to the skill of the blower. *Both lamps in the collection of William J. Elsholz; photograph by Leo Knight.*

Shallow bowl: 8¼ inches in diameter and 1¾ inches deep. Smaller pieces, mostly plates, are known with vaguely similar centers and shoulder patterns but this, in addition to being the largest of these related pieces on record, has an elaborate rose-and-thistle motif on its inner shoulder. Though the origin is unquestionably the eastern United States, it is not necessarily New England; there is some evidence, by no means conclusive, pointing to a source in the Philadelphia area. The period is apparently c. 1835 to 1840. *Duckworth collection; Lawrence photograph.*

Compote: 11 inches in diameter and 5⅝ inches high. While it is a truism that a stem and foot may be added to any bowl, such occurrences are, to say the least, infrequent. This particular bowl has not so far been published in compote form and is thus a find of major importance. The origin is New England about 1835. *Elsholz collection; Knight photograph.*

Large compote: 10½ inches in diameter, 6¼ inches high. Several bowls are known in this pattern, but the present specimen is the only one recorded in compote form. Its majestic size is not apparent in the illustration. Although its origin is almost certainly New England, c. 1835, it was found about thirty miles north of Pittsburgh—demonstrating the unreliability of attributions based on where a piece was found. *Elsholz collection; Knight photograph.*

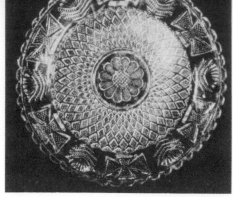

Plate: 7⁵⁄₁₆ inches in diameter. The strawberry diamonds of its cavetto are a well-known indication of early work. The curious shoulder pattern of alternating Maltese crosses and chevrons is, however, a new element in pre-lacy design, and the plate appears to be unique as of this writing. Presumably New England, early cap-ring period, c. 1830. *Collection of Preston R. Bassett.*

Shallow bowl: 6⅜ inches in diameter and 1¼ inches deep. The tulip pattern of the cavetto is, except for its eight-pointed-star center, well known to all collectors, but the continuous grapevine shoulder design is an unrecorded motif in such association. The origin is not certain but is perhaps New England somewhere close to 1840. *Elsholz collection.*

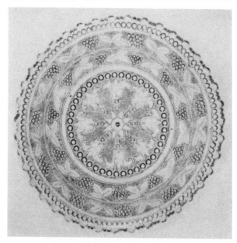

Rectangular dish: 6¾ inches long by 5¼ inches wide. This little dish with its geometric design may be unique. It was made somewhere in the Midwest, probably between 1835 and 1840. The tumbler with its Gothic arches is 2½ inches high and is an extremely rare survival, perhaps even unique. Pressed drinking glasses from the lacy period are virtually unknown. The best guess is that it was made in New England about 1830. The small handled mug is 2 inches high and seems to be the only other drinking glass on record from the lacy period. Unless Deming Jarves, who owned the patent on pressing handles in this fashion, leased his process to other factories, the mug is Sandwich, about 1835. One other heart mug is known, in the Ewing collection. *All three pieces in the collection of Louise S. Esterly; photograph by Patric P. Jacovidis.*

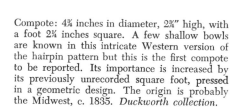

Compote: 4¾ inches in diameter, 2¾" high, with a foot 2¼ inches square. A few shallow bowls are known in this intricate Western version of the hairpin pattern but this is the first compote to be reported. Its importance is increased by its previously unrecorded square foot, pressed in a geometric design. The origin is probably the Midwest, c. 1835. *Duckworth collection.*

Candlestick: 14⅜ inches high, its base 4 inches square. As in the case of Mr. Duckworth's tall lamp, the puzzling feature here is the maker's foolhardy disregard of stability, a factor of major importance in a lighting device where overturn could have meant disaster. The pressed base occurs in at least three slightly varying forms, two of which are Eastern and one probably Western. This prohibits any dogmatic statements concerning origin, although the annulated knopping does suggest New England chair work. *Duckworth collection; Lawrence photograph.*

American lacy and pressed glass in the Toledo Museum of Art

BY JOHN W. KEEFE, *Assistant curator for European decorative arts, Art Institute of Chicago (formerly with the Toledo Museum of Art)*

Fig. 1. Most of these early examples indicate the dependence of the American designer upon the Anglo-Irish tradition of cut glass, as witnessed by the frequent use of strawberry-diamond and fan motifs. Exceptions which mark the beginning of purely American designs and motifs are the Industry bowl in the center here, the opalescent plate (above, right), and the elaborately patterned plate below that. *Clockwise, starting at top:* Clear lead-glass bowl, c. 1825-1835; New England area, perhaps New England Glass Company; diameter 6 inches. Greenish-opalescent lead-glass plate, c. 1825-1830; probably Boston & Sandwich Glass Company; diameter 5⅞ inches. Pale-green lead-glass plate, c. 1825-1835; probably New England Glass Company, perhaps Sandwich; diameter 5⅞ inches. Clear lead-glass plate, c. 1825-1835; probably New England Glass, perhaps Sandwich; diameter 5¾ inches. Clear lead-glass plate, c. 1825-1835; New England Glass; diameter 5⅞ inches. Light-green lead-glass plate with light red streaks, c. 1825-1835; probably New England Glass, perhaps Sandwich; diameter 5⅞ inches. *Center:* So-called Industry bowl, c. 1840; perhaps Sandwich, or New England Glass Company; diameter 6¼ inches. The log cabin and barrel were Whig symbols of the 1840 Presidential campaign, and the plowman represented Harrison, "the Cincinnatus of the West." Four variants of this bowl are recorded. *Except as noted, all of the objects illustrated are the gift of Mrs. Harold G. Duckworth to the Toledo Museum of Art.*

THE RICHNESS OF the American lacy and pressed glass collection at the Toledo Museum of Art is largely due to the generosity of a private collector, Mrs. Harold G. Duckworth. She and her husband began collecting early pressed glass in the mid-1920's and the result of their collecting acuity, presented to the museum after his death in a series of gifts beginning in 1964, is one of the most representative groups of these wares ever assembled. Inevitably, in telling of a collection of this size its actual scope will be somewhat distorted, for only the rarest objects or the rarest color variants have been chosen and certain forms such as cup plates and salts have been left out simply because they form specialized collections.

Pressing of glass had been employed as early as the

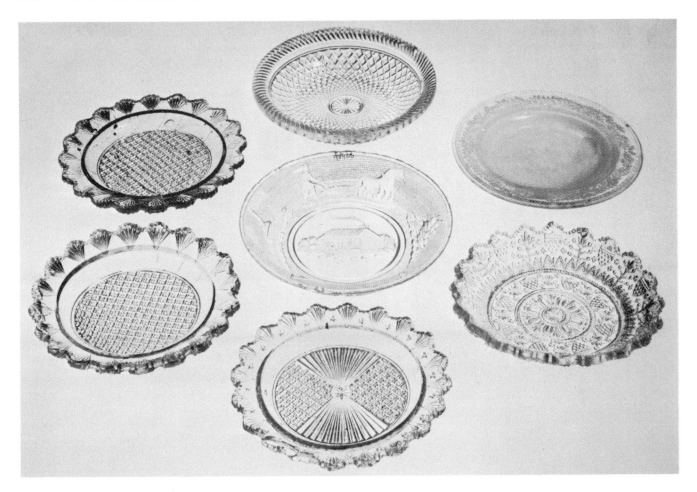

Fig. 2. Extremely rare bowl in Princess Feather medallion pattern alternating with Cross in Diamond, c. 1830; attributed to Sandwich; diameter 10 inches.

Fig. 3. All the glass objects here are attributed to Sandwich, and except as noted, all are in the Scrolled Peacock Eye pattern. Given the tendency to pirating among all designers of the period, there may be some question as to whether Sandwich or Meissen originated the popular Peacock Eye pattern; the variant plate at the right, however, shows how quickly designs were modified. *Left to right:* Plate, c. 1830-1835; diameter 6⅛ inches. Dish in unusual light blue, c. 1830-1850; diameter 4¼ inches. Rare covered mustard cup, c. 1835; height 3¼ inches (this has a matching plate 4⅜ inches in diameter). Meissen porcelain plate, Germany, c. 1830; pink cavetto with gold border; diameter 7⅞ inches. Plate with variant Star Medallion cavetto, c. 1835-1845; diameter 5¼ inches.

closing years of the eighteenth century in England and Holland for the feet of candlesticks, bowls, and glasses, and the technique was also used to shape mushroom and rayed stoppers for decanters; but until the 1820's it was not sufficiently mechanized to be commercially feasible for the production of larger objects.

Although Americans did not originate pressing, it is certain that its perfecting was largely the result of work by American inventors. The best known of these was Deming Jarves, a founder of both the New England and the Boston and Sandwich glass companies; Jarves held a number of important pressing patents and was extremely influential in promoting pressed-glass manufacture. Perhaps it was the connection of Jarves with the Boston and Sandwich Glass Company which led to the widely held belief that all lacy glass was produced at Sandwich. This is known today to be untrue, for the technique was not limited to any single manufacturer or region, and patents, recipes, and designs were consistently pirated. That both lacy and conventionally pressed (non-lacy) glass were produced in every major glassmaking area is attested by the regional variations which appear. In lacy glass, pieces made in the Midwest tend to exhibit relatively coarse stippling, and certain Midwestern plates and dishes stand

Fig. 4. *Left to right:* Shell and Leaf pattern plate with unique center treatment, c. 1825-1850; probably Sandwich; diameter 6⅛ inches. Extremely rare window pane, c. 1835-1840; probably Midwestern; height 6¹⁵⁄₁₆ inches. Extremely rare candlestick with ribbed and beaded socket and lacy base, c. 1840; probably Sandwich; height 5½ inches. Extremely rare dish in Pipes of Pan, or Devil, pattern, c. 1835-1845; New England area; length 8⅛ inches. Amethyst compote in Princess Feather medallion pattern, c. 1835-1840; probably Sandwich; height 6⅛ inches; rare form and color. Rare creamer in Gothic Arch and Sheaves (Palm) pattern below with Peacock Eye and Chain above, c. 1830-1835; perhaps Sandwich; height 4⅛ inches.

Fig. 5. Cake tray, c. 1835; attributed to Sandwich; length 11¾ inches. Pieces like this tray —an extremely rare form—were very difficult to press evenly, which frequently caused incomplete filling of the scalloped border and the handles. This is an exceptionally fine specimen.

on small round feet which appear in the pattern as a bead motif, while Eastern examples usually rest on a flat base or a rope ring.

The method for both lacy and conventionally pressed glass consisted of cutting a gather of molten glass from the pontil rod and dropping it into a mold. A shaped plunger was then brought down into the mold, forcing the molten glass into all its indentations and impressing the design into the glass. The technique produced a more distinct pattern than the soft contours of mold-blown glass and was therefore ideally suited to imitation of cut wares.

In spite of this relatively simple means of embellishment, the problems encountered by the early makers were considerable. Prior to the invention of the cap ring (some time before 1830), pieces tended to be of uneven thick-

ness; similarly, underfilling caused handles and borders to be left incomplete (see Fig. 5). More serious was the dull, cloudy effect caused by contact of the heated metal plunger with the molten glass, which could only be corrected by reheating. Obviously, this reheating would result in a loss of sharpness in both shape and pattern. The glassmakers' solution to this was to create over-all patterns which successfully masked the clouded quality of the glass. By using the stippling characteristic of lacy glass, the designer increased the refractive qualities of the material, imparting a silvery sheen.

Given these manufacturing handicaps, it is not surprising that early lacy and conventionally pressed wares relied heavily on the Anglo-Irish tradition of cut glass, which too was thick and geometrically patterned. Pressed glass fre-

Fig. 6. Pair of candlesticks with lacy sockets, molded double melon knops, and pressed stepped bases; c. 1830-1835; probably Sandwich; height 10 1/16 inches; this is a rare form, extremely rare in pairs. Amethyst spill holder in Bull's Eye, or Lawrence, pattern; c. 1850-1870; attributed to New England Glass; height 5 9/16 inches; rare form and pattern. Lamp with blown font and pressed classical base, in opaque white glass; c. 1835; attributed to New England Glass; height 10 3/16 inches; this form also occurs in clear glass. Candlestick with opaque blue socket composed of small dolphins, mounted on a square-based clam-broth dolphin stem; c. 1840-1850; New England area; height 8 5/8 inches; considered the rarest of the dolphin candlestick forms. Extremely rare lamp in single Tulip pattern with blue font, green shaft and base; c. 1840-1850; New England area; height 12 inches.

Fig. 7. Canary-yellow plate in Sandwich Plaid pattern, c. 1835-1845; Sandwich; diameter 8 1/16 inches; rare for its canary-yellow color, although the pattern is not so rare as the plain-edge Sandwich Plaid. Extremely rare opalescent glass claret goblet in Colonial pattern, c. 1840-1850; perhaps Sandwich; height 5 1/2 inches. Green plate in variant Roman Rosette pattern, c. 1835-1840; Midwestern area; diameter 5 11/16 inches; rare in any color. Light-amethyst goblet in Colonial pattern, c. 1840-1850; New England area; height 6 inches; rare in color.

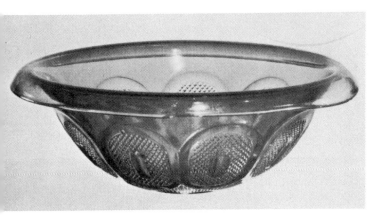

quently repeated its ribbing, strawberry-diamond, and fan motifs, as well as the diapered centers taken from slightly earlier English ceramics (Fig. 1). By 1830, however, these merely imitative patterns had begun to be eclipsed by designs incorporating scrolls, beaded and floral motifs, and figural designs which soon took on a distinctly national character (Fig. 2). It has been suggested that some of the American designs of this period borrowed from the Belgian and French, although the foreign prototypes show a more refined eclecticism and a stricter use of Gothic and Renaissance design elements. All glass designers consistently drew upon a variety of sources and used them in many combinations (Fig. 3). It cannot be overemphasized that this ability of the mold maker to create a greater variety than had previously been available made pressed glass the popular favorite. Until the closing years of the nineteenth century, pressed wares alone were able to keep up with the constant public demand for novelty of form and color (Figs. 4, 5).

By the mid-1840's, the buying public had begun to tire of stippled lacy types and to turn to pressed glass of a plain geometric character. This type of conventionally pressed glass took well to fire polishing, so cut glass could be more closely imitated. Popular motifs were panels, flutes, thumbprints, and diamonds (Fig. 6). By 1850,

lacy glass was out of fashion, and plain geometric patterns were the new favorites. Wares of this type were produced in an increasing variety of forms and colors to meet the demand for novelty. Today, the pressed-glass collector cherishes pieces in a rare color or shape, although these may have been design experiments which in their own day proved to be unpopular (frontispiece and Figs. 7, 8). Pressed objects of this heavier, rather monumental type were made in greater variety through the 1870's. With the invention of "lime" glass in West Virginia about 1864 these wares almost flooded the market, causing great economic problems for the manufacturers of lead glass and cut decoration.

By the late 1860's, however, there was another change in popular taste. Having moved from the intricate surfaces of the lacy variety to plain geometric patterns, the public was now receptive to more elaboration (Fig. 9). The pattern glass which resulted was made in large sets and included celeries, tumblers, plates, and covered dishes. Glass of this type had been made some fifteen years earlier, but it now reached a new level of favor. Basically, such patterns combined the plain geometric qualities of typical Middle-Period pressed glass with secondary motifs (Fig. 10).

The taste for more elaborate designs had its flowering in the exotic pressed glass which became popular from about 1870 on. From this period date such types as Three Face, Lion, and Westward-ho (originally Pioneer), the last of which boasts a crouching-Indian finial and elk and buffalo in high relief (Fig. 11). From this same period also came the late opaque-white wares known today as milk glass.

These pronounced shifts in taste were a significant comment upon the expanding American economy of the nineteenth century, which brought an unprecedented variety of goods before the buying public. Significant too was the fact that this type of glass, which had so severely threatened the market for cut and engraved wares, was in the last years of the century eclipsed by its more costly counterparts. At the Centennial Exhibition of 1876, pressed glass was less noticed by the public than the cut wares shown by the Boston and Sandwich, New England Glass, Dorflinger, and Gillinder companies.

No study of nineteenth-century American glass can be conducted without a knowledge of pressed glass. While other types existed contemporaneously, none was so popular or so well able to follow public demand. Lacy, conventionally pressed, and pattern wares did not include all of the nineteenth-century glass manufacture in America, but they constituted an important element; and not the least of their contributions was the fostering of glassmaking as an important national industry.

Fig. 10. Dark sapphire-blue cologne bottle in Bull's Eye, or Lawrence, pattern, with cut neck; c. 1850-1860; attributed to New England Glass; height 7 inches; rare in pattern, color, and form. Jade-green spill holder in Cable pattern with applied gilt decoration, c. 1860-1870; Sandwich; height 5¾ inches. Rare in any color; this particular color is extremely rare. The Cable pattern is said to commemorate the laying of the Atlantic cable in 1858. Cerulean-blue spoon holder in Ribbed Grape pattern, c. 1850 or later; probably Sandwich. Height 5¾ inches; this color may be unique in this pattern.

Fig. 11. Compote (one of a pair), celery vase, and pitcher in Westward-ho (Pioneer) pattern, c. 1870-1880; probably Gillinder; heights 11⅜ inches, 6⅝, and 7 inches. *Gift of Mr. and Mrs. Joseph S. Riegel.* Opaque white pitcher with design of swans and water plants on body, and beaded rim; c. 1880 or later; United States Glass Company, Gas City, Indiana; height 5¼ inches. *Gift of Mrs. E. M. Belknap.* All of these illustrate the very late Middle-Period taste for exotic patterns and finishes in pressed glass. In the 1890's pattern glass of this type was replaced in popular favor by brilliant-cut glass.

Lacy Hairpin in French and American glass

BY LOWELL INNES

COLLECTORS OF American lacy glass have too long looked at French lacy askance or with distaste. Nevertheless students have accepted the fact that many lacy salts and plates of identical patterns were made in France and America. The lacy Sandwich covered dish and the Meissen porcelain one which appear on Plates 151 and 152 of Ruth Webb Lee's *Sandwich Glass* (1947 ed.), as well as the lacy New England area bowl and the Meissen porcelain compote published as Numbers 239 and 242 in James H. Rose's *Story of American Pressed Glass of the Lacy Period* (catalogue of a 1954 Corning Museum exhibition), make it clear that German and American manufacturers were also using the same patterns (in these cases, variations on the Princess Feather). Recently several Meissen plates have been found in the pattern we call Roman Rosette (Fig. 1.) Since both these patterns are clearly far better suited to glass than to porcelain, it is now the consensus that the design originated here and was copied in Germany.

To find a long-accepted Midwestern lacy pattern in a French catalogue, however, is a bit unnerving. It ought to make collectors less dogmatic, more receptive, and more willing to admit that Continental lacy has merit. In 1831 a Paris firm, Barbier, Launay & Cie., was formed to distribute the products of Baccarat and St. Louis. The next year Barbier, Launay acquired the Cristallerie de St. Cloud but sold it four years later with the understanding that no more glass would be made there for fifty years. Soon after 1836 Choisy-le-Roi and the Cristallerie de Bercy came under the Launay firm, which by 1834 had

become Launay, Hautin & Cie.; it served as a distribution and advertising agent for Baccarat, St. Louis, Choisy-le-Roi, and Bercy. From time to time Launay, Hautin issued trade catalogues. Sometimes sections were reserved for each factory, sometimes different factory pieces pictured on the same page were identified by letters such as B for Baccarat and S*. L.* for St. Louis.

On page 30 in the second part of a Launay, Hautin & Cie. catalogue of about 1842, a saucerlike dish on a pedestal (Fig. 2) is shown. Its design was called *m: à perles* (pressed in beads) and its form, *Baguier f*. évasée* (flaring ring stand). In this country the pattern has long been called the Midwestern Hairpin and in fact the ring stand itself (Fig. 3) has been published as a compote, "probably Midwest" (ANTIQUES, February 1957, p. 162). Stem and base present a problem in technique as well as in design. The smooth stem, shaped in a mold, joins the saucer to a square base with small graduated diamonds on its underside. Probably stem and base were pressed in one operation. Nevertheless, the round shaft seems to have been fitted into a hole in the base just as lamp fonts were pegged. The part where the shaft emerges on the underside of the base has been polished. Clearly, the piece was pontil held for fire polishing.

The counterpart of this French ring stand, the five-inch American nappy shown in Figure 4 (right), lacks the brilliance achieved by skillful fire polishing. In the French piece the design was on the base mold; in the American, on the plunger. Another marked difference is the result of the use of the cap ring on the nappy. Such

Fig. 1. *Left:* Meissen plate in shades of pink, with gilding; c. 1850. Diameter 8½ inches. *Right:* opalescent lacy glass plate in Roman Rosette pattern; New England, c. 1845. Diameter 9¼ inches. This pattern was also produced in the Midwest. *Collection of Walter E. Simmons.*

Fig. 2. St. Louis *Baguier f*. *évasée* (flaring ring stand), as it appears in Part II, p. 30 of the Launay, Hautin & Cie. (Paris) catalogue, c. 1842. *Corning Museum of Glass.*

scalloped and pointed serrations occur frequently on Midwestern pieces. Though French and other Continental manufacturers seemed to prefer having the design of the shoulder a border for the whole, as in the ring stand, they also used the cap ring when it suited their purposes. The center design of both pieces is the so-called Midwestern Hairpin: in both it has a sixteen-rayed center; sixteen bordering lancets, each edged with thirty-four stippled dots; and finally, a border of sixteen medallions with rayed centers. Except for differences in technique of manufacture the center designs are identical.

In Lee and Rose's *American Glass Cup Plates*, Number 205 seems identical, except for its scalloped rim, to the French pattern, and on page 166 the authors say: "This is the only instance known to us of this peculiar rim. So far as we know, the only set so far discovered turned

Fig. 3. St. Louis ring stand, c. 1842. Diameter 4¾ inches, height 2¾. The square foot has graduated diamonds on the underside. This piece has been published as "probably Midwest" (ANTIQUES, February 1957, p. 162) because the pattern of the bowl is identical with the pattern known in this country as Midwestern Hairpin. *Toledo Museum of Art, Duckworth collection.*

Fig. 4. *Left:* bowl of the St. Louis ring stand. *Right:* American small bowl, c. 1840. Diameter 5⅛ inches, height 1 inch. The scallop-and-point rim pattern is also found on plates and cup plates from the Pittsburgh area. *Author's collection.*

Fig. 5. Pressed covered sweetmeat on Midwestern Hairpin base—a very rare piece; c. 1835. Both cover and bowl of this dish carry a design similar to that on the St. Louis ring stand. Height over all, 7¼ inches; diameter 6½. *Collection of William J. Elsholz.*

up in California, so distribution is no guide to origin." The cup plate has sixteen lancets, sixteen rays, and sixteen medallions, exactly like the St. Louis ring stand. It also has a turning pimple on the top center, which Lee and Rose "believe . . . to be a purely Midwestern trait." This need not, however, prevent us from considering the possibility that the cup plate is French.

In an article in ANTIQUES for March 1954 (p. 224) Mr. Rose shows two rarities with the lancet motif, a tray (Fig. 8a) and a covered sweetmeat (Fig. 5). The terraced cover of the sweetmeat carries practically the same Hairpin design as that on the ring stand. William J. Elsholz, who owns it, kindly let me have its statistics. The cover has eighteen center rays, eighteen lancets, and eighteen bordering medallions, where the ring stand has sixteen of each. The terraced line of the cover breaks the continuity somewhat, but a careful examination shows that the curves from the double lancets touch the medallions exactly as do those on the French piece, and the medallions include the same starlike blossoms. A marked difference, however, is the series of clear circles below the medallions. On the French piece it is a series of clear diamonds. As one looks down into the bowl of the sweetmeat he sees the cover pattern repeated.

The low, flaring Hairpin base on Mr. Elsholz' covered dish was widely used in the Midwest. It is impressive on blown sugar bowls with copper-wheel engraving (Fig. 6), and it also embellishes early blown candlesticks and lamp fonts (Figs. 7, 7a). Since it appears on late pressed compotes, too, we cannot date it with accuracy. The Hairpin base is a smaller version of the French piece and its American counterpart. Twenty rays, lancets, and medallions occur instead of sixteen. The stippling is less brilliant, and it lacks the artistic strength of larger examples of the lancet. The plain bull's eye in the medallion instead of the French design's rayed motif dulls the effect somewhat.

There has been little attempt to attribute the Midwestern Hairpin to one factory. On blown and pressed pieces like sugar bowls, candlesticks, and lamps the variety of styles forbids exact attribution. During the 1830's and 1840's at Pittsburgh, the Robinsons, the Curlings, Parke, Campbell and Hanna (Union Glass Works), and Bakewell were pressing excellent Midwestern lacy. So were the Ritchies of Wheeling. The Hairpin base could have been used by all of them on blown and pressed pieces. One pressed compote on the Hairpin base is in the Princess Feather pattern, the coarsened form that Bakewell made fairly late.

An interesting outgrowth of the Hairpin design is the

Fig. 6. Free-blown engraved sugar bowl on pressed Midwestern Hairpin base; c. 1835. Height 7 inches. Domed cover, galleried rim, panels at base of bowl, and generous proportions bespeak the Pittsburgh area, as does the leaf-and-fruit design executed in copper-wheel technique. *Henry Ford Museum, ex coll. McKearin.*

Fig. 7. Blown candlesticks
on pressed Midwestern Hairpin base; heights 8 and 8⅛ inches.
These candlesticks are attributed to the Pittsburgh area;
probably 1830's. *Corning Museum.*

Fig. 8. Pressed Midwestern casket, c. 1835. Both casket and tray (below)
utilize the lancet-and-leaf motif found on the Midwestern Hairpin base
and in the bowl of the St. Louis ring stand. Height over all, 5 inches;
dimensions at rim, 6⅜ by 3¹⁵⁄₁₆ inches. *Corning Museum.*

Fig. 8a. Tray matching Midwestern casket;
5¾ by 7¹³⁄₁₆ inches. *Corning Museum.*

Fig. 7a. Detail of Hairpin base
of candlestick in Fig. 7.

Fig. 9. Two Midwestern lacy plates from the Pittsburgh area, c. 1840. Centers in acorn-and-oak-leaf design; on shoulders, the lancet-and-leaf motif found on the Midwestern casket; in the French piece and in the Midwestern Hairpin base none of the lancets is stippled. *Left:* round plate with bull's-eye rim (38 eyes), an indication of Pittsburgh origin; diameter 5 inches. *Right:* octagonal plate with rim of thirty-two bull's eyes separated by stippled points; diameter 8 inches. This is illustrated on Pl. 143 (No. 3) of the McKearins' *American Glass;* No. 1 on that plate has the same distinctive rim. *Author's collection.*

Fig. 10. *Top:* unrecorded Pittsburgh lacy oval tray, c. 1840. Center shows large lancet and leaves almost out of proportion to the rest of the design, and the shoulders, arches with bisecting sunbursts; scallop-and-point rim. The pattern of fleurs-de-lis between the arches is found on some Midwestern octagonal vegetable dishes. Length 7⅞ inches, width 5⅜. *Bottom:* salt dish, c. 1840; top size, 2¾ by 2⅛ inches. In the Neals' *Pressed Glass Salt Dishes* (GA 3) this model, with its similar treatment of arches and emphasis on circles, is attributed to the Pittsburgh area. *Author's collection.*

wide use of the lancet in large pieces like the Midwestern casket and its tray (Figs. 8, 8a), the J. Grossman compote on a Roman Rosette base (Rose, *op. cit.,* No. 354), and the acorn-and-oak-leaf plates in Figure 9. Note that on these plates *the lancets are alternately clear and stippled,* rather than all clear like the ones on the French ring stand. On neither the round five-inch nor the larger octagonal acorn-and-oak-leaf plates are the lancets *edged with beads.* Sometimes the center of these plates is stippled, sometimes it is not. That difference bears no relationship to the alternate stippling of lancets or the absence of beads around the lancets. The clear lancets on the Midwestern casket and its tray and on the unrecorded tray in Figure 10, however, are bordered with beads.

The scarcity of American pieces in the exact design of the St. Louis piece strongly suggests that the Midwestern lacy Hairpin base came first and American designers borrowed and adapted lancets to become integral parts of a larger design, as on acorn plates, compotes, trays, and the Midwestern casket. If we accept the theory that the larger American pieces shown were pressed in the early thirties we can sustain no claims for the French as originators—unless other catalogue material exists.

We must admit, however, that if the French copied the Hairpin base, they also refined it. Their intertwining of medallion and lancet makes for unity and grace in the design. The Launay, Hautin & Cie. catalogue of the early forties also provides clear evidence of the excellence of St. Louis workmanship. But for the present, the exact relationship between French and American design must remain an enigma.

I am indebted to the Corning Museum of Glass for use of the Launay, Hautin & Cie. catalogue and to Paul N. Perrot for guidance and help.

232

Rarities in Pattern Glass

By RUTH WEBB LEE

Illustrations, except as noted, from the author's collection

THE value of antiques is determined not by one but by several considerations. Beauty of design, quality of workmanship, choice of material, rarity, usefulness, historical associations, all tend to influence appraisal, though the order of their importance varies with the preferences of individual collectors. The appeal, necessarily, is always to a particular temperament. There can be no just quarrel with those who set design above rarity, or historical association above usefulness.

It must be admitted today that a greater number of American collectors are interested in pressed pattern glass than in any other type of antiques. Throughout the depression the volume of sales and the range of prices of such glass actually rose. Dealers frankly agree that the passion for pattern glass helped to keep alive the regard for antiques in general. It brought customers to the shops. The reason is self-evident. Despite hard times, the desire to own antiques persisted, and collectors gratified it by purchasing pressed glass.

Research into the origin and age of various patterns, the establishment of an accepted nomenclature, the ascertaining of exactly how many forms are obtainable by those who desire to accumulate sets, all have helped. The reiterated objections of collectors who demand extreme age for their treasures — that pattern glass is not old enough to rank, for example, with Puritan furniture or colonial silver — has not checked the movement. As a matter of fact, there are pressed patterns collectible in sets that date back to the 1840's and possess, accordingly, a very respectable antiquity. Such glass harmonizes with still older furniture and surroundings. Great-grandmother was doubtless using just such glassware on a table that she inherited from *her* great-grandmother. And, by reason of its fragility, glass that belonged to grandmother is relatively more venerable than a Windsor chair, *circa* 1800.

The element of usefulness, another value-making factor of pressed glass,

Fig. 1 — "BELLFLOWER" OCTAGONAL SUGAR BOWL
A more complicated form than that usually encountered and suggesting a date in the 1840's. *Formerly in the collection of Mrs. C. C. Viall*

cannot be overlooked. Such glass is bought for practical as well as for sentimental reasons. It is enjoyed every day. It need not be enshrined in a cabinet. As an essentially American product, it "talks American" to lovers of American antiques. I have enjoyed exceptional facilities for noting the steady increase in the number of its collectors. Men, women, and children in all sections of the United States are today acquiring pressed glass. Even in Europe the contagion is spreading. Today's mail brought me a letter from a collector in Soviet Moscow!

The acquisitive yearning which is expressed in efforts to acquire a table service of *Ashburton, bellflower, comet,* or whatever the pattern may be need not subside with the completing of the set. Though scoffers may insist that the pattern lacks the element of rarity, there is a vast satisfaction in discovering the twelfth item of a sought-for dozen. And if this emotion is less intense than that experienced in unearthing an individual piece so unusual as to be almost unique, pressed glass still affords good hunting.

In many of the early patterns occur items apparently made in such limited quantity that very few specimens are obtainable today. The demand for these particular items may have been insufficient to justify continuing their manufacture, or the entire line may have been speedily discontinued for technical or commercial reasons, such as a too complicated mold, or too high production costs, or lack of appeal to the buying public. Again, some now desirable piece may have been made by a factory that did not remain long in business. Whatever the reason, all that collectors need realize is that pressed-glass rarities exist and that they are worth searching for and acquiring.

Bellflower

The earliest mention of the *bellflower* pattern that I have found appears in a catalogue of M'Kee Brothers of Pittsburgh. This pattern goes back to the late 1850's, and is listed as *R.L.,* presumably *ribbed leaf.* That some articles in this classification were

Fig. 2 — OPAQUE RIBBED COLOGNE BOTTLES, NOT TRUE "RIBBED LEAF"; "RIBBED IVY" CELERY VASE
The bottles are not true *bellflower* and may be of foreign origin. The celery vase in the *ivy* pattern is perhaps unique.
From the collection of George S. McKearin

Fig. 3 (above and centre) — "HORN OF PLENTY" OVAL COMPOTE AND ROUND COMPOTE
Both probably made at Sandwich. The oval form is very rare

Fig. 4 — "HORN OF PLENTY" CLARET
One of the handsomest of the pressed wine glasses

Fig. 5 — "HORN OF PLENTY" COVERED DISH

made at a still earlier date is indisputable. The rarest *bellflower* piece I believe to be the octagonal sugar bowl, shown in Figure 1. I know of one perfect specimen, from which the photograph was taken, and one other, complete but imperfect. Both were found in Western states. We are justified in surmising that this exceptional bowl was either an experiment on the part of a short-lived factory, or that the makers, finding that the round sugar bowl of the type usually found today was more easily and cheaply produced, discarded the eight-sided mold.

To a collector of *bellflower*, the quest for an octagonal bowl will furnish a fresh aim in life. Next in order of rarity in the same early pattern are the colored specimens, such as the amber egg cup, the opal egg cup, the sapphire-blue spoon holder and syrup jar, the milk-white syrup jars, and other forms. The clear cake plate on a standard is almost unobtainable today. The cologne bottles shown in Figure 2 I have always suspected of a foreign origin. The design is not the true *ribbed leaf*, though it comes very close to that. These bottles, marked as well as unmarked, are to be found in opaque white, opaque jade green, and so on. The *ribbed ivy* celery vase, shown in the same illustration, is the only one I have seen to date.

Horn of Plenty

The *horn of plenty*, so much in demand by collectors today, is rapidly becoming one of the scarcer patterns. In this group the oval compote on a standard is probably the most elusive item. One is shown in Figure 3. It is heavy, brilliant, and rather

suggests a large pickle dish. The standard has the heavy loops at the base, usually associated by collectors with Sandwich pieces. I strongly suspect that this compote may have come from the famous factory on the Cape. It should be noted that the disc design on the bowl is carried out on the base as well. To date only two of these dishes have come to my notice.

Next in rarity in this pattern is the small oblong covered dish shown in Figure 5. I have owned one and know of two others. It is undoubtedly one of the earliest pieces of this pattern. *Horn of plenty* claret glasses are so seldom found as to challenge the persistence of any collector. Tall and slender, with a delicate, graceful bowl, they are desirable for more reasons than their extreme rarity. Another noteworthy piece is the butter dish of which the cover knob is a head of Washington, queue and all. One has been found in clear yellow. Look for its twin if you specialize in what is hard to find. The *horn of plenty* spoon holder also may be obtained in opaque white and clear yellow. Six-inch compotes on a high standard, covered or open, were usually listed in the early catalogues as "sweet-meat dishes." They are rare in any early pattern, and particularly so in *horn of plenty*. It is well to note the petal standard and the waffle design in the base.

Egg Cups

Mrs. Wallace Hood of Danvers, Massachusetts, has gathered a remarkably interesting collection of those small objects originally termed "egg glasses." After assembling such of these as may be had in patterns collectible in sets, she turned her attention to exceptional specimens that sometimes are found not only in color but

Fig. 6 — "THREE-FACE" CHAMPAGNE
Here the stem is hollow — an unusual feature in a pressed item.
From the collection of Mrs. E. H. Bristol

what, today, are termed "spoon holders." These articles deserve the attention of rarity seekers. The examples shown in Figure 7 are early types. Many such vessels were originally made to match, in design, the bowls of whale-oil lamps. They were called "spill holders," and were dedicated to tapers or twisted paper spills which were used in lighting lamps, candles, and the wood in the fireplace at a time when matches were either expensive or unobtainable. Spill holders are of lead flint glass, some quite brilliant and others rather dull, but all of them heavy and squat. In the 1840's many of them were made and advertised as holders for cigars. Later, when spoon holders came into gen-

Fig. 7 — SPILL HOLDERS
Apparently of the 1840's, these were used for paper spills and for cigars. Subsequent spoon holders were deeper and mounted on taller stems.
From the collection of Mrs. Emma Fitts Bradford

covered. Two of the latter, both in opaque white, are shown in Figure 10. As an old glassworker once informed me, the covers were designed to keep the eggs warm as they were served. Covers were, however, gradually abandoned, perhaps because they broke so easily as to prove a liability instead of an asset. Thereafter egg cups came *sans* covers. A collection of these dainty cups is not only charming but well worthy of study.

Spoon Holders

I do not know of any collector who has devoted himself, or herself, exclusively to

eral use, a gradual change in form occurred. The bowls became deeper and the stems longer. The opal or milk-white specimen in Figure 11 is a good example of this transitional type.

Three Face

There are many rarities in the later patterns, even in those of the Centennial period. Mrs. E. H. Bristol, of Foxboro, Massachusetts, has the largest known collection in the *three-face* pattern, which is a product of the early 1870's. Among the unusual specimens that she has obtained is the hollow-stem champagne glass, shown in Figure 6, and another of the type known as a "saucer champagne," with a solid stem. Nearly all of the glasses of the early pressed period that are five or five and a half inches in height are listed in the old catalogues in my possession as "champagnes," and had solid glass stems. The pressed champagne glass with a hollow stem was apparently a later innovation. If you have any doubts about the rarity of the hollow-stem types, just try to find them today! Another rarity in the *three-face* design, in partly frosted and partly clear glass, is the tall, ribbed, covered biscuit jar illustrated in ANTIQUES for April 1933.

Lion Pattern

Of note in the *lion* pattern of the same period are oval salts and cologne bottles. The salts, both plain and engraved, are pictured in Figure 8, with the cologne bottles. The latter are the only specimens of their kind that have been found to date,

Fig. 8 — "LION" RARITIES
Salts of unusual form, one engraved; and perhaps unique pair of toilet bottles. Though the *lion* pattern is of the 1870's, it does not lack its rarities.
Salts from the collection of Joseph Makanna; bottles from the collection of Donald Lannin

Fig. 9 — "Morning-Glory" Pattern (*c. 1860 or later*)
Probably New England. Goblet, "champagne," and egg cup. The term "champagne" was rather indiscriminately applied to stemware of a certain height

orative of the dense white pieces of that period is the large swan dish with uplifted wings, pictured in Figure 12.

Morning-Glory

Those who would accumulate a rare pattern obtainable in sets, and who have the necessary patience and persistence, are advised to collect the *morning-glory* pattern, illustrated in Figure 9. To all appearances it is a product of the 1860's. I have never seen any documentary evidence conclusively identifying its source, though by many it

Fig. 10 — Covered Egg Cups in Opaque Glass (*c. 1850*)
Few of these glasses survive with covers, the making of the latter having been speedily discontinued.
From the collection of Mrs. Wallace Hood

in so far as I know, though there must be others somewhere. Look for them, if you seek that which is high odds against you.

Other Exceptional Pieces

Many interesting items in milk white, both early and late, are available to collectors who spurn easy finds. A pair of opal sweetmeat dishes in the *prism* pattern, shown in Figure 11, dates back to the 1850's, and possibly to the 1840's. They were probably made by M'Kee Brothers of Pittsburgh. The Liberty Bell cup in milk white

has been attributed to a New England factory.

Limitations of space preclude the enumeration or description of all the rarities in a number of other interesting patterns. Nevertheless, I hope that I have told enough to convince collectors who complain of insufficient excitement in pressed-glass hunting that they are sadly mistaken.

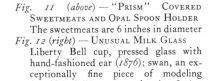

Fig. 11 (above) — "Prism" Covered Sweetmeats and Opal Spoon Holder
The sweetmeats are 6 inches in diameter
Fig. 12 (right) — Unusual Milk Glass
Liberty Bell cup, pressed glass with hand-fashioned ear (*1876*); swan, an exceptionally fine piece of modeling (*c. 1880*); *bellflower* syrup jug (*c. 1850*)

with the serpent handle was produced on the grounds of the Centennial Exposition in Philadelphia in 1876, by James Gillinger and Sons, in plain sight of the visitors. One of the rarest and most dec-

The Popular Ten in Pattern Glass

By RUTH WEBB LEE

Note. We concur with Mrs. Lee in decrying attempts to prepare numerically limited lists of the *best* items in any domain of collecting. The mere naming of presumably blue-ribbon specimens may quite easily convey the erroneous impression that specimens unnamed are, in some mysterious way, of inferior merit. It should therefore be noted that in the subjoined discussion Mrs. Lee carefully avoids consideration of good, better, and best, and confines herself exclusively to classifying certain designs in pattern glass on the basis of current popularity. In suggesting this new approach to an old topic we have been hopeful of accomplishing two ends: that of helping the non-specializing dealer to determine which of innumerable patterns he could most safely acquire for stock; and that of informing the collector of pattern glass as to the particular fields in which he may expect to encounter the most active competition from other ardent hunters. It is well to remember that majority sentiment is by no means invariably sound. The most successful collector may be the one who, after observing the direction followed by the crowd, turns toward another point of the compass and blazes a trail of his own.

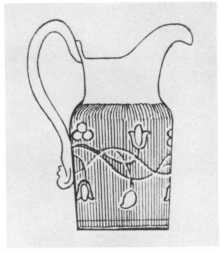 

Fig. 1 (left) — "BELLFLOWER"
Design believed to have originated prior to 1850. Produced by sundry factories. For ready reference illustrations are alphabetically arranged. For a complete list of items in each group see the author's book, *Early American Pressed Glass*

Fig. 2 (right) — "BLACKBERRY": OPAQUE WHITE
Design patented 1870 by William Leighton, Jr., of Wheeling, West Virginia

THE search for short-cuts to expert knowledge is as old as the desire to know, something born in all men, according to Aristotle. Lists of the ten "best" novels, or twelve "greatest" paintings, or six "wisest" philosophers have no value either educational or cultural; for at most they merely record the opinion of some individual or small group. Other opinions, quite different, may be fully as reliable. And after all, what the collector should do is to form his own independent conclusions based on his own observation and judgment. I have heard many criticisms of the "best" lists dealing with prints, cup plates, and so on. It is argued, not unreasonably, that such predigested material hinders rather than helps new collectors by tending to narrow their interest prematurely, and to discourage them before they are really under way. Among the "best" cup plates, for example, are many which are virtually unobtainable. Young collectors, finding that what began as a promising avocation turns into a disappointment, give up in despair. The veteran collector may be spurred on by the scarcity; but not the beginner.

Fortunately, there are not enough patterns of pressed glass to permit anyone to attempt a list of the one hundred "best" patterns collectible in sets. Selecting the "best" would provoke more debate than encourage agreement. At the same time, it *is* possible to comply with a request for a list of the ten patterns which are in the most active demand today, or which have maintained their popularity the longest. The vogue of pattern glass is not old. It began when discriminating eyes saw merit in some of the pressed American tableware displayed in antique shops. If the glass was by no means ancient, it was none the less attractive. As the vogue spread, a greater variety of patterns was carried by the dealers. Some patterns were inferior and tended to give a bad name to all pressed glass. It always was, of course, absurd to class the fine old patterns, dating from the 1840's, with ware produced in the 1890's or even later,

Fig. 3 — "DAISY AND BUTTON"
A pattern which was at the height of its popularity during the 1880's. Produced with variations by nearly every old factory specializing in tableware. *Daisy and button* is widely collected today

Fig. 4 — "HORN OF PLENTY"
Known to have been made at Sandwich and by M'Kee and Brothers, Pittsburgh, in the 1850's–1860's. The hand-expanded mouth and the hand-shaped and applied handle are indicative of early practice

Fig. 5 — "LION"
First produced in the 1870's by Gillinder & Sons of Philadelphia. Produced by a few others during a considerable period

and, in many instances, originally given away as a premium with soaps, teas, or baking powders.

In the six years since the first edition of *Early American Pressed Glass* was published, the popularity of all pattern glass has increased phenomenally. For this several reasons may be advanced. The increased ease of doing business by mail is one. Again, throughout the depression, pressed glass enabled thousands of persons to enjoy the pleasure of collecting without incurring bankruptcy. The demand for pattern glass has now reached such proportions that dealers all over the country depend upon its handling for a steady income. No sectionalism is observable among collectors of pressed glass. Everywhere the same patterns are sought, and those which today may be viewed as the leaders are the very ones most popular fifteen years ago.

Among the first patterns to win wide favor were *Ashburton* and *bellflower*. *Ashburton* has only recently reacquired its rightful name. For some years it was classed generically with *colonial*, a denomination that for a long time included several of the early, simple designs. *Ashburton* may claim to be a genuine antique, for it was produced and sold during the 1840's, nearly a hundred years ago. To the best of my knowledge, it was never offered as a premium of any kind. It occurs in a heavy flint glass of fine

quality. So popular was it from the start that it was copied by a number of factories.

Bellflower has been for years the commonly accepted name for the pattern originally listed as *R. L.* (presumably *Ribbed Leaf*), of which we have records going back to the 1850's. I think it was made even before 1850. That *bellflower* also was made almost simultaneously by a number of factories is evident from the many variants extant. No collector today need apologize for cherishing a pattern that has enjoyed popularity during so many years as *bellflower*.

Two later patterns, likewise widely collected fifteen years ago and still going strong, are *lion* and *wildflower*, both dating from the 1870's. *Lion* was made chiefly by the Gillinders of Philadelphia; and *wildflower* by Adams & Company of Pittsburgh. The long-enduring popularity of *wildflower* has been due to its decorative value, for it is obtainable in several attractive tints.

In order to determine — by investigation rather than by guesswork — the most popular pressed patterns today, I have gone to some trouble to learn from shops in all sections of the country just which ones are in such demand as to keep stocks at a low ebb. Confining my selection to those patterns which it is possible to collect in sets within a reasonable period, hence not necessarily the scarcest, I would name the following: *bellflower, horn of plenty, wildflower, thousand eye, lion, three face, westward-ho, rose in snow, milk-white blackberry,* and *daisy and button.*

It is fair to list an additional ten, which have enjoyed wide popularity but for certain reasons cannot be included in the first group. These are: *morning-glory, diamond thumbprint,* purple *marble* glass, *New England pineapple, tulip, star with dewdrop, thumbprint, inverted fern, Hamilton,* and *Baltimore pear.* The second choice calls for some explanation. *Morning-glory* would undoubtedly rate with the first ten in point of appearance and popularity except that examples are so seldom found that few dealers outside of New England, where the pattern originated, have ever seen a piece of it. *Diamond thumbprint* would also rank among the first ten but for the fact that the goblets are virtually unobtainable. The same holds true for the fluted goblet in *marble* glass, illustrated in the article *Mosaic Glass and Other Types* in ANTIQUES for February 1937. *New England pineapple* might displace some one among the first ten but, like *morning-glory,* it is too hard to find outside of New England. *Tulip* makes an attractive table setting, but has declined somewhat in popularity, perhaps because it is now rather scarce. It never was abundant.

Star with dewdrop, though undoubtedly one of the most brilliant and appealing patterns, lacks a true goblet approaching the quality of the plates. In assembling sets, collectors are compelled to substitute other goblets, usually the *popcorn.* *Thumbprint* is another widely known early pattern, with much to commend it. Like *tulip* it has been collected spasmodically. *Inverted fern* also is sufficiently in demand to deserve honorable mention. *Hamilton* is highly esteemed, especially among collectors who themselves bear that famous name; but its popularity does not quite entitle it to rank with the first ten. *Baltimore pear* runs even with *rose in snow.* Between these two, my own choice would be *rose in snow,* because it is the earlier and is the better in design and in quality of glass. First made during the 1870's, it has been widely known for years. *Baltimore pear* has enjoyed great popularity

Fig. 6 — "ROSE IN SNOW"
Manufactured by Bryce Brothers of Pittsburgh in the 1870's, and probably by others. Collectors should be wary of recent reproductions of this pattern

Fig. 7 — "THOUSAND EYE"
Made in the 1870's, and later. Adams & Company of Pittsburgh and Richards & Hartley of Tarentum, Pennsylvania, are known to have manufactured certain types

because, notwithstanding the poor quality of the glass, many people consider it highly decorative. This pattern made its first appearance in 1888. In writing my book, I tried to draw the line at patterns made after 1890.

There is little need to discuss in detail the reasons for choosing the first group of ten. Everyone knows the *bellflower* pattern. *Horn of plenty* is another very old favorite. *Thousand eye*, as well as *wildflower* in its various hues, has been collected from coast to coast. *Lion* and *westward-ho* have been known as far back as I can remember anything about glass. *Three face* has not been quite so well known for as long a period, but the demand for it has been steadily maintained. *Milk-white blackberry* has been sought for years. It was patented February 1, 1870, by the designer, William Leighton, Jr., and produced by Hobbs, Brockunier and Company of Wheeling,

Fig. 8 — "THREE FACE"
Made probably exclusively by George Duncan & Sons of Pittsburgh about 1875. The example pictured is a hollow-stem champagne, and rare

Fig. 9 — "WESTWARD-HO"
Issued by Gillinder & Sons of Philadelphia, about 1875. The *westward-ho* pattern has likewise been imitated, in goblets and sauce dishes

West Virginia. Let collectors who like rarities in pattern glass try to find a water pitcher like the one in Figure 2! *Rose in snow* has been consistently popular with the numerous collectors who like flowers. *Daisy and button* is the one pattern in the list which will develop differences of opinion. It is included because it is known and is being collected in every state of the Union. Other patterns may possess more merit; but this is the one on which most collectors cut their eyeteeth, before they turn to others. It is not expensive. Probably it is more generally collected than any other one pattern.

Statements regarding patterns most in demand are perhaps pointers for those collectors who like to follow where others lead. Hence let me warn the blindly trusting that goblets in *westward-ho*, *wildflower*, and *rose in snow* have been recently reproduced. I advise collectors to obtain one specimen which is undoubtedly "right," and keep it for purposes of comparison. Make sure that what is offered for sale *exactly* matches the genuine piece! Study, for example, the details of the design on a genuine *westward-ho* goblet. Note that the lips of the deer are closed, whereas on the reproduction they are slightly blurred, as if the animal were preparing to masticate. The original *wildflower* goblet has a full-inch fluted band around the base of the bowl, and the design is heavily stippled. On the reproduction the band measures three quarters of an inch, and the design is thinner and a trifle smaller. The imitative *rose in snow* goblet departs from the real in the design of flower and leaves as well as in the stem and in the appearance of the glass itself.

For the benefit of collectors who may seek rarities in pattern glass, I append a list of the rare articles in each of the first-named group of ten patterns:

1. Bellflower. Cake plate on standard; handled mug; colored pieces; whiskey tumbler; octagonal sugar bowl; 6-inch covered sweetmeat dish on high standard; 3-inch honey dish; footed tumbler; decanter with original *bellflower* stopper; celery vase; berry bowl; small-size water pitcher.

2. Horn of plenty. Oblong covered dish; butter dish with Washington's head forming knob to cover; claret glass; colored pieces; handled mug; large oval vegetable dish; 6-inch covered sweetmeat dish on high standard; oval salt.

3. Wildflower. Compote with square bowl, rounded at top, on high standard; oblong cake basket with wire handle; cordial and champagne; turtle salt.

4. Thousand eye. Champagne; cordial; egg cup.

5. Lion. Oval salt; cordial; all-frosted sauce dish without standard; syrup jug; covered cheese dish; miniature set; egg cup; cologne bottle; powder jar.

6. Three face. Champagne with hollow stem (the only one made in pattern glass); champagne with saucer bowl; cordial; cracker jar, covered.

7. Westward-ho. Cordial and wine; 5-inch covered compote on low standard (only one known to date); 5-inch covered compote on high standard.

8. Rose in snow. Toddy jar with plate; covered pickle jar; extra-large oval vegetable dish.

9. Milk-white blackberry. Water pitcher; celery vase; berry bowl not on standard.

10. Daisy and button. Egg cup; hat in largest size; pieces in amethyst color as well as in ruby red.

Of considerable interest is the finding within the past year of a *ribbed ivy* and a *bellflower* hat. These were apparently made in whiskey-tumbler molds, the top of the glass being rolled over and downward, forming a recognizable hat. Only one specimen of each is known at the present time.

Fig. 10 — "WILDFLOWER"
Made by Adams & Company of Pittsburgh in the 1870's

PRESIDENTIAL PORTRAITS
IN LATE GLASS

By HOMER EATON KEYES

Illustrations from the collection of Mrs. William Greig Walker

CUP-PLATE collectors reverently cherish those few "historicals" whose chief embellishment is a portrait of some well-known personage. In so far as I am aware, this category embraces only seven subjects: Washington, William Henry Harrison, Henry Clay, Major Ringgold, Queen Victoria, Victoria and Albert, the Prince and Princess of Wales. The actual number of designs is of course increased by sundry variants. Nevertheless, that so few likenesses in pressed ware were turned out between the Harrison campaign in 1840 and the marriage of Albert Edward, Prince of Wales, to Princess Alexandra of Denmark in 1863 is worth remarking. Furthermore, it may be observed that, with few exceptions, these cup-plate depictions of rulers and heroes are pretty feeble productions. In general they would be quite unrecognizable had the mold cutter failed to identify vague lineaments with easily decipherable labels.

What is true of portrait cup plates is almost equally true of the allied pictorials. At any rate, the latter exhibit no elaborate compositions, and no well-defined effects of light and shade achieved by modeling. As a matter of fact, the era of pictorial pressed glass did not really begin until the decade of the 1870's. It was to flourish during the rest of the century. Its end is not yet in sight.

This rather sudden manifestation in the domain of glassmaking must, I think, be ascribed in part to the perfecting of new methods of moldmaking. Apparently the patterns of the early molds employed for pressing, like those used for blowing articles in full size, were largely, if not entirely, hand cut. Deming Jarves is quoted to the effect that preparing the mold for the once famous Union Bowl, now lost, occupied the time of two men for six months. That certainly implies manual labor, to say nothing of high cost. This cost element was, I believe, primarily responsible for the shift from the lacy patterns of the 1830's and 1840's to the coarser forms and ornamental treatments that appeared in the 1850's. Molds for the latter could be satisfactorily produced by a process of casting. Since this involved the preliminary carving of a model in wood, it necessitated the elimination of intricately interlaced and delicate lines. (For wood models see ANTIQUES for March 1927, *p. 212.*)

The next step, taken, it would seem, shortly before 1876, permitted a return to the elaboration if not to the refinement of earlier glass. This consisted in casting the molds directly from plaster-of-Paris matrices, which had either been carved by hand, or, in their turn, cast from designs modeled in wax. Plaster of Paris is soft and easily cut in low relief. If when freshly mixed with water it is flowed over a wax sculpture and allowed to harden, it will retain the impression of every detail in the original.

The modeling in wax or plaster was of course the all-important part of this method of moldmaking. The Fostoria Glass Company tells me that it frequently engaged the talent of "well-known sculptors, as well as some who were destined to become famous."

The use of plaster-of-Paris matrices likewise permitted the accurate reproduction of glass items whose copying was considered desirable. In such instances plaster casts of the item were made in as many parts as were needed to deliver it from the mold. These sections were then sent to the foundry to be produced in iron. Thus we may perceive how readily imitations of popular pattern glass may be turned out. The only point at which the counterfeiter is likely to slip is in the final stage of his operation — that of *finishing* the cast-iron mold. This process must be accomplished by hand, and calls for the same expertness essential to die cutting and engraving. Only by observing the slight departures from verisimilitude that are almost certain to occur in hand finishing may certain current copies of older pattern glass be distinguished from the genuine.

According to the Westmoreland Glass Company, the *casting* of molds from plaster is advantageous when a complicated design is undertaken. But the iron employed is softer than that used for hand-cut molds and the results obtained are less brilliant than those accomplished by the latter type.

Concerning one phase of the process of translating a photographic or engraved likeness into a plaster model I am still in doubt. Some mechanical means must have

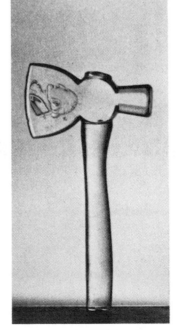

FIG. 1 (*above, left*) — WASHINGTON OVAL PLATE: BEAR-PAW HANDLES (*1876*)
Inscribed: on handles, *Centennial 1876;* around bust, *First in War, First in Peace, first in the hearts of his countrymen*

FIG. 2 (*above, right*) — WASHINGTON GLASS HATCHET (*1876*)
Inscription illegible; Washington profile on blade. A Centennial souvenir

FIG. 3 (*left*) — GRANT CIRCULAR PLATE: SERRATE LEAF BORDER (*1885*)

Inscribed: on border, *Let us have peace . . . U. S. Grant;* around bust, *Born April 27 1822 . . . Died July 23 1885*. A memorial piece

FIG. 4 (*right*) — GRANT RECTANGULAR PLATE WITH CHAMFERED CORNERS (*1885?*)

Circular medallion bust against faceted ground. Inscribed, around bust, *The patriot and soldier . . . Gen. Ulysses. S. Grant.* Probably a memorial piece

been relied upon, at least in many instances, to transfer the original picture to the plaster surface awaiting the carver's hand. I surmise that photography may have been requisitioned for this purpose. On the other hand, some tracing implement may have served.

So much for the outlines of a technique that opened new possibilities for the glass manufacturer and his market. Every imaginable kind of pictorial souvenir article in glass could now be turned out in quantities at prices attractive to the multitude. And turned out they were, to make thousands of homes happier and more hideous.

Manufacturers of domestic wares of many kinds have, for generations, been more concerned with technical progress than with æsthetic excellence. From the close of the Civil War until today they have been tireless in chemical research, in experimentation with mechanical improvements, and in search for skilled workmen. But only within recent years have any of them given serious thought to enlisting the aid of designers who could qualify as trained artists. Partly on this account, partly because, during the period from 1850 to 1900 or thereabouts, the best of world taste was pretty bad, the lively ingenuity devoted to creating eye-catchingly novel forms and colors in glassware, and to devising ways of turning them out in vast quantities, filled the country literally with tons of varied glassware, most of it of steadily declining æsthetic worth.

That generalization, with some exceptions, must, I fear, be accepted as the truth. But it may be countered with two questions: How would you define æsthetic worth in a domestic utensil? and, To what extent are collectors of such articles actuated in their selection by purely æsthetic considerations? I could answer neither to my own entire satisfaction or to that of anyone else. Perhaps the second question finds its own answer in the fact that within the past few years the collecting of the pictorial glasses made between 1876 and 1900 has gone forward at an ever-accelerating pace. This activity becomes somewhat more comprehensible when we realize that some of this glass is associated with specific events in United States history, and that historical objects are *ipso facto* certain to become collectibles as soon as they have accumulated a little dust.

The pictorial glasses in question may be roughly divided into three groups: I. Portraits of celebrities. II. Well-known scenes or reproductions of particular pictures — such as some of the Currier & Ives prints. III. Fanciful compositions like the *Westward-ho* pattern and its analogues. From the standpoint of the collector who has no intention of subjecting his glass to practical use on the table, the Portrait group is probably the most important. Save

perhaps for the actress items, portrait glass seldom occurs in complete sets. It is represented chiefly by individual plates and trays, some of which, however, are allied in detail to formal patterns. Portrait goblets or tumblers and portrait compotes occasionally turn up, but appear to be exceptions to the general rule. The group in question may again be divided into two sub-groups: *A*. Portraits of American presidents. *B*. Portraits of other celebrities. Of these the presidential pieces may be viewed as tops.

Under the circumstances it seems high time that all the significant items in the portrait group should be listed, so that the *omnium-gatherum* collector may have a distinct idea of the goal which he may hope to reach and the distance that he must travel in order to arrive. The purpose of these notes is to make a small beginning in that direction. I hope that interested persons throughout the country will fill inevitable gaps until a really comprehensive check list has been compiled. Hence I invite assistance in what may prove to be a large undertaking. In the present installment I shall confine myself to presidential items, leaving those representing other celebrities for subsequent consideration.

Apparently, American glassmakers of the last quarter of the 1800's did not at the outset think of issuing portrait glass in connection with campaigns for the presidency. If they had, the first candidates for such memorial treatment would doubtless have been Rutherford B. Hayes and his Democratic rival, Samuel J. Tilden, who were pitted against each other in the fall of 1876, the very year of the Philadelphia Centennial Exposition. Instead, President Washington appears to be the first first gentleman of the nation to figure in our late portrait group. His bust, quite well modeled, appears in the centre of an oval plate whose bear-paw handles are clearly marked *Centennial 1876* (*Fig. 1*). In the same year and to celebrate the same patriotic occasion the rare glass hatchet of Figure 2 was doubtless produced.

The blade of this implement carries an excellent relief of the Father of his Country. Iron hatchets of somewhat similar design were likewise made as Centennial souvenirs. The owner of one of these metal versions seriously maintains that it belonged to a restricted issue made for distinguished participants in Washington's inauguration in 1789. Such, alas, is human credulity.

Subject to welcome correction, I am inclined to believe that for some years presidential timber was not considered suitable for portrayal in glass until it had been felled by death. As I have already suggested, if Hayes was thus immortalized I am unaware of the fact. The two Ulysses S. Grant plates here pictured were — one certainly, the other probably — produced after the General's death in 1885, when his inadequacies as a president had

FIG. 5 *(left)* — GAR-
FIELD CIRCULAR
PLATE: STAR BOR-
DER WITH SHIELD
AND FLAGS *(1880–1881)*

Profile head, three quar-
ters bust. Inscribed, *James
A. Garfield*. Probably a
memorial piece

FIG. 6 *(right)* — GAR-
FIELD CIRCULAR
PLATE: INTEGRAL
HANDLES

Border: version of egg
and dart. Profile head,
three quarters bust. No
inscription. Probably a
memorial piece

FIG. 7 — GARFIELD
MEMORIAL
PLATES

Left, serrate rim, flowered drape border.
Head and bust three-
quarter view, sur-
rounded by stars. In-
scriptions: *We mourn
our nation's loss . . .
Born Nov. 19 1831
. . . Shot July 2 1881*

*. . . Died Sep 19 1881.
Right*, rim, irregular
small serrations. Bor-
der, laurel branches
against stippling. Pro-
file head, three quar-
ters bust. Inscribed,
Memorial. A somewhat
similar plate is illus-
trated by Ruth Webb
Lee, as cited in the
accompanying text

been long forgotten and only his greatness as a soldier was
remembered.

The next president after Hayes was James A. Garfield, whose
election in 1880 was followed in July of the next year by his assassination at the hands of the disgruntled office seeker Charles Jules
Guiteau. Of the five Garfield
items here illustrated three are
unquestionably memorials. I
incline to believe that the other
two belong in the same category. Yet I must admit the
possibility that they were issued
as campaign souvenirs.

The florid and amply side-
whiskered Vice President Chester
A. Arthur, who was unexpectedly pushed into the president's
chair by the death of his chief,
has been reported among the
glass portrayals.

The first indisputable campaign items in the group under
consideration present the countenances of James G. Blaine and
his running mate in the presidential race of 1884, John A.
Logan, better known as Black

Jack Logan. We know that the Blaine and Logan tray and plates
here illustrated are campaign pieces because the two aspirants to
office were defeated by Grover Cleveland and Thomas A. Hendricks. These two banner bearers for the Democratic party appear
on a tray whose border duplicates that of the Blaine and Logan
item (see Ruth Webb Lee's
Early American Pressed Glass,
Plate 165). A tray, or plaque,
exhibiting Benjamin Harrison
and Levi P. Morton, who defeated Cleveland and Thurman
in the election of 1888, is here
illustrated (*Fig. 11*). Four years
later Cleveland was returned to
office, thus defeating Harrison's
hope for a second term.

William McKinley, I am

FIG. 8 — GARFIELD OVAL
PLATE *(1881)*

Dotted serrate rim; leaf border.
Three laurel-framed medallions,
Garfield, Washington, Lincoln, in
order named; United States shield.
Inscribed below medallions, *God
reigns . . . First in peace . . .
Charity for all;* in border, *In
remembrance*

able to picture on two plates. One is either a campaign or a post-election product, since it carries the motto *Protection and plenty*. It is fair to assume that this plate was issued in 1896, since it was his position on the tariff and sound-money issues that won McKinley the election in that year. The other plate memorializes the president's assassination at the hands of Leon Czolgosz, September 6, 1901. In the campaigns of both 1896 and 1900 McKinley's opponent was William Jennings Bryan, who advocated bimetallism as a cure for all the economic ills of the masses. This accounts for the

Figure 15 are pictorial allusions to the man's exploits and personal peculiarities. The eagle, however, signifies his presidency. This plate was probably issued during or at the close of the campaign of 1904, when Roosevelt became president by popular election, and not by accident.

If it turns out that the presidential subjects in pressed glass here pictured and discussed are the only ones known, I shall be greatly surprised. I shall postpone attempting to make a check list until readers of ANTIQUES have had opportunity to inform me regarding additional subjects

FIG. 9 (*above*) — BLAINE AND LOGAN RECTANGULAR TRAY (*1884*)
Ivy-leaf border. Name of each candidate stamped on bust. A campaign item

FIG. 10 (*left and right*) — BLAINE AND LOGAN PLATES (*1884*)
Border, pointed daisy-and-button arches alternating with circular arches framing oak leaves. Finely modeled and well-placed three-quarter-view bust portraits

motto *The peoples money* above Bryan's portrayal on the bowl shown in Figure 13. Evidently it was produced at the same time and at the same place as an accompanying bowl revealing the bust of McKinley and the motto *Protection and prosperity*.

McKinley's untimely death brought Vice President Theodore Roosevelt to the White House. Roosevelt had already distinguished himself and his regiment of Rough Riders in the Spanish American War of 1898. He was known as an enthusiastic hunter of big game. As president he undertook various social and economic reforms under a "square deal" slogan. His somewhat autocratic methods of dealing with men and situations were satirically referred to as "wielding the big stick." The emblems on the rim of the Roosevelt oval plate in

FIG. 11 — HARRISON AND MORTON RECTANGULAR PLAQUE (*1888*)
Ivy-leaf border like that of Figure 9. Stiff bust portraits, each stamped with name of subject. Probably a campaign item

or to assure me that none are to be found. Whether or not a flask displaying the countenance of Franklin D. Roosevelt should be included I am not sure. It is a rather ghastly piece of work memorializing the president's first-term labors in behalf of prohibition repeal.

And that brings me to a brief consideration of the portrait items from the standpoint of quality. Here a wide diversity will be observed. Most of the models were, I think, cut in plaster instead of first modeled in wax. Their scratchy aspect suggests this opinion. In the group here pictured I consider two plates, one depicting Blaine, the other Logan, by far the best. They approach the precision of medalwork. The Bryan and McKinley covered cups or bowls win the booby prize hands down. They could hardly

FIG. 12 — McKINLEY CIRCULAR PLATE *(1896)*
Gadrooned rim, star-spangled border. Bust portrait framed by shield in circle. Inscribed, *Protection and plenty.* Probably a campaign item

FIG. 13 — BRYAN AND McKINLEY COVERED CUPS OR BOWLS *(1896)*
Left, inscribed, *The peoples money . . . W^m. J. Bryan.* Right, inscribed, *Protection and prosperity . . . Maj. Wm. McKinley*

be worse. Almost invariably the subsidiary decoration of these portrait items is either stiff and ungainly or overloaded with unrelated and coarsely executed motives. The stars surrounding one Garfield bust are, however, tastefully arranged, and those on one McKinley plate are not bad. The style of lettering employed is almost unfailingly atrocious.

Be that as it may, if I were instructing a class of highschool youngsters in United States history, I should gather all of these portrait glasses that I could find and set my pupils to work finding out the whys and wherefores of each design. Thus, I think, more than one precious jewel of learning might be borne to the head.

Note. In the preceding review I may seem to imply that the *Westward-ho* pattern was produced in cast-iron molds. James Gillinder assures me that this is not the case. On the contrary, it transpires that in the 1870's James Gillinder & Sons, Philadelphia glassmakers, had in their employ two exceptionally able die sinkers. One or both of these men cut by hand the iron molds for

the *Westward-ho* series, and for similar patterns. The labor involved must have been enormous.

I may also observe that a somewhat extended correspondence with manufacturers has revealed some differences of opinion. I have quoted two authorities who maintain that the molds for portrait glass were usually cast from plaster models. Manager K. R. Haley of the Overmyer Mould Company, Greensburg, Pennsylvania, believes that the designs were usually cut in the mold by means of chisels, hammers, and other hand-manipulated tools. Mr. Haley states that many of the old-time moldmakers could take a photograph or drawing and reproduce it accurately in iron. While casting from plaster models is widely in use, some artisans capable of cutting patterns by hand still survive. It seems reasonable to surmise that collaboration between accomplished designer and skilled craftsman might today develop unsuspected artistic capabilities in a technique hitherto dedicated primarily to commercial ends.

FIG. 14 *(left)* — McKINLEY OVAL PLATE
Laurel border. Full-length figure of the President. Inscribed, *It is Gods way . . . His will be done* [the dying man's own words]. *Born 1843 . . . Died 1901*

FIG. 15 *(right)* — THEODORE ROOSEVELT OVAL PLATE *(probably 1904)*
Rustic rim. Border of Teddy bears, military and hunting accoutrements, eagle, big sticks crossed. Inscribed, in border only, *A square deal.* Profile portrait in rustic frame

PORTRAITS IN LATE GLASS

By ELIZABETH GUNN

Except as noted, illustrations from the Walker collection

IN the latter half of the 1800's, and more particularly in the last twenty years of the century, glass manufacturers availed themselves of recently developed facilities for mass production of all manner of souvenir glassware. Of the pictorial pressed glass which they turned out in vast quantities and which was absorbed for domestic use by an enthusiastic public, the type of chief interest to present-day collectors is that decorated with portraits of notable personages. Portrait glass differs from conventional pattern glass in that it occurs mainly in plates, platters, or trays, only occasionally in tumblers, compotes, or goblets, and seldom if ever in complete sets. In ANTIQUES for November 1938 (*p. 240*), the late Homer Eaton Keyes discussed the mechanical processes by which this technically admirable — if not esthetically desirable — portrait glass was produced, and established a division of the category into two groups: portraits of American presidents, and portraits of other celebrities. His presentation of eighteen presidential items was offered as a start toward compiling a comprehensive check list. Eight additional items have now been reported, and are here reproduced. At the same time, I am illustrating thirteen portrait glasses depicting celebrities other than American presidents. For helpful information in regard to pieces in both groups I am indebted to Mrs. Lucien Nelson Lindsey and Mrs. William Greig Walker.

PORTRAITS OF PRESIDENTS

Five glass items portraying James A. Garfield have hitherto been

noted, three of them unquestionably memorials issued following Garfield's assassination in 1881 by Charles Jules Guiteau. To these may now be added a platter memorializing both Garfield and Lincoln (*Fig. 1*).

The majority of the other presidential items previously shown seem to have been campaign rather than memorial items. Certainly the tray with ivy-leaf border, portraying James G. Blaine and John A. Logan, was issued at the time of their unsuccessful campaign in 1884. It is worth noting that on this tray the name *Walter* appears in fine letters, partially identifying the designer of the original model for the portraits. Yet, though several American

FIG. 3 (*above*) — CLEVELAND AND HENDRICKS PLATES (*1884*)
Border of *classic* pattern. Finely modeled portraits. *Left, from the collection of Mrs. W. R. Marsh; right, from the collection of Mrs. Lucien Nelson Lindsey*

FIG. 4 (*left*) — BLAINE AND LOGAN PLATTER (*1884*)
Simple border, daisy-and-oak-leaf handles, notched rim. Finely modeled portrait busts. A campaign item

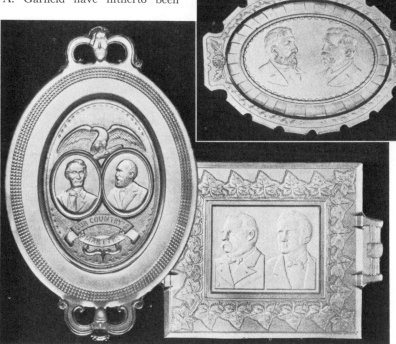

artists and sculptors of the name are recorded, none appears to have been flourishing in 1884. A matching tray, picturing the defeated candidates' opponents, Grover Cleveland and Thomas A. Hendricks, was reported by Mr. Keyes and is now illustrated (*Fig. 2*).

A similar impartiality on the part of the glassmaker is shown by other items produced for the same campaign, which was one of the most exciting in the nation's history. Counterparts of the round Blaine and Logan plates are two plates with identical border, portraying Cleveland and Hendricks (*Fig. 3*). This border, previously described as pointed daisy-and-button arches alternating with circular arches framing oak leaves, is listed by Ruth Webb Lee as *classic* pattern. The four plates in question are of particular interest because two of them are marked with the name of the artist, who doubtless executed the complete quartet. On the shoulder of Blaine and of Hendricks tiny letters spell the name *P. J. Jacobus, Scul*. Though who Jacobus was and what works he produced are not revealed in the annals of art history, Ruth Webb Lee in

FIG. 1 (*left*) — LINCOLN AND GARFIELD PLATTER (*1881*)
Bearded faces in handles perhaps intended to portray Garfield. A memorial item.
From the collection of Mrs. Lucien Nelson Lindsey

FIG. 2 (*right*) — CLEVELAND AND HENDRICKS TRAY (*1884*)
A campaign item, matching a Blaine and Logan tray

her *Early American Pressed Glass* says that the *westward-ho* pattern was designed by a German moldmaker named Jacobus. Quite possibly it was P. J. Jacobus who was responsible for the *westward-ho* molds and even the complete *classic* series. At all events, these portraits in glass were obviously executed by a competent sculptor; for that reason the revelation of his name alone is gratifying.

The 1884 campaign inspired the production of more portrait glass souvenirs than did any other electoral contest. Of not insignificant artistic merit are two more portraits of Blaine and Logan that appear *vis-à-vis* on an oval platter — another addition to our list (*Fig. 4*). Certain similarities in the modeling suggest the possibility that the original of these portraits might likewise have been prepared by Jacobus, though the work is not signed and nothing more than a guess may be hazarded.

A companion piece to the Harrison and Morton rectangular plaque previously illustrated depicts Grover Cleveland and Allen G. Thurman, defeated candidates in the campaign of 1888 (*Fig. 5*). Both plaques have an ivy-leaf border matching the Cleveland-Hendricks and Blaine-Logan trays of 1884. The portrait of Cleveland on the 1888 plate appears to be identical with that of the 1884 item. The thrifty glassmaker must have used the Cleveland half of the 1884 mold as model for the 1888 mold, unless perchance he actually used half of the old mold, welded to a new half portraying the new running mate.

The final Cleveland item is a round plate with a labeled portrait in the center, and the word *Reform* in the dewdrop border (*Fig. 6*). This is another campaign item, probably issued in connection with the election of 1884, though Cleveland was likewise Democratic candidate in 1888 and 1892. Throughout his political career his battle cry was reform, political and economic. In 1884, however, he was elected on a platform calling for radical reforms in the administrative departments, the civil service, the tariff, and national finances.

The only Bryan glass thus far noted is a covered cup, companion to a McKinley cup, issued in connection with the campaign of 1896. A second Bryan item, labeled with the words *Our Candidates*, portrays W. J. Bryan and J. W. Kern, an American

eagle, and a crowing cock (*Fig. 7*). John Worth Kern was Democratic candidate for vice president in 1908, running with Bryan in the latter's third unsuccessful attempt to win the presidency. This plate, then, portraying both candidates, with the national bird and the Democratic rooster, is one of the latest items in the group under consideration.

PORTRAITS OF OTHER CELEBRITIES

The non-presidential celebrities include naval and military heroes, foreign rulers, religious notables, and other figures who came momentarily or repeatedly before the public eye. Just as the presidential items may be classified as memorials and campaign items, this pictorial glass may be divided into two groups: memorials, issued following the death of the subject; and souvenirs, issued at the time of some event in which the subject was primarily involved. The number of Europeans commemorated on American glass is worth remarking — for there is little doubt that all the pieces here illustrated are of American manufacture. Like the presidential glass, they date from the 1880's and 1890's, with one late item of 1908.

Three heroes of the Spanish-American War found favor with the glass manufacturers. John Coalter Bates (*1842-1919*), who had served in the United States Infantry during the Civil War, was in May 1898 appointed brigadier general of volunteers for the war with Spain. In July of the same year he was promoted to the rank of major general in recognition of his services in the Santiago campaign, and in February 1899 was made military governor of the Cuban province of Santa Clara. He later gained distinction in the Philippines, where he was stationed from 1899 to 1906. It seems likely that the two-handled glass plate on which his portrait is framed in concentric borders signalized his achievement in Cuba in 1898 (*Fig. 8*).

Another Civil War veteran was the soldier and diplomat, Fitzhugh Lee (*1835-1905*), nephew of Robert E. Lee, who served the Confederacy until the end of the war, when he retired. From 1886 to 1890 he was governor of Virginia. In 1896 he became consul general to Cuba, and in 1898, major general of United States volunteers. Like General Bates, he was appointed military governor of a Cuban province after the war. His portrait on a round glass plate against a background of stars and stripes was probably likewise issued in 1898, in recognition of a Southerner's service to the Union (*Fig. 9*).

The hero of Manila Bay deserved a handsomer tribute than he received. Admiral Dewey's countenance appears on glass only once, so far as I have been able to discover. That is on a

FIG. 5 (*right*) — CLEVELAND AND THURMAN RECTANGULAR PLAQUE (*1888*)
Companion to Harrison and Morton plaque. Ivy-leaf border like that of Cleveland-Hendricks and Blaine-Logan trays. Each portrait stamped with subject's name. A campaign item. *From the collection of Mrs. Lucien Nelson Lindsey*

FIG. 6 — CLEVELAND PLATE (*1884*)
Stiff portrait bust. Dewdrop border. Probably a campaign item

FIG. 7 — BRYAN AND KERN PLATTER (*1896*)
Stars-and-stripes border. Bust portraits. American eagle and Democratic rooster. Obviously a campaign item. *From the collection of Mrs. Lucien Nelson Lindsey*

tumbler, whose stippled surface is likewise embellished with a spread eagle, American flags, and mounds of cannon balls (*Fig. 10*). This item, too, is almost certainly of 1898, the year of Dewey's Manila Bay achievement.

A final naval souvenir is an oval platter bearing portraits of Admirals Sperry and Evans above a watery waste traversed by a procession of battleships. The words *The Pacific Fleet/Souvenir 1908* in the border identify the dish (*Fig. 11*). In 1908 President Roosevelt sent the United States battleship fleet as "heralds of peace" on a round-the-world tour. Admiral Robley Dunglison Evans (*1846-1912*), affectionately known as "fighting Bob," started the

FIG. 8 (*left*) — GENERAL BATES TWO-HANDLED PLATE (*1898*)
Vine and beaded border. Bust portrait

FIG. 9 (*below, left*) — GENERAL LEE PLATE (*1898*)
Openwork border. Bust portrait against background of stars and stripes

FIG. 10 (*below, center*) — ADMIRAL DEWEY TUMBLER (*1898*)
Medallion portrait, framed in laurel wreath, surmounted by eagle; flags and cannon balls on either side. Body of tumbler stippled below rope border. No plate or platter commemorating the hero of Manila is known

FIG. 11 (*below, right*) — UNITED STATES FLEET PLATTER (*1908*)
Stippled border with laurel branches. Bust portraits of Admirals Sperry and Evans, who commanded the battleship fleet on its round-the-world good-will cruise in 1908.
From the collection of Mrs. Lucien Nelson Lindsey

voyage as commander-in-chief of the fleet. After rounding Cape Horn and reaching San Francisco, however, he was forced by ill health to relinquish his command. He was succeeded by Rear Admiral Charles Stillman Sperry (*1847–1911*), who had commanded the Second Squadron of the United States battleship fleet on the first lap of the round-the-world cruise under Evans' full command.

At least two foreign rulers were portrayed in glass, Kaiser Wilhelm I and Queen Victoria. Wilhelm, the first German emperor, was born in 1797, became seventh king of Prussia in 1861, and during the siege of Paris in 1871 was proclaimed emperor. It was doubtless following his death in 1888 that the glass memorial was issued (*Fig. 12*). Victoria, who was born in 1819 and throned in 1837, celebrated her long rule with a Golden Jubilee in 1887 and a Diamond Jubilee in 1897. The compote on which a medallion portrait of Victoria appears may have been made for either Jubilee, though probability favors the latter (*Fig. 13*). A more youthful portrait of the Queen appears on a bread plate whose border carries the arms of Great Britain, the thistle of Scotland, and the rose of England (*Fig. 14*). A variant of this plate was published in Antiques for October 1928 (*p. 354*).

Religious leaders, Protestant, Catholic, and Jewish, were commemorated on glass. The Henry Ward Beecher plate was probably issued in 1887, when the beloved Congregational minister died (*Fig. 15*). Born in 1813, he was from 1847 until his death pastor of Plymouth Congregational Church in Brooklyn, New York. His fame and influence were more than nation wide. Leo XIII was born in 1810, became Pope in 1878, and died in 1903. The plate bearing his portrait with papal emblems was probably, however, not produced in one of those years but in 1893 (*Fig. 16*). In that year Monsignor Satolli was appointed first permanent apostolic delegate to the United States, sent to quell opposition within the Catholic Church which had arisen following his two previous missions to this country. Sir Moses Montefiore, whose portrait appears on a third plate of religious significance, was a well-known Jewish philanthropist,

FIG. 12 (*above*) — WILHELM I PLATE (*1888*)
Square plate with notched corners. Laurel border

FIG. 13 (*above, right*) — VICTORIA JUBILEE COMPOTE (*probably 1897*)
Medallion portrait of Queen Victoria. Floral and beaded pattern

FIG. 14 (*right*) — VICTORIA JUBILEE TWO-HANDLED PLATE (*probably 1897*)
Youthful portrait of Queen Victoria in central sunburst medallion. Emblematic border.
From the collection of Mrs. Nathan Edstein

born in Italy in 1784 of a wealthy Anglo-Italian banking family. After retiring from business in 1824, he devoted himself to the Jewish cause. He worked chiefly in Poland, Russia, Roumania, and Damascus. In 1846 he was knighted and raised to a baronetcy. Still hale and hearty after a full century, he died in 1885 at the age of one hundred and one. His memorial plate bearing his portrait and name was probably produced shortly afterward (*Fig. 17*).

The year 1892 marked the four-hundredth anniversary of the discovery of America by Christopher Columbus. Quite naturally the occasion was observed by at least two glass manufacturers (*Fig. 19*). Both Columbus portrait items are marked with the dates *1492–1892* and the name *Columbus*. One of them is the only reported portrait piece that occurs in other than clear glass. It is found in milk white as well as blue.

The celebrity series is completed, so far as present information goes, by the Nellie Bly platter (*Fig. 18*). Nellie Bly was a pseudonym given Elizabeth Cochrane (*1867–1922*) by the managing editor of the Pittsburgh *Dispatch*, where she began her sensational journalistic career about 1881. After writing *Six Months in Mexico* and a series of articles on working girls' tribulations in Pittsburgh mills, she joined the staff of the New York *World*, and in 1887 startled the country with an exposé

FIG. 15 (*left*) — HENRY WARD BEECHER PLATE (*1887*)
Serrate rim; leaf border with initials *H.W.B.* A memorial item

FIG. 16 (*center*) — LEO XIII PLATE (*probably 1893*)
Profile bust. Beaded border with religious emblems in the reserves

FIG. 17 (*right*) — MONTEFIORE PLATE (*1885*)
Serrate rim; stippled border with leaves. A memorial plate

FIG. 18 — NELLIE BLY PLATTER (*1890*)
Commemorating her globe-circling trip

FIG. 19 — TWO COLUMBUS PLATES (*1892*)
Left, wheel border; profile bust portrait. *Right*, blue glass: the only colored item here illustrated; openwork border. Bust portrait. An apparently identical example in milk-white glass has likewise been reported, in the collection of Miss Elizabeth Meating of Appleton, Wisconsin

titled *Ten Days in the Mad House.* Six doctors had declared her insane and committed her to the insane ward at Blackwell's Island. Two years later her managing editor conceived the idea of beating the "record" of Jules Verne's Phileas Fogg by sending her around the world in less than eighty days. Her account of the trip, including an interview with Jules Verne in Amiens, France, built circulation for her newspaper. She herself became for a time a symbol of feminism, and mighty debates raged over the question of career versus home for women. "Nellie Bly" married Robert L. Seaman, aged and wealthy Brooklyn manufacturer, in 1895, and when he died in 1904 she assumed management of his properties. Later impoverished by protracted litigation, she returned to newspaper work on the New York *Journal*, which she continued until her death in 1922. An inscription on the glass platter summarizes her main achievement: *AROUND THE WORLD IN 72 D'S. 6 H'S. 11 M'S. NEW YORK NOV. 14, 89. SOUTHAMPTON NOV. 22. BRINDISI NOV. 24. SUEZ NOV. 27. COLOMBO DEC. 18. HONG KONG DEC. 23. YOKOHAMA DEC. 28. SAN FRANCISCO JAN. 21, 90. CHICAGO JAN. 24. PITTSBURG JAN. 25. NEW YORK JAN. 25.* The platter was undoubtedly issued in 1890, shortly after Nellie Bly's triumphal return to New York.

Among the Latest Things in Glass

From notes and illustrations supplied by NELLE B. ROBINSON

SLAG glass — more politely known as agate glass — has been favored for some years past by certain collectors of things Victorian. Such ware appears to have been manufactured by the Sowerbys at Gateshead near Newcastle, and at the Sandwich works on Cape Cod. Likewise, no doubt, the glasshouses in the Pittsburgh district, and farther to the westward, contributed to the general production.

According to Fredrick Carder, art director of the Corning Glass Works at Corning, New York, this type of glass was made from the slag acquired from blast iron furnaces or cupolas manufacturing cast iron. "Such slag," Mr. Carder writes, "was very fusible. When to some of this material was added cryolite and a little manganese, the mixture, when remelted, afforded a variety of curious color combinations.

"Cryolite, a soft, fusible fluoride, imparts to glass that dense whiteness apparent in American so-called 'cast porcelain'; 'vitro-porcelain' it was called in England. By employing cryolite to temper the shade of a dark material — black, brown, or red — various results could be obtained. Manganese with the white of cryolite would help give chocolate and reddish-brown tones."

That a variety of slag glass emphasizing the caramel and chocolate tints noted by Mr. Carder was made between the years 1900 and 1903 in Greentown, Indiana, has recently been discovered by Mrs. Nelle B. Robinson of Indianapolis, who spent no little time and trouble in verifying her facts. The combination of materials used in obtaining these particular caramel and chocolate effects, and the method of so handling them as to secure diverse chromatic intensities, were the invention of an old-time glassworker, Jacob Rosenthal by name. Mr. Rosenthal likewise suggested ideas for the patterns employed, though the actual making of these patterns was entrusted to one "Baldy" Jackson, recently deceased in Newark, Ohio.

Jacob Rosenthal was born in Pittsburgh, May 11, 1855, and began to learn his trade in that city at the early age of eleven years, when he found work in a glass factory operated by

Fig. 1 — CHOCOLATE BUTTER DISH
This and other pieces illustrated made at Greentown, Indiana, 1901–1903

Campbell, Jones and Company. In 1874, the year of his marriage, he was occupied at Bridgeport, Ohio, whence, in 1889, he went to Anderson, Indiana, to join forces with the American Glass Company. In 1899, following a merger of several glass concerns into the National Company, he was given the management of a factory at Greentown, where he remained until 1906. Thereafter, until his death not long ago, he lived in Williamstown, West Virginia.

It was during his stay in Greentown that Mr. Rosenthal, according to his own account, developed what he called "chocolate" and "golden agate" glass, from a secret formula. For two and one half years (*1901–1903*) three fourths of the Greentown factory output was chocolate glass, which was made in table sets, water sets, berry sets, creamers and sugar bowls, and such desirable novelty forms as toothpick and match holders in the shape of a dog's head, an old woman's head, a sheaf of wheat, a dolphin, and so on. Beer mugs were also on the novelty list. Following his retirement to Williamstown, where he was associated with the Fenton Glass Company, Mr. Rosenthal permitted the use of his chocolate formula, but the accompanying production was limited. The golden agate, never in copious supply, was made during a brief period only — about six months — and solely in Greentown.

Examples of the ware are almost unmistakable. But apart from the information secured by Mrs. Robinson, their dating would

Fig. 2 — GOLDEN-AGATE PITCHER AND CHOCOLATE COMPOTE

be virtually impossible. It is difficult to associate such forms and such ornament with the dawn of the twentieth century in America. Yet it must be remembered that these designs were not created by trained artists bent on finding patterns specially suited to a peculiar material, but by the factory folk themselves — a common practice today, as well as yesterday, in many American industries. While some details of ornament, notably in the cactus tumbler, betray a search for fresh motives, the majority recall the fancies of various earlier periods. Hence the confusion that examples of the glass in question might easily engender in the mind of the student of style.

Fig. 3 — CHOCOLATE MATCH HOLDER

Fig. 4 — TUMBLERS, PITCHER, CUP, AND BERRY DISH IN CHOCOLATE AND GOLDEN AGATE

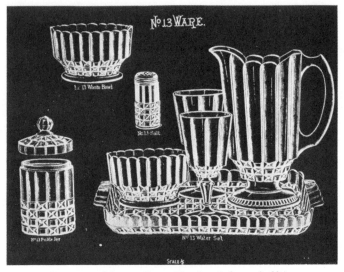

Fig. 1 — PATTERN IN MARBLE GLASS (*decades of 1870 and 1880*)
All illustrations are from the catalogue of Challinor, Taylor & Company.
Originally known as *mosaic*. Later listed merely as *No. 13 ware*

Fig. 2 — PATTERN IN MARBLE GLASS (*decades of 1870 and 1880*)
"Made in colors, crystal & mosaic," and in the dense white which was
called "opal" by the manufacturer

Mosaic Glass and Other Types

By RUTH WEBB LEE

Editor's Note. Glass vessels exhibiting irregular striations of white and colored metal resembling the veinings of agate were made long prior to the Christian era. A superb Roman urn of the type, probably dating from the first century A.D., was shown in the Metropolitan Museum special exhibition of glass held from October 13 to November 29, 1936. It is pictured as Number 5 in the catalogue of the event. Pazaurek in his *Gläser der Empire- und Biedermeierzeit* illustrates opposite 274 a vase of what he calls "lithyalinglas," which he ascribes to the 1830's. Probably a Bohemian product, the vase exhibits a blue-gray hue broken with agatelike streaks of yellow and russet whose aspect despite the vitreous material recalls the finely scroddled earthenware of Whieldon. The marble glass described by Mrs. Lee represents but a later phase of the same effort to produce a vitreous substance that would resemble a semiprecious stone.

The term "slag" by which the marbled glass material is often named is appropriate. On that topic ANTIQUES for August 1933 quoted from Frederick Carder, art director of the Corning Glass Works, to the following effect: The slag acquired from furnaces manufacturing cast iron is highly fusible. When to this slag were added cryolite and a little manganese, the mixture, when remelted, afforded a variety of curious color combinations. Cryolite imparts to glass that dense whiteness apparent in American so-called cast porcelain (the late type of

milk-white glass). Again, by employing cryolite to temper the shade of a dark material various results could be obtained.

By what technique the clearly marked stratifications of marbled glass were obtained no reference work at hand explains. The old-time agate or scroddled effects of earthenware were achieved by building up a loaf of clay layer by layer of different colors, then folding and refolding the loaf until these layers were satisfactorily intermingled. Slices were then cut from the slab and shaped according to the potter's fancy. Dribbling random portions of varicolored glass into a mold and subjecting the mass to piston pressure would obviously achieve a similar result.

For some reason, cryolite glass, either white or marbled, takes a much sharper impression from the mold than does so-called crystal of whatever quality. Of this fact American and English manufacturers of the 1870's and 1880's were well aware and, in consequence, achieved some patterns of real distinction. On the whole, it is surprising that present-day manufacturers of pressed wares have thus far failed to develop fresh possibilities in the same material.

As for the dates of the wares described by Mrs. Lee, they probably fall within the 1870's and 1880's. The registry mark on an English item of the type published in ANTIQUES for January 1934 (*p. 34*) is for the year 1877. —H. E. K.

F OR years past, many collectors have found much to admire in what they called *End of the Day* glass. They liked the ware itself, and they liked the romantic implications of the name. *End of the Day* glass, they devoutly believed, was the workman's own product, turned out after factory hours and owing its odd mixture of hues to the custom of throwing together the varied batches of unused metal remaining in the glass pots when the shop bell sounded quitting hour and the knell of parting day. That so charming a legend should be popularly accepted is by no means strange. That it is purely a figment of the imagination untainted by even the faintest trace of fact is also by no means strange. What would a host of collectors do if they were deprived of fairytales?

Now for the prosaic truth. The glass in question was made by Challinor, Taylor & Company of Tarentum, Pennsylvania, at one of the factories in what, during the 1880's, was known as "the old Pittsburgh glass district." The firm's name for the ware was *mosaic*. In course of time, however, this original trade designation was forgotten and mosaic glass became variously known in different sections of the country as *slag, calico, end of the day*, and *marble* glass. At present it is called *marble* by virtually all collectors and dealers. Unfortunately, it was not until after publishing the first edition of my *Early American Pressed Glass* that I found an old trade catalogue of Challinor, Taylor & Company

containing illustrations of this and other popular types of the period.

From the first, mosaic glass must have been highly esteemed or the number of pieces — the "line," as the old trade lists had it — would not have included so great a variety of forms. It was a difficult glass to manufacture. An old workman of the Tarentum factory assured me that considerable difficulty was encountered in making the purple part adhere to the white. Those familiar with this ware know how very brittle it is. Many dishes have been found with bubbles, sand, and other flaws. I have been told that some of the marble-glass goblets are prone to leak, not because of breakage of the pieces but because of a lack of cohesion in the material itself.

The *end of the day* legend should die a speedy death, since it is well known that the *mosaic* of the 1880's was a carefully prepared mixture of dense purple and dense white glass, which, in the process of heating, assumed the rich shadings now so popular. If leftover metal in the pots, with all its impurities, had been used, the result would not have been a combination of purple and white.

Marble glass has become extremely popular because of its decorative value in table settings. Indeed, the supply is inadequate to meet the demand, and the highest prices ever brought by goblets in American pattern glass are now being paid for the fluted marble pattern illustrated above in Figure 1.

Fig. 3 — OPAL WARE
A dense jadelike white, impressed with an exceptionally well-designed floral pattern of oriental implications

Fig. 4 — OPAL BARNYARD FOWL
These came with or without inserted eyes of colored glass. The same designs were naturalistically colored with thinly applied enamels

Marble glass was also made in England. In addition to the large, open-edged plate made by Challinor, Taylor & Company, there is an English eight-inch size, on the reverse of which appears the peacock head, mark of Sowerby, Neville, and Sowerby, now Sowerby's Ellison Glass Works, Ltd., near Newcastle, England. The English pieces may be recognized by peculiarities difficult to describe accurately. These consist chiefly in a special manner of shading the colors, probably due to a method of manufacture, differing from that employed in America. Many odd little English pieces in various marbleized effects are also to be found.

An all-over flowered pattern was also made during the same period by Challinor, Taylor & Company. A table set is shown in Figure 2. While this is an attractive design, it has not quite the charm of the fluted pattern, though a set of it makes an unusual table display. Challinor, Taylor & Company also turned out another all-over flowered pattern in milk white, so excellent in design and quality that for years it was attributed to English makers. However, it has been definitely established as an American product. In Figure 3 is pictured a bowl familiar to many collectors. It comes in opaque white painted in natural colors, as well as in color. A large round covered jar in opaque jade-green in the same design was recently found. When tapped, the glass responds with a clear bell tone, unusual in the general run of milk-white glass.

The catalogue referred to exhibits a number of large plates with open edges (*Figs. 5 and 6*). Some of these exhibit floral designs in color. I have been asked whether such plates can have been made in this country and then sent to Bristol, England, to receive their decoration.

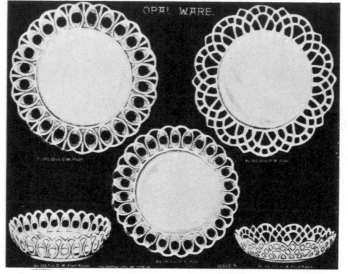

Fig. 5 — OPAL-WARE PLATES WITH OPEN-WORK BORDERS
Sometimes these plates were used as plaques adorned with homemade oil paintings, and made still more dreadful by a ribbon run through the open border. Hung on the parlor wall, they intensified the violence of the red or electric-blue plush furniture coverings

Fig. 6 — OPAL-WARE PLATE
Assorted decorations, either printed or printed in outline and hand colored

Since the applied patterns seem to be partly printed and partly hand-colored and of no special value from any standpoint, the possibility that they were executed outside the Tarentum factory may be dismissed without further consideration.

Gaily featured in the same catalogue is an assortment of barnyard fowl — roosters, swans, and ducks, in white as well as painted in flamboyant colors. The old turkey jar is also there, in clear glass as well as in clear glass with applied colors. Perfect reproductions of these turkey jars are in the market. I find no record that the bright-green and amber glass specimens now on sale were made in earlier days. It might be well to note here that the Challinor, Taylor & Company fowl illustrated are mostly in large sizes. The greatest number of the five-inch covered hen and rooster dishes were made by Charles West of the Westmoreland Glass Company in Grapeville, Pennsylvania. He sold them originally in carload lots, filled with prepared mustard, at ten cents apiece. One of these hen dishes bearing the label of the Westmoreland Specialty Company is in my collection.

Some of the earliest of the open-edge plates in both opaque-white and black glass were made by Challinor, Taylor & Company. Other factories also made them. At one time, they were called "stamp" plates, because the owners used to cover them with canceled postage stamps. Dealers also find them today with extraordinary decorations of flowers or animals painted in oils. A bath in a strong solution of sal soda overnight will remove the artist's efforts. Other early plates of this type during the 1870's came from the Atterbury Glass Company. These have an *A* embossed in the centre of the bottom.

GLASS AT WORLD'S FAIRS

By HELEN McKEARIN

FROM the beginning of glassblowing it has seemed little short of miraculous that from a molten mass of metal a blower's breath, nicety of judgment, manual dexterity, and feeling for form could create beautiful and useful objects. So it is scarcely remarkable that from the first World's Fair, London's *Industry of all Nations* held in 1851, to New York's 1939 *World of Tomorrow*, table and decorative wares and new, ingenious applications of glass have impressed a marveling public.

The miracle of the first World's Fair was the Crystal Palace itself. A building of glass would cause little comment today, but in 1851 it seemed a fascinating architectural innovation too fragile to be practical. "The first impression conveyed to the mind" was "a sense of insecurity arising from the apparent lightness of its supports compared with the vastness of its dimensions." Hence it was little wonder that a building whose ground floor area was 772,784 square feet and whose roof and walls were almost entirely of glass should arouse fears for its stability. But once it was realized that London Bridge was no safer, Britishers were calmly proud of their engineering achievement and visitors were conscious only of its "faerie" charm. Even more astounding to the public and glassmakers of the day was the almost unbelievable great crystal fountain manufactured by F. & C. Osler of Birmingham. *Four tons* of "pure crystal glass" were required to form its huge basin, two large dishes with their faceted canopies, and the central shaft, 27 feet in height. The annealing, transportation, and assembling of the fountain were in themselves a noteworthy accomplishment. Comments of the day indicate that this glass fountain became the symbol of the Fair of 1851 as the perisphere and trylon are of the Fair of 1939.

Literally hundreds of the 1851 exhibits included or consisted solely of glass. Almost every foreign country showed some glass, and England, where the industry was attaining new heights, had one hundred exhibits. One could see examples of nearly every type of article, method of manufacture, and decoration known at the time. Besides a "great variety of glass too tedious to insert" here, many items were shown which indicated trends modern enough to be surprising today. Among them were "patent pressed" clear and colored window glass; "patent model windows fitted with different qualities of perforated plate and sheet glass for ventilation"; a portable glass pavilion for lawns; pole fire screens; "panels for church altars, ceilings etc."; table tops; water pipes; "registered model of a percolator"; "opaque plates of glass, substitutes for marble in furniture etc."; chess tables, and Venetian blinds.

The majority of displays, however, were of table and ornamental wares in an amazing range of decorative effects, forms, and colors. One saw opal, alabaster, turquoise, amber, canary, topaz, chrysoprase, pink, blue, light and dark ruby, black, brown, green, purple, and Pomona green; crystal and ruby predominated. If one may judge from the quantity shown, glass ornamented either by cutting or engraving enjoyed the greatest popularity in 1851, and, according to English standards, was the most meritorious in design. Colorful cased (overlay) glass was a close second in favor. In this category, as might be expected, the examples of Bohemian glass from Austria were considered the most skillfully executed and spectacular. Gilded, painted, and enameled wares and frosted and Venetian glass shared about equal popularity. Two innovations attracted considerable attention. One was an exhibit by William Kidd, inventor and manufacturer, demonstrating "his new process for illuminating, embroidering and silvering flat surfaces in glass" whereby designs engraved on the underside of the glass appeared to be in high relief on the outer surface. The other, of "glass silvered by Hale Thompson's process, a recent development in glass making" was apparently of the type of glass we call mercury. Only one firm, Rice, Harris & Son, proprietors of the Islington Glass Works of Birmingham, showed pressed glass. Besides fine glass this firm displayed pressed tumblers, goblets, wines, sugar basins, butter coolers, salt cellars, honey pots and doorknobs.

At a time when our glass industry was expanding it seems unaccountable that among the many foreign exhibits there were only three of American glass. Perhaps the explanation lies in the fact that, unlike other foreign governments, ours gave no aid to exhibitors. Regarding this policy Benjamin P. Johnson, New York State agent to the exhibition, made this comment: "It is not by any means certain but that the influence of our exhibition has been far better upon the world, has more powerfully demonstrated the peculiar advantages of the energies of the people, than could have been done if the Government had made a large appropriation for the purpose of preparing articles especially for the exhibition . . . the character of our articles was such as to show the world that we worked for the great masses, not for the luxurious and privileged few."

Be that as it may, the jury on glass awarded a prize for "cut flint glass" to the Brooklyn Flint Glass Company. The basis for awards was not competitive, but comparative with a standard approved by the jury. One English critic remarked "The Brooklyn Flint Glass Company (American) have contributed creditable specimens of cut glass but the metal itself is not so pure as ours." Another said, "The American glass . . . was pre-eminent for its brillancy." And the pride of a native son found the expression in the account of Charles T. Rodgers of Louisiana, who wrote: "None exceed in beauty the contribution of the Brooklyn Flint Glass Company . . . What particularly distinguishes this is its surpassing whiteness which with its dazzling brillancy has given it, where elaborately cut articles are sought as proofs of taste and munificence, a fame that has conferred on the company quite a monopoly on this continent."

The other two American exhibitors were Cornelius & Company of Philadelphia and John Lee Chapman, of the Maryland Glass Works, Baltimore, established in 1849 for the manufacture of window glass and bottles. Cornelius & Company exhibited two chandeliers, 24 damask solar lamps, and 7 olive solar lamps. The compiler of the official catalogue gave no hint as to the nature of Chapman's contribution, but stated in connection with that of Cornelius & Company: "These castings and glasses are the product of a branch of manufacture less than 20 years old in the United States. Up to the year 1830 the whole trade in chandeliers was in the hands of foreign importers. These lamps are an American invention adapted to the use of lard and lard oil." The two chandeliers won praise but no prize. Nevertheless, for two exhibits out of three to receive high praise speaks well for American glass manufacture.

The tremendous success of the London international exhibition so impressed some adventurous American businessmen that by 1852, in spite of vigorous opposition, preparations for an American World's Fair were going on apace. It was argued that "one of the great lessons taught on that occasion was the capacity of the masses to appreciate and enjoy the pleasures which flow from refined culture in whatever direction." But the selling factor was the great financial success of the London venture. In expectation of large dividends the group persisted in the face of many discouragements, and July 14, 1853, a Crystal Palace in New York City was formally opened. It was a pocket edition of the London Crystal Palace — and a financial failure.

The exhibits of glass, while pitifully few in number compared with the hundreds in London, were comprehensive in content. More foreign glass manufactures were represented than American: Holland sent two window-glass exhibits; Germany, four displays consisting largely of fancy articles and small objects such as buttons, beads, hairpins; England, seven, mostly of window glass and industrial wares and just a few fine objects; France, six, of which

FIG. 1 — FIVE GLASS EXHIBITS AT WORLD'S FAIRS OF YESTERDAY

Left column, three prize-winning pieces exhibited in 1851 by the Brooklyn Flint Glass Works. According to the official catalogue, this firm "contributed a well-filled stand. . . . There is enough novelty of form in these works to assure us that our transatlantic brethren are fully aware of the mercantile value of Art." *Top right*, decanter shown at the 1853 Crystal Palace in New York City by Joseph Stouvenel & Company of New York. *Center*, "chili cup" of cut glass and silver exhibited at the 1876 Philadelphia exposition by Reed & Barton of Taunton, Massachusetts. It won a prize at the Chilean Exposition; hence the name. This epergne was described in the catalogue, "light and airy . . . filled with fruit and flowers, there could hardly be a more chaste or elegant centre-piece for a table." With which sentiments we beg to differ

Chili Cup: Reed & Barton, Taunton, Mass

two were of table and ornamental wares; and Austria, seven, of which only one consisted of fine wares and the others principally of small objects such as beads, buttons, and luster pendants. The finest table and ornamental glass was represented by the "noteworthy chandeliers" of Apsley Pellatt & Company, a famous English firm; the superb cut, engraved, cased, and gilded wares contributed by J. Maes, Gallerie de Clichy, France; and the "magnificent display of frosted, cased, and gilded glass" of E. Stanier, Austria. Had it not been for these exhibits it might have seemed that foreign guests were unaware that window glass was a common article of our manufacture and that we no longer needed such knickknacks as beads to trade with the Indians.

There were few American exhibits of glass. One showing in the United States group was by Berger & Walter, apparently a French firm with a branch in New York City. Also from New York were watch crystals shown by C. M. Bodine, Manufacturer; decorated and lettered wares especially for druggists by Frederick Hale & Company and A. G. Brandon; and a ruby-glass plate, cut with designs representing the arms of the United States contributed by Philip Smith. There were five exhibits of stained and painted glass — four of them individual items. "New machine engraved and etched ornamental window glass" manufactured by Cooper & Belcher, Camptown, New Jersey, was incorporated in the window of the west gallery. "Druggist glassware of all description, preserve and pickle jars, flasks; windowglass; ink bottles; wine bottles etc." were shown by Baker & Brothers of Baltimore; a firm of jobbers who early in 1853 had become manufacturers. Extensive displays of table and ornamental wares which not only maintained but enhanced our reputation for fine glass were contributed by Messrs. Joseph Stouvenel & Company of New York, the Brooklyn Flint Glass Company of Brooklyn, and the New England Glass Company of Boston. Clear, beautiful metal and skilled workmanship characterized the "great variety of glassware both pressed and cut from the manufactory of Messrs Joseph Stouvenel & Company." One is informed by contemporary critics that "The Brooklyn Flint Glass Company and the New England Glass Company are the largest manufactures, and their display of dioptric signal lamps, and of plain, pressed, and cut and decorated glass ware, is decidedly creditable to this country. The American flint glass is distinguished by its brilliancy and the purity of its color, and that of the New England Glass Company is the best pressed glass probably ever manufactured."

Although few in number the exhibits of table and decorative wares at New York's Crystal Palace were as representative of the types of articles, methods of manufacture, and various forms of ornamentation popular here and abroad as those of London's Crystal Palace. In fact, with very few exceptions, the forms, colors, and decoration were the same as those shown in 1851. No matter where it was made, the glass was "Victorian" in design.

Our next important World's Fair was the 1876 centennial celebration in Philadelphia. In the main building were over one hundred exhibits of glass, not including glass combined with metal. The groups of various types were so large that they were divided into classes: Class 214 — Glass used in construction and for mirrors, window glass, and plate glass; Class 215 — Chemical and pharmaceutical glassware, vials, and bottles; Class 216 — Decorated glassware.

The official catalogue of the fair lists 69 exhibits from 11 foreign countries: The Argentine Republic (1), Brazil (2), Norway (2), Sweden (2), Canada (1), Great Britain (6), France (6), Belgium (24), Austria (23), Portugal and Italy, the last two apparently including glass in their collective exhibits. Assorted glassware was contributed by the Burlington Glass Company of Hamilton, Canada. The decorative glassware of Argentina, Brazil, and Norway was represented by one exhibit from each country; three from France, and two from Belgium. England's fine glass was seen in small contributions from two firms, which, considering the importance of the industry, caused bitter comment among

Americans. Austria had seventeen large exhibits of fine table and decorative glass.

A discrepancy occurs between the official catalogue list of American exhibitors and the official list of awards, the latter including some firms not mentioned in the former. There were, however, at least forty-five displays of American glass. The list of awards is annoying in its lack of detailed descriptions but, since it contains interesting information, it is given here:

Albertson, J. M. Norristown, Pa.
Award for glass shades.

Atterbury & Co. Pittsburg
Award for lime glass lamp chimneys and globes.

Boston & Sandwich Glass Co. Manufacturers of cut glass.
Award. Showed "rich cut glass ware of every description including the 'Daniel Webster punch bowl',"

Bakewell, Pears & Co. Pittsburg, Pa.
Award for moulded glass tablewares. (Also showed blown crystal and opal glass ware.)

Central Glass Co. Wheeling, W. Virginia.
Award for lime glass pressed ware.

Cohansey Glass Manufacturing Co. Bridgeton, N. J.
Award. Showed cylinder window glass, bottles, vial and demijohns.

Dobleman, J. B. Greenpoint. (Long Island)
Award for flint cut and engraved tableware.

Dorflinger Glass Co. White Mills, Wayne Co., Pa.
Award for glass tablewares

Geo. Duncan & Sons, Pittsburg
Award for limeglass tablewares.

Excelsior Flint Glass Co. Pittsburg
Award. Showed lamp chimneys, silvered glass reflectors.

Fox, H. C. & Sons, Philadelphia
Award for druggist's and perfumers' glass wares.

Gillinder & Sons, Philadelphia
Award for flint glass ware

Hobbs, J. H. Brockunier & Co., Wheeling, W. Virginia.
Award for lime glass tablewares.

Keystone Flint Glass Co. Pittsburg
Award for pure lead lamp glasses. Showed silvered glassware also.

La Belle Glass Co., Bridgeport, Ohio
Award for glass tablewares moulded. Showed cut and engraved also.

Louisville Plate Glass Co. Louisville, Ky.
Award for plate glass.

Mount Washington Glass Works
Award for lime glass tablewares, chandeliers and bone glass.

C. Newman & Co. San Francisco, Cal.
Award for demijohns covered with packing.

New England Glass Co. Boston
Award for flint glass tablewares and decorative pieces.

O'Hara Glass Co. Pittsburg
Award for lime glass tablewares

Rochester Tumbler Co. Pittsburg
Award for tumblers.

Smith Bros. New Bedford, Mass.
Award for opal and bone glass lamp shades

Whitall, Tatum & Co. Millville, N. J.
Award for Chemists, Druggists and Perfumers wares of lime and green glass.

Among the American exhibits not receiving awards were two from old glasshouses — glass shades, monuments, and cylinders from the Union Glass Works, Somerville, Massachusetts, and "green and colored glass ware for druggists etc." from the factory of Whitney Brothers, Glassboro, New Jersey.

American table and ornamental glass, even though it received many awards, seems to have been far less exciting and impressive

to the historians of the Fair than the English cut and engraved crystal and the extensive Austrian exhibits. From the "elegant specimens" of cut glass of the Mount Washington Glass Works one writer did illustrate a candelabrum of a "prismatic character" showing the progress made in the "last thirty years." And several praised a glass chandelier by Mitchell Vance & Company of New York; likewise a chili cup and epergne of glass and silver and a lemonade set shown by Reed & Barton. The glass, undoubtedly of American manufacture, used in the overelaborated chili cup and epergne was deeply cut flint glass, while that of the lemonade set was of flint glass too richly ornamented with birds and flowers.

The Austrian glass commanded, as usual, the greatest attention and highest praise, but the crystal of James Green and Nephew of London and J. Millar & Company of Edinburgh made a deep and favorable impression on contemporary critics. The products of these two firms "excelled in quality of flint and skill in engraved and cut decoration." Extravagant praise was bestowed upon a chandelier and a crystal pitcher from the Green display elaborately engraved on one side with a depiction of Saint George and the Dragon and having a remarkable "filigree handle enameled and gilded." In better taste, according to present-day standards, were the crystal decanters and epergne, the latter "noteworthy for lightness and delicacy of design," from the Millar collection.

Among the Austrian exhibitors were Count Von Harrach, who exhibited, as in 1851, typical Bohemian glassware, and Heinrich Ullrich of Vienna, who showed "glass articles especially adapted for the United States of America." In the opinion of contemporary critics the outstanding glass not only of the Austrian groups but of the entire exhibition was that shown by J. & L. Lobmeyr of Vienna. Besides characteristic Bohemian styles of cased glass enhanced with gilding, this firm presented glass in the Venetian tradition and crystal, particularly engraved tableware which was considered unusually fine. The most incredible piece in their display was an elaborate vase and pedestal of chaste classical form, ruined, esthetically, by extravagant ornamentation — "richness of color, gilding, high relief and delicate tracery of intricate design."

A comparison of the glass of 1876 with that of 1851 and 1853 reveals a number of interesting and of deplorable developments. Production of industrial and commercial ware had increased by leaps and bounds, while that of fine wares suffered. In America there was great emphasis upon pressed glass and lime glass for tablewares, although flint was still considered the *fine* glass. In fact, in table and decorative wares one finds that the same colors and types — cut and engraved crystal and cased glass with rich ornamentation — enjoyed approximately the same proportional popularity as in 1851. But a taste for novelty had developed side by side with a trend toward the classical in shapes, and toward

FIG. 2 — WINE OF LEAD GLASS
Engraved "New Engl^d/Glass. C°./Boston," and on reverse side "Mass. Cent^l./Head Q^rs." Displayed at the 1876 Philadelphia Centennial Exhibition *Height, 4½ inches, top diameter, 2⅛ inches*

FIG. 3 — "LIBBEY GLASS CO.'S FACTORY, MIDWAY PLAISANCE"
At the 1893 World's Columbian Exposition, Chicago, "spinning wheels six feet in diameter . . . draw from glass rods melted before a blow-pipe the finest threads, which are put into a loom and woven into glass fabric," from which were made "dresses, napkins, bonnets, and the most beautiful lamp shades . . ." Visitors at the 1939 New York World's Fair are still fascinated by a demonstration of glass weaving at the Glass Center

ANTIQUES

a lamentable extravagance in decoration bordering often on the bizarre. Though an occasional piece appeared which might almost be termed a work of art, or a design in tableware which would be "good" in any period, the keynote of the time, for all countries, seems to have been extravagance in form and decoration, a nearly complete subordination of the beautiful metal itself to novelty and ornamentation.

In seventeen years between the Centennial Exhibition and Chicago's World's Columbian Exposition of 1893 science and ingenuity had contributed many new types of glass and found new uses for the metal. The general expansion is indicated by the number and contents of the classes devised for the exhibits: Class 589 — Plate glass; Class 590 — Blown glass, ordinary window glass, bottles, tubes, pipes, etc.; Class 591 — Pressed glass and glassware generally for the table and various purposes; skylights, insulators, etc.; Class 592 — Cut glassware for the table and various purposes, engraved and etched glass; Class 593 — Fancy glassware, plain iridescent, opalescent, colored, enameled, painted, beaded, gilded, etc., millefiori and aventurine glass; Class 594 — Crackled glass in layers, onyx glass, sculptured glass, and reproductions of ancient glassware; Class 595 — Glass mosaics, beads, *spun glass and glass fabrics.*

Eleven foreign countries sent exhibits. From Switzerland came *glass bricks for building purposes;* from Great Britain, two exhibits in Classes 590 and 591. Cut glassware, engraved and etched tableware were shown in two exhibits from Japan and one from the Diamond Glass Company of New Glasgow, Canada. Fancy scent bottles were sent from Siam. Cut, engraved, and etched glass and various of the fancy glasswares were in displays from Sweden, Germany, Belgium and Denmark. One of the exhibits from Denmark included a glass ceiling. Austria was again the largest exhibitor, with eighteen displays contributed by "all the famous factories of Bohemia" and "illustrative of the collective results of centuries of individual endeavor." Among the exhibitors were Count Harrach, Heinrich Ullrich, and J. & L. Lobmeyr who, as in 1876, had outstanding displays. Italy made a remarkable contribution in the miniature "palace of glass and mosaic" work erected by the Venice and Murano Company to house its display of *old* and *new* glass.

The American exhibits were few and, with two exceptions, not impressive in Classes 593 through 595. The list given in one official catalogue was as follows:

Geo. Macbeth & Co. optical and lamp glasses

Prugh, Conroy & Co. Mirrors

Wire Glass Co., Philadelphia. Wire glass

Diamond Plate Glass Co., Kokomo, Indiana. Plate glass

United States Glass Co., Pittsburg Misc. glass ware

F. M. Hicks & Co., Chicago. Ornamental flooring and skylights

Suess Co., Chicago. Beveled glass and enameled glass

Geo. E. Androvette & L. Strauss & Sons. Cut glass for table and ornaments

The Tiffany Glass & Decoration Co. Onyx glass, glass mosaics, incised and engraved glass, stained glass chapel including altar, reredos etc. designed by Louis Tiffany.

Libbey Glass Co., Toledo. Cut glass ware and glass fabrics.

J. Hoare & Co. Examples of engraving and rock crystal cutting.

The American exhibits which excited both public and critics were those of the Tiffany Glass & Decoration Company and the Libbey Glass Company. In the field of ornamental wares stress was laid on pieces demonstrating Tiffany's "new process in which glass of various colors is blown into a framework of silver and silver gilt, producing the effect of jewels, crystal and precious stones." The Libbey Company had its own building which was to the 1893 Fair what the Glass Center is to 1939. Besides its display of a great variety of cut-glass objects it had a glass factory in operation. Artisans demonstrated the art of engraving, etching, and cutting glass. But in the entire Fair the most amazing thing in the field of glass manufacture was the *spinning of fibers from glass rods and weaving of fabric.* However, even though various articles made from glass fabric were exhibited — a dress, "curtain portiers, decorations for ceiling and walls, lamp shades and other fancy articles beautifully painted" — the whole thing was considered by the public to be of little practical value.

The comments of contemporary writers indicate that little change had taken place since 1876 in designs of table and decorative ware. Except for the glass exhibited by J. & L. Lobmeyr, which was deemed superior in engraving and sculpturing, according to general opinion there was "much inferior work and but little calculated to interest the artist or art lover." Only the cut glass of the Libbey Glass Company seems to have merited any sort of praise, and that for the remarkable "accuracy and depth of cutting" which rendered the results "masterpieces of mechanical skill." In fact, with taste in decoration still at neap tide, progress in making decorated glassware seems to have been on the side of technical execution and mechanical perfection.

DORFLINGER GLASS

By JANET FOSTER NEWTON

ALTHOUGH WAYNE COUNTY, PENNSYLVANIA, during the nineteenth century was noted for its many glass-cutting establishments, there were only four factories which made the glass itself. Of these, the most successful was the Dorflinger Glass Works at White Mills. The other county plants flourished briefly, but Dorflinger glass, famous internationally for the excellent quality of its metal, continued to be produced and to maintain its high standards until 1921.

Christian Dorflinger (not Doerflinger, as often appears) was born March 16, 1828, in Rosteig, Canton Bitsch, Alsace, France. In 1837 he left his parents, Francis and Charlotte Clemens Dorflinger, to learn glassmaking with an uncle in St. Louis, Lorraine. There he mastered the fundamentals, but was especially interested in the methods of ornamenting glass — etching, engraving, enameling, and gold decorating. In 1845 his father died, and Christian in 1846 brought his mother, brothers, and sisters to America. The rest of the family went on to Indiana, but he stayed in Philadelphia working as a journeyman glassblower for a firm which manufactured druggist's bottles.

On one of his trips to New York, he became acquainted with his future wife, Elizabeth Hagen, who lived in Brooklyn. And on his visits to her, he used to stop at the Pacific Hotel in New York, kept by Captain Aaron Flower, a former seafaring captain. About 1850, when kerosene oil was giving a boom to the lamp business, Captain Flower and a group of men were discussing the idea of forming a company to make glass lamp chim-

neys. Flower remembered the young Alsatian, and sent for Christian Dorflinger to take charge of the business. The men put up the money, and in 1852 Christian began his first factory, the Long Island Flint Glass Works, Concord Street, Brooklyn. It began in a small way, with only one five-pot furnace. At that time Christian paid off the men who had financed the scheme and bought the business for himself. In 1858 he built a new factory at Plymouth and in 1860 he branched out again with a flint-glass factory, the Green Point Glass Works in Brooklyn, where he began the manufacture of the fine glassware he loved. In a short time the two plants were doing a business of about $300,000 a year.

In 1863, Christian, who had been living, eating, and breathing glass, became ill and his doctor told him to get out of Brooklyn and forget it. So he dutifully sold the Long Island Glass Works, leased the Green Point factory to E. P. Gleason, and retired to enjoy himself. Captain Flower sent him up to his farm in Wayne County for the summer, a spot on the east side of the Lackawaxen River near White Mills, through which the Delaware and Hudson Canal ran. Christian liked the place so well that in 1865 he bought the 300-acre farm. By this time, however, he was bored with retirement, and began plans to combine his doctor's orders with his own inclination by building a glassworks at White Mills. He first built a little plant in Indian Orchard, a farming center near-by, and later in the year built his glassworks at White Mills.

The White Mills plant started with a 5-pot furnace.

FIG. 1 — WAYNE COUNTY GLASS WORKS (1865-1921). Also called Dorflinger Glass Works, and, after 1881, C. Dorflinger & Sons. Located at White Mills, Pennsylvania. Goodrich's *History of Wayne County* (1886) says, "The glass produced there combines every degree of excellence and ornamentation. Specimens of the perfection of work were exhibited at the Centennial Exposition in Philadelphia in 1876, and were not excelled by the best work made at Pittsburg or elsewhere." The plant shown here burned in 1892, and was immediately replaced by a larger one. The Canal, going from Honesdale to Roundabout (Kingston) on the Hudson River, ran south of the picture in the present village of White Mills, where the Canal officials put in a special basin to take care of the Dorflinger boats. The building in the left foreground was the office. In addition to the numerous buildings erected for the business, Christian Dorflinger the first year built seven houses for his workmen, erected a large hotel in 1867, and a mansion in 1870. Eventually there were 75 homes for the workers built around the plant, of which Dorflinger owned 50, and for all of which he had put up the money. In 1886 about 300 people were employed, and the payroll amounted to $10,000 a month. At its peak the factory employed about 650. The row of houses along the back was called "Murderers' Row," because the Irish workmen who lived there usually had a big fight each Saturday night after pay day. *This and Figures 3 and 4 from prints in Matthew's "History of Wayne, Pike and Monroe Counties, Pennsylvania"* (1886).

FIG. 2 — PART OF A SET OF DORFLINGER GLASS DESIGNED FOR PRESIDENT LINCOLN. Fruit cup, finger bowl and saucer, and handled punch (height, 4 inches). Unlike most cut glass, which is heavy, this set is exceptionally thin, fine, and delicate. The Dorflingers made sets of tableware for all the Presidents from Lincoln to Wilson. The set for President Theodore Roosevelt included the first highball glasses ordered. All these pieces, of course, were engraved with the United States coat of arms, but each set had its distinctive pattern. *Figures 2, 5, 6, 7 from the collection of Miss Katherine Dorflinger.*

By the second year there were approximately a hundred men and boys at work. Most of them were local farm lads, trained by Christian, though he also had skilled workers from Brooklyn who had been trained in Europe. In 1867 the famous glass-cutting department was introduced. At that time the buildings comprised a glasshouse, and a "cutting" shop two stories high, later used as the packing department. A three-story wing was added a few years later, and also a building in which the great clay crucibles or pots were made.

Dorflinger spent as much time on the construction of these clay pots as on the actual glassmaking itself. They were made in a long, low room which was kept at a steady temperature so that the crucibles could become thoroughly and evenly seasoned. Most of the clay for the pots came from Germany, though clay from Missouri was sometimes used.

Later Dorflinger made further improvements in his plant. A new glasshouse was built, with a large basement of iron and stone extending under the whole building. It contained one eight-pot furnace and three annealing ovens. A three-story gray stone building for the increased cutting business was also built. On the second floor was a seventy-five horse-power engine to turn the hundred wheels in the cutting room below.

One of the most skilled glasscutters of the time was employed here. He was John S. O'Connor, born in Londonderry, Ireland, June 6, 1831. Before the Civil War he had worked for Turner & Lane and E. V. Houghwought & Co., both of New York City. After the War, in which he served, he returned to be superintendent of the Houghwought plant. The firm went out of business just as Christian Dorflinger was getting his glass-cutting department started, and O'Connor was hired by him as foreman of the White Mills cutting shop, starting glass-cutting with one frame. While there he invented many ma-chines for glasscutting that completely changed the cut-glass industry. One of them cut glass in circular lines instead of straight. One of his patented designs was the *Parisian*, which was copied by many other glasscutters. While O'Connor was with him, Dorflinger also brought out two other popular designs which were widely imitated, *Lorraine* and *Russian*, the latter used especially for stemware. In 1892 he left Dorflinger and started his own factory in Hawley, Pennsylvania.

Christian insisted that all processes necessary for a finished product be done at his plant, with the exception of the gold decorating. For this he sent the glass away, usually to an Austrian decorator in New York who did fine work. The volume of this business, however, increased so much that he needed a manager, and he got in touch with Carl F. Prosch from Vienna, an expert designer in etching and gold decoration, who had studied at Melk on the Danube in the school conducted there by the Benedictines. Prosch was in New York as the representative of an Austrian wholesale glass agency, Bawo and Dotter, whose factories were in Bohemia and whose main offices were in Kotzschenbroda bei Dresden. In 1900 Christian Dorflinger made an arrangement whereby Prosch was to do his type of decorating on Dorflinger glass exclusively, and the two men founded the Honesdale Decorating Company, with a factory located at Seelyville, a suburb of Honesdale. In 1915 Prosch bought out the Dorflinger interest and continued the business until 1932 under the old name.

Though Dorflingers furnished the blanks for twenty-two cutting shops in Wayne County, most of the glass made at their plant was shipped to their New York store at 915 Broadway, from which the goods were sold to Ovington, Tiffany, Gorham, and other New York retail stores, and also to shops in Washington, Chicago, Philadelphia, Boston, and San Francisco. Their New York office was located at 36 Murray Street. The variety of glass patterns and forms was wide. There were fancy dishes and bonbons in the *hobnail* cut with double star; punch bowls in *brilliante* cut with glass-handled ladles to match; table bells in various colors; lamps with dome shades; flower vases, decanters, cologne bottles, crystal and dark-green water bottles,

FIG. 4 *(below)* — UPPER FLOOR OF GLASSCUTTING DEPARTMENT, DORFLINGER GLASS WORKS. The machinery used here was originally planned by John S. O'Connor, and worked out by F. W. Farnham, who patented the brushes. The funnels held the water used both in cutting and polishing. In this room the three steps in the work were done. First was the "roughing" on an iron wheel, which the men at right are doing — the deep cutting of the pattern marked on the glass with red lead. The second process, smoothing, was done with fine stone wheels. Then came the polishing, done by the men at left, with wheel brushes and wooden wheels kept constantly smeared with "putty"—the plant name for a finely-ground oxide of zinc and lead.

FIG. 3 *(above)* — GLASSBLOWING DEPARTMENT AT THE DORFLINGER PLANT. The large square furnace is where the metal was made; each square opening had a pot for the melting. The smaller furnace at the right, called the glory hole, was used by the gaffer for finishing the glass after it was taken off the blowing iron. The gentleman in the foreground leaning on a cane is a slightly fictionalized portrait of Christian. There is a better portrait of him at the Wayne County Historical Society in Honesdale, and another owned by his daughter, Miss Katherine Dorflinger. The high quality of Dorflinger glass depended on the exceptional quality of the basic ingredients used. Christian at first insisted that the sand used be from Fontaine-bleau, France, and he had it brought here as ballast in sailing ships. The native product he favored was ground rock from the Berkshire Glass Sand Co., Cheshire, Massachusetts, and from the Pennsylvania Glass Sand Co., McVeigh, Pennsylvania. His special laboratory analyzed each new batch of sand to find the correct proportion of other ingredients to be mixed with it. For a batch of 600 pounds of sand, usually 400 pounds of oxide of lead were added, and 200 pounds of pearl ash. Into this went very small proportions of salt petre, arsenic, and manganese.

trade. There do exist many such items, made by the Dorflinger workmen in their spare time and for their own pleasure, but they were not put out with the line of Dorflinger products. For some reason, also, many people erroneously list chandeliers among Dorflinger products. At one time their New York store had two for decoration, but they were brought from France, and the Dorflingers never manufactured things of this kind.

Like the other big glassmakers of the period, the Dorflingers also made pressed glass, in such objects as knobs, lamp bases, stoppers, and silencers for chair legs. But this glass was inferior in quality to that made for the cut glass, and used lime instead of lead in the metal.

In 1881 Christian's sons, William, Louis J., and Charles, went into partnership with their father, and the firm became C. Dorflinger & Sons. Christian died in 1915. The plant continued operating until 1921, when it had to close for lack of the German potash used in their product, and also because the vogue for cut glass was on the wane.

and jugs (especially in *tusk* and *Flemish* patterns); trays, some with beautiful straight lines, with much the same style and simplicity of decoration as the most modern 1944 glassware; candlesticks, ice-cream sets, candy jars (one of which is now in the Cleveland Museum), and huge druggist-window bottles, a specialty of the Dorflinger firm.

The designers of these wares, with the exception of John O'Connor, are anonymous, and no record tells who should be credited with the work. The patterns were all given names when they first appeared on the market, though no list of them exists, for, unfortunately, most of the records of the plant were destroyed by fire. There is, however a pamphlet of the early 1900's, *Table Service, C. Dorflinger & Sons, New York City,* which illustrates various sets and gives the wholesale prices of the different pieces. Also there are a few people who know the glass well enough to have this information at hand. Dwight C. Dorflinger of Honesdale, Pennsylvania, a grandson of Christian and superintendent of the glassblowing department at White Mills for twenty-five years, is at work on a biography of his grandfather and a history of Dorflinger glass. He is thoroughly acquainted with all phases of his subject, and when the book is completed it should be a valuable contribution in the field of nineteenth-century American glass and its makers.

Contrary to a current popular belief, paper weights and glass canes were not part of the Dorflinger stock in

Dorflinger glass   Part I

BY KATHRYN HAIT DORFLINGER MANCHEE

This is the first of three articles on Christian Dorflinger and his glass. In it Mrs. Manchee tells of the founding and development of the Dorflinger glassworks in Brooklyn, New York, and White Mills, Pennsylvania, and shows some of their early products. Parts II and III will appear in coming months.

IN HER PIONEERING *Cut and Engraved Glass 1771-1905* (New York, 1950) Dorothy Daniel said of Christian Dorflinger that he was "one of the truly great glassmakers of America," and I am sure no serious student of nineteenth-century American glass would disagree with this judgment. Dorflinger's influence on the industry was profound, and his reputation was international. In the sixty-nine years (1852-1921) during which his Brooklyn, New York, and White Mills, Pennsylvania, factories were in operation they may well have turned out more glass of superlative quality than all other American factories combined. The range of his products was extensive: they came in hundreds of forms, patterns, cuttings, and engravings, and they won national and international awards. Yet the very name Dorflinger is known to few except students, museum curators, and knowledgeable collectors and dealers. Even ANTIQUES has published only one article about

the glass (January 1944, p. 27), and a comprehensive book on the subject has yet to be written.

A number of factors have contributed to this surprising obscurity. To begin with, Dorflinger was a modest man who shunned publicity and concentrated on one thing: the making of fine glassware. With negligible exceptions his glass was marked with only a small paper label, and inevitably very few pieces have retained these. The White Mills glassworks became one of the largest in the United States and perhaps in the world, but it was buried in the Pennsylvania mountains and the inaccessibility of its site has discouraged research which could more easily be done on factories near large cities or in less rugged country. Then, too, the skilled artisans Dorflinger imported from England and the Continent gave his glass an international flavor, and it can easily be mistaken for its European counterparts (an error sometimes encouraged by unscrupulous dealers who, according to Dorflinger's son William, even went so far as to ship Dorflinger glass to Europe and bring it back as an "imported" product which would bring higher prices—in those days!—than American glass). It is also true that many of those foreign craftsmen who left the White Mills works to be near big cities or to escape the harsh mountain winters made names for themselves in other factories turning out the same types of glassware they had made for Dorflinger, and this adds to the difficulty of attribution. Finally, there is a tremendous quantity of Dorflinger glass in existence that was supplied to cutters (the factory is said to have supplied nine-tenths of the cutting shops in the United States) who preferred it for its quality and blue-diamond brilliance—and who naturally signed the finished pieces with their own names.

I have had the good fortune to be closely associated with the Dorflinger family for many years, and to be acquainted with a number of the Dorflinger craftsmen as well. This account of Christian Dorflinger's career and the glass he made is based on family records and surviving factory documents, and on thoroughly authenticated examples of the glass itself.

Christian Dorflinger (1828-1915) was born in Alsace, France, in 1828. When he was ten an uncle associated with the renowned Cristalleries de Saint-Louis in Lorraine (founded in 1767) offered to teach his young nephew the art of fine glassmaking and for eight years Christian

Compote made at Christian Dorflinger's Long Island Flint Glass Works in Brooklyn, New York; c. 1856. This extremely rare piece exemplifies the simple cutting and sturdy forms of Dorflinger's earliest period. Of clear, brilliant lead glass, it is cut in flat panels alternating with sharp-diamond cutting. A sixteen-point star is cut on the foot. Height 7½ inches. *Corning Museum of Glass; gift of the author.*

was actively involved in every phase of this highly technical and delicate art, from the mixing of the raw material to the finished product. This intense training and exposure to the making of beautiful French glass gave him not only technical knowledge but an appreciation of fine glass and the discriminating taste which was to prove so valuable in his future career. At the end of these eight years his enthusiasm for his chosen work persuaded his widowed mother to bring her family to America to afford him greater opportunity.

Shortly after his arrival here, young Christian obtained employment in a glass factory in Camden, New Jersey. Because of his thorough knowledge of glassmaking he soon gained the admiration and respect of his associates. According to family memoirs and recollections, the youth was endowed with an exceptionally strong physique and endless drive and perseverance. He also manifested unusual business acumen for his age, and acquired a reputation for integrity and consideration of others which made him many devoted friends within and outside the industry.

By 1852, with his savings and the help of business friends and associates, he had established his own small glassworks on Plymouth Street in Brooklyn, New York. There he manufactured special lamp chimneys of his own design to complement the new kerosene oil burners. This business grew so rapidly that by 1853 the Long Island Flint Glass Works came into being to meet the ever-increasing demand for his products. He now broadened his line of merchandise and added a line of free-blown (the workmen call this off-hand) tablewares, plain, cut, and

Baby cup made for William Francis Dorflinger, first-born son of Christian Dorflinger; it carries his name and the date 1856. The only such cup Dorflinger ever made. Blown of heavy lead crystal, it is stone-wheel engraved and cut in a simple miter and silver-diamond design. Height 3 inches. *Except as noted, illustrations are from the author's collection.*

Compote and wineglass from the state service ordered from Dorflinger's Brooklyn glassworks and used in the White House by President and Mrs. Lincoln; 1861. Each piece is engraved with the United States coat of arms on a foliated and scrolled border. The lower portion of the bowl is cut in the Dorflinger silver-diamond design; the cut stem is tapered, enclosing a teardrop, and the base is cut in an eight-point star; the entire set is exceptionally thin and beautiful. Height of compote, 7½ inches; height of wineglass, 5 inches.

Celery glass, 1852-1861. Made at one of Dorflinger's Brooklyn factories, this shows the French influence apparent in much Dorflinger glass. Height 8¾ inches. *Newark Museum.*

Cologne bottle with paperweight stopper made by Nicholas Lutz at White Mills; 1867-1869. The stopper is cut of the most brilliant crystal, enclosing a deep blue flower. The slender bottle is blown, cut, and engraved; it has been in the possession of the Dorflinger family ever since Lutz worked in White Mills. Height 7 inches. Dorflinger brought this famous glassmaker from his native Lorraine in 1867; he had known him in the Cristalleries de Saint-Louis. After working in the White Mills factory for two years Lutz left to secure work in a less severe climate. Many of the items he made for Dorflinger he also made later at the Boston and Sandwich Glass Company.

engraved. In 1858, again needing more space, he moved to another Brooklyn site, on Concord Street; and in 1860 he built the Green Point Flint Glass Works on Commercial Street at the mouth of Newtown Creek. This gave him four times the space he had had earlier.

By 1861 Dorflinger's Brooklyn factories had gained such a reputation that he received through A. P. Zimandy and Company, his dealer in Washington, D.C., an order from President and Mrs. Lincoln for a complete service of tableware and accessories for the White House, each piece to be "rich cut & eng. with U.S. Coat of Arms." The cost was $1,500, and the order was signed by President and Mrs. Lincoln. This established Dorflinger's reputation as one of the leading makers of fine glass in America. From this time on, Dorflinger glass was used in the White House by eight Presidents, from Lincoln through Wilson.

At the age of thirty-three, nine years after the founding of his first glassworks, Dorflinger's gross annual sales amounted to over $300,000. However, this phenomenal success had taken its toll. His health was so impaired that

Porcelain plate with view of the White Mills glassworks, painted c. 1879 by a Swiss decorator who had a shop in White Mills for several years. The Delaware and Hudson Canal appears in the center, with the St. Charles Hotel at upper right. *Brooklyn Museum.*

his doctors advised a period of semi-retirement. Being a practical young man he heeded their warnings, and in 1863 he disposed of the Long Island Flint Glass Works and put the Green Point factory in the hands of trusted associates. In 1862 he had approached a good friend, Captain Aaron Flower, about purchasing the captain's summer home, a charming old farmhouse surrounded by three hundred acres of timberland (later expanded to fifteen hundred) in the mountains of Pennsylvania, just above the hamlet of White Mills. As Captain Flower wished to lessen his own responsibilities at this time, he consented to sell his entire holdings to his young friend. The following summer Dorflinger moved his family into their new home, which is still occupied by a member of the family.

Within two years, rest and invigorating mountain air had so restored Dorflinger's health that he became restive and felt the need for more activity, so early in 1865 he cleared a tract of land and built a small five-pot glass furnace at the edge of the Lackawaxen River. The following year he brought certain of his expert craftsmen from Brooklyn to train local farm lads in the art of glassmaking.

Again the Midas touch was evident. With a large capital and the income from his Brooklyn factory Dorflinger had ample funds for expansion, and the sleepy little village of White Mills grew into a thriving glass community. Dorflinger built over a hundred houses for his workers. Others built their own with his financial help. The plant itself grew rapidly. The Wayne County Glass Works, as it was called, required so much attention that Dorflinger decided to make White Mills his permanent home. So he sold his Brooklyn home and leased the glassworks which he later sold. The Delaware and Hudson Canal Company, whose canal ran through White Mills to Honesdale and

Goblet made for the 1869 wedding of Clothilde King to Eugene Dorflinger. The only such goblet made, this was used only once, at the wedding. It is exceptionally thin. The engraving includes a garland of ribbon and flowers entwined at the top from which are suspended three oval disks, one enclosing Clothilde's monogram and the others, delicate bouquets. Tiny dots are engraved over the entire bowl in clusters of three, giving it a lacy appearance; and the sixteen points of the star cutting on the foot alternate with engraved leaves and flowers. Height 6 inches. *Corning Museum; gift of the author.*

Pitcher, also made for Eugene and Clothilde Dorflinger; 1870-1875. Free-blown, cut, and engraved with the initial *D*. Height 10⅛ inches. *Everhart Museum; gift of the Museum Association of Scranton, Pennsylvania.*

on to Kingston on the Hudson River, built a large ship basin near the glassworks so the tremendous volume of glass that was blown, cut, and engraved in White Mills and the blanks (plain blown flint-glass shapes) for cutters throughout the country could be shipped. Barges returned from New York to White Mills loaded with sand from France, potash from Germany, and red lead from England which had been shipped as ballast. Dorflinger used only the finest raw materials. The furnace pots were built to his specifications of fine glazed brick from England. Later, sand was brought from the Berkshires and other parts of the United States. Coal, wood, and water were abundantly available. The Erie Railroad built a special spur and station to help accommodate shipments and passengers to and from the glassworks.

Dorflinger needed a place to entertain his guests and business associates, so in 1868 he started construction of a thirty-six-room hotel, complete with a large ballroom (this was 31 feet by 60). The handsome mansard-roofed building, constructed of local gray stone, was completed in 1870 and christened the St. Charles at a spectacular inaugural ball given May 25, 1870, for local prominent

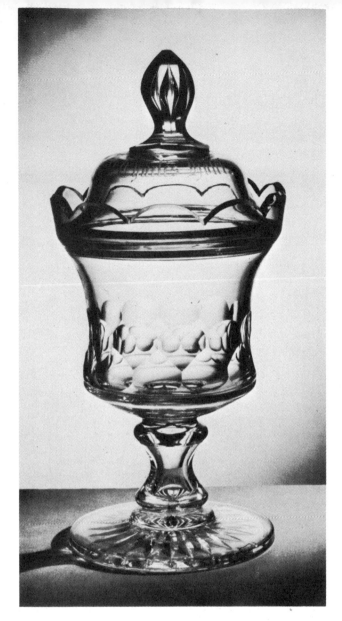

St. Charles Hotel is engraved on the domed cover of this graceful candy jar, made for the opening of the hotel built in White Mills by Dorflinger to accommodate visiting friends and business associates; 1869. Blown and cut of brilliant crystal, with the engraving left unpolished for contrast. The finial encloses a teardrop and is cut in six panels tapering to a point. Broad hollow-diamond cutting surrounds the base of the bowl, and there is a twenty-four-point star cut on the foot. Height 10½ inches. Always in the Dorflinger family. *Collection of June Dorflinger Hardy.*

Very thin and graceful goblet from a set once owned by Carlotta Dorflinger Atkinson, Christian's daughter. A wreath of leaves and flowers encircles the letter *D*. The stem is cut in panels and has a twenty-four-point star-cut base. Height 6½ inches. *Hardy collection.*

citizens and Dorflinger's friends from New York and Europe. By this time his land holdings had been increased to fifteen hundred acres. In 1872 a wing with seventeen marble fireplaces was added to the hotel, and Dorflinger moved his family from the farmhouse into it. It was occupied by members of the family until 1931. This elegant building became a well-known landmark. It stood until 1961, when the then owner of the property burned it down to clear the site for a new building. No sign of it remains today, but a beautiful iron fence and a long stone wall suggest the happy and almost feudal life lived there where so many distinguished guests had found a warm welcome when they came to visit the great glassworks or to attend balls and parties.

Dorflinger's four daughters were never allowed to step inside the factory, though it was only a few minutes away. It was not considered the thing for young ladies to do. I remember being surprised sometimes to find that they could not answer questions about the glass. They were sent to the best finishing schools and traveled extensively abroad. Their brothers went to schools and colleges in the United States and Europe.

Christian's own discriminating taste is apparent in the beauty and elegance of the glass he selected for his personal use. He was well aware of the growing demand for more elaborate cutting and engraving, but much of the Dorflinger glass remained relatively simple in form. Many of the most delicate pieces, even though produced in large services, have not survived. Owners of Dorflinger glass that is still extant may not be aware of where it was made and may attribute it to other American or to European glassworks. The glass illustrated in this article has been selected to show the quality and variety in form and design created even in the earliest days of the Dorflinger factories.

Dorflinger glass

Part II

BY KATHRYN HAIT DORFLINGER MANCHEE

In Part I of this article, which appeared in the April 1972 issue of ANTIQUES, Mrs. Manchee gave a brief biography of Christian Dorflinger and illustrated a number of pieces made in his factories' early years. Part III, which is to be published next month, will deal with identification of Dorflinger glass.

Decanter and two of thirty-eight wineglasses of the "Centennial Set," shown at the 1876 Centennial International Exhibition in Philadelphia and given at its conclusion to the City of Philadelphia. The oversized decanter has, in addition to spectacularly deep and intricate cutting, three engraved panels showing respectively the arms of the United States, the goddess of Liberty, and the crest of the City of Philadelphia with the name of its mayor and the year, 1876. The set was made with one wineglass for each of the thirty-eight states in the Union at that date, engraved with the state's coat of arms, the name of its governor, and the year. Over-all height of decanter, 16⅝ inches; height of wineglasses, 5 inches. *Philadelphia Museum of Art.*

IN 1876 OUR growing country celebrated its hundredth anniversary with the Philadelphia Centennial, and exhibitors from the United States and Europe had their finest products on view there. Included in the Dorflinger exhibit was the so-called Centennial Set shown here—a large decanter and thirty-eight wineglasses representing the thirty-eight states then in the Union. Not surprisingly, this tour-de-force in cut glass attracted a great deal of attention. The quality of the metal in the glass on display, as well as the skillful cutting, made an important impact on American glassmaking. Cut glass became the fashion, and Dorflinger glass became the status symbol of the carriage trade. It graced the tables of the Vanderbilts, Goulds, Reids, and others of America's foremost families. Queen Victoria and King Edward VII had special pieces made for Buckingham Palace. President Mario Menocal of Cuba selected it for the presidential palace in Havana. It also graced the special train used by the Prince of Wales when he toured the United States and Canada. Eight Presidents of the United States ordered it.

Dorflinger salesmen traveled extensively and the products of the White Mills glassworks were sold through leading jewelers and commercial houses throughout the country: E. G. Tiffany and Company, Gorham, Ovington's, Black Starr and Frost, New York City; and J. E. Caldwell, Bailey Banks and Biddle, Philadelphia.

In 1881, when Dorflinger took his three sons into the business, the firm name was changed to C. Dorflinger and Sons. William was responsible for the New York end of the business, where two stores had been opened: a retail shop at 915 Broadway (about 23rd Street), later moved to 3-5 West 19th Street (two doors from Fifth Avenue); and one for wholesale and display purposes occupying

1006

Candy jar, c. 1879-1880; the only such piece known to have been made at the White Mills glassworks. The elegance and grace of this simple form is reminiscent of Georgian silver design, as is the gadroonlike cutting at the base of the cover. The pointed finial encloses a teardrop; cover, base of bowl, and stem are cut in flat panels, and there is a star cutting on the foot. Over-all height, 16¾ inches. *Cleveland Museum of Art; given by Carlotta Dorflinger Atkinson in memory of her father, Christian Dorflinger.*

Goblet in the famous Parisian pattern—the first cut design to incorporate the curved miter cut. John S. O'Connor originated this design and patented it in 1886. assigning the patent to the Dorflinger firm. This particular goblet, with its intricately cut foot, was never put on the market. Height 5½ inches. *Collection of the author, currently on loan to the Corning Museum of Glass.*

three floors at 36 Murray Street. Louis stayed at White Mills in the financial end of the business, and Charles helped in the operation of the plants.

In 1886 John S. O'Connor Sr., an exceptionally skilled and original glass cutter who worked for the Dorflingers for twenty five years, from 1867 to 1892, patented the first cut design to have a curved line and assigned the patent to the Dorflinger company; the design was called Parisian. He left White Mills in 1892 to start his own cutting shop in Hawley, Pennsylvania.

In 1892 a disastrous fire destroyed many of the immense blowing and cutting shops and penetrated to most buildings, destroying many old records and directly or indirectly throwing almost a thousand people out of work. Undaunted, Dorflinger had one furnace operating within a month, and within a year the entire factory was rebuilt with the most modern equipment available.

For the next twenty years the company had its greatest prosperity. By 1903 there were twenty-seven factory buildings employing six hundred and fifty workers, and White Mills had grown to a community of some thirteen hundred people. It boasted three hotels, two churches, a public school, an opera house, a station on the Erie, several buildings of fraternal orders, a fire department, a baseball team, and a twenty-piece Dorflinger band, and it was a well-managed and happy place in which to live.

Dorflinger made numerous trips abroad to keep in touch with his family in Lorraine, to persuade skilled artisans in England, Ireland, and on the Continent to come to White Mills, and to keep up with the latest in European glassmaking. The craftsmen who came contributed a great deal to the factory's success: among them were Ralph Barber, who wrote me several years ago that "Mr. Dorflinger was the finest boss I ever had"; Nicholas

Two-handled vase cut in strawberry-diamond and fan pattern; c. 1886. This monumental piece (it is 12 inches in height) may also have been designed by O'Connor; it is thought to be the only one of its kind. *Ex coll.* Louis J. Dorflinger, one of Christian's sons. *Corning Museum of Glass; gift of the author.*

Pair of celery vases; 1880's. Exceptionally thin-blown and graceful, with copper-wheel-engraved fern design surrounding a heraldic device and the initial *C*. The flared bowl is edged with unusual cut notching, there is a tear drop in the baluster stem, and the foot is cut in a twenty-four-point star. Height 10¼ inches. *Author's collection.*

Spiral-cut wineglass; 1885-1890. A brilliant piece in one of the most difficult cuttings, this seems to be alive with light. A complete service, from goblets to cordials, was made in this design. The foot is cut in sixteen petals to form a flower. This spiral pattern was copied in pressed glass, but there it lacks the brilliance of the blown. Height 4½ inches. *Corning Museum; author's gift.*

Finger bowl in Russian pattern, from the 520-piece White House service made by Dorflinger for President Benjamin Harrison in 1889. In 1906 Theodore Roosevelt added 170 pieces to the set, including the first highball glasses bought for the White House, and fourteen dozen pieces were added by Woodrow Wilson; the set was in use until 1938. The Russian pattern was designed by Philip McDonald, one of the cutters working for the Hawkes firm in Corning, New York, and was used for a table service ordered by the Russian embassy in Washington—hence the name. Height 3½ inches. *Author's collection.*

Goblet from a 2300-piece set made for President Mario G. Menocal of Cuba in 1918. Cut in inverted Van Dyke pattern, the bell-shape bowl is engraved with the Cuban coat of arms. There were nineteen different sizes in the set, which cost $60,000. Louis C. Tiffany, who was responsible for the decoration of the presidential palace, gave Dorflinger the order. Height 6 inches. *Author's collection.*

Tumbler and plate from a set made for Henry Clay Pierce's yacht, *Yacona.* The sturdy, simple form was planned to withstand rough weather conditions. A rope design circles the rims, and on the tumbler crossed yachting flags are engraved above a ribbon bearing the name of the yacht. The bottom of the tumbler is decorated with a vertical "flash" miter cutting (with cuts of varying lengths), and its base is cut in a forty-eight-point flash star. *Yacona* was later sold, with all its furnishings, to the King of Portugal. *Author's collection.*

Champagnes. *Left:* Heavy flutes distinguish this hollow-stemmed glass, which is monogrammed and has a forty-eight-point star cut on the foot. Height 4¾ inches. *Right:* Hollow-stemmed saucer champagne, very thinly blown. Champagnes in this shape sometimes had engraving on the bowl. Height 5¾ inches. *Author's collection.*

Lutz, whom Dorflinger had known at the Cristalleries de Saint-Louis and who came to White Mills in 1867; O'Connor, who headed the cutting shop for many years; Carl F. Prosch, a Viennese whom Dorflinger persuaded to come to White Mills from New York; Johnny Johnson, who in 1914 left to work for Steuben; Joe Falk and his brother, who later also went to Steuben. Charles Northwood, Louis Aug, Oscar Levine, the Larsens, Hugo Liljequist, Art Firmstone (a cousin of Frederick Carder of Steuben), and scores of others were devoted and fine workers.

The factory's output included more than five hundred items, from apothecary jars, optical ware, and chemical wares to the highest grade of cut glass: "We make everything that is used in cut glass for the table—goblets, wine glasses, tumblers, finger bowls, carafes, decanters, oil and vinegar bottles, salad and punch bowls, berry dishes, bonbon and olive trays, ice cream sets, etc., etc. . . . We make also a large variety of useful ornamental pieces suitable for wedding and holiday presents such as cologne bottles, vases, flower globes, lamps, lemonade and water sets, etc., etc." Colors included canary yellow, ruby, cased ruby and crystal, shades of green, cased green and crystal, turquoise, the rare poppy color, amethyst, deep "Stiegel" blue to light blue, amber opalescent combinations, opaque white, and rose.

Paperweights and canes were not part of the Dorflinger line. They were fashioned by workmen in their time off.

The glass was cut and engraved at the factory on stone or copper wheels. Hand polishing on fine stone, brush, or felt wheels created a brilliance many glass men of the day considered impossible to achieve by the acid polishing used by other glassmakers; to my knowledge the glass made in White Mills was never polished by acid until after 1907. Etching was done on a less expensive line of tableware.

Silver was applied in filigree over the glass or as rims, tops, handles, and so forth. The name Dorflinger is found engraved on some of these silver mountings. I cannot account for the fact that some pieces were so engraved and others were not.

The glass was also decorated with gold. Especially notable is the goldwork by Prosch, one of the most skilled decorators of his time. Dorflinger helped Prosch set up a gold-decorating business, the Honesdale Decorating Company, in Seeleyville, Pennsylvania, not far from White Mills. There for many years Prosch decorated Dorflinger blanks exclusively. His work was marked on the bottom HONESDALE in gold, but many of the markings have worn off. Prosch bought out Dorflinger's interest in 1915 and continued to operate the Honesdale shop under his own name.

One of the best-known cutting shops was that of C. J. Hawkes of Corning, New York. Hawkes used a large volume of Dorflinger blanks on which he cut many prize-winning designs and which he signed with his own name. Charles Dorflinger, in charge of production at White Mills, had a dispute with Hawkes about inventory which ended with Hawkes' not buying Dorflinger glass for a period. However, he soon met Dorflinger's conditions because he found that he was unable to obtain blanks of equal quality anywhere else. The Dorflinger firm did not sell much to the Hawkes cutting shop after 1900.

In 1915 Christian Dorflinger, the founder of the great glassworks, died at the age of eighty-seven. He was active almost to the end of his life. Those who knew and worked for him loved him almost to the point of worship. His kindness, generosity, and fairness were renowned. He was highly respected for his thorough knowledge of glassmaking. He scrutinized and controlled every step from raw materials to the finished products, never compromising with the highest standards. During his entire career he demanded that his glass be as flawless as it could be made. The whole town mourned his death, as did his many friends in business both here and abroad.

With a brief interlude during which the plant was rented to another firm, Dorflinger's sons carried on the business until 1921; then they were forced to close the great works forever. A number of factors contributed to its demise. Christian, the glass genius with his great resourcefulness, had died. Then, it was extremely difficult to secure the best raw materials during the war: lead, which is so necessary in the making of fine glass, was almost impossible to obtain. Prohibition came in, so there was less demand for fine stemware.

The town's existence was entirely dependent on the glassworks, and when it closed the workers scattered to various other factories throughout the country. Some (*e.g.,* Johnny Johnson and his brother Siegfried) left about the time of Dorflinger's death. Many went to Corning, New York, where they made Corning and Steuben glass. I have been told that at one time practically every "gaffer" in the Steuben glassworks was a former Dorflinger workman. It was my privilege to know many of these workers personally, and I prize some pieces made for me at the Steuben glassworks by Dorflinger workers.

Today there is almost nothing left of the great glassworks in White Mills except a plaque on Route 6 and a few large solid gray-stone buildings which look as though they will endure forever.

Goblet combining strawberry-diamond and silver-diamond cuttings; 1870's. The charming over-all pattern is adapted to each form in the service; the foot is cut in a twenty-four-point star. Height 6½ inches. *Author's collection.*

Goblet with Dorflinger paper label still attached, the only one ever engraved in this elaborate over-all floral pattern; 1880's. It is very thinly blown and the engraving is correspondingly delicate. There is a teardrop in the panel-cut stem, and the foot is cut in a forty-eight-point flash star. Height 6 inches. *Author's collection.*

Dorflinger glass　　Part III

BY KATHRYN HAIT DORFLINGER MANCHEE

This is the final installment of a three-part article on the glass of Christian Dorflinger (1828-1915). Parts I and II, which appeared in ANTIQUES for April (p. 710) and June (p. 1006) of this year, gave a brief biography of Dorflinger, outlined the history of his factories, and illustrated a number of documented examples of his glass.

WHILE IT IS TRUE that the glass made at the Dorflinger factories (1852-1921) is not nearly so well known as that of other, less deserving makers, it is today gradually achieving the recognition which is its due. For instance, a magnificent piece of Dorflinger glass—a goblet blown and engraved in the factory's last years—was given to President Kennedy as a memento of the dedication of the Pinchot Institute in Pike County, Pennsylvania, in the fall of 1963. With this renewed appreciation the problem of identifying Dorflinger glass presents an increasing challenge.

In my earlier articles I showed some Dorflinger family pieces with unimpeachable records, as well as a number of other firmly documented examples—for instance, glass in the White House for which the order, signed by Mary and Abraham Lincoln, still exists. When there is such a record of the original purchase or a history of ownership by executives or workers in the Dorflinger factories and their descendants, there is of course no problem. But the Dorflinger output over the years was enormous, and authenticated pieces are relatively few.

How, then, can Dorflinger glass be identified? Marks are almost nonexistent. John Dorflinger (1880-1964), a relative, acid-etched a small DORFLINGER on some of the pieces from the factory's inventory which he sold after the factory closed, and a few pieces of bread-and-butter commercial ware have turned up with the name impressed on the base; but the fine glass itself, the bulk of the firm's output, was never marked except by a tiny paper label which was usually quickly discarded. The factory did produce some pieces with mountings of silver and on these the name DORFLINGER sometimes occurs—or even C.

DORFLINGER & SONS/NEW YORK, as in the case of the tantalus shown on page 100. These were not always so signed, however.

John Dorflinger did his best to keep alive and to further interest in Dorflinger glass at the small museum and store which he established in 1921 near the site of the old factory in White Mills, Pennsylvania, and maintained until his death in 1964. He gave lectures, answered questions, and kept on display some unusually fine and rare pieces from what had been the company's permanent exhibit. In 1950 Frederick Dorflinger Suydam, Christian's grandson, published a biography of his grandfather which contains much valuable information. Mr. Suydam spent many months in the preparation of this privately printed labor of love, but with modesty reminiscent of Christian himself he published it without a by-line, so some writers who have used his research have not credited their source. But in any event he did not include a discussion of patterns, or suggestions as to how to distinguish Dorflinger glass from other glass of the same period.

Here a consideration of just what types of glass Dorflinger produced should be helpful. In addition to the fine cut and engraved wares which were its principal output, the White Mills factory produced glass decorated in gold

Dorflinger paper label; actual size, ⅜ inch.
This was the only identification used on Dorflinger's fine wares from 1852 to 1921.
Except as noted, illustrations are from the author's collection.

One-of-a-kind goblet, blown and engraved at White Mills in 1917. Originally intended only for exhibition, this was given to President John F. Kennedy in the fall of 1963 as a memento of the dedication of the Pinchot Institute in Pike County, Pennsylvania.

C. DORFLINGER & SONS, NEW YORK.

Nappy and bowl in Mitre and Silver Diamond pattern;
diameter of nappy, 5 inches.
Miter cuts radiating from a pinpoint center, as in this pattern,
require exceptional skill in the cutting and polishing.

Nappy and butter dish in Mitre and Silver Diamond pattern;
from C. Dorflinger & Sons' Catalogue M (n.d.).

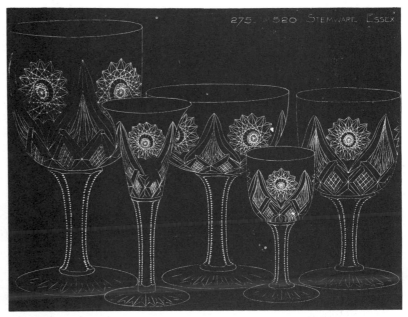

Goblet in Essex pattern; height 6⅛ inches.
This brilliant design was made
in table services which included goblets,
saucer champagnes, clarets, wines, cordials,
and finger bowls.

Stemware in Essex pattern, from a group of
undated working drawings found with Dorflinger factory records.

Three sizes of stemware in Heavy Flute pattern, 1919;
height of parfait glass (center), 6 inches.
This pattern was made for
the so-called royal train on which the then
Prince of Wales toured the United States and Canada.
Some ruby overlay was made in this pattern.

Green-and-crystal overlay two-piece footed punch bowl
in Montrose pattern, 1894; over-all height, 15 inches.
The matching silver ladle has a glass-tipped handle
and the name DORFLINGER engraved on the shaft.
A wedding gift to the mother of the owner.
*Collection of Catharine E. Lee; photograph by
courtesy of Corning Museum of Glass.*

No. 279ᴬ 519 STEMWARE
HEAVY FLUTE

Working drawing of stemware and a tumbler
in Heavy Flute pattern.

I.P.O. 798 FOOTED PUNCH BOWL
MONTROSE

Working drawing of footed punch bowl
in Montrose pattern.

by such great craftsmen as Carl Prosch. Cased glass, or overlay, in crystal and green or crystal and ruby, was a regular production item (examples can be seen in the Lincoln service in the White House and in museums and private collections). The colored glass items made were mentioned in Part II; and a less expensive line of etched tableware was also produced. Before the factory closed in 1921, reproductions of Italian glass were being made in color because of the difficulty of obtaining, during the war, the lead which is essential to the production of clear glass of high grade. At this time some fine copies of Stiegel and South Jersey types were made and sold as reproductions—to the confusion of collectors of early Americana!

Comparing a piece to patent office sketches, working drawings, or illustrations in company catalogues can of course be helpful, and the illustrations for this article have been chosen with the last two in mind. Sometimes the patterns vary from item to item to conform to differing shapes, but the original theme of the design can usually be traced. (There are hundreds of patterns, shapes, and items in my files of family records, and someday I hope to publish a picture book of this material.) Piracy, however, has always been prevalent among glassmakers, and there is no substitute for a study of the glass itself. If a piece is in a known Dorflinger pattern it may still not be Dorflinger glass unless it meets certain very definite criteria. Lack of any one of these is more significant than slight changes of pattern, which may have been made at the request of a buyer.

Dorflinger glass is skillfully made, with forms and designs harmoniously related. The cut wares, meticulously hand polished, are extremely brilliant, with great refractive qualities and a "blue-white diamond" look. When held to the light the glass is clear, almost entirely free of imperfections such as striations (appearing as tiny glass threads running through the body of the glass), stones (flecks of white clay which may have broken from the pot during the melting process), black flecks, or bubbles (air pockets). It has a beautiful bell-like ring when lightly struck, the tone depending on thickness and shape of the individual piece.

What I have been describing is, of course, glass of superlative quality, and that is just what Dorflinger glass is. So much of the fine handmade Dorflinger glass was produced that there must be quantities throughout the United States and some in Europe, in use or stored in cellars or attics, much of it hidden behind attributions to English, Irish, or French factories. I hope that the guidelines set forth here will help to identify it to its owners and enable them to prize it as the great product of American craftsmanship it truly is.

Brandy-and-soda tumbler in an unidentified pattern of lightly cut vertical panels; height 4½ inches.

Pattern identified (in pencil) as *No 1800 Cut* in C. Dorflinger & Sons' Catalogue C (n.d.).

Jug and brandy-and-soda tumbler in Old Colony pattern, an exceptionally brilliant design made in seventeen items.

Various items in Old Colony pattern, from Catalogue M.

Two-bottle tantalus set in Marlboro pattern (this also came with three bottles); case of American oak, with bar, lock, and trimmings of bronze, nickeled and lacquered. C. DORFLINGER & SONS/NEW YORK is engraved on the side of the case, and the letters *H H* under the handle. Over-all height of case, 12 inches.

Working drawing of tantalus set in Marlboro pattern.

Libbey cut and engraved glass

BY JOHN W. KEEFE, *Assistant curator, Toledo Museum of Art*

Fig. 1. Ice-cream plate in Kimberly pattern, c. 1890-1892; diameter 8 inches. This popular and beautiful pattern was named in honor of Charles G. Kimberly, a New Haven, Connecticut, dealer in crockery and glassware. *Except as noted, illustrations are from the Toledo Museum of Art.*

Fig. 2. Shallow bowl in Wedgemere pattern, c. 1900-1905; diameter 9 inches. Wedgemere was another popular Libbey pattern. This bowl is in a late variant of a design submitted to the patent office in July 1891. *Collection of Mr. and Mrs. Milton C. Zink.*

BY 1888, THE YEAR Edward Drummond Libbey moved his glass-manufacturing firm from East Cambridge, Massachusetts, to Toledo, Ohio, the deeply cut, ornate glass we know today as brilliant cut was an important part of the production of almost every table-glass firm. When it began operations the Libbey Glass Company (as Libbey rechristened his New England Glass Company) was not financially able to undertake its manufacture, but by 1893 it had become, and it remained, a leader in the field. In the last years of the "brilliant period" glass decorated with copper-wheel engraving was another outstanding product of the company.

The dates of the brilliant period in cut-glass production are generally given as from 1880 to about 1915. Although it did not become a national phenomenon until the 1880's, the new fashion was really introduced at the Philadelphia Centennial Exposition of 1876, and it remained in vogue to some extent down to 1925, so these dates, like those given for most style periods, should be understood as approximate.

Cut glass has always been costly, because a high grade of metal must be used if the glass is to withstand the pressure of cutting and because it involves a number of time-consuming procedures. The deep-miter cutting of the brilliant period was even more expensive than the fine-line cutting that had preceded it. The glass had to be heavier to take the deeper cuts; to achieve the desired sparkle it had to be of even, perfect quality throughout; the processes involved were still more complicated than those used for the earlier type.

Increasing American prosperity was responsible to a large degree for the popularity of the new wares. The panic of 1873 was but a memory; homes were larger, furnishings more ornate. Then, too, the formal living patterns of the late nineteenth and early twentieth centuries required elaborately correlated table settings, and the massive, costly cut glass was admirably suited to fill this need. An Edwardian comment on prevailing taste was that no table could be considered correctly set unless it had "cost a million and weighed a ton."

At the opening of the brilliant period technological developments had advanced to the point where the cutting lathes were driven by electric motors rather than by water or steam power. Finishing wheels of soft steel, which replaced those of cast iron, created a sharper, more brilliant cut and made deeper incisions possible. Improvement in the quality of the metal followed the introduction of natural gas as a furnace fuel: heat could be easily regulated and kept constant, fusion of the metal was more rapid, and annealing more perfect. The result was an exceptionally clear glass of considerable weight. It may truly be said that by the end of the nineteenth century American craftsmen were producing as fine a glass as the world had ever known.

Once the glass had been produced, it went through three further stages in the production of brilliant-cut

Fig. 3. Table in Neola pattern, 1902; height 32 inches. This monumental piece was probably cut by John Rufus Denman, one of the Libbey company's most skilled craftsmen. It was made for the company's display at the St. Louis World's Fair of 1904.

Fig. 4. Plate in Sultana pattern, c. 1897; diameter 12 inches. The border of this advertising piece is cut and the center is engraved with the Libbey sword mark and an advertising phrase; the phrase did not appear on the mark in normal use.

wares—a procedure fundamentally the same in the Libbey plant and in all the other glasshouses. When the blank of fine, heavy lead glass was completed, the pattern to be cut was drawn on the surface, usually in a mixture of red lead and turpentine. The cutter then roughed out his pattern with a wheel of iron or soft steel which was convex, flat, or V shape in profile, depending upon the cut desired. In the cutting of an ornate pattern the wheels might have to be changed a number of times.

The second step, the smoothing process, involved coating the wheel with a fine wet abrasive and deepening the cuts already made; these were then smoothed by sandstone wheels wet with water. Like the wheels used in the roughing, the sandstone ones varied in size from two to about eighteen inches and were changed according to the pattern being executed.

Polishing, the final stage, followed the smoothing. Traditionally, wooden wheels and a gentle abrasive such as putty powder were used for this process. A higher luster could be achieved by the use of felt wheels dusted with a rouge or a similar polishing agent. About 1890, a chemical process involving the dipping of the cut glass in an acid bath came into use, although old-time glassworkers deplored the change. Today, most experts feel that the finish acquired by the acid method cannot match the sparkle achieved by the earlier means.

Cutting is still done at the Libbey factory today, but the blanks are automatically blown and are relatively light in weight. The contemporary process differs from that of the brilliant period in that stone wheels rather than metal are now used to rough in the pattern. Stone wheels, or sometimes more rapidly cutting wheels of diamond and carborundum composition, are used for the smoothing process. Wooden wheels for polishing have been superseded by felt wheels using pumice. However, today most polishing is done by the acid method: the uncut portions are coated with wax; the piece is then dipped in an acid bath and dried, and the wax is melted off. Acid polishing is being replaced in some instances (chiefly in Europe) by a mechanical process in which brushes revolving at high speed do the work. This is cheaper, faster, and neater, but the machines are initially expensive.

The copper-wheel engraving which was used to decorate many pieces of Victorian glass involves an equally laborious process. Designs are created by copper disks of varying sizes revolving on a lathe. The most skillful engravers execute their designs freehand, while others draw them in a mixture of the aforementioned red lead and turpentine. Copper-wheel engraving is also an expensive process, since it, too, takes many hours and requires the finest lead glass.

The Libbey company hired the most highly skilled cutters and engravers available. William C. Anderson, who designed for the company from 1887 until 1906, was the creator of the beautiful and popular Kimberly (Fig. 1) and Wedgemere (Fig. 2) patterns as well as Neola, the pattern in which a spectacular glass table (Fig. 3) was cut for the 1904 St. Louis exposition.

William Marrett, another talented Libbey designer, worked for the company from 1897 until 1903. He cre-

ated the Chrysanthemum and Sultana (Fig. 4) patterns and designed the McKinley punch-bowl sets (see ANTIQUES, May 1968, p. 665). John Rufus Denman (1877-1956) was one of the company's most proficient cutters; he cut both of the McKinley bowls, as well as the twenty-five-inch St. Louis punch bowl now in the collection of the Toledo Museum of Art. Many other designers and cutters of skill were employed at the Ash Street plant in Toledo.

Before 1893 much fine American cut glass was presented to the public by prestige-conscious dealers as imported European ware. This, plus the enormous success of the Libbey pavilion at the 1893 Chicago Columbian Exposition, aroused the leading American glass manufacturers to undertake a massive advertising campaign. In succeeding years the advertisements of the Libbey company appeared in *Harper's, McClure's, Country Life,* and the *Ladies' Home Journal,* among other magazines. These did much to inform the public and to expand the market for the company's wares. So effective were they that fine cut glass, by Libbey and others, became the most prestigious gift of the period, and it was collected enthusiastically. However, as early as 1900 its popularity began to wane. Many designs lacked the clarity of patterns like the Kimberly or the Strawberry Diamond and Fan (Fig. 5). Some were confused and overly ornate. The best designs of the late brilliant period show deliberate restraint and patterns complement the form of the object on which they appear (Fig. 6).

Then, too, the public had simply tired of the glitter of a table set with cut glass. Costs within the factory itself had increased sharply, and designers began to look for patterns which would give the desired effect less expensively. After 1905, the so-called "buzz," or Pinwheel, pattern (Fig. 7) was produced in quantity; this created a glittering surface but was not so costly to produce.

Copper-wheel engraving, which had been eclipsed by deep-miter cutting, was reintroduced by Libbey and other firms in an attempt to revive the market for fine glass. Intaglio engraving of realistic flowers, fruit, and figures was executed from about 1900 to 1910; some fine ex-

amples were made through the 1920's (Fig. 8). However, after World War I increasing informality of living really spelled the end of popular interest in heavily ornamented glass. During the 1920's the Libbey company made simple, understated pieces (Fig. 9), frequently characterized by the use of colored glass and simple geometric patterns.

In 1931, the company hired A. Douglas Nash (1885-c. 1945) to design a new series decorated by cutting and engraving. Nash's father had been superintendent of the Tiffany Favrile Glass Works in Corona, Long Island, and he was well acquainted with fine glassmaking traditions.

Fig. 7. Footed punch bowl in Pinwheel pattern, c. 1900-1910; height 13 inches, diameter 10½. The "buzz," or Pinwheel, pattern was extensively used by the Libbey company in the late brilliant period because it produced the desired effect at some reduction in cost. *Zink collection.*

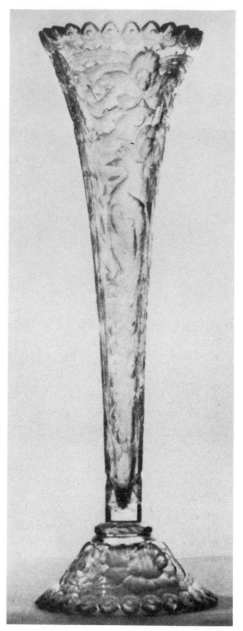

Fig. 8. Vase engraved with flowers, stylized leaves, and a peacock, on a mat surface; about 1905; height 20 inches. Copper-wheel engraving, revived in the first decade of this century, appealed to a public which had tired of the flashing, deep-miter-cut surface.

Fig. 9. Candlesticks and compote, geometric cutting and engraving; c. 1920-1925; heights 6¾ to 12¾ inches. These simple, elegant pieces were made by the Libbey Glass Company in combinations of clear, garnet, black, blue, and green glass, in some instances cased in the color and then cut or engraved through to the clear. The restraint of the decoration reflects the taste of the period.

Fig. 10. Group of goblets designed by A. Douglas Nash; cut or engraved, c. 1931-1935; heights 8 to 10 inches. The two on the left are in the Toledo pattern, that in the center is in the Oxford pattern, and the one on the far right is an experimental design not produced commercially.

Fig. 11. Goblet, cameo cut in Victoria pattern; c. 1931-1935; height 9¼ inches. Nash's most elaborate design, this spectacular goblet was triple-cased in pink, opal, and clear. Each piece took eighty hours to complete. *Collection of Mr. and Mrs. Carl U. Fauster.*

Fig. 12. Vases in the Modern American series, c. 1940-1945; heights 6 to 9 inches. The flute-cut vase in the center was called "my favorite piece" by Edwin W. Fuerst, who designed the line.

The new Nash line was characterized by beautiful form and intricate surface detail. The series specialized in formal stemware and matched centerpiece arrangements of candlesticks, bowls, and vases. The handsome Toledo pattern (Fig. 10, *left* and *center left*) was reminiscent of brilliant-period cutting; the pink-cased goblet in the Victoria pattern (Fig. 11), which was cameo cut, required eighty hours of cutting and retailed for a commensurately high figure. The Depression, however, destroyed the market for such expensive items, and the Nash line was discontinued in 1935.

In 1936 the Libbey Glass Company, now a division of the Owens-Illinois Glass Company, hired Edwin W. Fuerst (1903-   ) to design a series of heavy blown and mold-blown pieces, to be called Modern American. The new ware was presented to a few favored customers in 1939 and to the public in 1940. The beauty of the line depended upon the brilliance of the metal and the form of the article rather than upon decorative surface detail (Figs. 12, 13). Some of the vases were decorated by simple flute cuts or by copper-wheel engraving. The cutting was executed by Denman and the engraving by another highly skilled Libbey craftsman, Herman F. Hocke (1871-1944). Both techniques were used sparingly, and the copper-wheel engraving tended to draw upon contemporary subjects and stylized animals rather

than on mythological or elaborately realistic themes. The advent of World War II forced the discontinuation of this line in favor of war production. The Libbey company planned to produce Modern American after the war, but this was never done, and the line marked the end of Libbey's fine, completely handmade glass.

Since 1959 the Libbey company, as a segment of Owens-Illinois, Incorporated, has produced a line of tableware designed by Freda Diamond and called the 1818 series. All of the pieces in this line are automatically blown and then cut. This is the only Libbey glass still ornamented by cutting; copper-wheel engraving is not used at all.

Libbey trade-marks

The subject of trade-marks used by the Libbey Glass Company is a complex one. The company advertised that the Libbey signature was applied to every piece, but research has shown that this was not a consistent practice. Frequently marks of an earlier date than that of manufacture were applied. To compound the difficulty, the company often showed in its advertisements trade-marks which were not actually used.

The practice of affixing paper labels began around 1906, but for obvious reasons these rarely survive. The earliest of these Libbey labels was square in shape and bore the company name. Another was oval, with an open center and the company name printed in the perimeter. Labels of other shapes were used as well, but their dates are not known since the company did not register all its trade-marks.

Collectors and students should note that only the acid-etched mark on a piece of glass should be trusted: similarity of metal and an extensive use of nearly identical patterns often make attribution impossible without an acid mark or exact family history.

Following is a brief list of definitely established trade-marks and the approximate dates of their use by the Libbey Glass Company.

a. (1892-1896) Enameled, usually in red, and apparently stenciled.

b. (1896-1906) Here the L and the y are not connected. Note the sword under the whole.

c. (1901) Patented April 16, 1901, for use on pressed blanks sold to other companies for final cutting—which disproves the contention that Libbey never made pressed blanks.

d. (1906-c. 1913) In advertisements, the banner formed by the connection of the L and the y bore the phrase *The World's Best*. This was never included in the mark on actual pieces of glass. In the same period LIBBEY in an ovoid form was used, but here the L and y were not connected. This second mark is not common.

e. (1919-1930) Some authorities maintain that this trade-mark was first used in 1910, a contention that is open to debate.

f. (1933-1935) Paper label in blue and white. On some pieces of this period, the 1919-1930 mark is also found.

g. (1939-1945) Mark similar to the 1919-1930 version, but with a double-rimmed circle.

h. (1959-1968) Found on 1818 stemware; an adaptation of the old Libbey sword trade-mark.

Fig. 13.   Covered candy jar in the Modern American series, c. 1940-1945; height 9½ inches. Such simple stylized engraved decoration is typical of the period.

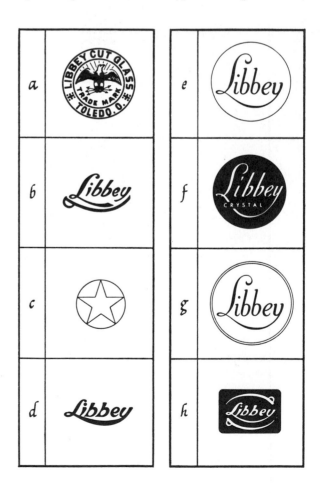

Louis Vaupel, master glass engraver

BY CARL U. FAUSTER

IN 1968 THE TOLEDO MUSEUM OF ART celebrated the hundred and fiftieth anniversary of the founding of the New England Glass Company by mounting an exhibition entitled *Libbey Glass, a tradition of 150 years.* (The New England Glass Company was founded in 1818 in Cambridge, Massachusetts; Edward Drummond Libbey moved it lock, stock, and barrel to Toledo in 1888, where its name was soon changed to Libbey Glass Company; and its lineal descendant today is the Libbey Products Division of Owens-Illinois, Inc.) The catalogue of that 1968 exhibition said of the superb presentation chalice shown here as color plate A that it represents "the high point in American Middle Period engraved glass"—an encomium which surely puts the man who engraved it at the top of his exacting craft.

The name of Louis Vaupel, the master craftsman who executed the chalice and all the other pieces illustrated here, is well known, but very little has been recorded about his life. There is at the Houghton Library at Harvard a 191-page journal kept by Vaupel covering the years 1824-1899 (he called it *Kurze Biographie Meiner Selbst,* which translates *Brief Autobiography*), but this is handwritten in German script and it has not been translated. I am indebted to Vaupel's grandson, John Leyson Vaupel, for the biographical material which follows.

Born on June 17, 1824, in the little German town of Schildhorst, Vaupel was the son of Georg Andreas Vaupel, a lifelong glass craftsman. (Incidentally, he used many versions of his name. He began life as Ludwig Heinrich Friedrich Vaupel, but by the time he arrived in the United States he was calling himself Louis Friedrich Vaupel and he often signed himself Louis F. Vaupel, L. F. Vaupel, L. H. F. Vaupel, or even H. F. Louis Vaupel.) He went to school at Freden, about four miles from Schildhorst, and by the time he was twelve he was working after school in the local glass factory, where his father was employed. It was not at all unusual at that time for very young boys to assist in the glass factory, and it was here that young Ludwig had his first chance to see how glass was blown and decorated. In 1836 the family moved to Breitenstein, near Stolberg, where Ludwig's father and his stepbrother, Karl, had established a glassworks of their own. Here he began work as a glass blower, studying all phases of glassmaking and becoming especially proficient in engraving.

Fig. 1. Clear-glass cup engraved by Louis Vaupel (1824-1903) with a design of love birds billing within a floral wreath, signed on the base *Louis,* inscribed *Minette* and *So inniglich liebe ich auch Dich* (So deeply do I love thee), and dated 1850—the year Vaupel migrated from Germany, leaving his sweetheart, Minette Kaufhold, behind. Four years later she joined him in America and they were married. *Except as noted, illustrations are from the Vaupel family collection.*

Fig. 2. Vaupel and his wife posed for this portrait by a Hannover photographer c. 1875, when they revisited Schildhorst, the small German town where both were born and where Vaupel had his earliest glassmaking experience.

Fig. 3. Two views of a clear-glass flask also apparently engraved before Vaupel left Germany. One side shows a pair of stags in a decorative wreath and is inscribed *Louis Vaupel/1850;* the other shows a group of buildings identified as *Glasfabrik/Schildhorst.* A cipher of Vaupel's initials is engraved on the base, evidently for use as a seal. Illustrated in ANTIQUES for December 1945 (p. 378). *Collection of Mrs. Henry G. Smith.*

When he was twenty-six and had served his time in the army he returned briefly to Schildhorst (see Fig. 3), and from there he migrated to America by way of Bremerhaven. Around 1850 Germany was experiencing a serious depression, and ready employment in American glasshouses awaited any talented glass craftsman. Four years after his arrival in America Ludwig (now Louis) was joined by his sister Louisa and by his fiancée, Minette Kaufhold, daughter of a Schildhorst glassmaker (Figs. 1, 2). The couple were married at Burlington, Massachusetts, on September 12, 1854.

By 1853 Vaupel had become an engraver for the New England Glass Company, the firm characterized by the McKearins (*Two Hundred Years of American Blown Glass,* 1950, p. 81) as "undoubtedly the leading house in New England in the production of the highest quality of glassware." The Cambridge city directory first lists Vaupel in 1860 as living at 125 Spring Street, within a few blocks of the glassworks. Vaupel was superintendent of the engraving department, which included, during the 1860's and 1870's, such highly skilled engravers as Henry S. Fillebrown and Henry Leighton, both of whom did exquisite work.

The remainder of Vaupel's working life was spent there. He retired in 1885, a few years before Edward Drummond Libbey moved the factory from Cambridge to Toledo. He was only sixty-one at the time, and this early retirement was probably due to the lessening demand for expertly engraved glass and the fact that the factory had fallen on troubled times. After retiring Vaupel lived on the income from several houses he owned in Cambridge. For a few years he accepted commissions to engrave glass

on the wheel he had set up in his home, but John Vaupel doubts that his grandfather did any such work after 1890, the year his wife died. Her protracted illness, involving frequent trips in search of medical help, had long been his major concern. Vaupel himself died in 1903 and is buried in Cambridge Cemetery on Coolidge Hill Road, where, John Vaupel says, "The family is all tucked in." The monument there was designed by Louis Vaupel.

During his long career Vaupel must have engraved hundreds of pieces of glass. His style naturally reflected the Bohemian influence which was paramount in Germany when he learned the art, and his earlier work was executed on thin, delicate glass. John Vaupel says that his grandfather used "a light, feathery cut, occasionally intaglio where that was called for, and usually in a wreath-like, flowery design with considerable detail on stem and leaf." Glass craftsmen were a sentimental lot, and following a common practice Vaupel often engraved a piece of glass for a member of the family, as a gift or to commemorate a special occasion; he even engraved some such pieces for himself (Figs. 3, 5, 6). His three children were named

A. Presentation chalice, Louis Vaupel's masterpiece; c. 1875-1880. Hollow-baluster, panel-cut stem; cut, scalloped foot; and cutting at base of bowl. Height 9 inches. The engraving encircling the bowl depicts forest scenes with several hunters, hounds, and a stag at bay. The work is so minutely detailed that a squirrel on a branch and a snake wriggling through the tall grass can be clearly seen. Exhibited publicly for the first time at the Toledo Museum of Art's 1968 exhibition *Libbey Glass, a tradition of 150 years.* The catalogue of that exhibition called this chalice "the high point in American Middle Period engraved glass."

A.

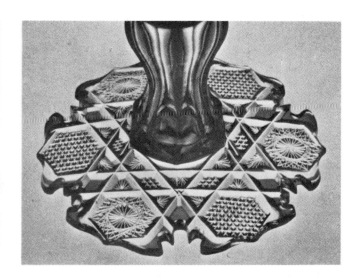

B.

C.

B. Goblet engraved with scene of wolves attacking a horse and, on the other side, lions and buffalo; c. 1875. Height 8⅛ inches. *Museum of Fine Arts, Boston; photograph by Milton C. Zink.*

C. This small beaker is one of several pieces Vaupel engraved and monogrammed *M N* for his married daughter. The beautifully executed engraving is typically Bohemian. Height 4½ inches; c. 1880-1890.

D. Flared beaker with patterned foot and cutting at base of bowl; height 4½ inches; c. 1880-1890. One of the few green pieces engraved by Vaupel: most of his cased pieces are ruby, with very few examples in green or blue.

D.

214

Fig. 4. Clear-glass compote engraved by Vaupel for his son, with monogram *L H W V* and design of grape clusters and floral garlands; height 9 inches. Utility pieces such as compotes, finger bowls, and decanters were engraved with names or monograms of members of the family to commemorate a birthday, anniversary, or similar event. The family collection currently includes twelve pieces so monogrammed.

Minette, Emilie, and Louis, and their initials occur on a number of the family pieces; it is sometimes difficult, however, to be sure which Minette or which Louis the initials stand for. The small red beaker (color plate C) monogrammed *M N* was certainly for his daughter: her married name was Newman.

It would of course be of great interest to know just which of the engraved pieces produced by the New England Glass Company during Vaupel's working years came from his hand. However, attributions of glass to a particular worker—or, for that matter, to a particular factory—are even trickier than attributions in other fields. For one thing, glass is rarely signed. It is possible to hazard an attribution on the ground of analogy to a documented piece, and for this purpose the objects illustrated here could hardly be improved on. Every one of them is either signed or firmly documented or both. All but four are still in the Vaupel family collection, and of those four one (Fig. 3) carries signature, date, and name of factory, and the other three (color plate B, Figs. 7, 8) were bequeathed to their present owner, the Museum of Fine Arts in Boston, by Vaupel's granddaughter.

Aside from their usefulness as a possible basis for attributions, the pieces shown here are of unusual interest to students and collectors of American engraved glass because they are, with one or two exceptions, quite unfamiliar. In his later years Vaupel refused to permit examples of his work which were still in the family to be exhibited in any museum, and he persuaded his son, L. H. W. Vaupel, to follow the same policy. I am particularly grateful, therefore, to the Vaupel family and to the Boston Museum of Fine Arts for permission to publish such an outstanding group from the work of Louis Vaupel.

Fig. 5. Goblet of clear glass, c. 1875-1880, engraved with floral motifs, heraldic device, and wreathed monogram *L V;* height 7 inches. Vaupel considered this "his" glass and it was reserved for his use. The heraldic device is a family coat of arms created by Vaupel; the original sketch is still in the family collection.

Fig. 6. Cruet engraved by Vaupel for his own use; height 7 inches; c. 1860-1870. Neck and stopper are elaborately faceted.

Fig. 7. The engraving on this small (4¾ inches high) beaker, pale ruby engraved to clear (c. 1865-1870), shows Venus and Cupid in a cartouche surrounded by flowers and foliage. Such a design is unusual in American glass of the period, but the style had long been familiar in Europe, where Vaupel learned his craft. The inscribed monogram *M V* identifies this as still another gift from Vaupel to his wife. *Museum of Fine Arts, Boston; all Vaupel pieces in the museum's collection were acquired by bequest of Dr. Minette D. Newman, Louis Vaupel's granddaughter.*

Fig. 8. Mercury, or silver-glass, goblet, engraved with flowers and foliage in a conventional repeat pattern resembling a textile or wallpaper design; signed *L V* under foot. Height 10 inches; 1860-1870. Engraving on such an exceptionally large silver-glass object is rare. *Museum of Fine Arts, Boston.*